Stata Reference Manual
Release 6
Volume 4 Su-Z

Stata Press
College Station, Texas

Stata Press, 702 University Drive East, College Station, Texas 77840

The suggested citation for this software is

StataCorp. 1999. *Stata Statistical Software: Release 6.0*. College Station, TX: Stata Corporation.

Title

summarize — Summary statistics

Syntax

$\big[$ by *varlist*: $\big]$ $\underline{\text{su}}$mmarize $\big[$*varlist*$\big]$ $\big[$*weight*$\big]$ $\big[$if *exp*$\big]$ $\big[$in *range*$\big]$ $\big[$, $\{$ detail | $\underline{\text{mean}}$only $\}$

$\underline{\text{f}}$ormat $\big]$

aweights and fweights are allowed.

The *varlist* following summarize may contain time-series operators; see [U] 14.4.3 Time-series varlists.

Description

summarize calculates and displays a variety of univariate summary statistics. If no *varlist* is specified, then summary statistics are calculated for all the variables in the dataset.

Also see [R] **ci** for calculating the standard error and confidence intervals of the mean.

Options

detail produces additional statistics, including skewness, kurtosis, the four smallest and largest values, and various percentiles.

meanonly, which is allowed only when detail is not specified, suppresses display of results and calculation of the variance. Ado-file writers will find this useful for fast calls.

format requests that the summary statistics be displayed using the display formats associated with the variables, rather than the default g display format; see [U] **15.5 Formats: controlling how data is displayed**.

Remarks

summarize can produce two different sets of summary statistics. Without the detail option, the number of nonmissing observations, the mean and standard deviation, and the minimum and maximum values are presented. With detail, the same information is presented along with the variance, skewness, and kurtosis; the four smallest and four largest values; and the 1st, 5th, 10th, 25th, 50th (median), 75th, 90th, 95th, and 99th percentiles.

▷ Example

You have data containing information on various automobiles, among which is the variable mpg, the mileage rating. We can obtain a quick summary of the mpg variable by typing

```
. summarize mpg
    Variable |     Obs      Mean    Std. Dev.      Min       Max
-------------+----------------------------------------------------
         mpg |      74   21.2973    5.785503       12        41
```

1

We see that we have 74 observations. The mean of `mpg` is 21.3 miles per gallon, and the standard deviation is 5.79. The minimum is 12 and the maximum is 41.

If we had not specified the variable (or variables) we wanted summarized, we would have obtained summary statistics on all the variables in the data:

```
. summarize
    Variable |     Obs        Mean    Std. Dev.       Min        Max
-------------+--------------------------------------------------------
        make |       0
       price |      74    6165.257    2949.496        3291      15906
         mpg |      74     21.2973    5.785503          12         41
       rep78 |      69    3.405797    .9899323           1          5
      weight |      74    3019.459    777.1936        1760       4840
     foreign |      74    .2972973    .4601885           0          1
```

Notice that there are only 69 observations on `rep78`, so some of the observations are missing. There are no observations on `make` since it is a string variable.

◁

▷ Example

The `detail` option provides all the information of a normal `summarize` and more. The format of the output also differs:

```
. summarize mpg, detail

                         Mileage (mpg)
-------------------------------------------------------------
      Percentiles      Smallest
 1%         12              12
 5%         14              12
10%         14              14       Obs                  74
25%         18              14       Sum of Wgt.          74

50%         20                       Mean            21.2973
                       Largest       Std. Dev.      5.785503
75%         25              34
90%         29              35       Variance       33.47205
95%         34              35       Skewness       .9487176
99%         41              41       Kurtosis       3.975005
```

As in the previous example, we see that the mean of `mpg` is 21.3 miles per gallon and the standard deviation is 5.79. We also see the various percentiles. The median of `mpg` (the 50th percentile) is 20 miles per gallon. The 25th percentile is 18 and the 75th percentile is 25.

When we performed the simple `summarize`, we learned that the minimum and maximum were 12 and 41, respectively. We now see that the four smallest values in our data are 12, 12, 14, and 14. The four largest values are 34, 35, 35, and 41. The skewness of the distribution is 0.95, and the kurtosis is 3.98. (A normal distribution would have skewness of 0 and kurtosis of 3.)

(*Skewness* is a measure of the lack of symmetry of a distribution. If the coefficient of skewness is 0, the distribution is symmetric. If the coefficient is negative, the median is usually greater than the mean and the distribution is said to be skewed left. If the coefficient is positive, the median is usually less than the mean and the distribution is said to be skewed right. *Kurtosis* (from the Greek kyrtosis meaning curvature) is a measure of peakedness of a distribution. The smaller the coefficient of kurtosis, the flatter the distribution. The normal distribution has a coefficient of kurtosis of 3 and provides a convenient benchmark.)

(On a historical note, see Plackett (1958) for a history of the concept of the mean.)

◁

▷ Example

summarize can usefully be combined with the by *varlist*: prefix. In our data we have a variable foreign that distinguishes foreign and domestic cars. We can obtain summaries of mpg and weight within each subgroup by typing

```
. by foreign: summarize mpg weight

-> foreign=Domestic
Variable |    Obs        Mean   Std. Dev.       Min        Max
---------+-----------------------------------------------------
     mpg |     52    19.82692    4.743297         12         34
  weight |     52    3317.115    695.3637       1800       4840

-> foreign= Foreign
Variable |    Obs        Mean   Std. Dev.       Min        Max
---------+-----------------------------------------------------
     mpg |     22    24.77273    6.611187         14         41
  weight |     22    2315.909    433.0035       1760       3420
```

Domestic cars in our data average 19.8 miles per gallon, whereas foreign cars average 24.8.

Since by *varlist*: can be combined with summarize, it can be combined with summarize, detail as well:

```
. by foreign: summarize mpg, detail

-> foreign=Domestic
                       Mileage (mpg)
-------------------------------------------------------------
        Percentiles     Smallest
  1%          12            12
  5%          14            12
 10%          14            14        Obs                 52
 25%         16.5           14        Sum of Wgt.         52

 50%          19                      Mean           19.82692
                        Largest       Std. Dev.      4.743297
 75%          22            28
 90%          26            29        Variance       22.49887
 95%          29            30        Skewness       .7712432
 99%          34            34        Kurtosis       3.441459

-> foreign= Foreign
                       Mileage (mpg)
-------------------------------------------------------------
        Percentiles     Smallest
  1%          14            14
  5%          17            17
 10%          17            17        Obs                 22
 25%          21            18        Sum of Wgt.         22

 50%         24.5                     Mean           24.77273
                        Largest       Std. Dev.      6.611187
 75%          28            31
 90%          35            35        Variance       43.70779
 95%          35            35        Skewness        .657329
 99%          41            41        Kurtosis        3.10734
```

◁

❏ Technical Note

summarize respects display formats if you specify the format option. When we type summarize price weight, we obtain

```
. summarize price weight
Variable |    Obs        Mean    Std. Dev.        Min        Max
---------+-------------------------------------------------------
   price |     74    6165.257    2949.496       3291      15906
  weight |     74    3019.459    777.1936       1760       4840
```

The display is accurate but is not as aesthetically pleasing as you may wish, particularly if you plan to use the output directly in published work. By placing formats on the variables, you can control how the table appears:

```
. format price weight %9.2fc
. summarize price weight, format
Variable |    Obs        Mean    Std. Dev.        Min        Max
---------+-------------------------------------------------------
   price |     74    6,165.26    2,949.50    3,291.00   15,906.00
  weight |     74    3,019.46      777.19    1,760.00    4,840.00
```

❏

If you specify a weight (see [U] **14.1.6 weight**), each observation is multiplied by the value of the weighting expression before the summary statistics are calculated, so that the weighting expression is interpreted as the discrete density of each observation.

▷ Example

You have 1980 Census data on each of the 50 states. Included among your variables is medage, the median age of the population of each state. If you type summarize medage, you obtain unweighted statistics:

```
. summarize medage
Variable |    Obs        Mean    Std. Dev.        Min        Max
---------+-------------------------------------------------------
  medage |     50       29.54    1.693445        24.2       34.7
```

Also among your variables is pop, the population in each state. Typing summarize medage [w=pop] produces population-weighted statistics:

```
. summarize medage [w=pop]
(analytic weights assumed)
Variable |    Obs      Weight       Mean    Std. Dev.        Min        Max
---------+-----------------------------------------------------------------
  medage |     50   225907472    30.11047     1.66933       24.2       34.7
```

The number listed under Weight is the sum of the weighting variable, pop. It indicates that there are roughly 226 million people in the U.S. The pop-weighted mean of medage is 30.11 (as compared with 29.54 for the unweighted statistic), and the weighted standard deviation is 1.67 (as compared with 1.69).

◁

▷ Example

You can obtain detailed summaries of weighted data as well. When you do this, *all* the statistics are weighted, including the percentiles.

```
. summarize medage [w=pop], detail
(analytic weights assumed)
```

```
                                Median age
-------------------------------------------------------------
          Percentiles      Smallest
    1%       27.1            24.2
    5%       27.7            26.1
   10%       28.2            27.1      Obs                   50
   25%       29.2            27.4      Sum of Wgt.    225907472
   50%       29.9                      Mean            30.11047
                            Largest    Std. Dev.       1.66933
   75%       30.9             32
   90%       32.1            32.1      Variance        2.786661
   95%       32.2            32.2      Skewness        .5281972
   99%       34.7            34.7      Kurtosis        4.494223
```

◁

❑ Technical Note

You are writing a program and need to access the mean of a variable. The `meanonly` option provides for fast calls. For example, suppose your program reads as follows:

```
program define mean
        summarize `1´, meanonly
        display "  mean = " r(mean)
end
```

The result of executing this is

```
. mean price
  mean = 6165.2568
```

❑

Saved Results

`summarize` saves in `r()`:

Scalars

r(N)	number of observations	r(p25)	25th percentile (detail only)
r(mean)	mean	r(p50)	50th percentile (detail only)
r(skewness)	skewness (detail only)	r(p75)	75th percentile (detail only)
r(min)	minimum	r(p90)	90th percentile (detail only)
r(max)	maximum	r(p95)	95th percentile (detail only)
r(sum_w)	sum of the weights	r(p99)	99th percentile (detail only)
r(p1)	1st percentile (detail only)	r(Var)	variance
r(p5)	5th percentile (detail only)	r(kurtosis)	kurtosis (detail only)
r(p10)	10th percentile (detail only)	r(sum)	sum of variable

Methods and Formulas

Let x denote the variable on which we want to calculate summary statistics, and let x_i, $i = 1, \ldots, n$, denote an individual observation on x. Let v_i be the weight, and if no weight is specified, define $v_i = 1$ for all i.

Define V as the *sum of the weight*:

$$V = \sum_{i=1}^{n} v_i$$

Define w_i to be v_i normalized to sum to n, $w_i = v_i(n/V)$.

The *mean*, $\overline{x}$, is defined as

$$\overline{x} = \frac{1}{n} \sum_{i=1}^{n} w_i x_i$$

The *variance*, s^2, is defined as

$$s^2 = \frac{1}{n-1} \sum_{i=1}^{n} w_i(x_i - \overline{x})^2$$

The *standard deviation*, s, is defined as $\sqrt{s^2}$.

Define m_r as the rth moment about the mean $\overline{x}$:

$$m_r = \frac{1}{n} \sum_{i=1}^{n} w_i(x_i - \overline{x})^r$$

The *coefficient of skewness* is then defined as $m_3 m_2^{-3/2}$. The *coefficient of kurtosis* is defined as $m_4 m_2^{-2}$.

Let $x_{(i)}$ refer to the x in ascending order, and let $w_{(i)}$ refer to the corresponding weights of $x_{(i)}$. The four smallest values are $x_{(1)}$, $x_{(2)}$, $x_{(3)}$, and $x_{(4)}$. The four largest values are $x_{(n)}$, $x_{(n-1)}$, $x_{(n-2)}$, and $x_{(n-3)}$.

To obtain the pth *percentile*, which we will denote as $x_{[p]}$, let $P = np/100$. Let

$$W_{(i)} = \sum_{j=1}^{i} w_{(j)}$$

Find the first index i such that $W_{(i)} > P$. The pth *percentile* is then

$$x_{[p]} = \begin{cases} \dfrac{x_{(i-1)} + x_{(i)}}{2} & \text{if } W_{(i-1)} = P \\ x_{(i)} & \text{otherwise} \end{cases}$$

References

Gleason, J. R. 1997. sg67: Univariate summaries with boxplots. *Stata Technical Bulletin* 36: 23–25. Reprinted in *Stata Technical Bulletin Reprints*, vol. 6, pp. 179–183.

Hamilton, L. C. 1996. *Data Analysis for Social Scientists*. Pacific Grove, CA: Brooks/Cole Publishing Company.

Plackett, R. L. 1958. The principle of the arithmetic mean. *Biometrika* 45: 130–135.

Stuart, A. and J. K. Ord. 1994. *Kendall's Advanced Theory of Statistics, Vol. I.* 6th ed. London: Edward Arnold.

Weisberg, H. F. 1992. *Central Tendency and Variability.* Newbury Park, CA: Sage Publications.

Also See

Related: [R] **centile**, [R] **cf**, [R] **ci**, [R] **codebook**, [R] **compare**, [R] **describe**, [R] **egen**,
[R] **inspect**, [R] **lv**, [R] **means**, [R] **pctile**, [R] **st stsum**, [R] **svymean**, [R] **table**,
[R] **tabsum**, [R] **xtsum**

Title

> **sureg** — Zellner's seemingly unrelated regression

Syntax

Basic syntax

> **sureg** ($depvar_1$ $varlist_1$) ($depvar_2$ $varlist_2$) ... ($depvar_N$ $varlist_N$)
>
> $[weight]$ $[\text{if } exp]$ $[\text{in } range]$

Full syntax

> **sureg** ($[eqname_1:]$ $depvar_{1a}$ $[depvar_{1b} \ldots =]$ $varlist_1$ $[$, **noconstant** $])$
>
> ($[eqname_2:]$ $depvar_{2a}$ $[depvar_{2b} \ldots =]$ $varlist_2$ $[$, **noconstant** $])$
>
> ...
>
> ($[eqname_N:]$ $depvar_{Na}$ $[depvar_{Nb} \ldots =]$ $varlist_N$ $[$, **noconstant** $])$ $[weight]$
>
> $[\text{if } exp]$ $[\text{in } range]$ $[$, **corr** **constraints**(*numlist*) **isure** **dfk** **dfk2** **small**
>
> **noheader** **notable** **level**(#) *maximize_options* $]$

aweights and **fweight**s are allowed; see [U] **14.1.6 weight**.

The *depvar*s and the *varlist*s may contain time-series operators; see [U] **14.4.3 Time-series varlists**.

sureg shares the features of all estimation commands; see [U] **23 Estimation and post-estimation commands**.

Explicit equation naming (eqname:) cannot be combined with multiple dependent variables in an equation specification.

Syntax for predict

> **predict** $[type]$ *newvarname* $[\text{if } exp]$ $[\text{in } range]$ $[$, **equation**(*eqno* $[,eqno])$
>
> **xb** **stdp** **difference** **stddp** **residuals** $]$

These statistics are available both in and out of sample; type **predict** ... **if** e(sample) ... if wanted only for the estimation sample.

Description

sureg estimates seemingly unrelated regression models (Zellner 1962, Zellner and Huang 1962, Zellner 1963). The acronyms SURE and SUR are often used for the estimator.

Options

noconstant omits the constant term (intercept) from the equation on which the option is specified.

8

corr displays the correlation matrix of the residuals between equations and performs a Breusch–Pagan test for independent equations; i.e., the disturbance covariance matrix is diagonal.

constraints(*numlist*) specifies by number the linear constraint(s) to be applied to the system. By default, sureg estimates an unconstrained system. See [R] **reg3** for an example using constraints with a system estimator.

isure specifies that sureg should iterate over the estimated disturbance covariance matrix and parameter estimates until the parameter estimates converge. Under seemingly unrelated regression, this iteration converges to the maximum likelihood results. If this option is not specified, sureg produces two-step estimates.

dfk specifies the use of an alternate divisor in computing the covariance matrix for the equation residuals. As an asymptotically justified estimator, sureg by default uses the number of sample observations (n) as a divisor. When the dfk option is set, a small-sample adjustment is made and the divisor is taken to be $\sqrt{(n - k_i)(n - k_j)}$, where k_i and k_j are the numbers of parameters in equations i and j respectively.

dfk2 specifies the use of an alternate divisor in computing the covariance matrix for the equation residuals. When the dfk2 option is set, the divisor is taken to be the mean of the residual degrees of freedom from the individual equations. This was the default divisor for sureg before version 6.0.

small specifies that small sample statistics are to be computed. It shifts the test statistics from chi-squared and Z statistics to F statistics and t statistics. While the standard errors from each equation are computed using the degrees of freedom for the equation, the degrees of freedom for the t statistics are all taken to be those for the first equation. Before version 6.0, sureg reported small-sample statistics.

noheader suppresses display of the table reporting F statistics, R-squared, and root mean square error above the coefficient table.

notable suppresses display of the coefficient table.

level(*#*) specifies the confidence level, in percent, for confidence intervals. The default is level(95) or as set by set level; see [U] **23.5 Specifying the width of confidence intervals**.

maximize_options control the maximization process; see [R] **maximize**. You should never have to specify them.

Options for predict

equation(*eqno*[,*eqno*]) specifies to which equation(s) you are referring.

equation() is filled in with one *eqno* for options xb, stdp, and residuals. equation(#1) would mean the calculation is to be made for the first equation, equation(#2) would mean the second, and so on. Alternatively, you could refer to the equations by their names. equation(income) would refer to the equation named income and equation(hours) to the equation named hours.

If you do not specify equation(), results are as if you specified equation(#1).

difference and stddp refer to between-equation concepts. To use these options, you must specify two equations; e.g., equation(#1,#2) or equation(income,hours). When two equations must be specified, equation() is not optional.

xb, the default, calculates the fitted values—the prediction of $x_j b$ for the specified equation.

stdp calculates the standard error of the prediction for the specified equation. It can be thought of as the standard error of the predicted expected value or mean for the observation's covariate pattern. This is also referred to as the standard error of the fitted value.

difference calculates the difference between the linear predictions of two equations in the system. With equation(#1,#2), difference computes the prediction of equation(#1) minus the prediction of equation(#2).

stddp is allowed only after you have previously estimated a multiple-equation model. The standard error of the difference in linear predictions $(\mathbf{x}_{1j}\mathbf{b} - \mathbf{x}_{2j}\mathbf{b})$ between equations 1 and 2 is calculated.

residuals calculates the residuals.

For more information on using predict after multiple-equation estimation commands, see [R] **predict**.

Remarks

Seemingly unrelated regression models are so called because they appear to be joint estimates of several regression models, each with its own error term. The regressions are related because the (contemporaneous) errors associated with the dependent variables may be correlated.

▷ Example

When you estimate models with the same set of right-hand-side variables, the seemingly unrelated regression results (in terms of coefficients and standard errors) are the same as estimating the models separately (using, say, regress). The same is true when the models are nested. Even in such cases, sureg is useful when you want to perform joint tests. For instance, let us assume that you think

$$\text{price} = \beta_0 + \beta_1\text{foreign} + \beta_2\text{length} + u_1$$
$$\text{weight} = \gamma_0 + \gamma_1\text{foreign} + \gamma_2\text{length} + u_2$$

Since the models have the same set of explanatory variables, you could estimate the two equations separately. Yet, you might still choose to estimate them with sureg because you want to perform the joint test $\beta_1 = \gamma_1 = 0$.

We use the small and dfk options to obtain small-sample statistics comparable to regress or mvreg.

```
. sureg (price foreign length) (weight foreign length), small dfk
Seemingly unrelated regression
-----------------------------------------------------------------------
Equation      Obs  Parms       RMSE    "R-sq"      F-Stat        P
-----------------------------------------------------------------------
price          74    2     2474.593   0.3154    16.35382    0.0000
weight         74    2     250.2515   0.8992    316.5447    0.0000
-----------------------------------------------------------------------
```

	Coef.	Std. Err.	t	P>|t|	[95% Conf. Interval]
price						
foreign	2801.143	766.117	3.656	0.000	1273.549	4328.737
length	90.21239	15.83368	5.697	0.000	58.64092	121.7839
_cons	-11621.35	3124.436	-3.720	0.000	-17851.3	-5391.401
weight						
foreign	-133.6775	77.47615	-1.725	0.089	-288.1605	20.80554
length	31.44455	1.601234	19.638	0.000	28.25178	34.63732
_cons	-2850.25	315.9691	-9.021	0.000	-3480.274	-2220.225

These two equation have a common set of regressors and we could have used a shorthand syntax to specify the equations:

```
. sureg (price weight = foreign length), small dfk
```

In this case, the results presented by **sureg** are the same as if we had estimated the equations separately:

```
. regress price foreign length
(output omitted )
. regress weight foreign length
(output omitted )
```

There is, however, a difference. We have allowed u_1 and u_2 to be correlated and have estimated the full variance–covariance matrix of the coefficients. **sureg** has estimated the correlations, but it does not report them unless we specify the **corr** option. We did not remember to specify **corr** when we estimated the model, but we can redisplay the results:

```
. sureg, notable noheader corr
Correlation matrix of residuals:

          price  weight
 price  1.0000
weight  0.5840  1.0000

Breusch-Pagan test of independence: chi2(1) =    25.237, Pr = 0.0000
```

The **notable** and **noheader** options prevented **sureg** from redisplaying the header and coefficient tables. We find that, for the same cars, the correlation of the residuals in the **price** and **weight** equations is .5840 and that we can reject the hypothesis that this correlation is zero.

We can perform a test that the coefficients on **foreign** are jointly zero in both equations—as we set out to do—by typing **test foreign**; see [R] **test**. When we type a variable without specifying the equation, that variable is tested for zero in all equations in which it appears:

```
. test foreign
 ( 1)  [price]foreign = 0.0
 ( 2)  [weight]foreign = 0.0

       F( 2,   71) =   17.99
           Prob > F =    0.0000
```

◁

▷ Example

When the models do not have the same set of explanatory variables and are not nested, **sureg** may lead to more efficient estimates than running the models separately as well as allowing joint tests. This time, let us assume you believe

$$\texttt{price} = \beta_0 + \beta_1 \texttt{foreign} + \beta_2 \texttt{mpg} + \beta_3 \texttt{displ} + u_1$$
$$\texttt{weight} = \gamma_0 + \gamma_1 \texttt{foreign} + \gamma_2 \texttt{length} + u_2$$

To estimate this model, you type

```
. sureg (price foreign mpg displ) (weight foreign length) , corr
Seemingly unrelated regression
------------------------------------------------------------------------
Equation        Obs  Parms       RMSE    "R-sq"       Chi2       P
------------------------------------------------------------------------
price            74     3     2165.321   0.4537    49.6383   0.0000
weight           74     2     245.2916   0.8990   661.8418   0.0000
------------------------------------------------------------------------

             |     Coef.   Std. Err.      z     P>|z|     [95% Conf. Interval]
-------------+----------------------------------------------------------------
price        |
     foreign |    3058.25   685.7357    4.460    0.000     1714.233    4402.267
         mpg |  -104.9591   58.47209   -1.795    0.073    -219.5623    9.644042
       displ |   18.18098   4.286372    4.242    0.000     9.779842    26.58211
       _cons |   3904.336   1966.521    1.985    0.047      50.0263    7758.645
-------------+----------------------------------------------------------------
weight       |
     foreign |  -147.3481   75.44314   -1.953    0.051    -295.2139     .517755
      length |   30.94905   1.539895   20.098    0.000     27.93091    33.96718
       _cons |  -2753.064   303.9336   -9.058    0.000    -3348.763   -2157.365
------------------------------------------------------------------------------

Correlation matrix of residuals:
          price  weight
price    1.0000
weight   0.3285  1.0000
Breusch-Pagan test of independence: chi2(1) =     7.984, Pr = 0.0047
```

By way of comparison, had we estimated the `price` model separately:

```
. regress price foreign mpg displ
    Source |       SS       df       MS              Number of obs =      74
-----------+------------------------------           F(  3,    70) =   20.13
     Model | 294104790       3   98034929.9          Prob > F      =  0.0000
  Residual | 340960606      70   4870865.81          R-squared     =  0.4631
-----------+------------------------------           Adj R-squared =  0.4401
     Total | 635065396      73   8699525.97          Root MSE      =  2207.0

       price |     Coef.   Std. Err.      t     P>|t|     [95% Conf. Interval]
-------------+----------------------------------------------------------------
     foreign |   3545.484   712.7763    4.974    0.000     2123.897    4967.072
         mpg |  -98.88559   63.17063   -1.565    0.122    -224.8754    27.10425
       displ |   22.40416   4.634239    4.834    0.000     13.16146    31.64686
       _cons |    2796.91   2137.873    1.308    0.195    -1466.943    7060.762
------------------------------------------------------------------------------
```

The coefficients are slightly different but the standard errors are uniformly larger. This would still be true if we specified the `dfk` option to make a small-sample adjustment to the estimated covariance of the disturbances.

◁

❏ Technical Note

Constraints can be applied to SURE models using Stata's standard syntax for constraints. For a general discussion of constraints, see [R] **constraint**; for examples similar to seemingly unrelated regression models, see [R] **reg3**.

❏

Saved Results

sureg saves in e():

Scalars

e(N)	number of observations
e(k_eq)	number of equations
e(mss_#)	model sum of squares for equation #
e(df_m#)	model degrees of freedom for equation #
e(rss_#)	residual sum of squares for equation #
e(df_r)	residual degrees of freedom
e(r2_#)	R-squared for equation #
e(F_#)	F statistic for equation # (small only)
e(rmse_#)	root mean square error for equation #
e(ll)	log likelihood
e(chi2_#)	χ^2 for equation #
e(p_#)	significance for equation #
e(chi2_bp)	Breusch–Pagan χ^2
e(df_bp)	degrees of freedom for Breusch–Pagan χ^2 test
e(ic)	number of iterations
e(cons_#)	1 when equation # has a constant; 0, otherwise

Macros

e(cmd)	sureg
e(depvar)	name(s) of dependent variable(s)
e(exog)	names of exogenous variables
e(eqnames)	names of equations
e(corr)	correlation structure
e(method)	requested estimation method
e(small)	small
e(predict)	program used to implement predict
e(dfk)	alternate divisor (dfk or dfk2 only)

Matrices

e(b)	coefficient vector
e(V)	variance–covariance matrix of the estimators
e(Sigma)	$\widehat{\Sigma}$ matrix

Functions

e(sample)	marks estimation sample

Methods and Formulas

sureg is implemented as an ado-file.

sureg uses the asymptotically efficient, feasible generalized least-squares algorithm described in Greene (1997, 674–688). The computing formulas are given on page 675.

The R-squared reported is the percent of variance explained by the predictors. It may be used for descriptive purposes, but R-squared is not a well-defined concept when GLS is used.

sureg will refuse to compute the estimators if (1) the same equation is named more than once or (2) the inverse covariance matrix of the residuals is singular.

The Breusch and Pagan (1980) χ^2 statistic—a Lagrange multiplier statistic—is given by

$$\lambda = T \sum_{m=1}^{M} \sum_{n=1}^{m-1} r_{mn}^2$$

where r_{mn} is the estimated correlation between the residuals of the M equations and T is the number of observations. It is distributed as χ^2 with $M(M-1)/2$ degrees of freedom.

References

Breusch, T. and A. Pagan. 1980. The LM test and its applications to model specification in econometrics. *Review of Economic Studies* 47: 239–254.

Greene, W. H. 1997. *Econometric Analysis*. 3d ed. Upper Saddle River, NJ: Prentice–Hall.

Zellner, A. 1962. An efficient method of estimating seeming unrelated regressions and tests for aggregation bias. *Journal of the American Statistical Association* 57: 348–368.

——. 1963. Estimators for seemingly unrelated regression equations: Some exact finite sample results. *Journal of the American Statistical Association* 58: 977–992.

Zellner, A. and D. S. Huang. 1962. Further properties of efficient estimators for seemingly unrelated regression equations. *International Economic Review* 3: 300–313.

Also See

Complementary:	[R] **lincom**, [R] **predict**, [R] **test**, [R] **testnl**, [R] **vce**
Related:	[R] **ivreg**, [R] **mvreg**, [R] **reg3**, [R] **regress**
Background:	[U] **16.5 Accessing coefficients and standard errors**,
	[U] **23 Estimation and post-estimation commands**

Title

| **svy** — Introduction to survey commands |

Description

The prefix svy refers to survey data, and all the commands for analyzing them begin with svy.

The svy commands are

svyreg	[R] **svy estimators**	Linear regression for survey data
svyivreg	[R] **svy estimators**	Instrumental variables regression for survey data
svyintrg	[R] **svy estimators**	Censored and interval regression for survey data
svylogit	[R] **svy estimators**	Logistic regression for survey data
svyprobt	[R] **svy estimators**	Probit models for survey data
svymlog	[R] **svy estimators**	Multinomial logistic regression for survey data
svyolog	[R] **svy estimators**	Ordered logistic regression for survey data
svyoprob	[R] **svy estimators**	Ordered probit models for survey data
svypois	[R] **svy estimators**	Poisson regression for survey data
svydes	[R] **svydes**	Describe strata and PSUs of survey data
svylc	[R] **svylc**	Estimate linear combinations of parameters (e.g., differences of means, regression coefficients)
svymean	[R] **svymean**	Estimation of population and subpopulation means
svyprop	[R] **svymean**	Estimation of population and subpopulation proportions
svyratio	[R] **svymean**	Estimation of population and subpopulation ratios
svytotal	[R] **svymean**	Estimation of population and subpopulation totals
svyset	[R] **svyset**	Set variables for survey data
svytab	[R] **svytab**	Two-way tables for survey data
svytest	[R] **svytest**	Hypotheses tests for survey data

Remarks

Data from sample surveys generally have three important characteristics:

1. sampling weights, also called probability weights—**pweight**s in Stata's syntax,
2. cluster sampling,
3. stratification.

The svy commands can be used when the sample has any or all of these features. For example, if the data are weighted, but the design did not involve clustering or stratification, this data can still be analyzed with the survey commands. The svy commands are also suitable for multistage sampling designs. For a general discussion of various aspects of survey designs and how to account for them in your analysis, see [U] **30 Overview of survey estimation**.

15

Several other estimation commands in Stata have features that make them suitable for certain limited designs. For example, `regress` handles sampling weights properly when `pweight`s are specified, and `regress` also has a `cluster()` option. However, the `svy` commands have capabilities that these other estimation commands do not have. Persons with bona fide survey data who care about getting all the details right should use the `svy` commands.

The `svy` commands compute the design effects deff and deft. The `svy` commands calculate adjusted Wald tests for the model F test. Using `svytest` after a `svy` estimation command, one can compute adjusted Wald tests and Bonferroni tests for other hypotheses. For survey data, `svytest` is used in place of `test`.

`svymean` is the sole command in Stata (other than setting up the estimation as a regression) that handles sampling weights properly for the estimation of means. Testing the differences of two means (the equivalent of a two-sample t test with sampling weights) can be done by running `svymean` with a `by()` option, and then running the command `svylc`.

`svylc` computes estimates of linear combinations of parameters, whether means, total, ratios, proportions, or regression coefficients after a `svy` estimation command. Used after `svylogit`, it can compute odds ratios for any covariate group relative to another. For survey data, `svylc` is used in place of `lincom` (see [R] **lincom**).

Persons wishing to use the `svy` commands should first glance at the `svyset` command described in [R] **svyset**. This allows you to set your `pweight`, strata, PSU (cluster), and FPC (finite population correction) variables at the outset rather than specifying them when you issue a command.

Programmers may want to use the `_robust` command to compute robust variance estimates for their own estimators; see [R] **_robust**. `svyreg` and the other `svy` estimation commands described in [R] **svy estimators** call this command to produce their variance estimates.

For more detailed introductions to complex survey data analysis, see, for example, Scheaffer et al. (1996), Stuart (1984), and Williams (1978). Advanced treatments and discussion of important special topics are given by Cochran (1977), Särndal et al. (1992), Skinner et al. (1989), Thompson (1992), and Wolter (1985).

Acknowledgment

The `svy` commands were developed in collaboration with John L. Eltinge, Department of Statistics, Texas A&M University. We thank him for his invaluable assistance.

References

Cochran, W. G. 1977. *Sampling Techniques*. 3d ed. New York: John Wiley & Sons.

Eltinge, J. L., and W. M. Sribney. 1996. svy1: Some basic concepts for design-based analysis of complex survey data. *Stata Technical Bulletin* 31: 3–6. Reprinted in *Stata Technical Bulletin Reprints*, vol. 6, pp. 208–213.

Kott, P. S. 1991. A model-based look at linear regression with survey data. *American Statistician* 45: 107–112.

Särndal, C.-E., B. Swensson, and J. Wretman. 1992. *Model Assisted Survey Sampling*. New York: Springer-Verlag.

Scheaffer, R. L., W. Mendenhall, and L. Ott. 1996. *Elementary Survey Sampling*. 5th ed. Boston: Duxbury Press.

Skinner, C. J., D. Holt, and T. M. F. Smith, eds. 1989. *Analysis of Complex Surveys*. New York: John Wiley & Sons.

Stuart, A. 1984. *The Ideas of Sampling*. 3d ed. New York: Macmillan.

Thompson, S. K. 1992. *Sampling*. New York: John Wiley & Sons.

Williams, B. 1978. *A Sampler on Sampling*. New York: John Wiley & Sons.

Wolter, K. M. 1985. *Introduction to Variance Estimation*. New York: Springer-Verlag.

Also See

Complementary:	[R] **svy estimators**, [R] **svydes**, [R] **svylc**, [R] **svymean**, [R] **svyset**, [R] **svytab**, [R] **svytest**
Related:	[R] **_robust**
Background:	[U] **30 Overview of survey estimation**

Title

svy estimators — Estimation commands for complex survey data

Syntax

svyreg *varlist* [*weight*] [if *exp*] [in *range*] [, *common_options*]

svyivreg *depvar* [*varlist*$_1$] (*varlist*$_2$ = *varlist*$_{iv}$) [*weight*] [if *exp*] [in *range*]

    [, *common_options*]

svyintrg *depvar*$_1$ *depvar*$_2$ [*indepvars*] [*weight*] [if *exp*] [in *range*]

    [, offset(*varname*) *maximize_options common_options*]

svylogit *varlist* [*weight*] [if *exp*] [in *range*] [, or offset(*varname*) asis

    maximize_options common_options]

svyprobt *varlist* [*weight*] [if *exp*] [in *range*] [, offset(*varname*) asis

    maximize_options common_options]

svymlog *varlist* [*weight*] [if *exp*] [in *range*] [, rrr basecategory(#)

    maximize_options common_options]

svyolog *varlist* [*weight*] [if *exp*] [in *range*] [, offset(*varname*)

    maximize_options common_options]

svyoprob *varlist* [*weight*] [if *exp*] [in *range*] [, offset(*varname*)

    maximize_options common_options]

svypois *varlist* [*weight*] [if *exp*] [in *range*] [, irr exposure(*varname*)

    offset(*varname*) *maximize_options common_options*]

The *common_options* are

    noconstant strata(*varname*) psu(*varname*) fpc(*varname*)

    subpop(*varname*) srssubpop noadjust

    eform level(#) prob ci deff deft

The commands typed without arguments redisplay previous results. The following options can be given when redisplaying results:

> or <u>rrr</u> <u>irr</u> <u>ef</u>orm level(*#*) prob ci deff deft

These commands allow pweights and iweights; see [U] **14.1.6 weight**.

These commands share the features of all estimation commands; see [U] **23 Estimation and post-estimation commands**.

Warning: Use of if or in restrictions will not produce correct variance estimates for subpopulations in many cases. To compute estimates for a subpopulation, use the subpop() option.

Syntax for predict

After svyreg and svyivreg, the syntax for predict is

> predict [*type*] *newvarname* [if *exp*] [in *range*] [, xb | <u>res</u>iduals | stbp]

After svyintrg, the syntax for predict is

> predict [*type*] *newvarname* [if *exp*] [in *range*] [, xb | stbp | <u>pr</u>(*a,b*)
> | e(*a,b*) | <u>ys</u>tar(*a,b*)]

After svylogit and svyprobt, the syntax for predict is

> predict [*type*] *newvarname* [if *exp*] [in *range*] [, { p | xb | stbp }
> <u>rules</u> asif <u>nooff</u>set]

After svymlog, svyolog, and svyoprob, the syntax for predict is

> predict [*type*] *newvarname(s)* [if *exp*] [in *range*] [, { p | xb | stbp }
> <u>ou</u>tcome(*outcome*) <u>nooff</u>set]

With the options xb and stdp, one new variable is specified. For svymlog, the options xb and stdp require outcome() to be specified. With p (which is the default), if outcome() is specified, then only one new variable is specified; if outcome() is not specified, then *k* new variables must be specified (where *k* is the total number of outcomes).

After svypois, the syntax for predict is

> predict [*type*] *newvarname* [if *exp*] [in *range*] [, { n | ir | xb | stbp }
> <u>nooff</u>set]

For all of the svy estimation commands, the statistics computed by predict are available both in and out of sample; type predict ... if e(sample) ... if wanted only for the estimation sample. For subpopulation estimates, further restriction to the subpopulation may be warranted.

Description

These commands estimate regression models for complex survey data. They are used in the same manner as the nonsurvey version of the command, so users should first familiarize themselves with the nonsurvey versions.

svyreg estimates linear regression; see [R] **regress**.

svyivreg estimates linear regression models with instrumental variables; see [R] **ivreg**.

svyintrg estimates linear regression models with censored or interval data; see intreg in [R] **tobit**.

svylogit estimates logistic regression; see [R] **logit**.

svyprobt estimates probit models; see [R] **probit**.

svymlog estimates multinomial logistic regression; see [R] **mlogit**.

svyolog estimates ordered logit models; see [R] **ologit**.

svyoprob estimates ordered probit models; see [R] **oprobit**.

svypois estimates Poisson regression; see [R] **poisson**.

All of these estimators except svyreg and svyivreg are estimated using pseudo-maximum-likelihood methods. That is, the point estimates are those from a weighted "ordinary" maximum-likelihood estimator. For complex survey data, however, this weighted "likelihood" is not the distribution function for the sample; hence, it is not a true likelihood. Thus, it is termed a pseudo-likelihood. One of the consequences of this is that standard likelihood-ratio tests are no longer valid. Since the pseudo-likelihood is not suitable for statistical inference in the standard manner, it is not displayed by the svy estimators. See Skinner (1989, Section 3.4.4) for a discussion of pseudo-MLEs.

These svy estimation commands allow any or all of the following: probability sampling weights, stratification, and clustering. Associated variance estimates and design effects (deff and deft) are computed. The subpop() option will give estimates for a single subpopulation. For a general discussion of various aspects of survey designs, including multistage designs, see [U] **30 Overview of survey estimation**.

Many of the options here are the same as those for the svymean, svytotal, and svyratio commands. See [R] **svymean** for a more thorough description of these shared svy command options.

To describe the strata and PSUs of your data and to handle the error message "stratum with only one PSU detected", see [R] **svydes**.

To estimate linear combinations of coefficients for any covariate group relative to another, see [R] **svylc**. svylc can also produce odds ratios after svylogit, relative risk ratios after svymlog, and incidence rate ratios after svypois.

To perform hypothesis tests, see [R] **svytest**.

See [R] **_robust** for a programmer's command that can compute variance estimates for survey data for a user-defined program.

Options

The *common_options* are

noconstant estimates a model without the constant term (intercept).

strata(*varname*) specifies the name of a variable (numeric or string) that contains stratum identifiers. strata() can also be specified with the svyset command; see the following examples and [R] **svyset**.

psu(*varname*) specifies the name of a variable (numeric or string) that contains identifiers for the primary sampling unit (i.e., the cluster). psu() can also be specified with the svyset command.

fpc(*varname*) requests a finite population correction for the variance estimates. If the variable specified has values less than or equal to 1, it is interpreted as a stratum sampling rate $f_h = n_h/N_h$, where n_h = number of PSUs sampled from stratum h and N_h = total number of PSUs in the population belonging to stratum h. If the variable specified has values greater than or equal to n_h, it is interpreted as containing N_h. fpc() can also be specified with the svyset command.

subpop(*varname*) specifies that estimates be computed for the single subpopulation defined by the observations for which *varname* $\neq 0$. Typically, *varname* $= 1$ defines the subpopulation, and *varname* $= 0$ indicates observations not belonging to the subpopulation. For observations whose subpopulation status is uncertain, *varname* should be set to missing ('.').

srssubpop can only be specified if subpop() is specified. srssubpop requests that deff and deft be computed using an estimate of simple-random-sampling variance for sampling within a subpopulation. If srssubpop is not specified, deff and deft are computed using an estimate of simple-random-sampling variance for sampling from the entire population. Typically, srssubpop would be given when computing subpopulation estimates by strata or by groups of strata.

noadjust specifies that the model Wald test be carried out as $W/k \sim F(k, d)$, where W is the Wald test statistic, k is the number of terms in the model excluding the constant term, $d = $ total number of sampled PSUs minus the total number of strata, and $F(k, d)$ is an F distribution with k numerator degrees of freedom and d denominator degrees of freedom. By default, an adjusted Wald test is conducted: $(d - k + 1)W/(kd) \sim F(k, d - k + 1)$. See Korn and Graubard (1990) for discussion of the Wald test and adjustments thereof.

The following options can be specified initially or when redisplaying results:

or (svylogit), rrr (svymlog), irr (svypois), and eform (after any of the commands) report the estimated coefficients transformed to, respectively, odds ratios, relative risk ratios, incidence rate ratios, and generic exponentiated coefficients; i.e., $\exp(\widehat{\beta})$ is displayed rather than $\widehat{\beta}$. Standard errors and confidence intervals are similarly transformed.

level(#) specifies the confidence level (i.e., nominal coverage rate), in percent, for confidence intervals. The default is level(95) or as set by set level; see [U] **23.5 Specifying the width of confidence intervals**.

prob requests that the t statistic and p-value be displayed. The degrees of freedom for the t statistic are $d = $ total number of sampled PSUs minus the total number of strata (regardless of the number of terms in the model). If no display options are specified, then, by default, the t statistic and p-value are displayed.

ci requests that confidence intervals be displayed. If no display options are specified, then, by default, confidence intervals are displayed.

deff requests that the design-effect measure deff be displayed; see [R] **svymean** for details.

deft requests that the design-effect measure deft be displayed; see [R] **svymean** for details.

The following options apply to only one or some of the commands:

offset(*varname*) specifies that *varname* is to be included in the model with coefficient constrained to be 1.

exposure(*varname*) (svypois only) is equivalent to specifying offset(ln(*varname*)).

asis, see [R] **probit**.

basecategory(*#*) (svymlog only) specifies the value of the dependent variable that is to be treated as the base category. The default is to choose the most frequent category.

maximize_options control the maximization process; see [R] **maximize**. You may want to specify the log option when estimating models on large datasets to view the progress of the maximum-likelihood estimation steps. You should never have to specify the other *maximize_options*.

Options for predict

See the entry for the nonsurvey version of the command for a description of the corresponding options for predict. Note that some of the options for predict after the nonsurvey version may not be available after the svy version.

Remarks

We illustrate a few of the svy estimation commands with some examples.

▷ Example

We use data from the Second National Health and Nutrition Examination Survey (NHANES II) (McDowell et al. 1981) as our example. First, we set the strata, psu, and pweight variables.

```
. svyset pweight leadwt
. svyset strata stratid
. svyset psu psuid
```

Once the strata, psu, and pweight variables are set, we can use svyreg just as we would regress with nonsurvey data. See [R] **svyset** for details on setting, unsetting, and displaying these variables.

```
. svyreg loglead age female black orace region2-region4 smsa1 smsa2
Survey linear regression

pweight:  leadwt                         Number of obs    =      4948
Strata:   stratid                        Number of strata =        31
PSU:      psuid                          Number of PSUs   =        62
                                         Population size   = 1.129e+08
                                         F(  9,     23)   =    134.62
                                         Prob > F          =    0.0000
                                         R-squared         =    0.2443

------------------------------------------------------------------------------
    loglead |      Coef.   Std. Err.       t    P>|t|     [95% Conf. Interval]
------------+-----------------------------------------------------------------
        age |   .0028425   .0004282      6.638   0.000     .0019691    .0037159
     female |  -.3641964   .0112612    -32.341   0.000    -.3871637   -.3412291
      black |   .1462126   .0277811      5.263   0.000     .0895527    .2028725
      orace |  -.0754489   .0370151     -2.038   0.050    -.1509418    .0000439
    region2 |  -.0206953   .0456639     -0.453   0.654    -.1138274    .0724369
    region3 |  -.1272598   .0528061     -2.410   0.022    -.2349586   -.0195611
    region4 |  -.0374591   .0422001     -0.888   0.382    -.1235268    .0486085
      smsa1 |   .1038586   .0432539      2.401   0.023     .0156417    .1920755
      smsa2 |   .0995561   .0365985      2.720   0.011     .0249129    .1741993
      _cons |   2.623901   .0421096     62.311   0.000     2.538018    2.709784
------------------------------------------------------------------------------
```

◁

If we wish to test joint hypotheses after the regression, we can use the svytest command; see [R] **svytest**.

Running logistic regressions with svylogit is as simple as running the logit command. Note that, just like logit, the dependent variable should be a 0/1 variable (or, more precisely, a zero/nonzero variable).

▷ Example

```
. svylogit highbp height weight age age2 female black
(sum of wgt is    1.1716e+08)
Survey logistic regression
```

pweight:	finalwgt	Number of obs	=	10351
Strata:	stratid	Number of strata =		31
PSU:	psuid	Number of PSUs	=	62
		Population size	=	1.172e+08
		F(6, 26)	=	87.70
		Prob > F	=	0.0000

highbp	Coef.	Std. Err.	t	P>|t|	[95% Conf. Interval]
height	-.0325996	.0058727	-5.551	0.000	-.0445771	-.0206222
weight	.049074	.0031966	15.352	0.000	.0425545	.0555936
age	.1541151	.0208709	7.384	0.000	.1115486	.1966815
age2	-.0010746	.0002025	-5.306	0.000	-.0014877	-.0006616
female	-.356497	.0885354	-4.027	0.000	-.537066	-.175928
black	.3429301	.1409005	2.434	0.021	.0555615	.6302986
_cons	-4.89574	1.159135	-4.224	0.000	-7.259813	-2.531668

We can redisplay the results expressed as odds ratios.

```
. svylogit, or
Survey logistic regression
```

pweight:	finalwgt	Number of obs	=	10351
Strata:	stratid	Number of strata =		31
PSU:	psuid	Number of PSUs	=	62
		Population size	=	1.172e+08
		F(6, 26)	=	87.70
		Prob > F	=	0.0000

highbp	Odds Ratio	Std. Err.	t	P>|t|	[95% Conf. Interval]
height	.967926	.0056843	-5.551	0.000	.9564019	.979589
weight	1.050298	.0033574	15.352	0.000	1.043473	1.057168
age	1.166625	.0243485	7.384	0.000	1.118008	1.217356
age2	.998926	.0002023	-5.306	0.000	.9985135	.9993386
female	.7001246	.0619858	-4.027	0.000	.5844605	.8386784
black	1.40907	.1985388	2.434	0.021	1.057134	1.878171

svylc can be used to estimate the sum of the coefficients for female and black.

```
. svylc female + black
( 1)  female + black = 0.0
```

highbp	Coef.	Std. Err.	t	P>|t|	[95% Conf. Interval]
(1)	-.0135669	.1653936	-0.082	0.935	-.3508894	.3237555

This result is more easily interpreted as an odds ratio.

```
. svylc female + black, or
 ( 1)  female + black = 0.0
```

highbp	Odds Ratio	Std. Err.	t	P>|t|	[95% Conf. Interval]
(1)	.9865247	.1631648	-0.082	0.935	.7040616 1.382309

The odds ratio 0.987 is an estimate of the ratio of the odds of having high blood pressure for black females over the odds for our reference category of nonblack males (controlling for height, weight, and age). You now know enough to use svylc for odds ratios; see [R] **svylc** for its other uses; see [R] **lincom** for more examples of odds ratios.

◁

▷ Example

To estimate a model for a subpopulation, the subpop() option is used:

```
. svylogit highlead age female, subpop(black) or
(sum of wgt is    1.0490e+07)
Survey logistic regression
```

pweight: leadwt	Number of obs = 4948
Strata: stratid	Number of strata = 31
PSU: psuid	Number of PSUs = 62
	Population size = 1.129e+08
Subpopulation no. of obs = 506	F(2, 30) = 13.32
Subpopulation size = 10490430	Prob > F = 0.0001

highlead	Odds Ratio	Std. Err.	t	P>|t|	[95% Conf. Interval]
age	1.015155	.0082557	1.850	0.074	.9984561 1.032133
female	.0281831	.0204156	-4.927	0.000	.0064322 .1234857

Note that this time we specified the **or** option when we first issued the command.

◁

The subpop(*varname*) option takes a 0/1 variable; the subpopulation of interest is defined by *varname* = 1. All other members of the sample not in the subpopulation are indicated by *varname* = 0.

If a person's subpopulation status is unknown, then *varname* should be set to missing ('.') and those observations will be omitted from the analysis as they should be. For instance, in the preceding example, if person's race is unknown, **race** should be coded as missing rather than as nonblack (**race** = 0).

Note that using 'if black==1' to model the subpopulation would not give the same result. All the discussion in the section *Warning about the use of if and in* in [R] **svymean** applies to the variance estimates for **svyreg**, **svylogit**, and **svyprobt** as well.

❑ Technical Note

Actually, the subpop(*varname*) option takes a zero/nonzero variable; the subpopulation of interest is defined by *varname* ≠ 0 and not missing. All other members of the sample not in the subpopulation are indicated by *varname* = 0. But 0, 1, and missing are typically the only values used for the subpop() variable.

❑

▷ Example

In the NHANES II dataset, we have a variable `health` containing self-reported health status, which takes on the values 1–5, with 1 being "poor" and 5 being "excellent". Since this is an ordered categorical variable, it makes sense to model it using `svyolog` or `svyoprob`. As predictors, we use basic demographic variables: `female` (1 if female, 0 if male), `black` (1 if black, 0 otherwise), `age`, and `age2` ($=$ age^2):

```
. svyolog health female black age age2
Survey ordered logistic regression
pweight:  finalwgt                        Number of obs    =       10335
Strata:   stratid                         Number of strata =          31
PSU:      psuid                           Number of PSUs   =          62
                                          Population size   = 1.170e+08
                                          F(  4,    28)    =      223.27
                                          Prob > F         =      0.0000
```

health	Coef.	Std. Err.	t	P>|t|	[95% Conf. Interval]	
female	-.1615219	.0523678	-3.084	0.004	-.2683266	-.0547171
black	-.986568	.0790276	-12.484	0.000	-1.147746	-.8253901
age	-.0119491	.0082974	-1.440	0.160	-.0288717	.0049736
age2	-.0003234	.000091	-3.552	0.001	-.000509	-.0001377
_cut1	-4.566229	.1632559	-27.970	0.000	-4.899192	-4.233266
_cut2	-3.057415	.1699943	-17.985	0.000	-3.404121	-2.710709
_cut3	-1.520596	.1714341	-8.870	0.000	-1.870238	-1.170954
_cut4	-.242785	.1703964	-1.425	0.164	-.5903107	.1047407

According to our model, females give self-reports of poorer health status than males, blacks report much poorer health status than nonblacks, and older people report worse health than younger.

If we model the categories of self-reported health status as unordered categories using `svymlog`, we get the following results:

(Continued on next page)

```
. svymlog health female black age age2
Survey multinomial logistic regression
pweight:   finalwgt                        Number of obs    =      10335
Strata:    stratid                         Number of strata =         31
PSU:       psuid                           Number of PSUs   =         62
                                           Population size  = 1.170e+08
                                           F(  16,      16) =      36.41
                                           Prob > F         =     0.0000
```

health	Coef.	Std. Err.	t	P>|t|	[95% Conf.	Interval]
poor						
female	-.1983735	.1072747	-1.849	0.074	-.4171617	.0204147
black	.8964694	.1797728	4.987	0.000	.5298203	1.263119
age	.0990246	.032111	3.084	0.004	.0335338	.1645155
age2	-.0004749	.0003209	-1.480	0.149	-.0011294	.0001796
_cons	-5.475074	.7468576	-7.331	0.000	-6.9983	-3.951848
fair						
female	.1782371	.0726556	2.453	0.020	.030055	.3264193
black	.4429445	.122667	3.611	0.001	.1927635	.6931256
age	.0024576	.0172236	0.143	0.887	-.0326702	.0375853
age2	.0002875	.0001684	1.707	0.098	-.0000559	.000631
_cons	-1.819561	.4018153	-4.528	0.000	-2.639069	-1.000053
good						
female	-.0458251	.074169	-0.618	0.541	-.1970938	.1054437
black	-.7532011	.1105444	-6.814	0.000	-.9786579	-.5277443
age	-.061369	.009794	-6.266	0.000	-.081344	-.0413939
age2	.0004166	.0001077	3.869	0.001	.000197	.0006363
_cons	1.815323	.1996917	9.091	0.000	1.408049	2.222597
excell						
female	-.222799	.0754205	-2.954	0.006	-.3766202	-.0689778
black	-.991647	.1238806	-8.005	0.000	-1.244303	-.7389909
age	-.0293573	.0137789	-2.131	0.041	-.0574595	-.001255
age2	-.0000674	.0001505	-0.448	0.657	-.0003744	.0002396
_cons	1.499683	.286143	5.241	0.000	.9160909	2.083276

```
(Outcome health==average is the comparison group)
```

We see an interesting pattern here. It suggests that females are less likely to report the extremes of health than males: females are less likely to report poor health and less likely to report excellent health. The results for blacks, on the other hand, are monotonic: the better the health rating, the less likely they are to report it, relative to nonblacks.

Just like mlogit, svymlog can display results as relative risk ratios, either at the time of estimation or when redisplaying results:

```
. svymlog, rrr
```
   (output omitted)

At the time of estimation, one can also specify the base category for the comparison:

```
. svymlog health female black age age2, base(1)
```
   (output omitted)

◁

Saved Results

The svy estimation commands save in e():

Scalars
e(N)	number of observations m
e(N_strata)	number of strata L
e(N_psu)	number of sampled PSUs n
e(N_pop)	estimate of population size $\widehat{M}$
e(N_subpop)	estimate of subpopulation size
e(N_sub)	subpopulation number of observations
e(df_m)	model degrees of freedom
e(df_r)	variance degrees of freedom $= n - L$
e(F)	model F statistic
e(k_cat)	number of categories (svymlog, svyolog, svyoprob)
e(basecat)	base category value of dependent variable (svymlog)
e(ibasecat)	base category number (svymlog)

Macros
e(cmd)	command name (e.g., svyreg)
e(depvar)	dependent variable name
e(wtype)	weight type
e(wexp)	weight variable or expression
e(strata)	strata() variable
e(psu)	psu() variable
e(fpc)	fpc() variable
e(offset)	offset() variable
e(predict)	program used to implement predict

Matrices
e(b)	vector of estimates $\widehat{\beta}$
e(V)	design-based (co)variance estimates $\widehat{V}$
e(V_srs)	simple-random-sampling-without-replacement (co)variance $\widehat{V}_{\mathrm{srswor}}$
e(V_srswr)	simple-random-sampling-with-replacement (co)variance $\widehat{V}_{\mathrm{srswr}}$ (only created when fpc() option is specified)
e(deff)	vector of deff estimates
e(deft)	vector of deft estimates
e(cat)	vector of category values (svymlog, svyolog, svyoprob)

Functions
e(sample)	marks estimation sample

Methods and Formulas

All of the svy estimators are implemented as ado-files that call _robust; see [R] _robust.

These commands use a variant on the basic weighted-point-estimation methods used by svytotal. They use "linearization"-based variance estimators that are natural extensions of the variance estimator used in svytotal. For general methodological background on regression and generalized-linear-model analyses of complex survey data, see, for example, Binder (1983), Cochran (1977), Fuller (1975), Godambe (1991), Kish and Frankel (1974), Särndal et al. (1992), Shao (1996), and Skinner (1989). The notation and development presented below is adapted from Binder (1983).

We use here the same notation as in the *Methods and Formulas* section of [R] **svymean**; that section should be read first.

Linear regression

We let (h, i, j) index the elements in the population, where $h = 1, \ldots, L$ are the strata, $i = 1, \ldots, N_h$ are the PSUs in stratum h, and $j = 1, \ldots, M_{hi}$ are the elements in PSU (h, i). The regression coefficients $\beta = (\beta_0, \beta_1, \ldots, \beta_k)$ are viewed as fixed finite-population parameters that we wish to estimate. These parameters are defined with respect to an outcome variable Y_{hij} and a $k+1$-dimensional row vector of explanatory variables $X_{hij} = (X_{hij0}, \ldots, X_{hijk})$. As in nonsurvey work, we often have X_{hij0} identically equal to unity, so that β_0 is an intercept coefficient. Within a finite-population context, we can formally define the regression coefficient vector β as the solution to the vector estimating equation

$$G(\beta) = X'Y - X'X\beta = 0 \tag{1}$$

where Y is the vector of outcomes for the full population and X is the matrix of explanatory variables for the full population. Assuming $(X'X)^{-1}$ exists, the solution to (1) is $\beta = (X'X)^{-1}X'Y$.

Given observations (y_{hij}, x_{hij}) collected through a complex sample design, we need to estimate β in a way that accounts for the sample design. To do this, note that the matrix factors $X'X$ and $X'Y$ can be viewed as matrix population totals. For example, $X'Y = \sum_{h=1}^{L} \sum_{i=1}^{N_h} \sum_{j=1}^{M_{hi}} X_{hij} Y_{hij}$. Thus, we estimate $X'X$ and $X'Y$ with the weighted estimators

$$\widehat{X'X} = \sum_{h=1}^{L} \sum_{i=1}^{n_h} \sum_{j=1}^{m_{hi}} w_{hij} x'_{hij} x_{hij} = X'_s W X_s$$

and

$$\widehat{X'Y} = \sum_{h=1}^{L} \sum_{i=1}^{n_h} \sum_{j=1}^{m_{hi}} w_{hij} x'_{hij} y_{hij} = X'_s W Y_s$$

where X_s is the matrix of explanatory variables for the sample, Y_s is the outcome vector for the sample, and $W = \text{diag}(w_{hij})$ is a diagonal matrix containing the sampling weights w_{hij}. The corresponding coefficient estimator is

$$\widehat{\beta} = (\widehat{X'X})^{-1} \widehat{X'Y} = (X'_s W X_s)^{-1} X'_s W Y_s \tag{2}$$

Note that equation (2) is what the **regress** command with **aweight**s or **iweight**s computes for point estimates.

The coefficient estimator $\widehat{\beta}$ can also be defined as the solution to the weighted sample estimating equation

$$\widehat{G}(\beta) = \widehat{X'Y} - \widehat{X'X}\beta = X'_s W Y_s - X'_s W X_s \beta = 0$$

We can write $\widehat{G}(\beta)$ as

$$\widehat{G}(\beta) = \sum_{h=1}^{L} \sum_{i=1}^{n_h} \sum_{j=1}^{m_{hi}} w_{hij} d_{hij} \tag{3}$$

where $d_{hij} = x'_{hij} e_{hij}$ and $e_{hij} = y_{hij} - x_{hij}\beta$ is the regression residual associated with sample unit (h, i, j). Thus, $\widehat{G}(\beta)$ can be viewed as a special case of a total estimator.

Our variance estimator for $\widehat{\beta}$ is based on the following "linearization" argument. A first-order Taylor expansion shows that

$$\widehat{\beta} - \beta \doteq -\left[\frac{\partial \widehat{G}(\beta)}{\partial \beta}\right]^{-1} \widehat{G}(\beta)$$

Thus, our variance estimator for $\widehat{\beta}$ is

$$\widehat{V}(\widehat{\beta}) = \left\{ \left[\frac{\partial \widehat{G}(\beta)}{\partial \beta} \right]^{-1} \widehat{V}(\widehat{G}(\beta)) \left[\frac{\partial \widehat{G}(\beta)}{\partial \beta} \right]^{-\mathrm{T}} \right\} \Bigg|_{\beta=\widehat{\beta}}$$

$$= [X_s' W X_s]^{-1} \widehat{V}(\widehat{G}(\beta)) \big|_{\beta=\widehat{\beta}} [X_s' W X_s]^{-1}$$

Viewing $\widehat{G}(\beta)$ as a total estimator according to equation (3), the variance estimator $\widehat{V}(\widehat{G}(\beta))\big|_{\beta=\widehat{\beta}}$ can be computed using equation (3) from [R] **svymean** with y_{hij} replaced by d_{hij} and with $\widehat{\beta}$ used to estimate e_{hij}.

Pseudo-maximum-likelihood estimators

To develop notation for our pseudo-maximum-likelihood estimators, suppose that we observed (Y_{hij}, X_{hij}) for the entire population, and that (Y_{hij}, X_{hij}) arose from a certain likelihood model (e.g., a logistic distribution). Let $l(\beta; Y_{hij}, X_{hij})$ be the associated "log-likelihood" under this model. Then, for our finite population, we define the parameter β by the vector estimating equation

$$G(\beta) = \sum_{h=1}^{L} \sum_{i=1}^{N_h} \sum_{j=1}^{M_{hi}} S(\beta; Y_{hij}, X_{hij}) = 0$$

where $S = \partial l / \partial \beta$ is the score vector; i.e., the first derivative with respect to β of $l(\beta; Y_{hij}, X_{hij})$. Then, the "pseudo-maximum-likelihood" estimator $\widehat{\beta}$ is the solution to the weighted sample estimating equation

$$\widehat{G}(\beta) = \sum_{h=1}^{L} \sum_{i=1}^{n_h} \sum_{j=1}^{m_{hi}} w_{hij} S(\beta; y_{hij}, x_{hij}) = 0 \tag{4}$$

Note that the solution $\widehat{\beta}$ of equation (4) is what the nonsurvey version of the command with `iweights` produces for point estimates.

Again, we use a first-order matrix Taylor series expansion to produce the variance estimator for $\widehat{\beta}$

$$\widehat{V}(\widehat{\beta}) = \left\{ \left[\frac{\partial \widehat{G}(\beta)}{\partial \beta} \right]^{-1} \widehat{V}(\widehat{G}(\beta)) \left[\frac{\partial \widehat{G}(\beta)}{\partial \beta} \right]^{-\mathrm{T}} \right\} \Bigg|_{\beta=\widehat{\beta}} = H^{-1} \widehat{V}(\widehat{G}(\beta)) \big|_{\beta=\widehat{\beta}} H^{-1}$$

where H is the Hessian for the weighted sample log-likelihood. We can write $\widehat{G}(\beta)$ as

$$\widehat{G}(\beta) = \sum_{h=1}^{L} \sum_{i=1}^{n_h} \sum_{j=1}^{m_{hi}} w_{hij} d_{hij}$$

where $d_{hij} = s_{hij} x_{hij}$ and s_{hij} is the score index for element (h, i, j). The term s_{hij} is computed by rewriting the sample log-likelihood $l(\beta; y_{hij}, x_{hij})$ as a function of $x_{hij}\beta$:

$$s_{hij} = \frac{\partial l(x_{hij}\beta; y_{hij})}{\partial (x_{hij}\beta)}$$

Thus, again, $\widehat{G}(\beta)$ can be viewed as a special case of a total estimator, and the variance estimator $\widehat{V}(\widehat{G}(\beta))|_{\beta=\widehat{\beta}}$ is computed using equation (3) from [R] **svymean** with y_{hij} replaced by d_{hij} and with $\widehat{\beta}$ used to estimate s_{hij}.

Acknowledgments

The `svyreg`, `svylogit`, and `svyprobt` commands were developed in collaboration with John L. Eltinge, Department of Statistics, Texas A&M University. We thank him for his invaluable assistance.

We thank Wayne Johnson of the National Center for Health Statistics for providing the NHANES II dataset.

References

Binder, D. A. 1983. On the variances of asymptotically normal estimators from complex surveys. *International Statistical Review* 51: 279–292.

Cochran, W. G. 1977. *Sampling Techniques*. 3d ed. New York: John Wiley & Sons.

Eltinge, J. L. and W. M. Sribney. 1996. svy4: Linear, logistic, and probit regressions for survey data. *Stata Technical Bulletin* 31: 26–31. Reprinted in *Stata Technical Bulletin Reprints*, vol. 6, pp. 239–245.

Fuller, W. A. 1975. Regression analysis for sample survey. *Sankhyā, Series C* 37: 117–132.

Godambe, V. P. ed. 1991. *Estimating Functions*. Oxford: Clarendon Press.

Gonzalez J. F., Jr., N. Krauss, and C. Scott. 1992. Estimation in the 1988 National Maternal and Infant Health Survey. In *Proceedings of the Section on Statistics Education, American Statistical Association*, 343–348.

Johnson, W. 1995. Variance estimation for the NMIHS. Technical document. National Center for Health Statistics, Hyattsville, MD.

Kish, L. and M. R. Frankel. 1974. Inference from complex samples. *Journal of the Royal Statistical Society* B 36: 1–37.

Korn, E. L., and B. I. Graubard. 1990. Simultaneous testing of regression coefficients with complex survey data: use of Bonferroni *t* statistics. *The American Statistician* 44: 270–276.

McDowell, A., A. Engel, J. T. Massey, and K. Maurer. 1981. Plan and operation of the Second National Health and Nutrition Examination Survey, 1976–1980. *Vital and Health Statistics* 15(1). National Center for Health Statistics, Hyattsville, MD.

Särndal, C.-E., B. Swensson, and J. Wretman. 1992. *Model Assisted Survey Sampling*. New York: Springer-Verlag.

Shao, J. 1996. Resampling methods for sample surveys (with discussion). *Statistics* 27: 203–254.

Skinner, C. J. 1989. Introduction to Part A. In *Analysis of Complex Surveys*, ed. C. J. Skinner, D. Holt, and T. M. F. Smith, 23–58. New York: John Wiley & Sons.

Also See

Complementary:	[R] **svydes**, [R] **svylc**, [R] **svymean**, [R] **svyset**, [R] **svytab**, [R] **svytest**
Related:	[R] **_robust**
Background:	[U] **30 Overview of survey estimation**,
	[R] **svy**

Title

svydes — Describe survey data

Syntax

svydes [*varlist*] [*weight*] [if *exp*] [in *range*] [, str̲ata(*varname*) psu(*varname*)

    fpc(*varname*) byp̲su]

pweights and iweights are allowed; see [U] **14.1.6 weight**.

Description

svydes displays a table that describes the strata and the primary sampling units for sample survey data.

Options

str̲ata(*varname*) specifies the name of a variable (numeric or string) that contains stratum identifiers. strata() can also be specified with the svyset command; see [R] **svyset**.

psu(*varname*) specifies the name of a variable (numeric or string) that contains identifiers for the primary sampling unit (i.e., the cluster). psu() can also be specified with the svyset command.

fpc(*varname*) can be set here or with the svyset command. If an fpc variable has been specified, svydes checks the fpc variable for missing values. Other than this, svydes does not use the fpc variable. See [R] **svymean** for details on fpc.

bypsu specifies that results be displayed for each PSU in the dataset; that is, a separate line of output is produced for every PSU. This option can only be used when a PSU variable has been specified using the psu() option or set with svyset.

Note: Weights are checked for missing values, but are not otherwise used by svydes.

Remarks

Sample-survey data are typically stratified. Within each stratum, there are primary sampling units (PSUs), which may be either clusters of observations or individual observations.

svydes displays a table that describes the strata and PSUs in the dataset. By default, one row of the table is produced for each stratum. Displayed for each stratum are the number of PSUs, the range and mean of the number of observations per PSU, and the total number of observations. If the bypsu option is specified, svydes will display the number of observations in each PSU for every PSU in the dataset.

If a *varlist* is specified, svydes will report the number of PSUs that contain at least one observation with complete data (i.e., no missing values) for all variables in the *varlist*. These are precisely the PSUs that would be used to compute estimates for the variables in *varlist* using the svy estimation commands: svymean, svytotal, svyratio, svyprop, svytab, or any of the commands described in [R] **svy estimators**.

The variance estimation formulas for the svy estimation commands require at least two PSUs per stratum. If there are some strata with only a single PSU, an error message is displayed:

```
. svymean x
stratum with only one PSU detected
r(499);
. svydes x
```

The stratum (or strata) with only one PSU can be located from the table produced by svydes x. After locating this stratum, it can be "collapsed" into an adjacent stratum, and then variance estimates can be computed. See the following examples for an illustration of the procedure.

For details on the svy estimation commands, see [R] **svymean** and [R] **svy estimators**.

▷ Example

We use data from the Second National Health and Nutrition Examination Survey (NHANES II) (McDowell et al. 1981) as our example. First, we set the strata, psu, and pweight variables.

```
. svyset strata stratid
. svyset psu psuid
. svyset pweight finalwgt
```

Typing svydes will show us the strata and PSU arrangement of the dataset.

```
. svydes
pweight:  finalwgt
Strata:   stratid
PSU:      psuid
```

Strata stratid	#PSUs	#Obs	#Obs per PSU		
			min	mean	max
1	2	380	165	190.0	215
2	2	185	67	92.5	118
3	2	348	149	174.0	199
4	2	460	229	230.0	231
5	2	252	105	126.0	147
6	2	298	131	149.0	167
7	2	476	206	238.0	270
8	2	338	158	169.0	180
9	2	244	100	122.0	144
10	2	262	119	131.0	143
11	2	275	120	137.5	155
12	2	314	144	157.0	170
13	2	342	154	171.0	188
14	2	405	200	202.5	205
15	2	380	189	190.0	191
16	2	336	159	168.0	177
17	2	393	180	196.5	213
18	2	359	144	179.5	215
20	2	285	125	142.5	160
21	2	214	102	107.0	112
22	2	301	128	150.5	173
23	2	341	159	170.5	182
24	2	438	205	219.0	233
25	2	256	116	128.0	140
26	2	261	129	130.5	132
27	2	283	139	141.5	144
28	2	299	136	149.5	163
29	2	503	215	251.5	288

```
      30          2        365        166      182.5        199
      31          2        308        143      154.0        165
      32          2        450        211      225.0        239
   --------   --------   --------   --------   --------   --------
      31         62      10351         67      167.0        288
```

Our NHANES II dataset has 31 strata (stratum 19 is missing) and 2 PSUs per stratum.

The variable hdresult contains serum levels of high-density lipoproteins (HDL). If we try to estimate the mean of hdresult, we get an error.

```
. svymean hdresult
stratum with only one PSU detected
r(499);
```

Running svydes with hdresult as its *varlist* will show us which stratum or strata have only one PSU.

```
. svydes hdresult

pweight:   finalwgt
Strata:    stratid
PSU:       psuid
                                    #Obs with  #Obs with    #Obs per included PSU
   Strata    #PSUs     #PSUs     complete    missing   ---------------------------
   stratid  included   omitted     data        data      min      mean       max
   --------  --------  --------  --------   --------  --------  --------  --------
       1          1         1        114        266       114      114.0       114
       2          1         1         98         87        98       98.0        98
       3          2         0        277         71       116      138.5       161
       4          2         0        340        120       160      170.0       180
       5          2         0        173         79        81       86.5        92
       6          2         0        255         43       116      127.5       139
       7          2         0        409         67       191      204.5       218
       8          2         0        299         39       129      149.5       170
       9          2         0        218         26        85      109.0       133
      10          2         0        233         29       103      116.5       130
      11          2         0        238         37        97      119.0       141
      12          2         0        275         39       121      137.5       154
      13          2         0        297         45       123      148.5       174
      14          2         0        355         50       167      177.5       188
      15          2         0        329         51       151      164.5       178
      16          2         0        280         56       134      140.0       146
      17          2         0        352         41       155      176.0       197
      18          2         0        335         24       135      167.5       200
      20          2         0        240         45        95      120.0       145
      21          2         0        198         16        91       99.0       107
      22          2         0        263         38       116      131.5       147
      23          2         0        304         37       143      152.0       161
      24          2         0        388         50       182      194.0       206
      25          2         0        239         17       106      119.5       133
      26          2         0        240         21       119      120.0       121
      27          2         0        259         24       127      129.5       132
      28          2         0        284         15       131      142.0       153
      29          2         0        440         63       193      220.0       247
      30          2         0        326         39       147      163.0       179
      31          2         0        279         29       121      139.5       158
      32          2         0        383         67       180      191.5       203
   --------  --------  --------  --------   --------  --------  --------  --------
      31         60         2       8720       1631        81      145.3       247
                                 ------------------
                                        10351
```

Both of stratid $= 1$ and stratid $= 2$ have only one PSU with nonmissing values of hdresult. Since this dataset has only 62 PSUs, the bypsu option will give a manageable amount of output:

```
. svydes hdresult, bypsu

pweight:  finalwgt
Strata:   stratid
PSU:      psuid
                         #Obs with  #Obs with
    Strata       PSU      complete    missing
    stratid     psuid       data       data
    --------   --------   --------   --------
         1          1          0        215
         1          2        114         51
         2          1         98         20
         2          2          0         67
         3          1        161         38
         3          2        116         33
(output omitted)
        32          1        180         59
        32          2        203          8
    --------   --------   --------   --------
        31         62       8720       1631
               -------------------
                             10351
```

It is rather striking that there are two PSUs without any values for hdresult. All other PSUs have only a moderate number of missing values. Obviously, in a case such as this, a data analyst should first try to ascertain the reason why these data are missing. The answer here (Johnson 1995) is that HDL measurements could not be collected until the third survey location. Thus, there are no hdresult data for the first two locations: stratid $= 1$, psuid $= 1$ and stratid $= 2$, psuid $= 2$.

Assuming that we wish to go ahead and analyze the hdresult data, we must "collapse" strata—that is, merge them together—so that every stratum has at least two PSUs with some nonmissing values. We can accomplish this by collapsing stratid $= 1$ into stratid $= 2$. To perform the stratum collapse, we create a new strata identifier newstr and a new PSU identifier newpsu. This is easy to do using basic commands in Stata.

```
. gen newstr = stratid
. gen newpsu = psuid
. replace newpsu = psuid + 2 if stratid==1
(380 real changes made)
. replace newstr = 2 if stratid==1
(380 real changes made)
```

We set the new strata and PSU variables.

```
. svyset strata newstr
. svyset psu newpsu
```

We use svydes to check what we have done.

```
. svydes hdresult, bypsu
pweight:  finalwgt
Strata:   newstr
PSU:      newpsu
                      #Obs with  #Obs with
     Strata     PSU   complete    missing
     newstr  newpsu       data       data
   --------  --------  --------   --------
          2        1        98         20
          2        2         0         67
          2        3         0        215
          2        4       114         51
          3        1       161         38
          3        2       116         33
```
(output omitted)
```
         32        1       180         59
         32        2       203          8
   --------  --------  --------   --------
         30       62      8720       1631
                      ------------------
                              10351
```

The new stratum, `newstr = 2`, has 4 PSUs, 2 of which contain some nonmissing values of `hdresult`. This is sufficient to allow us to estimate the mean of `hdresult`.

```
. svymean hdresult
Survey mean estimation
pweight:  finalwgt                    Number of obs   =       8720
Strata:   newstr                      Number of strata =        30
PSU:      newpsu                      Number of PSUs  =         60
                                      Population size = 98725345

------------------------------------------------------------------------
      Mean |   Estimate   Std. Err.   [95% Conf. Interval]       Deff
-----------+------------------------------------------------------------
  hdresult |   49.67141   .3830147   48.88919   50.45364    6.257131
------------------------------------------------------------------------
```
◁

Methods and Formulas

`svydes` is implemented as an ado-file.

References

Eltinge, J. L. and W. M. Sribney. 1996. svy3: Describing survey data: sampling design and missing data. *Stata Technical Bulletin* 31: 23–26. Reprinted in *Stata Technical Bulletin Reprints*, vol. 6, pp. 235–239.

Johnson, C. L. 1995. Personal communication.

McDowell, A., A. Engel, J. T. Massey, and K. Maurer. 1981. Plan and operation of the Second National Health and Nutrition Examination Survey, 1976–1980. *Vital and Health Statistics* 15(1). National Center for Health Statistics, Hyattsville, MD.

Also See

Complementary: [R] **svy estimators**, [R] **svylc**, [R] **svymean**, [R] **svyset**, [R] **svytab**, [R] **svytest**

Background: [U] **30 Overview of survey estimation**,
        [R] **svy**

Title

svylc — Estimate linear combinations after survey estimation

Syntax

svylc [*exp*] [, show or irr rrr eform level(#) deff deft meff meft]

Description

svylc produces estimates for linear combinations of parameters after a svy estimation command; i.e., any of the commands svymean, svytotal, svyratio, or the commands described in [R] svy estimators.

Estimating differences of subpopulation means, for example, can be done by running svymean with a by() option, and then running svylc. The svylc command computes estimates of linear combinations of parameters, whether means, total, ratios, proportions, or regression coefficients.

Used after svylogit, it will compute odds ratios for any covariate group relative to another. After svymlog, it can compute relative risk ratios, and after svypois, it can compute incident rate ratios. svylc is the equivalent of lincom for survey data. See [R] **lincom** for a thorough coverage of odds ratios.

Options

show requests that the labeling syntax for the previous svy estimates be displayed. This is useful when the svy estimation command produced estimates for subpopulations using the by() option. When show is specified, no expression *exp* is specified.

or, irr, rrr, and eform all do the same thing; they all report coefficient estimates as $\exp(\widehat{\beta})$ rather than $\widehat{\beta}$. Standard errors and confidence intervals are similarly transformed. The only difference is how the output is labeled: or gives "Odds Ratio" (appropriate for svylogit), rrr gives "Relative Rate Ratio" (appropriate for svymlog), irr gives "Incidence Rate Ratio" (appropriate for svypois), and eform gives a generic label.

level(#) specifies the confidence level (i.e., nominal coverage rate), in percent, for confidence intervals. The default is level(95) or as set by set level; see [U] **23.5 Specifying the width of confidence intervals**.

deff requests that the design-effect measure deff be displayed.

deft requests that the design-effect measure deft be displayed. See [R] **svymean** for a discussion of deff and deft.

meff requests that the meff measure of misspecification effects be displayed.

meft requests that the meft measure of misspecification effects be displayed. See [R] **svymean** for a discussion of meff and meft.

Remarks

Remarks are presented under the headings

> The use of svylc when there are no by() subpopulations
> Missing data: The complete and available options
> The use of svylc after svy model estimators
> Subpopulations with one by() variable
> Subpopulations with two or more by() variables
> The use of svylc after svyratio

By default, svylc computes the point estimate, standard error, t statistic, p-value, and confidence interval for the specified linear combination. Design effects (deff and deft) and misspecification effects (meff and meft) can be optionally displayed; see [R] **svymean** for a detailed description of these options.

The use of svylc when there are no by() subpopulations

▷ Example

We use data from the Second National Health and Nutrition Examination Survey (NHANES II) (McDowell et al. 1981) as our example. Suppose that we wish to estimate the difference of the means of systolic (variable bpsystol) and diastolic (variable bpdiast) blood pressures. First, we estimate the means, and then we use svylc.

```
. svymean bpsystol bpdiast

Survey mean estimation

pweight:  finalwgt                    Number of obs    =      10351
Strata:   stratid                     Number of strata =         31
PSU:      psuid                       Number of PSUs   =         62
                                      Population size  = 1.172e+08

------------------------------------------------------------------------
    Mean |  Estimate   Std. Err.   [95% Conf. Interval]       Deff
---------+--------------------------------------------------------------
bpsystol |  126.9458    .603462    125.715    128.1766     8.230475
 bpdiast |  81.01726   .5090314   79.97909    82.05544    16.38656
------------------------------------------------------------------------

. svylc bpsystol - bpdiast
 ( 1)  bpsystol - bpdiast = 0.0

------------------------------------------------------------------------
    Mean |  Estimate   Std. Err.      t     P>|t|    [95% Conf. Interval]
---------+--------------------------------------------------------------
     (1) |  45.92852   .2988395   153.690   0.000    45.31903    46.53801
------------------------------------------------------------------------
```

We can also specify any of the options deff, deft, meff, or meft, or change the confidence level (i.e., nominal coverage rate) of the confidence interval.

```
. svylc bpsystol - bpdiast, level(90) deff meff
( 1)  bpsystol - bpdiast = 0.0
```

Mean	Estimate	Std. Err.	t	P>|t|	[90% Conf. Interval]	
(1)	45.92852	.2988395	153.690	0.000	45.42183	46.43521

Mean	Deff	Meff
(1)	3.835532	3.087148

svylc works in the same manner after using the subpop option.

```
. svymean bpsystol bpdiast, subpop(female)

Survey mean estimation
```

pweight:	finalwgt		Number of obs	= 10351
Strata:	stratid		Number of strata =	31
PSU:	psuid		Number of PSUs =	62
Subpop.:	female==1		Population size	= 1.172e+08

Mean	Estimate	Std. Err.	[95% Conf. Interval]		Deff
bpsystol	124.2027	.7051858	122.7644	125.6409	5.162487
bpdiast	79.03227	.5207306	77.97023	80.09431	8.973799

```
. svylc bpsystol - bpdiast
( 1)  bpsystol - bpdiast = 0.0
```

Mean	Estimate	Std. Err.	t	P>|t|	[95% Conf. Interval]	
(1)	45.17039	.4040852	111.784	0.000	44.34625	45.99453

◁

Missing data: The complete and available options

The svymean, svytotal, and svyratio commands can handle missing data in two ways; see [R] **svymean**. The available option (which is the default when there are missing values and two or more variables) uses every available nonmissing value for each variable separately. The complete option (which is the default when there are no missing values or only one variable) uses only those observations with nonmissing values for all variables in the *varlist*. Here is an example where available is the default.

▷ Example

```
. svymean tcresult tgresult

Survey mean estimation
```

pweight:	finalwgt		Number of obs(*) =	10351
Strata:	stratid		Number of strata =	31
PSU:	psuid		Number of PSUs =	62
			Population size	= 1.172e+08

```
                ---------------------------------------------------------------------
           Mean |  Estimate    Std. Err.    [95% Conf. Interval]     Deff
        --------+------------------------------------------------------------
        tcresult |  213.0977    1.127252    210.7986    215.3967    5.602499
        tgresult |   138.576    2.071934    134.3503    142.8018    2.356968
                ---------------------------------------------------------------------
```

(*) Some variables contain missing values.

We redisplay the results using the `obs` option to see how many observations were used for each estimate.

```
. svymean, obs

Survey mean estimation

pweight:  finalwgt                        Number of obs(*) =      10351
Strata:   stratid                         Number of strata =         31
PSU:      psuid                           Number of PSUs    =         62
                                          Population size  = 1.172e+08

                ---------------------------------------------------------------------
           Mean |  Estimate    Std. Err.      Obs
        --------+------------------------------------------------------------
        tcresult |  213.0977    1.127252      10351
        tgresult |   138.576    2.071934       5050
                ---------------------------------------------------------------------
```

(*) Some variables contain missing values.

Because we estimated the mean of `tgresult` using a different set of observations than `tcresult`, we could not compute the covariance between the two, and hence, we cannot estimate the variance of the difference. So if we now ask `svylc` to estimate this difference, we get an error message.

```
. svylc tcresult - tgresult
must run svy command with "complete" option before using this command
r(301);
```

◁

We need not know in advance whether the default was **available** or **complete**. `svylc` will always tell us if we need to run the estimation command again with the **complete** option. With the **complete** option, only those observations that have nonmissing values for both **tgresult** and **tcresult** are used when we compute the means. When this option is specified, **svymean** computes the full covariance matrix.

▷ Example

```
. svymean tcresult tgresult, complete

Survey mean estimation

pweight:  finalwgt                        Number of obs    =       5050
Strata:   stratid                         Number of strata =         31
PSU:      psuid                           Number of PSUs    =         62
                                          Population size  = 56820832

                ---------------------------------------------------------------------
           Mean |  Estimate    Std. Err.    [95% Conf. Interval]     Deff
        --------+------------------------------------------------------------
        tcresult |  211.3975    1.252274    208.8435    213.9515    3.571411
        tgresult |   138.576    2.071934    134.3503    142.8018    2.356968
                ---------------------------------------------------------------------
```

Now we can estimate the variance of the difference.

```
. svylc tcresult - tgresult
 ( 1)  tcresult - tgresult = 0.0
```

Mean	Estimate	Std. Err.	t	P>|t|	[95% Conf. Interval]	
(1)	72.82146	2.039786	35.701	0.000	68.66129	76.98163

◁

The use of svylc after svy model estimators

svylc can be used after any of the commands described in [R] **svy estimators** to estimate a linear combination of the coefficients (i.e., the $\widehat{\beta}$'s).

Using svylc after svyreg is straightforward:

▷ Example

```
. svyreg tcresult bpsystol bpdiast age age2
Survey linear regression
```

pweight:	finalwgt		Number of obs	=	10351
Strata:	stratid		Number of strata	=	31
PSU:	psuid		Number of PSUs	=	62
			Population size	=	1.172e+08
			F(4, 28)	=	307.00
			Prob > F	=	0.0000
			R-squared	=	0.1945

tcresult	Coef.	Std. Err.	t	P>|t|	[95% Conf. Interval]	
bpsystol	.1060743	.0346796	3.059	0.005	.0353449	.1768038
bpdiast	.2966662	.0569594	5.208	0.000	.1804969	.4128356
age	3.35711	.2099842	15.987	0.000	2.928844	3.785375
age2	-.0247207	.0020795	-11.888	0.000	-.0289619	-.0204796
_cons	83.8242	5.649261	14.838	0.000	72.30246	95.34594

```
. svylc bpsystol - bpdiast
 ( 1)  bpsystol - bpdiast = 0.0
```

tcresult	Coef.	Std. Err.	t	P>|t|	[95% Conf. Interval]	
(1)	-.1905919	.0818056	-2.330	0.027	-.3574354	-.0237483

◁

Note that the svy commands in [R] **svy estimators** always use only complete cases, so that the covariance is always computed, and svylc can always be run afterward.

▷ Example

The variable `highbp` is 1 if a person has high blood pressure and 0 otherwise. We can model it using logistic regression.

```
. svylogit highbp height weight age age2 female black
(sum of wgt is   1.1716e+08)
Survey logistic regression
pweight:  finalwgt                               Number of obs    =      10351
Strata:   stratid                                Number of strata =         31
PSU:      psuid                                  Number of PSUs   =         62
                                                 Population size   = 1.172e+08
                                                 F(   6,     26)  =      87.70
                                                 Prob > F         =     0.0000
------------------------------------------------------------------------------
     highbp |    Coef.    Std. Err.       t     P>|t|     [95% Conf. Interval]
------------+-----------------------------------------------------------------
     height |  -.0325996   .0058727    -5.551   0.000    -.0445771   -.0206222
     weight |   .049074    .0031966    15.352   0.000     .0425545    .0555936
        age |   .1541151   .0208709     7.384   0.000     .1115486    .1966815
       age2 |  -.0010746   .0002025    -5.306   0.000    -.0014877   -.0006616
     female |  -.356497    .0885354    -4.027   0.000    -.537066    -.175928
      black |   .3429301   .1409005     2.434   0.021     .0555615    .6302986
      _cons |  -4.89574    1.159135    -4.224   0.000    -7.259813   -2.531668
------------------------------------------------------------------------------
```

We can redisplay the results expressed as odds ratios.

```
. svylogit, or
Survey logistic regression
pweight:  finalwgt                               Number of obs    =      10351
Strata:   stratid                                Number of strata =         31
PSU:      psuid                                  Number of PSUs   =         62
                                                 Population size   = 1.172e+08
                                                 F(   6,     26)  =      87.70
                                                 Prob > F         =     0.0000
------------------------------------------------------------------------------
     highbp | Odds Ratio  Std. Err.       t     P>|t|     [95% Conf. Interval]
------------+-----------------------------------------------------------------
     height |   .967926    .0056843    -5.551   0.000     .9564019    .979589
     weight |  1.050298    .0033574    15.352   0.000    1.043473    1.057168
        age |  1.166625    .0243485     7.384   0.000    1.118008    1.217356
       age2 |   .998926    .0002023    -5.306   0.000     .9985135    .9993386
     female |   .7001246   .0619858    -4.027   0.000     .5844605    .8386784
      black |  1.40907     .1985388     2.434   0.021    1.057134    1.878171
------------------------------------------------------------------------------
```

`svylc` can be used to estimate the sum of the coefficients for `female` and `black`.

```
. svylc female + black
 ( 1)  female + black = 0.0

------------------------------------------------------------------------------
     highbp |    Coef.    Std. Err.       t     P>|t|     [95% Conf. Interval]
------------+-----------------------------------------------------------------
        (1) |  -.0135669   .1653936    -0.082   0.935    -.3508894    .3237555
------------------------------------------------------------------------------
```

This result is more easily interpreted as an odds ratio.

```
. svylc female + black, or
 ( 1)  female + black = 0.0
```

```
--------------------------------------------------------------------------
  highbp | Odds Ratio   Std. Err.       t    P>|t|     [95% Conf. Interval]
---------+----------------------------------------------------------------
     (1) |  .9865247    .1631648    -0.082   0.935     .7040616    1.382309
--------------------------------------------------------------------------
```

The odds ratio 0.987 is an estimate of the ratio of the odds of having high blood pressure for black females over the odds for our reference category of nonblack males (controlling for height, weight, and age).

See [R] **lincom** for more examples of odds ratios.

◁

Using `svylc` after estimators that estimate multiple-equation models is a little trickier, but still straightforward. Users merely need to refer to the coefficients using the syntax for multiple equations; see [U] **16.5 Accessing coefficients and standard errors** for a description and [R] **test** for examples of its use.

▷ Example

In the NHANES II data, we have a variable `health` containing self-reported health status, which takes on the values 1–5, with 1 being "poor" and 5 being "excellent". Since this is an ordered categorical variable, it makes sense to model it using `svyolog` or `svyoprob`. We will do so in the next example, but we will first use `svymlog` since it is a good example of a multiple-equation estimator at its simplest.

So, we estimate a multinomial logistic regression model:

```
. svymlog health female black age age2
Survey multinomial logistic regression

pweight:  finalwgt                       Number of obs    =       10335
Strata:   stratid                        Number of strata =          31
PSU:      psuid                          Number of PSUs   =          62
                                         Population size   = 1.170e+08
                                         F( 16,     16)   =       36.41
                                         Prob > F         =      0.0000

--------------------------------------------------------------------------
  health |    Coef.     Std. Err.       t    P>|t|     [95% Conf. Interval]
---------+----------------------------------------------------------------
poor     |
  female | -.1983735    .1072747    -1.849   0.074    -.4171617    .0204147
   black |  .8964694    .1797728     4.987   0.000     .5298203    1.263119
     age |  .0990246    .032111      3.084   0.004     .0335338    .1645155
    age2 | -.0004749    .0003209    -1.480   0.149    -.0011294    .0001796
   _cons | -5.475074    .7468576    -7.331   0.000      -6.9983   -3.951848
---------+----------------------------------------------------------------
fair     |
  female |  .1782371    .0726556     2.453   0.020      .030055    .3264193
   black |  .4429445    .122667      3.611   0.001     .1927635    .6931256
     age |  .0024576    .0172236     0.143   0.887    -.0326702    .0375853
    age2 |  .0002875    .0001684     1.707   0.098    -.0000559     .000631
   _cons | -1.819561    .4018153    -4.528   0.000    -2.639069   -1.000053
---------+----------------------------------------------------------------
good     |
  female | -.0458251    .074169     -0.618   0.541    -.1970938    .1054437
   black | -.7532011    .1105444    -6.814   0.000    -.9786579   -.5277443
     age |  -.061369    .009794     -6.266   0.000     -.081344   -.0413939
    age2 |  .0004166    .0001077     3.869   0.001      .000197    .0006363
   _cons |  1.815323    .1996917     9.091   0.000     1.408049    2.222597
```

```
---------+----------------------------------------------------------------
excell   |
  female |   -.222799    .0754205    -2.954   0.006    -.3766202   -.0689778
   black |   -.991647    .1238806    -8.005   0.000    -1.244303   -.7389909
     age |  -.0293573    .0137789    -2.131   0.041    -.0574595    -.001255
    age2 |  -.0000674    .0001505    -0.448   0.657    -.0003744    .0002396
   _cons |   1.499683     .286143     5.241   0.000     .9160909    2.083276
---------+----------------------------------------------------------------
```

(Outcome health==average is the comparison group)

One might want to calculate the estimate for black females for the "excellent" category:

```
. svylc [excell]female + [excell]black
( 1)  [excell]female + [excell]black = 0.0

---------------------------------------------------------------------
  health |      Coef.    Std. Err.       t     P>|t|    [95% Conf. Interval]
---------+-----------------------------------------------------------
    (1)  |  -1.214446    .1428188    -8.503   0.000    -1.505727   -.9231652
---------------------------------------------------------------------
```

This result might be better interpreted as a relative risk ratio. Since the estimate was negative, one could reverse signs to get a relative risk ratio that is greater than one:

```
. svylc -[excell]female - [excell]black, rrr
( 1)  - [excell]female - [excell]black = 0.0

---------------------------------------------------------------------
  health |       RRR    Std. Err.       t     P>|t|    [95% Conf. Interval]
---------+-----------------------------------------------------------
    (1)  |  3.368427    .4810747     8.503   0.000     2.517245    4.507429
---------------------------------------------------------------------
```

RRR = 3.37 is the ratio of relative risk for nonblack males to black females, with "relative risk" being the probability of being in the "excellent" category divided by the probability of being in the "average" base category. Hence, this relative risk ratio is

$$\text{RRR} = \frac{\Pr(\text{excellent} \mid \text{nonblack male})/\Pr(\text{average} \mid \text{nonblack male})}{\Pr(\text{excellent} \mid \text{black female})/\Pr(\text{average} \mid \text{black female})}$$

We now estimate the same model using svyolog:

```
. svyolog health female black age age2
Survey ordered logistic regression
pweight: finalwgt                    Number of obs    =      10335
Strata:  stratid                     Number of strata =         31
PSU:     psuid                       Number of PSUs   =         62
                                     Population size  = 1.170e+08
                                     F(  4,    28)    =     223.27
                                     Prob > F         =     0.0000

---------------------------------------------------------------------
  health |      Coef.    Std. Err.       t     P>|t|    [95% Conf. Interval]
---------+-----------------------------------------------------------
  female |  -.1615219    .0523678    -3.084   0.004    -.2683266   -.0547171
   black |   -.986568    .0790276   -12.484   0.000    -1.147746   -.8253901
     age |  -.0119491    .0082974    -1.440   0.160    -.0288717    .0049736
    age2 |  -.0003234     .000091    -3.552   0.001     -.000509   -.0001377
---------+-----------------------------------------------------------
   _cut1 |  -4.566229    .1632559   -27.970   0.000    -4.899192   -4.233266
   _cut2 |  -3.057415    .1699943   -17.985   0.000    -3.404121   -2.710709
   _cut3 |  -1.520596    .1714341    -8.870   0.000    -1.870238   -1.170954
   _cut4 |   -.242785    .1703964    -1.425   0.164    -.5903107    .1047407
---------------------------------------------------------------------
```

Although `svyolog` and `svyoprob` are multiple-equation estimators, one can refer to the estimates in the first equation using single-equation syntax:

```
. svylc female + black
( 1)  [health]female + [health]black = 0.0
```

health	Coef.	Std. Err.	t	P>|t|	[95% Conf. Interval]
(1)	-1.14809	.1008367	-11.386	0.000	-1.353748 -.942432

The single-equation syntax does not work when referring to the cutpoints:

```
. svylc _cut1 - _cut2
_cut1 not found
r(111);
```

When in doubt, always use the **show** option. It will show you exactly how the equations are labeled.

```
. svylc, show
```

health	Coef.	Std. Err.	t	P>|t|	[95% Conf. Interval]
health					
female	-.1615219	.0523678	-3.084	0.004	-.2683266 -.0547171
black	-.986568	.0790276	-12.484	0.000	-1.147746 -.8253901
age	-.0119491	.0082974	-1.440	0.160	-.0288717 .0049736
age2	-.0003234	.000091	-3.552	0.001	-.000509 -.0001377
_cut1					
_cons	-4.566229	.1632559	-27.970	0.000	-4.899192 -4.233266
_cut2					
_cons	-3.057415	.1699943	-17.985	0.000	-3.404121 -2.710709
_cut3					
_cons	-1.520596	.1714341	-8.870	0.000	-1.870238 -1.170954
_cut4					
_cons	-.242785	.1703964	-1.425	0.164	-.5903107 .1047407

The output of `svyolog` and `svyoprob` is actually quite deceiving. The first equation contains all the coefficient estimates, but then there is one equation for each cutpoint. To estimate differences of the cutpoints, use the multiple-equation syntax:

```
. svylc [_cut2]_cons - [_cut1]_cons
( 1) - [_cut1]_cons + [_cut2]_cons = 0.0
```

health	Coef.	Std. Err.	t	P>|t|	[95% Conf. Interval]
(1)	1.508814	.0501686	30.075	0.000	1.406495 1.611134

◁

Subpopulations with one by() variable

The svymean, svytotal, and svyratio commands allow a by() option which produces estimates for subpopulations; see [R] **svymean**. Frequently, one wishes to compute estimates for differences of subpopulation estimates. It is easy to use svylc to compute estimates for differences or any other linear combination of estimates. The only thing one must know is the proper syntax for referencing the subpopulation estimates. In this and the next two sections, we illustrate the syntax with a series of examples.

▷ Example

Suppose that we wish to get an estimate of the difference in mean vitamin C levels (variable vitaminc) between males and females. First, we compute the means of vitaminc by sex.

```
. svymean vitaminc, by(sex)

Survey mean estimation

pweight:  finalwgt                       Number of obs    =       9973
Strata:   stratid                        Number of strata =         31
PSU:      psuid                          Number of PSUs   =         62
                                         Population size  = 1.129e+08

------------------------------------------------------------------------
Mean      Subpop. |  Estimate   Std. Err.   [95% Conf. Interval]    Deff
----------------+-------------------------------------------------------
vitaminc          |
           Male | .9312051    .0169297    .8966768   .9657333    4.926449
         Female | 1.12753     .0173704    1.092103   1.162957    5.028652
------------------------------------------------------------------------
```

Then we use the svylc command.

```
. svylc [vitaminc]Male - [vitaminc]Female
 ( 1)  [vitaminc]Male - [vitaminc]Female = 0.0

------------------------------------------------------------------------
    Mean |   Estimate   Std. Err.      t    P>|t|     [95% Conf. Interval]
---------+--------------------------------------------------------------
     (1) |  -.1963252    .015981   -12.285   0.000    -.2289186   -.1637318
------------------------------------------------------------------------
```

When svymean or svytotal is used with a by() option, the syntax for referencing the subpopulation estimates is

   [*varname*] *subpop_label*

For example, we use [vitaminc]Male to refer to the subpopulation estimates. This is the same syntax that is used with the test command when there are multiple equations; see [R] **test** for full details.

Be sure to type the variable names and subpopulation labels exactly as they are displayed in the output. Remember that Stata is case-sensitive.

```
. svylc [vitaminc]male - [vitaminc]female
male not found
r(111);
```

If there are no subpopulation labels, simply use the numbers displayed in the output.

```
. svymean vitaminc, by(sex) nolabel
```

Survey mean estimation

```
pweight:  finalwgt                    Number of obs    =      9973
Strata:   stratid                     Number of strata =        31
PSU:      psuid                       Number of PSUs   =        62
                                      Population size  = 1.129e+08
```

Mean	Subpop.	Estimate	Std. Err.	[95% Conf. Interval]		Deff
vitaminc						
	sex==1	.9312051	.0169297	.8966768	.9657333	4.926449
	sex==2	1.12753	.0173704	1.092103	1.162957	5.028652

```
. svylc [vitaminc]1 - [vitaminc]2
 ( 1)  [vitaminc]1 - [vitaminc]2 = 0.0
```

Mean	Estimate	Std. Err.	t	P>|t|	[95% Conf. Interval]	
(1)	-.1963252	.015981	-12.285	0.000	-.2289186	-.1637318

◁

Subpopulations with two or more by() variables

If there are two or more by() variables, you must refer to the subpopulations by numbers (1, 2, 3, ...) when using svylc.

▷ Example

```
. svymean vitaminc, by(sex race)
```

Survey mean estimation

```
pweight:  finalwgt                    Number of obs    =      9973
Strata:   stratid                     Number of strata =        31
PSU:      psuid                       Number of PSUs   =        62
                                      Population size  = 1.129e+08
```

Mean	Subpop.		Estimate	Std. Err.	[95% Conf. Interval]		Deff
vitaminc							
Male	White		.9475117	.0168982	.9130475	.9819758	4.646413
Male	Black		.7382045	.0477521	.6408135	.8355955	2.165885
Male	Other		1.021363	.0521427	.915017	1.127708	1.739788
Female	White		1.151125	.0168117	1.116838	1.185413	4.032603
Female	Black		.9222313	.0348224	.8512105	.993252	2.915009
Female	Other		1.0804	.0412742	.9962202	1.164579	1.00135

You can see the numbering scheme by running `svylc` with the `show` option.

```
. svylc, show

------------------------------------------------------------------------
    Mean |     Coef.   Std. Err.       t    P>|t|     [95% Conf. Interval]
---------+--------------------------------------------------------------
vitaminc |
       1 |   .9475117   .0168982    56.072   0.000      .9130475   .9819758
       2 |   .7382045   .0477521    15.459   0.000      .6408135   .8355955
       3 |   1.021363   .0521427    19.588   0.000       .915017   1.127708
       4 |   1.151125   .0168117    68.472   0.000      1.116838   1.185413
       5 |   .9222313   .0348224    26.484   0.000      .8512105    .993252
       6 |     1.0804   .0412742    26.176   0.000      .9962202   1.164579
------------------------------------------------------------------------
```

So if we want to test the hypothesis that vitamin C levels are the same in white females and black females, we need to test subpopulation 4 versus subpopulation 5.

```
. svylc [vitaminc]4 - [vitaminc]5
 ( 1)  [vitaminc]4 - [vitaminc]5 = 0.0

------------------------------------------------------------------------
    Mean |   Estimate   Std. Err.       t    P>|t|     [95% Conf. Interval]
---------+--------------------------------------------------------------
     (1) |   .2288941   .0337949     6.773   0.000      .1599688   .2978193
------------------------------------------------------------------------
```

◁

The use of svylc after svyratio

Using `svylc` after `svyratio` is a little more complicated. But, again, the `show` option on `svylc` will guide you.

▷ Example

```
. svyratio y1/x1 y2/x2
Survey ratio estimation
pweight:  finalwgt              Number of obs    =      10351
Strata:   stratid               Number of strata =         31
PSU:      psuid                 Number of PSUs   =         62
                                Population size   = 1.172e+08

------------------------------------------------------------------------
         Ratio |  Estimate   Std. Err.   [95% Conf. Interval]       Deff
---------------+--------------------------------------------------------
         y1/x1 |  .9918905   .0102386    .9710087   1.012772    1.647415
         y2/x2 |  .9962729   .0083088    .9793269   1.013219      1.0771
------------------------------------------------------------------------

. svylc, show

------------------------------------------------------------------------
   Ratio |     Coef.   Std. Err.       t    P>|t|     [95% Conf. Interval]
---------+--------------------------------------------------------------
y1       |
      x1 |   .9918905   .0102386    96.878   0.000      .9710087   1.012772
---------+--------------------------------------------------------------
y2       |
      x2 |   .9962729   .0083088   119.905   0.000      .9793269   1.013219
------------------------------------------------------------------------
```

```
. svylc [y1]x1 - [y2]x2
( 1)  [y1]x1 - [y2]x2 = 0.0
```

Ratio	Estimate	Std. Err.	t	P>|t|	[95% Conf. Interval]
(1)	-.0043824	.0125921	-0.348	0.730	-.0300641 .0212993

◁

The following examples illustrate the syntax when there are by() subpopulations.

▷ Example

```
. svyratio y1/x1, by(race)
Survey ratio estimation
```

pweight:	finalwgt			Number of obs	=	10351
Strata:	stratid			Number of strata	=	31
PSU:	psuid			Number of PSUs	=	62
				Population size	=	1.172e+08

Ratio	Subpop.	Estimate	Std. Err.	[95% Conf. Interval]		Deff
y1/x1						
	White	.995116	.0116867	.9712807	1.018951	1.879759
	Black	.9525558	.0381059	.8748384	1.030273	2.242268
	Other	1.026876	.0447707	.9355659	1.118187	.8308877

```
. svylc, show
```

Ratio	Coef.	Std. Err.	t	P>|t|	[95% Conf. Interval]	
1						
White	.995116	.0116867	85.149	0.000	.9712807	1.018951
Black	.9525558	.0381059	24.998	0.000	.8748384	1.030273
Other	1.026876	.0447707	22.936	0.000	.9355659	1.118187

```
. svylc [1]White - [1]Black
( 1)  [1]White - [1]Black = 0.0
```

Ratio	Estimate	Std. Err.	t	P>|t|	[95% Conf. Interval]
(1)	.0425602	.0439945	0.967	0.341	-.0471671 .1322875

```
. svyratio y1/x1, by(sex race)
```

Survey ratio estimation

pweight:	finalwgt	Number of obs = 10351
Strata:	stratid	Number of strata = 31
PSU:	psuid	Number of PSUs = 62
		Population size = 1.172e+08

Ratio	Subpop.	Estimate	Std. Err.	[95% Conf. Interval]		Deff
y1/x1						
Male	White	1.000215	.0150805	.9694585	1.030972	1.460442
Male	Black	.9726418	.0486307	.8734589	1.071825	1.426839
Male	Other	1.000358	.0732775	.850907	1.149808	1.266913
Female	White	.9904237	.0169396	.9558752	1.024972	2.109029
Female	Black	.9362548	.0409748	.8526861	1.019823	1.619815
Female	Other	1.056553	.082305	.8886906	1.224415	1.228803

```
. svylc, show
```

Ratio	Coef.	Std. Err.	t	P>|t|	[95% Conf. Interval]	
1						
1	1.000215	.0150805	66.325	0.000	.9694585	1.030972
2	.9726418	.0486307	20.001	0.000	.8734589	1.071825
3	1.000358	.0732775	13.652	0.000	.850907	1.149808
4	.9904237	.0169396	58.468	0.000	.9558752	1.024972
5	.9362548	.0409748	22.850	0.000	.8526861	1.019823
6	1.056553	.082305	12.837	0.000	.8886906	1.224415

```
. svylc [1]1 - [1]4
 ( 1)  [1]1 - [1]4 = 0.0
```

Ratio	Estimate	Std. Err.	t	P>|t|	[95% Conf. Interval]	
(1)	.0097916	.0221119	0.443	0.661	-.0353058	.054889

◁

Saved Results

svylc saves in r():

Scalars

r(est)	point estimate of linear combination
r(se)	standard error (square root of design-based variance estimate)
r(N_strata)	number of strata
r(N_psu)	number of sampled PSUs
r(deff)	deff
r(deft)	deft
r(meft)	meft

Methods and Formulas

svylc is implemented as an ado-file.

svylc estimates $\eta = C\theta$, where θ is a $q \times 1$ vector of parameters (e.g., population means or population regression coefficients), and C is any $1 \times q$ vector of constants. The estimate of η is $\widehat{\eta} = C\widehat{\theta}$, and the estimate of its variance is

$$\widehat{V}(\widehat{\eta}) = C\widehat{V}(\widehat{\theta})C'$$

Similarly, the simple-random-sampling variance estimator used in the computation of deff and deft is $\widehat{V}_{\mathrm{srs}}(\widetilde{\eta}_{\mathrm{srs}}) = C\widehat{V}_{\mathrm{srs}}(\widetilde{\theta}_{\mathrm{srs}})C'$. And the variance estimator used in the computation of meff and meft is $\widehat{V}_{\mathrm{msp}}(\widehat{\eta}_{\mathrm{msp}}) = C\widehat{V}_{\mathrm{msp}}(\widehat{\theta}_{\mathrm{msp}})C'$. See the *Methods and Formulas* section of [R] **svymean** for details on the computation of deff, deft, meff, and meft.

References

Eltinge, J. L. and W. M. Sribney. 1996. svy5: Estimates of combinations and hypothesis tests for survey data. *Stata Technical Bulletin* 31: 31–42. Reprinted in *Stata Technical Bulletin Reprints*, vol. 6, pp. 246–259.

McDowell, A., A. Engel, J. T. Massey, and K. Maurer. 1981. Plan and operation of the Second National Health and Nutrition Examination Survey, 1976–1980. *Vital and Health Statistics* 15(1). National Center for Health Statistics, Hyattsville, MD.

Also See

Complementary:	[R] **svy estimators**, [R] **svydes**, [R] **svymean**, [R] **svyset**, [R] **svytest**
Related:	[R] **lincom**
Background:	[U] **16.5 Accessing coefficients and standard errors**,
	[U] **30 Overview of survey estimation**,
	[R] **svy**

Title

> **svymean** — Estimate means, totals, ratios, and proportions for survey data

Syntax

svymean *varlist* [*weight*] [if *exp*] [in *range*] [, *common_options*]

svytotal *varlist* [*weight*] [if *exp*] [in *range*] [, *common_options*]

svyratio *varname* [/] *varname* [*varname* [/] *varname* ...] [*weight*] [if *exp*] [in *range*]
    [, *common_options*]

svyprop *varlist* [*weight*] [if *exp*] [in *range*] [, strata(*varname*) psu(*varname*)
    fpc(*varname*) by(*varlist*) subpop(*varname*) nolabel format(%*fmt*)]

The *common_options* for svymean, svytotal, and svyratio are

    strata(*varname*) psu(*varname*) fpc(*varname*) by(*varlist*)

    subpop(*varname*) srssubpop nolabel { complete | available }

    level(*#*) ci deff deft meff meft obs size

svymean, svyratio, and svytotal typed without arguments redisplay previous results. Any of the
following options can be used when redisplaying results:

    level(*#*) ci deff deft meff meft obs size

All these commands allow pweights and iweights; see [U] **14.1.6 weight**.

Warning: Use of if or in restrictions will not produce correct variance estimates for subpopulations in many cases.
To compute estimates for subpopulations, use the by() or subpop() options.

Description

svymean, svytotal, svyratio, and svyprop produce estimates of finite-population means,
totals, ratios, and proportions. Associated variance estimates, design effects (deff and deft), and
misspecification effects (meff and meft) are also computed.

Estimates for multiple subpopulations can be obtained using the by() option. The subpop()
option will give estimates for a single subpopulation.

To describe the strata and PSUs of your data and to handle the error message "stratum with only
one PSU detected", see [R] **svydes**.

To estimate differences (and other linear combinations) of means, totals, and ratios, see [R] **svylc**.
To perform hypothesis tests, see [R] **svytest**.

Options

strata(*varname*) specifies the name of a variable (numeric or string) that contains stratum identifiers. strata() can also be specified with the svyset command; see the following examples and [R] **svyset**.

psu(*varname*) specifies the name of a variable (numeric or string) that contains identifiers for the primary sampling unit (i.e., the cluster). psu() can also be specified with the svyset command.

fpc(*varname*) requests a finite population correction for the variance estimates. If the variable specified has values less than or equal to 1, it is interpreted as a stratum sampling rate $f_h = n_h/N_h$, where n_h = number of PSUs sampled from stratum h and N_h = total number of PSUs in the population belonging to stratum h. If the variable specified has values greater than or equal to n_h, it is interpreted as containing N_h. fpc() can also be specified with the svyset command.

by(*varlist*) specifies that estimates be computed for the subpopulations defined by different values of the variable(s) in the by *varlist*.

subpop(*varname*) specifies that estimates be computed for the single subpopulation defined by the observations for which *varname* $\neq 0$ Typically, *varname* $= 1$ defines the subpopulation, and *varname* $= 0$ indicates observations not belonging to the subpopulation. For observations whose subpopulation status is uncertain, *varname* should be set to missing ('.').

srssubpop can only be specified if by() or subpop() is specified. srssubpop requests that deff and deft be computed using an estimate of simple-random-sampling variance for sampling within a subpopulation. If srssubpop is not specified, deff and deft are computed using an estimate of simple-random-sampling variance for sampling from the entire population. Typically, srssubpop would be given when computing subpopulation estimates by strata or by groups of strata.

nolabel can only be specified if by() is specified. nolabel requests that numeric values rather than value labels be used to label output for subpopulations. By default, value labels are used.

{ complete | available } specifies how missing values are to be handled. complete specifies that only observations with complete data should be used; i.e., any observation that has a missing value for any of the variables in the *varlist* is omitted from the computation. available specifies that all available nonmissing values be used for each estimate.

If neither complete nor available is specified, available is the default when there are missing values and there are two or more variables in the *varlist* (or four or more for svyratio). If there are missing values and two or more variables (or four or more for svyratio), complete must be specified to compute the covariance or to use svytest (for hypothesis tests) or svylc (estimates for linear combinations) after running the command; see [R] **svylc** and [R] **svytest**.

format(%*fmt*) (svyprop only) specifies the display format for the proportion estimates and their standard errors. The default is %9.6f.

The following options can be specified initially or when redisplaying results:

level(*#*) specifies the confidence level (i.e., nominal coverage rate), in percent, for confidence intervals. The default is level(95) or as set by set level; see [U] **23.5 Specifying the width of confidence intervals**.

ci requests that confidence intervals be displayed. If no display options are specified, then, by default, confidence intervals are displayed.

deff requests that the design-effect measure deff be displayed. If no display options are specified, then, by default, deff is displayed.

deft requests that the design-effect measure deft be displayed. See the following section, *Some fine points about deff and deft*, for a discussion of deff and deft.

meff requests that the meff measure of misspecification effects be displayed.

meft requests that the meft measure of misspecification effects be displayed. See the following section, *Misspecification effects: meff and meft*, for a discussion of meff and meft.

obs requests that the number of observations used for the computation of the estimate be displayed for each row of estimates.

size requests that the estimate of the (sub)population size be displayed for each row of estimates. The (sub)population size estimate equals the sum of the weights for those observations used for the mean/total/ratio estimate.

Remarks

Remarks are presented under the headings

> *Setting the strata, psu, fpc, and pweight variables*
> *Estimates for subpopulations*
> *Warning about the use of if and in*
> *Options for displaying results: ci deff deft meff meft obs size*
> *Using svytotal and svyratio*
> *Estimating proportions*
> *Changing the strata, psu, fpc, and pweight variables*
> *Finite population correction (FPC)*
> *Some fine points about deff and deft*
> *Misspecification effects: meff and meft*

The svy commands are designed for use with complex survey data. The survey design may or may not be stratified. Depending on the original sample design, primary sampling units (PSUs) may consist of clusters of observations (e.g., counties or city blocks) or the PSUs may be individual observations.

Typically, there are sampling weights proportional to the inverse of the probability of being selected. In Stata syntax, sampling weights are referred to as pweights—short for "probability weights".

For a general discussion of various aspects of survey designs, including multistage designs, see [U] **30 Overview of survey estimation.**

Setting the strata, psu, fpc, and pweight variables

For our first example, we use data from the National Maternal and Infant Health Survey (NMIHS) (Gonzalez et al. 1992, Johnson 1995). This dataset has a stratification variable stratan. Primary sampling units are mothers; i.e., PSUs are individual observations—there is no separate PSU variable. The sampling weights are given by the variable finwgt. We do not include a finite population correction for this analysis.

We use the svyset command to set the stratification variable and the pweight variable.

```
. svyset strata stratan
. svyset pweight finwgt
```

Typing svyset alone shows what has been set.

```
. svyset
strata is stratan
pweight is finwgt
```

If we save the dataset, these settings will be remembered next time we use this dataset.

```
. save nmihs, replace
file nmihs.dta saved
. use nmihs, clear
. svyset
strata is stratan
pweight is finwgt
```

We can now use the `svy` commands without having to specify explicitly the `pweight`s and the `strata()` option.

```
. svymean birthwgt

Survey mean estimation

pweight:  finwgt              Number of obs    =       9946
Strata:   stratan            Number of strata =          6
PSU:      <observations>     Number of PSUs   =       9946
                             Population size  = 3895561.7
```

Mean	Estimate	Std. Err.	[95% Conf. Interval]		Deff
birthwgt	3355.452	6.402741	3342.902	3368.003	1.142614

Alternatively, we could have set the `pweight`s and `strata` when we issued the command.

```
. svymean birthwgt [pweight=finwgt], strata(stratan)
```

No matter which of these methods are used initially to set `pweight`s and `strata`, the settings are remembered and do not have to be specified in subsequent use of any of the `svy` commands. We will illustrate the other features of the `svyset` command in later examples; see [R] **svyset** for a syntax diagram.

Estimates for subpopulations

Estimates for subpopulations can be obtained using the `by()` option.

```
. svymean birthwgt, by(race)

Survey mean estimation

pweight:  finwgt              Number of obs    =       9946
Strata:   stratan            Number of strata =          6
PSU:      <observations>     Number of PSUs   =       9946
                             Population size  = 3895561.7
```

Mean	Subpop.	Estimate	Std. Err.	[95% Conf. Interval]		Deff
birthwgt						
	nonblack	3402.32	7.609532	3387.404	3417.236	1.443763
	black	3127.834	6.529814	3115.035	3140.634	.1720408

Note: One may wish to specify the `srssubpop` option for the computation of deff in this case; see the section *Some fine points about deff and deft* which appears later in this entry.

Any number of variables can be used in the `by()` option.

```
. svymean birthwgt, by(race marital)

Survey mean estimation

pweight:  finwgt                              Number of obs    =      9946
Strata:   stratan                             Number of strata =         6
PSU:      <observations>                      Number of PSUs   =      9946
                                              Population size   = 3895561.7

--------------------------------------------------------------------------
Mean        Subpop. |   Estimate   Std. Err.   [95% Conf. Interval]    Deff
------------------+-------------------------------------------------------
birthwgt            |
nonblack     single |   3291.045   20.18795    3251.472    3330.617  1.684919
nonblack    married |   3426.407   8.379497    3409.982    3442.833  1.477145
   black     single |   3073.122   8.752553    3055.965    3090.279   .1954712
   black    married |   3221.616   12.42687    3197.257    3245.975   .2368791
--------------------------------------------------------------------------
```

In this example, the variables `race` and `marital` have value labels. `race` has the value 0 labeled "nonblack" (i.e., white and other) and 1 labeled "black"; `marital` has the value 0 labeled "single" and 1 labeled "married". Value labels on the `by` variables make for better-looking and more readable output when producing estimates for subpopulations. See [U] **15.6.3 Value labels** for information on creating value labels.

The `subpop()` option can be used to specify a single subpopulation.

```
. svymean birthwgt, subpop(race)

Survey mean estimation

pweight:  finwgt                              Number of obs    =      9946
Strata:   stratan                             Number of strata =         6
PSU:      <observations>                      Number of PSUs   =      9946
Subpop.:  race==1                             Population size   = 3895561.7

--------------------------------------------------------------------------
    Mean |   Estimate   Std. Err.   [95% Conf. Interval]      Deff
---------+----------------------------------------------------------------
birthwgt |   3127.834   6.529814    3115.035    3140.634    .1720408
--------------------------------------------------------------------------
```

The `subpop(varname)` option takes a 0/1 variable; the subpopulation of interest is defined by *varname* = 1. All other members of the sample not in the subpopulation are indicated by *varname* = 0.

If a person's subpopulation status is unknown, then *varname* should be set to missing ('.') and those observations will be omitted from the analysis as they should be. For instance, in the preceding example, if person's race is unknown, `race` should be coded as missing rather than as nonblack (`race` = 0).

Missing values for `by()` variables are also treated in this manner. Observations with missing values for any of the `by()` variables are automatically omitted from the analysis.

❑ Technical Note

Actually, the `subpop(varname)` option takes a zero/nonzero variable; the subpopulation of interest is defined by *varname* ≠ 0 and not missing. All other members of the sample not in the subpopulation are indicated by *varname* = 0. But 0, 1, and missing are typically the only values used for the `subpop()` variable.

❑

You can combine `subpop()` with `by()`.

```
. gen white = (race==0) if race~=.
. svymean birthwgt, subpop(white) by(marital age20)
```

Survey mean estimation

pweight:	finwgt	Number of obs	=	9946
Strata:	stratan	Number of strata	=	6
PSU:	<observations>	Number of PSUs	=	9946
Subpop.:	white==1	Population size	=	3895561.7

Mean	Subpop.	Estimate	Std. Err.	[95% Conf. Interval]		Deff
birthwgt						
single	age20+	3312.012	24.2869	3264.405	3359.619	1.635331
single	age<20	3244.709	36.85934	3172.457	3316.961	1.876781
married	age20+	3434.923	8.674633	3417.919	3451.927	1.487806
married	age<20	3287.301	34.15988	3220.341	3354.262	1.585084

This time we wanted means for the marital status and age < 20 or > 20 subpopulations for the nonblack race only. To use the `subpop()` option, we must specify a variable that is 1 for the nonblacks and 0 otherwise, so we create the variable `white`. Note that we carefully define `white` so that it is missing when `race` is missing. If we omitted the `if race~=.` in our `generate` statement, `white` would be 0 when `race` was missing. This would improperly assume that all persons with `race` missing were black and cause our results to have incorrect standard errors.

Warning about the use of if and in

One might be tempted to use the following standard Stata syntax to get subpopulation estimates:

```
. svymean birthwgt if highbp==1
```

Survey mean estimation

pweight:	finwgt	Number of obs	=	595
Strata:	stratan	Number of strata	=	6
PSU:	<observations>	Number of PSUs	=	595
		Population size	=	186196.71

Mean	Estimate	Std. Err.	[95% Conf. Interval]		Deff
birthwgt	3202.483	28.7201	3146.077	3258.89	1.060747

The above, however, gives incorrect variance estimates for this study design. One should use `by()` or `subpop` to get subpopulation estimates in this case.

```
. svymean birthwgt, subpop(highbp)
```

Survey mean estimation

pweight:	finwgt	Number of obs	=	9946
Strata:	stratan	Number of strata	=	6
PSU:	<observations>	Number of PSUs	=	9946
Subpop.:	highbp==1	Population size	=	3895561.7

Mean	Estimate	Std. Err.	[95% Conf. Interval]		Deff
birthwgt	3202.483	33.29483	3137.219	3267.748	1.140812

The different variance estimates are due to the way if works in Stata. For all commands in Stata, using if is equivalent to deleting all observations that do not satisfy the if expression and then running the commands. In contrast with this, the svy commands compute subpopulation variance estimates in a way that accounts for which sample units were and were not contained in the subpopulation of interest. Thus, the svy commands must also have access to those observations not in the subpopulation to compute the variance estimates. The survey literature refers to these variance estimators as "unconditional" variance estimators. See, e.g., Cochran (1977, Section 2.13) for a further discussion of these unconditional variance estimators and some alternative "conditional" variance estimators.

For survey data, there are only a few circumstances that necessitate the use of if. For example, if one suspected laboratory error for a certain set of measurements, then it might be proper to use if to omit these observations from the analysis.

Options for displaying results: ci deff deft meff meft obs size

We now use data from the Second National Health and Nutrition Examination Survey (NHANES II) (McDowell et al. 1981) as our example. First, we set the strata, psu, and pweight variables.

```
. svyset strata stratid
. svyset psu psuid
. svyset pweight finalwgt
```

We will estimate the population means for total serum cholesterol (tcresult) and serum triglycerides (tgresult).

```
. svymean tcresult tgresult

Survey mean estimation

pweight:  finalwgt                    Number of obs(*) =      10351
Strata:   stratid                     Number of strata =         31
PSU:      psuid                       Number of PSUs   =         62
                                      Population size  = 1.172e+08
```

Mean	Estimate	Std. Err.	[95% Conf. Interval]		Deff
tcresult	213.0977	1.127252	210.7986	215.3967	5.602499
tgresult	138.576	2.071934	134.3503	142.8018	2.356968

(*) Some variables contain missing values.

If we want to see how many nonmissing observations there are for each variable, we can redisplay the results specifying the obs option.

```
. svymean, obs

Survey mean estimation

pweight:  finalwgt                    Number of obs(*) =      10351
Strata:   stratid                     Number of strata =         31
PSU:      psuid                       Number of PSUs   =         62
                                      Population size  = 1.172e+08
```

Mean	Estimate	Std. Err.	Obs
tcresult	213.0977	1.127252	10351
tgresult	138.576	2.071934	5050

(*) Some variables contain missing values.

The svymean, svytotal, and svyratio commands allow you to display any or all of the
following: ci (confidence intervals), deff, deft, meff, meft, obs, and size (estimated (sub)
population size).

```
. svymean, ci deff deft meff meft obs size

Survey mean estimation

pweight:  finalwgt                         Number of obs(*) =      10351
Strata:   stratid                          Number of strata =         31
PSU:      psuid                            Number of PSUs   =         62
                                           Population size  = 1.172e+08

--------------------------------------------------------------------------------
      Mean |   Estimate    Std. Err.   [95% Conf. Interval]        Deff
-----------+--------------------------------------------------------------------
  tcresult |   213.0977    1.127252    210.7986    215.3967    5.602499
  tgresult |    138.576    2.071934    134.3503    142.8018    2.356968
--------------------------------------------------------------------------------


--------------------------------------------------------------------------------
      Mean |      Deff        Meff        Meft         Obs    Pop. Size
-----------+--------------------------------------------------------------------
  tcresult |   2.36696     5.39262    2.322202       10351    1.172e+08
  tgresult |  1.535242    2.328208    1.525847        5050     56820832
--------------------------------------------------------------------------------

(*) Some variables contain missing values.
```

If none of these options are specified, ci and deff are the default. Note that there is no control over
the order in which the options are displayed; they are always displayed in the order shown here.

We can also give display options when we first issue a command.

```
. svymean tcresult tgresult, deff meff obs
```

Using svytotal and svyratio

All our examples to this point have used svymean. The svytotal command has exactly the same
syntax.

In our NHANES II dataset, heartatk is a variable that is 1 if a person has ever had a heart attack
and 0 otherwise. We estimate the total numbers of persons who have had heart attacks by sex in the
population represented by our data.

```
. svytotal heartatk, by(sex)

Survey total estimation

pweight:  finalwgt                         Number of obs    =      10349
Strata:   stratid                          Number of strata =         31
PSU:      psuid                            Number of PSUs   =         62
                                           Population size  = 1.171e+08

--------------------------------------------------------------------------------
Total  Subpop. |   Estimate    Std. Err.   [95% Conf. Interval]        Deff
---------------+----------------------------------------------------------------
heartatk       |
          Male |    2304839    200231.3     1896465     2713213    1.567611
        Female |    1178437    109020.5    956088.2     1400786    .9000898
--------------------------------------------------------------------------------
```

The syntax for the svyratio command only differs from svymean and svytotal in the way the
varlist can be specified. All the options are the same.

In our NHANES II dataset, the variable `tcresult` contains total serum cholesterol and the variable `hdresult` contains serum levels of high-density lipoproteins (HDL). We can use `svyratio` to estimate the ratio of the total of `hdresult` to the total of `tcresult`.

```
. svyratio hdresult/tcresult

Survey ratio estimation

pweight: finalwgt                          Number of obs    =      8720
Strata:  newstr                            Number of strata =        30
PSU:     newpsu                            Number of PSUs   =        60
                                           Population size  =  98725345

------------------------------------------------------------------------
         Ratio  |  Estimate   Std. Err.   [95% Conf. Interval]     Deff
----------------+-------------------------------------------------------
hdresult/tcresult |  .2336173   .0024621    .228589    .2386457   7.724248
------------------------------------------------------------------------
```

Out of the 10351 NHANES II subjects with a `tcresult` reading, only 8720 had an `hdresult` reading. Consequently, `svyratio` used only the 8720 observations that had nonmissing values for both variables. In your own datasets, if you encounter substantial missing-data rates, it is generally a good idea to look into the reasons for the missing-data phenomenon, and to consider the potential for problems with nonresponse bias in your analysis.

Note that the slash / in the *varlist* for `svyratio` is optional. We could have typed

```
. svyratio hdresult tcresult
```

`svyratio` or `svymean` can be used to estimate means for subpopulations. Consider the following example.

In our NHANES II dataset, we have a variable `female` (equal to 1 if female and 0 otherwise) and a variable `iron` containing iron levels. Suppose that we wish to estimate the ratio of total iron levels in females to total number of females in the population. We can do this by first creating a new variable `firon` that represents iron levels in females; i.e., the variable equals iron level if the subject is female and zero if male. We can then use `svyratio` to estimate the ratio of the total of `firon` to the total of `female`.

```
. gen firon = female*iron

. svyratio firon/female

Survey ratio estimation

pweight: finalwgt                          Number of obs    =     10351
Strata:  stratid                           Number of strata =        31
PSU:     psuid                             Number of PSUs   =        62
                                           Population size  = 1.172e+08

------------------------------------------------------------------------
         Ratio  |  Estimate   Std. Err.   [95% Conf. Interval]     Deff
----------------+-------------------------------------------------------
  firon/female  |  97.16247   .6743344    95.78715   98.53778   2.014025
------------------------------------------------------------------------
```

This estimate can be obtained more easily using `svymean` with the `subpop` option. The computation that is carried out is identical.

```
. svymean iron, subpop(female)

Survey mean estimation

pweight:  finalwgt                         Number of obs    =     10351
Strata:   stratid                          Number of strata =        31
PSU:      psuid                            Number of PSUs   =        62
Subpop.:  female==1                        Population size  = 1.172e+08
```

```
--------------------------------------------------------------------------
    Mean |  Estimate    Std. Err.   [95% Conf. Interval]        Deff
---------+----------------------------------------------------------------
    iron |  97.16247    .6743344    95.78715    98.53778     2.014025
--------------------------------------------------------------------------
```

Estimating proportions

Estimating proportions can be done using the `svymean` or `svyprop` commands.

The mean of `heartatk` (`heartatk` equals 1 if a person has ever had a heart attack and 0 otherwise) is an estimate of the proportion of persons who have had heart attacks.

```
. svymean heartatk

Survey mean estimation

pweight:  finalwgt                           Number of obs    =     10349
Strata:   stratid                            Number of strata =        31
PSU:      psuid                              Number of PSUs   =        62
                                             Population size  = 1.171e+08

--------------------------------------------------------------------------
    Mean |  Estimate    Std. Err.   [95% Conf. Interval]        Deff
---------+----------------------------------------------------------------
heartatk |  .0297383    .0018484    .0259684    .0335081     1.225296
--------------------------------------------------------------------------
```

We could have also obtained this estimate using `svyprop`.

```
. svyprop heartatk

--------------------------------------------------------------------------
pweight:  finalwgt                           Number of obs    =     10349
Strata:   stratid                            Number of strata =        31
PSU:      psuid                              Number of PSUs   =        62
                                             Population size  = 1.171e+08
--------------------------------------------------------------------------

Survey proportions estimation
  heartatk      _Obs    _EstProp    _StdErr
         0      9873    0.970262    0.001848
         1       476    0.029738    0.001848
```

The `svymean` command produces more output than `svyprop`—it calculates covariance, deff, meff, etc. In order to do these computations, `svymean` requires that you specify a separate dummy (0/1) variable for each proportion you wish to estimate. With `svyprop`, we do not have to create dummy variables, nor does the command create them internally. `svyprop` will estimate proportions for all the categories defined by the unique values of the variables in its *varlist*. It can handle any number of categories, but provides less output.

```
. svyprop race agegrp

--------------------------------------------------------------------------
pweight:  finalwgt                           Number of obs    =     10351
Strata:   stratid                            Number of strata =        31
PSU:      psuid                              Number of PSUs   =        62
                                             Population size  = 1.172e+08
--------------------------------------------------------------------------

Survey proportions estimation
   race     agegrp      _Obs    _EstProp    _StdErr
  White    age20-29     1975    0.241082    0.006800
  White    age30-39     1411    0.178603    0.006491
  White    age40-49     1120    0.148661    0.004936
```

White	age50-59	1129	0.147948	0.006418
White	age60-69	2552	0.120860	0.004560
White	age 70+	878	0.042001	0.003132
Black	age20-29	286	0.031459	0.004918
Black	age30-39	179	0.020485	0.002754
Black	age40-49	124	0.015115	0.001964
Black	age50-59	140	0.015160	0.002668
Black	age60-69	260	0.009703	0.001380
Black	age 70+	97	0.003583	0.000753
Other	age20-29	59	0.007917	0.002237
Other	age30-39	32	0.005213	0.002072
Other	age40-49	28	0.004587	0.001669
Other	age50-59	22	0.004052	0.002168
Other	age60-69	48	0.002926	0.002152
Other	age 70+	11	0.000645	0.000540

svyprop also allows the by() and subpop() options for subpopulation estimates.

```
. svyprop agegrp, by(race)
```

```
-------------------------------------------------------------------------------
pweight:  finalwgt                         Number of obs      =       10351
Strata:   stratid                          Number of strata   =          31
PSU:      psuid                            Number of PSUs     =          62
                                           Population size     = 1.172e+08
-------------------------------------------------------------------------------
```

Survey proportions estimation

-> race=White

agegrp	_Obs	_EstProp	_StdErr
age20-29	1975	0.274220	0.007286
age30-39	1411	0.203153	0.006602
age40-49	1120	0.169096	0.004680
age50-59	1129	0.168285	0.005908
age60-69	2552	0.137473	0.004102
age 70+	878	0.047774	0.003265

-> race=Black

agegrp	_Obs	_EstProp	_StdErr
age20-29	286	0.329388	0.019606
age30-39	179	0.214495	0.012963
age40-49	124	0.158266	0.013822
age50-59	140	0.158738	0.012046
age60-69	260	0.101601	0.007740
age 70+	97	0.037513	0.005293

-> race=Other

agegrp	_Obs	_EstProp	_StdErr
age20-29	59	0.312426	0.047763
age30-39	32	0.205729	0.027031
age40-49	28	0.181028	0.019953
age50-59	22	0.159901	0.024910
age60-69	48	0.115473	0.038194
age 70+	11	0.025442	0.011067

Changing the strata, psu, fpc, and pweight variables

The NHANES II dataset contains a special sampling weight for use with the lead variable. We can change the pweight by setting it again using svyset.

```
. svyset pweight leadwt
```

```
. svymean lead, by(sex race)

Survey mean estimation

pweight:  leadwt                          Number of obs    =       4948
Strata:   stratid                         Number of strata =         31
PSU:      psuid                           Number of PSUs   =         62
                                          Population size   = 1.129e+08

----------------------------------------------------------------------------
Mean         Subpop. |  Estimate   Std. Err.   [95% Conf. Interval]     Deff
---------------------+------------------------------------------------------
lead                 |
     Male    White   |  16.78945   .3010539   16.17544   17.40345   4.641307
     Male    Black   |  19.70286   .7448225   18.18379   21.22194   1.950369
     Male    Other   |  16.16566   .9394023   14.24973   18.08158   1.293194
   Female    White   |  11.80468   .2447241   11.30556   12.30379   5.920213
   Female    Black   |  12.92722   .5255033   11.85545   13.99899   3.946779
   Female    Other   |  11.74192    .655919   10.40417   13.07968   1.492849
----------------------------------------------------------------------------
```

To change the pweight back to `finalwgt`, we type

```
. svyset pweight finalwgt
```

Remember that typing `svyset` alone displays the settings.

```
. svyset
strata is stratid
psu is psuid
pweight is finalwgt
```

Finite population correction (FPC)

A finite population correction (FPC) accounts for the reduction in variance that occurs when we sample *without* replacement from a finite population, as compared with sampling *with* replacement. The `fpc()` option of the `svy` commands computes an FPC for cases of simple random sampling or stratified random sampling; i.e., for sample designs that use simple random sampling without replacement of PSUs within each stratum with no subsampling within PSUs. The `fpc()` option is not intended for use with designs that involve subsampling within PSUs.

Consider the following dataset.

```
. list
        stratid    psuid    weight      nh       Nh        x
   1.        1        1        3        5       15       2.8
   2.        1        2        3        5       15       4.1
   3.        1        3        3        5       15       6.8
   4.        1        4        3        5       15       6.8
   5.        1        5        3        5       15       9.2
   6.        2        1        4        3       12       3.7
   7.        2        2        4        3       12       6.6
   8.        2        3        4        3       12       4.2
```

We first set the `strata`, `psu`, and `pweight`s.

```
. svyset strata stratid

. svyset psu psuid

. svyset pweight weight
```

In this dataset, the variable nh is the number of PSUs per stratum that were sampled, Nh is the total number of PSUs per stratum in the sampling frame (i.e., the population), and x is our survey item of interest. If we wish to use a finite population correction in our computations, we set fpc to Nh, the variable representing the total number of PSUs per stratum in the population.

```
. svyset fpc Nh

. svyset
strata is stratid
psu is psuid
pweight is weight
fpc is Nh

. svymean x

Survey mean estimation

pweight:  weight                          Number of obs    =        8
Strata:   stratid                         Number of strata =        2
PSU:      psuid                           Number of PSUs   =        8
FPC:      Nh                              Population size   =       27

------------------------------------------------------------------------
     Mean |   Estimate   Std. Err.   [95% Conf. Interval]      Deff
----------+-------------------------------------------------------------
        x |   5.448148   .6160407    3.940751    6.955545    .9853061
------------------------------------------------------------------------

Finite population correction (FPC) assumes simple random sampling without
replacement of PSUs within each stratum with no subsampling within PSUs.
```

If we want to redo the computation without an FPC, we must clear the fpc using svyset and run the estimation command again.

```
. svyset fpc, clear

. svymean x

Survey mean estimation

pweight:  weight                          Number of obs    =        8
Strata:   stratid                         Number of strata =        2
PSU:      psuid                           Number of PSUs   =        8
                                          Population size   =       27

------------------------------------------------------------------------
     Mean |   Estimate   Std. Err.   [95% Conf. Interval]      Deff
----------+-------------------------------------------------------------
        x |   5.448148   .7412683    3.63433     7.261966    1.003906
------------------------------------------------------------------------
```

Including an FPC always reduces the variance estimate. However, when the N_h are large relative to the n_h, the reduction in estimated variance due to the FPC is small.

Rather than having a variable that represents the total number of PSUs per stratum in the sampling frame, we sometimes have a variable that represents a sampling rate $f_h = n_h/N_h$. If we have a variable that represents a sampling rate, we set it the same way to get an FPC. The commands are smart; if the fpc variable is less than or equal to 1, it is interpreted as a sampling rate; if it is greater than or equal to n_h, it is interpreted as containing N_h.

Some fine points about deff and deft

The ratio deff (Kish 1965) is intended to compare the variance obtained under our complex survey design with the variance that we would have obtained if we had collected our observations through simple random sampling. deff is defined as

$$\text{deff} = \widehat{V}/\widehat{V}_{\text{srswor}}$$

where $\widehat{V}$ is the design-based estimate of variance (i.e., this is what the svy commands compute—the displayed standard error is the square root of $\widehat{V}$) and $\widehat{V}_{\text{srswor}}$ is an estimate of what the variance would be if a similar survey were conducted using simple random sampling (srs) without replacement (wor) with the same number of sample elements as in the actual survey. In other words, $\widehat{V}_{\text{srswor}}$ is an estimate of the variance for a hypothetical simple-random-sampling design in place of the complex design that we actually used; i.e., in place of our actual weighted/stratified/clustered design.

deft is defined as (Kish 1995)

$$\text{deft} = \sqrt{\widehat{V}/\widehat{V}_{\text{srswr}}}$$

where $\widehat{V}_{\text{srswr}}$ is computed in the same way as $\widehat{V}_{\text{srswor}}$ except now the hypothetical simple-random-sampling design is with replacement (wr).

Computationally, $\widehat{V}_{\text{srswor}} = (1 - m/\widehat{M})\widehat{V}_{\text{srswr}}$, where m is the number of sampled elements (i.e., the number of observations in the dataset) and $\widehat{M}$ is the estimated total number of elements in the population. For many surveys, the term $(1 - m/\widehat{M})$ is very close to 1, so that in these cases $\widehat{V}_{\text{srswor}}$ and $\widehat{V}_{\text{srswr}}$ are almost equal. Furthermore, if the fpc() option is not specified or set with svyset, we do not compute any finite population corrections, so the estimates produced for $\widehat{V}_{\text{srswor}}$ and $\widehat{V}_{\text{srswr}}$ are exactly equal. To summarize: deft is exactly the square root of deff when fpc is not set, and it is somewhat smaller than the square root of deff when the user sets an fpc.

The srssubpop option for deff and deft with subpopulations

When there are subpopulations, the svy commands can compute design effects with respect to one of two different hypothetical simple random sampling designs. The first hypothetical design is one in which simple random sampling is conducted across the full population. This scheme is the default for deff and deft computed by the svy commands. The second hypothetical design is one in which the simple random sampling is conducted entirely within the subpopulation of interest. This second scheme is used for deff and deft when the srssubpop option is specified.

Deciding which scheme is preferable depends on the nature of the subpopulations. If one reasonably can imagine identifying members of the subpopulations prior to sampling them, then the second scheme is preferable. This case arises primarily when the subpopulations are strata or groups of strata. Otherwise, one may prefer to use the first scheme.

Here is an example of using the first scheme (i.e., the default) with the NHANES II data.

```
. svymean iron, by(sex)

Survey mean estimation

pweight:  finalwgt                      Number of obs    =    10351
Strata:   stratid                       Number of strata =       31
PSU:      psuid                         Number of PSUs   =       62
                                        Population size  = 1.172e+08

-------------------------------------------------------------------------------
Mean    Subpop. |  Estimate   Std. Err.  [95% Conf. Interval]      Deff
----------------+--------------------------------------------------------------
iron            |
          Male  | 104.7969    .557267    103.6603   105.9334    1.360971
        Female  | 97.16247    .6743344   95.78715   98.53778    2.014025
-------------------------------------------------------------------------------
```

Here is the same example rerun using the second scheme; i.e., specifying the srssubpop option.

```
. svymean iron, by(sex) srssubpop
Survey mean estimation
pweight: finalwgt                          Number of obs    =       10351
Strata:  stratid                           Number of strata =          31
PSU:     psuid                             Number of PSUs   =          62
                                           Population size  = 1.172e+08
-------------------------------------------------------------------------------
Mean    Subpop. |  Estimate    Std. Err.    [95% Conf. Interval]      Deff
----------------+--------------------------------------------------------------
iron            |
         Male   |  104.7969    .557267     103.6603    105.9334     1.348002
         Female |  97.16247    .6743344    95.78715    98.53778     2.031321
-------------------------------------------------------------------------------
```

Because the NHANES II did not stratify on sex, we consider it problematic to consider design effects with respect to simple random sampling of the female (or male) subpopulation. Consequently, we would prefer to use the first scheme here, although the values of deff differ little between the two schemes in this case.

For other examples (generally involving heavy oversampling or undersampling of specified subpopulations), the differences in deff for the two schemes can be much more dramatic.

Consider the NMIHS data and compute the mean of `birthwgt` by `race`:

```
. svymean birthwgt, by(race) deff obs
Survey mean estimation
pweight: finwgt                            Number of obs    =        9946
Strata:  stratan                           Number of strata =           6
PSU:     <observations>                    Number of PSUs   =        9946
                                           Population size  = 3895561.7
-------------------------------------------------------------------------------
Mean    Subpop. |  Estimate    Std. Err.      Deff          Obs
----------------+--------------------------------------------------------------
birthwgt        |
        nonblack|  3402.32     7.609532     1.443763       4724
        black   |  3127.834    6.529814     .1720408       5222
-------------------------------------------------------------------------------

. svymean birthwgt, by(race) deff obs srssubpop
Survey mean estimation
pweight: finwgt                            Number of obs    =        9946
Strata:  stratan                           Number of strata =           6
PSU:     <observations>                    Number of PSUs   =        9946
                                           Population size  = 3895561.7
-------------------------------------------------------------------------------
Mean    Subpop. |  Estimate    Std. Err.      Deff          Obs
----------------+--------------------------------------------------------------
birthwgt        |
        nonblack|  3402.32     7.609532     .8268418       4724
        black   |  3127.834    6.529814     .5289629       5222
-------------------------------------------------------------------------------
```

Since the NMIHS survey was stratified on race, marital status, age, and birthweight, we consider it plausible to consider design effects computed with respect to simple random sampling within an individual race group. Consequently, in this case, we would recommend the second scheme; i.e., we would use the `srssubpop` option.

Misspecification effects: meff and meft

Misspecification effects are used to assess biases in variance estimators that are computed under the wrong assumptions. The survey literature (e.g., Scott and Holt 1982, p. 850; Skinner 1989) defines misspecification effects with respect to a general set of "wrong" variance estimators. The current svy commands consider only one specific form: variance estimators computed under the incorrect assumption that our *observed* sample was selected through simple random sampling.

The resulting "misspecification effect" measure is informative primarily in cases for which an unweighted point estimator is approximately unbiased for the parameter of interest. See Eltinge and Sribney (1996a) for a detailed discussion of extensions of misspecification effects that are appropriate for *biased* point estimators.

Note that the definition of misspecification effect is in contrast with the earlier definition of design effect. For a design effect, we compare our complex-design-based variance estimate with an estimate of the true variance that we would have obtained under a hypothetical true simple random sample.

The svy commands use the following definitions for meff_c and meft_c:

$$\text{meff}_c = \widehat{V}/\widehat{V}_{\text{msp}}$$

$$\text{meft}_c = \sqrt{\text{meff}_c}$$

where $\widehat{V}$ is the appropriate design-based estimate of variance and $\widehat{V}_{\text{msp}}$ is the variance estimate computed with a misspecified design—namely, ignoring the sampling weights, stratification, and clustering. In other words, $\widehat{V}_{\text{msp}}$ is what the ci command used without weights would naively compute.

Here we request that the misspecification effects be displayed for the estimation of mean zinc levels using our NHANES II data.

```
. svymean zinc, by(sex) meff meft

Survey mean estimation

pweight:  finalwgt                    Number of obs     =      9202
Strata:   stratid                     Number of strata  =        31
PSU:      psuid                       Number of PSUs    =        62
                                      Population size  = 1.043e+08

--------------------------------------------------------------------
Mean    Subpop. |  Estimate   Std. Err.      Meff       Meft
----------------+---------------------------------------------------
zinc            |
         Male   |  90.74543   .5850741    6.282539    2.506499
        Female  |   83.8635   .4689532    6.326477    2.515249
--------------------------------------------------------------------
```

If we run ci without weights, we get the standard errors that are $(\widehat{V}_{\text{msp}})^{1/2}$.

```
. ci zinc, by(sex)

-> sex=Male
Variable |     Obs        Mean   Std. Err.     [95% Conf. Interval]
---------+----------------------------------------------------------
   zinc  |    4375    89.53143   .2334228      89.0738    89.98906

-> sex=Female
Variable |     Obs        Mean   Std. Err.     [95% Conf. Interval]
---------+----------------------------------------------------------
   zinc  |    4827    83.76652    .186444      83.40101   84.13204
```

```
. di .5850741/.2334228
2.5064994
. di (.5850741/.2334228)^2
6.2825391
. di .4689532/.186444
2.5152496
. di (.4689532/.186444)^2
6.3264806
```

Saved Results

svymean, svytotal, svyratio save in e():

Scalars
e(N)	number of observations m
e(N_strata)	number of strata L
e(N_psu)	number of sampled PSUs n
e(N_pop)	estimate of population size $\widehat{M}$
e(n_by)	number of subpopulations

Macros
e(cmd)	command name (e.g., svymean)
e(depv)	Mean, Total, or Ratio
e(by)	by() *varlist*
e(subpop)	subpop() criterion
e(label)	label indicator or labels
e(wtype)	weight type
e(wexp)	weight variable or expression
e(strata)	strata() variable
e(psu)	psu() variable
e(fpc)	fpc() variable

Matrices
e(est)	vector of mean, total, or ratio estimates
e(V_db)	design-based (co)variance estimates $\widehat{V}$
e(V_msp)	misspecification (co)variance $\widehat{V}_{\mathrm{msp}}$
e(V_srs)	simple-random-sampling-without-replacement (co)variance $\widehat{V}_{\mathrm{srswor}}$
e(V_srswr)	simple-random-sampling-with-replacement (co)variance $\widehat{V}_{\mathrm{srswr}}$ (only created when fpc() option is specified)
e(deff)	vector of deff estimates
e(deft)	vector of deft estimates
e(meft)	vector of meft estimates
e(_N_subp)	vector of subpopulation size estimates
e(_N)	vector of numbers of nonmissing observations
e(_N_str)	vector of numbers of strata
e(_N_psu)	vector of numbers of sampled PSUs

Functions
e(sample)	marks estimation sample (complete option only)

Methods and Formulas

svymean, svytotal, svyratio, and svyprop are implemented as ado-files.

The current svy commands use the relatively simple variance estimators outlined below. See, for example, Cochran (1977) and Wolter (1985) for some methodological background on these variance estimators. In some cases, some authors prefer to use other variance estimators that, for example, account separately for variance components at different stages of sampling, use finite population corrections with some unequal-probability and multistage designs, and include other special design features.

In addition, the current svy commands use "linearization" based variance estimators for nonlinear functions like sample ratios. Alternative variance estimators that use replication methods—for example, jackknifing or balanced repeated replication—may be included in future svy versions.

Totals

All the computations done by the svytotal, svymean, svyratio, and svyprop commands are essentially based on the formulas for totals.

Let $h = 1, \ldots, L$ enumerate the strata in the survey, and let (h, i) denote the ith primary sampling unit (PSU) in stratum h for $i = 1, \ldots, N_h$, where N_h is the total number of PSUs in stratum h in the population. Let M_{hi} be the number of elements in PSU (h, i), and let $M = \sum_{h=1}^{L} \sum_{i=1}^{N_h} M_{hi}$ be the total number of elements in the population.

Let Y_{hij} be a survey item for element j in PSU (h, i) in stratum h; e.g., Y_{hij} might be income for adult j in block i in county h. The associated population total is

$$Y = \sum_{h=1}^{L} \sum_{i=1}^{N_h} \sum_{j=1}^{M_{hi}} Y_{hij} \tag{1}$$

Let y_{hij} be the items for those elements selected in our sample; here $h = 1, \ldots, L$; $i = 1, \ldots, n_h$; and $j = 1, \ldots, m_{hi}$. The total number of elements in the sample (i.e., the number of observations in the dataset) is $m = \sum_{h=1}^{L} \sum_{i=1}^{n_h} m_{hi}$.

Our estimator $\widehat{Y}$ for the population total Y is

$$\widehat{Y} = \sum_{h=1}^{L} \sum_{i=1}^{n_h} \sum_{j=1}^{m_{hi}} w_{hij} y_{hij} \tag{2}$$

where w_{hij} are the user-specified sampling weights (pweights or iweights). Our estimator $\widehat{M}$ for the total number of elements in the population is simply the sum of the weights:

$$\widehat{M} = \sum_{h=1}^{L} \sum_{i=1}^{n_h} \sum_{j=1}^{m_{hi}} w_{hij}$$

$\widehat{M}$ is labeled "Population size" on the output of the commands.

To compute an estimate of the variance of $\widehat{Y}$, we first define z_{yhi} and $\overline{z}_{yh}$ by

$$z_{yhi} = \sum_{j=1}^{m_{hi}} w_{hij} y_{hij} \qquad \text{and} \qquad \overline{z}_{yh} = \frac{1}{n_h} \sum_{i=1}^{n_h} z_{yhi}$$

Our estimate for the variance of $\widehat{Y}$ is

$$\widehat{V}(\widehat{Y}) = \sum_{h=1}^{L} (1 - f_h) \frac{n_h}{n_h - 1} \sum_{i=1}^{n_h} (z_{yhi} - \overline{z}_{yh})^2 \tag{3}$$

The factor $(1 - f_h)$ is the finite population correction. If the user does not set an `fpc` variable, $f_h = 0$ is used in the formula. If an `fpc` variable is set and is greater than or equal to n_h, the variable is assumed to contain the values of N_h, and f_h is given by $f_h = n_h/N_h$. If the `fpc` variable is less than or equal to 1, it is assumed to contain the values of f_h. As discussed earlier, nonzero values of f_h in formula (3) are intended for use *only* with simple random sampling or stratified random sampling with no subsampling within PSUs.

If the *varlist* given to `svytotal` contains two or more variables and the `complete` option is specified or is the default, the covariance of the variables is computed. For estimated totals $\widehat{Y}$ and $\widehat{X}$ (notation for X is defined similarly to that of Y), our covariance estimate is

$$\widehat{\text{Cov}}(\widehat{Y}, \widehat{X}) = \sum_{h=1}^{L} (1 - f_h) \frac{n_h}{n_h - 1} \sum_{i=1}^{n_h} (z_{yhi} - \overline{z}_{yh})(z_{xhi} - \overline{z}_{xh}) \tag{4}$$

Ratios, means, and proportions

Let $R = Y/X$ be a population ratio that we wish to estimate, where Y and X are population totals defined as in (1). Our estimate for R is $\widehat{R} = \widehat{Y}/\widehat{X}$. Using the delta method (i.e., a first-order Taylor expansion), the variance of the approximate distribution of $\widehat{R}$ is

$$\frac{1}{X^2} \left[V(\widehat{Y}) - 2R \, \text{Cov}(\widehat{Y}, \widehat{X}) + R^2 \, V(\widehat{X}) \right]$$

Direct substitution of $\widehat{X}$, $\widehat{R}$, and expressions (3) and (4) lead to the variance estimator

$$\widehat{V}(\widehat{R}) = \frac{1}{\widehat{X}^2} \left[\widehat{V}(\widehat{Y}) - 2\widehat{R} \, \widehat{\text{Cov}}(\widehat{Y}, \widehat{X}) + \widehat{R}^2 \, \widehat{V}(\widehat{X}) \right] \tag{5}$$

If we define the following "ratio residual"

$$d_{hij} = \frac{1}{\widehat{X}} (y_{hij} - \widehat{R} \, x_{hij}) \tag{6}$$

and replace y_{hij} with d_{hij} in our variance formula (3), we get the right-hand side of equation (7) below. Simple algebra shows that this is identical to (5).

$$\widehat{V}(\widehat{R}) = \sum_{h=1}^{L} (1 - f_h) \frac{n_h}{n_h - 1} \sum_{i=1}^{n_h} (z_{dhi} - \overline{z}_{dh})^2 \tag{7}$$

To extend our variance estimators from ratios to other parameters, note that means are simply ratios with $X_{hij} = 1$ and proportions are simply means with Y_{hij} equal to a $0/1$ variable. Similarly, estimates for a subpopulation S are obtained by computing estimates for $Y_{Shij} = I_{(h,i,j) \in S} Y_{hij}$ and $X_{Shij} = I_{(h,i,j) \in S} X_{hij}$ where $I_{(h,i,j) \in S}$ equals 1 if element (h, i, j) is a member of subpopulation S and 0 otherwise.

Weights

When computing finite population corrections (i.e., when an fpc variable is set) or when estimating totals, the svy commands assume your weights are the weights appropriate for estimation of a population total. For example, the sum of your weights should equal an estimate of the size of the relevant population. When an fpc is not set, the commands svymean, svyratio, and svyprop are invariant to the scale of the weights; i.e., these commands give the same results no matter what the scale of weights.

Confidence intervals

Let $n = \sum_{h=1}^{L} n_h$ be the total number of PSUs in the sample. The customary "degrees of freedom" attributed to our test statistic are $d = n - L$. Hence, under regularity conditions, an approximate $100(1 - \alpha)\%$ confidence interval for a parameter θ (e.g., θ could be a total Y or ratio R) is $\widehat{\theta} \pm t_{1-\alpha/2,d} \, [\widehat{V}(\widehat{\theta})]^{1/2}$.

Cochran (1977, Section 2.8) and Korn and Graubard (1990) give some theoretical justification for the use of $d = n - L$ in computation of univariate confidence intervals and p-values. However, for some cases, inferences based on the customary $n - L$ degrees-of-freedom calculation may be excessively liberal. For example, the resulting confidence intervals may have coverage rates substantially less than the nominal $1 - \alpha$. This problem generally is of greatest practical concern when the population of interest has a very skewed or heavy-tailed distribution, or is concentrated in a small number of PSUs. In some of these cases, the user may want to consider constructing confidence intervals based on alternative degrees-of-freedom terms based on the Satterthwaite (1941, 1946) approximation and modifications thereof; see, e.g., Cochran (1977, 96) and Jang and Eltinge (1995).

deff and deft

deff is estimated as (Kish 1965)

$$\text{deff} = \frac{\widehat{V}(\widehat{\theta})}{\widetilde{V}_{\text{srswor}}(\widetilde{\theta}_{\text{srs}})}$$

where $\widehat{V}(\widehat{\theta})$ is the design-based estimate of variance from formula (3) for a parameter θ, and $\widehat{V}_{\text{srswor}}(\widetilde{\theta}_{\text{srs}})$ is an estimate of the variance for an estimator $\widetilde{\theta}_{\text{srs}}$ that would be obtained from a similar hypothetical survey conducted using simple random sampling (srs) without replacement (wor) with the same number of sample elements m as in the actual survey. If θ is a total Y, we calculate

$$\widehat{V}_{\text{srswor}}(\widetilde{\theta}_{\text{srs}}) = (1 - f) \frac{\widehat{M}}{m - 1} \sum_{h=1}^{L} \sum_{i=1}^{n_h} \sum_{j=1}^{m_{hi}} w_{hij} \left(y_{hij} - \widehat{\overline{Y}} \right)^2 \tag{8}$$

where $\widehat{\overline{Y}} = \widehat{Y}/\widehat{M}$. The factor $(1 - f)$ is a finite population correction. If the user sets an fpc, we use $f = m/\widehat{M}$; if the user does not specify an fpc, $f = 0$ is used. If θ is a ratio R, we replace y_{hij} in (8) with d_{hij} from (6). Note that $\sum_{h=1}^{L} \sum_{i=1}^{n_h} \sum_{j=1}^{m_{hi}} w_{hij} d_{hij} = 0$, so that $\widehat{\overline{Y}}$ is replaced with zero.

deft is estimated as (Kish 1995)

$$
\text{deft} = \sqrt{\frac{\widehat{V}(\theta)}{\widehat{V}_{\text{srswr}}(\widetilde{\theta}_{\text{srs}})}}
$$

where $\widehat{V}_{\text{srswr}}(\widetilde{\theta}_{\text{srs}})$ is an estimate of the variance for an estimator $\widetilde{\theta}_{\text{srs}}$ obtained from a similar survey conducted using simple random sampling (srs) with replacement (wr). $\widehat{V}_{\text{srswr}}(\widetilde{\theta}_{\text{srs}})$ is computed using (8) with $f = 0$.

When we are computing estimates for a subpopulation $\mathcal{S}$ and the srssubpop option is *not* specified (i.e., the default), formula (8) is used with $y_{\mathcal{S}hij} = I_{(h,i,j)\in\mathcal{S}}\, y_{hij}$ in place of y_{hij}. Note that the sums in (8) are still calculated over all elements in the sample regardless of whether they belong to the subpopulation. This is because we assume, by default, that the simple random sampling is done across the full population.

When the srssubpop option is specified, we assume that the simple random sampling is carried out within subpopulation $\mathcal{S}$. In this case, we use (8) with the sums restricted to those elements belonging to the subpopulation; m is replaced with $m_{\mathcal{S}}$, the number of sample elements from the subpopulation; $\widehat{M}$ is replaced with $\widehat{M}_{\mathcal{S}}$, the sum of the weights from the subpopulation; and $\widehat{\overline{Y}} = \widehat{Y}/\widehat{M}$ is replaced with $\widehat{\overline{Y}}_{\mathcal{S}} = \widehat{Y}_{\mathcal{S}}/\widehat{M}_{\mathcal{S}}$, the weighted mean across the subpopulation.

meff and meft

meff_{c} and meft_{c} are estimated as

$$
\text{meff}_{\text{c}} = \frac{\widehat{V}(\theta)}{\widehat{V}_{\text{msp}}(\widehat{\theta}_{\text{msp}})}
$$

$$
\text{meft}_{\text{c}} = \sqrt{\text{meff}_{\text{c}}}
$$

where $\widehat{V}(\theta)$ is the design-based estimate of variance from formula (3) for a parameter θ. In addition, $\widehat{\theta}_{\text{msp}}$ and $\widehat{V}_{\text{msp}}(\widehat{\theta}_{\text{msp}})$ are the point estimator and variance estimator based on the incorrect assumption that our observations were obtained through simple random sampling with replacement—in other words, they are the estimators obtained by simply ignoring weights, stratification, and clustering. When θ is a mean $\overline{Y}$, the estimator and its variance estimate are computed using the standard formulas for an unweighted mean:

$$
\widehat{\overline{Y}}_{\text{msp}} = \frac{1}{m}\sum_{h=1}^{L}\sum_{i=1}^{n_h}\sum_{j=1}^{m_{hi}} y_{hij}
$$

$$
\widehat{V}_{\text{msp}}(\widehat{\overline{Y}}_{\text{msp}}) = \frac{1}{m(m-1)}\sum_{h=1}^{L}\sum_{i=1}^{n_h}\sum_{j=1}^{m_{hi}}\left(y_{hij} - \widehat{\overline{Y}}_{\text{msp}}\right)^2
$$

When θ is a total Y, $\widehat{Y}_{\text{msp}} = \widehat{M}\,\widehat{\overline{Y}}_{\text{msp}}$ and $\widehat{V}_{\text{msp}}(\widehat{Y}_{\text{msp}}) = \widehat{M}^2\,\widehat{V}_{\text{msp}}(\widehat{\overline{Y}}_{\text{msp}})$. When θ is a ratio $R = Y/X$, $\widehat{R}_{\text{msp}} = \widehat{\overline{Y}}_{\text{msp}}/\widehat{\overline{X}}_{\text{msp}}$ and the estimator (5) with $\widehat{V}_{\text{msp}}(\widehat{\overline{Y}}_{\text{msp}})$, etc., is used to compute $\widehat{V}_{\text{msp}}(\widehat{R}_{\text{msp}})$.

When we compute meff and meft for a subpopulation, we simply restrict our sums to those elements belonging to the subpopulation and use $m_\mathcal{S}$ and $\widehat{M}_\mathcal{S}$ in place of m and $\widehat{M}$.

Acknowledgments

The `svymean`, `svytotal`, `svyratio`, and `svyprop` commands were developed in collaboration with John L. Eltinge, Department of Statistics, Texas A&M University. We thank him for his invaluable assistance.

We thank Wayne Johnson of the National Center for Health Statistics for providing the NMIHS and NHANES II datasets.

References

Cochran, W. G. 1977. *Sampling Techniques.* 3d ed. New York: John Wiley & Sons.

Eltinge, J. L. and W. M. Sribney. 1996a. Accounting for point-estimation bias in assessment of misspecification effects, confidence-set coverage rates and test sizes. Unpublished manuscript. Department of Statistics, Texas A & M University.

——. 1996b. svy2: Estimation of means, totals, rations, and proportions for survey data. *Stata Technical Bulletin* 31: 6–23. Reprinted in *Stata Technical Bulletin Reprints*, vol. 6, pp. 213–235.

Gonzalez, J. F., Jr., N. Krauss, and C. Scott. 1992. Estimation in the 1988 National Maternal and Infant Health Survey. In *Proceedings of the Section on Statistics Education, American Statistical Association*, 343–348.

Jang, D. S. and J. L. Eltinge. 1995. Empirical assessment of the stability of variance estimators based on a two-clusters-per-stratum design. Technical Report #225, Department of Statistics, Texas A&M University. Submitted for publication.

Johnson, W. 1995. Variance estimation for the NMIHS. Technical document. National Center for Health Statistics, Hyattsville, MD.

Kish, L. 1965. *Survey Sampling.* New York: John Wiley & Sons.

——. 1995. Methods for design effects. *Journal of Official Statistics* 11: 55–77.

Korn, E. L., and B. I. Graubard. 1990. Simultaneous testing of regression coefficients with complex survey data: use of Bonferroni t statistics. *The American Statistician* 44: 270–276.

McDowell, A., A. Engel, J. T. Massey, and K. Maurer. 1981. Plan and operation of the Second National Health and Nutrition Examination Survey, 1976–1980. *Vital and Health Statistics* 15(1). National Center for Health Statistics, Hyattsville, MD.

Satterthwaite, F. E. 1941. Synthesis of variance. *Psychometrika* 6: 309–316.

——. 1946. An approximate distribution of estimates of variance components. *Biometrics Bulletin* 2: 110–114.

Scott, A. J. and D. Holt. 1982. The effect of two-stage sampling on ordinary least squares methods. *Journal of the American Statistical Association* 77: 848–854.

Skinner, C. J. 1989. Introduction to Part A. In *Analysis of Complex Surveys*, ed. C. J. Skinner, D. Holt, and T. M. F. Smith, 23–58. New York: John Wiley & Sons.

Wolter, K. M. 1985. *Introduction to Variance Estimation.* New York: Springer-Verlag.

Also See

Complementary:	[R] **svy estimators**, [R] **svydes**, [R] **svylc**, [R] **svyset**, [R] **svytab**, [R] **svytest**
Related:	[R] **ci**
Background:	[U] **30 Overview of survey estimation**,
	[R] **svy**

Title

svyset — Set variables for survey data

Syntax

svyset [*thing_to_set* [*varname*]] [, clear]

Description

svyset associates a variable with an option or weight for the svy commands.

You can set any or all of the following:

thing_to_set	Sets	Description
strata	strata(*varname*) option	strata identifier variable *varname*
psu	psu(*varname*) option	PSU (cluster) identifier variable *varname*
fpc	fpc(*varname*) option	finite population correction variable *varname*
pweight	[pweight=*varname*]	sampling (probability) weight variable *varname*

Settings made by svyset are saved with a dataset. So if a dataset is saved after a *thing_to_set* has been set, it does not have to be set again.

Current settings can be displayed by typing svyset without arguments. Settings can be changed simply by setting a different variable. Settings can be erased using the clear option.

Options

clear clears the current setting of *thing_to_set* if *thing_to_set* is specified. If svyset, clear is typed, all settings are cleared.

Remarks

▷ Example

We use the svyset command to set the stratification variable and the pweight variable.

```
. svyset strata stratan
. svyset pweight finwgt
```

Typing svyset alone shows what has been set.

```
. svyset
strata is stratan
pweight is finwgt
```

73

If we save the dataset, these settings will be remembered next time we use this dataset.

```
. save nmihs, replace
file nmihs.dta saved
. use nmihs, clear
. svyset
strata is stratan
pweight is finwgt
```

We can now use the svy commands without having to specify explicitly the pweights and the strata() option.

```
. svymean birthwgt

Survey mean estimation

pweight:  finwgt                    Number of obs     =        9946
Strata:   stratan                   Number of strata  =           6
PSU:      <observations>            Number of PSUs    =        9946
                                    Population size    = 3895561.7

---------------------------------------------------------------------------
      Mean |   Estimate   Std. Err.   [95% Conf. Interval]      Deff
---------+-----------------------------------------------------------------
  birthwgt |   3355.452    6.402741    3342.902   3368.003    1.142614
---------------------------------------------------------------------------
```

Alternatively, we could have set the pweights and strata when we issued the command.

```
. svymean birthwgt [pweight=finwgt], strata(stratan)
```
(*output omitted*)
```
. svyset
strata is stratan
pweight is finwgt
```

Specifying the pweights and strata() option has exactly the same effect as using svyset. No matter which of these methods are used initially to set pweights and strata, the settings are remembered and do not have to be specified in subsequent use of any of the svy commands.

The settings can be changed by setting another variable.

```
. svyset pweight adjwgt
```

Typing svyset shows the settings.

```
. svyset
strata is stratan
pweight is adjwgt
```

Settings can be erased using the clear option. Either a single setting can be erased:

```
. svyset strata, clear
. svyset
pweight is adjwgt
```

Or all settings can be erased:

```
. svyset, clear
. svyset
no variables have been set
```

◁

Methods and Formulas

svyset is implemented as an ado-file.

Also See

Complementary: [R] **svy estimators**, [R] **svydes**, [R] **svylc**, [R] **svymean**, [R] **svytab**, [R] **svytest**

Background: [U] **30 Overview of survey estimation**,
                        [R] **svy**

Title

svytab — Tables for survey data

Syntax

svytab *varname₁* *varname₂* [*weight*] [in *exp*] [in *range*] [,

    strata(*varname*) psu(*varname*) fpc(*varname*) subpop(*varname*) srssubpop

    tab(*varname*) missing

    cell count row column obs se ci deff deft

    { proportion | percent } nolabel nomarginals format(%*fmt*) vertical level(#)

    pearson lr null wald llwald noadjust]

pweights and iweights are allowed; see [U] **14.1.6 weight**.

When any of se, ci, deff, or deft are specified, only one of cell, count, row, or column can be specified. If none of se, ci, deff, or deft are specified, any or all of cell, count, row, and column can be specified.

svytab is implemented as an estimation command; as such, it shares the features of all estimation commands; see [U] **23 Estimation and post-estimation commands**. In particular, svytab typed without arguments redisplays previous results. Any of the options on the last three lines of the syntax diagram (cell through noadjust) can be specified when redisplaying with the following exception: wald must be specified at run time.

Warning: Use of if or in restrictions will not produce correct statistics and variance estimates for subpopulations in many cases. To compute estimates for a subpopulation, use the subpop() option.

Description

svytab produces two-way tabulations with tests of independence for complex survey data or for other clustered data.

Despite the long list of options for svytab, it is a simple command to use. Using the svytab command is just like using tabulate to produce two-way tables for ordinary data. The main difference is that svytab will compute a test of independence that is appropriate for a complex survey design or for clustered data.

The test of independence that is displayed by default is based on the usual Pearson χ^2 statistic for two-way tables. To account for the survey design, the statistic is turned into an F statistic with noninteger degrees of freedom using a second-order Rao and Scott (1981, 1984) correction. Although the theory behind the Rao and Scott correction is complicated, the p-value for the corrected F statistic can be interpreted in the same way as a p-value for the Pearson χ^2 statistic for "ordinary" data (i.e., data that are assumed independent and identically distributed).

svytab will, in fact, compute four statistics for the test of independence with two variants of each, for a total of eight statistics. The options that give these eight statistics are pearson (the default), lr, null (a toggle for displaying variants of the pearson and lr statistics), wald, llwald, and noadjust (a toggle for displaying variants of the wald and llwald statistics). The options wald and llwald with noadjust yield the statistics developed by Koch et al. (1975), which have been implemented in the CROSSTAB procedure of the SUDAAN software (Shah et al. 1997, Release 7.5).

These eight statistics along with other variants have been evaluated in simulations (Sribney 1998). Based on these simulations, we advise researchers to use the default statistic (the `pearson` option) in all situations. We recommend that the other statistics only be used for comparative or pedagogical purposes. Sribney (1998) gives a detailed comparison of the statistics; a summary of his conclusions is provided later in this entry.

Other than the survey design options (the first row of options in the syntax diagram) and the test statistic options (the last row of options in the diagram), most of the other options of `svytab` simply relate to different choices for what can be displayed in the body of the table. By default, cell proportions are displayed, but it is likely that in most circumstances, it makes more sense to view either row or column proportions or weighted counts.

Standard errors and confidence intervals can optionally be displayed for weighted counts or cell, row, or column proportions. The confidence intervals are constructed using a logit transform so that their endpoints always lie between 0 and 1. Associated design effects (deff and deft) can be viewed for the variance estimates. The mean generalized deff (Rao and Scott 1984) is also displayed when `deff` or `deft` is requested. The mean generalized deff is essentially a design effect for the asymptotic distribution of the test statistic; see the *Methods and Formulas* section at the end of this entry.

Options

The survey design options `strata()`, `psu()`, `fpc()`, `subpop()`, and `srssubpop` are the same as those for the `svymean` command; see [R] **svyset** and [R] **svymean** for a description of these options.

`tab`(*varname*) specifies that counts should instead be cell totals of this variable and proportions (or percentages) should be relative to (i.e., weighted by) this variable. For example, if this variable denotes income, then the cell "counts" are instead totals of income for each cell, and the cell proportions are proportions of income for each cell.

`missing` specifies that missing values of *varname*$_1$ and *varname*$_2$ are to be treated as another row or column category, rather than be omitted from the analysis (the default).

`cell` requests that cell proportions (or percentages) be displayed. This is the default if none of `count`, `row`, or `column` are specified.

`count` requests that weighted cell counts be displayed.

`row` or `column` requests that row or column proportions (or percentages) be displayed.

`obs` requests that the number of observations for each cell be displayed.

`se` requests that the standard errors of either cell proportions (the default), weighted counts, or row or column proportions be displayed. When `se` (or `ci`, `deff`, or `deft`) is specified only one of `cell`, `count`, `row`, or `column` can be selected. The standard error computed is the standard error of the one selected.

`ci` requests confidence intervals for either cell proportions, weighted counts, or row or column proportions.

`deff` or `deft` requests that the design-effect measure deff or deft be displayed for either cell proportions, counts, or row or column proportions. See [R] **svymean** for details. The mean generalized deff is also displayed when `deff` or `deft` is requested; see *Methods and Formulas* for an explanation.

`proportion` or `percent` requests that proportions (the default) or percentages be displayed.

`nolabel` requests that variable labels and value labels be ignored.

`nomarginals` requests that row and column marginals not be displayed.

format(%*fmt*) specifies a format for the items in the table. The default is %6.0g. See [U] **15.5 Formats: controlling how data is displayed**.

vertical requests that the endpoints of confidence intervals be stacked vertically on display.

level(#) specifies the confidence level (i.e., nominal coverage rate), in percent, for confidence intervals. The default is level(95) or as set by set level; see [U] **23.5 Specifying the width of confidence intervals**.

pearson requests that the Pearson χ^2 statistic be computed. By default, this is the test of independence that is displayed. The Pearson χ^2 statistic is corrected for the survey design using the second-order correction of Rao and Scott (1984) and converted into an F statistic. One term in the correction formula can be calculated using either observed cell proportions or proportions under the null hypothesis (i.e., the product of the marginals). By default, observed cell proportions are used. If the null option is selected, then a statistic corrected using proportions under the null is displayed as well. See the following discussion for details.

lr requests that the likelihood-ratio test statistic for proportions be computed. Note that this statistic is not defined when there are one or more zero cells in the table. The statistic is corrected for the survey design using exactly the same correction procedure that is used with the pearson statistic. Again, either observed cell proportions or proportions under the null can be used in the correction formula. By default, the former is used; specifying the null option gives both the former and the latter. Neither variant of this statistic is recommended for sparse tables. For nonsparse tables, the lr statistics are very similar to the corresponding pearson statistics.

null modifies the pearson and lr options only. If it is specified, two corrected statistics are displayed. The statistic labeled "D-B (null)" ("D-B" stands for design-based) uses proportions under the null hypothesis (i.e., the product of the marginals) in the Rao and Scott (1984) correction. The statistic labeled merely "Design-based" uses observed cell proportions. If null is not specified, only the correction that uses observed proportions is displayed. See the following discussion for details.

wald requests a Wald test of whether observed weighted counts equal the product of the marginals (Koch et al. 1975). By default, an adjusted F statistic is produced; an unadjusted statistic can be produced by specifying noadjust. The unadjusted F statistic can yield extremely anticonservative p-values (i.e., p-values that are too small) when the degrees of freedom of the variance estimates (the number of sampled PSUs minus the number of strata) are small relative to the $(R-1)(C-1)$ degrees of freedom of the table (where R is the number of rows and C is the number of columns). Hence, the statistic produced by wald and noadjust should not be used for inference except when it is essentially identical to the adjusted statistic.

llwald requests a Wald test of the log-linear model of independence (Koch et al. 1975). Note that the statistic is not defined when there are one or more zero cells in the table. The adjusted statistic (the default) can produce anticonservative p-values, especially for sparse tables, when the degrees of freedom of the variance estimates are small relative to the degrees of freedom of the table. Specifying noadjust yields a statistic with more severe problems. Neither the adjusted nor the unadjusted statistic is recommended for inference; the statistics are only made available for comparative and pedagogical purposes.

noadjust modifies the wald and llwald options only. It requests that an unadjusted F statistic be displayed in addition to the adjusted statistic.

Note: svytab uses the tabdisp command (see [R] **tabdisp**) to produce the table. Only five items can be displayed in the table at one time. If too many items are selected, a warning will appear immediately. To view additional items, redisplay the table while specifying different options.

Remarks

Most of svytab's options deal with choices for the items that can be displayed in the body of the table. We will illustrate these options in a series of examples.

▷ Example

We use data from the Second National Health and Nutrition Examination Survey (NHANES II) (McDowell et al. 1981). The strata, psu, and pweight variables are first set using the svyset command rather than specifying them as options to svytab; see [R] svyset for details.

```
. svyset strata stratid
. svyset psu psuid
. svyset pweight finalwgt
. svytab race diabetes
-------------------------------------------------------------------------------
pweight:  finalwgt                      Number of obs     =      10349
Strata:   stratid                       Number of strata  =         31
PSU:      psuid                         Number of PSUs    =         62
                                        Population size    = 1.171e+08
-------------------------------------------------------------------------------

----------+--------------------------
          |        Diabetes
    Race  |    no      yes     Total
----------+--------------------------
   White  |   .851    .0281    .8791
   Black  |  .0899    .0056    .0955
   Other  |  .0248   5.2e-04   .0253
          |
   Total  |  .9658    .0342       1
----------+--------------------------
 Key:  cell proportions

 Pearson:
   Uncorrected   chi2(2)         =   21.3483
   Design-based  F(1.52,47.26)   =   15.0056      P = 0.0000
```

The default table displays only cell proportions, and this makes it very difficult to compare the incidence of diabetes in white versus black versus "other" racial groups. It would be better to look at row proportions. This can be done by redisplaying the results (i.e., the command is reissued without specifying any variables) with the row option.

```
. svytab, row
-------------------------------------------------------------------------------
pweight:  finalwgt                      Number of obs     =      10349
Strata:   stratid                       Number of strata  =         31
PSU:      psuid                         Number of PSUs    =         62
                                        Population size    = 1.171e+08
-------------------------------------------------------------------------------

----------+--------------------
          |      Diabetes
    Race  |   no     yes   Total
----------+--------------------
   White  |  .968   .032      1
   Black  |  .941   .059      1
   Other  | .9797  .0203      1
          |
   Total  | .9658  .0342      1
----------+--------------------
```

```
Key:  row proportions
Pearson:
  Uncorrected   chi2(2)          =    21.3483
  Design-based  F(1.52,47.26)    =    15.0056     P = 0.0000
```

This table is much easier to interpret. A larger proportion of blacks have diabetes than do whites or persons in the "other" racial category. Note that the test of independence for a two-way contingency table is equivalent to the test of homogeneity of row (or column) proportions. Hence, we can conclude that there is a highly significant difference between the incidence of diabetes among the three racial groups.

We may now wish to compute confidence intervals for the row proportions. If we try to redisplay specifying `ci` along with `row`, we get the following result:

```
. svytab, row ci
confidence intervals are only available for cells
to compute row confidence intervals, rerun command with row and ci options
r(111);
```

There are limits to what `svytab` can redisplay. Basically, any of the options relating to variance estimation (i.e., `se`, `ci`, `deff`, and `deft`) must be specified at run time along with the single item (i.e., `count`, `cell`, `row`, or `column`) for which one wants standard errors, confidence intervals, deff, or deft. So to get confidence intervals for row proportions, one must rerun the command. We do so below requesting not only `ci` but also `se`.

```
. svytab race diabetes, row se ci format(%7.4f)
```

```
------------------------------------------------------------------------------
pweight:  finalwgt                        Number of obs      =      10349
Strata:   stratid                         Number of strata   =         31
PSU:      psuid                           Number of PSUs     =         62
                                          Population size    = 1.171e+08
------------------------------------------------------------------------------

----------+--------------------------------------------------------
          |                   Diabetes
   Race   |          no              yes            Total
----------+--------------------------------------------------------
  White   |      0.9680           0.0320           1.0000
          |     (0.0020)         (0.0020)
          |  [0.9638,0.9718]  [0.0282,0.0362]
          |
  Black   |      0.9410           0.0590           1.0000
          |     (0.0061)         (0.0061)
          |  [0.9271,0.9523]  [0.0477,0.0729]
          |
  Other   |      0.9797           0.0203           1.0000
          |     (0.0076)         (0.0076)
          |  [0.9566,0.9906]  [0.0094,0.0434]
          |
  Total   |      0.9658           0.0342           1.0000
          |     (0.0018)         (0.0018)
          |  [0.9619,0.9693]  [0.0307,0.0381]
----------+--------------------------------------------------------
  Key:  row proportions
        (standard errors of row proportions)
        [95% confidence intervals for row proportions]

  Pearson:
    Uncorrected   chi2(2)          =    21.3483
    Design-based  F(1.52,47.26)    =    15.0056     P = 0.0000
```

In the above table, we specified a `%7.4f` format rather than use the default `%6.0g` format. Note that the single format applies to every item in the table. If you do not want to see the marginal totals, you can omit them by specifying nomarginal. If the above style for displaying the confidence intervals is obtrusive—and it can be in a wider table—you can use the vertical option to stack the endpoints of the confidence interval one over the other and omit the brackets (the parentheses around the standard errors are also omitted when vertical is specified). If you would rather have results expressed as percentages, like the tabulate command (see [R] **tabulate**), use the percent option. If you want to play around with these display options until you get a table that you are satisfied with, first try making changes to the options on redisplay (i.e., omit the cross-tabulated variables when you issue the command). This will be much faster if you have a large dataset.

◁

❏ Technical Note

The standard errors computed by svytab are exactly the same as those produced by the other svy commands that can compute proportions: namely, svymean, svyratio, and svyprop. Indeed, svytab calls the same driver program that svymean and svyratio use.

Continuing with the previous example, we note that the estimate of the proportion of African-Americans with diabetes (the second proportion in the second row of the preceding table) is simply a ratio estimate; hence, we can also obtain the same estimates using svyratio:

```
gen black = (race==2) if race~=.
. gen diablk = diabetes*black
(2 missing values generated)

. svyratio diablk/black

Survey ratio estimation

pweight:  finalwgt                        Number of obs      =      10349
Strata:   stratid                         Number of strata   =         31
PSU:      psuid                           Number of PSUs     =         62
                                          Population size    = 1.171e+08

-------------------------------------------------------------------------
          Ratio  |  Estimate   Std. Err.   [95% Conf. Interval]     Deff
-----------------+-------------------------------------------------------
    diablk/black |  .0590349   .0061443   .0465035    .0715662   .6718049
-------------------------------------------------------------------------
```

Although the standard errors are exactly the same (which they must be since the same driver program computes both), the confidence intervals are slightly different. The svytab command produced the confidence interval $[0.0477, 0.0729]$, and svyratio gave $[0.0465, 0.0716]$. The difference is due to the fact that svytab uses a logit transform to produce confidence intervals whose endpoints are always between 0 and 1. This transformation also shifts the confidence intervals slightly toward the null (i.e., 0.5), which is beneficial since the untransformed confidence intervals tend to be, on average, biased away from the null. See the *Methods and Formulas* section at the end of this entry for details.

❏

The tab option

The tab() option allows one to compute proportions relative to a certain variable. For example, suppose one wishes to compare the proportion of total income among different racial groups in males with that of females. We do so below with fictitious data:

```
. svytab gender race, tab(income) row

--------------------------------------------------------------------------
pweight:  samwgt                          Number of obs    =      5479
Strata:   samstr                          Number of strata =         4
PSU:      sampsu                          Number of PSUs   =        76
                                          Population size  =   1986683
--------------------------------------------------------------------------


----------+--------------------------
          |          Race
 Gender   | White  Black  Other  Total
----------+--------------------------
    Male  | .8857  .0875  .0268      1
  Female  | .884   .094   .022       1
          |
   Total  | .8848  .0909  .0243      1
----------+--------------------------
Tabulated variable:  income

Key:  row proportions

Pearson:
  Uncorrected   chi2(2)         =    3.6241
  Design-based  F(1.91,59.12)   =    0.8626     P = 0.4227
```

The Rao and Scott correction

svytab can produce eight different statistics for the test of independence. By default, svytab displays the Pearson χ^2 statistic with the Rao and Scott (1981, 1984) second-order correction. Based on simulations (Sribney 1998), we recommend that researchers use this statistic in all situations. The statistical literature, however, contains several alternatives, along with other possibilities for the implementation of the Rao and Scott correction. Hence, for comparative or pedagogical purposes, one may want to view some of the other statistics computed by svytab. We briefly describe the differences among these statistics; for a more detailed discussion, see Sribney (1998).

Two statistics commonly used for independent, identically distributed (iid) data for the test of independence of $R \times C$ tables (R rows and C columns) are the Pearson χ^2 statistic

$$X_{\mathrm{P}}^2 = n \sum_{r=1}^{R} \sum_{c=1}^{C} (\widehat{p}_{rc} - \widehat{p}_{0rc})^2 / \widehat{p}_{0rc}$$

and the likelihood-ratio χ^2 statistic

$$X_{\mathrm{LR}}^2 = 2n \sum_{r=1}^{R} \sum_{c=1}^{C} \widehat{p}_{rc} \ln (\widehat{p}_{rc} / \widehat{p}_{0rc})$$

where n is the total number of observations, $\widehat{p}_{rc}$ is the estimated proportion for the cell in the rth row and cth column of the table, and $\widehat{p}_{0rc}$ is the estimated proportion under the null hypothesis of independence; i.e., $\widehat{p}_{0rc} = \widehat{p}_{r.}\widehat{p}_{.c}$, the product of the row and column marginals: $\widehat{p}_{r.} = \sum_{c=1}^{C} \widehat{p}_{rc}$ and $\widehat{p}_{.c} = \sum_{r=1}^{R} \widehat{p}_{rc}$.

For iid data, both of these statistics are distributed asymptotically as $\chi_{(R-1)(C-1)}^2$. Note that the likelihood-ratio statistic is not defined when one or more of the cells in the table are empty. The Pearson statistic, however, can be calculated when one or more cells in the table are empty—the statistic may not have good properties in this case, but the statistic still has a computable value.

For survey data, X_P^2 and X_{LR}^2 can be computed using weighted estimates of $\widehat{p}_{rc}$ and $\widehat{p}_{0rc}$. However, for a complex sampling design, one can no longer claim that they are distributed as $\chi^2_{(R-1)(C-1)}$. But one can estimate the variance of $\widehat{p}_{rc}$ under the sampling design. For instance, in Stata, this variance can be estimated using linearization methods using svymean or svyratio.

Rao and Scott (1981, 1984) derived the asymptotic distribution of X_P^2 and X_{LR}^2 in terms of the variance of $\widehat{p}_{rc}$. Unfortunately, the result (see equation (1) in *Methods and Formulas*) is not computationally feasible, but it can be approximated using correction formulas. svytab uses the second-order correction developed by Rao and Scott (1984). By default or when the pearson option is specified, svytab displays the second-order correction of the Pearson statistic. The lr option gives the second-order correction of the likelihood-ratio statistic. Because it is the default of svytab, we refer to the correction computed with $\widehat{p}_{rc}$ as the default correction.

The Rao and Scott papers, however, left some details outstanding about the computation of the correction. One term in the correction formula can be computed using either $\widehat{p}_{rc}$ or $\widehat{p}_{0rc}$. Since under the null hypothesis both are asymptotically equivalent, theory offers no guidance about which is best. By default, svytab uses $\widehat{p}_{rc}$ for the corrections of the Pearson and likelihood-ratio statistics. If the null option is specified, the correction is computed using $\widehat{p}_{0rc}$. For nonsparse tables, these two correction methods yield almost identical results. However, in simulations of sparse tables, Sribney (1998) found that the null-corrected statistics were extremely anticonservative for 2×2 tables (i.e., under the null, "significance" was declared too often) and too conservative for other tables. The default correction, however, had better properties. Hence, we do not recommend use of the null option.

For the computational details of the Rao and Scott corrected statistics, see the *Methods and Formulas* section at the end of this entry.

Wald statistics

Prior to the work by Rao and Scott (1981, 1984), Wald tests for the test of independence for two-way tables were developed by Koch et al. (1975). Two Wald statistics have been proposed. The first is similar to the Pearson statistic in that it is based on

$$\widehat{Y}_{rc} = \widehat{N}_{rc} - \widehat{N}_{r.}\widehat{N}_{.c}/\widehat{N}_{..}$$

where $\widehat{N}_{rc}$ is the estimated weighted count for the r, cth cell. The delta-method can be used to approximate the variance of $\widehat{Y}_{rc}$, and a Wald statistic can be calculated in the usual manner. A second Wald statistic can be constructed based on a log-linear model for the table. Like the likelihood-ratio statistic, this statistic is undefined when there is a zero proportion in the table.

These Wald statistics are initially χ^2 statistics, but they have better properties when converted into F statistics with denominator degrees of freedom that account for the degrees of freedom of the variance estimator. They can be converted to F statistics in one of two ways. One method is the standard manner: divide by the χ^2 degrees of freedom $d_0 = (R-1)(C-1)$ to get an F statistic with d_0 numerator degrees of freedom and $\nu = n_{PSU} - L$ denominator degrees of freedom. This is the form of the F statistic suggested by Koch et al. (1975) and implemented in the CROSSTAB procedure of the SUDAAN software (Shah et al. 1997, Release 7.5), and it is the method used by svytab when the noadjust option is specified along with wald or llwald.

Another technique is to adjust the F statistic by using

$$F_{\text{adj}} = (\nu - d_0 + 1)W/(\nu d_0) \qquad \text{with} \qquad F_{\text{adj}} \sim F(d_0, \nu - d_0 + 1)$$

This is the adjustment that is done by default by `svytab`. Note that `svytest` and the other `svy` estimation commands produce adjusted F statistics by default, using exactly the same adjustment procedure. See Korn and Graubard (1990) for a justification of the procedure.

The adjusted F statistic is identical to the unadjusted F statistic when $d_0 = 1$; that is, for 2×2 tables.

As Thomas and Rao (1987) point out (also see Korn and Graubard, 1990), the unadjusted F statistics can become extremely anticonservative as d_0 increases when ν is small or moderate; i.e., under the null, the statistics are "significant" far more often than they should be. Because the unadjusted statistics behave so poorly for larger tables when ν is not large, their use can only be justified for small tables or when ν is large. But when the table is small or when ν is large, the unadjusted statistic is essentially identical to the adjusted statistic. Hence, for the purpose of statistical inference, there is no point in looking at the unadjusted statistics.

The adjusted "Pearson" Wald F statistic behaves reasonably under the null in most cases. However, even the adjusted F statistic for the log-linear Wald test tends to be moderately anticonservative when ν is not large (Thomas and Rao 1987, Sribney 1998).

▷ Example

With the NHANES II data, we tabulate, for the male subpopulation, high blood pressure (`highbp`) versus a variable (`sizplace`) that indicates the degree of urban/ruralness. We request that all eight statistics for the test of independence be displayed.

```
. gen male = (sex==1) if sex~=.

. svytab highbp sizplace, subpop(male) col obs pearson lr null wald llwald noadj
-------------------------------------------------------------------------------
pweight:  finalwgt                        Number of obs      =      10351
Strata:   stratid                         Number of strata   =         31
PSU:      psuid                           Number of PSUs     =         62
                                          Population size    = 1.172e+08
Subpop.:  male==1                         Subpop. no. of obs =       4915
                                          Subpop. size       =   56159480
-------------------------------------------------------------------------------


----------+--------------------------------------------------------------------
Blood     |              Urban/rural: 1=urban,..., 8=rural
pressure  |    1      2      3      4      5      6      7      8   Total
----------+--------------------------------------------------------------------
not high  | .8489  .8929  .9213  .8509  .8413  .9242  .8707  .8674  .8764
          |   927   1143   1201    809    433    485    718   3300   9016
          |
    high  | .1511  .1071  .0787  .1491  .1587  .0758  .1293  .1326  .1236
          |   167    160    122    147     77     47    112    503   1335
          |
   Total  |    1      1      1      1      1      1      1      1      1
          |  1094   1303   1323    956    510    532    830   3803  1.0e+04
----------+--------------------------------------------------------------------
  Key:  column proportions
        number of observations
```

```
Pearson:
    Uncorrected    chi2(7)          =    64.4581
    D-B (null)     F(5.30,164.45)   =     2.2078     P = 0.0522
    Design-based   F(5.54,171.87)   =     2.6863     P = 0.0189

Likelihood ratio:
    Uncorrected    chi2(7)          =    68.2365
    D-B (null)     F(5.30,164.45)   =     2.3372     P = 0.0408
    Design-based   F(5.54,171.87)   =     2.8437     P = 0.0138

Wald (Pearson):
    Unadjusted     chi2(7)          =    21.2704
    Unadjusted     F(7,31)          =     3.0386     P = 0.0149
    Adjusted       F(7,25)          =     2.4505     P = 0.0465

Wald (log-linear):
    Unadjusted     chi2(7)          =    25.7644
    Unadjusted     F(7,31)          =     3.6806     P = 0.0052
    Adjusted       F(7,25)          =     2.9683     P = 0.0208
```

The p-values from the null-corrected Pearson and likelihood-ratio statistics (lines labeled "D-B (null)"; "D-B" stands for "design-based") are bigger than the corresponding default-corrected statistics (lines labeled "Design-based"). Simulations (Sribney 1998) show that the null-corrected statistics are overly conservative for many sparse tables (except 2×2 tables); this appears to be the case here— although this table is hardly sparse. The default-corrected Pearson statistic has good properties under the null for both sparse and nonsparse tables; hence, the smaller p-value for it should be considered reliable.

The default-corrected likelihood-ratio statistic is usually similar to the default-corrected Pearson statistic except for very sparse tables, when it tends to be anticonservative. This example follows this pattern, with its p-value being slightly smaller than that of the default-corrected Pearson statistic.

For tables of these dimensions (2×8), the unadjusted "Pearson" Wald and log-linear Wald F statistics are extremely anticonservative under the null when the variance degrees of freedom are small. Here the variance degrees of freedom are only 31 (62 PSUs minus 31 strata), so it is expected that the unadjusted Wald F statistics yield smaller p-values than the adjusted F statistics. Because of their poor behavior under the null for small variance degrees of freedom, they cannot be trusted in this case. Simulations show that although the adjusted "Pearson" Wald F statistic has good properties under the null, it is often less powerful than the default Rao-and-Scott corrected statistics. That is likely the explanation for the larger p-value for the adjusted "Pearson" Wald F statistic than that for the default-corrected Pearson and likelihood-ratio statistics.

The p-value for the adjusted log-linear Wald F statistic is about the same as that for the trustworthy default-corrected Pearson statistic. However, that is likely due to the anticonservatism of the log-linear Wald under the null balancing out its lower power under alternative hypotheses.

Note that the "uncorrected" χ^2 Pearson and likelihood-ratio statistics displayed in the table are misspecified statistics; that is, they are based on an iid assumption, which is not valid for complex survey data. Hence, they are not correct, even asymptotically. The "unadjusted" Wald χ^2 statistics, on the other hand, are completely different. They are valid asymptotically as the variance degrees of freedom become large.

◁

Properties of the statistics

We briefly summarize here the properties of the eight statistics computed by svytab. For details, see Sribney (1998), Rao and Thomas (1989), Thomas and Rao (1987), and Korn and Graubard (1990).

pearson is the Rao and Scott (1984) second-order corrected Pearson statistic, computed using $\widehat{p}_{rc}$ in the correction (default correction). It is displayed by default. Simulations show it to have good properties under the null for both sparse and nonsparse tables. Its power is similar to the lr statistic in most situations. It appears to be more powerful than the adjusted "Pearson" Wald F statistic (wald option) in many situations, especially for larger tables. We recommend the use of this statistic in all situations.

pearson null is the Rao and Scott (1984) second-order corrected Pearson statistic, computed using $\widehat{p}_{0rc}$ in the correction. It is numerically similar to the pearson statistic for nonsparse tables. For sparse tables, it can be erratic. Under the null, it can be anticonservative for sparse 2×2 tables, but conservative for larger sparse tables.

lr is the Rao and Scott second-order corrected likelihood-ratio statistic, computed using $\widehat{p}_{rc}$ in the correction (default correction). The correction is identical to that for pearson. It is numerically similar to the pearson statistic for nonsparse tables. It can be anticonservative (p-values too small) in very sparse tables. If there is a zero cell, it cannot be computed.

lr null is the Rao and Scott second-order corrected likelihood-ratio statistic, computed using $\widehat{p}_{0rc}$ in the correction. The correction is identical to that for pearson null. It is numerically similar to the lr statistic for nonsparse tables. For sparse tables, it can be overly conservative. If there is a zero cell, it cannot be computed.

wald statistic is the adjusted "Pearson" Wald F statistic. It has good properties under the null for nonsparse tables. It can be erratic for sparse 2×2 tables and some sparse large tables. The pearson statistic appears to be more powerful in many situations.

wald noadjust is the unadjusted "Pearson" Wald F statistic. It can be extremely anticonservative under the null when the table degrees of freedom (number of rows minus one times the number of columns minus one) approach the variance degrees of freedom (number of sampled PSUs minus the number of strata). It is exactly the same as the adjusted wald statistic for 2×2 tables. It is similar to the adjusted wald statistic for small tables and/or large variance degrees of freedom.

llwald statistic is the adjusted log-linear Wald F statistic. It can be anticonservative for both sparse and nonsparse tables. If there is a zero cell, it cannot be computed.

llwald noadjust statistic is the unadjusted log-linear Wald F statistic. Like wald noadjust, it can be extremely anticonservative under the null when the table degrees of freedom approach the variance degrees of freedom. It also suffers from the same general anticonservatism of the llwald statistic. If there is a zero cell, it cannot be computed.

Saved Results

svytab saves in e():

Scalars

e(N)	number of observations	e(N_subpop)	estimate of subpopulation size
e(N_strata)	number of strata	e(df_r)	variance degrees of freedom
e(N_psu)	number of sampled PSUs	e(r)	number of rows
e(N_pop)	estimate of population size	e(c)	number of columns
e(total)	weighted sum of tab variable	e(mgdeff)	mean generalized deff
e(N_sub)	subpopulation number of observations	e(cvgdeff)	c.v. of generalized deff eigenvalues
e(F_Pear)	default-corrected Pearson F	e(F_Penl)	null-corrected Pearson F
e(df1_Pear)	numerator d.f. for e(F_Pear)	e(df1_Penl)	numerator d.f. for e(F_Penl)
e(df2_Pear)	denominator d.f. for e(F_Pear)	e(df2_Penl)	denominator d.f. for e(F_Penl)
e(p_Pear)	p-value for e(F_Pear)	e(p_Penl)	p-value for e(F_Penl)
e(cun_Pear)	uncorrected Pearson χ^2		
e(F_LR)	default-corrected likelihood-ratio F	e(F_LRnl)	null-corrected likelihood-ratio F
e(df1_LR)	numerator d.f. for e(F_LR)	e(df1_LRnl)	numerator d.f. for e(F_LRnl)
e(df2_LR)	denominator d.f. for e(F_LR)	e(df2_LRnl)	denominator d.f. for e(F_LRnl)
e(p_LR)	p-value for e(F_LR)	e(p_LRnl)	p-value for e(F_LRnl)
e(cun_LR)	uncorrected likelihood-ratio χ^2		
e(F_Wald)	adjusted "Pearson" Wald F	e(F_LLW)	adjusted log-linear Wald F
e(p_Wald)	p-value for e(F_Wald)	e(p_LLW)	p-value for e(F_LLW)
e(Fun_Wald)	unadjusted "Pearson" Wald F	e(Fun_LLW)	unadjusted log-linear Wald F
e(pun_Wald)	p-value for e(Fun_Wald)	e(pun_LLW)	p-value for e(Fun_LLW)
e(cun_Wald)	unadjusted "Pearson" Wald χ^2	e(cun_LLW)	unadjusted log-linear Wald χ^2

Macros

e(cmd)	svytab	e(rowvar)	row variable
e(strata)	strata() variable	e(colvar)	column variable
e(psu)	psu() variable	e(wtype)	weight type
e(fpc)	fpc() variable	e(wexp)	weight expression
e(tab)	tab() variable	e(subpop)	subpop() criterion
e(setype)	std. error computed for this item		

Matrices

e(prop)	matrix of cell proportions	e(obs)	matrix of observation counts
e(b)	vector of e(setype) items	e(deff)	deff vector for e(setype) items
e(V)	variance matrix for e(setype) items	e(deft)	deft vector for e(setype) items

Functions

e(sample)	marks estimation sample

Methods and Formulas

We assume here that readers are familiar with the *Methods and Formulas* section of the [R] **svymean** entry.

For a table of R rows by C columns with cells indexed by r, c, let

$$y_{(rc)hij} = \begin{cases} 1 & \text{if the } hij\text{th element of the data is in the } r, c \text{ th cell} \\ 0 & \text{otherwise} \end{cases}$$

where $h = 1, \ldots, L$, indexes strata; $i = 1, \ldots, n_h$, indexes PSUs; and $j = 1, \ldots, m_{hi}$, indexes elements in the PSU. Weighted cell counts (the count option) are

$$\widehat{N}_{rc} = \sum_{h=1}^{L} \sum_{i=1}^{n_h} \sum_{j=1}^{m_{hi}} w_{hij}\, y_{(rc)hij}$$

where w_{hij} are the weights, if any. If a variable x_{hij} is specified with the tab() option, $\widehat{N}_{rc}$ becomes

$$\widehat{N}_{rc} = \sum_{h=1}^{L} \sum_{i=1}^{n_h} \sum_{j=1}^{m_{hi}} w_{hij}\, x_{hij}\, y_{(rc)hij}$$

Let

$$\widehat{N}_{r\cdot} = \sum_{c=1}^{C} \widehat{N}_{rc}, \qquad \widehat{N}_{\cdot c} = \sum_{r=1}^{R} \widehat{N}_{rc}, \qquad \text{and} \qquad \widehat{N}_{\cdot\cdot} = \sum_{r=1}^{R} \sum_{c=1}^{C} \widehat{N}_{rc}$$

Estimated cell proportions are $\widehat{p}_{rc} = \widehat{N}_{rc}/\widehat{N}_{\cdot\cdot}$. Estimated row proportions (row option) are $\widehat{p}_{\text{row }rc} = \widehat{N}_{rc}/\widehat{N}_{r\cdot}$. Estimated column proportions (column option) are $\widehat{p}_{\text{col }rc} = \widehat{N}_{rc}/\widehat{N}_{\cdot c}$. Estimated row marginals are $\widehat{p}_{r\cdot} = \widehat{N}_{r\cdot}/\widehat{N}_{\cdot\cdot}$. Estimated column marginals are $\widehat{p}_{\cdot c} = \widehat{N}_{\cdot c}/\widehat{N}_{\cdot\cdot}$.

$\widehat{N}_{rc}$ is a total and the proportion estimators are ratios, and their variances can be estimated using linearization methods as outlined in [R] **svymean**. **svytab** computes the variance estimates using the same driver program that **svymean**, **svyratio**, and **svytotal** use. Hence, **svytab** produces exactly the same standard errors as these commands would.

Confidence intervals for proportions are calculated using a logit transform so that the endpoints lie between 0 and 1. Let $\widehat{p}$ be an estimated proportion and $\widehat{s}$ an estimate of its standard error. Let $f(\widehat{p}) = \ln(\widehat{p}/(1 - \widehat{p}))$ be the logit transform of the proportion. In this metric, an estimate of the standard error is $f'(\widehat{p})\widehat{s} = \widehat{s}/\widehat{p}(1 - \widehat{p})$. Thus, a $100(1 - \alpha)\%$ confidence interval in this metric is $\ln(\widehat{p}/(1 - \widehat{p})) \pm t_{1-\alpha/2,\nu}\,\widehat{s}/\widehat{p}(1 - \widehat{p})$, where $t_{1-\alpha/2,\nu}$ is the $(1 - \alpha/2)$th quantile of Student's t distribution. The endpoints of this confidence interval are transformed back to the proportion metric using $f^{-1}(y) = \exp(y)/(1 + \exp(y))$. Hence, the displayed confidence intervals for proportions are

$$f^{-1}\left(\ln\left(\frac{\widehat{p}}{1 - \widehat{p}} \right) \pm \frac{t_{1-\alpha/2,\nu}\,\widehat{s}}{\widehat{p}(1 - \widehat{p})} \right)$$

Confidence intervals for weighted counts are untransformed and are identical to the intervals produced by **svytotal**.

The uncorrected Pearson χ^2 statistic is

$$X_{\text{P}}^2 = n \sum_{r=1}^{R} \sum_{c=1}^{C} \left(\widehat{p}_{rc} - \widehat{p}_{0rc} \right)^2 / \widehat{p}_{0rc}$$

and the uncorrected likelihood-ratio χ^2 statistic is

$$X_{\text{LR}}^2 = 2n \sum_{r=1}^{R} \sum_{c=1}^{C} \widehat{p}_{rc} \ln\left(\widehat{p}_{rc}/\widehat{p}_{0rc} \right)$$

where n is the total number of observations, $\widehat{p}_{rc}$ is the estimated proportion for the cell in the rth row and cth column of the table as defined earlier, and $\widehat{p}_{0rc}$ is the estimated proportion under the null hypothesis of independence; i.e., $\widehat{p}_{0rc} = \widehat{p}_{r.}\widehat{p}_{.c}$, the product of the row and column marginals.

Rao and Scott (1981, 1984) showed that, asymptotically, X_{P}^2 and X_{LR}^2 are distributed as

$$X^2 \sim \sum_{k=1}^{(R-1)(C-1)} \delta_k W_k \tag{1}$$

where the W_k are independent χ_1^2 variables and the δ_k are the eigenvalues of

$$\Delta = (\widetilde{\mathbf{X}}_2' \mathbf{V}_{\mathrm{srs}} \widetilde{\mathbf{X}}_2)^{-1} (\widetilde{\mathbf{X}}_2' \mathbf{V} \widetilde{\mathbf{X}}_2) \tag{2}$$

where $\mathbf{V}$ is the variance of the $\widehat{p}_{rc}$ under the survey design and $\mathbf{V}_{\mathrm{srs}}$ is the variance of the $\widehat{p}_{rc}$ that one would have if the design were simple random sampling; namely, $\mathbf{V}_{\mathrm{srs}}$ has diagonal elements $p_{rc}(1 - p_{rc})/n$ and off-diagonal elements $-p_{rc}p_{st}/n$.

$\widetilde{\mathbf{X}}_2$ is calculated as follows. Rao and Scott do their development in a log-linear modeling context, so consider $[\,\mathbf{1} \mid \mathbf{X_1} \mid \mathbf{X_2}\,]$ as predictors for the cell counts of the $R \times C$ table in a log-linear model. The $\mathbf{X_1}$ matrix of dimension $RC \times (R + C - 2)$ contains the $R - 1$ "main effects" for the rows and the $C - 1$ "main effects" for the columns. The $\mathbf{X_2}$ matrix of dimension $RC \times (R-1)(C-1)$ contains the row and column "interactions". Hence, fitting $[\,\mathbf{1} \mid \mathbf{X_1} \mid \mathbf{X_2}\,]$ gives the fully saturated model (i.e., fits the observed values perfectly) and $[\,\mathbf{1} \mid \mathbf{X_1}\,]$ gives the independence model. The $\widetilde{\mathbf{X}}_2$ matrix is the projection of $\mathbf{X}_2$ onto the orthogonal complement of the space spanned by the columns of $\mathbf{X}_1$, where the orthogonality is defined with respect to $\mathbf{V}_{\mathrm{srs}}$; i.e., $\widetilde{\mathbf{X}}_2' \mathbf{V}_{\mathrm{srs}} \mathbf{X}_1 = \mathbf{0}$.

See Rao and Scott (1984) for the proof justifying equations (1) and (2). However, even without a full understanding, one can get a feeling for Δ. It is like a "ratio" (although remember that it is a matrix) of two variances. The variance in the "numerator" involves the variance under the true survey design, and the variance in the "denominator" involves the variance assuming that the design was simple random sampling. Recall that the design effect deff for the estimated proportions is defined as $\mathrm{deff} = V(\widehat{p}_{rc})/V_{\mathrm{srs}}(\widehat{p}_{rc})$ (see the *Methods and Formulas* section of [R] **svymean**. Hence, Δ can be regarded as a design effects matrix, and Rao and Scott call its eigenvalues, the δ_k's, the "generalized design effects".

It is easy to compute an estimate for Δ using estimates for $\mathbf{V}$ and $\mathbf{V}_{\mathrm{srs}}$. Rao and Scott (1984) derive a simpler formula for $\widehat{\Delta}$:

$$\widehat{\Delta} = \left(\mathbf{C}' \mathbf{D}_{\widehat{\mathbf{p}}}^{-1} \widehat{\mathbf{V}}_{\mathrm{srs}} \mathbf{D}_{\widehat{\mathbf{p}}}^{-1} \mathbf{C}\right)^{-1} \left(\mathbf{C}' \mathbf{D}_{\widehat{\mathbf{p}}}^{-1} \widehat{\mathbf{V}} \mathbf{D}_{\widehat{\mathbf{p}}}^{-1} \mathbf{C}\right)$$

Here $\mathbf{C}$ is a contrast matrix that is any $RC \times (R-1)(C-1)$ full-rank matrix that is orthogonal to $[\,\mathbf{1} \mid \mathbf{X}_1\,]$; i.e., $\mathbf{C}'\mathbf{1} = \mathbf{0}$ and $\mathbf{C}'\mathbf{X}_1 = \mathbf{0}$. $\mathbf{D}_{\widehat{\mathbf{p}}}$ is a diagonal matrix with the estimated proportions $\widehat{p}_{rc}$ on the diagonal. Note that when one of the $\widehat{p}_{rc}$ is zero, the corresponding variance estimate is also zero; hence, the corresponding element for $\mathbf{D}_{\widehat{\mathbf{p}}}^{-1}$ is immaterial for the computation of $\widehat{\Delta}$.

Unfortunately, equation (1) is not practical for the computation of a p-value. However, one can compute simple first-order and second-order corrections based on it. A first-order correction is based on downweighting the iid statistics by the average eigenvalue of $\widehat{\Delta}$; namely, one computes

$$X_{\mathrm{P}}^2(\widehat{\delta}_.) = X_{\mathrm{P}}^2/\widehat{\delta}_. \quad \text{and} \quad X_{\mathrm{LR}}^2(\widehat{\delta}_.) = X_{\mathrm{LR}}^2/\widehat{\delta}_.$$

where $\widehat{\delta}.$ is the mean generalized deff

$$\widehat{\delta}. = \frac{1}{(R-1)(C-1)} \sum_{k=1}^{(R-1)(C-1)} \delta_k$$

These corrected statistics are asymptotically distributed as $\chi^2_{(R-1)(C-1)}$. Thus, to first-order, one can view the iid statistics X^2_P and X^2_{LR} as being "too big" by a factor of $\widehat{\delta}.$ for true survey design.

A better second-order correction can be obtained by using the Satterthwaite approximation to the distribution of a weighted sum of χ^2_1 variables. Here the Pearson statistic becomes

$$X^2_P(\widehat{\delta}., \widehat{a}) = \frac{X^2_P}{\widehat{\delta}.(\widehat{a}^2 + 1)} \tag{3}$$

where $\widehat{a}$ is the coefficient of variation of the eigenvalues:

$$\widehat{a}^2 = \frac{\sum \widehat{\delta}_k^2}{(R-1)(C-1)\widehat{\delta}^2} - 1$$

Since $\sum \widehat{\delta}_k = \text{tr}\,\widehat{\Delta}$ and $\sum \widehat{\delta}_k^2 = \text{tr}\,\widehat{\Delta}^2$, equation (3) can be written in an easily computable form as

$$X^2_P(\widehat{\delta}., \widehat{a}) = \frac{\text{tr}\,\widehat{\Delta}}{\text{tr}\,\widehat{\Delta}^2} X^2_P$$

These corrected statistics are asymptotically distributed as χ^2_d with

$$d = \frac{(R-1)(C-1)}{\widehat{a}^2 + 1} = \frac{(\text{tr}\,\widehat{\Delta})^2}{\text{tr}\,\widehat{\Delta}^2}$$

i.e., a χ^2 with, in general, noninteger degrees of freedom. The likelihood-ratio X^2_{LR} statistic can also be given this second-order correction in an identical manner.

We would be done if it were not for two outstanding issues. First, there are two possible ways to compute the variance estimate $\widehat{V}_{srs}$, which is used in the computation of $\widehat{\Delta}$. V_{srs} has diagonal elements $p_{rc}(1 - p_{rc})/n$ and off-diagonal elements $-p_{rc}p_{st}/n$; but note that here p_{rc} is the true, not estimated, proportion. Hence, the question is, what to use to estimate p_{rc}: the observed proportions $\widehat{p}_{rc}$ or the proportions estimated under the null hypothesis of independence $\widehat{p}_{0rc} = \widehat{p}_{r.}\widehat{p}_{.c}$? Rao and Scott (1984, 53) leave this as an open question.

Because of the question of whether to use $\widehat{p}_{rc}$ or $\widehat{p}_{0rc}$ to compute $\widehat{V}_{srs}$, svytab can compute both corrections. By default, when the null option is not specified, only the correction based on $\widehat{p}_{rc}$ is displayed. If null is specified, two corrected statistics and corresponding p-values are displayed, one computed using $\widehat{p}_{rc}$ and the other using $\widehat{p}_{0rc}$.

The second outstanding issue concerns the degrees of freedom resulting from the variance estimate $\widehat{V}$ of the cell proportions under the survey design. The customary degrees of freedom for t statistics resulting from this variance estimate are $\nu = n_{PSU} - L$, where n_{PSU} is the total number of PSUs in the sample and L is the total number of strata.

Rao and Thomas (1989) suggest turning the corrected χ^2 statistic into an F statistic by dividing it by its degrees of freedom $d_0 = (R-1)(C-1)$. The F statistic is then taken to have numerator degrees of freedom equal to d_0, and denominator degrees of freedom equal to νd_0. Hence, the corrected Pearson F statistic is

$$F_{\mathrm{P}} = \frac{X_{\mathrm{P}}^2}{\operatorname{tr} \widehat{\Delta}} \quad \text{with} \quad F_{\mathrm{P}} \sim F(d, \nu d) \quad \text{where} \quad d = \frac{(\operatorname{tr} \widehat{\Delta})^2}{\operatorname{tr} \widehat{\Delta}^2} \quad \text{and} \quad \nu = n_{\mathrm{PSU}} - L \qquad (4)$$

This is the corrected statistic that `svytab` displays by default or when the `pearson` option is specified. When the `lr` option is specified, an identical correction is produced for the likelihood-ratio statistic X_{LR}^2. When `null` is specified equation (4) is also used. For the statistic labeled "D-B (null)", $\widehat{\Delta}$ is computed using $\widehat{p}_{0rc}$. For the statistic labeled "Design-based", $\widehat{\Delta}$ is computed using $\widehat{p}_{rc}$.

The Wald statistics computed by `svytab` with the `wald` and `llwald` options were developed by Koch et al. (1975). The statistic given by the `wald` option is similar to the Pearson statistic since it is based on

$$\widehat{Y}_{rc} = \widehat{N}_{rc} - \widehat{N}_{r.}\widehat{N}_{.c}/\widehat{N}_{..}$$

where $r = 1, \ldots, R-1$ and $c = 1, \ldots, C-1$. The delta-method can be used to estimate the variance of $\widehat{\mathbf{Y}}$ (which is $\widehat{Y}_{rc}$ stacked into a vector), and a Wald statistic can be constructed in the usual manner:

$$W = \widehat{\mathbf{Y}}' \big(\mathbf{J_N} \widehat{\mathbf{V}}(\widehat{\mathbf{N}}) \mathbf{J_N}' \big)^{-1} \widehat{\mathbf{Y}} \quad \text{where} \quad \mathbf{J_N} = \partial \widehat{\mathbf{Y}} / \partial \widehat{\mathbf{N}}'$$

The statistic given by the `llwald` option is based on the log-linear model with predictors $[\mathbf{1} | \mathbf{X}_1 | \mathbf{X}_2]$ that was mentioned earlier. This Wald statistic is

$$W_{\mathrm{LL}} = \big(\mathbf{X}_2' \ln \widehat{\mathbf{p}} \big)' \big(\mathbf{X}_2' \mathbf{J_p} \widehat{\mathbf{V}}(\widehat{\mathbf{p}}) \mathbf{J_p}' \mathbf{X}_2 \big)^{-1} \big(\mathbf{X}_2' \ln \widehat{\mathbf{p}} \big)$$

where $\mathbf{J_p}$ is the matrix of first derivatives of $\ln \widehat{\mathbf{p}}$ with respect to $\widehat{\mathbf{p}}$, which is, of course, just a matrix with $\widehat{p}_{rc}^{-1}$ on the diagonal and zero elsewhere. Note that this log-linear Wald statistic is undefined when there is a zero cell in the table.

Unadjusted F statistics (`noadjust` option) are produced using

$$F_{\mathrm{unadj}} = W/d_0 \quad \text{with} \quad F_{\mathrm{unadj}} \sim F(d_0, \nu)$$

Adjusted F statistics are produced using

$$F_{\mathrm{adj}} = (\nu - d_0 + 1)W/(\nu d_0) \quad \text{with} \quad F_{\mathrm{adj}} \sim F(d_0, \nu - d_0 + 1)$$

The other `svy` estimators also use this adjustment procedure for F statistics. See Korn and Graubard (1990) for a justification of the procedure.

References

Fuller, W. A., W. Kennedy, D. Schnell, G. Sullivan, H. J. Park. 1986. *PC CARP*. Ames, IA: Statistical Laboratory, Iowa State University.

Koch, G. G., D. H. Freeman, Jr., and J. L. Freeman. 1975. Strategies in the multivariate analysis of data from complex surveys. *International Statistical Review* 43: 59–78.

Korn, E. L. and B. I. Graubard. 1990. Simultaneous testing of regression coefficients with complex survey data: use of Bonferroni t statistics. *The American Statistician* 44: 270–276.

McDowell, A., A. Engel, J. T. Massey, and K. Maurer. 1981. Plan and operation of the Second National Health and Nutrition Examination Survey, 1976–1980. *Vital and Health Statistics* 15(1). National Center for Health Statistics, Hyattsville, MD.

Rao, J. N. K. and A. J. Scott. 1981. The analysis of categorical data from complex sample surveys: chi-squared tests for goodness of fit and independence in two-way tables. *Journal of the American Statistical Association* 76: 221–230.

——. 1984. On chi-squared tests for multiway contingency tables with cell proportions estimated from survey data. *Annals of Statistics* 12: 46–60.

Rao, J. N. K. and D. R. Thomas. 1989. Chi-squared tests for contingency tables. In *Analysis of Complex Surveys*, ed. C. J. Skinner, D. Holt, and T. M. F. Smith, Ch. 4, 89–114. New York: John Wiley & Sons.

Shah, B. V., B. G. Barnwell, and G. S. Bieler. 1997. *SUDAAN User's Manual, Release 7.5*. Research Triangle Park, NC: Research Triangle Institute.

Sribney, W. M. 1998. svy7: Two-way contingency tables for survey or clustered data. *Stata Technical Bulletin* 45: 33–49.

Thomas, D. R. and J. N. K. Rao. 1987. Small-sample comparisons of level and power for simple goodness-of-fit statistics under cluster sampling. *Journal of the American Statistical Association* 82: 630–636.

Also See

Complementary:	[R] **svydes**, [R] **svymean**, [R] **svyset**
Related:	[R] **svy estimators**, [R] **svytest**, [R] **tabulate**
Background:	[U] **30 Overview of survey estimation**, [R] **svy**

Title

svytest — Test linear hypotheses after survey estimation

Syntax

The command svytest can be used with three different syntaxes:

(1) svytest *exp* = *exp*   [, noadjust accumulate notest]

(2) svytest *coefficientlist*   [, noadjust accumulate notest]

(3) svytest [*varlist* | *coefficientlist*] , bonferroni

In the above, *exp* is a linear expression that is valid for the test command; *exp* = *exp* is a linear equation that is valid for the test command; and *coefficientlist* is a valid coefficient list for the test command; see [R] test.

Description

svytest tests multidimensional linear hypotheses after a svy estimation command. See [R] svymean and [R] svy estimators for an introduction to the svy estimation commands.

In addition to computing point estimates for linear combinations, svylc computes t statistics and p-values; see [R] svylc Thus, svylc can be used for testing one-dimensional hypotheses; it gives the same results as svytest.

Syntax (1) for svytest allows you to build up a multidimensional hypothesis consisting of any number of linear equations. Syntax (2) tests hypotheses of the form $\beta_1 = 0$, $\beta_2 = 0$, $\beta_3 = 0$, etc.

Syntax (3) is only available after the svy commands described in [R] svy estimators. It computes a Bonferroni adjustment for hypotheses of the form $\beta_1 = 0$, $\beta_2 = 0$, $\beta_3 = 0$, etc. See the following examples and the *Methods and Formulas* section for details.

By default, svytest used with syntax (1) or (2) carries out an adjusted Wald test. Specifically, it uses the approximate F statistic $(d - k + 1)W/(kd)$, where W is the Wald test statistic, k is the dimension of the hypothesis test, and $d = $ total number of sampled PSUs minus the total number of strata. Under the null hypothesis, $(d - k + 1)W/(kd) \sim F(k, d - k + 1)$, where $F(k, d - k + 1)$ is an F distribution with k numerator degrees of freedom and $d - k + 1$ denominator degrees of freedom.

Options

noadjust specifies that the Wald test be carried out as $W/k \sim F(k, d)$ (notation as described above). This gives the same result as the test command.

accumulate allows a hypothesis to be tested jointly with the previously tested hypotheses.

notest suppresses the output. This option is useful when you are interested only in the joint test of a number of hypotheses.

bonferroni can be specified only after estimating a model with any of the svy estimation commands described in [R] **svy estimators**. When this option is specified, svytest displays adjusted p-values for each of the specified coefficients. Adjusted p-values are computed as $p_{\mathrm{adj}} = \min(kp, 1)$, where k is the number of coefficients specified, and p is the unadjusted p-value (i.e., the p-value shown in the output of the estimation command) obtained from the statistic $t = \widehat{\beta}/[\widehat{V}(\widehat{\beta})]^{1/2}$ which is assumed to have a t distribution with d degrees of freedom. If no argument list is specified with the bonferroni option, adjustments are made for all terms in the model excluding the constant term(s) and any ancillary parameters.

Remarks

Testing hypotheses with svytest

Joint hypothesis tests can be performed after svy estimation commands using the svytest command. Here we estimate a linear regression of loglead (log of blood lead).

▷ Example

```
. svyreg loglead age female black orace region2-region4

Survey linear regression

pweight:  leadwt                         Number of obs   =        4948
Strata:   stratid                        Number of strata =         31
PSU:      psuid                          Number of PSUs  =          62
                                         Population size  = 1.129e+08
                                         F(   7,      25) =      186.18
                                         Prob > F         =      0.0000
                                         R-squared        =      0.2321

------------------------------------------------------------------------------
 loglead |    Coef.    Std. Err.      t     P>|t|    [95% Conf. Interval]
---------+--------------------------------------------------------------------
     age |  .0027842   .0004318     6.448   0.000    .0019036    .0036649
  female | -.3645445   .0110947   -32.857   0.000   -.3871724   -.3419167
   black |  .1783735   .0321995     5.540   0.000    .1127022    .2440447
   orace | -.0473781   .0383677    -1.235   0.226   -.1256295    .0308733
 region2 | -.0242082   .0384767    -0.629   0.534   -.1026819    .0542655
 region3 | -.1646067   .0549628    -2.995   0.005    -.276704   -.0525094
 region4 | -.0361289   .0377054    -0.958   0.345   -.1130296    .0407717
   _cons |  2.696084   .0236895   113.809   0.000    2.647769    2.744399
------------------------------------------------------------------------------
```

We can use svytest to test the joint significance of the region dummies: region1 is the Northeast, region2 is the Midwest, region3 is the South, and region4 is the West. We test the hypothesis that region2 = 0, region3 = 0, and region4 = 0.

```
. svytest region2 region3 region4

Adjusted Wald test
 ( 1)  region2 = 0.0
 ( 2)  region3 = 0.0
 ( 3)  region4 = 0.0

      F(  3,     29) =     2.97
            Prob > F =   0.0480
```

The noadjust option on svytest produces an unadjusted Wald test.

```
. svytest region2 region3 region4, noadjust
Unadjusted Wald test
 ( 1)   region2 = 0.0
 ( 2)   region3 = 0.0
 ( 3)   region4 = 0.0
        F(  3,     31) =      3.18
              Prob > F =    0.0377
```

Note that for one-dimensional tests, the adjusted and unadjusted F statistics are identical, but for higher dimensional tests, they differ. Using the noadjust option is not recommended since the unadjusted F statistic can produce extremely anticonservative p-values (i.e., p-values that are too small) when the variance degrees of freedom (equal to the number of sampled PSUs minus the number of strata) are not large relative to the dimension of the test.

Bonferroni-adjusted p-values can also be computed:

```
. svytest region2 region3 region4, bonferroni
Bonferroni adjustment for 3 comparisons

----------------------------------------------------------------------
 loglead |      Coef.   Std. Err.        t     Adj. P
---------+------------------------------------------------------------
 region2 |  -.0242082   .0384767    -0.629     1.0000
 region3 |  -.1646067   .0549628    -2.995     0.0161 *
 region4 |  -.0361289   .0377054    -0.958     1.0000
----------------------------------------------------------------------
```

The smallest adjusted p-value is a p-value for a test of the same joint hypothesis that we tested before; namely, region2 $= 0$, region3 $= 0$, and region4 $= 0$.

See Korn and Graubard (1990) for a discussion of these three different procedures for conducting joint hypothesis tests.

◁

The examples given above show how to use svytest to test hypotheses for which the coefficients are jointly hypothesized to be zero. We will now illustrate the use of svytest to test general hypotheses.

▷ Example

Let us run the same regression model as in the previous example, only this time we will include the other region dummy region1 and omit the constant term.

(Continued on next page)

```
. svyreg loglead age female black orace region1-region4, nocons
Survey linear regression
pweight:  leadwt                          Number of obs    =     4948
Strata:   stratid                         Number of strata =       31
PSU:      psuid                           Number of PSUs   =       62
                                          Population size  = 1.129e+08
                                          F(  8,   24)     = 5148.74
                                          Prob > F         =   0.0000
                                          R-squared        =   0.9806

------------------------------------------------------------------------
 loglead |    Coef.   Std. Err.     t      P>|t|    [95% Conf. Interval]
---------+--------------------------------------------------------------
     age |  .0027842   .0004318    6.448    0.000    .0019036   .0036649
  female | -.3645445   .0110947  -32.857    0.000   -.3871724  -.3419167
   black |  .1783735   .0321995    5.540    0.000    .1127022   .2440447
   orace | -.0473781   .0383677   -1.235    0.226   -.1256295   .0308733
 region1 |  2.696084   .0236895  113.809    0.000    2.647769   2.744399
 region2 |  2.671876   .0420415   63.553    0.000    2.586132    2.75762
 region3 |  2.531477   .0601017   42.120    0.000    2.408899   2.654055
 region4 |  2.659955   .0405778   65.552    0.000    2.577196   2.742714
------------------------------------------------------------------------
```

In order to test the joint hypothesis that **region1 = region2 = region3 = region4**, we must enter the equations of the hypothesis one at a time and use the **accumulate** option.

```
. svytest region1 = region2
Adjusted Wald test
 ( 1)  region1 - region2 = 0.0
       F(  1,   31) =    0.40
           Prob > F =  0.5338

. svytest region2 = region3, accum
Adjusted Wald test
 ( 1)  region1 - region2 = 0.0
 ( 2)  region2 - region3 = 0.0
       F(  2,   30) =    4.41
           Prob > F =  0.0209

. svytest region3 = region4, accum
Adjusted Wald test
 ( 1)  region1 - region2 = 0.0
 ( 2)  region2 - region3 = 0.0
 ( 3)  region3 - region4 = 0.0
       F(  3,   29) =    2.97
           Prob > F =  0.0480
```

As expected, we get the same answer as before. Note that the Bonferroni adjustment procedure is not available for use with the above syntax. The **svytest** command can only use the Bonferroni procedure to test whether a group of coefficients are simultaneously equal to zero.

◁

Using **svytest** after estimators that estimate multiple-equation models is straightforward. Users merely need to refer to the coefficients using the syntax for multiple equations; see [U] **16.5 Accessing coefficients and standard errors** for a description and [R] **test** for examples of its use.

▷ Example

Here we estimate a multiple-equation model using `svymlog`:

```
. svymlog health female black age age2

Survey multinomial logistic regression

pweight:  finalwgt                       Number of obs    =      10335
Strata:   stratid                        Number of strata =         31
PSU:      psuid                          Number of PSUs   =         62
                                         Population size   = 1.170e+08
                                         F( 16,     16)    =      36.41
                                         Prob > F          =     0.0000

------------------------------------------------------------------------------
     health |     Coef.    Std. Err.      t     P>|t|     [95% Conf. Interval]
------------+-----------------------------------------------------------------
poor        |
     female |  -.1983735   .1072747    -1.849   0.074    -.4171617    .0204147
      black |   .8964694   .1797728     4.987   0.000     .5298203   1.263119
        age |   .0990246   .032111      3.084   0.004     .0335338   .1645155
       age2 |  -.0004749   .0003209    -1.480   0.149    -.0011294   .0001796
      _cons |  -5.475074   .7468576    -7.331   0.000     -6.9983   -3.951848
------------+-----------------------------------------------------------------
fair        |
     female |   .1782371   .0726556     2.453   0.020     .030055    .3264193
      black |   .4429445   .122667      3.611   0.001     .1927635   .6931256
        age |   .0024576   .0172236     0.143   0.887    -.0326702   .0375853
       age2 |   .0002875   .0001684     1.707   0.098    -.0000559   .000631
      _cons |  -1.819561   .4018153    -4.528   0.000    -2.639069  -1.000053
------------+-----------------------------------------------------------------
good        |
     female |  -.0458251   .074169     -0.618   0.541    -.1970938   .1054437
      black |  -.7532011   .1105444    -6.814   0.000    -.9786579  -.5277443
        age |  -.061369    .009794     -6.266   0.000    -.081344   -.0413939
       age2 |   .0004166   .0001077     3.869   0.001     .000197    .0006363
      _cons |   1.815323   .1996917     9.091   0.000     1.408049   2.222597
------------+-----------------------------------------------------------------
excell      |
     female |  -.222799    .0754205    -2.954   0.006    -.3766202  -.0689778
      black |  -.991647    .1238806    -8.005   0.000    -1.244303  -.7389909
        age |  -.0293573   .0137789    -2.131   0.041    -.0574595  -.001255
       age2 |  -.0000674   .0001505    -0.448   0.657    -.0003744   .0002396
      _cons |   1.499683   .286143      5.241   0.000     .9160909   2.083276
------------------------------------------------------------------------------
(Outcome health==average is the comparison group)
```

Suppose we want to do a joint test of whether the coefficients for **female** and **black** are the same for the "good" and "excellent" categories. We do so, using first the **notest** option to suppress the output, and then **accum** to add the second equation to the test.

```
. svytest [good]female = [excell]female, notest

 ( 1)  [good]female - [excell]female = 0.0

. svytest [good]black = [excell]black, accum

Adjusted Wald test

 ( 1)  [good]female - [excell]female = 0.0
 ( 2)  [good]black - [excell]black = 0.0

       F(  2,     30) =     4.32
            Prob > F =    0.0225
```

◁

The `svytest` command can also be used after `svymean`, `svytotal`, and `svyratio`. `svytest` and `svylc` use the same syntax to reference the estimates. The only difference is that you use `svytest` with a full equation (i.e., you include an equal sign and a right-hand side for the equation), or with a list of estimates that you wish to test simultaneously equal to zero. Here is an example of the former.

▷ Example

```
. svymean bpsystol bpdiast, by(rural)

Survey mean estimation

pweight:  finalwgt                      Number of obs     =      10351
Strata:   stratid                       Number of strata  =         31
PSU:      psuid                         Number of PSUs    =         62
                                        Population size  = 1.172e+08

---------------------------------------------------------------------------
Mean    Subpop. |   Estimate   Std. Err.   [95% Conf. Interval]     Deff
---------------+-----------------------------------------------------------
bpsystol        |
      rural==0 |   126.6065    .5503138   125.4841   127.7289   4.655704
      rural==1 |   127.6753   1.261624    125.1022   130.2484   11.52492
---------------+-----------------------------------------------------------
bpdiast         |
      rural==0 |   80.90864    .4990564   79.89081   81.92648   10.94774
      rural==1 |   81.25081    .9476732   79.31802   83.1836    17.36593
---------------------------------------------------------------------------

. svytest [bpsystol]0 = [bpsystol]1

Adjusted Wald test

 ( 1)  [bpsystol]0 - [bpsystol]1 = 0.0

        F(  1,    31) =     0.71
             Prob > F =     0.4064

. svytest [bpdiast]0 = [bpdiast]1, accumulate

Adjusted Wald test

 ( 1)  [bpsystol]0 - [bpsystol]1 = 0.0
 ( 2)  [bpdiast]0 - [bpdiast]1 = 0.0

        F(  2,    30) =     0.65
             Prob > F =     0.5300
```

◁

Saved Results

`svytest` saves in `r()`:

Scalars
     `r(df)` F numerator degrees of freedom (i.e., dimension of hypothesis test)
     `r(df_r)` F denominator degrees of freedom (or t statistic degrees of freedom for `bonferroni`)
     `r(F)` F statistic (or maximal t statistic for `bonferroni`)

Methods and Formulas

svytest is implemented as an ado-file.

svytest tests the null hypothesis H_0: $C\theta = c$, where θ is a $q \times 1$ vector of parameters, C is any $k \times q$ matrix of constants, and c is a $k \times 1$ vector of constants. The Wald test statistic is

$$W = (C\theta - c)'(C\widehat{V}(\theta)C')^{-1}(C\theta - c)$$

By default, svytest uses

$$\frac{d - k + 1}{kd} W \sim F(k, d - k + 1)$$

to compute the p-value. Here d = total number of sampled PSUs minus the total number of strata, and $F(k, d - k + 1)$ is an F distribution with k numerator degrees of freedom and $d - k + 1$ denominator degrees of freedom. If the noadjust option is specified, the p-value is computed using $W/d \sim F(k, d)$. Note that the noadjust option gives the same results as the test command.

When the bonferroni option is specified, svytest displays adjusted p-values for each of the coefficients corresponding to the specified variables. Adjusted p-values are computed as $p_{\text{adj}} = \min(kp, 1)$, where k is the number of variables specified, and p is the unadjusted p-value (i.e., the p-value shown in the output of the estimation command) obtained from the statistic $t = \widehat{\beta}/[\widehat{V}(\widehat{\beta})]^{1/2}$ which is assumed to have a t distribution with d degrees of freedom.

See Korn and Graubard (1990) for a detailed description of the Bonferroni adjustment technique and a discussion of the relative merits of it and of the adjusted and unadjusted Wald tests.

Acknowledgment

The svytest command was developed in collaboration with John L. Eltinge, Department of Statistics, Texas A&M University.

References

Eltinge, J. L. and W. M. Sribney. 1996. svy5: Estimates of linear combinations and hypothesis tests for survey data. *Stata Technical Bulletin* 31: 31–42. Reprinted in *Stata Technical Bulletin Reprints*, vol. 6, pp. 246–259.

Korn, E. L. and B. I. Graubard. 1990. Simultaneous testing of regression coefficients with complex survey data: use of Bonferroni t statistics. *The American Statistician* 44: 270–276.

Also See

Complementary:	[R] **lincom**, [R] **svy estimators**, [R] **svydes**, [R] **svylc**, [R] **svymean**
Related:	[R] **test**
Background:	[U] **30 Overview of survey estimation**, [R] **svy**

Title

> **sw** — Stepwise maximum-likelihood estimation

Syntax

sw *estimation_command term* $\begin{bmatrix} term & [\ldots] \end{bmatrix}$ $\begin{bmatrix} weight \end{bmatrix}$ $\begin{bmatrix} \texttt{if} \ exp \end{bmatrix}$ $\begin{bmatrix} \texttt{in} \ range \end{bmatrix}$,

$\left\{ \texttt{pr}(\#) \,|\, \texttt{pe}(\#) \,|\, \texttt{pr}(\#) \ \texttt{pe}(\#) \right\}$ $\begin{bmatrix} \underline{\texttt{forward}} \ \texttt{lr} \ \texttt{hier} \ \underline{\texttt{lock}}\texttt{term1} \ cmd\_options \end{bmatrix}$

where *term* is $\left\{ varname \,|\, (varlist) \right\}$ and where *estimation_command* is

cloglog | cnreg | cox | ereg | gamma | glm | gompertz | hetprob | llogist | lnormal |

logistic | logit | ologit | oprobit | poisson | probit | qreg | <u>regress</u> | scobit |

tobit | weibull

For example,

. sw regress mpg weight displ, pr(.2)

would perform backward-selection linear regression.

Weights are allowed if *estimation_command* allows them; see [U] **14.1.6 weight**.

sw shares the features of all estimation commands; see [U] **23 Estimation and post-estimation commands**.

predict after sw behaves the same as predict after *estimation_command*; see the *Syntax for predict* section in the manual entry for *estimation_command*.

Description

sw performs stepwise estimation; the flavor of which is determined by the options specified:

backward selection	pr(#)
backward hierarchical selection	pr(#) hier
backward stepwise	pr(#) pe(#)
forward selection	pe(#)
forward hierarchical selection	pe(#) hier
forward stepwise	pr(#) pe(#) forward

Options

pr(#) specifies the significance level for removal from the model; terms with $p \geq \texttt{pr}()$ are eligible for removal.

pe(#) specifies the significance level for addition to the model; terms with $p < \texttt{pe}()$ are eligible for addition.

forward specifies the forward-stepwise method and may only be specified when both pr() and pe() are also specified. Specifying both pr() and pe() without forward results in backward stepwise. Note that specifying only pr() results in backward selection, and specifying only pe() results in forward selection.

lr specifies the test of term significance is to be the likelihood-ratio test. The default is the less computationally expensive Wald test (i.e., the test is based on the estimated variance–covariance matrix of the estimators).

hier specifies hierarchical selection.

lockterm1 specifies that the first term is to be included in the model and not subjected to the selection criteria.

cmd_options refers to any of the options of *estimation_command*. sw operates by iterating the estimation command to obtain results.

Remarks

sw performs stepwise estimation, the flavor of which is determined by the options specified:

backward selection	pr(*#*)
backward hierarchical selection	pr(*#*) hier
backward stepwise	pr(*#*) pe(*#*)
forward selection	pe(*#*)
forward hierarchical selection	pe(*#*) hier
forward stepwise	pr(*#*) pe(*#*) forward

Typing

```
. sw regress y1 x1 x2 d1 d2 d3 x4 x5, pr(.10)
```

performs a backward selection search for the regression model y1 on x1, x2, d1, d2, d3, x4, and x5. In this search, each explanatory variable is said to be a term. Typing

```
. sw regress y1 x1 x2 (d1 d2 d3) (x4 x5), pr(.10)
```

performs a similar backward selection search, but the variables d1, d2, and d3 are treated as a single term as are x4 and x5. That is, d1, d2, and d3 may or may not appear in the final model, but they appear or not together.

▷ Example

Using the automobile data, we estimate a backward selection model of mpg:

```
. gen weight2 = weight*weight
. sw regress mpg weight weight2 displ gratio turn hdroom foreign price, pr(.2)
                   begin with full model
p = 0.7116 >= 0.2000  removing hdroom
p = 0.6138 >= 0.2000  removing displ
p = 0.3278 >= 0.2000  removing price
    Source |       SS       df       MS                  Number of obs =      74
---------+------------------------------                 F(  5,    68) =   33.39
     Model | 1736.31455      5  347.262911              Prob > F      =  0.0000
  Residual |  707.144906     68  10.3991898              R-squared     =  0.7106
---------+------------------------------                 Adj R-squared =  0.6893
     Total | 2443.45946      73  33.4720474              Root MSE      =  3.2248
```

```
     mpg |     Coef.   Std. Err.       t    P>|t|      [95% Conf. Interval]
---------+----------------------------------------------------------------
  weight |  -.0158002   .0039169    -4.034   0.000     -.0236162   -.0079842
 weight2 |   1.77e-06   6.20e-07     2.862   0.006      5.37e-07    3.01e-06
 foreign |  -3.615107   1.260844    -2.867   0.006     -6.131082   -1.099131
   gratio |   2.011674   1.468831     1.370   0.175     -.9193319    4.94268
    turn |  -.3087038   .1763099    -1.751   0.084     -.6605248    .0431172
   _cons |   59.02133    9.3903      6.285   0.000      40.28328    77.75938
```

In this estimation, each variable was treated as its own term and so considered separately. The engine displacement and gear ratio should really be considered together:

```
. sw regress mpg weight weight2 (displ gratio) turn hdroom foreign price, pr(.2)
                     begin with full model
p = 0.7116 >= 0.2000  removing hdroom
p = 0.3944 >= 0.2000  removing displ gratio
p = 0.2798 >= 0.2000  removing price
   Source |       SS       df       MS               Number of obs =      74
---------+------------------------------             F(  4,    69) =   40.76
    Model |  1716.80842     4   429.202105           Prob > F      =  0.0000
 Residual |  726.651041    69   10.5311745           R-squared     =  0.7026
---------+------------------------------             Adj R-squared =  0.6854
    Total |  2443.45946    73   33.4720474           Root MSE      =  3.2452

     mpg |     Coef.   Std. Err.       t    P>|t|      [95% Conf. Interval]
---------+----------------------------------------------------------------
  weight |  -.0160341   .0039379    -4.072   0.000     -.0238901   -.0081782
 weight2 |   1.70e-06   6.21e-07     2.733   0.008      4.58e-07    2.94e-06
 foreign |  -2.758668   1.101772    -2.504   0.015     -4.956643   -.5606926
    turn |  -.2862724   .176658     -1.620   0.110     -.6386955    .0661507
   _cons |   65.39216   8.208778     7.966   0.000      49.0161     81.76823
```

◁

Search logic for a step

Before giving the complete search logic, let's consider the logic for a step—the first step—in detail. The other steps follow the same logic. If you type

```
. sw regress y1 x1 x2 (d1 d2 d3) (x4 x5), pr(.20)
```

the logic is

1. Estimate the model y on x1 x2 d1 d2 d3 x4 x5.
2. Consider dropping x1.
3. Consider dropping x2.
4. Consider dropping d1 d2 d3.
5. Consider dropping x4 x5.
6. Find the term above that is least significant. If its significance level is $\geq .20$, remove that term.

If you typed

```
. sw regress y1 x1 x2 (d1 d2 d3) (x4 x5), pr(.20) hier
```

the logic is different because the `hier` option states the terms are ordered. The initial logic becomes

1. Estimate the model `y` on `x1 x2 d1 d2 d3 x4 x5`.
2. Consider dropping `x4 x5`—the last term.
3. If the significance of this last term is $\geq$ .20, remove the term.

The process would then stop or continue. It would stop if `x4 x5` were not dropped and otherwise `sw` would continue to consider the significance of the next-to-last term, `d1 d2 d3`.

Specifying `pe()` rather than `pr()` switches to forward estimation. If you typed

```
. sw regress y1 x1 x2 (d1 d2 d3) (x4 x5), pe(.20)
```

`sw` performs forward selection search. The logic for the first step is

1. Estimate a model of `y` on nothing (meaning a constant).
2. Consider adding `x1`.
3. Consider adding `x2`.
4. Consider adding `d1 d2 d3`.
5. Consider adding `x4 x5`.
6. Find the term above that is most significant. If its significance level is $<$ .20, add that term.

As with backward estimation, if you specified `hier`,

```
. sw regress y1 x1 x2 (d1 d2 d3) (x4 x5), pe(.20) hier
```

the search for the most significant term is restricted to the next term:

1. Estimate a model of `y` on nothing (meaning a constant).
2. Consider adding `x1`—the first term.
3. If the significance is $<$ .20, add the term.

If `x1` were added, `sw` would next consider `x2`; otherwise, the search process would stop.

`sw` can also employ a stepwise selection logic where it alternates between adding and removing terms. The full logic for all the possibilities is given below.

(Continued on next page)

Full search logic

Option	Logic
`pr()` (backward selection)	Estimate full model on all explanatory variables. While the least significant term is "insignificant", remove it and reestimate.
`pr() hier` (backward hierarchical selection)	Estimate full model on all explanatory variables. While the last term is "insignificant", remove it and reestimate.
`pr() pe()` (backward stepwise)	Estimate full model on all explanatory variables. If least significant term is "insignificant", remove it and reestimate; otherwise stop. Do that again: If least significant term is "insignificant", remove it and reestimate; otherwise stop. Repeatedly, if most significant excluded term is "significant", add it and reestimate; if least significant included term is "insignificant", remove it and reestimate; until neither is possible.
`pe()` (forward selection)	Estimate "empty" model. While the most significant excluded term is "significant", add it and reestimate.
`pe() hier` (forward hierarchical selection)	Estimate "empty" model. While the next term is "significant", add it and reestimate.
`pr() pe() forward` (forward stepwise)	Estimate "empty" model. If most significant excluded term is "significant", add it and reestimate; otherwise stop. If most significant excluded term is "significant", add it and reestimate; otherwise stop. Repeatedly, if least significant included term is "insignificant", remove it and reestimate; if most significant excluded term is "significant", add it and reestimate; until neither is possible.

Examples

The following two statements are equivalent; both include solely one-variable terms:

```
. sw reg price mpg weight displ, pr(.2)
. sw reg price (mpg) (weight) (displ), pr(.2)
```

The following two statements are equivalent; the last term in each is r1, ..., r4:

```
. sw reg price mpg weight displ (r1-r4), pr(.2) hier
. sw reg price (mpg) (weight) (displ) (r1-r4), pr(.2) hier
```

If one also wished to group variables weight and displ into a single term, one might type

~~. sw reg price mpg (weight displ) (r1-r4), pr(.2) hier~~

sw can be used with commands other than regress, for instance

```
. sw logit outcome (sex weight) treated1 treated2, pr(.2)
. sw logistic outcome (sex weight) treated1 treated2, pr(.2)
```

Either statement would estimate the same model because logistic and logit both estimate maximum-likelihood logistic regression; they differ only in how they report results; see [R] **logit** and [R] **logistic**.

If one wished that variables treated1 and treated2 be included in the model no matter what, one could type

```
. sw logistic outcome (treated1 treated2) ..., pr(.2) lockterm1
```

After sw estimation, you can type sw without arguments to redisplay results

```
. sw
(output from logistic appears)
```

or you can type the underlying estimation command:

```
. logistic
(output from logistic appears)
```

At estimation time, you may specify options unique to the command being stepped:

```
. sw logit outcome (sex weight) treated1 treated2, pr(.2) or
```

or is logit's option to report odds ratios rather than coefficients; see [R] **logit**.

Estimation sample considerations

Whether you use backward or forward estimation, sw forms an estimation sample by taking observations with nonmissing values of all the variables specified. The estimation sample is held constant throughout the stepping. Thus, if you type

```
. sw regress amount sk edul sval, pr(.2) hier
```

and variable sval is missing in half the data, that half of the data will not be used in the reported model even if sval is not included in the final model.

The function e(sample) identifies the sample that was used. e(sample) contains 1 for observations used and 0 otherwise. If e(sample) is defined, it is dropped and recreated. For instance, if you type

```
. sw logistic outcome x1 x2 (x3 x4) (x5 x6 x7), pr(.2) pe(.10)
```

and the final model is outcome on **x1**, **x5**, **x6**, and **x7**, you could recreate the final regression by typing

```
. logistic outcome x1 x5 x6 x7 if e(sample)
```

You could obtain summary statistics within the estimation sample of the independent variables by typing

```
. summarize x1 x5 x6 x7 if e(sample)
```

If you estimate another model, **e(sample)** will automatically be redefined. Typing

```
. sw logistic outcome (x1 x2) (x3 x4) (x5 x6 x7), lock pr(.2)
```

would automatically drop **e(sample)** and recreate it.

Messages

Informatory message: _____ dropped due to collinearity

Each term is checked for collinearity and variables within the term dropped if collinearity is found. For instance, you type

```
. sw regress y x1 x2 (r1-r4) (x3 x4), pr(.2)
```

and assume variables **r1** through **r4** are mutually exclusive and exhaustive dummy variables—perhaps **r1**, ..., **r4** indicate in which of four regions the subject resides. One of the **r1**, ..., **r4** variables will be automatically dropped to identify the model.

This message should cause you no concern.

Error message: between-term collinearity, variable _____

After removing any within-term collinearity, if **sw** still finds collinearity between terms, it refuses to continue. For instance, assume you type

```
. sw regress y1 x1 x2 (d1-d8) (r1-r4), pr(.2)
```

Assume **r1**, ..., **r4** identify in which of four regions the subject resides and that **d1**, ..., **d8** identify the same sort of information, but more finely. **r1**, say, amounts to **d1** and **d2**; **r2** to **d3**, **d4**, **d5**; **r3** to **d6** and **d7**; and **r4** to **d8**. One can estimate the **d*** variables or the **r*** variables, but not both.

It is your responsibility to specify noncollinear terms.

Informatory message: _____ dropped due to estimability and _____ obs. dropped due to estimability

You probably received this message in estimating a logistic or probit model. Regardless of estimation strategy, **sw** checks that the full model can be estimated. The indicated variable had a 0 or infinite standard error.

In the case of logistic, logit, and probit, this is typically caused by one-way causation. Assume you type

```
. sw logistic outcome (x1 x2 x3) d1, pr(.2)
```

and assume variable d1 is an indicator (dummy) variable. Further assume that whenever d1 = 1, outcome = 1 in the data. Then the coefficient on d1 is infinite. One (conservative) solution to this problem is to drop the d1 variable and the d1==1 observations. The underlying estimation commands probit, logit, and logistic report the details of the difficulty and solution; sw simply accumulates such problems and reports the above summary messages. Thus, if you see this message, you could type

```
. logistic outcome x1 x2 x3 d1
```

to see the details. While you should think carefully about such situations, Stata's solution of dropping the offending variables and observations is, in general, appropriate.

Saved Results

sw saves whatever is saved by the underlying estimation command.

Methods and Formulas

sw is implemented as an ado-file.

Some statisticians do not recommend stepwise procedures; see Sribney (1998) for a summary.

References

Beale, E. M. L. 1970. Note on procedures for variable selection in multiple regression. *Technometrics* 12: 909–914.

Bendel, R. B. and A. A. Afifi. 1977. Comparison of stopping rules in forward "stepwise" regression. *Journal of the American Statistical Association* 72: 46–53.

Berk, K. N. 1978. Comparing subset regression procedures. *Technometrics* 20: 1–6.

Draper, N. and H. Smith. 1998. *Applied Regression Analysis*. 3d ed. New York: John Wiley & Sons.

Efroymson, M. A. 1960. Multiple regression analysis. In *Mathematical Methods for Digital Computers*, ed. A. Ralston and H. S. Wilf, 191–203. New York: John Wiley & Sons.

Gorman, J. W. and R. J. Toman. 1966. Selection of variables for fitting equations to data. *Technometrics* 8: 27–51.

Hocking, R. R. 1976. The analysis and selection of variables in linear regression. *Biometrics* 32: 1–50.

Hosmer, D. W., Jr., and S. Lemeshow. 1989. *Applied Logistic Regression*. New York: John Wiley & Sons.

Kennedy, W. J. and T. A. Bancroft. 1971. Model-building for prediction in regression based on repeated significance tests. *Annals of Mathematical Statistics* 42: 1273–1284.

Mantel, N. 1970. Why stepdown in variable selection. *Technometrics* 12: 621–625.

——. 1971. More on variable selection and an alternative approach (letter to the editor). *Technometrics* 13: 455–457.

Sribney, W. M. 1998. FAQ: What are some problems with stepwise regression? *http://www.stata.com/support/faqs/stat.*

Also See

Complementary:	[R] **cloglog**, [R] **cox**, [R] **glm**, [R] **hetprob**, [R] **logistic**, [R] **logit**, [R] **ologit**, [R] **oprobit**, [R] **poisson**, [R] **probit**, [R] **qreg**, [R] **regress**, [R] **scobit**, [R] **tobit**, [R] **weibull**
Background:	[U] **16.5 Accessing coefficients and standard errors**, [U] **23 Estimation and post-estimation commands**

Title

> **swilk** — Shapiro–Wilk and Shapiro–Francia tests for normality

Syntax

swilk *varlist* [if *exp*] [in *range*] [, l̲normal no̲ties g̲enerate(*newvar*)]

sfrancia *varlist* [if *exp*] [in *range*]

Description

swilk performs the Shapiro–Wilk W and sfrancia performs the Shapiro–Francia W' tests for normality. swilk can be used with $7 \leq n \leq 2000$ observations and sfrancia can be used with $5 \leq n \leq 5000$ observations; see [R] **sktest** for a test allowing a larger number of observations.

Options

l̲normal specifies the test is to be for 3-parameter lognormality, meaning $\ln(X - k)$ is tested for normality, where k is calculated from the data as the value that makes the skewness coefficient zero. When simply testing $\ln(X)$ for normality, do not specify this option. See [R] **lnskew0** for estimation of k.

no̲ties suppresses use of averaged ranks for tied values when calculating the W test coefficients.

g̲enerate(*newvar*) creates new variable *newvar* containing the W test coefficients.

Remarks

▷ Example

Using our automobile data, we will test whether the variables **mpg** and **trunk** are normally distributed:

```
. swilk mpg trunk
                   Shapiro-Wilk W test for normal data
    Variable |    Obs          W          V           z    Pr > z
    ---------+-----------------------------------------------------
         mpg |     74      0.94821      3.335       2.627   0.00430
       trunk |     74      0.97921      1.339       0.637   0.26215

. sfrancia mpg trunk
                  Shapiro-Francia W´ test for normal data
    Variable |    Obs          W´         V´          z     Pr>z
    ---------+-----------------------------------------------------
         mpg |     74      0.94872      3.629       2.490   0.00639
       trunk |     74      0.98446      1.100       0.190   0.42477
```

We can reject that `mpg` is normally distributed but cannot reject that `trunk` is normally distributed.

The values reported under W and W' are the Shapiro–Wilk and Shapiro–Francia test statistics. The tests also report V and V', which are more appealing indexes for departure from normality. The median values of V and V' are 1 for samples from normal populations. Large values indicate nonnormality. The 95% critical values of V (V'), which depend on the sample size, are between 1.2 and 2.4 (2.0 and 2.8); see Royston (1991a). (There is no additional information in V (V') than in W (W')—one is just the transform of the other.)

◁

▷ Example

You have data on a variable called `chol` which you suspect is distributed lognormally:

```
. generate lchol = ln(chol)
. swilk lchol
                  Shapiro-Wilk W test for normal data
    Variable |    Obs         W          V           z     Pr > z
-------------+-------------------------------------------------------
       lchol |     78     0.84530    10.401       5.124   0.00000
```

You can reject the lognormal assumption. Note that you do *not* specify the `lnnormal` option when testing for log normality. The `lnnormal` option is for *3-parameter* log normality.

◁

▷ Example

Having discovered that $\ln(\texttt{chol})$ is not distributed normally, you now test that $\ln(\texttt{chol} - k)$ is normally distributed, where k is chosen so that the resulting skewness is zero. You obtain the estimate for k from `lnskew0`; see [R] **lnskew0**:

```
. lnskew0 lcholk = chol, level(95)
        Transform |        k      [95% Conf. Interval]      Skewness
------------------+-------------------------------------------------
      ln(chol-k)  | 4.984322     4.566498   5.069748        .0000399
. swilk lcholk, lnnormal
              Shapiro-Wilk W test for 3-parameter lognormal data
    Variable |    Obs         W          V           z     Pr > z
-------------+-------------------------------------------------------
      lcholk |     78     0.98316     1.132       0.770   0.22053
```

You cannot reject that $\ln(\texttt{chol} - 4.98)$ is distributed normally. Note that you do specify the `lnnormal` option when using an estimated value of k.

◁

Saved Results

`swilk` and `sfrancia` save in `r()`:

Scalars

r(N)	number of observations	r(W)	W or W'
r(p)	significance	r(V)	V or V'
r(z)	z statistic		

Methods and Formulas

`swilk` and `sfrancia` are implemented as ado-files.

The Shapiro–Wilk test is based on Shapiro and Wilk (1965) with a new approximation accurate for $3 \leq n \leq 2000$ (Royston 1992). The interested reader is directed to the original papers for a discussion of the theory behind the test. The calculations made by `swilk` are based on Royston (1982, 1992, 1993).

The Shapiro–Francia test (Shapiro and Francia, 1972; Royston 1983) is an approximate test that is similar to the Shapiro–Wilk test for very large samples.

Acknowledgment

`swilk` and `sfrancia` were written by Patrick Royston of the Imperial College School of Medicine, London.

References

Gould, W. W. 1992. sg3.7: Final summary of tests of normality. *Stata Technical Bulletin* 5: 10–11. Reprinted in *Stata Technical Bulletin Reprints*, vol. 1, pp. 114–115.

Royston, P. 1982. An extension of Shapiro and Wilk's *W* test for normality to large samples. *Applied Statistics* 31: 115–124.

——. 1983. A simple method for evaluating the Shapiro–Francia *W'* test of nonnormality. *Applied Statistics* 32: 297–300.

——. 1991a. Estimating departure from normality. *Statistics in Medicine* 10: 1283–1293.

——. 1991b. sg3.2: Shapiro–Wilk and Shapiro–Francia tests. *Stata Technical Bulletin* 3: 19. Reprinted in *Stata Technical Bulletin Reprints*, vol. 1, p. 105.

——. 1992. Approximating the Shapiro–Wilk *W*-test for non-normality. *Statistics and Computing* 2: 117–119.

——. 1993. A toolkit for testing for non-normality in complete and censored samples. *Statistician* 42: 37–43.

Shapiro, S. S. and R. S. Francia. 1972. An approximate analysis of variance test for normality. *Journal of the American Statistical Association* 67: 215–216.

Shapiro, S. S. and M. B. Wilk. 1965. An analysis of variance test for normality (complete samples). *Biometrika* 52: 591–611.

Also See

Related: [R] **lnskew0**, [R] **lv**, [R] **sktest**

Title

symmetry — Symmetry and marginal homogeneity tests

Syntax

symmetry *casevar controlvar* [*weight*] [if *exp*] [in *range*] [, notable contrib

    exact mh trend cc]

symmi $\#_{11}$ $\#_{12}$ [...] \ $\#_{21}$ $\#_{22}$ [...] [\...] [if *exp*] [in *range*] [, notable

    contrib exact mh trend cc]

fweights are allowed; see [U] **14.1.6 weight**.

Description

symmetry performs asymptotic symmetry and marginal homogeneity tests, and an exact symmetry test on $K \times K$ tables where there is a 1-to-1 matching of cases and controls (nonindependence). This is used to analyze matched-pair case–control data with multiple discrete levels of the exposure (outcome) variable. In genetics, the test is known as the Transmission/Disequilibrium test (TDT) and is used to test the association between transmitted and nontransmitted parental marker alleles to an affected child (Spieldman, McGinnis, and Ewens 1993). In the case of 2×2 tables, the asymptotic test statistics reduce to the McNemar test statistic and the exact symmetry test produces an exact McNemar test; see [R] **epitab**. For numeric exposure variables, symmetry can optionally perform a test for linear trend in the log relative risk.

symmetry expects the data to be in the wide format, that is, each observation contains the matched case and control values in variables *casevar* and *controlvar*. Variables can be numeric or string.

symmi is the immediate form of symmetry. The symmi command uses the values specified on the command line; rows are separated by '\'; options are the same as for symmetry. See [U] **22 Immediate commands** for a general introduction to immediate commands.

Options

notable suppresses the output of the contingency table. By default, symmetry displays the $n \times n$ contingency table at the top of the output.

contrib reports the contribution of each off-diagonal cell-pair to the overall symmetry χ^2.

exact performs an exact test of table symmetry. This option is recommended for sparse tables. CAUTION: the exact test requires substantial amounts of time and computer memory for large tables.

mh performs two marginal homogeneity tests that do not require the inversion of the variance–covariance matrix.

By default, **symmetry** produces the Stuart–Maxwell test statistic which requires the inversion of the nondiagonal variance–covariance matrix, $\mathbf{V}$. When the table is sparse, the matrix may not be of full rank and, in that case, the command substitutes a generalized inverse $\mathbf{V}^*$ for $\mathbf{V}^{-1}$. mh calculates optional marginal homogeneity statistics that do not require the inversion of the variance–covariance matrix. These tests may be preferred in certain situations. See *Methods and formulas*, and Bickenböller and Clerget-Darpoux (1995) for details on these test statistics.

trend performs a test for linear trend in the (log) relative risk (**RR**). This option is only allowed for numeric exposure (outcome) variables and its use should be restricted to measurements on the ordinal or the interval scales.

cc specifies that the continuity correction be used when calculating the test for linear trend. This correction should only be specified when the levels of the exposure variable are equally spaced.

Remarks

symmetry and **symmi** may be used to analyze 1-to-1 matched case–control data with multiple discrete levels of the exposure (outcome) variable.

▷ Example

Consider a survey of 344 individuals (BMDP 1990, 267–270), who were asked in October 1986 whether they agreed with President Reagan's handling of foreign affairs. In January 1987, after the "Iran-Contra" affair became public, these same individuals were surveyed again and asked the same question. We would like to know if public opinion changed over this time period.

We first describe the data and list a few observations.

```
. describe
Contains data from iran.dta
  obs:           344
  vars:            2                          2 Sep 1998 09:27
  size:         2,064 (99.9% of memory free)
-------------------------------------------------------------------------------
    1. before     byte    %8.0g      vlab     Public Opinion before IC
    2. after      byte    %8.0g      vlab     Public Opinion after IC
-------------------------------------------------------------------------------
Sorted by:
. list in 1/5
            before     after
    1.       agree     agree
    2.       agree  disagree
    3.       agree    unsure
    4.    disagree     agree
    5.    disagree  disagree
```

Each observation corresponds to one of the 344 individuals. The data is in wide form so that each observation has a before and an after measurement. We now perform the test without options.

```
. symmetry before after

----------+-------------------------------------------
Public    |
Opinion   |         Public Opinion after IC
before IC |   agree   disagree   unsure      Total
----------+-------------------------------------------
    agree |      47        56       38         141
 disagree |      28        61       31         120
   unsure |      26        47       10          83
          |
    Total |     101       164       79         344
----------+-------------------------------------------

                                      Chi-Squared    df    Prob>chi2
                             ---------+----------------------------------
Symmetry (asymptotic)                 |     14.87      3      0.0019
Marginal homogeneity (Stuart-Maxwell) |     14.78      2      0.0006
                             ---------+----------------------------------
```

The test first tabulates the data in a $K \times K$ table and then performs Bowker's (1948) test for table symmetry, and the Stuart–Maxwell (Stuart 1955, Maxwell 1970) test for marginal homogeneity.

Both the symmetry test and the marginal homogeneity test are highly significant, thus indicating a shift in public opinion.

An exact test of symmetry is provided for use on sparse tables. This test is computationally intensive and so should not be used on large tables. Since we are working on a fast computer, we will run the symmetry test again, and this time include the **exact** option. We will suppress the output of the contingency table by specifying **notable**, and also include the **contrib** option so that we may further examine the cells responsible for the significant result.

```
. symmetry before after, contrib exact mh notable
                    Contribution
                     to symmetry
     Cells            chi-squared
  --------------     --------------
  n1_2 & n2_1            9.3333
  n1_3 & n3_1            2.2500
  n2_3 & n3_2            3.2821
                                      Chi-Squared    df    Prob>chi2
                             ---------+----------------------------------
Symmetry (asymptotic)                 |     14.87      3      0.0019
Marginal homogeneity (Stuart-Maxwell) |     14.78      2      0.0006
Marginal homogeneity (Bickenboller)   |     13.53      2      0.0012
Marginal homogeneity (no diagonals)   |     15.25      2      0.0005
                             ---------+----------------------------------
Symmetry (exact significance probability)              0.0018
```

The largest contribution to the symmetry χ^2 is due to cells n_{12} and n_{21}. These correspond to changes between the agree and disagree categories. Of the 344 individuals, 56 (16.3%) changed from the agree to the disagree response while only 28 (8.1%) changed in the opposite direction.

For this data, the results from the exact test are similar to those from the asymptotic test.

◁

▷ Example

Breslow and Day (1980, 163) reprinted data from Mack et al. (1976) from a case–control study of the effect of exogenous estrogen on the risk of endometrial cancer. The data consist of 59 elderly women diagnosed with endometrial cancer and 59 disease-free controls living in the same community as the cases. Cases and controls were matched on age, marital status, and time living in the community. The data collected included information on the daily dose of conjugated estrogen therapy. Breslow and Day analyzed these data by creating four levels of the dose variable. Here is the data as entered into a Stata dataset:

```
. list, noobs
        case    control     count
           0          0         6
           0  0.1-0.299       2
           0  0.3-0.625       3
           0       626+        1
   0.1-0.299          0         9
   0.1-0.299  0.1-0.299       4
   0.1-0.299  0.3-0.625       2
   0.1-0.299       626+        1
   0.3-0.625          0         9
   0.3-0.625  0.1-0.299       2
   0.3-0.625  0.3-0.625       3
   0.3-0.625       626+        1
        626+          0        12
        626+  0.1-0.299       1
        626+  0.3-0.625       2
        626+       626+        1
```

This data is in a different format than the previous example. Instead of each observation representing a single matched pair, each observation represents possibly multiple pairs indicated by the count variable. For instance, the first observation corresponds to 6 matched pairs where neither the case nor the control was on estrogen; the second observation corresponds to 2 matched pairs where the case was not on estrogen and the control was on 0.1 to 0.299 mg/day; etc.

In order to use symmetry to analyze this data, we must specify fweight to indicate that in our data there are observations corresponding to more than one matched pair.

```
. symmetry case contrib [fweight=count]
----------+------------------------------------------------------
          |                        control
     case |    0      0.1-0.299  0.3-0.625   0.626+     Total
----------+------------------------------------------------------
        0 |    6          2          3          1         12
0.1-0.299 |    9          4          2          1         16
0.3-0.625 |    9          2          3          1         15
   0.626+ |   12          1          2          1         16
          |
    Total |   36          9         10          4         59
----------+------------------------------------------------------

                                       Chi-Squared    df    Prob>chi2
--------------------------------------+---------------------------------
Symmetry (asymptotic)                 |     17.10      6       0.0089
Marginal homogeneity (Stuart-Maxwell) |     16.96      3       0.0007
--------------------------------------+---------------------------------
```

Both the test of symmetry and the test of marginal homogeneity are highly significant, thus leading us to reject the null hypothesis that there is no effect of exposure to estrogen on the risk of endometrial cancer.

Breslow and Day perform a test for trend assuming that the estrogen exposure levels were equally spaced by recoding the exposure levels as 1, 2, 3, and 4.

We can easily reproduce their results by recoding our data in this way and by specifying the `trend` option. Two new numeric variables were created, `ca` and `co`, corresponding to the variables `case` and `control` respectively. Below, we list some of the data and our results from `symmetry`:

```
. list in 1/4, noobs
     case    control     count      ca       co
        0          0         6       1        1
        0    0.1-0.299      2       1        2
        0    0.3-0.625      3       1        3
        0      0.626+       1       1        4

. symmetry ca co [fw=count], notable trend cc
```

		Chi-Squared	df	Prob>chi2
Symmetry (asymptotic)	|	17.10	6	0.0089
Marginal homogeneity (Stuart-Maxwell)	|	16.96	3	0.0007
Linear trend in the (log) RR	|	14.43	1	0.0001

Note that we requested the continuity correction by specifying `cc`. This is appropriate because our coded exposure levels are equally spaced.

The test for trend was highly significant indicating an increased risk of endometrial cancer with increased dosage of conjugated estrogen.

You must be cautious: the way in which you code the exposure variable affects the linear trend statistic. If instead of coding the levels as 1, 2, 3 and 4, we had used 0, .2, .46, and .7 (roughly the midpoint in the range of each level) we would have obtained a χ^2 statistic of 11.19 for this data.

◁

Saved Results

`symmetry` saves in `r()`:

Scalars

`r(N_pair)`	number of matched pairs
`r(chi2)`	asymptotic symmetry χ^2
`r(df)`	asymptotic symmetry degrees of freedom
`r(p)`	asymptotic symmetry p-value
`r(chi2_sm)`	MH (Stuart–Maxwell) χ^2
`r(df_sm)`	MH (Stuart–Maxwell) degrees of freedom
`r(p_sm)`	MH (Stuart–Maxwell) p-value
`r(chi2_b)`	MH (Bickenböller) χ^2
`r(df_b)`	MH (Bickenböller) degrees of freedom
`r(p_b)`	MH (Bickenböller) p-value
`r(chi2_nd)`	MH (no diagonals) χ^2
`r(df_nd)`	MH (no diagonals) degrees of freedom
`r(p_nd)`	MH (no diagonals) p-value
`r(chi2_t)`	χ^2 for linear trend
`r(p_trend)`	p-value for linear trend
`r(p_exact)`	exact symmetry p-value

Methods and Formulas

`symmetry` is implemented as an ado-file.

Asymptotic tests

Consider a square table with K exposure categories, that is, K rows and K columns. Let n_{ij} be the count corresponding to row i and column j of the table, $N_{ij} = n_{ij} + n_{ji}$, for $i, j = 1, 2, \ldots, K$, and $n_{i.}$ and $n_{.j}$ be the marginal totals for row i and column j respectively. Asymptotic tests for symmetry and marginal homogeneity for this $K \times K$ table are calculated as follows.

The null hypothesis of complete symmetry $p_{ij} = p_{ji}$, $i \neq j$, is tested by calculating the test statistic (Bowker 1948)

$$T_{\text{cs}} = \sum_{i<j} \frac{(n_{ij} - n_{ji})^2}{n_{ij} + n_{ji}}$$

which is asymptotically distributed as χ^2 with $K(K-1)/2 - R$ degrees of freedom, where R is the number of off-diagonal cells with $N_{ij} = 0$.

The null hypothesis of marginal homogeneity, $p_{i.} = p_{.i}$, is tested by calculating the Stuart–Maxwell test statistic (Stuart 1955, Maxwell 1970)

$$T_{\text{sm}} = \mathbf{d}' \mathbf{V}^{-1} \mathbf{d}$$

where $\mathbf{d}$ is a column vector with elements equal to the differences $d_i = n_{i.} - n_{.i}$ for $i = 1, 2, \ldots, K$, and $\mathbf{V}$ is the variance–covariance matrix with elements:

$$v_{ii} = n_{i.} + n_{.i} - 2n_{ii}$$
$$v_{ij} = -(n_{ij} + n_{ji}), \quad i \neq j$$

T_{sm} is asymptotically χ^2 with $K - 1$ degrees of freedom.

This test statistic properly accounts for the dependence between the table's rows and columns. When the matrix $\mathbf{V}$ is not of full rank a generalized inverse $\mathbf{V}^*$ is substituted for $\mathbf{V}^{-1}$.

The Bickenböller and Clerget-Darpoux (1995) marginal homogeneity test statistic is calculated by

$$T_{\text{mh}} = \sum_i \frac{(n_{i.} - n_{.i})^2}{n_{i.} + n_{.i}}$$

This statistic is asymptotically distributed, under the assumption of marginal independence, as χ^2 with $K - 1$ degrees of freedom.

The marginal homogeneity (no diagonals) test statistic T_{mh}^0 is calculated in the same way as T_{mh} except that the diagonal elements do not enter into the calculation of the marginal totals. Unlike the previous test statistic, T_{mh}^0 reduces to a McNemar test statistic for 2×2 tables. The test statistic $[(K-1)/2]T_{\text{mh}}^0$ is asymptotically distributed as χ^2 with $K - 1$ degrees of freedom (Cleves et al. 1997, Spieldman and Ewens 1996).

Breslow and Day's test statistic for linear trend in the (log) of relative risk

$$\frac{\left(\sum_{i<j}(n_{ij} - n_{ji})(X_j - X_i) - cc \right)^2}{\sum_{i<j}(n_{ij} + n_{ji})(j - i)^2}$$

where the X_j are the "doses" associated with the various levels of exposure and cc is the continuity correction; it is asymptotically distributed as χ^2 with 1 degree of freedom.

The continuity correction option is only applicable when the levels of the exposure variable are equally spaced.

Exact symmetry test

The exact test is based on a permutation algorithm applied to the null distribution. The distribution of the off-diagonal elements n_{ij}, $i \neq j$, conditional on the sum of the complementary off-diagonal cells, $N_{ij} = n_{ij} + n_{ji}$, can be written as the product of $K(K-1)/2$ binomial random variables:

$$P(\mathbf{n}) = \prod_{i<j} \binom{N_{ij}}{n_{ij}} \pi_{ij}{}^{n_{ij}} (1 - \pi_{ij})^{n_{ij}}$$

where $\mathbf{n}$ is a vector with elements n_{ij} and $\pi_{ij} = E(n_{ij}/N_{ij}|N_{ij})$. Under the null hypothesis of complete symmetry, $\pi_{ij} = \pi_{ji} = 1/2$, and thus the permutation distribution is given by

$$P_0(\mathbf{n}) = \prod_{i<j} \binom{N_{ij}}{n_{ij}} \left(\frac{1}{2}\right)^{N_{ij}}$$

The exact significance test is performed by evaluating

$$P_{\text{cs}} = \sum_{n \in p} P_0(\mathbf{n})$$

where $p = \{n : P_0(\mathbf{n}) < P_0(\mathbf{n}^*)\}$ and $\mathbf{n}^*$ is the observed contingency table data vector. The algorithm evaluates p_{cs} exactly.

References

Bickenböller, H. and F. Clerget-Darpoux. 1995. Statistical properties of the allelic and genotypic transmission/disequilibrium test for multiallelic markers. *Genetic Epidemiology* 12: 865–870.

BMDP. 1990. *BMDP statistical software manual*. Example 4F2.9. Los Angeles: BMDP Statistical Software, Inc.

Bowker, A. H. 1948. A test for symmetry in contingency tables. *Journal of the American Statistical Association* 43: 572–574.

Breslow, N. E. and N. E. Day. 1980. *Statistical Methods in Cancer Research*, vol. 1, 182–198. Lyon: International Agency for Research on Cancer.

Cleves, M. A. 1997. sg74: Symmetry and marginal homogeneity test/TDT. *Stata Technical Bulletin* 40: 23–27. Reprinted in *Stata Technical Bulletin Reprints*, vol. 7, pp. 193–197.

Cleves, M. A., J. M. Olson, and K. B. Jacobs. 1997. Exact transmission–disequilibrium tests with multiallelic markers. *Genetic Epidemiology* 14: 337–347.

Mack, T. M., M. C. Pike, B. E. Henderson, R. I. Pfeffer, V. R. Gerkins, B. S. Arthur, and S. E. Brown. 1976. Estrogens and endometrial cancer in a retirement community. *New England Journal of Medicine* 294: 1262–1267.

Maxwell, A. E. 1970. Comparing the classification of subjects by two independent judges. *British Journal of Psychiatry* 116: 651–655.

Spieldman, R. S. and W. J. Ewens. 1996. The TDT and other family-based tests for linkage disequilibrium and association. *American Journal of Human Genetics* 59: 983–989.

Spieldman, R. S., R. E. McGinnis, and W. J. Ewens. 1993. Transmission test for linkage disequilibrium: The insulin gene region and insulin-dependents diabetes mellitus. *American Journal of Human Genetics* 52: 506–516.

Stuart, A. 1955. A test for homogeneity of the marginal distributions in a two-way classification. *Biometrika* 42: 412–416.

Also See

Related: [R] **epitab**

Title

---

syntax — Parse Stata syntax

Syntax

> **args** *macroname1* [*macroname2* [*macroname3* ...]]
>
> **syntax** *description_of_syntax*

Description

There are two ways that a Stata program can interpret what the user types:

1. positionally, meaning first argument, second argument, and so on;

2. according to a grammar such as standard Stata syntax.

args does the first. The first argument is assigned to *macroname1*, the second to *macroname2*, and so on. In the program, you subsequently refer to the contents of the macros by enclosing their names in single quotes: `macroname1´, `macroname2´, ...:

```
program define myprog
        args varname dof beta
        (the rest of the program would be coded in terms of `varname´, `dof´, and `beta´)
        ...
end
```

syntax does the second. You specify the new command's syntax on the **syntax** command; for instance, you might code

```
program define myprog
        syntax varlist [if] [in] [, DOF(integer 50) Beta(real 1.0)]
        (the rest of the program would be coded in terms of `varlist´, `if´, `in´, `dof´, and `beta´)
        ...
end
```

syntax examines what the user typed and attempts to match it to the syntax diagram. If it does not match, an error message is issued and the program is stopped (a nonzero return code is returned). If it does match, the individual components are stored in particular local macros where you can subsequently access them. In the example above, the result would be to define the local macros `varlist´, `if´, `in´, `dof´, and `beta´.

For an introduction to Stata programming, see [U] **21 Programming Stata** and especially [U] **21.4 Program arguments**.

Syntax, continued

The *description_of_syntax* allowed by `syntax` includes

description_of_varlist:

type	*nothing*
or	
optionally type	[
then type one of	`varlist` `varname` `newvarlist` `newvarname`
optionally type	(*varlist_specifiers*)
type	] (if you typed [at the start)

varlist_specifiers are `default=none` `min=#` `max=#` numeric string ts
  generate   (`newvarlist` and `newvarname` only)

Examples:
```
syntax varlist ...
syntax [varlist] ...
syntax varlist(min=2) ...
syntax varlist(max=4) ...
syntax varlist(min=2 max=4 numeric) ...
syntax varlist(default=none) ...

syntax newvarlist(max=1) ...

syntax varname ...
syntax [varname] ...
```

If you type nothing, then the command does not allow a varlist.

Typing [and] means the varlist is optional.

`default=` specifies how the varlist is to be filled in when the varlist is optional and the user does not specify it. The default is to fill it in with all the variables. If `default=none` is specified, it is left empty.

`min=` and `max=` specify the minimum and maximum number of variables that may be specified. Typing `varname` is equivalent to typing `varlist(max=1)`.

`numeric` and `string` restrict the specified varlist to consist of entirely numeric or entirely string variables.

`ts` allows the varlist to contain time-series operators.

`generate` specifies, in the case of `newvarlist` or `newvarname`, that the new variables are to be created and filled in with missing values.

After the `syntax` command, the resulting varlist is returned in `` `varlist' ``. If there are new variables (you coded `newvarname` or `newvarlist`), the macro `` `typlist' `` is also defined containing the storage type of each of the new variables, listed one after the other.

description_of_if:

type	*nothing*
or	
optionally type	[
type	if
optionally type	/
type	] (if you typed [at the start)

Examples:
```
syntax ... if ...
syntax ... [if] ...
syntax ... [if/] ...
syntax ... if/ ...
```

If you type nothing, then the command does not allow an if *exp*.

Typing [and] means the if *exp* varlist is optional.

After the `syntax` command, the resulting if *exp* is returned in `` `if' ``. The macro contains if followed by the expression unless you specified /, in which case the macro contains just the expression.

description_of_in:

type	*nothing*	
or		
optionally type	[	
type	in	
optionally type	/	
type	]	(if you typed [at the start)

Examples:
```
syntax ... in ...
syntax ... [in] ...
syntax ... [in/] ...
syntax ... in/ ...
```

If you type nothing, then the command does not allow an in *range*.

Typing [and] means the in *range* is optional.

After the syntax command, the resulting in *range* is returned in `in´. The macro contains in followed by the range unless you specified /, in which case the macro contains just the range.

description_of_using:

type	*nothing*	
or		
optionally type	[	
type	using	
optionally type	/	
type	]	(if you typed [at the start)

Examples:
```
syntax ... using ...
syntax ... [using] ...
syntax ... [using/] ...
syntax ... using/ ...
```

If you type nothing, then the command does not allow using *filename*.

Typing [and] means the using *filename* is optional.

After the syntax command, the resulting filename is returned in `using´. The macro contains using followed by the filename in quotes unless you specified /, in which case the macro contains just the filename and without quotes.

description_of_=exp:

type	*nothing*	
or		
optionally type	[	
type	=	
optionally type	/	
type	exp	
type	]	(if you typed [at the start)

Examples:
```
syntax ... =exp ...
syntax ... [=exp] ...
syntax ... [=/exp] ...
syntax ... =/exp ...
```

If you type nothing, then the command does not allow an *=exp*.

Typing [and] means the *=exp* is optional.

After the syntax command, the resulting expression is returned in `exp´. The macro contains =, a space, and the expression unless you specified /, in which case the macro contains just the expression.

description_of_weights:

type	*nothing*
or	
type	[
type any of	<u>f</u>weight <u>a</u>weight <u>p</u>weight <u>i</u>weight
optionally type	/
type	]

Examples: `syntax ... [fweight] ...`
`syntax ... [fweight pweight] ...`
`syntax ... [pweight fweight] ...`
`syntax ... [fweight pweight iweight/] ...`

If you type nothing, then the command does not allow weights. A command may not allow both a weight and =*exp*.

~~You must type [and]; they are not optional.~~ Weights are always optional.

The first weight specified is the default weight type.

After the `syntax` command, the resulting weight and expression are returned in `weight` and `exp`. `weight` contains the weight type or nothing if no weights were specified. `exp` contains =, a space, and the expression unless you specified /, in which case the macro contains just the expression.

description_of_options:

type	*nothing*	
or		
type	[,	
type	*option_descriptors*	(these options will be optional)
optionally type	*	
type	]	
or		
type	,	
type	*option_descriptors*	(these options will be required)
optionally type	[	
optionally type	*option_descriptors*	(these options will be optional)
optionally type	*	
optionally type	]	

Examples: `syntax ... [, MYopt Thisopt]`
`syntax ..., MYopt Thisopt`
`syntax ..., MYopt [Thisopt]`
`syntax ... [, MYopt Thisopt *]`

If you type nothing, then the command does not allow options.

The brackets distinguish optional from required options. All options can be optional, all options required, or some can be optional and others be required.

After the `syntax` command, options are returned to you in local macros based on the first 7 letters of each option's name. If you also specify *, any remaining options are collected and placed, one after the other, in `options`. If you do not specify *, then if the user specifies any options that you do not list, an error is returned.

option_descriptors are documented below.

(Continued on next page)

option_descriptor optionally_on:
    type   OPname   (capitalization indicates minimal abbreviation)

                    Examples: syntax ..., ... replace ...
                                        syntax ..., ... REPLACE ...
                                        syntax ..., ... detail ...
                                        syntax ..., ... Detail ...
                                        syntax ..., ... CONStant ...

The result of the option is returned in a macro name formed by the first 7 letters of the option's name. Thus, option `replace` is returned in local macro `` `replace' ``, option `detail` in local macro `` `detail' ``, but option `constant` in local macro `` `constan' ``.

The macro contains nothing if not specified or else it contains the macro's name, fully spelled out.

Warning: be careful if the first two letters of the option's name are `no`, such as the option called `notice`. You must capitalize at least the `N` in such cases.

---

option_descriptor optionally_off:
    type   no
    type   OPname   (capitalization indicates minimal abbreviation)

                    Examples: syntax ..., ... noreplace ...
                                      syntax ..., ... noREPLACE ...
                                      syntax ..., ... nodetail ...
                                      syntax ..., ... noDetail ...
                                      syntax ..., ... noCONStant ...

The result of the option is returned in a macro name formed by the first 7 letters of the option's name excluding the `no`. Thus, option `noreplace` is returned in local macro `` `replace' ``, option `nodetail` in local macro `` `detail' ``, and option `noconstant` in local macro `` `constan' ``.

The macro contains nothing if not specified or else it contains the macro's name, fully spelled out, with a `no` prefixed. That is, in the `noREPLACE` example above, macro `` `replace' `` contains nothing or it contains `noreplace`.

---

option_descriptor optional_integer_value:
    type   OPname   (capitalization indicates minimal abbreviation)
    type   (integer
    type   # (unless the option is required)   (the default integer value)
    type   )

                    Examples: syntax ..., ... Count(integer 3) ...
                                        syntax ..., ... SEQuence(integer 1) ...
                                        syntax ..., ... dof(integer -1) ...

The result of the option is returned in a macro name formed by the first 7 letters of the option's name.

The macro contains the integer specified by the user or else it contains the default value.

---

option_descriptor optional_real_value:
    type   OPname   (capitalization indicates minimal abbreviation)
    type   (real
    type   # (unless the option is required)   (the default value)
    type   )

                    Examples: syntax ..., ... Mean(real 2.5) ...
                                        syntax ..., ... SD(real -1) ...

The result of the option is returned in a macro name formed by the first 7 letters of the option's name.

The macro contains the integer specified by the user or else it contains the default value.

option_descriptor optional_numlist:

type	OPname	(capitalization indicates minimal abbreviation)
type	(numlist	
type	<u>ascending</u> or <u>descending</u> or *nothing*	
optionally type	<u>integer</u>	
optionally type	<u>missingokay</u>	
optionally type	min=#	
optionally type	max=#	
optionally type	># or >=# or *nothing*	
optionally type	<# or <=# or *nothing*	
optionally type	sort	
type	)	

Examples:
```
syntax ..., ... VALues(numlist) ...
syntax ..., ... VALues(numlist max=10 sort) ...
syntax ..., ... TIME(numlist >0) ...
syntax ..., ... FREQuency(numlist >0 integer) ...
syntax ..., ... OCCur(numlist missingokay >=0 <1e+9) ...
```

The result of the option is returned in a macro name formed by the first 7 letters of the option's name.

The macro contains the values specified by the user, but listed out, one after the other. For instance, the user might specify `time(1(4),10)` and then the local macro `time` would contain "1 2 3 4 10".

`min` and `max` specify the minimum and maximum number of elements that may be in the list.

`<`, `<=`, `>`, and `>=` specify the range of elements allowed in the list.

`integer` indicates the user may specify integer values only.

`missingokay` indicates the user may specify missing (a single period) as a list element.

`ascending` specifies the user must give the list in ascending order without repeated values. `descending` specifies the user must give the list in descending order and without repeated values.

`sort` specifies that the list be sorted before being returned. Distinguish this from modifier `ascending`. `ascending` states the user must type the list in ascending order. `sort` says the user may type the list in any order but it is to be returned in ascending order. `ascending` states the list may have no repeated elements. `sort` places no such restriction on the list.

---

option_descriptor optional_varlist:

type	OPname	(capitalization indicates minimal abbreviation)
type	(varlist or (varname	
optionally type	<u>numeric</u> or <u>string</u>	
optionally type	min=#	
optionally type	max=#	
optionally type	ts	
type	)	

Examples:
```
syntax ..., ... ROW(varname) ...
syntax ..., ... BY(varlist) ...
syntax ..., ... Counts(varname numeric) ...
syntax ..., ... TItlevar(varname string) ...
syntax ..., ... Sizes(varlist numeric min=2 max=10) ...
```

The result of the option is returned in a macro name formed by the first 7 letters of the option's name.

The macro contains the variables specified by the user, unabbreviated, listed one after the other.

`min` indicates the minimum number of variables to be specified if the option is given. `min=1` is the default.

`max` indicates the maximum number of variables that may be specified if the option is given. `max=800` is the default for `varlist` (you may set it to be larger) and `max=1` is the default for `varname`.

`numeric` specifies that the variable list must be comprised entirely of numeric variables; `string` specifies string variables.

`ts` indicates the variable list may contain time-series operators.

option_descriptor optional_string:

type	OPname	(capitalization indicates minimal abbreviation)
type	(<u>string</u>	
optionally type	asis	
type	)	
	Examples:	syntax ..., ... Title(string) ...
		syntax ..., ... XTRAvars(string) ...
		syntax ..., ... SAVing(string asis) ...

The result of the option is returned in a macro name formed by the first 7 letters of the option's name.

The macro contains the string specified by the user or else it contains nothing.

asis is rarely specified; if specified, the option's arguments are returned just as the user typed them, without quotes stripped and with leading and trailing blanks. If you specify this modifier, be sure to use compound double quotes when referring to the macro.

option_descriptor optional_passthru:

type	OPname	(capitalization indicates minimal abbreviation)
type	(passthru)	
	Examples:	syntax ..., ... Title(passthru) ...
		syntax ..., ... SAVing(passthru) ...

The result of the option is returned in a macro name formed by the first 7 letters of the option's name.

The macro contains the full option—unabbreviated option name, parentheses, and argument—as specified by the user or else it contains nothing. For instance, were the user to type ti("My Title") the macro would contain title("My Title").

Remarks

Stata is programmable and that makes it possible to implement new commands. This is done with program define:

```
program define newcmd
        ...
end
```

The first duty of the program is to parse the arguments it receives.

Programmers use positional argument passing for subroutines and for some new commands with exceedingly simple syntax. They do this because it is so easy to program. If program myprog is to receive a variable name (call it varname) and two numeric arguments (call them dof and beta), all they need code is

```
program define myprog
        args varname dof beta
        (the rest of the program would be coded in terms of `varname´, `dof´, and `beta´)
        ...
end
```

The disadvantage of this is from the caller's side: Heaven forbid the caller get the arguments in the wrong order, or not spell out the variable name, etc.

The alternative is to use standard Stata syntax. `syntax` makes it easy to make new command `myprog` have syntax

> `myprog` *varname* $\left[\, ,\ \underline{d}of(\#)\ \underline{b}eta(\#)\, \right]$

and even to have defaults for `dof()` and `beta()`:

```
program define myprog
        syntax varlist(max=1) [, Dof(integer 50) Beta(real 1.0)]
        (the rest of the program would be coded in terms of `varlist', `dof', and `beta')
        . . .
end
```

The args command

`args` splits what the user typed into words and places the first word in the first macro specified, the second in the second macro specified, and so on:

```
program define myprog
        args arg1 arg2 arg3 . . .
        do computations using local macros 'arg1', 'arg2', 'arg3', . . .
end
```

`args` never produces an error. If the user specified more arguments than macros specified, the extra arguments are ignored. If the user specified fewer arguments than macros specified, the extra macros are set to contain `""`.

A better version of this program would read

```
program define myprog
        version 6.0                                      ← new
        args arg1 arg2 arg3 . . .
        do computations using local macros 'arg1', 'arg2', 'arg3', . . .
end
```

Placing `version 6.0` as the first line of the program ensures that the command will continue to work even with future versions of Stata; see [U] **19.1.1 Version** and [R] **version**. We will include the `version` line from now on.

▷ Example

The following command displays the three arguments it receives:

```
. program define argdisp
  1.            version 6.0
  2.            args first second third
  3.            display "1st argument = `first'"
  4.            display "2nd argument = `second'"
  5.            display "3rd argument = `third'"
  6. end
. argdisp cat dog mouse
1st argument = cat
2nd argument = dog
3rd argument = mouse

. argdisp 3.456 2+5-12 X*3+cat
1st argument = 3.456
2nd argument = 2+5-12
3rd argument = X*3+cat
```

Note that arguments are defined by the spaces that separate them. "X*3+cat" is one argument but, had we typed "X*3 + cat", that would have been three arguments.

If the user specifies fewer arguments than expected by **args**, the additional local macros are set to being empty. By the same token, if the user specifies too many, they are ignored:

```
. argdisp cat dog
1st argument = cat
2nd argument = dog
3rd argument =
. argdisp cat dog mouse cow
1st argument = cat
2nd argument = dog
3rd argument = mouse
```
◁

❏ Technical Note

When a program is invoked, what the user typed just as the user typed it is stored in the macro `0´. In addition, the first word of that is also stored in `1´, the second in `2´, and so on. **args** merely copies the `1´, `2´, ..., macros. Coding

```
args arg1 arg2 arg3
```

is no different from coding

```
local arg1 `"`1´"´
local arg2 `"`2´"´
local arg3 `"`3´"´
```
❏

The syntax command

syntax is easy to use. **syntax** parses standard Stata syntax, which is

command varlist **if** *exp* **in** *range* [*weight*] **using** *filename*, *options*

The basic idea is that you code a **syntax** command describing which parts of standard Stata syntax you expect to see. For instance, you might code

```
syntax varlist if in, title(string) adjust(real 1)
```

or code

```
syntax [varlist] [if] [in] [, title(string) adjust(real 1)]
```

In the first example, you are saying that everything is required. In the second, everything is optional. You can make some elements required and others optional:

```
syntax varlist [if] [in], adjust(real) [title(string)]
```

or

```
syntax varlist [if] [in] [, adjust(real 1) title(string)]
```

or lots of other possibilities. Square brackets denote optional. Put them around what you wish.

Anyway, you code what you expect the user to type. **syntax** then compares that with what the user actually did type and, if there is a mismatch, **syntax** issues an error message. Otherwise, **syntax** processes what the user typed and stores the pieces, broken out into categories, in macros. These macros are named the same as the syntactical piece:

The varlist specified	will go into `` `varlist' ``
The if *exp*	will go into `` `if' ``
The in *range*	will go into `` `in' ``
The adjust() option's contents	will go into `` `adjust' ``
The title() option's contents	will go into `` `title' ``

Go back to the section *Syntax, continued.* Where each element is stored is explicitly stated. When a piece is not specified by the user, the corresponding macro is cleared.

▷ **Example**

The following program simply displays the pieces:

```
. program define myprog
1. version 6.0
2. syntax varlist [if] [in] [, adjust(real 1) title(string)]
3. display "varlist contains |`varlist'|"
4. display "     if contains |`if'|"
5. display "     in contains |`in'|"
6. display " adjust contains |`adjust'|"
7. display "  title contains |`title'|"
8. end

. myprog
varlist required
r(100);
```

Well that should not surprise us; we said the varlist was required in the **syntax** command, so when we tried **myprog** without explicitly specifying a varlist, Stata complained.

```
. myprog mpg weight
varlist contains |mpg weight|
     if contains ||
     in contains ||
 adjust contains |1|
  title contains ||

. myprog mpg weight if foreign
varlist contains |mpg weight|
     if contains |if foreign|
     in contains ||
 adjust contains |1|
  title contains ||

. myprog mpg weight in 1/20
varlist contains |mpg weight|
     if contains ||
     in contains |in 1/20|
 adjust contains |1|
  title contains ||

. myprog mpg weight in 1/20 if foreign
varlist contains |mpg weight|
     if contains |if foreign|
     in contains |in 1/20|
 adjust contains |1|
  title contains ||
```

```
. myprog mpg weight in 1/20 if foreign, title("My Results")
varlist contains |mpg weight|
     if contains |if foreign|
     in contains |in 1/20|
 adjust contains |1|
  title contains |My Results|
. myprog mpg weight in 1/20 if foreign, title("My Results") adjust(2.5)
varlist contains |mpg weight|
     if contains |if foreign|
     in contains |in 1/20|
 adjust contains |2.5|
  title contains |My Results|
```

That is all there is to it.

◁

▷ Example

With this in hand, it would not be difficult to actually make `myprog` do something. For want of a better example, we will change `myprog` to display the mean of each variable, said mean multiplied by `adjust()`:

```
program define myprog
        version 6.0
        syntax varlist [if] [in] [, adjust(real 1) title(string)]
        display
        if "`title'" ~= "" {
                display "`title':"
        }
        tokenize `varlist'
        while "`1'" ~= "" {
                quietly summarize `1' `if' `in'
                display %9s "`1'" "  " %9.0g r(mean)*`adjust'
                macro shift
        }
end

. myprog mpg weight
     mpg    21.2973
  weight   3019.459
. myprog mpg weight if foreign==1
     mpg   24.77273
  weight   2315.909
. myprog mpg weight if foreign==1, title("My title")
My title:
     mpg   24.77273
  weight   2315.909
. myprog mpg weight if foreign==1, title("My title") adjust(2)
My title:
     mpg   49.54545
  weight   4631.818
```

◁

❏ Technical Note

myprog is hardly deserving of any further work given what little it does, but let's illustrate two things using it.

First, learn about the marksample command; see [R] **mark**. A common mistake is to use one sample in one part of the program and a different sample in another part. The solution is to create a variable at the outset that contains 1 if the observation is to be used and 0 otherwise. marksample will do this and do it correctly because marksample knows what syntax has just parsed:

```
program define myprog
        version 6.0
        syntax varlist [if] [in] [, adjust(real 1) title(string)]
        marksample touse                                ← new
        display
        if "`title'" ~= "" {
                display "`title':"
        }
        tokenize `varlist'
        while "`1'" ~= "" {
                quietly summarize `1' if `touse'        ← changed
                display %9s "`1'" "  " %9.0g r(mean)*`adjust'
                macro shift
        }
end
```

The second thing we will do is modify our program so that what is done with each variable is done by a subroutine. Pretend, in this, that we are doing something more involved than calculating and displaying a mean.

We want to make this modification to show you the right and proper use of the **args** command. Passing arguments by position to subroutines is convenient and there is no chance of error due to arguments being out of order, or at least there is no chance assuming we wrote our program properly:

```
program define myprog
        version 6.0
        syntax varlist [if] [in] [, adjust(real 1) title(string)]
        marksample touse
        display
        if "`title'" ~= "" {
                display "`title':"
        }
        tokenize `varlist'
        while "`1'" ~= "" {
                doavar `touse' `1' `adjust'
                macro shift
        }
end
program define doavar
        version 6.0
        args touse name value
        qui summarize `name' if `touse'
        display %9s "`name'" "  " %9.0g r(mean)*`value'
end
```

❏

Also See

Complementary:	[R] **mark**, [R] **numlist**, [R] **program**
Related:	[R] **gettoken**, [R] **tokenize**, [R] **tsrevar**, [R] **unab**
Background:	[U] **14 Language syntax**,
	[U] **19.1.1 Version**,
	[U] **21 Programming Stata**,
	[U] **21.3.1 Local macros**,
	[U] **21.3.5 Double quotes**

Title

sysdir — Set system directories

Syntax

sysdir [list]

sysdir set *codeword* ["]*path*["]

adopath

adopath + *path_or_codeword*

adopath ++ *path_or_codeword*

adopath - {*path_or_codeword* | #}

set adosize # $10 \leq \# \leq 500$

where *codeword* is { STATA | UPDATES | BASE | SITE | STBPLUS | PERSONAL | OLDPLACE }

Description

sysdir lists and resets the identities of Stata's system directories.

adopath provides a convenient way to examine and manipulate the ado-file path stored in the global macro S_ADO.

set adosize sets the maximum amount of memory in kilobytes that automatically loaded do-files may consume. The default is set adosize 65 for Intercooled Stata and 15 for Small Stata.

These commands have to do with technical aspects of Stata's implementation. With the exception of sysdir list, you should never have to use them.

Remarks

sysdir

Stata expects to find various parts of itself in various directories (folders). Rather than describe these directories as C:\stata\ado\base or /usr/local/stata/ado, these places are referenced by codewords. Here are the definitions of the codewords on a particular Windows computer:

```
. sysdir
    STATA:  C:\STATA\
  UPDATES:  C:\STATA\ado\updates\
     BASE:  C:\STATA\ado\base\
     SITE:  C:\STATA\ado\site\
  STBPLUS:  C:\ado\stbplus\
 PERSONAL:  C:\ado\personal\
 OLDPLACE:  C:\ado\
```

Even if you are using Stata for Windows, when you type `sysdir`, you might see different directories listed.

The `sysdir` command allows you to obtain the correspondence between codeword and actual directory and it allows you to change the mapping. Each of the directories serves a particular purpose:

STATA refers to the directory where the Stata executable is to be found.

UPDATES is where the updates to the official ado-files that were shipped with Stata are installed. The `update` command places files in this directory; see [R] **update**.

BASE is where the original official ado-files that were shipped with Stata are installed. This directory was written when Stata was installed and thereafter the contents are never changed.

SITE is relevant only on networked computers. It is where administrators may place ado-files for sitewide use on networked computers. No Stata command writes in this directory, but administrators may move files into the directory or they may obtain ado-files using `net` and choose to install them into this directory; see [R] **net**.

STBPLUS is relevant on all systems. It is where ado-files written by other people that you obtain using the `net` command are installed; by default, `net` installs files to this directory; see [R] **net**.

PERSONAL is where you are to copy ado-files that you write and that you wish to use no matter what your current directory when you use Stata. (The alternative is to put ado-files in your current directory and then they will only be available when you are in that directory.)

OLDPLACE is included for backwards compatibility. Old Stata users used to put ado-files here, both the personal ones and the ones written by others. Nowadays they are supposed to put their personal files in PERSONAL and the ones written by others in STBPLUS.

Do not change the definitions of UPDATES or BASE, You may want to change the definitions of SITE, PERSONAL, STBPLUS, or especially OLDPLACE. For instance, if you wanted to change the definition of OLDPLACE to be `d:\ado`, type

```
. sysdir set OLDPLACE "d:\ado"
```

Resetting a system directory affects only the current session; the next time you enter Stata, the system directories will be set back to being as they originally were. If you want to reset a system directory permanently, place the `sysdir set` command in your `profile.do`; see [GSW] **A.7 Executing commands every time Stata is started**, [GSW] **B.7 Executing commands every time Stata is started**, [GSM] **A.6 Executing commands every time Stata is started**, or [GSU] **A.7 Executing commands every time Stata is started**.

adopath

`adopath` displays and resets the contents of the global macro S_ADO, the path over which Stata searches for ado-files. The default search path is

```
. adopath
  [1]  (UPDATES)   "C:\STATA\ado\updates"
  [2]  (BASE)      "C:\STATA\ado\base"
  [3]  (SITE)      "C:\STATA\ado\site"
  [4]              "."
  [5]  (PERSONAL)  "C:\ado\personal"
  [6]  (STBPLUS)   "C:\ado\stbplus"
  [7]  (OLDPLACE)  "C:\ado"
```

In reading the above, you want to focus on the codewords on the left. `adopath` mentions the actual directories but, were you to change the meaning of a codeword using `sysdir`, that change would affect `adopath`.

The above states that, when Stata looks for an ado-file, first it looks in UPDATES. If the ado-file is found, that copy is used. If it is not found, Stata next looks in BASE and, if it is found there, that copy is used. And so the process continues. Note that at the fourth step, Stata looks in the current directory (for which there is no codeword).

`adopath` merely presents the information in S_ADO in a more readable form:

```
. macro list S_ADO
S_ADO:     UPDATES;BASE;SITE;.;PERSONAL;STBPLUS;OLDPLACE
```

`adopath` can also change the contents of the path. In general, you should not do this unless you are sure of what you are doing. You should not because many features of Stata will stop working if you change the path incorrectly. At worst, however, you might have to exit and reenter Stata, so you cannot do any permanent damage. Moreover, it is safe to add to the end of the path.

The path may include actual directory names, such as `c:\myprogs`, or codewords, such as PERSONAL, STBPLUS, and OLDPLACE. If you wanted to add `c:\myprogs` to the end of the path, you type

```
. adopath + c:\myprogs
  [1]  (UPDATES)    "C:\STATA\ado\updates"
  [2]  (BASE)       "C:\STATA\ado\base"
  [3]  (SITE)       "C:\STATA\ado\site"
  [4]               "."
  [5]  (PERSONAL)   "C:\ado\personal"
  [6]  (STBPLUS)    "C:\ado\stbplus"
  [7]  (OLDPLACE)   "C:\ado"
  [8]               "c:\myprogs"
```

If later you wished to remove `c:\myprogs` from the ado path, you could type `adopath - c:\myprogs`, but easier is

```
. adopath - 8
  [1]  (UPDATES)    "C:\STATA\ado\updates"
  [2]  (BASE)       "C:\STATA\ado\base"
  [3]  (SITE)       "C:\STATA\ado\site"
  [4]               "."
  [5]  (PERSONAL)   "C:\ado\personal"
  [6]  (STBPLUS)    "C:\ado\stbplus"
  [7]  (OLDPLACE)   "C:\ado"
```

When followed by a number, 'adopath -' removes that element from the path. If you cannot remember what the numbers are, you can first type `adopath` without arguments.

❑ Technical Note

`adopath ++` *path* works like `adopath +` *path* except that it adds to the beginning rather than to the end of the path. Our recommendation is that you not do this. When looking for *name*.ado, Stata loads the first file it encounters as it searches along the path. If you did not like our implementation of the command `ci`, for instance, even if you wrote your own and stored it in `ci.ado`, Stata would continue to use the one in the Stata directory because that is the directory listed earlier in the path. To force Stata to use yours rather than ours, you would have to put at the front of the path the name of the directory where your ado-file resides.

You should not, however, name any of your ado-files the same as we have named ours. If you add to the front of the path, you assume exclusive responsibility for the Stata commands working as documented in this manual.

❏

set adosize

Stata keeps track of the ado-commands you use and discards from memory commands that have not been used recently. Stata discards old commands to keep the amount of memory consumed by such commands below `adosize`. The default value of 65 means the total amount of memory consumed by ado-commands is not to exceed 65K. When an ado-command has been discarded, Stata will have to reload the command the next time you use it.

You can increase `adosize`. Typing `set adosize 80` would allow up to 80K to be allocated to ado-commands. This would improve performance slightly if you happened to use one of the not-recently-used commands, but at the cost of some memory no longer being available for your data. In practice, there is little reason to increase `adosize`.

`adosize` must be between 10 and 500.

Methods and Formulas

`adopath` is implemented as an ado-file.

Also See

Complementary: [R] **net**, [R] **query**, [R] **update**

Background: [U] **20.5 Where does Stata look for ado-files?**

Title

tabdisp — Display tables

Syntax

tabdisp *rowvar* [*colvar* [*supercolvar*]] [if *exp*] [in *range*], <u>c</u>ellvar(*varname(s)*)

   [by(*superrowvar(s)*) <u>f</u>ormat(%*fmt*) <u>cen</u>ter <u>l</u>eft <u>con</u>cise <u>m</u>issing <u>to</u>tals

   <u>cell</u>width(*#*) <u>csep</u>width(*#*) <u>scsep</u>width(*#*) <u>stub</u>width(*#*)]

Rows, columns, supercolumns, and superrows are defined

			supercol 1		supercol 2	
			col 1	col 2	col 1	col 2
row 1	.		.	.	.	.
row 2	.		.	.	.	.

	col 1	col 2
row 1	.	.
row 2	.	.

	supercol 1		supercol 2	
	col 1	col 2	col 1	col 2
superrow 1:				
row 1	.	.	.	.
row 2	.	.	.	.
superrow 2:				
row 1	.	.	.	.
row 2	.	.	.	.

Description

tabdisp displays data in a table. tabdisp calculates no statistics and is intended for use by programmers.

For the corresponding command that calculates statistics and displays them in a table, see [R] **table**.

Although tabdisp is intended for programming applications, it can be used interactively for listing data.

Options

cellvar(*varname(s)*) is not optional; it specifies the numeric or string variables containing the values to be displayed in the table's cells. Up to 5 variable names may be specified.

by(*superrowvar(s)*) specifies numeric or string variables to be treated as superrows. Up to four variables may be specified in *varlist*.

format(%*fmt*) specifies the display format for presenting numbers in the table's cells. format(%9.0g) is the default; format(%9.2f) is a popular alternative. The width of the format you specify does not matter except that %*fmt* must be valid. The width of the cells is chosen by tabdisp to be what it thinks looks best. Option cellwidth() allows you to override tabdisp's choice.

center specifies results are to be centered in the table's cells. The default is to right align results. For centering to work well, you typically need to specify a display format as well. center format(%9.2f) is popular.

left specifies that column labels are to be left aligned. The default is to right align column labels to distinguish them from supercolumn labels, which are left aligned. If you specify left, both column and supercolumn labels are left aligned.

concise specifies that rows with all missing entries are not to be displayed.

missing specifies that missing cells are to be shown in the table as periods (Stata's missing-value indicator). The default is that missing entries are left blank.

totals specifies that observations where *rowvar*, *colvar*, *supercolvar*, and/or *superrowvar(s)* contain missing are to be interpreted as containing the corresponding totals of cellvar(). Missing is interpreted as numeric missing value or "" depending on variable type. If totals is not specified, missing values in *rowvar*, *colvar*, *supercolvar*, and *superrowvar(s)* are given no special interpretation.

cellwidth(#) specifies the width of the cell in units of digit widths; 10 means the space occupied by 10 digits, which is 1234567890. The default cellwidth() is not a fixed number but a number chosen by tabdisp to spread the table out while presenting a reasonable number of columns across the page.

csepwidth(#) specifies the separation between columns in units of digit widths. The default is not a fixed number but a number chosen by tabdisp according to what it thinks looks best.

scsepwidth(#) specifies the separation between supercolumns in units of digit widths. The default is not a fixed number but a number chosen by tabdisp according to what it thinks looks best.

stubwidth(#) specifies the width, in units of digit widths, to be allocated to the left stub of the table. The default is not a fixed number but a number chosen by tabdisp according to what it thinks looks best.

Limits

Up to 4 variables may be specified in the by(), so with the three row, column, and supercolumn variables, seven-way tables may be displayed.

Up to 5 variables may be displayed in each cell of the table.

The sum of the number of rows, columns, supercolumns, and superrows is called the number of margins. A table may contain up to 3,000 margins. Thus, a one-way table may contain 3,000 rows. A two-way table could contain 2,998 rows and 2 columns, 2,997 rows and 3 columns, ..., 1,500 rows and 1,500 columns, ..., 2 rows and 2,998 columns. A three-way table is similarly limited by the sum of the number of rows, columns, and supercolumns. A $r \times c \times d$ table is feasible if $r + c + d \leq 3{,}000$. Note that the limit is set in terms of the sum of the rows, columns, supercolumns, and superrows and not, as you might expect, their product.

Remarks

If you have not read [R] **table**, please do so. Then understand that `tabdisp` is what `table` uses to display the tables.

`tabdisp` calculates nothing. `tabdisp` instead displays the data in memory. In this, think of `tabdisp` as an alternative to `list`. Consider the following little dataset:

```
. list

          a         b         c
 1.       0         1        15
 2.       0         2        26
 3.       0         3        11
 4.       1         1        14
 5.       1         2        12
 6.       1         3         7
```

We can use `tabdisp` to list it:

```
. tabdisp a b, cell(c)
----------+------------------
          |         b
        a |    1     2     3
----------+------------------
        0 |   15    26    11
        1 |   14    12     7
----------+------------------
```

`tabdisp` is merely an alternative way to list the data. It is when the data in memory are statistics by category that `tabdisp` becomes really useful. `table` provides one prepackaging of that idea.

Unlike `list`, `tabdisp` is unaffected by the order of the data. Here is the same data in a different order:

```
. list

          a         b         c
 1.       1         3         7
 2.       0         3        11
 3.       1         2        12
 4.       1         1        14
 5.       0         1        15
 6.       0         2        26
```

and yet the output of `tabdisp` is unaffected.

```
. tabdisp a b, cell(c)
----------+------------------
          |         b
        a |    1     2     3
----------+------------------
        0 |   15    26    11
        1 |   14    12     7
----------+------------------
```

Nor does `tabdisp` care if one of the cells is missing in the data.

```
. drop in 6
(1 observation deleted)
```

```
. tabdisp a b, cell(c)
----------+-----------------
          |         b
        a |    1     2     3
----------+-----------------
        0 |   15    26    11
        1 |   14    12
----------+-----------------
```

On the other hand, `tabdisp` assumes that each value combination of the row, column, superrow, and supercolumn variables occurs only once. If that is not so, `tabdisp` displays the earliest value occurring:

```
. input

              a         b         c
6.  0 1 99
7. end

. list

              a         b         c
1.            1         3         7
2.            0         3        11
3.            1         2        12
4.            1         1        14
5.            0         1        15
6.            0         1        99

. tabdisp a b, cell(c)
----------+-----------------
          |         b
        a |    1     2     3
----------+-----------------
        0 |   15    26    11
        1 |   14    12
----------+-----------------

. drop in 6
```

Thus, our previous claim that `tabdisp` was unaffected by sort order has this one exception.

Finally, `tabdisp` uses variable and value labels when they are defined:

```
. label var a "Sex"
. label define sex 0 male 1 female
. label values a sex
. label var b "Treatment Group"
. label def tg 1 "controls" 2 "low dose" 3 "high dose"
. label values b tg
. tabdisp a b, cell(c)
----------+-------------------------------
          |         Treatment Group
      Sex | controls    low dose  high dose
----------+-------------------------------
     male |       15          26         11
   female |       14          12
----------+-------------------------------
```

There are two things you can do with `tabdisp`.

You can use it to list data, but be certain you have a unique identifier. In the automobile data, the variable `make` is unique:

```
. list make mpg weight displ rep78
      make                    mpg    weight    displ    rep78
  1. AMC Concord              22     2,930      121       3
  2. AMC Pacer                17     3,350      258       3
  3. AMC Spirit               22     2,640      121       .
  (output omitted )
 74. Volvo 260                17     3,170      163       5
. tabdisp make, cell(mpg weight displ rep78)
------------------+---------------------------------------------------------
   Make and Model | Mileage (mpg)  Weight (lbs.)        displ        rep78
------------------+---------------------------------------------------------
      AMC Concord |          22          2,930          121            3
        AMC Pacer |          17          3,350          258            3
        AMC Spirit |         22          2,640          121
  (output omitted )
        Volvo 260 |          17          3,170          163            5
------------------+---------------------------------------------------------
```

Mostly, however, tabdisp is intended for use when you have a dataset of statistics that you want to display:

```
. collapse (mean) mpg, by(foreign rep78)
. list
       rep78   foreign       mpg
  1.       1   Domestic        21
  2.       2   Domestic    19.125
  3.       3   Domestic        19
  4.       4   Domestic   18.44444
  5.       5   Domestic        32
  6.       .   Domestic     23.25
  7.       3   Foreign    23.33333
  8.       4   Foreign    24.88889
  9.       5   Foreign    26.33333
 10.       .   Foreign         14
. tabdisp foreign rep78, cell(mpg)
----------+-------------------------------------------------------------
          |                    Repair Record 1978
 Car type |      1         2         3         4         5         .
----------+-------------------------------------------------------------
 Domestic |     21    19.125        19  18.44444        32     23.25
  Foreign |                   23.33333  24.88889  26.33333        14
----------+-------------------------------------------------------------
. drop if rep78==.
(2 observations deleted)
. label define repair 1 Poor 2 Fair 3 Average 4 Good 5 Excellent
. label values rep78 repair
. tabdisp foreign rep78, cell(mpg) format(%9.2f) center
----------+--------------------------------------------------------
          |                    Repair Record 1978
 Car type |   Poor      Fair    Average     Good   Excellent
----------+--------------------------------------------------------
 Domestic |  21.00     19.12     19.00     18.44     32.00
  Foreign |            23.33     24.89     26.33
----------+--------------------------------------------------------
```

Treatment of string variables

The variables specifying the rows, columns, supercolumns, and superrows may be numeric or string. In addition, the variables specified for inclusion in the table may be numeric or string. In the example below, all variables are strings, including `reaction`:

```
. tabdisp agecat sex party, c(reaction) center

----------+----------------------------------------------------------------------
          |                   Party Affiliation and Sex
Age       | ---------- Democrat ----------      --------- Republican ---------
category  |    Female          Male               Female          Male
----------+----------------------------------------------------------------------
      Old |   Disfavor      Indifferent           Favor      Strongly Favor
    Young |   Disfavor       Disfavor           Indifferent       Favor
----------+----------------------------------------------------------------------
```

Treatment of missing values

The `cellvar()` variable(s) specified for inclusion in the table may contain missing values and whether the variable contains a missing value or the observation is missing altogether makes no difference:

```
. list

          sex    response        pop
    1.     0         0            12
    2.     0         1            20
    3.     0         2             .
    4.     1         0            15
    5.     1         1            11

. tabdisp sex response, cell(pop)

----------+------------------
          |     Response
      Sex |   0     1     2
----------+------------------
        0 |  12    20
        1 |  15    11
----------+------------------
```

In the above output, the $(1,3)$ cell is empty because the observation for `sex` $= 0$ and `response` $= 2$ has a missing value for `pop`. The $(2,3)$ is empty because there is no observation for `sex` $= 1$ and `response` $= 2$.

If you specify the option `missing`, rather than cells being left blank, a period is placed in them:

```
. tabdisp sex response, cell(pop) missing

----------+------------------
          |     Response
      Sex |   0     1     2
----------+------------------
        0 |  12    20     .
        1 |  15    11     .
----------+------------------
```

Missing values of the row, column, superrow, and supercolumn variables are allowed and, by default, given no special meaning. The output below is from a different dataset:

```
. list
              sex    response          pop
     1.        0           0            15
     2.        0           1            11
     3.        0           .            26
     4.        1           0            20
     5.        1           1            24
     6.        1           .            44
     7.        .           .            70
     8.        .           0            35
     9.        .           1            35

. tabdisp sex response, cell(pop)
  ----------+-----------------
            |     response
      sex   |    0      1      .
  ----------+-----------------
        0   |   15     11     26
        1   |   20     24     44
        .   |   35     35     70
  ----------+-----------------
```

If you specify the option `total`, however, the missing values are labeled as reflecting totals:

```
. tabdisp sex response, cell(pop) total
  ----------+--------------------
            |     response
      sex   |    0      1   Total
  ----------+--------------------
        0   |   15     11     26
        1   |   20     24     44
            |
    Total   |   35     35     70
  ----------+--------------------
```

It is important to understand that `tabdisp` did not calculate the totals; it merely labeled the results as being totals. The number 70 appears in the lower right because there happens to be an observation in the dataset where both `sex` and `response` contain a missing value and `pop` = 70.

In this example, the row and column variables were numeric. Had they been strings, the option `total` would have given the special interpretation to `sex` = " " and `response` = " ".

Also See

Related: [R] **table**, [R] **tabulate**

Title

> **table** — Tables of summary statistics

Syntax

> table *rowvar* [*colvar* [*supercolvar*]] [if *exp*] [in *range*] [*weight*] [, contents(*clist*)
>
> by(*superrowvarlist*) cw row col scol replace name(*string*)
>
> format(%*fmt*) center left concise missing
>
> cellwidth(#) csepwidth(#) scsepwidth(#) stubwidth(#)]

where the elements of *clist* may be

freq	frequency	median *varname*	median
mean *varname*	mean of *varname*	p1 *varname*	1st percentile
sd *varname*	standard deviation	p2 *varname*	2nd percentile
sum *varname*	sum	...	3rd–49th percentiles
rawsum *varname*	sums ignoring optionally specified weight	p50 *varname*	50th percentile (median)
count *varname*	count of nonmissing observations	...	51st–97th percentiles
n *varname*	same as count	p98 *varname*	98th percentile
max *varname*	maximum	p99 *varname*	99th percentile
min *varname*	minimum	iqr *varname*	interquartile range

fweights, aweights, iweights, and pweights are allowed; see [U] **14.1.6 weight**. sd (standard deviation) is not allowed with pweights.

Rows, columns, supercolumns, and superrows are defined

				supercol 1		supercol 2	
				col 1	col 2	col 1	col 2
row 1	.		row 1	.	.	.	.
row 2	.		row 2	.	.	.	.

				supercol 1		supercol 2	
				col 1	col 2	col 1	col 2
			superrow 1:				
			row 1	.	.	.	.
	col 1	col 2	row 2	.	.	.	.
			superrow 2:				
row 1	.	.	row 1	.	.	.	.
row 2	.	.	row 2	.	.	.	.

Description

table calculates and displays tables of statistics.

Options

contents(*clist*) specifies the contents of the table's cells; if not specified, contents(freq) is used by default. contents(freq) produces a table of frequencies. contents(mean mpg) produces a table of the means of variable mpg. contents(freq mean mpg sd mpg) produces a table of frequencies together with the mean and standard deviation of variable mpg. Up to five statistics may be specified.

by(*superrowvarlist*) specifies numeric or string variables to be treated as superrows. Up to four variables may be specified in *varlist*.

cw specifies casewise deletion. If not specified, all observations possible are used to calculate each of the specified statistics. cw is relevant only when you request a table containing statistics on multiple variables. For instance, contents(mean mpg mean weight) would produce a table reporting the means of variables mpg and weight. Consider an observation in which mpg is known but weight is missing. Should that observation be used in the calculation of the mean of mpg? By default, it will be. Specify cw and the observation will be excluded in the calculation of the means of both mpg and weight.

row specifies a row is to be added to the table reflecting the total across the rows.

col specifies a column is to be added to the table reflecting the total across columns.

scol specifies a supercolumn is to be added to the table reflecting the total across supercolumns.

replace specifies the data in memory is to be replaced with data containing one observation per cell (row, column, supercolumn, and superrow) and with variables containing the statistics designated in contents().

This option is rarely specified. If you do not specify this option, the data in memory remains unchanged.

If you do specify this option, the first statistic will be named table1, the second table2, and so on. For instance, if contents(mean mpg sd mpg) was specified, the means of mpg would be in variable table1 and the standard deviations in table2.

name(*string*) is relevant only if you specify replace. name() allows changing the default stub name replace uses to name the new variables associated with the statistics. Specify name(stat) and the first statistic will be placed in variable stat1, the second in stat2, and so on.

format(%*fmt*) specifies the display format for presenting numbers in the table's cells. format(%9.0g) is the default; format(%9.2f) and format(%9.2fc) are popular alternatives. The width of the format you specify does not matter except that %*fmt* must be valid. The width of the cells is chosen by table to be what it thinks looks best. Option cellwidth() allows you to override table's choice.

center specifies results are to be centered in the table's cells. The default is to right align results. For centering to work well, you typically need to specify a display format as well. center format(%9.2f) is popular.

left specifies that column labels are to be left aligned. The default is to right align column labels to distinguish them from supercolumn labels, which are left aligned. If you specify left, both column and supercolumn labels are left aligned.

concise specifies that rows with all missing entries are not to be displayed.

missing specifies that missing statistics are to be shown in the table as periods (Stata's missing-value indicator). The default is that missing entries are left blank.

cellwidth(#) specifies the width of the cell in units of digit widths; 10 means the space occupied by 10 digits, which is 1234567890. The default cellwidth() is not a fixed number but a number chosen by table to spread the table out while presenting a reasonable number of columns across the page.

csepwidth(#) specifies the separation between columns in units of digit widths. The default is not a fixed number but a number chosen by table according to what it thinks looks best.

scsepwidth(#) specifies the separation between supercolumns in units of digit widths. The default is not a fixed number but a number chosen by table according to what it thinks looks best.

stubwidth(#) specifies the width, in units of digit widths, to be allocated to the left stub of the table. The default is not a fixed number but a number chosen by table according to what it thinks looks best.

Limits

Up to 4 variables may be specified in the by(), so with the three row, column, and supercolumn variables, seven-way tables may be displayed.

Up to 5 statistics may be displayed in each cell of the table.

The sum of the number of rows, columns, supercolumns, and superrows is called the number of margins. A table may contain up to 3,000 margins. Thus, a one-way table may contain 3,000 rows. A two-way table could contain 2,998 rows and 2 columns, 2,997 rows and 3 columns, ..., 1,500 rows and 1,500 columns, ..., 2 rows and 2,998 columns. A three-way table is similarly limited by the sum of the number of rows, columns, and supercolumns. A $r \times c \times d$ table is feasible if $r + c + d \leq 3,000$. Note that the limit is set in terms of the sum of the rows, columns, supercolumns, and superrows and not, as you might expect, their product.

Remarks

One-way tables

Using the automobile data, here is a simple one-way table:

```
. table rep78, contents(mean mpg)
----------+-----------
Repair    |
Record    |
1978      |  mean(mpg)
----------+-----------
        1 |        21
        2 |    19.125
        3 |  19.43333
        4 |  21.66667
        5 |  27.36364
----------+-----------
```

We are not limited to including only a single statistic:

```
. table rep78, c(n mpg  mean mpg  sd mpg  median mpg)
----------+-----------------------------------------------
Repair    |
Record    |
1978      |    N(mpg)   mean(mpg)     sd(mpg)    med(mpg)
----------+-----------------------------------------------
       1 |         2          21     4.24264         21
       2 |         8      19.125    3.758324         18
       3 |        30    19.43333    4.141325         19
       4 |        18    21.66667     4.93487       22.5
       5 |        11    27.36364    8.732385         30
----------+-----------------------------------------------
```

Note we abbreviated `contents()` as `c()`. The `format()` option will allow us to better format the numbers in the table:

```
. table rep78, c(n mpg  mean mpg  sd mpg  median mpg) format(%9.2f)
----------+-----------------------------------------------
Repair    |
Record    |
1978      |    N(mpg)   mean(mpg)     sd(mpg)    med(mpg)
----------+-----------------------------------------------
       1 |         2       21.00        4.24      21.00
       2 |         8       19.12        3.76      18.00
       3 |        30       19.43        4.14      19.00
       4 |        18       21.67        4.93      22.50
       5 |        11       27.36        8.73      30.00
----------+-----------------------------------------------
```

And the `center` option will center the results under the headings:

```
. table rep78, c(n mpg  mean mpg  sd mpg  median mpg) format(%9.2f) center
----------+-----------------------------------------------
Repair    |
Record    |
1978      |    N(mpg)    mean(mpg)    sd(mpg)    med(mpg)
----------+-----------------------------------------------
       1 |         2       21.00        4.24      21.00
       2 |         8       19.12        3.76      18.00
       3 |        30       19.43        4.14      19.00
       4 |        18       21.67        4.93      22.50
       5 |        11       27.36        8.73      30.00
----------+-----------------------------------------------
```

Two-way tables

When we typed 'table rep78, ...', we obtained a one-way table. If we type 'table rep78 foreign, ...', we obtain a two-way table:

```
. table rep78 foreign, c(mean mpg)
----------+-------------------
Repair    |
Record    |       Car type
1978      | Domestic    Foreign
----------+-------------------
       1 |       21
       2 |   19.125
       3 |       19   23.33333
       4 | 18.44444   24.88889
       5 |       32   26.33333
----------+-------------------
```

Note the missing cells. Certain combinations of repair record and car type do not exist in our data.

As with one-way tables, we can specify a display format for the cells and center the numbers within the cells if we wish.

```
. table rep78 foreign, c(mean mpg) format(%9.2f) center

----------+--------------------
Repair    |
Record    |       Car type
1978      | Domestic   Foreign
----------+--------------------
       1  |   21.00
       2  |   19.12
       3  |   19.00     23.33
       4  |   18.44     24.89
       5  |   32.00     26.33
----------+--------------------
```

We can obtain row totals by specifying the `rowtotal` option and column totals by specifying the `coltotal` option. We specify both below and abbreviate the options `row` and `col`:

```
. table rep78 foreign, c(mean mpg) format(%9.2f) center row col

----------+------------------------------
Repair    |
Record    |            Car type
1978      | Domestic   Foreign    Total
----------+------------------------------
       1  |   21.00                21.00
       2  |   19.12                19.12
       3  |   19.00     23.33      19.43
       4  |   18.44     24.89      21.67
       5  |   32.00     26.33      27.36
          |
   Total  |   19.54     25.29      21.29
----------+------------------------------
```

`table` can display multiple statistics within cells but, once we move beyond one-way tables, the table becomes busy:

```
. table foreign rep78, c(mean mpg  n mpg) format(%9.2f) center

----------+----------------------------------
          |        Repair Record 1978
Car type  |   1      2      3      4      5
----------+----------------------------------
Domestic  | 21.00  19.12  19.00  18.44  32.00
          |    2      8     27      9      2
          |
 Foreign  |               23.33  24.89  26.33
          |                  3      9      9
----------+----------------------------------
```

This two-way table with two statistics per cell works well in this case. That was, in part, helped along by us interchanging the rows and columns. We turned the table around by typing `table foreign rep78` rather than `table rep78 foreign`.

Another way we can display two-way tables is to specify a row and superrow rather than a row and column. We do that below and display three statistics per cell:

```
. table foreign, by(rep78) c(mean mpg  sd mpg  n mpg) format(%9.2f) center
----------+-------------------------------------
Repair    |
Record    |
1978 and  |
Car type  |  mean(mpg)    sd(mpg)     N(mpg)
----------+-------------------------------------
1         |
Domestic  |   21.00        4.24          2
 Foreign  |
----------+-------------------------------------
2         |
Domestic  |   19.12        3.76          8
 Foreign  |
----------+-------------------------------------
3         |
Domestic  |   19.00        4.09         27
 Foreign  |   23.33        2.52          3
----------+-------------------------------------
4         |
Domestic  |   18.44        4.59          9
 Foreign  |   24.89        2.71          9
----------+-------------------------------------
5         |
Domestic  |   32.00        2.83          2
 Foreign  |   26.33        9.37          9
----------+-------------------------------------
```

Three-way tables

We have data on the prevalence of byssinosis, a form of pneumoconiosis to which workers exposed to cotton dust are subject. The data is on 5,419 workers in a large cotton mill. We know whether each worker smokes, his or her race, and the dustiness of the work area. The categorical variables are

smokes	Smoker or nonsmoker in the last five years.
race	White or other.
wrkplace	1 (most dusty), 2 (less dusty), 3 (least dusty).

Moreover, this data includes a frequency-weight variable pop. Here is a three-way table showing the fraction of workers with byssinosis:

```
. table wrkplace smokes race [fw=pop], c(mean prob)
----------+-------------------------------------------
Dustiness |              Race and Smokes
of        | ------ other -----    ------ white -----
workplace |     no       yes          no       yes
----------+-------------------------------------------
    least | .0107527  .0101523    .0081549  .0162774
    less  |      .02  .0081633    .0136612  .0143149
    most  | .0820896  .1679105    .0833333  .2295082
----------+-------------------------------------------
```

This table would look better if we showed the fraction to four digits:

```
. table wrkplace smokes race [fw=pop], c(mean prob) format(%9.4f)
----------+---------------------------------
Dustiness |        Race and Smokes
of        | ---- other ---    ---- white ---
workplace |   no     yes        no     yes
----------+---------------------------------
   least  | 0.0108  0.0102    0.0082  0.0163
   less   | 0.0200  0.0082    0.0137  0.0143
   most   | 0.0821  0.1679    0.0833  0.2295
----------+---------------------------------
```

In this table, the rows are the dustiness of the workplace, the columns are whether the worker smokes, and the supercolumns are race.

Here is what happens if we request that the table include the supercolumn totals, which we request by specifying the option sctotal, which we can abbreviate sc:

```
. table wrkplace smokes race [fw=pop], c(mean prob) format(%9.4f) sc
----------+--------------------------------------------------------
Dustiness |              Race and Smokes
of        | ---- other ---    ---- white ---    ---- Total ---
workplace |   no     yes        no     yes        no     yes
----------+--------------------------------------------------------
   least  | 0.0108  0.0102    0.0082  0.0163    0.0090  0.0145
   less   | 0.0200  0.0082    0.0137  0.0143    0.0159  0.0123
   most   | 0.0821  0.1679    0.0833  0.2295    0.0826  0.1929
----------+--------------------------------------------------------
```

The supercolumn total is the total over **race** and divided into its columns based on **smokes**. Here is the table with the column rather than the supercolumn totals:

```
. table wrkplace smokes race [fw=pop], c(mean prob) format(%9.4f) col
----------+--------------------------------------------------------
Dustiness |                Race and Smokes
of        | -------- other -------    -------- white -------
workplace |   no     yes    Total      no     yes    Total
----------+--------------------------------------------------------
   least  | 0.0108  0.0102  0.0104    0.0082  0.0163  0.0129
   less   | 0.0200  0.0082  0.0135    0.0137  0.0143  0.0140
   most   | 0.0821  0.1679  0.1393    0.0833  0.2295  0.1835
----------+--------------------------------------------------------
```

And here is the table with both the column and supercolumn totals:

```
. table wrkplace smokes race [fw=pop], c(mean prob) format(%9.4f) sc col
-------+------------------------------------------------------------------------
Dustin |
ess of |                        Race and Smokes
workpl | -------- other -------  -------- white -------  -------- Total -------
ace    |   no     yes    Total     no     yes    Total     no     yes    Total
-------+------------------------------------------------------------------------
 least | 0.0108  0.0102  0.0104  0.0082  0.0163  0.0129  0.0090  0.0145  0.0122
 less  | 0.0200  0.0082  0.0135  0.0137  0.0143  0.0140  0.0159  0.0123  0.0138
 most  | 0.0821  0.1679  0.1393  0.0833  0.2295  0.1835  0.0826  0.1929  0.1570
-------+------------------------------------------------------------------------
```

Note that **table** is struggling to keep this table from becoming too wide—notice how it divided the words in the title in the top-left stub. In this case, if the table had more columns or we demanded more digits, **table** would be forced to segment the table and present it in pieces, which it would do:

```
. table wrkplace smokes race [fw=pop], c(mean prob) format(%9.6f) sc col
----------+-----------------------------------------------------------------
Dustiness |                        Race and Smokes
of        | ----------- other ----------    ----------- white ----------
workplace |      no        yes     Total         no        yes     Total
----------+-----------------------------------------------------------------
    least | 0.010753  0.010152  0.010417    0.008155  0.016277  0.012949
    less  | 0.020000  0.008163  0.013483    0.013661  0.014315  0.014035
    most  | 0.082090  0.167910  0.139303    0.083333  0.229508  0.183521
----------+-----------------------------------------------------------------


----------+----------------------------
Dustiness |     Race and Smokes
of        | ----------- Total ----------
workplace |      no        yes     Total
----------+----------------------------
    least | 0.008990  0.014471  0.012174
    less  | 0.015901  0.012262  0.013846
    most  | 0.082569  0.192905  0.156951
----------+----------------------------
```

In this case, three digits is probably enough, so here is the table including all the row, column, and supercolumn totals:

```
. table wrkplace smokes race [fw=pop], c(mean prob) format(%9.3f) sc col row
----------+----------------------------------------------------------------------
Dustiness |                          Race and Smokes
of        | ------ other ------    ------ white ------    ------ Total ------
workplace |   no    yes   Total      no    yes   Total      no    yes   Total
----------+----------------------------------------------------------------------
    least | 0.011  0.010  0.010    0.008  0.016  0.013    0.009  0.014  0.012
    less  | 0.020  0.008  0.013    0.014  0.014  0.014    0.016  0.012  0.014
    most  | 0.082  0.168  0.139    0.083  0.230  0.184    0.083  0.193  0.157
          |
    Total | 0.025  0.048  0.038    0.014  0.035  0.026    0.018  0.039  0.030
----------+----------------------------------------------------------------------
```

If we wish, we can show multiple statistics:

```
. table wrkplace smokes race [fw=pop], c(mean prob  n prob) format(%9.3f)
    sc col row
----------+----------------------------------------------------------------------
Dustiness |                          Race and Smokes
of        | ------ other ------    ------ white ------    ------ Total ------
workplace |   no    yes   Total      no    yes   Total      no    yes   Total
----------+----------------------------------------------------------------------
    least | 0.011  0.010  0.010    0.008  0.016  0.013    0.009  0.014  0.012
          |   465    591   1056      981   1413   2394     1446   2004   3450
          |
    less  | 0.020  0.008  0.013    0.014  0.014  0.014    0.016  0.012  0.014
          |   200    245    445      366    489    855      566    734   1300
          |
    most  | 0.082  0.168  0.139    0.083  0.230  0.184    0.083  0.193  0.157
          |   134    268    402       84    183    267      218    451    669
          |
    Total | 0.025  0.048  0.038    0.014  0.035  0.026    0.018  0.039  0.030
          |   799   1104   1903     1431   2085   3516     2230   3189   5419
----------+----------------------------------------------------------------------
```

Four-way and higher-dimensional tables

Let's pretend our byssinosis data also recorded each worker's sex (it does not and we have made up this extra information). We obtain a four-way table just as we would a three-way table but specify the fourth variable as a superrow by including it in the `by()` option:

```
. table wrkplace smokes race [fw=pop], by(sex) c(mean prob) format(%9.3f)
  sc col row

----------+-----------------------------------------------------------------
Sex and   |
Dustiness |                       Race and Smokes
of        | ------ other ------    ------ white ------     ------ Total ------
workplace |    no    yes  Total       no    yes  Total        no    yes  Total
----------+-----------------------------------------------------------------
Female    |
    least | 0.006  0.009  0.008    0.009  0.021  0.016     0.009  0.018  0.014
     less | 0.020  0.008  0.010    0.015  0.015  0.015     0.016  0.012  0.014
     most | 0.057  0.154  0.141                            0.057  0.154  0.141
          |
    Total | 0.017  0.051  0.043    0.011  0.020  0.016     0.012  0.032  0.024
----------+-----------------------------------------------------------------
Male      |
    least | 0.013  0.011  0.012    0.006  0.007  0.006     0.009  0.008  0.009
     less | 0.020  0.000  0.019    0.000  0.013  0.011     0.016  0.013  0.014
     most | 0.091  0.244  0.136    0.083  0.230  0.184     0.087  0.232  0.167
          |
    Total | 0.029  0.041  0.033    0.020  0.056  0.043     0.025  0.052  0.039
----------+-----------------------------------------------------------------
```

If our data also included work group and we wanted a five-way table, we could include both the sex and work-group variables in the `by()` option. You may include up to four variables in `by()` and so produce up to 7-way tables.

Methods and Formulas

`table` is implemented as an ado-file. The contents of cells are calculated by `collapse` and displayed by `tabdisp`; see [R] **collapse** and [R] **tabdisp**.

Also See

Related: [R] **adjust**, [R] **collapse**, [R] **tabdisp**, [R] **tabulate**

Background: [U] **15.6 Dataset, variable, and value labels**,
[U] **28 Commands for dealing with categorical variables**

Title

tabsum — One- and two-way tables of summary statistics

Syntax

$\big[$ by *varlist*: $\big]$ <u>ta</u>bulate *varname*$_1$ $\big[$ *varname*$_2$ $\big]$ $\big[$ *weight* $\big]$ $\big[$ if *exp* $\big]$ $\big[$ in *range* $\big]$

, <u>s</u>ummarize(*varname*$_3$) $\big[$ $\big[\underline{no}\big]$ <u>mean</u>s $\big[\underline{no}\big]$ <u>st</u>andard $\big[\underline{no}\big]$ <u>freq</u> $\big[\underline{no}\big]$ obs

<u>wr</u>ap <u>nol</u>abel <u>miss</u>ing $\big]$

aweights and fweights are allowed; see [U] **14.1.6 weight**.

Description

tabulate, summarize() produces one- and two-way tables (breakdowns) of means and standard deviations. See [R] **tabulate** for frequency tables. See [R] **table** for a more flexible command that produces one-, two-, and n-way tables of frequencies and a wide variety of summary statistics. table is better but tabulate, summarize() is faster.

Options

summarize(*varname*$_3$) identifies the name of the variable for which summary statistics are to be reported. If you do not specify this option, then a table of frequencies is produced; see [R] **tabulate**. The description here concerns tabulate when this option is specified.

[no]means includes only or suppresses only the means from the table.

The summarize() table normally includes the mean, standard deviation, frequency, and, if the data is weighted, the number of observations. Individual elements of the table may be included or suppressed by the [no]means, [no]standard, [no]freq, and [no]obs options. For example, typing

    tabulate category, summarize(myvar) means standard

produces a summary table by category containing only the means and standard deviations of myvar. You could also achieve the same result by typing

    tabulate category, summarize(myvar) nofreq

[no]standard includes only or suppresses only the standard deviations from the table; see [no]means option above.

[no]freq includes only or suppresses only the frequencies from the table; see [no]means option above.

[no]obs includes only or suppresses only the reported number of observations from the table. If the data is not weighted, the number of observations is identical to the frequency and by default only the frequency is reported. If the data is weighted, the frequency refers to the sum of the weights. See [no]means option above.

wrap requests no action be taken on wide tables to make them readable. Unless wrap is specified, wide tables are broken into pieces to enhance readability.

nolabel causes the numeric codes to be displayed rather than any label values.

missing requests that missing values of *varname₁* and *varname₂* be treated as categories rather than as observations to be omitted from the analysis.

Remarks

tabulate with the summarize() option produces one- and two-way tables of summary statistics. When combined with the by prefix, it can produce *n*-way tables as well.

One-way tables

▷ Example

You have data on 74 automobiles. Included in your data are the variables foreign, which marks domestic and foreign cars, and mpg, the car's mileage rating. If you type tabulate foreign, you obtain a breakdown of the number of observations you have by the values of the foreign variable.

```
. tabulate foreign
   Car type |      Freq.     Percent        Cum.
------------+-----------------------------------
   Domestic |         52       70.27       70.27
    Foreign |         22       29.73      100.00
------------+-----------------------------------
      Total |         74      100.00
```

You discover that you have 52 domestic cars and 22 foreign cars in your data. If you add the summarize(*varname*) option, however, tabulate produces a table of summary statistics for *varname*:

```
. tabulate foreign, summarize(mpg)
            |      Summary of Mileage (mpg)
   Car type |       Mean   Std. Dev.       Freq.
------------+-----------------------------------
   Domestic |      19.83        4.74          52
    Foreign |      24.77        6.61          22
------------+-----------------------------------
      Total |      21.30        5.79          74
```

In addition to discovering that you have 52 domestic and 22 foreign cars in your data, you discover that the average gas mileage for domestic cars is about 20 mpg and the average foreign is almost 25 mpg. Overall, the average is 21 mpg in your data.

◁

❑ Technical Note

You might now wonder if the difference in gas mileage between foreign and domestic cars is statistically significant. You can use the oneway command to find out; see [R] **oneway**. You obtain an analysis-of-variance table of mpg on foreign by typing

```
. oneway mpg foreign
                        Analysis of Variance
     Source              SS          df      MS            F     Prob > F
------------------------------------------------------------------------
Between groups      378.153515        1   378.153515    13.18     0.0005
Within groups       2065.30594       72   28.6848048
------------------------------------------------------------------------
     Total          2443.45946       73   33.4720474

Bartlett's test for equal variances:  chi2(1) =   3.4818  Prob>chi2 = 0.062
```

The F statistic is 13.18 and the difference between foreign and domestic cars' mileage ratings is significant at the 0.05% level.

There are a number of ways that we could have statistically compared mileage ratings—see, for instance, [R] **anova**, [R] **oneway**, [R] **regress**, and [R] **ttest**—but oneway seemed the most convenient.

❏

Two-way tables

▷ Example

tabulate, summarize can be used to obtain two-way as well as one-way breakdowns. For instance, we obtained summary statistics on mpg decomposed by foreign by typing tabulate foreign, summarize(mpg). We can specify up to two variables before the comma:

```
. tabulate wgtcat foreign, summarize(mpg)
        Means, Standard Deviations and Frequencies of Mileage (mpg)
            | Car type
    wgtcat |   Domestic     Foreign |      Total
-----------+----------------------+----------
         1 |      28.29       27.06 |      27.43
           |       3.09        5.98 |       5.23
           |          7          16 |         23
-----------+----------------------+----------
         2 |      21.75       19.60 |      21.24
           |       2.41        3.44 |       2.76
           |         16           5 |         21
-----------+----------------------+----------
         3 |      17.26       14.00 |      17.12
           |       1.86        0.00 |       1.94
           |         23           1 |         24
-----------+----------------------+----------
         4 |      14.67           . |      14.67
           |       3.33           . |       3.33
           |          6           0 |          6
-----------+----------------------+----------
     Total |      19.83       24.77 |      21.30
           |       4.74        6.61 |       5.79
           |         52          22 |         74
```

In addition to giving the means, standard deviations, and frequencies for each weight-mileage cell, also reported are the summary statistics by weight, by mileage, and overall. For instance, the last row of the table reveals that the average mileage of domestic cars is 19.83 and of foreign cars is 24.77—domestic cars yield poorer mileage than foreign cars. But we now see that domestic cars yield better gas mileage within weight class—the reason domestic cars yield poorer gas mileage is because they are, on average, heavier.

◁

▷ Example

When you do not specify the statistics to be included in a table, **tabulate** reports the mean, standard deviation, and frequency. You can specify the statistics you want to see using the **means**, **standard**, and **freq** options:

```
. tabulate wgtcat foreign, summarize(mpg) means
                    Means of Mileage (mpg)
           | Car type
   wgtcat  | Domestic    Foreign  |    Total
-----------+----------------------+----------
        1  |    28.29      27.06  |    27.43
        2  |    21.75      19.60  |    21.24
        3  |    17.26      14.00  |    17.12
        4  |    14.67          .  |    14.67
-----------+----------------------+----------
    Total  |    19.83      24.77  |    21.30
```

When we specify one or more of the **means**, **standard**, and **freq** options, solely those statistics are displayed. Thus, we could obtain a table containing just the means and standard deviations by typing **means standard** after the **summarize(mpg)** option.

We can also suppress selected statistics by placing a **no** in front of the option name. Another way of obtaining solely the means and standard deviations is to type the **nofreq** option:

```
. tabulate wgtcat foreign, summarize(mpg) nofreq
         Means and Standard Deviations of Mileage (mpg)
           | Car type
   wgtcat  | Domestic    Foreign  |    Total
-----------+----------------------+----------
        1  |    28.29      27.06  |    27.43
           |     3.09       5.98  |     5.23
-----------+----------------------+----------
        2  |    21.75      19.60  |    21.24
           |     2.41       3.44  |     2.76
-----------+----------------------+----------
        3  |    17.26      14.00  |    17.12
           |     1.86       0.00  |     1.94
-----------+----------------------+----------
        4  |    14.67          .  |    14.67
           |     3.33          .  |     3.33
-----------+----------------------+----------
    Total  |    19.83      24.77  |    21.30
           |     4.74       6.61  |     5.79
```

◁

Also See

Related: [R] **adjust**, [R] **oneway**, [R] **table**, [R] **tabulate**

Background: [U] **15.6 Dataset, variable, and value labels**,
                  [U] **28 Commands for dealing with categorical variables**

Title

> **tabulate** — One- and two-way tables of frequencies

Syntax

One-way tables

$\bigl[$by *varlist*:$\bigr]$ <u>ta</u>bulate *varname* $\bigl[$*weight*$\bigr]$ $\bigl[$if *exp*$\bigr]$ $\bigl[$in *range*$\bigr]$

$\bigl[$, <u>g</u>enerate(*varname*) matcell(*matname*) matcol(*matname*) matrow(*matname*)

<u>m</u>issing <u>nof</u>req <u>nol</u>abel <u>p</u>lot subpop(*varname*) $\bigr]$

tab1 *varlist* $\bigl[$*weight*$\bigr]$ $\bigl[$if *exp*$\bigr]$ $\bigl[$in *range*$\bigr]$ $\bigl[$, <u>m</u>issing <u>nol</u>abel <u>p</u>lot $\bigr]$

Two-way tables

$\bigl[$by *varlist*:$\bigr]$ <u>ta</u>bulate *varname$_1$* *varname$_2$* $\bigl[$*weight*$\bigr]$ $\bigl[$if *exp*$\bigr]$ $\bigl[$in *range*$\bigr]$

$\bigl[$, <u>a</u>ll <u>c</u>ell <u>ch</u>i2 <u>c</u>olumn <u>e</u>xact gamma <u>lr</u>chi2 matcell(*matname*)

matcol(*matname*) matrow(*matname*) <u>m</u>issing <u>nof</u>req <u>w</u>rap

<u>nol</u>abel <u>r</u>ow <u>t</u>aub V $\bigr]$

tab2 *varlist* $\bigl[$*weight*$\bigr]$ $\bigl[$if *exp*$\bigr]$ $\bigl[$in *range*$\bigr]$ $\bigl[$, *tabulate_options* $\bigr]$

tabi *#$_{11}$* *#$_{12}$* $\bigl[\ldots\bigr]$ \ *#$_{21}$* *#$_{22}$* $\bigl[\ldots\bigr]$ $\bigl[$\ $\ldots\bigr]$ $\bigl[$, replace *tabulate_options* $\bigr]$

fweights, aweights, and iweights are allowed by tabulate. fweights are allowed by tab1 and tab2. See [U] **14.1.6 weight**.

Description

tabulate produces one- and two-way tables of frequency counts along with various measures of association, including the common Pearson χ^2, the likelihood-ratio χ^2, Cramér's V, Fisher's exact test, Goodman and Kruskal's gamma, and Kendall's τ_b.

tab1 produces a one-way tabulation for each variable specified in *varlist*.

tab2 produces all possible two-way tabulations of the variables specified in *varlist*.

tabi displays the $r \times c$ table using the values specified; rows are separated by '\'. If no options are specified, it is as if **exact** were specified for 2×2 tables and chi2 were specified otherwise. See [U] **22 Immediate commands** for a general description of immediate commands. Specifics for tabi can be found toward the end of [R] **tabulate**.

Also see [R] **table** if you want one-, two-, or n-way tables of frequencies and a wide variety of summary statistics. See [R] **tabsum** for a description of tabulate with the summarize() option; it produces tables (breakdowns) of means and standard deviations. table is better than tabulate, summarize(), but tabulate, summarize() is faster. See [R] **epitab** for 2×2 tables with statistics of interest to epidemiologists.

Options

all is equivalent to specifying chi2 lrchi2 V gamma taub. Note the omission of exact. When all is specified, no may be placed in front of the other options. all noV requests all measures of association but Cramér's V (and Fisher's exact). all exact requests all association measures including Fisher's exact test. all may not be specified if aweights or iweights are specified.

cell displays the relative frequency of each cell in a two-way table.

chi2 calculates and displays Pearson's χ^2 for the hypothesis that the rows and columns in a two-way table are independent. chi2 may not be specified if aweights or iweights are specified.

column displays in each cell of a two-way table the relative frequency of that cell within its column.

exact displays the significance calculated by Fisher's exact test and may be applied to $r \times c$ as well as 2×2 tables. In the case of 2×2 tables, both one- and two-sided probabilities are displayed. exact may not be specified if aweights or iweights are specified.

gamma displays Goodman and Kruskal's gamma along with its asymptotic standard error. gamma is appropriate only when both variables are ordinal. gamma may not be specified if aweights or iweights are specified.

generate(*varname*) creates a set of indicator variables reflecting the observed values of the tabulated variable.

lrchi2 displays the likelihood-ratio χ^2 statistic. The request is ignored if any cell of the table contains no observations. lrchi2 may not be specified if aweights or iweights are specified.

matcell(*matname*) saves the reported frequencies in *matname*. This option is for use by programmers.

matcol(*matname*) saves the numeric values of the $1 \times c$ column stub in *matname*. This option is for use by programmers. matcol() may not be specified if the column variable is a string.

matrow(*matname*) saves the numeric values of the $r \times 1$ row stub in *matname*. This option is for use by programmers. matrow() may not be specified if the row variable is a string.

missing requests that missing values be treated like other values in calculations of counts, percentages, and other statistics.

nofreq suppresses the printing of the frequencies.

nolabel causes the numeric codes to be displayed rather than the value labels.

plot produces a bar chart of the relative frequencies in a one-way table. (Also see [G] **histogram**.)

replace indicates that the immediate data specified as arguments to the tabi command are to be left as the current data in place of whatever data was there.

row displays in each cell of a two-way table the relative frequency of that cell within its row.

subpop(*varname*) excludes observations for which *varname* $= 0$ in tabulating frequencies. The mathematical results of tabulate ..., subpop(myvar) are the same as tabulate ... if myvar~=0, but the table may be presented differently. The identities of the rows and columns will be determined from all the data, including the myvar $= 0$ group and so there may be entries in the table with frequency 0.

Consider tabulating `answer`, a variable that takes on values 1, 2, and 3, but consider tabulating it just for the `male==1` subpopulation. Assume `answer` is never 2 in this group. `tabulate answer if male==1` will produce a table with two rows: one for answer 1 and one for answer 3. There will be no row for answer 2 because answer 2 was never observed. `tabulate answer, subpop(male)` produces a table with three rows. The row for answer 2 will be shown as having 0 frequency.

`taub` displays Kendall's τ_b along with its asymptotic standard error. `taub` is appropriate only when both variables are ordinal. `taub` may not be specified if `aweights` or `iweights` are specified.

`V` (note capitalization) displays Cramér's V. `V` may not be specified if `aweights` or `iweights` are specified.

`wrap` requests that Stata take no action on wide, two-way tables to make them readable. Unless `wrap` is specified, wide tables are broken into pieces to enhance readability.

Limits

One-way tables may have a maximum of 3,000 rows (Intercooled Stata) or 500 rows (Small Stata).

Two-way tables may have a maximum of 300 rows and 20 columns (Intercooled Stata) or 150 rows and 20 columns (Small Stata). If larger tables are needed, see [R] **table**.

Remarks

Remarks are presented under the headings

> *One-way tables*
> *Two-way tables*
> *Measures of association*
> *N-way tables*
> *Weighted data*
> *Tables with immediate data*
> *tab1 and tab2*

For each value of a specified variable (or a set of values for a pair of variables), `tabulate` reports the number of observations with that value. The number of times a value occurs is called its *frequency*.

One-way tables

▷ Example

You have data summarizing the speed limit, the number of access points (on-ramps and off-ramps) per mile, and the accident rate per million vehicle miles along various Minnesota highways in 1973. The variable containing the speed limit is called `spdlimit`. If you `summarize` the variable, you obtain its mean and standard deviation:

```
. summarize spdlimit
    Variable |       Obs        Mean    Std. Dev.       Min        Max
-------------+--------------------------------------------------------
    spdlimit |        39          55    5.848977         40         70
```

The average speed limit is 55 miles per hour. We can learn more about this variable by tabulating it:

```
. tabulate spdlimit
Speed Limit |      Freq.     Percent        Cum.
------------+-----------------------------------
         40 |          1        2.56        2.56
         45 |          3        7.69       10.26
         50 |          7       17.95       28.21
         55 |         15       38.46       66.67
         60 |         11       28.21       94.87
         65 |          1        2.56       97.44
         70 |          1        2.56      100.00
------------+-----------------------------------
      Total |         39      100.00
```

We see that one highway has a speed limit of 40 miles per hour, three have speed limits of 45, 7 of 50, and so on. The column labeled **Percent** shows the percent of highways in the data that have the indicated speed limit. For instance, 38.46% of highways in our data have a speed limit of 55 miles per hour. The final column shows the cumulative percent. We see that 66.67% of highways in our data have a speed limit of 55 miles per hour or less.

◁

▷ Example

The **plot** option places a sideways histogram alongside the table:

```
. tabulate spdlimit, plot
Speed Limit |      Freq.
------------+-------------+----------------------------------------------------
         40 |          1 |*
         45 |          3 |***
         50 |          7 |*******
         55 |         15 |***************
         60 |         11 |***********
         65 |          1 |*
         70 |          1 |*
------------+-------------+----------------------------------------------------
      Total |         39
```

Of course, **graph** can produce better-looking histograms; see [G] **histogram**.

◁

▷ Example

tabulate labels tables using *variable* and *value labels* if they exist. To demonstrate how this works, let's add a new variable to our data that categorizes **spdlimit** into three categories. We will call this new variable **spdcat**:

```
. generate spdcat=recode(spdlimit,50,60,70)
```

The **recode()** function divides **spdlimit** into 50 or below, 51–60, and above 60 miles per hour; see [U] **16.3.6 Special functions**. We specified the break points in the arguments (**spdlimit,50,60,70**). The first argument is the variable to be recoded. The second argument is the first break point, the third argument the second break point, and so on. We can specify as many break points as we wish.

recode() used our arguments not only as the break points, but to label the results as well. If **spdlimit** is less than or equal to 50, **spdcat** is set to 50; if **spdlimit** is between 51 and 60, **spdcat** is 60; otherwise, **spdcat** is arbitrarily set to 70. (See [U] **28 Commands for dealing with categorical variables**.)

Since we just created the variable `spdcat`, it is not yet labeled. When we make a table using this variable, `tabulate` uses the variable's name to label it:

```
. tabulate spdcat
     spdcat |      Freq.     Percent        Cum.
------------+-----------------------------------
         50 |         11       28.21       28.21
         60 |         26       66.67       94.87
         70 |          2        5.13      100.00
------------+-----------------------------------
      Total |         39      100.00
```

Even through the table is not well labeled, `recode()`'s coding scheme provides us with clues as to the table's meaning. The first line of the table corresponds to 50 miles per hour and below, the next to 51 through 60 miles per hour, and the last to above 60 miles per hour.

We can improve this table by labeling the values and variables:

```
. label define scat 50 "40 to 50" 60 "55 to 60" 70 "Above 60"
. label values spdcat scat
. label variable spdcat "Speed Limit Category"
```

We define a *value label* called `scat` that attaches labels to the numbers 50, 60, and 70 using the `label define` command; see [U] **15.6.3 Value labels**. We label the value 50 as '40 to 50', since we looked back at our original tabulation in the first example and saw that the speed limit was never less than 40. Similarly, we could have labeled the last category '65 to 70' since the speed limit is never greater than 70 miles per hour.

Next, we told Stata that it was to label the values of the new variable `spdcat` using the value label `scat`. Finally, we labeled our variable `Speed Limit Category`. We are now ready to `tabulate` the result:

```
. tabulate spdcat
Speed Limit |
   Category |      Freq.     Percent        Cum.
------------+-----------------------------------
   40 to 50 |         11       28.21       28.21
   55 to 60 |         26       66.67       94.87
   Above 60 |          2        5.13      100.00
------------+-----------------------------------
      Total |         39      100.00
```

◁

▷ Example

If you have missing values in your data, `tabulate` ignores them unless you explicitly indicate otherwise. We have no missing data in our example, so let's put some in:

```
. replace spdcat=. in 1
(1 real change made)
```

We changed the first observation on `spdcat` to *missing*. Let's now `tabulate` the result:

```
. tabulate spdcat

Speed Limit |
   Category |      Freq.      Percent         Cum.
------------+-----------------------------------
   40 to 50 |         11        28.95        28.95
   55 to 60 |         26        68.42        97.37
   Above 60 |          1         2.63       100.00
------------+-----------------------------------
      Total |         38       100.00
```

If you compare this output with that in the previous example, you will find that the total frequency count is now one less than it was—38 rather than 39. You will also find that the 'Above 60' category now has only one observation where it used to have two, so we evidently changed a road with a high speed limit.

If you want `tabulate` to treat missing values just as it treats numbers, specify the `missing` option:

```
. tabulate spdcat, missing

Speed Limit |
   Category |      Freq.      Percent         Cum.
------------+-----------------------------------
   40 to 50 |         11        28.21        28.21
   55 to 60 |         26        66.67        94.87
   Above 60 |          1         2.56        97.44
          . |          1         2.56       100.00
------------+-----------------------------------
      Total |         39       100.00
```

We now see our missing value—the last category, labeled '.', shows a frequency count of 1. The table sum is once again 39.

Let's put our data back as it was originally:

```
. replace spdcat=70 in 1
(1 real change made)
```

◁

❏ Technical Note

`tabulate` has another useful feature—the ability to automatically create indicator variables from categorical variables. We will briefly review that capability here, but see [U] **28 Commands for dealing with categorical variables** for a complete description. Let's begin by describing our highway data:

```
. describe

Contains data from hiway.dta
  obs:           39                          Minnesota Highway Data, 1973
  vars:           5                          20 Aug 1998 06:58
  size:         936 (99.6% of memory free)
-------------------------------------------------------------------------------
  1. acc_rate  float  %9.0g                  Accident rate
  2. spdlimit  float  %9.0g                  Speed limit
  3. acc_pts   float  %9.0g                  Access points per mile
  4. rate      float  %9.0g           rcat   Accident rate per million
                                                vehicle miles
  5. spdcat    float  %9.0g           scat   Speed Limit Category
-------------------------------------------------------------------------------
Sorted by:
    Note:  dataset has changed since last saved
```

Our data contains five variables. We will type `tabulate spdcat, generate(spd)`, `describe` our data, and then explain what happened.

```
. tabulate spdcat, generate(spd)

Speed Limit |
   Category |      Freq.      Percent       Cum.
------------+-----------------------------------
   40 to 50 |         11        28.21       28.21
   55 to 60 |         26        66.67       94.87
   Above 60 |          2         5.13      100.00
------------+-----------------------------------
      Total |         39       100.00

. describe

Contains data from hiway.dta
  obs:            39                          Minnesota Highway Data, 1973
 vars:             8                          20 Aug 1998 06:58
 size:         1,053 (99.6% of memory free)
-------------------------------------------------------------------------
  1. acc_rate    float   %9.0g                Accident rate
  2. spdlimit    float   %9.0g                Speed limit
  3. acc_pts     float   %9.0g                Access points per mile
  4. rate        float   %9.0g        rcat    Accident rate per million
                                                vehicle miles
  5. spdcat      float   %9.0g        scat    Speed Limit Category
  6. spd1        byte    %8.0g                spdcat==40 to 50
  7. spd2        byte    %8.0g                spdcat==55 to 60
  8. spd3        byte    %8.0g                spdcat==Above 60
-------------------------------------------------------------------------
Sorted by:
      Note:  dataset has changed since last saved
```

When we typed `tabulate` with the `generate()` option, Stata responded by producing a one-way frequency table, so it appeared that the option did nothing. Yet when we `describe` our data, we find that we now have *eight* variables instead of the original five. The new variables are named `spd1`, `spd2`, and `spd3`.

When you specify the `generate()` option, you are telling Stata not only to produce the table but also to create a set of indicator variables that correspond to that table. Stata adds a numeric suffix to the name you specify in the parentheses. `spd1` refers to the first line of the table, `spd2` to the second line, and so on. In addition, Stata labels the variables so that you know what they mean. `spd1` is an indicator variable that is *true* (takes on the value 1) when `spdcat` is between 40 and 50; otherwise, it is zero. (There is an exception: If `spdcat` is missing, so are the `spd1`, `spd2`, and `spd3` variables. This did not happen in our data.)

We want to prove our claim to you. Since we have not yet introduced two-way tabulations, we will use the `summarize` statement:

```
. summarize spdlimit if spd1==1

Variable |       Obs        Mean    Std. Dev.       Min        Max
---------+--------------------------------------------------------
spdlimit |        11    47.72727    3.437758         40         50

. summarize spdlimit if spd2==1

Variable |       Obs        Mean    Std. Dev.       Min        Max
---------+--------------------------------------------------------
spdlimit |        26    57.11538    2.519157         55         60

. summarize spdlimit if spd3==1

Variable |       Obs        Mean    Std. Dev.       Min        Max
---------+--------------------------------------------------------
spdlimit |         2        67.5    3.535534         65         70
```

Notice the indicated minimum and maximum in each of the tables above. When we restrict the sample to `spd1`, `spdlimit` is between 40 and 50; when we restrict the sample to `spd2`, `spdlimit` is between 55 and 60; when we restrict the sample to `spd3`, `spdlimit` is between 65 and 70.

Thus, `tabulate` provides an easy way to create indicator (sometimes called dummy) variables. We could now use these variables in, for instance, regression analysis. See [U] **28 Commands for dealing with categorical variables** for an example of such use.

❑

Two-way tables

▷ Example

`tabulate` will make two-way tables if you specify two variables following the word `tabulate`. In our highway data, we have a variable called `rate` that divides the accident rate into three categories: below 4, 4–7, and above 7 per million vehicle miles. Let's make a table of the speed limit category and the accident rate category:

```
. tabulate spdcat rate

    Speed |    Accident rate per million
    Limit |          vehicle miles
 Category |   Below 4       4-7    Above 7 |     Total
----------+---------------------------------+----------
 40 to 50 |        3         5         3 |        11
 55 to 60 |       19         6         1 |        26
 Above 60 |        2         0         0 |         2
----------+---------------------------------+----------
    Total |       24        11         4 |        39
```

The table indicates that 3 stretches of highway have an accident rate below 4 and a speed limit of 40 to 50 miles per hour. The table also shows the row and column sums (called the *marginals*). The number of highways with a speed limit of 40 to 50 miles per hour is 11, which is the same result we obtained in our previous one-way tabulations.

Stata can present this basic table in a number of ways — 16, to be precise — and we will show just a few below. It might be easier to read the table if we included the row-percentages. For instance, out of 11 highways in the lowest speed limit category, there are 3 in the lowest accident rate category as well. Three-elevenths amounts to some 27.3%. We can ask Stata to fill in this information for us by using the `row` option:

```
. tabulate spdcat rate, row
    Speed |    Accident rate per million
    Limit |          vehicle miles
 Category |   Below 4       4-7    Above 7 |     Total
----------+---------------------------------+----------
 40 to 50 |        3         5         3 |        11
          |    27.27     45.45     27.27 |    100.00
----------+---------------------------------+----------
 55 to 60 |       19         6         1 |        26
          |    73.08     23.08      3.85 |    100.00
----------+---------------------------------+----------
 Above 60 |        2         0         0 |         2
          |   100.00      0.00      0.00 |    100.00
----------+---------------------------------+----------
    Total |       24        11         4 |        39
          |    61.54     28.21     10.26 |    100.00
```

The number listed below each frequency is the percentage of cases that each cell represents out of its row. That is easy to remember because we see 100% listed in the "Total" column. The bottom row is also informative. We see that 61.54% of all the highways in our data fall into the lowest accident rate category, that 28.21% are in the middle category, and that 10.26% are in the highest.

tabulate can calculate column percentages and cell percentages as well. It does so when you specify the column or cell options, respectively. You can even specify them together. Below we make a table that includes everything:

```
. tabulate spdcat rate, row column cell
    Speed |       Accident rate per million
    Limit |              vehicle miles
 Category |   Below 4         4-7     Above 7 |      Total
----------+---------------------------------+----------
 40 to 50 |        3           5           3 |         11
          |    27.27       45.45       27.27 |     100.00
          |    12.50       45.45       75.00 |      28.21
          |     7.69       12.82        7.69 |      28.21
----------+---------------------------------+----------
 55 to 60 |       19           6           1 |         26
          |    73.08       23.08        3.85 |     100.00
          |    79.17       54.55       25.00 |      66.67
          |    48.72       15.38        2.56 |      66.67
----------+---------------------------------+----------
 Above 60 |        2           0           0 |          2
          |   100.00        0.00        0.00 |     100.00
          |     8.33        0.00        0.00 |       5.13
          |     5.13        0.00        0.00 |       5.13
----------+---------------------------------+----------
    Total |       24          11           4 |         39
          |    61.54       28.21       10.26 |     100.00
          |   100.00      100.00      100.00 |     100.00
          |    61.54       28.21       10.26 |     100.00
```

The number at the top of each cell is the frequency count. The second number is the row percentage—they sum to 100% going across the table. The third number is the column percentage—they sum to 100% going down the table. The bottom number is the cell percentage—they sum to 100% going down all the columns and across all the rows. For instance, highways with a speed limit above 60 miles per hour and in the lowest accident rate category account for 100% of highways with a speed limit above 60 miles per hour; 8.33% of highways in the lowest accident rate category; and 5.13% of all our data.

There is a fourth option you will find useful—nofreq. That option tells Stata not to print the frequency counts. If we wish to construct a table consisting only of row percentages, we type

```
. tabulate spdcat rate, row nofreq
    Speed |       Accident rate per million
    Limit |              vehicle miles
 Category |   Below 4         4-7     Above 7 |      Total
----------+---------------------------------+----------
 40 to 50 |    27.27       45.45       27.27 |     100.00
 55 to 60 |    73.08       23.08        3.85 |     100.00
 Above 60 |   100.00        0.00        0.00 |     100.00
----------+---------------------------------+----------
    Total |    61.54       28.21       10.26 |     100.00
```

◁

Measures of association

▷ Example

tabulate will calculate the Pearson χ^2 test for the independence of the rows and columns if you specify the chi2 option. Suppose you have 1980 Census data on 956 cities in the U.S. and wish to compare the age distribution across regions of the country. Assume that agecat is the median age in each city and that region denotes the region of the country in which the city is located.

```
. tabulate region agecat, chi2
Census |            agecat
Region |     19-29       30-34        35+ |     Total
-----------+---------------------------------+----------
    NE |        46          83         37 |       166
N Cntrl |       162          92         30 |       284
 South |       139          68         43 |       250
  West |       160          73         23 |       256
-----------+---------------------------------+----------
 Total |       507         316        133 |       956
        Pearson chi2(6) =   61.2877   Pr = 0.000
```

We obtain the standard two-way table and, at the bottom, a summary of the χ^2 test. Stata informs us that the χ^2 associated with this table has 6 degrees of freedom and is 61.29. The observed differences are quite significant.

The table is, perhaps, easier to understand if we suppress the frequencies and print just the row percentages:

```
. tabulate region agecat, row nofreq chi2
Census |            agecat
Region |     19-29       30-34        35+ |     Total
-----------+---------------------------------+----------
    NE |     27.71       50.00      22.29 |    100.00
N Cntrl |     57.04       32.39      10.56 |    100.00
 South |     55.60       27.20      17.20 |    100.00
  West |     62.50       28.52       8.98 |    100.00
-----------+---------------------------------+----------
 Total |     53.03       33.05      13.91 |    100.00
        Pearson chi2(6) =   61.2877   Pr = 0.000
```

◁

▷ Example

You have data on dose level and outcome for a set of patients and wish to evaluate the association between the two variables. You can obtain all the association measures by specifying the all and exact options:

(Table on next page)

```
. tabulate dose function, all exact

            | Function
    Dosage |    < 1 hr      1 to 4         4+ |      Total
-----------+--------------------------------+----------
     1/day |        20          10          2 |         32
     2/day |        16          12          4 |         32
     3/day |        10          16          6 |         32
-----------+--------------------------------+----------
     Total |        46          38         12 |         96

              Pearson chi2(4) =   6.7780   Pr = 0.148
     likelihood-ratio chi2(4) =   6.9844   Pr = 0.137
                  Cramer's V =   0.1879
                       gamma =   0.3689   ASE = 0.129
             Kendall's tau-b =   0.2378   ASE = 0.086
               Fisher's exact =              0.145
```

We find evidence of association, but not yet enough to be truly convincing.

Had we not also specified the **exact** option, we would not have obtained Fisher's exact test. Stata can calculate this statistic not only for 2×2 tables but also for $r \times c$. For 2×2 tables, the calculation is almost instant. On more general tables, however, the calculation can take a long time. In this case, on a 60 MHz Pentium, the calculation took 9.4 seconds. On a 25 MHz 80386 with an 80387, the calculation took 1.5 minutes. That is why **all** does not imply **exact**—you must explicitly request it.

Note that we carefully constructed our example so that **all** would be meaningful. Kendall's τ_b and Goodman and Kruskal's gamma are relevant only when both dimensions of the table can be ordered, say low-to-high or worst-to-best. The other statistics, however, are applicable in all cases.

◁

❑ Technical Note

You are warned that calculation of Fisher's exact test can not only run into the minutes, it can run into the hours for big tables. Using the older 25 MHz 80386 computer, a 9×2 table containing 40 observations took 30 seconds, but a 5×4 containing 29 observations took 49 minutes (5.1 minutes on a 60 MHz Pentium)!

❑

N-way tables

If you need more than two-way tables, your best alternative to is use **table**, not **tabulate**; see [R] **table**.

In the technical note below, we show you how to trick **tabulate** into doing a sequence of two-way tables that together form, in effect, a three-way table, but using **table** is easy and produces prettier results:

(Table on next page)

```
. table birthcat region agecat, c(freq)
```

| | agecat and Census Region | | | | | | | |
| | ------------ 19-29 ------------ | | | | ------------ 30-34 ------------ | | | |
birthcat	NE	N Cntrl	South	West	NE	N Cntrl	South	West
29-136	11	23	11	11	34	27	10	8
137-195	31	97	65	46	48	58	45	42
196-529	4	38	59	91	1	3	12	21

| | agecat and Census Region | | | |
| | ------------ 35+ ------------ | | | |
birthcat	NE	N Cntrl	South	West
29-136	34	26	27	18
137-195	3	4	7	4
196-529			4	

❏ Technical Note

You can make *n*-way tables by combining the **by** *varlist*: prefix with **tabulate**. Continuing with the dataset of 956 cities, say we want to make a table of age category by birth rate category by region of the country. The birth rate category variable is named **birthcat** in our data. Below we make separate tables for each age category.

```
. sort agecat
. by agecat: tabulate birthcat region
-> agecat=    19-29
```

| | Census Region | | | | |
birthcat	NE	N Cntrl	South	West	Total
29-136	11	23	11	11	56
137-195	31	97	65	46	239
196-529	4	38	59	91	192
Total	46	158	135	148	487

```
-> agecat=    30-34
```

| | Census Region | | | | |
birthcat	NE	N Cntrl	South	West	Total
29-136	34	27	10	8	79
137-195	48	58	45	42	193
196-529	1	3	12	21	37
Total	83	88	67	71	309

```
-> agecat=    35+
```

| | Census Region | | | | |
birthcat	NE	N Cntrl	South	West	Total
29-136	34	26	27	18	105
137-195	3	4	7	4	18
196-529	0	0	4	0	4
Total	37	30	38	22	127

❏

Weighted data

▷ Example

tabulate can process weighted as well as unweighted data. As with all Stata commands, you indicate the weight by specifying the [*weight*] modifier; see [U] **14.1.6 weight**.

Continuing with our dataset of 956 cities, we also have a variable called pop, the population of each city. We can make a table of region by age category, weighted by population, by typing

```
. tabulate region agecat [freq=pop]
   Census |            Age Category
   region |     19-29       30-34         35+ |      Total
----------+---------------------------------+----------
       NE |   4257167    17290828     5015443 |   26563438
   N Cntrl |  17161373     5548927     1348988 |   24059288
    South |  17607696     4809089     2612535 |   25029320
     West |  12862832     9089231     1856258 |   23808321
----------+---------------------------------+----------
    Total |  51889068    36738075    10833224 |   99460367
```

If we specify the cell, column, or row options, they will also be appropriately weighted. Below we repeat the table, suppressing the counts and substituting row percentages:

```
. tabulate region agecat [freq=pop], nofreq row
   Census |            Age Category
   region |     19-29       30-34         35+ |      Total
----------+---------------------------------+----------
       NE |     16.03       65.09       18.88 |     100.00
   N Cntrl |    71.33       23.06        5.61 |     100.00
    South |     70.35       19.21       10.44 |     100.00
     West |     54.03       38.18        7.80 |     100.00
----------+---------------------------------+----------
    Total |     52.17       36.94       10.89 |     100.00
```

◁

Tables with immediate data

▷ Example

tabi ignores the data in memory and uses as the table the values you specify on the command line:

```
. tabi 30 18 \ 38 14
          | col
      row |         1          2 |      Total
----------+----------------------+----------
        1 |        30         18 |         48
        2 |        38         14 |         52
----------+----------------------+----------
    Total |        68         32 |        100

          Fisher's exact =                 0.289
  1-sided Fisher's exact =                 0.179
```

You may specify any of the options of `tabulate` and are not limited to 2×2 tables:

```
. tabi 30 18 38 \ 13 7 22, chi2 exact
          | col
     row  |        1          2         3 |     Total
----------+---------------------------------+----------
       1  |       30         18        38 |        86
       2  |       13          7        22 |        42
----------+---------------------------------+----------
   Total  |       43         25        60 |       128

          Pearson chi2(2) =   0.7967   Pr = 0.671
          Fisher's exact =                0.707

. tabi 30 13 \ 18 7 \ 38 22, all exact col
          | col
     row  |        1          2 |     Total
----------+---------------------+----------
       1  |       30         13 |        43
          |    34.88      30.95 |     33.59
----------+---------------------+----------
       2  |       18          7 |        25
          |    20.93      16.67 |     19.53
----------+---------------------+----------
       3  |       38         22 |        60
          |    44.19      52.38 |     46.88
----------+---------------------+----------
   Total  |       86         42 |       128
          |   100.00     100.00 |    100.00

               Pearson chi2(2) =   0.7967   Pr = 0.671
      likelihood-ratio chi2(2) =   0.7985   Pr = 0.671
                   Cramer's V =   0.0789
                        gamma =   0.1204   ASE = 0.160
              Kendall's tau-b =   0.0630   ASE = 0.084
               Fisher's exact =                0.707
```

Note that, for 2×2 tables, both the one- and two-sided Fisher's exact probabilities are displayed; this is true of both `tabulate` and `tabi`. See *Cumulative incidence data* and *Case-control data* in [R] **epitab** for more discussion on the relationship between one- and two-sided probabilities.

◁

❑ Technical Note

   `tabi`, as with all immediate commands, leaves any data in memory undisturbed. With the `replace` option, however, the data in memory is replaced by the data from the table:

```
. tabi 30 18 \ 38 14, replace
          | col
     row  |        1          2 |     Total
----------+---------------------+----------
       1  |       30         18 |        48
       2  |       38         14 |        52
----------+---------------------+----------
   Total  |       68         32 |       100

               Fisher's exact =              0.289
       1-sided Fisher's exact =              0.179
```

```
. list
          row       col       pop
     1.     1         1        30
     2.     1         2        18
     3.     2         1        38
     4.     2         2        14
```

With this data, one could recreate the above table by typing

```
. tabulate row col [freq=pop], exact
           | col
       row |         1         2 |     Total
-----------+----------------------+----------
         1 |        30        18 |        48
         2 |        38        14 |        52
-----------+----------------------+----------
     Total |        68        32 |       100
                 Fisher's exact =                 0.289
         1-sided Fisher's exact =                 0.179
```

❑

tab1 and tab2

tab1 and tab2 are convenience tools. Typing

```
. tab1 myvar thisvar thatvar, plot
```

is equivalent to typing

```
. tabulate myvar, plot
. tabulate thisvar, plot
. tabulate thatvar, plot
```

Typing

```
. tab2 myvar thisvar thatvar, chi2
```

is equivalent to typing

```
. tabulate myvar thisvar, chi2
. tabulate myvar thatvar, chi2
. tabulate thisvar thatvar, chi2
```

Saved Results

tabulate, tab1, tab2, and tabi save in r():

Scalars

r(N)	number of observations	r(p_exact)	Fisher's exact p
r(r)	number of rows	r(chi2_lr)	likelihood-ratio χ^2
r(c)	number of columns	r(p_lr)	significance of likelihood-ratio χ^2
r(chi2pear)	Pearson's χ^2	r(CramersV)	Cramér's V
r(p_pear)	significance of Pearson's χ^2	r(ase_gam)	ASE of gamma
r(gamma)	gamma	r(ase_taub)	ASE of τ_b
r(p1_exact)	one-sided Fisher's exact p	r(taub)	τ_b

r(p1_exact) is defined only for 2×2 tables. In addition, the matrow(), matcol(), and matcell() options allow you to obtain the row values, column values, and frequencies, respectively.

Methods and Formulas

`tab1`, `tab2`, and `tabi` are implemented as ado-files.

Let n_{ij}, $i = 1, \ldots, I$, $j = 1, \ldots, J$, be the number of observations in the ith row and jth column. If the data is not weighted, n_{ij} is just a count. If the data is weighted, n_{ij} is the sum of the weights of all data corresponding to the (i, j) cell.

Define the row and column marginals as

$$n_{i.} = \sum_{j=1}^{J} n_{ij}, \qquad\qquad n_{.j} = \sum_{i=1}^{I} n_{ij}$$

and let $n = \sum_i \sum_j n_{ij}$ be the overall sum. Also define the concordance and discordance as

$$A_{ij} = \sum_{k>i}\sum_{l>j} n_{kl} + \sum_{k<i}\sum_{l<j} n_{kl}, \qquad\qquad D_{ij} = \sum_{k>i}\sum_{l<j} n_{kl} + \sum_{k<i}\sum_{l>j} n_{kl}$$

along with twice the number of concordances $P = \sum_i \sum_j n_{ij} A_{ij}$ and twice the number of discordances $Q = \sum_i \sum_j n_{ij} D_{ij}$.

The Pearson χ^2 statistic with $(I-1)(J-1)$ degrees of freedom (so called because it is based on Pearson 1900; see Conover 1980, 159 and Fienberg 1980, 9) is defined as

$$X^2 = \sum_i \sum_j \frac{(n_{ij} - m_{ij})^2}{m_{ij}}$$

where $m_{ij} = n_{i.} n_{.j} / n$.

The likelihood-ratio χ^2 statistic with $(I-1)(J-1)$ degrees of freedom (Fienberg 1980, 40) is defined as

$$G^2 = 2 \sum_i \sum_j n_{ij} \ln(n_{ij}/m_{ij})$$

Cramér's V (Cramér 1946; also see Agresti 1984, 23–24) is a measure of association designed so that the attainable upper bound is 1. For 2×2 tables, $-1 \leq V \leq 1$, and otherwise $0 \leq V \leq 1$.

$$V = \begin{cases} (n_{11} n_{22} - n_{12} n_{21})/(n_{1.} n_{2.} n_{.1} n_{.2})^{1/2} & \text{for } 2 \times 2 \\ \left[(X^2/n)/\min(I-1, J-1)\right]^{1/2} & \text{otherwise} \end{cases}$$

Gamma (Goodman and Kruskal 1954, 1959, 1963, 1972; also see Agresti 1984, 159–161) ignores tied pairs and is based only on the number of concordant and discordant pairs of observations, $-1 \leq \gamma \leq 1$:

$$\gamma = (P - Q)/(P + Q)$$

with asymptotic variance

$$16 \sum_i \sum_j n_{ij} (Q A_{ij} - P D_{ij})^2 / (P + Q)^4$$

Kendall's τ_b (Kendall 1945; also see Agresti 1984, 161–163), $-1 \leq \tau_b \leq 1$, is similar to gamma except that it uses a correction for ties:

$$\tau_b = (P - Q)/(w_r w_c)^{1/2}$$

with asymptotic variance

$$\frac{\sum_i \sum_j n_{ij}(2w_r w_c d_{ij} + \tau_b v_{ij})^2 - n^3 \tau_b^2 (w_r + w_c)^2}{(w_r w_c)^4}$$

where

$$w_r = n^2 - \sum_i n_{i\cdot}^2$$

$$w_c = n^2 - \sum_j n_{\cdot j}^2$$

$$d_{ij} = A_{ij} - D_{ij}$$

$$v_{ij} = n_{i\cdot}w_c + n_{\cdot j}w_r$$

Fisher's exact test (Fisher 1935; Finney 1948; and see Zelterman and Louis 1992, 293–301, for the 2×2 case) yields the probability of observing a table that gives at least as much evidence of association as the one actually observed under the assumption of no association. Holding row and column marginals fixed, the hypergeometric probability P of every possible table A is computed and the

$$P = \sum_{T \in A} \Pr(T)$$

where A is the set of all tables with the same marginals as the observed table, $T^\star$, such that $\Pr(T) \leq \Pr(T^\star)$. In the case of 2×2 tables, the one-sided probability is calculated by further restricting A to tables in the same tail as $T^\star$. The first algorithm extending this calculation to $r \times c$ tables was Pagano and Halvorsen (1981); the one implemented here is a search-tree clipping method based on the ideas of Mehta and Patel (1983).

References

Agresti, A. 1984. *Analysis of Ordinal Categorical Data*. New York: John Wiley & Sons.

Conover, W. J. 1980. *Practical Nonparametric Statistics*. 2d ed. New York: John Wiley & Sons.

Cox, N. J. 1996. sg57: An immediate command for two-way tables. *Stata Technical Bulletin* 33: 7–9. Reprinted in *Stata Technical Bulletin Reprints*, vol. 6, pp. 140–143.

Cramér, H. 1946. *Mathematical Methods of Statistics*. Princeton, NJ: Princeton University Press.

Fienberg, S. E. 1980. *The Analysis of Cross-Classified Categorical Data*. 2d ed. Cambridge: MIT Press.

Finney, D. J. 1948. The Fisher–Yates test of significance in 2×2 contingency tables. *Biometrika* 35: 145–156.

Fisher, R. A. 1935. The logic of inductive inference. *Journal of the Royal Statistical Society*, Series A 98: 39–54.

Goodman, L. A. and W. H. Kruskal. 1954. Measures of association for cross classifications. *Journal of the American Statistical Association* 49: 732–764.

——. 1959. Measures of association for cross classifications II: further discussion and references. *Journal of the American Statistical Association* 54: 123–163.

——. 1963. Measures of association for cross classifications III: approximate sampling theory. *Journal of the American Statistical Association* 58: 310–364.

——. 1972. Measures of association for cross classifications IV: simplification of asymptotic variances. *Journal of the American Statistical Association* 67: 415–421.

Judson, D. H. 1992. sg12: Extended tabulate utilities. *Stata Technical Bulletin* 10: 22–23. Reprinted in *Stata Technical Bulletin Reprints*, vol. 2, pp. 140–141.

Kendall, M. G. 1945. The treatment of ties in rank problems. *Biometrika* 33: 239–251.

Mehta, C. R. and N. R. Patel. 1983. A network algorithm for performing Fisher's exact test in $r \times c$ contingency tables. *Journal of the American Statistical Association* 78: 427–434.

Pagano, M. and K. Halvorsen. 1981. An algorithm for finding the exact significance levels of $r \times c$ tables. *Journal of the American Statistical Association* 76: 931–934.

Pearson, K. 1900. On the criterion that a given system of deviations from the probable in the case of a correlated system of variables is such that it can be reasonably supposed to have arisen from random sampling. *Philosophical Magazine*, Series 5, 50: 157–175.

Selvin, S. 1995. *Practical Biostatistical Methods*. Belmont, CA: Duxbury Press.

Zelterman, D. and T. A. Louis. 1992. Contingency tables in medical studies. In *Medical Uses of Statistics*, ed. J. C. Bailar III and F. Mosteller, 293–310. 2d ed. Boston: New England Journal of Medicine Books.

Also See

Complementary:	[R] **encode**
Related:	[R] **epitab**, [R] **table**, [R] **tabsum**, [R] **xtdes**, [R] **xttab**
Background:	[U] **15.6.3 Value labels**,
	[U] **22 Immediate commands**,
	[U] **28 Commands for dealing with categorical variables**

Title

> **test** — Test linear hypotheses after model estimation

Syntax

(1) <u>test</u> $\left[\mathit{exp} = \mathit{exp}\right]$ $\left[\,,\ \underline{a}\text{ccumulate}\ \underline{\text{not}}\text{est}\,\right]$

(2) <u>test</u> $\left[\mathit{coefficientlist}\right]$ $\left[\,,\ \underline{a}\text{ccumulate}\ \underline{\text{not}}\text{est}\,\right]$

(3) <u>test</u> $\left[\mathit{term}\ \left[\mathit{term}\ \left[\ldots\right]\right]\right]$ $\left[/\ \mathit{term}\ \left[\mathit{term}\ \left[\ldots\right]\right]\right]$ $\left[\,,\ \underline{\text{s}}\text{ymbolic}\right]$

(4) testparm *varlist* $\left[\,,\ \underline{\text{e}}\text{qual}\,\right]$

Syntax 1 is available after all estimation commands. Syntax 2 is available after all estimation commands except **anova**. Syntax 3 is available only after **anova**. Syntax 4 is available after all estimation commands except **anova** and multiple-equation estimation commands such as **mlogit** or **mvreg**.

coefficientlist is one of

>> *coefficient* $\left[\mathit{coefficient}\ \ldots\right]$
>> [*eqno*] : *coef* $\left[\mathit{coef}\ \ldots\right]$
>> [*eqno*]
>> [$\mathit{eqno}_1\mathit{=eqno}_2$] : *coef* $\left[\mathit{coef}\ \ldots\right]$
>> [$\mathit{eqno}_1\mathit{=eqno}_2$]

coefficient is

>> *coef*
>> [*eqno*]*coef*

coef is

>> *varname*
>> _b[*varname*]
>> or something more complicated in the case of **anova**

eqno is

>> # #
>> #
>> *name*

term is

>> $\mathit{varname}\left[\left\{\ *\ |\ |\ \right\}\mathit{varname}\left[\ldots\right]\right]$

Distinguish between [ ], which are to be typed, and $\left[\ \right]$, which indicate optional arguments.

Description

test tests linear hypotheses about the estimated parameters from the most recently estimated model using a Wald test. Without arguments, **test** redisplays the results of the last test.

testparm provides a useful alternative to **test** that permits *varlist* rather than just a list of coefficients (which is often nothing more than a list of variables), allowing use of standard Stata notation including '-' and '*', which are given the *ex*pression interpretation by **test**.

For likelihood-ratio tests, see [R] **lrtest**. For tests of nonlinear hypotheses; see [R] **testnl**. To display estimates for one-dimensional tests, see [R] **lincom**. If you have estimated a model with one of the **svy** commands, you should use **svytest** rather than **test**; see [R] **svytest**.

Options

accumulate allows a hypothesis to be tested jointly with the previously tested hypotheses.

notest suppresses the output. This option is useful when you are interested only in the joint test of a number of hypotheses.

symbolic requests the symbolic form of the test rather than the test statistic and is allowed only after anova estimation. When this option is specified without any *terms* (test, symbolic), the symbolic form of the estimable functions is displayed.

equal tests that the variables appearing in *varlist* that also appear in the previously estimated model are equal to each other rather than jointly equal to zero.

Remarks

test performs F or χ^2 tests of linear restrictions applied to the most recently estimated model (e.g., anova, regress, ... in the linear regression case; cox, logit, ... in the single-equation maximum-likelihood case; mlogit, mvreg, ... in the multiple-equation maximum-likelihood case). test may be used after *any* estimation command, although in the case of maximum likelihood techniques, the test is performed on the inverse-matrix-of-second-partials estimate of the covariance matrix—you may prefer to use the more computationally expensive likelihood-ratio test; see [U] **23 Estimation and post-estimation commands** and [R] **lrtest**.

There are three variations on the syntax for test. The first syntax

$$\text{test } exp = exp$$

is allowed after any form of estimation, although it is not that useful after anova unless you wish to concoct your own test. The anova case is discussed in [R] **anova**, so we will ignore it. Putting aside anova, after estimating a model of depvar on x1, x2, and x3, typing test x1+x2=x3 tests the restriction that the coefficients on x1 and x2 sum to the coefficient on x3. The expressions can be arbitrarily complicated, for instance, typing test x1+2*(x2+x3)=x2+3*x3 is the same as typing test x1+x2=x3.

Note that test understands that when you type x1, you are referring to the coefficient on x1. You could also (and more explicitly) type test _b[x1]+_b[x2]=_b[x3] (or test _coef[x1]+_coef[x2]=_coef[x3] or test [#1]x1+[#1]x2= [#1]x3 or many other things since there is more than one way to refer to an estimated coefficient; see [U] **16.5 Accessing coefficients and standard errors**). The shorthand involves less typing. On the other hand, you must be more explicit after estimation of multiple-equation models since there may be more than one coefficient associated with an independent variable. You might type, for instance, test [#2]x1+[#2]x2=[#2]x3 to test the constraint in equation 2 or, more readably, test [ford]x1+[ford]x2=[ford]x3, meaning to test the constraint on the equation corresponding to ford, which might be equation 2. (ford would be an equation name after, say, sureg or, after mlogit, ford would be one of the outcomes. In the case of mlogit, you could also type test [2]x1+[2]x2=[2]x3—note the lack of the #—meaning not equation 2 but the equation corresponding to the numeric outcome 2.) You can even test constraints across equations: test [ford]x1+[ford]x2=[buick]x3.

The second syntax

$$\text{test } coefficientlist$$

is available after all estimation commands except anova and is a convenient way to test that multiple coefficients are zero following estimation. A *coefficientlist* can simply be a list of variable names

$$\text{test } varname \ \big[varname \ \dots\big]$$

and it is most often specified that way. After estimating a model of depvar on x1, x2, and x3, typing test x1 x3 tests that the coefficients on x1 and x3 are jointly zero. After multiple-equation estimation, this would test that the coefficients on x1 and x3 are zero in all equations that contain them. Alternatively, you can be more explicit and type, for instance, test [ford]x1 [ford]x3 to test that the coefficients on x1 and x3 are zero in the equation corresponding to ford.

In the multiple-equation case, there are more alternatives. You could also test that the coefficients on x1 and x3 are zero in the equation corresponding to ford by typing test [ford]: x1 x3. You could test that all coefficients except the coefficient on the constant are zero in the equation corresponding to ford by typing test [ford]. You could test that the coefficients on x1 and x3 in the equation corresponding to ford are equal to the corresponding coefficients in the equation corresponding to buick by typing test[ford=buick]: x1 x3. You could test that all the corresponding coefficients except the constant are equal by typing test [ford=buick].

testparm is much like the second syntax of test except it cannot be used after multiple-equation commands and, like the second syntax, cannot be used after anova. Its usefulness will be demonstrated below.

Finally, syntax 3 of test is used for testing effects after anova models. It will not be discussed here; see [R] **anova**.

In the examples below we will use **regress**, but what is said is equally applicable after any single-equation estimation command (such as **logistic**, etc.). It is also applicable after multiple-equation estimation commands if you bear in mind that references to coefficients must be qualified with an equation name or number in square brackets placed before them. The convenient syntaxes for dealing with tests of many coefficients in multiple-equation models are demonstrated in *Special syntaxes after multiple-equation estimation*, below.

▷ Example

You have 1980 Census data on the 50 states recording the birth rate in each state (brate), the median age (medage) and its square, (medagesq), and the region of the country in which each state is located.

The variable reg1 is 1 if the state is located in the Northeast and zero otherwise, whereas reg2 marks the North Central, reg3 the South, and reg4 the West. You estimate the following regression:

```
. regress brate medage medagesq reg2-reg4

    Source |       SS       df       MS                  Number of obs =      50
-----------+------------------------------              F(  5,    44) =  100.63
     Model | 38803.419        5  7760.68381              Prob > F      =  0.0000
  Residual | 3393.40096      44  77.1227491              R-squared     =  0.9196
-----------+------------------------------              Adj R-squared =  0.9104
     Total | 42196.82        49  861.159592              Root MSE      =   8.782

-------------------------------------------------------------------------------
     brate |      Coef.   Std. Err.       t     P>|t|     [95% Conf. Interval]
-----------+-------------------------------------------------------------------
    medage | -109.0957   13.52452     -8.066    0.000    -136.3526   -81.83886
  medagesq |   1.635208    .2290536     7.139    0.000     1.173581    2.096835
      reg2 |   15.00284   4.252068      3.528    0.001     6.433365    23.57233
      reg3 |   7.366435   3.953336      1.863    0.069    -.6009897    15.33386
      reg4 |   21.39679   4.650602      4.601    0.000     12.02412    30.76946
     _cons |    1947.61   199.8405      9.746    0.000     1544.858    2350.362
-------------------------------------------------------------------------------
```

test can now be used to perform a variety of statistical tests. We can test the hypothesis that the coefficient on reg3 is zero by typing

```
. test reg3=0
 ( 1)  reg3 = 0.0
       F(  1,    44) =    3.47
            Prob > F =    0.0691
```

The F statistic with 1 numerator and 44 denominator degrees of freedom is 3.47. The significance level of the test is 6.91%—we can reject the hypothesis at the 10% level but not at the 5% level.

This test result, obtained by using **test**, is identical to a test result presented in the output from **regress**. That output indicates that the t statistic on the **reg3** coefficient is 1.863 and that its significance level is 0.069. The t statistic presented in the output tests the hypothesis that the corresponding coefficient is zero, although it states the test in slightly different terms. The F distribution with 1 numerator degree of freedom is, however, identical to the t^2 distribution. We note that $1.863^2 \approx 3.47$. We also note that the significance levels associated with each test agree, although one extra digit is presented by the **test** command.

◁

❑ Technical Note

After all estimation commands, even maximum likelihood, the result reported by **test** of whether a single variable is zero is identical to the result reported by the command's output. The tests are performed in the same way—using the information matrix. If the estimation command reports significance levels and confidence intervals using z rather than t statistics, **test** will report results using the χ^2 rather than the F statistic.

❑

▷ Example

If that were all **test** could do, it would be useless. We can use **test**, however, to perform other tests. For instance, we can **test** the hypothesis that the coefficient on **reg2** is 21 by typing

```
. test reg2=21
 ( 1)  reg2 = 21.0
       F(  1,    44) =    1.99
            Prob > F =    0.1654
```

We find that we cannot reject that hypothesis, or at least cannot reject it at any significance level below 16.5%.

◁

▷ Example

The previous test is useful, but we could almost as easily perform it by hand using the results presented in the regression output—if we were well read on our statistics. We could type

```
. display fprob(1,44,((_coef[reg2]-21)/4.252068)^2)
.16544976
```

So now let's **test** something a bit more difficult. Let's test whether the coefficient on **reg2** is the same as the coefficient on **reg4**:

```
. test reg2=reg4
 ( 1)  reg2 - reg4 = 0.0
       F(  1,    44) =    2.84
            Prob > F =    0.0989
```

We find that we cannot reject the equality hypothesis at the 5% level, but we can at the 10%.

◁

▷ Example

You may notice that when we tested the equality of the **reg2** and **reg4** coefficients, Stata rearranged our algebra. When Stata repeated the test, it indicated that we were testing whether **reg2** *minus* **reg4** is zero. The rearrangement is innocuous and, in fact, offers an advantage. Stata can perform much more complicated algebra; for instance:

```
. test 2*(reg2-3*(reg3-reg4))=reg3+reg2+6*(reg4-reg3)
 ( 1)   reg2 - reg3 = 0.0
       F(  1,    44) =    5.06
            Prob > F =    0.0295
```

Although we requested what appeared to be a lengthy hypothesis, once Stata simplified the algebra it realized that all we wanted to do was test whether the coefficient on **reg2** is the same as the coefficient on **reg3**.

◁

❑ Technical Note

Stata's ability to simplify and test complex hypotheses is limited to *linear* hypotheses. If you attempt to **test** a nonlinear hypothesis, you will be told that it is not possible:

```
. test reg2/reg3=reg2+reg3
not possible with test
r(131);
```

If you want to test a nonlinear hypothesis, see [R] **testnl**.

❑

▷ Example

The real power of **test** is demonstrated when we test *joint* hypotheses. Perhaps we wish to test whether the region variables, taken as a whole, are significant. This amounts to a test of whether the coefficients on **reg2**, **reg3**, and **reg4** are simultaneously zero. To perform tests of this kind, specify each constraint and **accumulate** it with the previous constraints:

```
. test reg2=0
 ( 1)   reg2 = 0.0
       F(  1,    44) =   12.45
            Prob > F =    0.0010
. test reg3=0, accumulate
 ( 1)   reg2 = 0.0
 ( 2)   reg3 = 0.0
       F(  2,    44) =    6.42
            Prob > F =    0.0036
. test reg4=0, accumulate
 ( 1)   reg2 = 0.0
 ( 2)   reg3 = 0.0
 ( 3)   reg4 = 0.0
       F(  3,    44) =    8.85
            Prob > F =    0.0001
```

We will show you a more convenient way to perform tests of this kind in the next example, but you should first understand this one. We tested the hypothesis that the coefficient on reg2 was zero by typing test reg2=0. We then tested whether the coefficient on reg3 was *also* zero by typing test reg3=0, accumulate. The accumulate option told Stata that this was not the start of a new test but a continuation of a previous one. Stata responded by showing us the two equations and reporting an F statistic of 6.42. The significance level associated with those two coefficients being zero is 0.36%.

When we added the last constraint test reg4=0, accumulate, we discover that the three region variables are quite significant.

◁

❏ Technical Note

If all we wanted was the overall significance and we did not want to bother seeing the interim results, we could have used the notest option:

```
. test reg2=0, notest
 ( 1)   reg2 = 0.0
. test reg3=0, accumulate notest
 ( 1)   reg2 = 0.0
 ( 2)   reg3 = 0.0
. test reg4=0, accumulate
 ( 1)   reg2 = 0.0
 ( 2)   reg3 = 0.0
 ( 3)   reg4 = 0.0
        F(  3,    44) =    8.85
             Prob > F =    0.0001
```

❏

▷ Example

Typing separate test commands for each constraint can be tiresome. The second syntax allows us to perform our last test more conveniently:

```
. test reg2 reg3 reg4
 ( 1)   reg2 = 0.0
 ( 2)   reg3 = 0.0
 ( 3)   reg4 = 0.0
        F(  3,    44) =    8.85
             Prob > F =    0.0001
```

◁

▷ Example

We will now show you the use of testparm. In its second syntax, test accepts a list of variable names, but not a *varlist*.

```
. test reg2-reg4
- not found
r(111);
```

In a *varlist*, reg2-reg3 means variables reg2 and reg3 and all the variables in between. Yet we received an error. test is mightily confused because the – has two meanings: it means subtraction in an expression and "through" in a *varlist*. Similarly, '*' means "any set of characters" in a *varlist* and multiplication in an expression. testparm avoids this confusion—it allows only a *varlist*.

```
. testparm reg2-reg4

 ( 1)   reg2 = 0.0
 ( 2)   reg3 = 0.0
 ( 3)   reg4 = 0.0

      F(  3,    44) =    8.85
           Prob > F =    0.0001
```

testparm has another advantage. We have five variables in our data that start with the characters reg: region, reg1, reg2, reg3, and reg4. reg* thus means those five variables:

```
. describe reg*

   1. region    int     %8.0g        region    Census Region
   2. reg1       byte    %9.0g                  region==NE
   3. reg2       byte    %9.0g                  region==N Cntrl
   4. reg3       byte    %9.0g                  region==South
   5. reg4       byte    %9.0g                  region==West
```

We cannot type test reg* because in an expression, '*' means multiplication, but here is what would happen if we attempted to test all the variables that begin with reg:

```
. test region reg1 reg2 reg3 reg4
region not found
r(111);
```

The variable region was not included in our model and so was not found. However, with testparm:

```
. testparm reg*

 ( 1)   reg2 = 0.0
 ( 2)   reg3 = 0.0
 ( 3)   reg4 = 0.0

      F(  3,    44) =    8.85
           Prob > F =    0.0001
```

That is, testparm took reg* to mean all variables that start with reg that were in our model.

◁

❑ Technical Note

Actually, reg* means what it always does—all variables in our dataset that begin with reg—in this case, region reg1 reg2 reg3 reg4. testparm just ignores any variables you specify that are not in the model.

❑

▷ Example

We just used test (testparm, actually, but it does not matter) to test the hypothesis that reg2, reg3, and reg4 are jointly zero. We can resee the results of our last test by typing test without arguments:

```
. test
( 1)   reg2 = 0.0
( 2)   reg3 = 0.0
( 3)   reg4 = 0.0
         F(  3,    44) =    8.85
              Prob > F =    0.0001
```

◁

❏ Technical Note

test does not care how you build joint hypotheses; you may freely mix syntax 1 and syntax 2. (You can even start with testparm, but you cannot use it thereafter because it does not have an accumulate option.)

Say we type test reg2 reg3 reg4 to test that the coefficients on our region dummies are jointly zero. We could then add a fourth constraint, say that medage = 100, by typing test medage=100, accumulate. Or, if we had introduced the medage constraint first (our first test command had been test medage=100), we could then add the region dummy test by typing test reg2 reg3 reg4, accumulate.

Remember that all previous tests are cleared when you do not specify the accumulate option. No matter what tests we performed in the past, if we type test medage medagesq, omitting the accumulate option, we would test that medage and medagesq are jointly zero.

❏

▷ Example

Let's test the hypothesis that all the included regions have the *same* coefficient—that it is the Northeast which is significantly different from the rest of the nation:

```
. test reg2=reg4
( 1)   reg2 - reg4 = 0.0
         F(  1,    44) =    2.84
              Prob > F =    0.0989
. test reg3=reg4, accum
( 1)   reg2 - reg4 = 0.0
( 2)   reg3 - reg4 = 0.0
         F(  2,    44) =    8.23
              Prob > F =    0.0009
```

We find that they are not all the same. We performed this test by imposing two constraints: Region 2 has the same coefficient as region 4 and region 3 has the same coefficient as region 4. Alternatively, we could have tested that the coefficients on regions 2 and 3 are the same and that the coefficients on regions 3 and 4 are the same. We would obtain the same results in either case.

◁

▷ Example

This test is even easier with the testparm command. When you include the equal option, testparm tests that all the variables specified are equal:

```
. testparm reg*, equal
( 1)  - reg2 + reg3 = 0.0
( 2)  - reg2 + reg4 = 0.0
      F(  2,    44) =    8.23
          Prob > F =    0.0009
```
◁

❏ Technical Note

If you specify a set of inconsistent constraints, test will tell you by dropping the constraint or constraints that led to the inconsistency. For instance, let's test that the coefficients on region 2 and region 4 are the same, add the test that the coefficient on region 2 is 20, and finally add the test that the coefficient on region 4 is 21:

```
. test reg2==reg4
( 1)  reg2 - reg4 = 0.0
      F(  1,    44) =    2.84
          Prob > F =    0.0989

. test reg2=20, accumulate
( 1)  reg2 - reg4 = 0.0
( 2)  reg2 = 20.0
      F(  2,    44) =    1.63
          Prob > F =    0.2076

. test reg4=21, accumulate
( 1)  reg2 - reg4 = 0.0
( 2)  reg2 = 20.0
( 3)  reg4 = 21.0
      Constraint 2 dropped
      F(  2,    44) =    1.82
          Prob > F =    0.1737
```

Note that when we typed test reg4=21, accumulate, test informed us that it was dropping constraint 2. All three equations cannot be simultaneously true, so test drops whatever it takes to get back to something that makes sense.

❏

Special syntaxes after multiple-equation estimation

Everything said above about tests after single-equation estimation applies to tests after multiple-equation estimation as long as you remember to specify the equation name. By way of demonstration, let's estimate a seemingly unrelated regression using sureg; see [R] sureg.

(Continued on next page)

```
. sureg (price foreign mpg displ) (weight foreign length)
Seemingly unrelated regression
-----------------------------------------------------------------------
Equation      Obs   Parms         RMSE    "R-sq"        Chi2        P
-----------------------------------------------------------------------
price          74      3       2165.321   0.4537      49.6383   0.0000
weight         74      2       245.2916   0.8990     661.8418   0.0000
-----------------------------------------------------------------------

              |     Coef.    Std. Err.       z    P>|z|    [95% Conf. Interval]
--------------+--------------------------------------------------------
price         |
      foreign |    3058.25    685.7357     4.460   0.000     1714.233   4402.267
          mpg |  -104.9591    58.47209    -1.795   0.073    -219.5623   9.644042
        displ |   18.18098    4.286372     4.242   0.000     9.779842   26.58211
        _cons |   3904.336    1966.521     1.985   0.047     50.0263    7758.645
--------------+--------------------------------------------------------
weight        |
      foreign |  -147.3481    75.44314    -1.953   0.051    -295.2139   .517755
       length |   30.94905    1.539895    20.098   0.000     27.93091   33.96718
        _cons |  -2753.064    303.9336    -9.058   0.000    -3348.763  -2157.365
-----------------------------------------------------------------------
```

If we wanted to test the significance of `foreign` in the `price` equation,

```
. test [price]foreign
 ( 1)  [price]foreign = 0.0
          chi2(  1) =    19.89
        Prob > chi2 =     0.0000
```

which is the same result reported by `sureg`: $4.460^2 \approx 19.89$. If we wanted to test `foreign` in both equations, we could type

```
. test [price]foreign [weight]foreign
 ( 1)  [price]foreign = 0.0
 ( 2)  [weight]foreign = 0.0
          chi2(  2) =    31.61
        Prob > chi2 =     0.0000
```

or

```
. test foreign
 ( 1)  [price]foreign = 0.0
 ( 2)  [weight]foreign = 0.0
          chi2(  2) =    31.61
        Prob > chi2 =     0.0000
```

This last syntax—typing the variable name by itself—tests the coefficients in all equations in which they appear. The variable `length` appears in only the `weight` equation, so typing

```
. test length
 ( 1)  [weight]length = 0.0
          chi2(  1) =   403.94
        Prob > chi2 =     0.0000
```

yields the same result as typing `test [weight]length`. We may also specify a linear expression rather than a list of coefficients:

```
. test mpg=displ
 ( 1)  [price]mpg - [price]displ = 0.0
          chi2(  1) =     4.85
        Prob > chi2 =     0.0277
```

or

```
. test [price]mpg = [price]displ
 ( 1)  [price]mpg - [price]displ = 0.0

            chi2(  1) =    4.85
          Prob > chi2 =    0.0277
```

A variation on this syntax can be used to test cross-equation constraints:

```
. test [price]foreign = [weight]foreign
 ( 1)  [price]foreign - [weight]foreign = 0.0

            chi2(  1) =    23.07
          Prob > chi2 =    0.0000
```

Typing an equation name in square brackets by itself tests all the coefficients except the intercept in that equation:

```
. test [price]
 ( 1)  [price]foreign = 0.0
 ( 2)  [price]mpg = 0.0
 ( 3)  [price]displ = 0.0

            chi2(  3) =    49.64
          Prob > chi2 =    0.0000
```

Typing an equation name in square brackets, a colon, and a list of variable names tests those variables in the specified equation:

```
. test [price]: foreign displ
 ( 1)  [price]foreign = 0.0
 ( 2)  [price]displ = 0.0

            chi2(  2) =    25.19
          Prob > chi2 =    0.0000
```

test [$eqname_1$=$eqname_2$] tests that all the coefficients in the two equations are equal. We cannot use that syntax here because we have different variables in our model:

```
. test [price=weight]
[weight]mpg not found
r(111);
```

This syntax is, however, useful after mvreg or mlogit, where all the equations do share the same independent variables. We can, however, use a modification of this syntax with our model if we also type a colon and the names of the variables we want to test:

```
. test [price=weight]: foreign
 ( 1)  [price]foreign - [weight]foreign = 0.0

            chi2(  1) =    23.07
          Prob > chi2 =    0.0000
```

We have only one variable in common between our two equations, but if there had been more, we could have listed them.

Finally, you may use the accum and notest options just as you do after single-equation estimation. Earlier, we tested the joint significance of foreign by typing test foreign. We could also have typed

```
. test [price]foreign, notest
( 1)  [price]foreign = 0.0
. test [weight]foreign, accum
( 1)  [price]foreign = 0.0
( 2)  [weight]foreign = 0.0
           chi2(  2) =    31.61
         Prob > chi2 =     0.0000
```

Saved Results

test and testparm save in r():

Scalars

r(p)	two-sided p-value		r(chi2)	χ^2
r(F)	F statistic		r(ss)	model sum of squares
r(df)	test constraint(s) degrees of freedom		r(rss)	residual sum of squares
r(df_r)	residual degrees of freedom			

r(ss) and r(rss) are defined only when test is used for testing effects after anova.

Methods and Formulas

testparm is implemented as an ado-file.

test and testparm perform Wald tests. Let the estimated coefficient vector be **b** and the estimated variance–covariance matrix be **V**. Let $\mathbf{Rb} = \mathbf{r}$ denote the set of q linear hypotheses to be tested jointly.

The Wald test statistic is (Judge et al. 1985, 20–28)

$$W = (\mathbf{Rb} - \mathbf{r})'(\mathbf{RVR}')^{-1}(\mathbf{Rb} - \mathbf{r})$$

If the estimation command reports its significance levels using Z statistics, a chi-squared distribution with q degrees of freedom

$$W \sim \chi^2_q$$

is used for computation of the significance level of the hypothesis test.

If the estimation command reports its significance levels using t statistics with d degrees of freedom, an F statistic

$$F = \frac{1}{q}W$$

is computed, and an F distribution with q numerator degrees of freedom and d denominator degrees of freedom is used to compute the significance level of the hypothesis test.

References

Beale, E. M. L. 1960. Confidence regions in nonlinear estimation. *Journal of the Royal Statistical Society*, Series B 22: 41–88.

Judge, G. G., W. E. Griffiths, R. C. Hill, H. Lütkepohl, and T.-C. Lee. 1985. *The Theory and Practice of Econometrics*. 2d ed. New York: John Wiley & Sons.

Also See

Related:	[R] **anova**, [R] **lincom**, [R] **linktest**, [R] **lrtest**, [R] **svytest**, [R] **testnl**
Background:	[U] **16.5 Accessing coefficients and standard errors**,
	[U] **23 Estimation and post-estimation commands**

Title

testnl — Test nonlinear hypotheses after model estimation

Syntax

testnl *exp=exp* $\left[\, , \; \mathbf{g}(matname_1) \; \mathbf{r}(matname_2) \,\right]$

testnl *(exp=exp)* $\left[\, (exp=exp) \; ... \right]$ $\left[\, , \; \mathbf{g}(matname_1) \; \mathbf{r}(matname_2) \,\right]$

The second syntax means that if more than one equation is specified, each must be surrounded by parentheses.

Description

testnl tests (linear or nonlinear) hypotheses about the estimated parameters from the most recently estimated model.

Options

g(*matname_1*) supplies a matrix name to be created containing $\mathbf{G}$, the matrix of derivatives of $R(\mathbf{b})$ with respect to $\mathbf{b}$; see *Methods and Formulas* below. This option is intended for programmers needing an internal ingredient of the calculation.

r(*matname_2*) supplies a matrix name to be created containing $R(\mathbf{b}) - \mathbf{q}$; see *Methods and Formulas* below. This option is intended for programmers needing an internal ingredient of the calculation.

Remarks

▷ Example

We have just estimated an earnings model on cross-sectional time-series data using one of Stata's more sophisticated estimators:

```
. xtgee ln_w grade age age2, i(id) t(t) corr(unstr) nolog
GEE population-averaged model            Number of obs      =      1326
Group and time vars:          idcode t   Number of groups   =       269
Link:                         identity   Obs per group: min =         1
Family:                       Gaussian                  avg =       4.9
Correlation:              unstructured                  max =         9
                                         Wald chi2(3)       =    282.58
Scale parameter:               .0980824  Prob > chi2        =    0.0000

------------------------------------------------------------------------
 ln_wage |    Coef.   Std. Err.      z     P>|z|    [95% Conf. Interval]
---------+--------------------------------------------------------------
   grade |   .074266   .0067065   11.074   0.000    .0611215    .0874105
     age |  .1190881   .0276476    4.307   0.000    .0648998    .1732763
    age2 | -.0018859    .000559   -3.373   0.001   -.0029817   -.0007902
   _cons | -.9835956    .32578    -3.019   0.003   -1.622113   -.3450786
------------------------------------------------------------------------
```

An implication of this model is that peak earnings occur at age $-\_b[age]/(2*\_b[age2])$, which here is equal to 33.1. Pretend we have a theory that peak earnings should occur at age $16 + 1/\_b[grade]$ (we do not, but pretend we do).

```
. testnl -_b[age]/(2*_b[age2]) = 16 + 1/_b[grade]

 (1)  -_b[age]/(2*_b[age2]) = 16 + 1/_b[grade]

            chi2(1) =        0.62
          Prob > chi2 =      0.4306
```

This data does not reject our theory.

◁

Using testnl to perform linear tests

testnl may be used to test linear constraints, but test is faster; see [R] **test**. You could type

```
. testnl _b[x4] = _b[x1]
```

but it would take less computer time if you typed

```
. test _b[x4] = _b[x1]
```

Specifying constraints

The algebraic form in which you specify the constraint does not matter; you could type

```
. testnl _b[mpg]*_b[weight] = 1
```

or

```
. testnl _b[mpg] = 1/_b[weight]
```

or you could express the constraint any other way you wished. You must, however, exercise one caution: Users of test often refer to the coefficient on a variable by specifying the variable name, for example:

```
. test mpg = 0
```

More formally, they should type

```
. test _b[mpg] = 0
```

but test allows the _b[] surrounding the variable name to be omitted. testnl does not allow this shorthand. Typing

```
. testnl mpg=0
```

specifies the constraint that the value of variable mpg in the first observation is zero. If you make this mistake, in some cases testnl will catch it:

```
. testnl mpg=0
equation (1) contains reference to X rather than _b[X]
r(198);
```

In other cases testnl may not catch the mistake; in that case, the constraint will be dropped because it does not make sense:

```
. testnl mpg=0
Constraint (1) dropped
```

(There are reasons other than this for constraints being dropped.) The worst case, however, is

> . testnl _b[weight]*mpg = 1

when what you mean is not that _b[weight] equals the reciprocal of the value of mpg in the first observation, but rather

> . testnl _b[weight]*_b[mpg] = 1

Sometimes this mistake will be caught by the "contains reference to X rather than _b[X]" error and sometimes not. Be careful.

testnl, like test, can be used after any Stata estimation command. When used after a multiple-equation command such as mlogit or heckman, you refer to coefficients using Stata's standard syntax: [eqname]_b[varname].

Stata's single-equation estimation output looks like

```
             |    Coef   ...
-----------+----------  ...
   weight  |   12.27   ...      <-  coefficient is   _b[weight]
      mpg  |    3.21   ...
-----------------------  ...
```

Stata's multiple-equation output looks like

```
             |    Coef   ...
-----------+----------  ...
cat1        |           ...
   weight  |   12.27   ...      <-  coefficient is   [cat1]_b[weight]
      mpg  |    3.21   ...
-----------+----------  ...
8           |           ...
   weight  |    5.83   ...      <-  coefficient is   [8]_b[weight]
      mpg  |    7.43   ...
-----------------------  ...
```

Dropped constraints

testnl automatically drops constraints when

1. They are nonbinding, e.g., _b[mpg]=_b[mpg]. More subtle cases include

   ```
   _b[mpg]*_b[weight] = 4
   _b[weight] = 2
   _b[mpg] = 2
   ```

   In this example, the 3rd constraint is nonbinding since it is implied by the first two.

2. They are contradictory, e.g., _b[mpg]=2 and _b[mpg]=3. More subtle cases include

   ```
   _b[mpg]*_b[weight] = 4
   _b[weight] = 2
   _b[mpg] = 3
   ```

   The 3rd constraint contradicts the first two.

Output

testnl reports the constraints being tested followed by a F or χ^2 test:

```
. regress price mpg weight weightsq foreign
(output omitted)
. testnl (39*_b[mpg]^2 = _b[foreign]) (_b[mpg]/_b[weight] = 4)

 (1)  39*_b[mpg]^2 = _b[foreign]
 (2)  _b[mpg]/_b[weight] = 4

          F(2, 69) =          0.08
          Prob > F =        0.9195

. logit foreign price weight mpg
(output omitted)
. testnl (45*_b[mpg]^2 = _b[price]) (_b[mpg]/_b[weight] = 4)

 (1)  45*_b[mpg]^2 = _b[price]
 (2)  _b[mpg]/_b[weight] = 4

           chi2(2) =          2.44
       Prob > chi2 =        0.2946
```

Saved Results

testnl saves in r():

Scalars
  r(df)   degrees of freedom
  r(df_r)   residual degrees of freedom
  r(chi2) χ^2
  r(F) F statistic

Methods and Formulas

testnl is implemented as an ado-file.

You have estimated a model. Define **b** as the resulting $1 \times k$ parameter vector and **V** as the $k \times k$ covariance matrix. The (linear or nonlinear) hypothesis is given by $R(\mathbf{b}) = \mathbf{q}$, where R is a function returning a $j \times 1$ vector. The Wald test formula is (Greene 1997, 163)

$$W = \left(R(\mathbf{b}) - \mathbf{q} \right)' \left[\mathbf{GVG}' \right]^{-1} \left(R(\mathbf{b}) - \mathbf{q} \right)$$

where **G** is the derivative matrix of $R(\mathbf{b})$ with respect to **b**. W is distributed as χ^2 if **V** is an asymptotic covariance matrix. $F = W/j$ is distributed as F in the case of linear regression.

References

Gould, W. W. 1996. crc43: Wald test of nonlinear hypotheses after model estimation. *Stata Technical Bulletin* 29: 2–4. Reprinted in *Stata Technical Bulletin Reprints*, vol. 5, pp. 15–18.

Greene, W. H. 1997. *Econometric Analysis*. 3d ed. Upper Saddle River, NJ: Prentice–Hall.

Also See

Related: [R] **lincom**, [R] **lrtest**, [R] **test**

Background: [U] **23 Estimation and post-estimation commands**

Title

> **tobit** — Tobit, censored-normal, and interval regression

Syntax

> <u>tob</u>it *depvar* [*indepvars*] [*weight*] [if *exp*] [in *range*] , ll[(#)] ul[(#)] [<u>l</u>evel(#)
>
>   <u>off</u>set(*varname*) *maximize_options*]
>
> <u>cnr</u>eg *depvar* [*indepvars*] [*weight*] [if *exp*] [in *range*] , <u>cen</u>sored(*varname*) [<u>l</u>evel(#)
>
>   <u>off</u>set(*varname*) *maximize_options*]

>   intreg *depvar*₁ *depvar*₂ [*indepvars*] [*weight*] [if *exp*] [in *range*] [, <u>nocon</u>stant
>
>   <u>r</u>obust <u>cl</u>uster(*varname*) <u>sc</u>ore(*newvar*₁ *newvar*₂) <u>l</u>evel(#)
>
>   <u>off</u>set(*varname*) *maximize_options*]

aweights and fweights are allowed by all three commands; intreg also allows pweights and iweights; see [U] **14.1.6 weight**.

These commands share the features of all estimation commands; see [U] **23 Estimation and post-estimation commands**.

tobit and cnreg may be used with sw to perform stepwise estimation; see [R] **sw**.

Syntax for predict

>   predict [*type*] *newvarname* [if *exp*] [in *range*] [, *statistic* <u>nooff</u>set]

where *statistic* is

xb	$x_j b$, fitted values (the default)
<u>pr</u>(a,b)	$\Pr(a < y_j < b)$
e(a,b)	$E(y_j \mid a < y_j < b)$
<u>y</u>star(a,b)	$E(y_j^*)$, $y_j^* = \max(a, \min(y_j, b))$
stdp	standard error of the prediction
stdf	standard error of the forecast

where *a* and *b* may be numbers or variables; *a* equal to '.' means $-\infty$; *b* equal to '.' means $+\infty$.

These statistics are available both in and out of sample; type predict ... if e(sample) ... if wanted only for the estimation sample.

Description

tobit estimates a model of *depvar* on *indepvars* where the censoring values are fixed.

cnreg estimates a model of *depvar* on *indepvars* where *depvar* contains both observations and censored observations on the process. Censoring values may vary from observation to observation.

intreg estimates a model of $y = [\,depvar_1,\,depvar_2\,]$ on *indepvars*, where y for each observation is either point data, interval data, left-censored data, or right-censored data.

depvar$_1$ and *depvar*$_2$ should have the following form:

type of data		*depvar*$_1$	*depvar*$_2$
point data	$a = [\,a, a\,]$	a	a
interval data	$[\,a, b\,]$	a	b
left-censored data	$(-\infty, b\,]$	.	b
right-censored data	$[\,a, +\infty)$	a	.

Options

ll(#) and ul(#) indicate the censoring points in tobit. You may specify one or both. ll() indicates the lower limit for left censoring. Observations with *depvar* $\leq$ ll() are left-censored; observations with *depvar* $\geq$ ul() are right-censored; remaining observations are not censored. You do not have to specify the censoring values at all. It is enough to type ll, ul, or both. When you do not specify a censoring value, tobit assumes that the lower limit is the minimum observed in the data (if ll is specified) and the upper limit is the maximum (if ul is specified).

censored(*varname*) is not optional for cnreg. *varname* is a variable indicating if *depvar* is censored and, if so, whether the censoring is left or right. 0 indicates that *depvar* is not censored. -1 indicates left censoring; the true value is known only to be less than or equal to the value recorded in *depvar*. $+1$ indicates right censoring; the true value is known only to be greater than or equal to the value recorded in *depvar*.

level(#) specifies the confidence level, in percent, for confidence intervals. The default is level(95) or as set by set level; see [U] **23.5 Specifying the width of confidence intervals**.

offset(*varname*) specifies that *varname* is to be included in the model with coefficient constrained to be 1.

noconstant (intreg only) suppresses the constant term (intercept) in the estimation.

robust (intreg only) specifies that the Huber/White/sandwich estimator of the variance is to be used in place of the conventional MLE variance estimator. robust combined with cluster() further allows observations which are not independent within cluster (although they must be independent between clusters).

If you specify pweights, robust is implied. See [U] **23.11 Obtaining robust variance estimates**.

cluster(*varname*) (intreg only) specifies that the observations are independent across groups (clusters) but not necessarily independent within groups. *varname* specifies to which group each observation belongs. cluster() affects the estimated standard errors and variance–covariance matrix of the estimators (VCE), but not the estimated coefficients. cluster() can be used with pweights to produce estimates for unstratified cluster-sampled data.

cluster() implies robust; that is, specifying robust cluster() is equivalent to typing cluster() by itself.

score(*newvar*$_1$ *newvar*$_2$) (intreg only) creates two new variables containing, respectively, $u_{1j} = \partial \ln L_j / \partial (\mathbf{x}_j \boldsymbol{\beta})$ and $u_{2j} = \partial \ln L_j / \partial \sigma$ for each observation j in the sample, where L_j is the jth observation's contribution to the likelihood. The jth observation's contribution to the score vector is thus $[\,\partial \ln L_j / \partial \boldsymbol{\beta} \;\; \partial \ln L_j / \partial \sigma\,] = [\,u_{1j} \mathbf{x}_j \;\; u_{2j}\,]$. The score vector can be obtained by summing over j. See [U] **23.12 Obtaining scores**.

maximize_options control the maximization process; see [R] **maximize**. You should never have to specify them. Unlike most maximum likelihood commands, however, `cnreg` and `tobit` default to `nolog`—they suppress the iteration log (see *Methods and Formulas* below). `log` will display the iteration log.

Options for predict

`xb`, the default, calculates the linear prediction.

`pr(a,b)` calculates $\Pr(a < \mathbf{x}_j\mathbf{b} + u_j < b)$, the probability that $y_j|\mathbf{x}_j$ would be observed in the interval (a, b).

> *a* and *b* may be specified as numbers or variable names; *lb* and *ub* are variable names;
> `pr(20,30)` calculates $\Pr(20 < \mathbf{x}_j\mathbf{b} + u_j < 30)$;
> `pr(lb,ub)` calculates $\Pr(lb < \mathbf{x}_j\mathbf{b} + u_j < ub)$;
> and `pr(20,ub)` calculates $\Pr(20 < \mathbf{x}_j\mathbf{b} + u_j < ub)$.
>
> $a = .$ means $-\infty$; `pr(.,30)` calculates $\Pr(\mathbf{x}_j\mathbf{b} + u_j < 30)$;
> `pr(lb,30)` calculates $\Pr(\mathbf{x}_j\mathbf{b} + u_j < 30)$ in observations for which $lb = .$
> (and calculates $\Pr(lb < \mathbf{x}_j\mathbf{b} + u_j < 30)$ elsewhere).
>
> $b = .$ means $+\infty$; `pr(20,.)` calculates $\Pr(\mathbf{x}_j\mathbf{b} + u_j > 20)$;
> `pr(20,ub)` calculates $\Pr(\mathbf{x}_j\mathbf{b} + u_j > 20)$ in observations for which $ub = .$
> (and calculates $\Pr(20 < \mathbf{x}_j\mathbf{b} + u_j < ub)$ elsewhere).

`e(a,b)` calculates $E(\mathbf{x}_j\mathbf{b} + u_j \mid a < \mathbf{x}_j\mathbf{b} + u_j < b)$, the expected value of $y_j|\mathbf{x}_j$ conditional on $y_j|\mathbf{x}_j$ being in the interval (a, b), which is to say, $y_j|\mathbf{x}_j$ is censored. *a* and *b* are specified as they are for `pr()`.

`ystar(a,b)` calculates $E(y_j^*)$ where $y_j^* = a$ if $\mathbf{x}_j\mathbf{b} + u_j \leq a$, $y_j^* = b$ if $\mathbf{x}_j\mathbf{b} + u_j \geq b$, and $y_j^* = \mathbf{x}_j\mathbf{b} + u_j$ otherwise, which is to say, y_j^* is truncated. *a* and *b* are specified as they are for `pr()`.

`stdp` calculates the standard error of the prediction. It can be thought of as the standard error of the predicted expected value or mean for the observation's covariate pattern. This is also referred to as the standard error of the fitted value.

`stdf` calculates the standard error of the forecast. This is the standard error of the point prediction for a single observation. It is commonly referred to as the standard error of the future or forecast value. By construction, the standard errors produced by `stdf` are always larger than those by `stdp`; see [R] **regress** *Methods and Formulas*.

`nooffset` is relevant only if you specified `offset(`*varname*`)`. It modifies the calculations made by `predict` so that they ignore the offset variable; the linear prediction is treated as $\mathbf{x}_j\mathbf{b}$ rather than $\mathbf{x}_j\mathbf{b} + \text{offset}_j$.

Remarks

Remarks are presented under the headings

> *tobit*
> *cnreg*
> *intreg*

tobit

Tobit estimation was originally developed by Tobin (1958). A consumer durable was purchased if a consumer's desire was high enough, where desire was measured by the dollar amount spent by the purchaser. If no purchase was made, the measure of desire was censored at zero.

▷ Example

We will demonstrate `tobit` using a more artificial example which, in the process, will allow us to emphasize the assumptions underlying the estimation. We have a dataset containing the mileage ratings and weights of 74 cars. There are no censored variables in this data, but we are going to create one. Before that, however, the relationship between mileage and weight in our complete data is

```
. gen wgt = weight/1000

. regress mpg wgt

    Source |       SS       df       MS              Number of obs =      74
-----------+------------------------------           F(  1,    72) =  134.62
     Model | 1591.99024       1  1591.99024          Prob > F      =  0.0000
  Residual | 851.469221      72  11.8259614          R-squared     =  0.6515
-----------+------------------------------           Adj R-squared =  0.6467
     Total | 2443.45946      73  33.4720474          Root MSE      =  3.4389

------------------------------------------------------------------------------
       mpg |      Coef.   Std. Err.       t    P>|t|     [95% Conf. Interval]
-----------+------------------------------------------------------------------
       wgt |  -6.008687   .5178782    -11.602   0.000    -7.041058   -4.976316
     _cons |   39.44028   1.614003     24.436   0.000     36.22283    42.65774
------------------------------------------------------------------------------
```

(We divided `weight` by 1,000 simply to make discussing the resulting coefficients easier. We find that each additional 1,000 pounds of weight reduces mileage by 6 mpg.)

mpg in our data ranges from 12 to 41. Let us now pretend that our data was censored in the sense that we could not observe a mileage rating below 17 mpg. If the true mpg is 17 or less, all we know is that the mpg is less than or equal to 17:

```
. replace mpg=17 if mpg<=17
(14 real changes made)

. tobit mpg wgt, ll

Tobit estimates                                Number of obs    =      74
                                               LR chi2(1)       =   72.85
                                               Prob > chi2      =  0.0000
Log likelihood = -164.25438                    Pseudo R2        =  0.1815

------------------------------------------------------------------------------
       mpg |      Coef.   Std. Err.       t    P>|t|     [95% Conf. Interval]
-----------+------------------------------------------------------------------
       wgt |   -6.87305   .7002559     -9.815   0.000    -8.268658   -5.477442
     _cons |   41.49856   2.05838      20.161   0.000     37.39621    45.6009
-----------+------------------------------------------------------------------
       _se |   3.845701   .3663309           (Ancillary parameter)
------------------------------------------------------------------------------

Obs. summary:        18 left-censored observations at mpg<=17
                     56 uncensored observations
```

The `replace` before estimation was not really necessary—we remapped all the mileage ratings below 17 to 17 merely to reassure you that `tobit` was not somehow using uncensored data. We typed `ll` after `tobit` to inform `tobit` that the data was left-censored. `tobit` found the minimum of mpg in our data and assumed that was the censoring point. Alternatively, we could have dispensed with `replace` and typed `ll(17)`, informing `tobit` that all values of the dependent variable 17 and below are really censored at 17. In either case, at the bottom of the table, we are informed that there are, as a result, 18 left-censored observations.

On this data, our estimate is now a reduction of 6.9 mpg per 1,000 extra pounds of weight as opposed to 6.0. The parameter reported as `_se` is the estimated standard error of the regression; the resulting 3.8 is comparable to the estimated root mean square error reported by `regress` of 3.4.

◁

❑ Technical Note

It should be understood that one would never want to throw away information—which is to say, purposefully censor variables. The `regress` estimates are in every way preferable to those of `tobit`. Our example is solely designed to illustrate the relationship between `tobit` and `regress`. If you have uncensored data, use `regress`. If your data is censored, however, you have no choice but to use `tobit`.

❑

▷ Example

`tobit` can also estimate models that are censored from above. This time, let's assume that we do not observe the actual mileage rating of cars yielding 24 mpg or better—we know only that it is at least 24. (Also assume that we have undone the change to `mpg` we made in the previous example.)

```
. tobit mpg wgt, ul(24)

Tobit estimates                                Number of obs   =       74
                                               LR chi2(1)      =    90.72
                                               Prob > chi2     =   0.0000
Log likelihood =  -129.8279                    Pseudo R2       =   0.2589

------------------------------------------------------------------------------
       mpg |      Coef.   Std. Err.       t    P>|t|     [95% Conf. Interval]
-----------+------------------------------------------------------------------
       wgt | -5.080645     .43493    -11.682   0.000    -5.947459   -4.213831
     _cons |  36.08037    1.432056    25.195   0.000     33.22628    38.93445
-----------+------------------------------------------------------------------
       _se |  2.385357    .2444604             (Ancillary parameter)
------------------------------------------------------------------------------

Obs. summary:        51 uncensored observations
                     23 right-censored observations at mpg>=24
```

◁

(Continued on next page)

▷ **Example**

tobit can also estimate models which are censored from both sides, the so-called two-limit tobit:

```
. tobit mpg wgt, ll(17) ul(24)
```

Tobit estimates				Number of obs	=	74
				LR chi2(1)	=	77.60
				Prob > chi2	=	0.0000
Log likelihood = -104.25976				Pseudo R2	=	0.2712

mpg	Coef.	Std. Err.	t	P>|t|	[95% Conf. Interval]
wgt	-5.764448	.7245417	-7.956	0.000	-7.208457 -4.320438
_cons	38.07469	2.255917	16.878	0.000	33.57865 42.57072
_se	2.886337	.3952143		(Ancillary parameter)	

```
Obs. summary:        18 left-censored observations at mpg<=17
                     33 uncensored observations
                     23 right-censored observations at mpg>=24
```

◁

cnreg

cnreg is a generalization of tobit. Rather than there being a constant lower- and/or upper-censoring point, each observation is allowed to be censored at a different point. With cnreg, you specify censored(*varname*) rather than the ll(*#*) and/or ul(*#*) options. *varname* records a 0 if the observation is not censored, a -1 if it is left-censored, and a $+1$ if it is right-censored.

▷ **Example**

You are estimating an earnings model. The data is censored from above in that, if the respondent's income was $60,000 or above, the interviewer recorded simply "in excess of $60,000". You might estimate the model using tobit, specifying ul(60000) (or, if you are working in natural logs, ul(11)). Later, you get another dataset to merge with your current data. In the second survey earnings were again censored, but this time at $100,000. You can no longer use tobit since some observations are censored at $60,000 and others at $100,000. You could, however

```
. gen cens=0
. replace cens=1 if survey==1 & earnings==60000
. replace cens=1 if survey==2 & earnings==100000
. cnreg earnings etc., censored(cens)
```

◁

▷ **Example**

Censored-normal regression has been used to estimate duration-time models, but such use has now declined in favor of models with more "reasonable" assumptions (e.g., exponential or Weibull; see [R] **st streg**); or no assumption except proportionality among groups (see [R] **st stcox**). There are, however, occasions when a normally distributed time variable may be reasonable.

You have (fictional) data on the date various newspapers adopted VDT (video display terminal) editing stored in `date` as days since 1/1/60. You also know the newspaper's circulation (`lncltn`) and whether the newspaper is a subsidiary or family-owned (`famown`). Your data begins in 1982 and ends in 1991. You have left censoring if the paper adopted VDT editing before 1982. You have right censoring if the paper had not adopted VDT editing by 1991.

In your data, `date` is recorded as missing if the paper is still not using VDTs or if it began before 1982. The variable `before82` is 1 if the paper started using VDTs before 1982:

```
. gen cnsrd=0                                           (nobody censored yet)
. replace cnsrd=-1 if before82
(24 real changes made)
. replace date=mdy(1,1,1982) if before82
(24 real changes made)
. replace cnsrd=1 if date==.
(11 real changes made)
. replace date =mdy(1,1,1991) if date==.
(11 real changes made)
. cnreg date lncltn famown, censored(cnsrd)

Censored normal regression                   Number of obs   =         100
                                             LR chi2(2)      =      201.09
                                             Prob > chi2     =      0.0000
Log likelihood = -519.74678                  Pseudo R2       =      0.1621

------------------------------------------------------------------------------
     date |      Coef.   Std. Err.       t    P>|t|     [95% Conf. Interval]
----------+-------------------------------------------------------------------
   lncltn | -1377.138   76.92723    -17.902   0.000    -1529.797   -1224.478
   famown |  576.8444   185.5287      3.109   0.002     208.6687    945.0201
    _cons |  24439.46   815.7107     29.961   0.000     22820.71    26058.21
----------+-------------------------------------------------------------------
      _se |  607.9846   53.19381             (Ancillary parameter)
------------------------------------------------------------------------------

Obs. summary:       24 left-censored observations
                    65 uncensored observations
                    11 right-censored observations
```

You estimate that family-owned newspapers adopted VDT editing 577 days later than nonfamily-owned newspapers (but remember, the data is fictional).

◁

❏ Technical Note

Censored-normal regression and tobit models achieve their results by assuming that the distribution of the error term is normal. This is a rather standard assumption but, in the case of these two models, it is vital. Results from censored-normal regression and tobit are not robust to other distributions of the errors; see Goldberger (1983). Moreover, heteroscedastic error terms can wreak havoc on such models; see Hurd (1979).

◁

intreg

intreg is an obvious generalization of the models estimated by cnreg and tobit. For censored data, their likelihoods contain terms of the form $\Pr(Y_j \leq y_j)$ for left-censored data and $\Pr(Y_j \geq y_j)$ for right-censored data, where y_j is the observed censoring value and Y_j denotes the random variable representing the dependent variable in the model. This can be extended to include interval data. If we know that the value for the jth individual is somewhere in the interval $[y_{1j}, y_{2j}]$, then the likelihood contribution from this individual is simply $\Pr(y_{1j} \leq Y_j \leq y_{2j})$.

Hence, intreg can estimate models for data where each observation represents either interval data, left-censored data, right-censored data, or point data. Regardless of the type of observation, the data should be stored in the dataset as interval data; that is, two dependent variables, *depvar*$_1$ and *depvar*$_2$, are used to hold the endpoints of the interval. If the data is left-censored, the lower endpoint is $-\infty$ and is represented by a missing value '.' in *depvar*$_1$. If the data is right-censored, the upper endpoint is $+\infty$ and is represented by a missing value '.' in *depvar*$_2$. Point data is represented by the two endpoints being equal.

type of data		*depvar*$_1$	*depvar*$_2$
point data	$a = [a, a]$	a	a
interval data	$[a, b]$	a	b
left-censored data	$(-\infty, b]$	.	b
right-censored data	$[a, +\infty)$	a	.

Note: Truly missing values of the dependent variable must be represented by missing values in both *depvar*$_1$ and *depvar*$_2$.

Interval data arises naturally in many contexts. One common one is wage data. Often you only know that, for example, a person's salary is between $30,000 and $40,000. Below we give an example for wage data, and show how to set up *depvar*$_1$ and *depvar*$_2$.

▷ Example

We have a dataset that contains the yearly wages of working women. Women were asked via a questionnaire to indicate a category for their yearly income from employment. The categories were less than 5,000, 5,001–10,000, ..., 25,001–30,000, 30,001–40,000, 40,001–50,000, and above 50,000. The wage categories are stored in the variable wagecat.

```
. tab wagecat

Wage      |
category  |
($1000s)  |     Freq.      Percent        Cum.
----------+-----------------------------------
       5 |        14         2.87        2.87
      10 |        83        17.01       19.88
      15 |       158        32.38       52.25
      20 |       107        21.93       74.18
      25 |        57        11.68       85.86
      30 |        30         6.15       92.01
      40 |        19         3.89       95.90
      50 |        14         2.87       98.77
      51 |         6         1.23      100.00
----------+-----------------------------------
   Total |       488       100.00
```

A value of 5 for `wagecat` represents the category less than 5,000, a value of 10 represents 5,001–10,000, ..., and a value of 51 represents greater than 50,000.

To use `intreg`, we must create two variables `wage1` and `wage2` containing the lower and upper endpoints of the wage categories. Here's one way to do it. We first create a little dataset containing just the nine wage categories. Then we lag the wage categories into `wage1`, then we match-merge this dataset with nine observations back into the main one.

```
. sort wagecat

. save womenwage
file womenwage.dta saved

. quietly by wagecat: keep if _n==1

. gen wage1 = wagecat[_n-1]
(1 missing value generated)

. keep wagecat wage1

. save lagwage
file lagwage.dta saved

. use womenwage, clear
(Wages of women)

. merge wagecat using lagwage

. tab _merge
    _merge |      Freq.     Percent        Cum.
-----------+-----------------------------------
         3 |        488      100.00      100.00
-----------+-----------------------------------
     Total |        488      100.00

. drop _merge
```

The variable `_merge` created by `merge` indicates that all the observations in the merge were matched (you should always check this; see [R] **merge** for more information).

Now we create the upper endpoint:

```
. gen wage2 = wagecat

. replace wage2 = . if wagecat == 51
(6 real changes made, 6 to missing)
```

Let's list the new variables:

```
. sort age

. list wage1 wage2 in 1/10

          wage1     wage2
  1.          5        10
  2.          .         5
  3.         10        15
  4.          5        10
  5.         10        15
  6.         10        15
  7.         10        15
  8.          5        10
  9.         10        15
 10.          5        10
```

We can now run `intreg`:

```
. intreg wage1 wage2 age age2 nev_mar rural school tenure
Fitting constant-only model:
Iteration 0:  log likelihood = -967.24956
Iteration 1:  log likelihood =  -967.1368
Iteration 2:  log likelihood =  -967.1368
Fitting full model:
Iteration 0:  log likelihood = -856.65324
Iteration 1:  log likelihood = -856.33293
Iteration 2:  log likelihood = -856.33293
Iteration 3:  log likelihood = -856.33293
```

```
Interval regression                      Number of obs =      488
                                         Model chi2(6) =   221.61
Log likelihood = -856.33293              Prob > chi2   =   0.0000
```

	Coef.	Std. Err.	z	P>|z|	[95% Conf. Interval]	
age	.7914438	.4433604	1.785	0.074	-.0775265	1.660414
age2	-.0132624	.0073028	-1.816	0.069	-.0275757	.0010509
nev_mar	-.2075022	.8119581	-0.256	0.798	-1.798911	1.383906
rural	-3.043044	.7757324	-3.923	0.000	-4.563452	-1.522637
school	1.334721	.1357873	9.829	0.000	1.068583	1.600859
tenure	.8000664	.1045077	7.656	0.000	.5952351	1.004898
_cons	-12.70238	6.367117	-1.995	0.046	-25.1817	-.2230585
_sigma	7.299626	.2529633	28.856	0.000	6.803827	7.795425

```
       Obs. summary:          0 uncensored observations
                             14 left-censored observations
                              6 right-censored observations
                            468 interval observations
```

We could also model this data using an ordered probit model. We do so running `oprobit`:

```
. oprobit wagecat age age2 nev_mar rural school tenure
Iteration 0:  log likelihood =  -881.1491
Iteration 1:  log likelihood = -764.31729
Iteration 2:  log likelihood = -763.31191
Iteration 3:  log likelihood = -763.31049
```

```
Ordered probit estimates                 Number of obs   =      488
                                         LR chi2(6)      =   235.68
                                         Prob > chi2     =   0.0000
Log likelihood = -763.31049              Pseudo R2       =   0.1337
```

wagecat	Coef.	Std. Err.	z	P>|z|	[95% Conf. Interval]	
age	.1674519	.0620333	2.699	0.007	.0458689	.289035
age2	-.0027983	.0010214	-2.740	0.006	-.0048001	-.0007964
nev_mar	-.0046417	.1126736	-0.041	0.967	-.225478	.2161946
rural	-.5270036	.1100448	-4.789	0.000	-.7426875	-.3113197
school	.2010587	.0201189	9.994	0.000	.1616263	.2404911
tenure	.0989916	.0147887	6.694	0.000	.0700063	.127977
_cut1	2.650637	.8957242	(Ancillary parameters)			
_cut2	3.941018	.8979164				
_cut3	5.085205	.9056579				
_cut4	5.875534	.912093				
_cut5	6.468723	.9181166				
_cut6	6.922726	.9215452				
_cut7	7.34471	.9237624				
_cut8	7.963441	.9338878				

We can directly compare the log likelihoods for the `intreg` and `oprobit` models since both likelihoods are discrete. If we had point data in our `intreg` estimation, the likelihood would be a mixture of discrete and continuous terms and we could not compare it directly with the `oprobit` likelihood.

In this case, the `oprobit` log likelihood is significantly larger (i.e., less negative), and thus, it fits better than the `intreg` model. The `intreg` model assumes normality. But the distribution of wages is skewed and definitely nonnormal. Normality is more closely approximated if we model the log of wages.

```
. gen logwage1 = log(wage1)
(14 missing values generated)
. gen logwage2 = log(wage2)
(6 missing values generated)
```

```
. intreg logwage1 logwage2 age age2 nev_mar rural school tenure

Fitting constant-only model:
Iteration 0:   log likelihood = -889.23647
Iteration 1:   log likelihood = -889.06346
Iteration 2:   log likelihood = -889.06346

Fitting full model:
Iteration 0:   log likelihood = -773.81968
Iteration 1:   log likelihood = -773.36565
Iteration 2:   log likelihood = -773.36563
Iteration 3:   log likelihood = -773.36563

Interval regression                             Number of obs   =      488
                                                Model chi2(6)   =   231.40
Log likelihood = -773.36563                     Prob > chi2     =   0.0000
```

	Coef.	Std. Err.	z	P>|z|	[95% Conf. Interval]	
age	.0645589	.0249954	2.583	0.010	.0155689	.1135489
age2	-.0010812	.0004115	-2.627	0.009	-.0018878	-.0002746
nev_mar	-.0058151	.0454867	-0.128	0.898	-.0949674	.0833371
rural	-.2098361	.0439454	-4.775	0.000	-.2959675	-.1237047
school	.0804832	.0076783	10.482	0.000	.0654341	.0955323
tenure	.0397144	.0058001	6.847	0.000	.0283464	.0510825
_cons	.7084023	.3593192	1.972	0.049	.0041495	1.412655
_sigma	.403738	.0143838	28.069	0.000	.3755463	.4319297

```
Obs. summary:        0 uncensored observations
                    14 left-censored observations
                     6 right-censored observations
                   468 interval observations
```

The log likelihood of this `intreg` model is very close to the `oprobit` log likelihood, and the z statistics for both models are very similar.

◁

(*Continued on next page*)

Saved Results

tobit and cnreg save in e():

Scalars

e(N)	number of observations	e(df_r)	residual degrees of freedom
e(N_unc)	number of uncensored observations	e(r2_p)	pseudo R-squared
e(N_lc)	number of left-censored observations	e(F)	F statistic
e(N_rc)	number of right-censored observations	e(ll)	log likelihood
e(df_m)	model degrees of freedom	e(ll_0)	log likelihood, constant-only model

Macros

e(cmd)	tobit or cnreg	e(chi2type)	Wald or LR; type of model χ^2 test
e(depvar)	name of dependent variable	e(offset)	offset
e(wtype)	weight type	e(predict)	program used to implement predict
e(wexp)	weight expression		

Matrices

e(b)	coefficient vector	e(V)	variance–covariance matrix of the estimators

Functions

e(sample)	marks estimation sample

intreg saves in e():

Scalars

e(N)	number of observations	e(ll)	log likelihood
e(N_unc)	number of uncensored observations	e(ll_0)	log likelihood, constant-only model
e(N_lc)	number of left-censored observations	e(N_clust)	number of clusters
e(N_rc)	number of right-censored observations	e(chi2)	χ^2
e(N_int)	number of interval observations	e(sigma)	estimate of sigma
e(df_m)	model degrees of freedom	e(se_sigma)	standard error of sigma

Macros

e(cmd)	intreg	e(clustvar)	name of cluster variable
e(depvar)	name(s) of dependent variable(s)	e(vcetype)	covariance estimation method
e(wtype)	weight type	e(offset)	offset
e(wexp)	weight expression	e(predict)	program used to implement predict

Matrices

e(b)	coefficient vector	e(V)	variance–covariance matrix of the estimators

Functions

e(sample)	marks estimation sample

Methods and Formulas

cnreg and tobit are built-in commands. intreg is implemented as an ado-file using the ml commands (see [R] **ml**); its robust variance computation is performed by _robust (see [R] **_robust**).

Let $\mathbf{y} = \mathbf{X}\boldsymbol{\beta} + \boldsymbol{\epsilon}$ be the model. $\mathbf{y}$ represents continuous outcomes—either observed or not observed. Our model assumes $\boldsymbol{\epsilon} \sim N(\mathbf{0}, \sigma^2 \mathbf{I})$.

We will describe the likelihood for `intreg` as it subsumes the `tobit` and `cnreg` models. For observations $j \in C$, we observe y_j; i.e., point data. Observations $j \in L$ are left-censored; we know only that the unobserved y_j is less than or equal to y_{Lj}, a censoring value that we do know. Similarly, observations $j \in R$ are right-censored; we know only that the unobserved y_j is less than or equal to y_{Rj}. Observations $j \in I$ are intervals; we know only that the unobserved y_j is in the interval $[y_{1j}, y_{2j}]$.

The log likelihood is

$$
L = -\frac{1}{2} \sum_{j \in C} w_j \left[\left(\frac{y_j - \mathbf{x}\boldsymbol{\beta}}{\sigma} \right)^2 + \log 2\pi\sigma^2 \right]
$$
$$
+ \sum_{j \in L} w_j \log \Phi \left(\frac{y_{Lj} - \mathbf{x}\boldsymbol{\beta}}{\sigma} \right)
$$
$$
+ \sum_{j \in R} w_j \log \left[1 - \Phi \left(\frac{y_{Rj} - \mathbf{x}\boldsymbol{\beta}}{\sigma} \right) \right]
$$
$$
+ \sum_{j \in I} w_j \log \left[\Phi \left(\frac{y_{2j} - \mathbf{x}\boldsymbol{\beta}}{\sigma} \right) - \Phi \left(\frac{y_{1j} - \mathbf{x}\boldsymbol{\beta}}{\sigma} \right) \right]
$$

where $\Phi()$ is the standard cumulative normal, and w_j is the weight for the jth observation, normalized to sum to N if `aweight`s are specified and otherwise not normalized; if no weights are specified, $w_j = 1$.

Maximization is as described in [R] **maximize**; the estimate reported as _se or _sigma is $\hat{\sigma}$. See [U] **23.11 Obtaining robust variance estimates** and [R] **_robust** for a description of the computation performed when `robust` is specified as an option to `intreg`.

See Tobin (1958) for the original derivation of the tobit model and Amemiya (1973) for a generalization to variable but known cutoffs. An introductory description of the tobit model can be found in, for instance, Johnston and DiNardo (1997, 436–441), Kmenta (1997, 562–566), Long (1997, 196–210), and Maddala (1992, 338–342).

References

Amemiya, T. 1973. Regression analysis when the dependent variable is truncated Normal. *Econometrica* 41: 997–1016.

——. 1984. Tobit models: a survey. *Journal of Econometrics* 24: 3–61.

Goldberger, A. S. 1983. Abnormal selection bias. In *Studies in Econometrics, Time Series, and Multivariate Statistics*, ed. S. Karlin, T. Amemiya, and L. A. Goodman, 67–84. New York: Academic Press.

Hurd, M. 1979. Estimation in truncated samples when there is heteroscedasticity. *Journal of Econometrics* 11: 247–258.

Johnston, J. and J. DiNardo. 1997. *Econometric Methods*. 4th ed. New York: McGraw–Hill.

Kendall, M. G. and A. Stuart. 1973. *The Advanced Theory of Statistics*, vol. 2. New York: Hafner.

Kmenta, J. 1997. *Elements of Econometrics*. 2d ed. Ann Arbor: University of Michigan Press.

Long, J. S. 1997. *Regression Models for Categorical and Limited Dependent Variables*. Thousand Oaks, CA: Sage Publications.

Maddala, G. S. 1992. *Introduction to Econometrics*. 2d ed. New York: Macmillan.

McDonald, J. and R. Moffitt. 1980. The use of tobit analysis. *Review of Economics and Statistics* 62: 318–321.

Stewart, M. B. 1983. On least squares estimation when the dependent variable is grouped. *Review of Economic Studies* 50: 737–753.

Tobin, J. 1958. Estimation of relationships for limited dependent variables. *Econometrica* 26: 24–36.

Also See

Complementary:	[R] **linktest**, [R] **lrtest**, [R] **predict**, [R] **sw**, [R] **test**, [R] **testnl**, [R] **vce**, [R] **xi**
Related:	[R] **heckman**, [R] **oprobit**, [R] **regress**, [R] **_robust**, [R] **svy estimators**, [R] **xtintreg**, [R] **xttobit**
Background:	[U] **16.5 Accessing coefficients and standard errors**, [U] **23 Estimation and post-estimation commands**, [U] **23.11 Obtaining robust variance estimates**, [U] **23.12 Obtaining scores**

Title

> **tokenize** — Divide strings into tokens

Syntax

<u>tokenize</u> ["] [*string*] ["] [, <u>p</u>arse("*pchars*")]

Description

tokenize divides *string* into tokens, storing the result in `` `1´ ``, `` `2´ ``, ... (the positional local macros). Tokens are determined based on the parsing characters *pchars* which defaults to a space if not specified.

Options

parse("*pchars***")** specifies the parsing characters. If **parse()** is not specified, **parse(" ")** is assumed, and thus *string* is split into words.

Remarks

tokenize may be used as an alternative or supplement to the **syntax** command for parsing command line arguments. Most often, it is used to further process the local macros created by **syntax** as shown below.

```
program define myprog
        version 6.0
        syntax [varlist] [if] [in]
        marksample touse

        tokenize `varlist´
        local first `1´
        macro shift
        local rest `*´

        ...

end
```

▷ Example

We interactively apply **tokenize** and then display several of the numbered macros to illustrate how the command works.

```
. tokenize some words
. di "1=|`1´|, 2=|`2´|, 3=|`3´|"
1=|some|, 2=|words|, 3=||
. tokenize "some more words"
. di "1=|`1´|, 2=|`2´|, 3=|`3´|, 4=|`4´|"
1=|some|, 2=|more|, 3=|words|, 4=||
. local str "A strange++string"
. tokenize `str´
```

```
. di "1=|`1´|, 2=|`2´|, 3=|`3´|"
1=|A|, 2=|strange++string|, 3=||

. tokenize `str´, parse(" +")

. di "1=|`1´|, 2=|`2´|, 3=|`3´|, 4=|`4´|, 5=|`5´|, 6=|`6´|"
1=|A|, 2=|strange|, 3=|+|, 4=|+|, 5=|string|, 6=||

. tokenize `str´, parse("+")

. di "1=|`1´|, 2=|`2´|, 3=|`3´|, 4=|`4´|, 5=|`5´|, 6=|`6´|"
1=|A strange|, 2=|+|, 3=|+|, 4=|string|, 5=||, 6=||

. tokenize

. di "1=|`1´|, 2=|`2´|, 3=|`3´|"
1=||, 2=||, 3=||
```

These examples illustrate that the quotes surrounding the string are optional; the space parsing character is not saved in the numbered macros; non-space parsing characters are saved in the numbered macros together with the tokens being parsed; and more than one parsing character may be specified. Also, when called with no string argument, tokenize resets the local numbered macros to empty.

◁

Also See

Complementary:	[R] **syntax**
Related:	[R] **gettoken**, [R] **macro**
Background:	[U] **21 Programming Stata**

Title

> **touch** — Change a file's type and creator (Macintosh only)

Syntax

touch $\left[\,"\,\right]$ *filename*$_1$ $\left[\,"\,\right]$, like($\left[\,"\,\right]$ *filename*$_2$ $\left[\,"\,\right]$)

Description

The **touch** command sets the characteristics of *filename*$_1$ to be the same as those of *filename*$_2$. These characteristics control what happens when you double-click on a file.

This command is rarely used. On the Macintosh, file characteristics are set automatically when the file is created. When you copy files from other systems—such as a Windows computer—you may wish to set the characteristics by hand.

See [GSM] **D. More on Stata for Macintosh** for an alternative method for changing file characteristics.

Options

like(*filename*$_2$) specifies that the characteristics of *filename*$_1$ are to be the same as those for *filename*$_2$. You must specify this option.

Remarks

This command is exceedingly technical and exceedingly powerful. Most Macintosh users will never need it. If you copy files from other computers, however, it will allow you to set the characteristics that are otherwise not available.

▷ Example

Perhaps you use SoftPC on your Macintosh to run DOS programs. A friend of yours, also a Stata user, has created a dataset called **hisdata.dta** on his DOS computer and gives you a DOS diskette. Using SoftPC, you copy the file to your hard disk. Outside of SoftPC, when you look at your disk, you note that **hisdata.dta** has the SoftPC icon attached to it. You wish it had the Stata **.dta** icon and also wish that double-clicking on the file's icon would invoke Stata. You have another dataset in the folder called **mydata.dta** that was created on the Macintosh and so has the correct icon. From inside Stata, you type

```
. touch hisfile.dta, like(myfile.dta)
```

The file's characteristics are now changed, although the Finder will not notice the change until the next time the folder is opened. So, if the folder is already open, you must close and reopen it to see the new icon.

◁

Also See

Background:　　[U] **14.6 File-naming conventions,**

　　　　　　　　　　[GSM] **D. More on Stata for Macintosh**

Title

---

tsreport — Report time-series aspects of dataset or estimation sample

---

Syntax

tsreport [if *exp*] [in *range*] [, report report0 list panel]

tsreport typed without options produces no output, but does provide its standard saved results.

Description

tsreport reports on time gaps in a sample of observations. A one-line statement displaying a count of the gaps is provided by the report option and a full list of records that follow gaps is provided by the list option. A return value r(N_gaps) is always set to the number of gaps in the sample.

Options

report specifies that a count of the number of gaps in the time series be reported, if any gaps exist.

report0 specifies that the count of gaps be reported even if there are no gaps.

list specifies that a tabular list of gaps be displayed.

panel specifies that panel changes are not to be counted as gaps. Whether panel changes are counted as gaps usually depends on how the calling command handles panels.

Remarks

Time-series commands sometimes require that observations be on a fixed time interval with no gaps, or that the behavior of the command might be different if the time series contains gaps. tsreport provides a tool for reporting the gaps in a sample.

▷ Example

The following monthly panel data has two panels and a missing month (March) in the second panel.

```
. list edlevel month income

        edlevel     month    income
  1.          1    1998m1       687
  2.          1    1998m2       783
  3.          1    1998m3       790
  4.          2    1998m1      1435
  5.          2    1998m2      1522
  6.          2    1998m4      1532
```

Invoking `tsreport` without the `panel` option, we get the following report:

```
. tsreport, report
Number of gaps in sample:  2   (gap count includes panel changes)
```

We could get a list of gaps and better see what has been counted as a gap by using the `list` option:

```
. tsreport, report list
Number of gaps in sample:  2   (gap count includes panel changes)
Observations with preceding time gaps
(gaps include panel changes)
----------+----------------------
   Record |    edlevel       month
----------+----------------------
        4 |          2      1998m1
        6 |          2      1998m4
----------+----------------------
```

We now see why `tsreport` is reporting two gaps. It is counting the known gap in March of the second panel and also counting the change from the first to the second panel. (If we are programmers writing a procedure that does not account for panels, a change from one panel to the next represents a break in the time series just as a gap in the data does.)

We may prefer that the changes in panels not be counted as gaps. We obtain a count without the panel change by using the `panel` option:

```
. tsreport, report panel
Number of gaps in sample:  1
```

Or, to obtain a fuller report, we type

```
. tsreport, report list panel
Number of gaps in sample:  1
Observations with preceding time gaps
----------+----------------------
   Record |    edlevel       month
----------+----------------------
        6 |          2      1998m4
----------+----------------------
```

◁

Saved Results

`tsreport` saves in `r()`:

Scalars
    `r(N_gaps)`   number of gaps in sample

Also See

Complementary: [R] **tsset**

Background: [U] **14.4.3 Time-series varlists,**
                [U] **15.5.3 Time-series formats,**
                [U] **27.3 Time series,**
                [U] **29.12 Models with time-series data**

Title

tsrevar — Time-series operator programming command

Syntax

tsrevar $\left[varlist\right]$ $\left[\text{if } exp\right]$ $\left[\text{in } range\right]$ $\left[, \text{substitute list}\right]$

tsrevar is for use with time-series data. You must tsset your data before using tsrevar; see [R] **tsset**.

Description

tsrevar, substitute takes a variable list that might contain *op.varname* combinations and substitutes real variables that are equivalent for the combinations. For instance, the original *varlist* might be "gnp L.gnp r" and tsrevar, substitute would create *newvar = L.gnp* and create the equivalent varlist "gnp *newvar* r". This new varlist could then be used with commands that do not otherwise support time-series operators or it could be used in a program to make execution faster at the expense of using more memory.

tsrevar, substitute might create no new variables, one new variable, or many new variables, depending on the number of *op.varname* combinations appearing in *varlist*. Any new variables created are temporary variables. The new, equivalent varlist is returned in r(varlist). Note that the new varlist has a one-to-one correspondence with the original *varlist*.

tsrevar, list does something different. It returns in r(varlist) the list of base variable names of *varlist* with the time-series operators removed. tsrevar, list creates no new variables. For instance, if the original *varlist* were "gnp l.gnp l2.gnp r l.cd", then r(varlist) would contain "gnp r cd". This is useful for programmers who might want, in their programs, to keep just the variables corresponding to *varlist*.

Options

substitute specifies that tsrevar is to resolve *op.varname* combinations by creating temporary variables as described above. substitute is the default action taken by tsrevar; you do not need to specify the option.

list specifies that tsrevar is return in r(varname) the list of base names.

▷ Example

```
. tsrevar l.gnp d.gnp r
```

creates two new temporary variables containing the values for l.gnp and d.gnp. The variable r appears in the new variable list, but does not require a temporary variable.

The resulting variable list is

```
. di "`r(varlist)'"
__00014P __00014Q r
```

213

We can see the results by listing the new variables alongside the original value of **gnp**.

```
. list gnp `r(varlist)´  in 1/5
         gnp    __00014P   __00014Q        r
  1.     128          .          .      3.2
  2.     135        128          7      3.8
  3.     132        135         -3      2.6
  4.     138        132          6      3.9
  5.     145        138          7      4.2
```

Remember that temporary variables automatically vanish when the program concludes.

If we had needed only the base variable names, we could have specified

```
. tsrevar l.gnp d.gnp r, list
. di "`r(varlist)´"
gnp r
```

The ordering of the list will probably be different from the original list; base variables are listed only once and will be listed in the order in which they appear in the dataset.

◁

□ Technical Note

tsrevar, substitute is smart and avoids creating duplicate variables. Consider

```
. tsrevar gnp l.gnp r cd l.cd l.gnp
```

Note that **l.gnp** appears twice in the varlist. **tsrevar** will create only one new variable for **l.gnp** and the use that new variable twice in the resulting **r(varlist)**. Moreover, **tsrevar** will even do this across multiple calls:

```
. tsrevar gnp l.gnp cd l.cd
. tsrevar cpi l.gnp
```

Note that **l.gnp** appears in two separate calls. At the first call, **tsrevar** will create a temporary variable corresponding to **l.gnp**. At the second call, **tsrevar** will remember what it has done and use that same, previously created temporary variable for **l.gnp** again.

□

Saved Results

tsrevar saves in **r()**:

Macros
    r(varlist)   the modified variable list or list of base variable names

Also See

Related: [R] **syntax**, [R] **unab**

Background: [U] **14 Language syntax**,
                   [U] **14.4.3 Time-series varlists**,
                   [U] **21 Programming Stata**

Title

> **tsset** — Declare dataset to be time-series data

Syntax

> tsset [*panelvar*] *timevar* [, <u>f</u>ormat(%*fmt*)
>
>   { <u>d</u>aily | <u>w</u>eekly | <u>m</u>onthly | <u>q</u>uarterly | <u>h</u>alfyearly | <u>y</u>early | <u>g</u>eneric }]
>
> tsset
>
> tsset, clear
>
> tsfill [, <u>f</u>ull]

Description

    tsset declares the data a time series and designates that *timevar* represents time. *timevar* must take on integer values. If *panelvar* is also specified, the dataset is declared to be a cross section of time series (e.g., time series of different countries). **tsset** must be used before time-series operators may be used in expressions and varlists. After **tsset**, the data will be sorted on *timevar* or on *panelvar timevar*.

    If you have annual data with the variable **year** representing time, using **tsset** is as simple as

    . tsset year, yearly

although you could omit the **yearly** option because it affects only how results are displayed.

    tsset without arguments displays how the data is currently **tsset** and it re-sorts the data on *timevar* or on *panelvar timevar* if it is sorted differently than that.

    tsset, clear is a rarely used programmer's command to declare that the data is no longer a time series.

    tsfill is for use after **tsset** to fill in missing times with missing observations. For instance, perhaps observations for *timevar* = 1, 3, 5, 6, ..., 22 exist. **tsfill** would create observations for *timevar* = 2 and *timevar* = 4 containing all missing values. There is seldom reason to do this because Stata's time-series operators work on the basis of *timevar* and not observation number. Referring to **L.gnp** to obtain lagged **gnp** values would correctly produce a missing value for *timevar* = 3 even if the data were not filled in. Referring to **L2.gnp** would correctly return the value of **gnp** in the first observation for *timevar* = 3 even if the data were not filled in.

Options

    format(%*fmt*), **daily**, **weekly**, **monthly**, **quarterly**, **halfyearly**, **yearly**, and **generic** deal with how *timevar* will be subsequently displayed—which **%t** format, if any, will be placed on *timevar*. Whether *timevar* is formatted is optional; all **tsset** requires is that *timevar* take on integer values.

The optional format states how *timevar* is measured (for instance, *timevar* = 5 might mean the fifth day of January 1960, or the fifth week of January 1960, or the fifth something else) and how you want it displayed (*timevar* = 5 might be displayed 05jan1960, 1960–5, or in a host of other ways.) In addition, the format makes the `tin()` and `twithin()` selection functions work so that later, after `tsset`ing the data, you can type things like `regress ... if tin(1jan1998,1apr1998)` to run the regression on the subsample 1jan1998 ≤ *timevar* ≤ 1apr1998.

Formatting is accomplished by placing a `%t` format on *timevar*. You can do it yourself or you can ask `tsset` to do it.

The time scales `%t` understands are daily (`%td`, 0 = 1jan1960), weekly (`%tw`, 0 = 1960w1), monthly (`%tm`, 0 = 1960m1), quarterly (`%tq`, 0 = 1960q1), halfyearly (`%th`, 0 = 1960h1), yearly (`%ty`, 1960 = 1960), and generic (`%tg`, 0 = ?).

Say *timevar* is recorded in Stata-quarterly units, meaning 0 = 1960q1, 1 = 1960q2, etc. (Perhaps your data starts in 1990q1; then the first observation has *timevar* = 120.) You could format *timevar* and then `tsset` your data,

. `format` *timevar* `%tq`

. `tsset` *timevar*

or you could `tsset` your data and then format *timevar*,

. `tsset` *timevar*

. `format` *timevar* `%tq`

or you could `tsset` your data specifying `tsset`'s `format()` option,

. `tsset` *timevar*, `format(%tq)`

or you could `tsset` your data specifying `tsset`'s `quarterly` option

. `tsset` *timevar*, `quarterly`

These alternatives yield the same result; use whichever appeals. See [U] **27.3 Time series** and [U] **15.5.3 Time-series formats** for more information on the `%t` format and the advantages of setting it.

`clear` is for use with `tsset`; `tsset, clear` is a rarely used programmer's command to declare that the data is no longer a time series.

`full` is for use with `tsfill` and affects the outcome only if a *panelvar* has been previously `tsset`.

By default with panel data, `tsfill` fills in observations for each panel according to the minimum and maximum values of *timevar* for the panel. Thus, if the first panel spanned the times 5–20 and the second panel the times 1–15, after `tsfill` they would still span the same time periods; observations would be created to fill in any missing times from 5 through 20 in the first panel and from 1 through 15 in the second.

If `full` is specified, observations will be created so that both panels span the period 1 through 20, the overall minimum and maximum of *timevar* across panels.

Remarks

`tsset` sets *timevar* so that time-series operated variables such as `l.gnp` are understood in varlists and expressions. When you refer to `l.gnp`, you are referring to the value of `gnp` one time unit before the current observation, which is not necessarily the same as referring to the previous observation because the previous time might be missing entirely from the dataset. There are two requirements you must satisfy for operators such as `l.gnp` to work:

1. the data must be `tsset`, and

2. the data must be sorted by *timevar* or, if it is a cross-sectional time-series dataset, by *panelvar timevar*.

`tsset` handles both requirements. As you use Stata, however, you may later use a command that re-sorts that data and, if you do, the time-series operators will refuse to work:

```
. tsset time
(output omitted )
. regress y x l.x
(output omitted )
. (you continue to use Stata and, sometime later:)
. regress y x l.x
not sorted
r(5);
```

In that case, typing `tsset` without arguments will reestablish the sort order:

```
. tsset
(output omitted )
. regress y x l.x
(output omitted )
```

In this case, typing `tsset` is the same as typing `sort time`. Had we previously `tsset country time`, however, typing `tsset` would be the same as typing `sort country time`. You can type the `sort` command or type `tsset` without arguments; it makes no difference.

▷ Example

You have monthly data on personal income. Variable `month` records the time of an observation:

```
. list
              t     income
  1.          1       1153
  2.          2       1181
(output omitted )
  9.          9       1282
. tsset t
        time variable:  t, 1 to 9
. regress income l.income
(output omitted )
```

◁

▷ Example

In the above example, it is not important that `t` start at 1. The `t` variable could just as well be recorded 21, 22, ..., 29, or 426, 427, ..., 434, or any other way we liked. What is important is that the difference in `t` between observations when there are no gaps is 1.

Although how time is measured makes no difference, Stata has formats to display time prettily if it is recorded in certain ways. In particular, Stata likes time variables with 1jan1960 recorded as 0. In our example above, if our first observation is July 1995, such that $t = 1$ corresponds to July 1995, then we could make a time variable that fits Stata's preference by typing

```
. gen newt = m(1995m7) + t - 1
```

`m()` is the function that returns month equivalent; `m(1995m6)` evaluates to the constant 425, meaning 425 months after January 1960. We now have variable `newt` containing

```
. list t newt income

              t     newt    income
  1.          1      426      1153
  2.          2      427      1181
  3.          3      428      1208
(output omitted)
  9.          9      434      1282
```

If we put a `%tm` format on `newt`, it will list more prettily:

```
. format newt %tm

. list t newt income

              t     newt    income
  1.          1   1995m7      1153
  2.          2   1995m8      1181
  3.          3   1995m9      1208
(output omitted)
  9.          9   1996m3      1282
```

We could now `tsset newt` rather than `t`:

```
. tsset newt
        time variable:  newt, 1995m7 to 1996m3
```

◁

▷ Example

Perhaps we have the same time-series data but with no time variable at all:

```
. list income

        income
  1.      1153
  2.      1181
  3.      1208
  4.      1272
  5.      1236
  6.      1297
  7.      1265
  8.      1230
  9.      1282
```

Pretend we know that the first observation corresponds to July 1995 and continues without gaps. We can create a monthly time variable and format it by typing

```
. gen t = m(1995m7) + _n - 1
. format t %tm
```

We can now `tsset` our data and `list` it:

```
. tsset t
        time variable:  t, 1995m7 to 1996m3
```

```
. list t income

            t       income
   1.    1995m7       1153
   2.    1995m8       1181
   3.    1995m9       1208
   4.   1995m10       1272
   (output omitted )
   9.    1996m3       1282
```
◁

❑ Technical Note

Your data does not have to be monthly. Stata understands daily, weekly, monthly, quarterly, halfyearly, and yearly data. Correspondingly, there are the d(), w(), m(), q(), h(), and y() functions and there are the %td, %tw, %tm, %tq, %th, and %ty formats. Here is what we would have typed in the above examples had our data been on a different time scale:

Daily: pretend your t variable had t=1 corresponding to 15mar1993
```
. gen newt = d(15mar1993) + t - 1
. format newt %td
. tsset newt
```

Weekly: pretend your t variable had t=1 corresponding to 1994w1:
```
. gen newt = w(1994w1) + t - 1
. format newt %tw
. tsset newt
```

Monthly: pretend your t variable had t=1 corresponding to 2004m7:
```
. gen newt = m(2004m7) + t - 1
. format newt %tm
. tsset newt
```

Quarterly: pretend your t variable had t=1 corresponding to 1994q1:
```
. gen newt = q(1994q1) + t - 1
. format newt %tq
. tsset newt
```

Halfyearly: pretend your t variable had t=1 corresponding to 1921h2:
```
. gen newt = h(1921h2) + t - 1
. format newt %th
. tsset newt
```

Yearly: pretend your t variable had t=1 corresponding to 1842:
```
. gen newt = y(1842) + t - 1
. format newt %ty
. tsset newt
```

In each of the above examples, we subtracted one from our time variable in constructing the new time variable newt because we assumed that our starting time value was 1. For the quarterly example, if our starting time value had been 5 and that corresponded to 1994q1 we would have typed

```
. gen newt = q(1994q1) + t - 5
```

Had our initial time value been $t = 742$ and this corresponded to 1994q1, we would have typed

```
. gen newt = q(1994q1) + t - 742
```

The %td, %tw, %tm, %tq, %th, and %ty formats can display the date in the form you want; when you type, for instance, %td, you are specify the *default* daily format, which produces dates of the form 15apr2002. If you wanted that to be displayed as "April 15, 2002", %td can do that; see [U] **27.3 Time series**. Similarly, all the other %t formats can be modified to produce the results you want.

❑

▷ Example

Your data might include a time variable that is encoded into a string. Below, each monthly observation is identified by string variable `yrmo` containing the year and month of the observation, sometimes with punctuation in between:

```
. list yrmo income

             yrmo     income
  1.        1995 7      1153
  2.        1995 8      1181
  3.        1995,9      1208
  4.       1995 10      1272
  5.       1995/11      1236
  6.       1995,12      1297
  7.        1996-1      1265
  8.        1996.2      1230
  9.      1996 Mar      1282
```

The first step is to convert the string to a numeric representation. That is easy using the `monthly()` function; see [U] **27.3 Time series**.

```
. gen mdate = monthly(yrmo, "ym")
. list yrmo mdate income

             yrmo    mdate    income
  1.        1995 7      426      1153
  2.        1995 8      427      1181
  3.        1995,9      428      1208
(output omitted )
  9.      1996 Mar      434      1282
```

Our new variable, `mdate`, contains the number of months from January, 1960. Now having numeric variable `mdate`, we can `tsset` the data:

```
. format mdate %tm
. tsset mdate
        time variable:  mdate, 1995m7 to 1996m3
```

In fact, we can combine the two and type

```
. tsset mdate, format(%tm)
        time variable:  mdate, 1995m7 to 1996m3
```

or, even easier type

```
. tsset mdate, monthly
        time variable:  mdate, 1995m7 to 1996m3
```

We do not have to bother to format the time variable at all, but formatting makes it display more prettily:

```
. list yrmo mdate income

             yrmo     mdate    income
  1.        1995 7    1995m7      1153
  2.        1995 8    1995m8      1181
  3.        1995,9    1995m9      1208
  4.       1995 10   1995m10      1272
  5.       1995/11   1995m11      1236
  6.       1995,12   1995m12      1297
  7.        1996-1    1996m1      1265
  8.        1996.2    1996m2      1230
  9.      1996 Mar    1996m3      1282
```

◁

❑ Technical Note

In addition to the `monthly()` function for translating strings to monthly dates, Stata has `daily()`, `weekly()`, `quarterly()`, `halfyearly()`, and `yearly()`. Stata also has the `yw()`, `ym()`, `yq()`, and `yh()` functions to convert from two numeric time variables to a Stata time variable. For example, `gen qdate = yq(year,qtr)` takes the variable `year` containing year values, and the variable `qtr` containing quarter values (1–4), and produces the variable `qdate` containing the number of quarters since 1960q1. See [U] **27.3 Time series**.

❑

▷ Example

Gaps in the time series cause no difficulties:

```
. list yrmo income

                yrmo     income
1.              1995 7     1153
2.              1995 8     1181
3.             1995/11     1236
4.             1995,12     1297
5.             1996-1      1265
6.            1996 Mar     1282
. gen mdate = monthly(yrmo,"ym")

. tsset mdate, monthly
        time variable:  mdate, 1995m7 to 1996m3, but with gaps
```

Once the data have been `tsset`, we can use the time-series operators. The D operator specifies first (or higher order) differences:

```
. list mdate income d.income

      mdate    income   D.income
1.    1995m7     1153          .
2.    1995m8     1181         28
3.    1995m11    1236          .
4.    1995m12    1297         61
5.    1996m1     1265        -32
6.    1996m3     1282          .
```

You can use the operators in an expression or varlist context; you do not have to create a new variable to hold `D.income`. You can use `D.income` with the `list` command, or with the `regress` command, or with any other Stata command that allows time-series varlists.

◁

▷ Example

We stated above that gaps were no problem and that is true as far as operators are concerned. You might, however, need to fill in the gaps for some analysis, say by interpolation. This is easy to do with `tsfill` and `ipolate`. `tsfill` will create the missing observations and then `ipolate` (see [R] **ipolate**) will fill them in. Staying with the example above, we can fill in the time series by typing

```
. tsfill
```

```
. list mdate income

          mdate     income
  1.      1995m7       1153
  2.      1995m8       1181
  3.      1995m9          .              ← new
  4.     1995m10          .              ← new
  5.     1995m11       1236
  6.     1995m12       1297
  7.      1996m1       1265
  8.      1996m2          .              ← new
  9.      1996m3       1282
```

We listed the data after `tsfill` just to show you the role `tsfill` plays in this. `tsfill` created the observations. We can now use `ipolate` to fill them in:

```
. ipolate income mdate, gen(ipinc)
. list mdate income ipinc

          mdate     income      ipinc
  1.      1995m7       1153       1153
  2.      1995m8       1181       1181
  3.      1995m9          .   1199.333
  4.     1995m10          .   1217.667
  5.     1995m11       1236       1236
  6.     1995m12       1297       1297
  7.      1996m1       1265       1265
  8.      1996m2          .     1273.5
  9.      1996m3       1282       1282
```

◁

Panel data

▷ Example

Now let us assume that we have time series on annual income and that we have the series for two groups: individuals who have not completed high school (`edlevel` = 1) and individuals who have (`edlevel` = 2).

```
. list edlevel year income

        edlevel      year     income
  1.          1      1988      14500
  2.          1      1989      14750
  3.          1      1990      14950
  4.          1      1991      15100
  5.          2      1989      22100
  6.          2      1990      22200
  7.          2      1992      22800
```

We declare the data to be a panel by typing

```
. tsset edlevel year, yearly
       panel variable:  edlevel, 1 to 2
        time variable:  year, 1988 to 1992, but with a gap
```

Having `tsset` the data, we can now use time-series operators. The difference operator, for example, can be used to list annual changes in income:

```
. list edlevel year income d.income

         edlevel       year      income   D.income
  1.           1        1988       14500        .
  2.           1        1989       14750       250
  3.           1        1990       14950       200
  4.           1        1991       15100       150
  5.           2        1989       22100        .
  6.           2        1990       22200       100
  7.           2        1992       22800        .
```

We see that in addition to producing missing values due to missing times, the difference operator correctly produced a missing value at the start of each panel. Once we have **tsset** our panel data, we can use time-series operators and be assured that they will handle missing time periods and panel changes correctly.

◁

▷ Example

As with nonpanel time series, we can use **tsfill** to fill in gaps in a panel time series. Continuing with our example data:

```
. tsfill

. list edlevel year income

         edlevel       year      income
  1.           1        1988       14500
  2.           1        1989       14750
  3.           1        1990       14950
  4.           1        1991       15100
  5.           2        1989       22100
  6.           2        1990       22200
  7.           2        1991         .        ← new
  8.           2        1992       22800
```

We could instead ask **tsfill** to produce fully balanced panels using the **full** option:

```
. tsfill, full

. list edlevel year income

          edlevel      year      income
  1.           1        1988       14500
  2.           1        1989       14750
  3.           1        1990       14950
  4.           1        1991       15100
  5.           1        1992         .        ← new
  6.           2        1988         .        ← new
  7.           2        1989       22100
  8.           2        1990       22200
  9.           2        1991         .        ← new
 10.           2        1992       22800
```

◁

Saved Results

tsset saves in r():

Scalars

r(tmin)	minimum time	r(imin)	minimum panel id
r(tmax)	maximum time	r(imax)	maximum panel id

Macros

r(timevar)	time variable	r(tmins)	formatted minimum time
r(panelvar)	panel variable	r(tmaxs)	formatted maximum time

Also See

Background: [U] **14.4.3 Time-series varlists**,
[U] **15.5.3 Time-series formats**,
[U] **27.3 Time series**,
[U] **29.12 Models with time-series data**

Title

ttest — Mean comparison tests

Syntax

ttest *varname* = # [if *exp*] [in *range*] [, level(*#*)]

ttest *varname*$_1$ = *varname*$_2$ [if *exp*] [in *range*] [, unequal unpaired welch
  level(*#*)]

ttest *varname* [if *exp*] [in *range*], by(*groupvar*) [unequal welch level(*#*)]

ttesti #$_{obs}$ #$_{mean}$ #$_{sd}$ #$_{val}$ [, level(*#*)]

ttesti #$_{obs,1}$ #$_{mean,1}$ #$_{sd,1}$ #$_{obs,2}$ #$_{mean,2}$ #$_{sd,2}$ [, unequal welch level(*#*)]

Description

ttest performs *t* tests on the equality of means. In the first form, ttest tests that *varname* has a mean of #. In the second form, ttest tests that *varname*$_1$ and *varname*$_2$ have the same mean. Data are assumed to be paired, but unpaired changes this assumption. In the third form, ttest tests that *varname* has the same mean within the two groups defined by *groupvar*.

ttesti is the immediate form of ttest; see [U] **22 Immediate commands**.

For the equivalent of a two-sample *t* test with sampling weights (pweights), use the svymean command with the by() option and then use svylc; see [R] **svymean** and [R] **svylc**.

Options

unequal indicates that the unpaired data are not to be assumed to have equal variances.

unpaired indicates that the data are to be treated as unpaired.

welch indicates that the approximate degrees of freedom for the test should be obtained from Welch's formula rather than Satterthwaite's approximation formula (1946), which is the default when unequal is specified. This option is not appropriate unless unequal is specified.

level(*#*) specifies the confidence level, in percent, for confidence intervals. The default is level(95) or as set by set level; see [U] **23.5 Specifying the width of confidence intervals**.

Remarks

▷ Example

In the first form, ttest tests whether the mean of the sample is equal to a known constant under the assumption of unknown variance. Assume you have a sample of 74 automobiles. For each automobile you know its average mileage rating. You wish to test whether the overall average for the sample is 20 miles per gallon.

```
. ttest mpg=20

One-sample t test

------------------------------------------------------------------------------
Variable |    Obs        Mean    Std. Err.   Std. Dev.   [95% Conf. Interval]
---------+--------------------------------------------------------------------
     mpg |     74     21.2973    .6725511    5.785503     19.9569    22.63769
------------------------------------------------------------------------------
Degrees of freedom: 73
                              Ho: mean(mpg) = 20
       Ha: mean < 20               Ha: mean ~= 20             Ha: mean > 20
         t =   1.9289                t =   1.9289               t =   1.9289
     P < t =   0.9712            P > |t| =   0.0576         P > t =   0.0288
```

The test indicates that the underlying mean is not 20 with a significance level of 5.8%.

◁

▷ Example

You are testing the effectiveness of a new fuel additive. You run an experiment with 12 cars. You run the cars without and with the fuel treatment. The results of the experiment are

Without Treatment	With Treatment	Without Treatment	With Treatment
20	24	18	17
23	25	24	28
21	21	20	24
25	22	24	27
18	23	23	21
17	18	19	23

Creating two variables called mpg1 and mpg2 representing mileage without and with the treatment, respectively, we can test the equality of means by typing

```
. ttest mpg1=mpg2

Paired t test

------------------------------------------------------------------------------
Variable |    Obs        Mean    Std. Err.   Std. Dev.   [95% Conf. Interval]
---------+--------------------------------------------------------------------
    mpg1 |     12          21    .7881701    2.730301    19.26525    22.73475
    mpg2 |     12       22.75    .9384465    3.250874    20.68449    24.81551
---------+--------------------------------------------------------------------
    diff |     12       -1.75    .7797144     2.70101    -3.46614   -.0338602
------------------------------------------------------------------------------
                 Ho: mean(mpg1 - mpg2) = mean(diff) = 0
    Ha: mean(diff) < 0           Ha: mean(diff) ~= 0         Ha: mean(diff) > 0
         t =  -2.2444                t =  -2.2444               t =  -2.2444
     P < t =   0.0232            P > |t| =   0.0463         P > t =   0.9768
```

You find that the means are statistically different from each other at any level greater than 4.6%.

◁

▷ Example

Let's pretend that the preceding data was collected not by running 12 cars but 24 cars: 12 cars with the additive and 12 without. Although you might be tempted to enter the data in the same way, you should not (see the technical note below). Instead, you enter the data as 24 observations on mpg with an additional variable, treated, taking on 1 if the car received the fuel treatment and 0 otherwise:

```
. ttest mpg, by(treated)
Two-sample t test with equal variances
------------------------------------------------------------------------------
   Group |     Obs       Mean    Std. Err.   Std. Dev.   [95% Conf. Interval]
---------+--------------------------------------------------------------------
       0 |      12         21    .7881701    2.730301    19.26525    22.73475
       1 |      12      22.75    .9384465    3.250874    20.68449    24.81551
---------+--------------------------------------------------------------------
combined |      24     21.875    .6264476    3.068954    20.57909    23.17091
---------+--------------------------------------------------------------------
    diff |                -1.75   1.225518               -4.291568    .7915684
------------------------------------------------------------------------------
Degrees of freedom: 22
                      Ho: mean(0) - mean(1) = diff = 0

  Ha: diff < 0               Ha: diff ~= 0               Ha: diff > 0
    t =  -1.4280               t =  -1.4280                t =  -1.4280
P < t =   0.0837      P > |t| =   0.1673        P > t =   0.9163
```

This time you do not find a statistically significant difference.

If you were not willing to assume that the variances were equal and you wanted to use Welch's formula, you could type

```
. ttest mpg, by(treated) unequal welch
Two-sample t test with unequal variances
------------------------------------------------------------------------------
   Group |     Obs       Mean    Std. Err.   Std. Dev.   [95% Conf. Interval]
---------+--------------------------------------------------------------------
       0 |      12         21    .7881701    2.730301    19.26525    22.73475
       1 |      12      22.75    .9384465    3.250874    20.68449    24.81551
---------+--------------------------------------------------------------------
combined |      24     21.875    .6264476    3.068954    20.57909    23.17091
---------+--------------------------------------------------------------------
    diff |                -1.75   1.225518               -4.28369     .7836901
------------------------------------------------------------------------------
Welch's degrees of freedom:  23.2465
                      Ho: mean(0) - mean(1) = diff = 0

  Ha: diff < 0               Ha: diff ~= 0               Ha: diff > 0
    t =  -1.4280               t =  -1.4280                t =  -1.4280
P < t =   0.0833      P > |t| =   0.1666        P > t =   0.9167
```

◁

❑ Technical Note

In two-group randomized designs, subjects will sometimes refuse the assigned treatment but still be measured for an outcome. In this case, care must be taken to specify the group properly. One might be tempted to let *varname* contain missing where the subject refused and thus let ttest drop such observations from the analysis. Zelen (1979) argues that it would be better to specify that the subject belongs to the group in which he or she was randomized even though such inclusion will dilute the measured effect.

❑

❑ Technical Note

There is a second, inferior way the data could have been organized in the preceding example. Remember, we ran a test on 24 cars, 12 without the additive and 12 with. Nevertheless, we could have entered the data in the same way as we did when we had 12 cars, each run without and with the additive; we could have created two variables—mpg1 and mpg2.

This is inferior because it suggests a connection that is not there. In the case of the 12-car experiment, there was most certainly a connection—it was the same car. In the 24-car experiment, however, it is arbitrary which mpg results appear next to which. Nevertheless, if your data is organized like this, ttest can accommodate you.

```
. ttest mpg1=mpg2, unpaired
Two-sample t test with equal variances
-------------------------------------------------------------------------
Variable |    Obs       Mean    Std. Err.   Std. Dev.  [95% Conf. Interval]
---------+---------------------------------------------------------------
   mpg1 |     12         21    .7881701    2.730301    19.26525   22.73475
   mpg2 |     12      22.75    .9384465    3.250874    20.68449   24.81551
---------+---------------------------------------------------------------
combined |     24     21.875    .6264476    3.068954    20.57909   23.17091
---------+---------------------------------------------------------------
   diff |              -1.75    1.225518                -4.291568    .7915684
-------------------------------------------------------------------------
Degrees of freedom: 22
                 Ho: mean(mpg1) - mean(mpg2) = diff = 0

  Ha: diff < 0                 Ha: diff ~= 0                 Ha: diff > 0
    t =  -1.4280                 t =  -1.4280                 t =  -1.4280
  P < t =   0.0837          P > |t| =   0.1673           P > t =   0.9163
```

❑

▷ Example

ttest can be used to test the equality of a pair of means; see [R] **oneway** for testing the equality of more than two means.

Suppose you have data on the 50 states. The data contains the median age of the population (medage) and the region of the country (region) for each state. Region 1 refers to the Northeast, region 2 to the North Central, region 3 to the South, and region 4 to the West. Using oneway, you can test the equality of all four means.

```
. oneway medage region
                     Analysis of Variance
    Source              SS         df      MS            F     Prob > F
-----------------------------------------------------------------------
Between groups      46.3961903      3    15.4653968     7.56    0.0003
Within groups       94.1237947     46    2.04616945
-----------------------------------------------------------------------
    Total          140.519985      49    2.8677548
Bartlett's test for equal variances:  chi2(3) =  10.5757  Prob>chi2 = 0.014
```

You find that the means are different. You, however, are only interested in testing whether the means for the East (region==1) and West (region==4) are different. You could use oneway:

```
. oneway medage region if region==1 | region==4
                        Analysis of Variance
     Source              SS          df       MS            F      Prob > F
--------------------------------------------------------------------------
Between groups       46.241247        1    46.241247      20.02    0.0002
Within groups        46.1969169      20    2.30984584
--------------------------------------------------------------------------
     Total           92.4381638      21    4.40181733
Bartlett's test for equal variances:  chi2(1) =   2.4679  Prob>chi2 = 0.116
```

Or you could use `ttest`:

```
. ttest medage if region==1 | region==4, by(region)
Two-sample t test with equal variances
```

Group	Obs	Mean	Std. Err.	Std. Dev.	[95% Conf. Interval]
NE	9	31.23333	.3411581	1.023474	30.44662 32.02005
West	13	28.28462	.4923577	1.775221	27.21186 29.35737
combined	22	29.49091	.4473059	2.098051	28.56069 30.42113
diff		2.948718	.6590372		1.57399 4.323445

```
Degrees of freedom: 20
                       Ho: mean(NE) - mean(West) = diff = 0

   Ha: diff < 0                Ha: diff ~= 0                Ha: diff > 0
     t =   4.4743               t =   4.4743                 t =   4.4743
   P < t =  0.9999           P > |t| =  0.0002            P > t =  0.0001
```

Note that the significance levels of both tests are the same.

⊲

Immediate form

▷ Example

`ttesti` is like `ttest` except that you specify summary statistics rather than variables as arguments. For instance, you are reading an article which reports the mean number of sunspots per month as 62.6 with a standard deviation of 15.8. There are 24 months of data. You wish to test whether the mean is 75:

```
. ttesti 24 62.6 15.8 75
One-sample t test
```

	Obs	Mean	Std. Err.	Std. Dev.	[95% Conf. Interval]
x	24	62.6	3.225161	15.8	55.92825 69.27175

```
Degrees of freedom: 23
                          Ho: mean(x) = 75

   Ha: mean < 75              Ha: mean ~= 75              Ha: mean > 75
     t =  -3.8448               t =  -3.8448                t =  -3.8448
   P < t =   0.0004          P > |t| =   0.0008          P > t =   0.9996
```

⊲

▷ Example

There is no immediate form of **ttest** with paired data since the test is also a function of the covariance, a number unlikely to be reported in any published source. For nonpaired data, however:

```
. ttesti 20 20 5  32 15 4

Two-sample t test with equal variances

---------------------------------------------------------------------------
         |    Obs      Mean    Std. Err.   Std. Dev.   [95% Conf. Interval]
---------+-----------------------------------------------------------------
       x |     20        20    1.118034           5    17.65993    22.34007
       y |     32        15    .7071068           4    13.55785    16.44215
---------+-----------------------------------------------------------------
combined |     52  16.92308    .6943785    5.007235    15.52905     18.3171
---------+-----------------------------------------------------------------
    diff |                 5    1.256135                2.476979    7.523021
---------------------------------------------------------------------------

Degrees of freedom: 50

                    Ho: mean(x) - mean(y) = diff = 0

     Ha: diff < 0               Ha: diff ~= 0               Ha: diff > 0
        t =   3.9805               t =   3.9805                t =   3.9805
    P < t =   0.9999          P > |t| =   0.0002           P > t =   0.0001
```

Had we typed **ttesti 20 20 5 32 15 4, unequal**, the test would have been under the assumption of unequal variances.

◁

Saved Results

ttest and **ttesti** save in **r()**:

Scalars

r(N_1)	sample size n_1	r(t)	t statistic
r(N_2)	sample size n_2	r(sd_1)	standard deviation for first variable
r(p_l)	lower one-sided p-value	r(sd_2)	standard deviation for second variable
r(p_u)	upper one-sided p-value	r(mu_1)	$\bar{x}_1$ mean for population 1
r(p)	two-sided p-value	r(mu_2)	$\bar{x}_2$ mean for population 2
r(se)	estimate of standard error	r(df_t)	degrees of freedom

Methods and Formulas

ttest and **ttesti** are implemented as ado-files.

See, for instance, Hoel (1984, 140–161) or Dixon and Massey (1983, 121–130) for an introduction and explanation of the calculation of these tests.

The test for $\mu = \mu_0$ for unknown σ is given by

$$t = \frac{(\bar{x} - \mu_0)\sqrt{n}}{s}$$

The statistic is distributed as Student's t with $n - 1$ degrees of freedom (Gosset 1908).

The test for $\mu_x = \mu_y$ when σ_x and σ_y are unknown but $\sigma_x = \sigma_y$ is given by

$$t = \frac{\overline{x} - \overline{y}}{\sqrt{\frac{(n_x - 1)s_x^2 + (n_y - 1)s_y^2}{n_x + n_y - 2}}\sqrt{\frac{1}{n_x} + \frac{1}{n_y}}}$$

The result is distributed as Student's t with $n_x + n_y - 2$ degrees of freedom.

One could perform `ttest` (without the `unequal` option) in a regression setting given that regression assumes a homoscedastic error model. In order to compare with the `ttest` command, denote the underlying observations on x and y by x_j, $j = 1, \ldots, n_x$, and y_j, $j = 1, \ldots, n_y$. In a regression framework, `ttest` without the `unequal` option is equivalent to creating a new variable z_j representing the stacked observations on x and y (so that $z_j = x_j$ for $j = 1, \ldots, n_x$ and $z_{n_x + j} = y_j$ for $j = 1, \ldots, n_y$) and then estimating the equation $z_j = \beta_0 + \beta_1 d_j + \epsilon_j$, where $d_j = 0$ for $j = 1, \ldots, n_x$ and $d_j = 1$ for $j = n_x + 1, \ldots, n_x + n_y$ (i.e., $d_j = 0$ when the z observations represent x, and $d_j = 1$ when the z observations represent y). The estimated value of β_1, b_1, will equal $\overline{y} - \overline{x}$ and the reported t statistic will be the same t statistic as given by the formula above.

The test for $\mu_x = \mu_y$ when σ_x and σ_y are unknown and $\sigma_x \neq \sigma_y$ is given by

$$t = \frac{\overline{x} - \overline{y}}{\sqrt{s_x^2/n_x + s_y^2/n_y}}$$

The result is distributed as Student's t with ν degrees of freedom, where ν is given by (using Satterthwaite's formula)

$$\frac{\left(s_x^2/n_x + s_y^2/n_y\right)^2}{\frac{\left(s_x^2/n_x\right)^2}{n_x - 1} + \frac{\left(s_y^2/n_y\right)^2}{n_y - 1}}$$

Or using Welch's formula (1947), the number of degrees of freedom is given by

$$-2 + \frac{\left(\frac{s_x^2}{n_x} + \frac{s_y^2}{n_y}\right)^2}{\frac{\left(\frac{s_x^2}{n_x}\right)^2}{n_x + 1} + \frac{\left(\frac{s_y^2}{n_y}\right)^2}{n_y + 1}}$$

The test for $\mu_x = \mu_y$ for matched observations (also known as paired observations, or correlated pairs or permanent components) is given by

$$t = \frac{\overline{d}\sqrt{n}}{s_d}$$

where $\overline{d}$ represents the mean of $x_i - y_i$ and s_d represents the standard deviation. The test statistic t is distributed as Student's t with $n - 1$ degrees of freedom.

Note that `ttest` without the `unpaired` option may also be performed in a regression setting since a paired comparison includes the assumption of constant variance. The `ttest` with unequal variance assumption does not lend itself to an easy representation in regression settings and is not discussed here. $\left(x_j - y_j\right) = \beta_0 + \epsilon_j$.

References

Dixon, W. J. and F. J. Massey, Jr. 1983. *Introduction to Statistical Analysis.* 4th ed. New York: McGraw–Hill.

Gosset, W. S. [Student, pseud.] 1908. The probable error of a mean. *Biometrika* 6: 1–25.

Hoel, P. G. 1984. *Introduction to Mathematical Statistics.* 5th ed. New York: John Wiley & Sons.

Satterthwaite, F. E. 1946. An approximate distribution of estimates of variance components. *Biometrics Bulletin* 2: 110–114.

Welch, B. L. 1947. The generalization of Student's problem when several different population variances are involved. *Biometrika* 34: 28–35.

Zelen, M. 1979. A new design for randomized clinical trials. *New England Journal of Medicine* 300: 1242–1245.

Also See

Related:	[R] **bitest**, [R] **ci**, [R] **hotel**, [R] **oneway**, [R] **sdtest**, [R] **signrank**, [R] **svylc**, [R] **svymean**
Background:	[U] **22 Immediate commands**

Title

> **tutorials** — Quick reference for Stata tutorials

Syntax

`tutorial` *name*

Description

`tutorial intro` presents an introductory tutorial to Stata.

`tutorial contents` lists the available official Stata tutorials.

`tutorial` followed by the name of a tutorial file presents that particular tutorial.

Remarks

Stata tutorials are introduced in [U] **9 Stata's on-line tutorials and sample datasets** and a list of the available official tutorials (as of the time of manual printing) is provided there. A current listing of official tutorials can be obtained with the `tutorial contents` command.

The tutorial command can also be used to execute tutorials written by others. For instance, Verbeek and Weesie (1998) provide a tutorial demonstrating Gaussian and Cauchy random walks. Since this tutorial was presented in the *Stata Technical Bulletin* you can easily obtain it; see [R] **net**.

Tutorial files end in the suffix `.tut` and must be placed in the Stata directory. You can determine the Stata directory by typing the command `sysdir`; see [R] **sysdir**. The Stata directory is the first one listed. Of course Stata's official tutorials are already in this directory. You only need to be concerned with this detail if you are installing additional tutorials.

Acknowledgments

We thank Jeroen Weesie, Utrecht University, Netherlands for making public the random walk tutorial of the late Albert Verbeek. Albert Verbeek contributed a great deal to the early development of Stata for which he will always be remembered.

References

Newton, H. J. and J. L. Harvill. 1997. *StatConcepts: A Visual Tour of Statistical Ideas*. Pacific Grove, CA: Duxbury Press.

Verbeek, A. and J. Weesie. 1998. tt7: Random walk tutorial. *Stata Technical Bulletin* 41: 46. Reprinted in *Stata Technical Bulletin Reprints*, vol. 7, p. 301.

Also See

Background: [U] **9 Stata's on-line tutorials and sample datasets**

Title

> **type** — Display contents of files

Syntax

$\underline{\text{type}}$ $\left[" \right]$ *filename* $\left[" \right]$ $\left[, \underline{\text{showtabs}} \right]$

Note: On Stata for Windows and Stata for Macintosh, double quotes must be used to enclose *filename* if the name contains blanks.

Description

type lists the contents of a file stored on disk. This command is similar to the DOS TYPE and Unix **more**(1) or **pg**(1) commands.

In Stata for Unix, **cat** is a synonym for **type**.

Options

showtabs requests that any tabs be displayed.

Remarks

> ▷ Example

You have raw data containing the level of Lake Victoria Nyanza and the number of sunspots during the years 1902–1921 stored in a file called **sunspots.raw**. You want to read this data into Stata using **infile**, but you cannot remember the order in which you entered the variables. You can find out by typing the data:

```
. type sunspots.raw
1902 -10    5    1903   13 24    1904   18 42
1905   15  63    1906   29 54    1907   21 62
1908   10  49    1909    8 44    1910    1 19
1911   -7   6    1912  -11  4    1913   -3  1
1914   -2  10    1915    4 47    1916   15 57
1917   35 104    1918   27 81    1919    8 64
1920    3  38    1921   -5 25
```

Looking at this output, you now remember that the variables are entered year, level, and number of sunspots. You can read this data by typing **infile year level spots using sunspots**.

If you had wanted to see the tabs in **sunspots.raw**, you could have typed

```
. type sunspots.raw, showtabs
1902 -10    5<T>1903   13 24<T>1904   18 42
1905   15  63<T>1906   29 54<T>1907   21 62
1908   10  49<T>1909    8 44<T>1910    1 19
1911   -7   6<T>1912  -11  4<T>1913   -3  1
1914   -2  10<T>1915    4 47<T>1916   15 57
1917   35 104<T>1918   27 81<T>1919    8 64
1920    3  38<T>1921   -5 25
```

◁

Also See

Related: [R] **cd**, [R] **copy**, [R] **dir**, [R] **erase**, [R] **mkdir**, [R] **shell**

Background: [U] **14.6 File-naming conventions**

Title

---
unab — Unabbreviate variable list

Syntax

Standard variable lists

> unab *lmacname* : [*varlist*] [, min(*#*) max(*#*) name(*string*)]

Variable lists that may contain time-series operators

> tsunab *lmacname* : [*varlist*] [, min(*#*) max(*#*) name(*string*)]

Description

unab expands and unabbreviates a *varlist* (see [U] **14.4 varlists**) of existing variables placing the result in the local macro *lmacname*. unab is a low-level parsing command. The syntax command is a high-level parsing command that, among other things, also unabbreviates variable lists; see [R] **syntax**.

The difference between unab and tsunab is that tsunab will allow time-series operators to modify the variables in *varlist*; see [U] **14.4.3 Time-series varlists**.

Options

min(*#*) specifies the minimum number of variables allowed. The default is min(1).

max(*#*) specifies the maximum number of variables allowed. The default is max(32000).

name(*string*) provides a label that is used when printing error messages.

Remarks

In most cases, the syntax command will automatically handle the unabbreviating of variable lists; see [R] **syntax**. In a few cases, unab will be needed to obtain unabbreviated variable lists.

▷ Example

The separate command (see [R] **separate**) provides an example of the use of unab. Its required option by(*byvar* | *exp*) takes either a variable name or an expression. This is not handled automatically by the syntax command.

In this case, the syntax command for separate takes the form

```
syntax varname [if] [in], BY(string) [ other options]
```

After syntax performs the command line parsing, the local variable by contains what the user entered for the option. We now need to determine if it is an existing variable name or an expression and if it is a variable name, we may need to expand it.

```
capture confirm var `by´
if _rc == 0 {
        unab by: `by´, max(1) name(by())
}
else {
        ( parse `by´ as an expression )
}
```

◁

▷ Example

We interactively demonstrate the **unab** command with the auto dataset.

```
. unab x : mpg wei for, name(myopt())
. display "`x´"
mpg weight foreign
. unab x : junk
junk not found
r(111);
. unab x : mpg wei, max(1) name(myopt())
myopt():  too many variables specified
          1 variable required
r(103);
. unab x : mpg wei, max(1) name(myopt()) min(0)
myopt():  too many variables specified
          0 or 1 variables required
r(103);
. unab x : mpg wei, min(3) name(myopt())
myopt():  too few variables specified
          3 or more variables required
r(102);
. unab x : mpg wei, min(3) name(myopt()) max(10)
myopt():  too few variables specified
          3 - 10 variables required
r(102);
. unab x : mpg wei, min(3) max(10)
mpg weight:
too few variables specified
r(102);
```

◁

▷ Example

If we created a time variable and used **tsset** to declare the dataset as time series, we can also expand time-series variable lists.

```
. gen time = _n
. tsset time
. tsunab mylist : l(1/3).mpg
. display "`mylist´"
L.mpg L2.mpg L3.mpg
. tsunab mylist : l(1/3).(price turn displ)
. di "`mylist´"
L.price L2.price L3.price L.turn L2.turn L3.turn L.displ L2.displ L3.displ
```

◁

Also See

Related: [R] syntax

Background: [U] **14 Language syntax,**
                  [U] **21 Programming Stata**

Title

> **update** — Update Stata

Syntax

update

update from *location*

update query [, from(*location*)]

update ado [, from(*location*) into(*dirname*)]

update executable [, from(*location*) into(*dirname*) force]

update all [, from(*location*)]

Description

The **update** command reports on the current update level and installs official updates to Stata. Official updates are updates to Stata as it was originally shipped from StataCorp, not the additions to Stata published in, for instance, the *Stata Technical Bulletin* (STB). Those additions are installed using the **net** command; see [R] **net**.

update without arguments reports on the update level of the currently installed Stata.

update from sets an update source. *location* is a directory name or URL. If you are on the Internet, type 'update from http://www.stata.com'. Updates may also be obtained from STB diskettes. In that case, type 'update from a:' (Windows) or 'update from :diskette:' (Macintosh). If you do not type **update from**, results for subsequent **update** commands are as if you typed **update from** http://www.stata.com.

update query compares the update level of the currently installed Stata with that available from the update source and displays a report.

update ado compares the update level of the official ado-files of the currently installed Stata with those available from the update source. If the currently installed ado-files need updating, **update ado** copies and installs files from the update source necessary to bring the ado-files up to date.

update executable compares the update level of the currently installed Stata executable with that available from the update source. If the currently installed Stata needs updating, **update executable** copies the new executable from the update source but the last step of the installation—erasing the old executable and renaming the new executable—is left for the user to perform. **update executable** displays instructions on how to do this.

update all does the same as **update ado** followed by **update executable**.

Options

from(*location*) specifies the location of the update source. The from() option may be specified on the individual **update** commands or it may be set by the **update from** command. Which you do makes no difference.

into(*dirname*) specifies the name of the directory into which the updates are to be copied. *dirname* may be specified as a directory name or as a `sysdir` codeword such as `UPDATES` or `STATA`; see [R] **sysdir**.

In the case of `update ado`, the default is `into(UPDATES)`, the official update directory. Network computer managers might want to specify `into()` if they want to copy down the updates but leave the last step—copying the files into the official directory—to do themselves.

In the case of `update executable`, the default is `into(STATA)`, the official Stata directory. Network computer managers might want to specify `into()` so that they could copy the update into another, more accessible directory. In that case, the last step of copying the new executable over the existing executable would be left for them to perform.

force is used with `update executable` to force downloading a new executable even if, based on the date comparison, Stata does not think it necessary. There is seldom a reason to specify this option. There is no such option for `update ado` because, if one wanted to force the reinstallation of all ado-file updates, one need only erase the `UPDATES` directory. You can type `sysdir list` to see where the `UPDATES` directory is on your computer; see [R] **sysdir**.

Remarks

update is used to update the two official components of Stata, its binary executable and its ado-files, from either of two official sources: *http://www.stata.com* or from an official STB diskette. Jumping ahead of the story, the easiest thing to do if you are connected to the Internet, is to type

```
. update all
```

and follow the instructions. If you are up to date, `update all` will do nothing. Otherwise, it will download whatever is necessary and display detailed instructions on what, if anything, needs to be done next. If you want to know what `update all` would do beforehand, type

```
. update query
```

update query will present a report comparing what you have installed with what is available and recommend that you do nothing or that you type `update ado` or that you type `update executable` or that you type `update all`.

If you want just a report on what you have installed without comparing to what is available, type

```
. update
```

update will show you what you have installed and where it is installed and recommend you type `update query` to compare that with what is available.

Before doing any of this, you can type

```
. update from http://www.stata.com
```

but that is not really necessary because *http://www.stata.com* is the default location. Updates are also available on official STB diskettes which can be obtained from Stata Corporation. If you are using an STB diskette, insert the diskette and type

```
. update from a:              Windows 98/95/NT
. update from :diskette:      Macintosh
```

Unix users can also update from diskette; see [GSU] **17 Updating Stata**.

Users of all operating systems may use the `update` command. In addition, Stata for Windows and Stata for Macintosh users may pull down **Help** and select **Official Updates**. The menu item does the same thing as the command, but it does not provide the file redirection option `into()`, which managers of networked computers may wish to use so that they can download the updates and then copy the files to the official locations for themselves.

For examples of using `update`, see

Windows 98/95/NT		
	from *http://www.stata.com*	[GSW] **19 Using the Internet** and
		[U] **32 Using the Internet to keep up to date**
	from diskette	[GSW] **20 Updating Stata**
Windows 3.1		
	from *http://www.stata.com*	(not possible)
	from diskette	[GSW] **20 Updating Stata**
Power Mac		
	from *http://www.stata.com*	[GSM] **19 Using the Internet** and
		[U] **32 Using the Internet to keep up to date**
	from diskette	[GSM] **20 Updating Stata**
Macintosh 680x0		
	from *http://www.stata.com*	(not possible)
	from diskette	[GSM] **20 Updating Stata**
Unix		
	from *http://www.stata.com*	[GSU] **16 Using the Internet** and
		[U] **32 Using the Internet to keep up to date**
	from diskette	[GSU] **17 Updating Stata**

Notes for multi-user system administrators

There are two types of updates that `update` downloads: ado-file updates and the binary executable update. Typically, there are only ado-file updates, but sometimes there are both and even more occasionally, there is only a binary update.

By default, `update` handles installation of the ado-file updates. There can be lots of small files associated with an ado-file update. `update` is very careful about how it does this. First, it downloads all the files you need to a temporary place, then it closes the connection to *http://www.stata.com*, then it checks them to make sure the files are complete, and only after all that does `update` copy them to the official place, which is the UPDATES directory; see [R] **sysdir**. This is all designed so that, should anything go wrong at any step along the way, no damage is done.

Updated binary executables, on the other hand, are just copied down and then it is left to the user to (1) exit Stata; (2) rename the current executable; (3) rename the updated executable; (4) try Stata; and (5) erase the old executable. `update` displays detailed instructions on how to do this and, as you can imagine, those instructions are simple.

In order for `update` to work as it typically would, however, `update` must have write access to both the STATA and UPDATES directories. The names of these directories can be obtained by typing `sysdir`. As system administrator, you must decide whether you are going to fire up Stata with such permissions (Unix users could first become superuser) and trust Stata to do the right thing. That is what we recommend you do, but we provide the `into()` option for those who do not trust our recommendation.

If you wish to perform the final copying by hand, obtain the new executable, if any, by typing

```
. update executable, into(.)
```

That will place the new executable in the current directory. You need no special permissions to do this step. Later, you can copy the file into the appropriate place and give it the appropriate name. Type update without arguments; the default output will make it clear where the file goes and what its name must be. When you copy the file, be sure to make it executable by everybody.

To obtain the ado-file updates, make a new, empty directory, and then place the updates into it.

```
. mkdir mydir
. update ado, into(mydir)
```

In this example, we chose to place the new, empty directory in the current directory under the name mydir. You need no special permissions to perform this step. Later, you can copy all the files in mydir to the official place. Type update without arguments; the default output will make it clear where the files go. When you copy the files, be sure to copy all of them and to make all of them readable by everybody.

Also See

Related:	[R] **net**, [R] **sysdir**
Background:	[U] **32 Using the Internet to keep up to date**,
	[GSW] **19 Using the Internet**,
	[GSW] **20 Updating Stata**,
	[GSM] **19 Using the Internet**,
	[GSM] **20 Updating Stata**,
	[GSU] **16 Using the Internet**,
	[GSU] **17 Updating Stata**

Title

> **vce** — Display covariance matrix of the estimators

Syntax

vce [, <u>c</u>orr <u>r</u>ho]

Description

vce displays the variance–covariance matrix of the estimators (VCE) after model estimation. vce may be used after any estimation command.

To obtain a copy of the covariance matrix for manipulation, type `matrix V = e(V)`.

vce merely displays the matrix; it does not fetch it.

Options

corr and rho are synonyms. They display the matrix as a correlation matrix rather than a covariance matrix.

Remarks

▷ Example

Using the automobile data, we run a regression of mpg on weight and displ.

```
. regress mpg weight displ

      Source |       SS       df       MS              Number of obs =      74
-------------+------------------------------           F(  2,    71) =   66.79
       Model |  1595.40969     2  797.704846           Prob > F      =  0.0000
    Residual |  848.049768    71  11.9443629           R-squared     =  0.6529
-------------+------------------------------           Adj R-squared =  0.6432
       Total |  2443.45946    73  33.4720474           Root MSE      =  3.4561

------------------------------------------------------------------------------
         mpg |      Coef.   Std. Err.       t    P>|t|     [95% Conf. Interval]
-------------+----------------------------------------------------------------
      weight |  -.0065671   .0011662     -5.631   0.000    -.0088925   -.0042417
       displ |   .0052808   .0098696      0.535   0.594    -.0143986    .0249602
       _cons |   40.08452    2.02011     19.843   0.000     36.05654    44.11251
------------------------------------------------------------------------------
```

To display the covariance matrix:

```
. vce

             |   weight      displ      _cons
-------------+------------------------------
      weight |  1.4e-06
       displ |  -.00001    .000097
       _cons |  -.002075   .011884   4.08085
```

To display the correlation matrix:

```
. vce, corr
        |   weight    displ    _cons
--------+---------------------------
 weight|   1.0000
  displ|  -0.8949   1.0000
  _cons|  -0.8806   0.5960   1.0000
```

◁

Methods and Formulas

vce is implemented as an ado-file.

Also See

Related: [R] **saved results**

Background: [U] **23 Estimation and post-estimation commands**

Title

version — Version control

Syntax

version [#]

Description

version sets the command interpreter to an internal version number # or, if # is not specified, shows the current internal version number to which the command interpreter is set.

For information on external version control, see [R] **which**.

Remarks

version ensures that programs written under an older release of Stata will continue to work under newer releases of Stata. If you do not write programs and if you use only the programs distributed by us, you can ignore version. If you do write programs, see [U] **21.11.1 Version** for guidelines to follow to ensure compatibility of your programs across future releases of Stata.

❑ Technical Note

If you have upgraded to the current release (6.0) from a release of Stata prior to Stata 3.0, read this technical note; otherwise, don't bother. With the release of Stata 3.0, changes were introduced to the Stata language, changes serious enough to cause programs written in Stata's language prior to 3.0 not to work. version resurrects such programs. If you have old programs or do-files you have written or obtained from the STB (see [U] **2.4 The Stata Technical Bulletin**) prior to the Stata 3.0 release, version will make them work. In addition, if you will use the version command in all new do- and ado-files you write, you will never again be faced with this incompatibility problem.

To make old do- and ado-files work, edit these files to include the line version 2.1 immediately after any program define command.

❑

❑ Technical Note

The details of how version works are as follows. When Stata is invoked, it sets its internal version number to the current version of Stata, which is 6.0 at the time this was written. Typing version without arguments shows the current value of the internal version number:

```
. version
version 6.0
```

One way to make old programs work is to set the internal version number interactively to that of a previous release:

```
. version 2.1
. version
version 2.10
```

Now Stata's default interpretation of a program is the same as it was for Stata 2.1. In point of fact, Stata 3.0 is the first instance of an inconsistency in the language being introduced, so setting the version to any number below 3.0 has the same effect—it reestablishes the old interpretation. In the future, however, version 3.0 might differ from version 7.0 and, if it does, setting the version to 3.0 would reestablish the 3.0 interpretation of programs.

You cannot set the version to a number higher than the current version. Since we are using Stata 6.0, we cannot set the version number to 7.0.

```
. version 7.0
version 7.0 not supported
r(9);
```

❏

❏ Technical Note

We strongly recommend that all ado- and do-files begin with a version command. In the case of programs (ado-files), the version command should appear immediately following the program define command:

```
program define myprog
        version 6.0
        ( etc.)
end
```

❏

Also See

Related: [R] **display**, [R] **which**

Background: [U] **21.11.1 Version**

Title

> **vwls** — Variance-weighted least squares

Syntax

vwls *depvar* [*indepvars*] [*weight*] [if *exp*] [in *range*] [, sd(*varname*) noconstant

level(*#*)]

fweights are allowed; see [U] **14.1.6 weight**.

vwls shares the features of all estimation commands; see [U] **23 Estimation and post-estimation commands**.

Syntax for predict

predict [*type*] *newvarname* [if *exp*] [in *range*] [, xb stdp]

These statistics are available both in and out of sample; type predict ... if e(sample) ... if wanted only for the estimation sample.

Description

vwls estimates a linear regression using variance-weighted least squares. It is different from ordinary least squares (OLS) regression in that homogeneity of variance is not assumed, but the conditional variance of *depvar* must be estimated prior to the regression. The estimated variance need not be constant across observations. vwls treats the estimated variance as if it were the true variance when it computes the standard errors of the coefficients.

An estimate of the conditional standard deviation of *depvar* must be supplied to vwls using the sd(*varname*) option; or else you must have grouped data with the groups defined by the *indepvars* variables. In the latter case, all *indepvars* are treated as categorical variables; the mean and standard deviation of *depvar* are computed separately for each subgroup; and the regression of the subgroup means on *indepvars* is computed.

regress with analytic weights can be used to produce another kind of "variance-weighted least squares"; see the following remarks for an explanation of the difference.

Options

sd(*varname*) is an estimate of the conditional standard deviation of *depvar* (that is, it can vary observation by observation). All values of *varname* must be > 0. If sd() is specified, fweights cannot be used.

If sd() is not given, the data will be grouped by *indepvars*. In this case, *indepvars* are treated as categorical variables, and the means and standard deviations of *depvar* for each subgroup are calculated and used for the regression. Any subgroup for which the standard deviation is zero is dropped.

noconstant suppresses the constant term (intercept) in the regression.

level(*#*) specifies the confidence level, in percent, for confidence intervals. The default is level(95) or as set by set level; see [U] **23.5 Specifying the width of confidence intervals**.

Options for predict

xb, the default, calculates the linear prediction.

stdp calculates the standard error of the linear prediction.

Remarks

The vwls command is intended for use with two special—and very different—types of data. The first is data consisting of measurements from physical science experiments in which (1) all error is due solely to measurement errors, and (2) the sizes of the measurement errors are known.

Variance-weighted least squares linear regression can also be used for certain problems in categorical data analysis. It can be used when all the independent variables are categorical and the outcome variable is either continuous or a quantity that can sensibly be averaged. If each of the subgroups defined by the categorical variables contains a reasonable number of subjects, then the variance of the outcome variable can be estimated independently within each subgroup. For the purposes of estimation, each subgroup is treated as a single observation with the dependent variable being the subgroup mean of the outcome variable.

The vwls command estimates the model

$$y_i = \mathbf{x}_i \boldsymbol{\beta} + \varepsilon_i$$

where the errors ε_i are independent normal random variables with the distribution $\varepsilon_i \sim N(0, \nu_i)$. The independent variables $\mathbf{x}_i$ are assumed to be known without error.

As described above, we assume that we already have estimates s_i^2 for the variances ν_i. The error variance is not estimated in the regression. The estimates s_i^2 are used for the computation of the standard errors of the coefficients; see *Methods and Formulas* below.

In comparison, weighted ordinary least squares regression assumes that the errors have the distribution $\varepsilon_i \sim N(0, \sigma^2/w_i)$, where the w_i are known weights and σ^2 is an unknown parameter that is estimated in the regression. This is the difference from variance-weighted least squares: in weighted OLS, the magnitude of the error variance is estimated in the regression using all the data.

▷ Example

An artificial, but informative, example illustrates the difference between variance-weighted least squares and weighted OLS.

An experimenter measures the quantities x_i and y_i, and estimates that the standard deviation of y_i is s_i. He enters the data into Stata:

```
. input x y s

              x         y         s
  1.          1        1.2       0.5
  2.          2        1.9       0.5
  3.          3        3.2       1
  4.          4        4.3       1
  5.          5        4.9       1
  6.          6        6.0       2
  7.          7        7.2       2
  8.          8        7.9       2
  9. end
```

Since the experimenter wants observations with smaller variance to carry larger weight in the regression, he computes an OLS regression with analytic weights proportional to the inverse of the squared standard deviations:

```
. regress y x [aweight=s^(-2)]
(sum of wgt is   1.1750e+01)

    Source |       SS       df       MS                Number of obs =       8
-----------+------------------------------             F(  1,      6) =  702.26
     Model | 22.6310183      1  22.6310183             Prob > F      =  0.0000
  Residual | .193355117      6  .032225853             R-squared     =  0.9915
-----------+------------------------------             Adj R-squared =  0.9901
     Total | 22.8243734      7  3.26062477             Root MSE      =  .17952

-------------------------------------------------------------------------------
         y |      Coef.   Std. Err.       t    P>|t|     [95% Conf. Interval]
-----------+-------------------------------------------------------------------
         x |   .9824683   .0370739    26.500   0.000     .8917517    1.073185
     _cons |   .1138554   .1120078     1.016   0.349    -.1602179    .3879288
-------------------------------------------------------------------------------
```

If he computes a variance-weighted least-squares regression using vwls, he gets the same results for the coefficient estimates, but very different standard errors:

```
. vwls y x, sd(s)
Variance-weighted least-squares regression        Number of obs   =       8
Goodness-of-fit chi2(6)     =     0.28             Model chi2(1)   =   33.24
Prob > chi2                 =   0.9996             Prob > chi2     =  0.0000
-------------------------------------------------------------------------------
         y |      Coef.   Std. Err.       z    P>|z|     [95% Conf. Interval]
-----------+-------------------------------------------------------------------
         x |   .9824683    .170409     5.765   0.000     .6484728    1.316464
     _cons |   .1138554     .51484     0.221   0.825    -.8952124    1.122923
-------------------------------------------------------------------------------
```

Despite the fact that the values of y_i were nicely linear with x_i, the vwls regression used the experimenter's large estimates for the standard deviations to compute large standard errors for the coefficients. For weighted OLS regression, however, the scale of the analytic weights has no effect on the standard errors of the coefficients—only the relative proportions of the analytic weights affect the regression.

If the experimenter is sure of the sizes of his error estimates for y_i, then the use of vwls is valid. However, if he can only estimate the relative proportions of error among the y_i, then vwls is not appropriate.

◁

▷ Example

Let us now consider an example of the use of vwls with categorical data. Suppose that we have blood pressure data for $n = 400$ subjects, categorized by gender and race (black or white). Here is a description of the data:

(Continued on next page)

```
. table gender race, s(mean bp sd bp freq) row col format(%8.1f)
----------+--------------------
          |        Race
   Gender | White  Black  Total
----------+--------------------
   Female | 117.1  118.5  117.8
          |  10.3   11.6   10.9
          |   100    100    200
          |
     Male | 122.1  125.8  124.0
          |  10.6   15.5   13.3
          |   100    100    200
          |
    Total | 119.6  122.2  120.9
          |  10.7   14.1   12.6
          |   200    200    400
----------+--------------------
```

Performing a variance-weighted regression using **vwls** gives

```
. vwls bp gender race
Variance-weighted least-squares regression       Number of obs   =      400
Goodness-of-fit chi2(1)    =      0.88             Model chi2(2)   =    27.11
Prob > chi2                =    0.3486             Prob > chi2     =   0.0000
------------------------------------------------------------------------------
       bp |     Coef.   Std. Err.      z     P>|z|      [95% Conf. Interval]
----------+-------------------------------------------------------------------
   gender |  5.876522   1.170241     5.022   0.000      3.582892    8.170151
     race |  2.372818   1.191683     1.991   0.046      .0371631    4.708473
    _cons |  116.6486    .9296297   125.479  0.000      114.8266    118.4707
------------------------------------------------------------------------------
```

By comparison, an OLS regression gives the following result:

```
. regress bp gender race
    Source |       SS       df       MS              Number of obs =      400
-----------+------------------------------           F(  2,   397) =    15.24
     Model |  4485.66639     2  2242.83319           Prob > F      =   0.0000
  Residual |  58442.7305   397  147.210908           R-squared     =   0.0713
-----------+------------------------------           Adj R-squared =   0.0666
     Total |  62928.3969   399   157.71528           Root MSE      =   12.133

------------------------------------------------------------------------------
       bp |     Coef.   Std. Err.      t     P>|t|      [95% Conf. Interval]
----------+-------------------------------------------------------------------
   gender |    6.1775   1.213305     5.091   0.000      3.792194    8.562806
     race |    2.5875   1.213305     2.133   0.034      .2021939    4.972806
    _cons |  116.4862   1.050753   110.860   0.000      114.4205     118.552
------------------------------------------------------------------------------
```

Note the larger value for the **race** coefficient (and smaller *p*-value) in the OLS regression. The assumption of homogeneity of variance in OLS means that the mean for black men is allowed to pull the regression line higher than in the **vwls** regression, which takes into account the larger variance for black men and reduces its effect on the regression.

◁

Saved Results

vwls saves in e():

Scalars
e(N)	number of observations
e(df_m)	model degrees of freedom
e(chi2)	model χ^2
e(df_gf)	goodness-of-fit degrees of freedom
e(chi2_gf)	goodness-of-fit χ^2

Macros
e(cmd)	vwls
e(depvar)	name of dependent variable

Matrices
e(b)	coefficient vector
e(V)	variance–covariance matrix of the estimators

Functions
e(sample)	marks estimation sample

Methods and Formulas

vwls is implemented as an ado-file.

Let $\mathbf{y} = (y_1, y_2, \ldots, y_n)'$ be the vector of observations of the dependent variable, where n is the number of observations. For the case when sd() is specified, let s_1, s_2, ..., s_n be the standard deviations supplied by sd(). For categorical data, when sd() is not given, the means and standard deviations of y for each subgroup are computed, and n becomes the number of subgroups, $\mathbf{y}$ is the vector of subgroup means, and s_i are the standard deviations for the subgroups.

Let $\mathbf{V} = \mathrm{diag}(s_1^2, s_2^2, \ldots, s_n^2)$ denote the estimate of the variance of $\mathbf{y}$. Then the estimated regression coefficients are

$$\mathbf{b} = (\mathbf{X'V^{-1}X})^{-1}\mathbf{X'V^{-1}y}$$

and their estimated covariance matrix is

$$\widehat{\mathrm{Cov}}(\mathbf{b}) = (\mathbf{X'V^{-1}X})^{-1}$$

A statistic for the goodness of fit of the model is

$$Q = (\mathbf{y} - \mathbf{Xb})' \mathbf{V}^{-1}(\mathbf{y} - \mathbf{Xb})$$

where Q has a χ^2 distribution with $n - k$ degrees of freedom (k is the number of independent variables plus the constant, if any).

References

Grizzle, J. E., C. F. Starmer, and G. G. Koch. 1969. Analysis of categorical data by linear models. *Biometrics* 25: 489–504.

Press, W. H., S. A. Teukolsky, W. T. Vetterling, and B. P. Flannery. 1992. *Numerical Recipes in C: The Art of Scientific Computing*. 2d ed. Cambridge: Cambridge University Press.

Also See

Complementary:	[R] **lincom**, [R] **predict**, [R] **test**, [R] **testnl**, [R] **vce**
Related:	[R] **regress**
Background:	[U] **16.5 Accessing coefficients and standard errors**, [U] **23 Estimation and post-estimation commands**

Title

weibull — Estimate Weibull and other parametric survival-time models

Syntax

{ weibull | ereg } *depvar* [*varlist*] [*weight*] [if *exp*] [in *range*] [, hazard hr

    tr dead(*varname*) t0(*varname*) robust cluster(*varname*) score(*newvar(s)*)

    noconstant level(#) nocoef noheader *maximize_options*]

{ lnormal | llogist | gamma } *depvar* [*varlist*] [*weight*] [if *exp*] [in *range*]

    [, tr dead(*varname*) t0(*varname*) robust cluster(*varname*) score(*newvar(s)*)

    noconstant level(#) nocoef noheader *maximize_options*]

gompertz *depvar* [*varlist*] [*weight*] [if *exp*] [in *range*] [, hr dead(*varname*)

    t0(*varname*) robust cluster(*varname*) score(*newvar(s)*) noconstant

    level(#) nocoef noheader *maximize_options*]

fweights, pweights, and iweights are allowed; see [U] **14.1.6 weight**.

These commands share the features of all estimation commands; see [U] **23 Estimation and post-estimation commands**.

These commands may be used with **sw** to perform stepwise estimation; see [R] **sw**.

Syntax for predict

predict [*type*] *newvarname* [if *exp*] [in *range*] [, *statistic*]

where *statistic* is

time	predicted survival time (the default, except for Gompertz)
lntime	predicted ln(survival time)
hazard	predicted hazard (the default for Gompertz)
hr	predicted hazard ratio
xb	linear prediction $x_j b$
stdp	standard error of the linear prediction; $SE(x_j b)$
surv	predicted S(*depvar*) or S(*depvar* | t0)
csnell	(partial) Cox–Snell residuals
mgale	(partial) martingale-like residuals

These statistics are available both in and out of sample; type predict ... if e(sample) ... if wanted only for the estimation sample.

When no option is specified the predicted survival time is calculated for all models except Gompertz, in which case the predicted hazard is calculated. The predicted hazard ratio option hr is only available for the exponential, Weibull and Gompertz models. The time and lntime options are not available for the Gompertz model.

Description

weibull estimates maximum-likelihood Weibull distribution (survival time) models. ereg estimates maximum-likelihood exponential distribution (survival time) models. lnormal estimates maximum-likelihood lognormal distribution (survival time) models. llogist estimates maximum-likelihood log-logistic distribution (survival time) models. gamma estimates maximum-likelihood generalized log-gamma distribution (survival time) models. gompertz estimates maximum-likelihood Gompertz distribution (survival time) models. See [R] **st streg** for a detailed discussion of these parametric survival models.

In all cases, the dependent variable *depvar* represents the time of failure or censoring and *varlist* represents the independent variables. These commands allow estimation with fixed or time-varying covariates, allow for left truncation (delayed entry) and gaps, and may be used with single- or multiple-failure data.

We advise use of **streg** over these commands but only because we think using the st commands is easier; the choice is yours. If you take our advice, see [R] **st streg** and skip reading this entry altogether.

streg produces the same results and this is assured because the **streg** command calls the commands in this entry to perform the estimation.

Also see [R] **st stcox** (or [R] **cox**) for estimation of proportional hazards models.

Options

hazard specifies that the model be estimated according to the log hazard rate parameterization rather than the default log time (accelerated failure time) parameterization is to be displayed.

hr reports the estimated coefficients transformed to hazard ratios, i.e., e^b rather than b, and implies hazard if issued at estimation time. Standard errors and confidence intervals are similarly transformed. Hazard estimates may be redisplayed in either form.

tr reports the estimated coefficients transformed to time ratios, i.e., e^b rather than b, and may not be combined with hazard. Standard errors and confidence intervals are similarly transformed. Time-to-failure estimates may be redisplayed in either form.

dead(*varname*) specifies the name of a variable recording 0 if the observation is censored and a value other than 0—typically 1—if the observation represents a failure.

t0(*varname*) specifies the variable that indicates when the observation became at risk. t0() can be used to handle left truncation, gaps, time-varying covariates, and recurring failures.

In the following data, each subject has only one record, but the third subject was observed starting at time 5, not 0:

id	t0	t	d	x1	x2
55	0	12	0	3	0
56	0	30	1	2	1
57	5	22	1	1	0
58	0	16	0	2	0

The interpretation of this data is that subject 55 had x1 = 3 and x2 = 0 over the interval $(0, 12]$ and then, at time 12, was lost due to censoring; subject 56 had x1 = 2 and x2 = 1 over the interval $(0, 30]$ and then, at time 30, failed; subject 57 had x1 = 1 and x2 = 0 over the interval $(5, 22]$ and then, at time 22, failed.

One could estimate a Weibull regression on this data by typing

```
. weibull t x1 x2, dead(d) t0(t0)
```

In the following data, covariate x1 varies over time:

id	t0	t	d	x1	x2
91	0	15	0	2	1
91	15	22	0	1	1
91	22	31	1	3	1
92	0	11	0	3	0
92	11	52	0	.	0
92	52	120	1	2	0

The interpretation here is that subject 91 had x1 = 2 over the interval $(0, 15]$, x1 = 1 over the interval $(15, 22]$, and x1 = 3 over the interval $(22, 31]$; the value of x2 never varied from 1; and at time 31 a failure was observed.

While one could estimate a Weibull regression by typing the same thing as before

```
. weibull t x1 x2, dead(d) t0(t0)
```

we would strongly recommend

```
. weibull t x1 x2, dead(d) t0(t0) robust cluster(id)
```

That is because the observations are no longer independent. This issue is discussed under the `cluster()` option below.

Note the missing value of x1 in subject 92's second record. That causes no difficulty.

In the following data, some subjects fail more than once (and have time-varying regressors):

id	t0	t	d	x1	x2
23	0	12	1	2	1
23	12	18	0	1	1
23	18	22	1	3	1
24	0	8	1	3	0
24	8	22	1	1	0
24	22	31	1	2	0

Subject 23 has x2 = 1 at all times. Between $(0, 12]$, x1 = 2 and a failure is observed at time 12. Between $(12, 18]$, x1 = 1 and no failure is observed. Between $(18, 22]$, x1 = 3 and a failure is observed at time 22.

Again, the estimation command is the same

```
. weibull t x1 x2, dead(d) t0(t0) robust cluster(id)
```

and note that again, since subjects appear more than once in the data, we also specified options `robust` and `cluster(id)`.

robust specifies that the robust method of calculating the variance–covariance matrix is to be used instead of the conventional inverse-matrix-of-second-derivatives method.

cluster(*varname*) implies robust and specifies a variable on which clustering is to be based. By default, each observation in the data is assumed to represent a cluster. Consider the following data:

t0	t	d	x1	x2
0	15	0	2	1
15	22	0	1	1
22	31	1	3	1

Does this represent three subjects or just one? Perhaps three subjects were observed: one over $(0, 15]$, another from $(15, 22]$, and a third from $(22, 31]$. In that case, the three observations are presumably independent and the conventional variance calculation is appropriate, as is the robust calculation. If you wanted the robust estimate of variance, you would specify robust but not cluster().

On the other hand, if the data is

id	t0	t	d	x1	x2
91	0	15	0	2	1
91	15	22	0	1	1
91	22	31	1	3	1

that is, if it represents the same subject, then these records do not amount to independent observations. The conventional variance calculation is inappropriate. To obtain the robust standard errors, you would specify robust and cluster(id), although you could omit the robust because cluster() implies robust.

score(*newvar(s)*) requests that *newvar(s)* be created containing the score function(s). One new variable is specified in the case of ereg, two are specified in the case of weibull, lnormal, llogist and gompertz, and three are specified in the case of gamma.

The first new variable will contain $\partial(\ln L_j)/\partial(\mathbf{x}_j\boldsymbol{\beta})$.

The second and third new variables, if they exist, will contain $\partial(\ln L_j)$ with respect to the second and third ancillary parameters. See Table 1 in [R] **st streg** for a list of ancillary parameters.

noconstant suppresses the constant term (intercept) in the model.

level(*#*) specifies the confidence level, in percent, for confidence intervals. The default is level(95) or as set by set level; see [U] **23.5 Specifying the width of confidence intervals**.

nocoef is for use by programmers. It prevents the displaying of results but still allows the display of the iteration log.

noheader is for use by programmers. It causes the display of the coefficient table only; the table above the coefficients reporting chi-squared tests and the like is suppressed. The code for streg, for instance, uses this option, since streg wants to substitute its own (more informative) header.

maximize_options control the maximization process; see [R] **maximize**. You should never have to specify them.

Options for predict

time calculates the predicted survival time. Note that this is the prediction from time 0 conditional on constant covariates. When no option is specified the predicted survival time is calculated for all models except Gompertz, in which case the predicted hazard is calculated. This option is not available for the gompertz command.

lntime calculates the ln() of what time produces. This option is not available for the gompertz command.

hazard calculates the predicted hazard. This is the default for the Gompertz distribution.

hr calculates the hazard ratio. This option is valid only for models having a proportional hazard parameterization. i.e., Weibull, exponential, and Gompertz.

xb calculates the linear prediction from the estimated model. That is, all models can be thought of as estimating a set of parameters $b_1, b_2, \cdots, b_k$, and the linear prediction is $\widehat{y}_j = b_1 x_{1j} + b_2 x_{2j} + \ldots + b_k x_{kj}$, often written in matrix notation as $\widehat{y}_j = \mathbf{x}_j \mathbf{b}$.

It is important to understand that $x_{1j}, x_{2j}, \ldots, x_{kj}$ used in the calculation are obtained from the data currently in memory and do not have to correspond to the data on the independent variables used in estimating the model (obtaining the $b_1, b_2, \ldots, b_k$).

stdp calculates the standard error of the prediction; that is, the standard error of $\widehat{y}_j$.

surv calculates each observation's predicted survivor probability $S(t|t_0)$. If you did not specify t0() when you estimated the model, t0=0 and thus surv calculates the predicted survivor function at the time of failure or censoring, $S(t)$. Otherwise, it is the probability of surviving through t given survival through t_0. In such cases, you may wish to also see help for streg.

csnell calculates the (partial) Cox–Snell residual. If you have single observations per subject, then csnell calculates the usual Cox–Snell residual. Otherwise, csnell calculates the additive contribution of this observation to the subject's overall Cox–Snell residual. In such cases, you may wish to also see help for streg.

mgale calculates the (partial) martingale-like residual. The issues are the same as with csnell above.

Remarks

See [R] **st streg** for a discussion appropriate to these commands.

streg uses the commands in this entry to perform the estimation but has an easier-to-use syntax. In reading the streg entry, it is just a matter of translating from one syntax to the other.

In [R] **st streg**, if you see an example such as

    . streg drug age, dist(weibull)

the equivalent weibull command might be

    . weibull *timevar* drug age

or it might be

    . weibull *timevar* drug age, dead(*failvar*)

or it might be

    . weibull *timevar* drug age, dead(*failvar*) t0(*t0var*)

depending on context.

streg fills in the identities of the time-of-censoring or failure variable (*timevar*), the outcome variable (*failvar*), and the entry-time variable (*t0var*) for you. Users of streg first stset their data and that is how the commands know what to fill in.

Another difference between these commands and streg concerns an implied cluster() option when you specify robust. With the commands in this entry it is your responsibility to specify clustering if you want it. With streg specifying robust implies cluster() if a subject-id variable has been set.

The final difference concerns the default metric for the Weibull and exponential models. weibull and ereg default to the accelerated time (log expected time) metric but will, if hazard is specified, use the log relative hazard metric. With streg, it is the other way around. They default to the log relative hazard metric but will, if another option is specified—time—use the log expected time metric.

Saved Results

These commands save in e():

Scalars

e(N)	number of observations	e(chi2)	χ^2
e(k)	number of parameters	e(p)	significance
e(k_eq)	number of equations	e(ic)	number of iterations
e(k_dv)	number of dependent variables	e(sigma)	ancillary parameter (gamma, lnormal)
e(df_m)	model degrees of freedom	e(kappa)	ancillary parameter (gamma)
e(ll)	log likelihood	e(aux_p)	ancillary parameter (weibull)
e(ll_0)	log likelihood, constant-only model	e(gamma)	ancillary parameter (llogist, gompertz)
e(rc)	return code		

Macros

e(cmd)	name of command	e(t0)	name of variable marking entry time
e(dead)	variable indicating failure	e(frm2)	hazard or time
e(depvar)	name of dependent variable	e(user)	name of likelihood-evaluator program
e(title)	title in estimation output	e(opt)	type of optimization
e(wtype)	weight type	e(chi2type)	LR; type of model χ^2 test
e(wexp)	weight expression	e(predict)	program used to implement predict

Matrices

e(b)	coefficient vector	e(V)	variance–covariance matrix of the estimators

Functions

e(sample)	marks estimation sample

Methods and Formulas

See [R] **st streg**.

References

See [R] **st streg**.

Also See

Complementary: [R] **lincom**, [R] **linktest**, [R] **lrtest**, [R] **ltable**, [R] **predict**, [R] **sw**, [R] **test**, [R] **testnl**, [R] **vce**

Related: [R] **st streg**; [R] **st stcox**; [R] **cox**, [R] **glm**, [R] **_robust**

Background: [U] **16.5 Accessing coefficients and standard errors**,
[U] **23 Estimation and post-estimation commands**,
[U] **23.11 Obtaining robust variance estimates**,
[U] **23.12 Obtaining scores**

Title

> **which** — Display location and version for an ado-file

Syntax

which *ado_command*

Description

which searches the S_ADO path for *command_name*.ado and, if found, displays the full path and filename together with all lines in the file that begin with "*!" in the first column. If *command_name*.ado is not found, the message "file not found" is displayed and the return code is set to 111.

For information on internal version control, see [R] **version**.

Remarks

If you write programs, you know that you make changes to the programs over time. If you are like us, you also end up with multiple versions of the program stored on your disk, perhaps in different directories. It is even possible that you have given copies of your programs to other Stata users. This leads to the problem of knowing which version of a program you or your friends are using. The which command helps you solve this problem.

▷ Example

Lines that start with an '*' are comments—Stata ignores them—so Stata also ignores lines that begin with '*!'. Such lines, however, are of special interest to which. The notes command, described in [R] **notes**, is an ado-file written by StataCorp. Here is what happens when we type which notes:

```
. which notes
c:\stata\ado\base\n\notes.ado
*! version 1.0.1  04feb1998
```

which informs us that notes, if executed, would be obtained from c:\stata\ado\base\n. There is now no question as to which notes, if we had more than one, Stata would choose to execute. The second line is from the notes.ado file: when we revised notes, we included a line that read '*! version 1.0.1 04feb1998'. This is how we, at StataCorp, do version control—see [U] **21.11.1 Version** for an explanation of our version control numbers.

You, however, can be less formal. Anything typed after lines that begin with '*!' will be displayed by which. For instance, you might write myprog.ado:

```
. which myprog
.\myprog.ado
*! first written 1/03/97
*! bug fix on 1/05/97 (no variance case)
*! updated 1/24/97 to include nocons option
*! still suspicious if variable takes on only two values
```

It does not matter where in the program the lines beginning with *! are—they will be listed (in particular, our "still suspicious" comment was buried about fifty lines down in the code). All that is important is that the *! marker appear in the first two columns of a line.

◁

▷ Example

If we type which *command*, where *command* is not an ado-file, Stata responds with the following message:

```
. which regress
ado-file for regress not found
r(111);
```

regress is a built-in command.

◁

Also See

Related: [R] **version**

Background: [U] **20 Ado-files**,
                 [U] **21.11.1 Version**

Title

> **while** — Looping

Syntax

```
while exp {
        stata_commands
}
```

Description

while evaluates *exp* and, if it is true (nonzero), executes the commands enclosed in the braces. It then repeats the process until *exp* evaluates to false (zero). whiles may be nested within whiles. If the *exp* refers to any variables, their values in the first observation are used unless explicit subscripts are specified; see [U] **16.7 Explicit subscripting**.

Remarks

while may be used interactively, but it is most frequently used in programs. See [U] **21 Programming Stata** for a complete description of programs.

▷ Example

The *stata_commands* enclosed in the braces may be executed once, many times, or not at all. For instance:

```
. program define demo
        local i = `1'
        while `i'>0 {
                display "i is now `i'"
                local i = `i' - 1
        }
        display "done"
end
. demo 2
i is now 2
i is now 1
done
. demo 0
done
```

◁

▷ Example

Here is an example of while used interactively. We want to generate several variables filled with random numbers. We first initialize the loop:

```
. local i = 1
```

We then type the opening `while ` i ´ < 4`, together with the opening left brace. Stata will automatically prompt us with program line numbers until we type the closing right brace, and then Stata will execute the loop:

```
. while `i´ < 4 {
  2. gen u`i´ = uniform()
  3. local i = `i´ + 1
  4. }
```

We use **summarize** on the generated variables to show that they were indeed created.

```
. summ u*
Variable |     Obs        Mean   Std. Dev.       Min        Max
---------+----------------------------------------------------------
     u1 |      74    .4773226    .2930084    .0369273   .9746088
     u2 |      74    .5078113    .2663548    .0057233   .9844069
     u3 |      74    .5079178    .3032114     .014819   .9640535
```

This is a silly example since only three **generate** commands are needed. However, imagine needing to do this or some other Stata commands a large number of times. In these cases, **while** becomes a more serious tool.

◁

If you accidentally create an endless **while** loop, you can press the *Break* key (see [U] **12 The Break key**) to exit the loop.

Also See

Related: [R] **for**, [R] **if**

Background: [U] **16 Functions and expressions**,
                    [U] **21 Programming Stata**

Title

> **window** — Programming menus, dialogs, and windows (Windows and Macintosh only)

Description

The **window** commands allow Stata programmers to create menus and dialogs. Below we provide an overview of the commands. In the entries that follow, we fill in the details.

Remarks

The **window** commands are organized as follows:

1. **window menu** creates menu hierarchies; see [R] **window menu**.

2. **window dialog** creates and invokes dialog boxes for obtaining input from the user; see [R] **window dialog**.

   a. **window control** places controls on dialog boxes; see [R] **window control**.

   b. **window fopen** and **window fsave** invoke two standard dialog boxes; see [R] **window fopen**.

3. **window stopbox** displays message boxes; see [R] **window stopbox**.

4. **window manage** minimizes windows, brings them forward, etc.; see [R] **window manage**.

Taken as a whole, this can be an overwhelming amount of material.

Dialog boxes

Dialog boxes—**window dialog** and **window control**—can be understood in isolation. A dialog box is nothing more than a way of obtaining input from the user. A dialog box contains controls, meaning fields where a user might type, buttons that a user might click, or check boxes a user might check.

Although you may think of dialog boxes and menus together—one pulls down a menu, makes a selection, and a dialog box appears—in fact any Stata program (command) can make use of dialog boxes. One could write a program called **myprog** that, after the user typed

```
. myprog
```

displayed a dialog box to obtain more information and then acted on that information. Here is how the dialog-box process works:

1. Your program defines the fields of a dialog box using **window control**.

2. Your program displays the dialog box using **window dialog**.

3. The user interacts with your dialog box. The user fills in any edit fields, checks any checkboxes, etc., and eventually clicks some button. Each button that the user might click invokes some command, which might be a program or a return (**exit**) statement. You specified how this works when you defined the dialog box.

4. Eventually the user clicks a button that you defined as closing the dialog box and control is returned to the calling program (**myprog**).

Thus, a dialog system might consist of one or more programs. In a one-program system, the program defines the dialog box, setting all the actions to return. In a multiple-program system, one program defines the dialog box and the other programs serve as subroutines to be invoked when the user clicks here or there.

Menus

A menu system is just a logical hierarchy. Think about the pull-downs on the Stata menu bar. Those are called popout menus and Stata, by default, has popout menus called **File**, **Edit**, **Prefs**, etc.

Pull any one of those popout menus down and you are presented with a list of more choices. Choose any one and you might (1) be presented with even more choices or (2) cause something to happen (such as a dialog box to appear).

That is, menus are lists and each item in the list invokes another list or causes something to happen. The way this happens is that each menu item invokes another menu list or executes a Stata program (command).

`window menu` allows you to

1. create menus, which is to say, create lists of menu entries and associated actions,

    a. set an action to display yet another menu list,

    b. set an action to execute a Stata program (command).

2. specify a menu list is to be added to Stata's top-level menu bar or to another menu list.

A menu system might involve writing no Stata programs whatsoever. Imagine you wanted to add a pull-down to Stata's top-level menu-bar labeled **Descriptions**. When the user pulled down **Descriptions**, the user would be presented with two choices: **Describe** and **Summarize**. Choose one, and Stata will `describe` the data, choose the other, and Stata will `summarize` the data. Here is how you would do that.

You could first create a menu list called **Descriptions** appended to `sysmenu`, Stata's name for its top-level menu bar. Menu list **Descriptions** would contain two entries, one labeled **Describe** and the other labeled **Summarize**. The actions associated with each would be the Stata commands "`summarize`" and "`describe`".

You could do all of that interactively by typing

```
. window menu clear
. window menu append popout "sysmenu" "Descriptions"
. window menu append string "Descriptions" "Describe" "describe"
. window menu append string "Descriptions" "Summarize" "summarize"
. window menu set "sysmenu"
```

It might be easier, however, to put these commands in a program called `addesc` and then just type `addesc`.

Now say that you decide to add another item to **Description**'s list. You wish to add **Other** and, if the user selects that, another menu is to appear with the choices **Letter Value** and **Codebook**, going to Stata's `lv` and `codebook` commands.

You would create another menu hierarchy called **Other** appended to **Descriptions**. **Other** would contain two items, **Letter Value** and **Codebook** with associated actions "`lv`" and "`codebook`". Now when the user pulled down **Descriptions** from the top level, there would be a third choice. Here is the additional code to do that:

```
. window menu append popout "Descriptions" "Other"
. window menu append string "Other" "Letter Value" "lv"
. window menu append string "Other" "Codebook" "codebook"
. window menu set "sysmenu"
```

Putting menus and dialog boxes together

The action associated with a menu item need not be an existing Stata command. It can be a command you write, such as `myprog`. `myprog` might invoke a dialog box. The whole thing then appears to the user as if pulling down a menu and making a selection causes a dialog to appear. The user is never aware that he or she is running something called `myprog`.

Also See

Complementary: [R] **window control**, [R] **window dialog**, [R] **window fopen**,
[R] **window manage**, [R] **window menu**, [R] **window push**,
[R] **window stopbox**

Title

window control — Create dialog-box controls (Windows and Macintosh only)

Syntax

$\underline{\text{win}}$dow $\underline{\text{c}}$ontrol button *"label"* x_{offset} y_{offset} x_{extent} y_{extent} *macroname*

[default escape help]

$\underline{\text{win}}$dow $\underline{\text{c}}$ontrol check *"text"* x_{offset} y_{offset} x_{extent} y_{extent} *macroname*

[left | right]

$\underline{\text{win}}$dow $\underline{\text{c}}$ontrol edit x_{offset} y_{offset} x_{extent} y_{extent} *macroname*

[maxlen #] [password]

$\underline{\text{win}}$dow $\underline{\text{c}}$ontrol static *text_macroname* x_{offset} y_{offset} x_{extent} y_{extent}

[{left | right | center} blackframe]

$\underline{\text{win}}$dow $\underline{\text{c}}$ontrol radbegin *"text"* x_{offset} y_{offset} x_{extent} y_{extent} *macroname*

$\underline{\text{win}}$dow $\underline{\text{c}}$ontrol radio   *"text"* x_{offset} y_{offset} x_{extent} y_{extent} *macroname*

$\underline{\text{win}}$dow $\underline{\text{c}}$ontrol radend   *"text"* x_{offset} y_{offset} x_{extent} y_{extent} *macroname*

$\underline{\text{win}}$dow $\underline{\text{c}}$ontrol ssimple *list_macroname* x_{offset} y_{offset} x_{extent} y_{extent} *macroname*

[parse(*parse_character*)]

$\underline{\text{win}}$dow $\underline{\text{c}}$ontrol msimple *list_macroname* x_{offset} y_{offset} x_{extent} y_{extent} *macroname*

[parse(*parse_character*)]

$\underline{\text{win}}$dow $\underline{\text{c}}$ontrol scombo *list_macroname* x_{offset} y_{offset} x_{extent} y_{extent} *macroname*

[parse(*parse_character*)]

$\underline{\text{win}}$dow $\underline{\text{c}}$ontrol mcombo *list_macroname* x_{offset} y_{offset} x_{extent} y_{extent} *macroname*

[parse(*parse_character*)]

$\underline{\text{win}}$dow $\underline{\text{c}}$ontrol clear

where x_{offset}, y_{offset}, x_{extent}, and y_{extent} are literal numbers (#).

$(x_{\text{offset}}, y_{\text{offset}})$ specifies the upper-left corner of the control relative to the upper-left corner of the dialog box. $(x_{\text{extent}}, y_{\text{extent}})$ specifies the control's size. Units of measurement are approximately one-fifth the width of a character horizontally and one-eighth the height of a character vertically.

266

Description

window control defines controls on dialog boxes. Controls include for example, buttons, check boxes, and the like. When the user accesses a control (presses a button or checks a box), either a command is executed or a global macro is defined.

Remarks

Remarks are presented under the headings

> *The command button control*
> *The check box control*
> *The edit control*
> *The static control*
> *The radio-button control group*
> *List box controls*
> *Combo box controls*
> *Clearing old controls*
> *Putting it all together*
> *Defining global macros*

The command button control

window control button "*label*" x_{offset} y_{offset} x_{extent} y_{extent} *macroname*

$\left[\texttt{default escape help}\right]$

Command buttons are used to perform an action and are typically labeled OK or Cancel.

macroname is a global macro that contains the command to be executed when the user clicks the button.

default marks this button as the default button for the dialog; if users press *Enter* it will be as if they clicked this button. escape marks this button as associated with the *Escape* key on the keyboard; if users press *Escape*, it will be as if they clicked this button. help marks this button as associated with the *F1* key on the keyboard; if users press *F1*, it will be as if they clicked this button. The specifications default, escape, and help may be included in any combination. An obvious command to assign a button with the help specification is the whelp *topic* command, see [R] **help**.

Example:

```
window control button "OK" 10 10 30 10 DB_ok
```

defines a button labeled OK and executes $DB_ok when the user clicks the button.

The check box control

window control check "*text*" x_{offset} y_{offset} x_{extent} y_{extent} *macroname*

$\left[\texttt{left right}\right]$

Check boxes are used to obtain input concerning Boolean options.

macroname is a global macro. If, at the outset, *macroname* is undefined or contains 0, the box is unchecked; otherwise it is checked. Later, *macroname* contains 0 if the box is unchecked and 1 if it is checked.

left and right specify whether the text labeling the check box is to be to the left or right of the box. right is the default and left is allowed under Windows only. For portability reasons, we recommend against specifying left.

Example:

```
window control check "Robust" 10 10 35 10 DB_chk
```

defines global macro DB_chk to contain 1 if the user checks the box and a 0 otherwise.

The edit control

window control edit x_{offset} y_{offset} x_{extent} y_{extent} *macroname*

$\left[\text{maxlen } \#\right]$ $\left[\text{password}\right]$

Edit controls are used to obtain text input.

macroname is a global macro. At the outset, *macroname* contains what is to be preloaded into the edit field; *macroname* may be undefined. Later, *macroname* contains what the user typed.

password replaces the characters that the user types with $*$ characters in the edit field. maxlen $\#$ prevents the user from typing more than $\#$ characters.

Example:

```
window control edit 10 10 100 10 DB_edit
```

defines global macro DB_edit to contain the input from the user.

The static control

window control static *text_macroname* x_{offset} y_{offset} x_{extent} y_{extent}

$\left[\text{left right center blackframe}\right]$

Static controls are used to display text information or draw frames. They differ from edit controls in that the user may not change the static text.

text_macroname is a global macro that contains the text to be displayed.

blackframe draws a frame (rectangle) defined by the $(x_{\text{offset}}, y_{\text{offset}})$ and $(x_{\text{extent}}, y_{\text{extent}})$. When the blackframe specification is used, the contents of *text_macroname* are ignored. left specifies that the text should be left-justified, right that it be right-justified, and center that it be centered. left is the default.

Example:

```
window control static DB_stat 10 10 100 10
```

displays the contents of global macro DB_stat on the dialog.

Much later, when the dialog box is displayed by window dialog you can change the contents of global macro DB_stat and those changes will be reflected in the open dialog box, but sometimes with a lag. To make the changes appear instantly, use window dialog update; see [R] **window dialog**.

The radio-button control group

<u>win</u>dow <u>c</u>ontrol radbegin *"text"* x_{offset} y_{offset} x_{extent} y_{extent} *macroname*

<u>win</u>dow <u>c</u>ontrol radio   *"text"* x_{offset} y_{offset} x_{extent} y_{extent} *macroname*

<u>win</u>dow <u>c</u>ontrol radend   *"text"* x_{offset} y_{offset} x_{extent} y_{extent} *macroname*

A radio-button control group allows the user to choose one of several alternatives.

You must specify the same global macro *macroname* for all commands in a group. At the outset, *macroname* contains which button is selected (1, 2, 3, ...). If *macroname* is undefined, button 1 is selected. Later, *macroname* is redefined to contain the button number actually selected.

A radio-button control group has at least two choices that are defined using the `radbegin` and `radend` commands. Additional choices are defined by the `radio` commands that appear in between.

Example:

```
window control radbegin "Unpaired and unequal" 10 10 90 10 DB_rad
window control radio     "Unpaired and equal"   10 20 90 10 DB_rad
window control radend    "Paired"               10 30 90 10 DB_rad
```

defines macro `DB_rad` to contain 1, 2, or 3 depending on which button the user selects.

List box controls

<u>win</u>dow <u>c</u>ontrol ssimple *list_macroname* x_{offset} y_{offset} x_{extent} y_{extent} *macroname*

$\big[$parse*(parse_character)*$\big]$

<u>win</u>dow <u>c</u>ontrol msimple *list_macroname* x_{offset} y_{offset} x_{extent} y_{extent} *macroname*

$\big[$parse*(parse_character)*$\big]$

A list box presents an edit field on top of a list. The user may type in the edit field and/or choose one or more items from the list. The list box will automatically include a scroll bar if the number of choices is large. When users click on an item in the list, that item is copied to the edit field. If users then click on a second item, `ssimple` list boxes replace the contents of the edit field with the new selection. `msimple` list boxes append the second choice to the first with a space in between.

macroname is a global macro. As with an edit control, at the outset *macroname* contains the initial contents of the edit field (*macroname* may be undefined) and is redefined to contain what the user types.

At the outset, *list_macroname* (a global macro) contains the choices to be filled into the list. The choices are the words recorded in *list_macroname*, each word being a choice. That is convenient for most purposes but, if individual choices contain multiple words, that will not work. In such cases, you may use any choice-separation character you wish and then include the parse*(parse_character)* specification.

Example:

```
window control ssimple DB_list 10 10 30 100 DB_sl
window control msimple DB_list 60 20 30 100 DB_ml
```

uses the contents of `DB_list` to fill in two different list boxes. The choices will then be accessible to the programmer as `$DB_sl` and `$DB_ml`.

Combo box controls

<u>win</u>dow <u>c</u>ontrol scombo *list_macroname* x_{offset} y_{offset} x_{extent} y_{extent} *macroname*

$\big[$parse(*parse_character*)$\big]$

<u>win</u>dow <u>c</u>ontrol mcombo *list_macroname* x_{offset} y_{offset} x_{extent} y_{extent} *macroname*

$\big[$parse(*parse_character*)$\big]$

A combo box is like a list box—an edit field in which the user may type with an associated list from which the user may choose. The difference is that the list does not show. Instead, the edit field has a down-arrow button and, if the user clicks that, the list pops down. The list box will automatically include a scroll bar if the number of choices is large.

When users click on an item in the list, that item is copied to the edit field. If users then click on a second item, scombo list boxes replace the contents of the edit field with the new selection. mcombo list boxes append the second choice to the first with a blank in between.

macroname is a global macro. As with a list box, *macroname* contains the initial text (if any) and is redefined to contain what the user types.

list_macroname (a global macro) works in the same way as it does for a list box.

Note that even though combo box controls display only the edit box, you define y_{extent} to include the space you want for the drop-down list box.

Example:

```
window control scombo DB_list 10 10 30 100 DB_sc
window control mcombo DB_list 60 20 30 100 DB_mc
```

will use the contents of DB_list to fill in two different list boxes. The choices will then be accessible to the programmer as $DB_sc and $DB_mc.

Clearing old controls

window control clear erases from Stata's memory any previously defined dialog controls. Controls are automatically cleared from memory when the dialog box is closed.

The window control clear command is useful when you are programming a dialog box in Stata. If a do-file has defined several controls but then exits due to an error, you should correct the error in the do-file. Type window control clear to clear the controls the do-file defined, and then re-execute the do-file. Better would be to make window control clear appear before any other window control commands in your do-file.

Putting it all together

Here we present a sample dialog that contains all the previously mentioned controls. You may need to resize the Stata window to see all of the controls on the dialog box.

(*Continued on next page*)

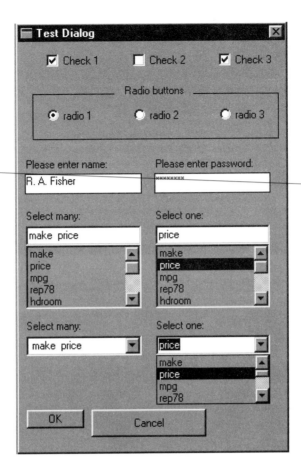

To run the example, run the do-file below and then type `mycmd` to the Stata prompt. In the figure above, we had `auto.dta` loaded when we ran `mycmd`.

———————————————————————————————————— top of dialog.do ————

```
macro drop DB*
capture program drop mycmd
program define mycmd
        version 6.0
        * Check boxes
        global DB_chk1 = 0
        global DB_chk2 = 0
        global DB_chk3 = 0
        window control check "Check 1"  20 5 50 10 DB_chk1
        window control check "Check 2"  80 5 50 10 DB_chk2
        window control check "Check 3" 140 5 50 10 DB_chk3

        * Frame with title
        global DB_rad "Radio buttons"
        window control static DB_rad 10 28 172 25 blackframe
        window control static DB_rad 65 25  55 12 center

        * Radio button group defaults to option 1
        global DB_rval = 1
        window control radbegin "radio 1"  20 35 35 10 DB_rval
```

```
        window control radio    "radio 2"  80 35 35 10 DB_rval
        window control radend    "radio 3" 140 35 35 10 DB_rval

        global DB_nval ""
        global DB_eval ""
        global DB_pval ""

        global DB_name "Please enter name:"
        window control static DB_name 5 60 80  9
        window control edit            5 70 80 10 DB_nval

        global DB_pass "Please enter password:"
        window control static DB_pass 95 60 80  9
        window control edit           95 70 80 10 DB_pval password maxlen 8

        global DB_many "Select many:"
        global DB_one  "Select one:"

        window control static  DB_many 5  90 80  9
        window control msimple DB_var  5 100 80 50 DB_ms

        window control static  DB_one 95  90 80  9
        window control ssimple DB_var 95 100 80 50 DB_ss

        window control static  DB_many 5 150 80  9
        window control mcombo  DB_var  5 160 80 40 DB_mc

        window control static  DB_one 95 150 80  9
        window control scombo  DB_var 95 160 80 40 DB_sc

        window control button "OK"      5 200 40 10 DB_ok default
        window control button "Cancel" 50 200 80 15 DB_ca

        global DB_ok "showvals"
        global DB_ca "exit 3000"

        syntax [varlist]
        global DB_var "`varlist'"
        wdlg "Test Dialog" 10 10 190 235
end
capture program drop showvals
program define showvals
        display
        if $DB_chk1 {
                display "You checked check box 1"
        }
        else { display "You did not check check box 1" }
        if $DB_chk2 {
                display "You checked check box 2"
        }
        else { display "You did not check check box 2" }
        if $DB_chk3 {
                display "You checked check box 3"
        }
        else { display "You did not check check box 3" }
        display "You selected choice $DB_rval from the radio buttons"
        display "You entered the name $DB_nval"
        display "You entered the password $DB_pval"
        display "You selected $DB_ms from the select many list box"
        display "You selected $DB_ss from the select one list box"
        display "You selected $DB_mc from the select many combo box"
        display "You selected $DB_sc from the select one combo box"
end
```

——— end of dialog.do —————————

Defining global macros

When you write code for defining the controls on a dialog box, note that the global macros that are used as input for the controls do not have to be defined when the control is defined. You can define them before you use the **window dialog** command, or you can define them after the dialog is running and then refresh the controls using the **window dialog update** command.

References

Newton, H. J. 1997. ip16: Using dialog boxes to vary program parameters. *Stata Technical Bulletin* 36: 11–14. Reprinted in *Stata Technical Bulletin Reprints*, vol. 6, pp. 77–81.

Also See

Complementary:	[R] **window dialog**, [R] **window menu**
Background:	[R] **window**

Title

---
window dialog — Create dialog box (Windows and Macintosh only)

Syntax

<u>win</u>dow <u>d</u>ialog *"description"* $\left\{ x_{\text{offset}} \ y_{\text{offset}} \ \middle| \ . \ . \right\}$ $x_{\text{extent}} \ y_{\text{extent}}$

<u>win</u>dow <u>d</u>ialog update

where *description* is the words to appear as the title of the dialog and $(x_{\text{offset}}, y_{\text{offset}})$ specifies the upper-left corner of the dialog box relative to the Stata window. x_{offset} may be specified as . as may be y_{offset}, meaning the default location for dialog boxes. $(x_{\text{extent}}, y_{\text{extent}})$ specifies the dialog box's size. Units of measurement are approximately one-fifth the width of a character horizontally and one-eighth the height of a character vertically.

Description

window dialog displays a dialog box with the controls that have previously been defined by window control.

window dialog update redraws the controls.

Remarks

window dialog is the second step in programming a dialog box. First, you define the dialog box's controls using window control. Then you display it—open it—using window dialog.

Remarks are presented under the headings

> Opening (displaying) a dialog box
> Working with an open dialog box
> Closing the dialog box
> User-preferred positioning of dialog boxes
> Updating information on the open dialog box

Opening (displaying) a dialog box

Once the dialog box's controls have been defined by window control statements, you use window dialog to open it. For example, a program might contain the statements

```
window control button "OK" 10 10 30 18 DB_ok
window control button "Cancel" 50 10 30 18 DB_ca
global DB_ok ...
global DB_ca ...
window dialog "Sample dialog" . . 100 55
```

The example above is overly simplified because it does not deal with handling the dialog's requests. That is covered below.

Working with an open dialog box

Consider the following dialog-box program:

```
program define ex1
        version 6.0
        window control button "Sum" 10 10 30 18 DB_sum
        window control button "Error" 50 10 30 18 DB_er
        window control button "Cancel" 90 10 30 18 DB_ca
        global DB_sum "summarize mpg"
        global DB_er "exit 111"
        global DB_ca "exit 3000"
        window dialog "Sample dialog" . . 140 55
end
```

Type `ex1` to Stata's prompt and this code displays a dialog box with three buttons, labeled **Sum**, **Error**, and **Cancel**. If you click **Sum**, it executes the command 'summarize mpg'. If you click **Cancel**, it executes 'exit 3000', which will cause the `window dialog` command to exit with return code 3000 and hence `ex1` to terminate with the same return code. We will explain the **Error** button momentarily.

You should try this example. When you click **Sum**, Stata will `summarize mpg` and the dialog box will remain open. Click **Sum** again and Stata will `summarize mpg` again. Click **Sum** with no data in memory and `summarize` will produce an error message but the dialog box will still remain open. Only when you click **Cancel** will the dialog box go away.

Dialog boxes, evidently, do not vanish easily. Errors in the commands they execute, such as `summarize mpg` when there is no `mpg`, do not cause them to close. If you think carefully about this, you will be surprised. `summarize mpg` when there is no `mpg`, for instance, produces a return code of 111. Note that our **Error** button also returns 111. Try the button. Nothing happens! The dialog stays open. Yet clicking **Cancel** causes the dialog to exit (with return code 3000).

One button executes `exit 111` and the other `exit 3000` and yet they have very different outcomes.

Dialog boxes close only when the return code is between 3000 and 3099. Nothing else will cause them to close (except clicking on the Close box, which is just like `exit 3000`).

Why do dialog boxes do this? Because there will be occasions where you want a dialog box to remain open while commands are executing and those commands might fail. If you really want a dialog box to exit, the command must return a return code in the range 3000 to 3099.

Closing the dialog box

When you want a dialog box to close, the action invoked must return a return code in the range 3000 to 3099.

Any dialog box that you design should contain at least two command buttons, one that does something (often labeled **OK**) and another which calls the whole thing off and which should be labeled **Cancel**. Here is a program that does nothing while the dialog box is up but does something after it closes:

```
program define ex2
      version 6.0
      window control button "OK" 10 10 30 18 DB_ok
      window control button "Cancel" 50 10 30 18 DB_ca
      global DB_ok "exit 3001"
      global DB_ca "exit 3000"
      capture noisily window dialog "Sample dialog" . . 100 55
      if _rc==3001 {              /* user clicked okay */
              display "user clicked OK"
      }
      /* Just exit if the user clicked cancel */
end
```

This is a very common dialog-box control program and it differs importantly, if subtly, from ex1. ex1 did something while the dialog box was up. This one waits until the dialog box closes. You can use either style or even combine them.

For most applications, the ex2 style is preferable. You should use the ex1 style only when the result is truly interactive. For instance, perhaps you have a histogram up and, as the user clicks a button, the number of bins is incremented or decremented by 1. That would be coded using the ex1 style. If instead the dialog box is just gathering information to execute some request, the ex2 style is preferable.

Note that a dialog box could have more than one action:

```
program define ex2v2
      version 6.0
      window control button "Sum" 10 10 30 18 DB_sum
      window control button "Describe" 50 10 30 18 DB_des
      window control button "Cancel" 90 10 30 18 DB_ca
      global DB_ca "exit 3000"
      global DB_sum "exit 3001"
      global DB_des "exit 3002"
      capture noisily window dialog "Sample dialog" . . 140 55
      if _rc==3001 {
              summarize
      }
      else if _rc==3002 {
              describe
      }
      /* Just exit if the user clicked cancel */
end
```

Just remember, the return codes 3000 to 3099 are special. No other Stata command returns them. They are reserved for dialog-box communication.

User-preferred positioning of dialog boxes

Users often move dialog boxes after they are displayed. You should honor this preference. The easiest way to do that is to use '. .' to represent the x_{offset} and y_{offset}. In the examples above, you have seen us code statements like

```
      window dialog "Sample dialog" . . 140 55
```

This means the dialog box is to appear wherever the user likes (based on where he or she last moved the previous dialog) and that its size is 140×55.

Alternatively, if you want to force the position of a dialog box, you can code statements like,

```
      window dialog "Sample dialog" 30 40 140 55
```

window dialog saves the final position of the dialog box in r(x) and r(y).

Updating information on the open dialog box

As dialog box controls are manipulated, the associated global macros are automatically updated.

If a dialog box stays open and calls a Stata program, however, and if that program wishes to change the contents of the macros and have those changes immediately reflected on the screen, you code 'window dialog update'. You only need code this if you want the change immediately reflected in the dialog box. The dialog box will be automatically updated when the subprogram returns.

Saved Results

window dialog (not window dialog update) saves in r():

Scalars
$r(x)$ x offset of dialog box
$r(y)$ y offset of dialog box

References

Schmidt, T. J. 1997. ip15: A dialog box layout manager for Stata. *Stata Technical Bulletin* 35: 16–20. Reprinted in *Stata Technical Bulletin Reprints*, vol. 6, pp. 71–77.

Also See

Complementary:	[R] **window control**, [R] **window menu**, [R] **window push**, [R] **window stopbox**
Background:	[R] **window**

Title

> **window fopen** — Display open/save dialog box (Windows and Macintosh only)

Syntax

<u>win</u>dow {<u>fop</u>en | <u>fs</u>ave} *macroname* *"title"* *"filter"* [*extension*]

Description

`window fopen` and `window fsave` allow Stata programmers to use standard **File-Open** and **File-Save** dialog boxes in their programs.

Remarks

`window fopen` and `window fsave` call forth the operating system's standard **File-Open** and **File-Save** dialog boxes. The commands do not themselves open or save any files; they merely obtain from the user the name of the file to be opened or saved and return it to you. The filename returned is guaranteed to be valid and includes the full path.

The filename is returned in the global macro *macroname*. In addition, if *macroname* is defined at the outset, its contents will be used to fill in the default filename selection.

title is displayed as the title of the file-open or file-save dialog.

filter is relevant only with Windows; it is ignored by Stata for Macintosh but it still must be specified. One possible specification is "", meaning no filter. Alternatively, *filter* consists of pairs of descriptions and wildcard file selection strings separated by '|', such as

    "Stata Graphs|*.gph|All Files|*.*"

Stata for Windows uses the filter to restrict the files the user sees. The above example allows the user either to see Stata graph files or to see all files. Windows will display a drop-down list from which the user can select a file type (extension). The first item of each pair (`Stata Graphs` and `All Files`) will be listed as the choices in the drop-down list. The second item of each pair restricts the files displayed in the dialog box to those that match the wildcard description. For instance, if the user selects `Stata Graphs` from the list box, only files with extension `.gph` will be displayed in the file dialog box.

Finally, *extension* is optional. It may contain a string of characters to be added to the end of filenames by default. For example, if the *extension* were specified as `xyz`, and the user typed a filename of `abc` in the file dialog box, `abc.xyz` would be returned in *macroname*.

In Windows, the default *extension* is ignored if a *filter* other than `*.*` is in effect. For example, if the user's current filter is `*.gph`, the default extension will be `.gph` regardless of what *extension* was specified.

❑ **Technical Note**

Since Windows 98, 95, and NT allow long filenames, *extension* can lead to unexpected results. For example, if *extension* were specified as `xyz` and the user typed a filename of `abc.def`, Windows 98, 95 or NT would append `.xyz` before returning the filename to Stata, so the resulting filename is `abc.def.xyz`. Windows 98, 95, or NT users should be aware that if they want to specify an extension different from the default, then they must enter a filename in the file dialog box enclosed in double quotes: `"abc.def"`. This applies to all programs, not just Stata.   ❑

If the user presses the **Cancel** button on the file dialog, `window fopen` and `window fsave` set *macroname* to be empty and exit with a return code of 601. Programmers should use the `capture` command to prevent the 601 return code from appearing to the user.

▷ Example

———————————————————————————————— top of gphview.ado ————————

```
program define gphview
        version 6.0
        capture window fopen D_gph "Select a graph to view:" /*
                */ "Stata Graphs (*.gph)|*.gph|All Files (*.*)|*.*" gph ;
        if _rc==0 {
                display "User chose $D_gph as the filename."
                graph using "$D_gph"
        }
end
```

———————————————————————————————— end of gphview.ado ————————

```
. gphview
```

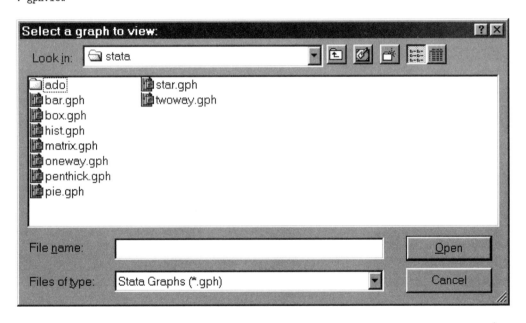

◁

Also See

Complementary:	[R] **window control**, [R] **window dialog**, [R] **window menu**, [R] **window stopbox**
Background:	[R] **window**

Title

> **window manage** — Manage window characteristics (Windows and Macintosh only)

Syntax

<u>win</u><u>man</u>age minimize

<u>win</u><u>man</u>age restore

<u>win</u><u>man</u>age prefs {load | save | default}

<u>win</u><u>man</u>age update variable

<u>win</u><u>man</u>age print {graph | log}

<u>win</u><u>man</u>age forward *window-name*

where *window-name* can be command, dialog, doeditor, graph, help, log, results, review, or variables.

Description

window manage gives Stata programs the ability to invoke features from Stata's main menu.

Remarks

window manage accesses various parts of Stata's windowed interface that would otherwise be available only interactively. For instance, say a program wanted to ensure that the graph window was brought to the front. An interactive user would do that by pulling down **Window** and choosing **Graph**. A Stata program could do the same thing by coding 'window manage forward graph'.

Remarks are presented under the headings

> *Minimizing the main Stata window*
> *Restoring the main Stata window (Windows only)*
> *Windowing preferences*
> *Refreshing the Variables window*
> *Printing Graphs and Logs*
> *Bringing windows forward*

Minimizing the main Stata window

window manage minimize minimizes (hides) the Stata window. With Stata for Windows, this has the same effect as clicking on the minimize button on Stata's title bar. With Stata for Macintosh, this has the same effect as pulling down the Application menu (the little Stata icon in the upper-right corner) and choosing **Hide Stata**.

Example:

```
window manage minimize
```

minimizes the overall Stata window if you are using Stata for Windows and hides Stata's windows if you are using Stata for Macintosh.

Restoring the main Stata window (Windows only)

`window manage restore` restores the Stata window if necessary. This command is allowed only with Stata for Windows.

With Stata for Windows 98/95/NT, this command has the same effect as clicking the Stata button on the taskbar.

With Stata for Windows 3.1, this command has the same effect as double-clicking on the Stata icon at the bottom of your screen after you have minimized Stata.

Example:

```
window manage restore
```

restores Stata's overall window to its normal, nonminimized state.

Windowing preferences

`window manage prefs` { `load` | `save` | `default` } loads, saves, and restores windowing preferences.

Stata for Macintosh allows only `window manage prefs default`, which is equivalent to **Prefs–Restore Defaults**.

Stata for Windows allows `load`, `save`, or `default`. `window manage prefs save` is equivalent to pulling down **Prefs–Save Windowing Preferences**. `window manage prefs load` is equivalent to pulling down **Prefs–Load Windowing Preferences**. `window manage prefs default` is equivalent to pulling down **Prefs–Default Windowing**.

Example:

```
window manage prefs default
```

restores Stata's windows to their "factory" appearance.

Refreshing the Variables window

`window manage update variable` forces an update of Stata's Variables window, the window that displays the currently loaded variable names and their labels. Stata normally updates this window between interactive commands only. If you run a long do- or ado-file which changes the data in a way which would affect the Variables window, the change will not be visible until the do- or ado-file completes.

`window manage update variable` allows a do- or ado-file to force an early update of the Variables window to reflect any changes.

Example:

```
————————————————————————————————————————— top of vars.do ————————
    use auto
    drop make
    window manage update variable
    drop price
    window manage update variable
    drop mpg
    window manage update variable
    label variable weight "Weight of car"
    window manage update variable
————————————————————————————————————————————— end of vars.do ————————
```

If you were to run the above do-file and there were no `window manage update variable` commands in it, you would not see the changes made to the variables until after the do-file completed.

Printing Graphs and Logs

`window manage print { graph | log }` invokes the actions of the **File–Print Graph** and **File–Print Log** menu items. If there is no current graph or log, `window manage print` does nothing; it does not return an error.

Example:

```
window manage print graph
```

displays the print dialog box just as if you pulled down **File–Print Graph**.

Bringing windows forward

`window manage forward` *window-name* brings the specified window to the top of all other Stata windows. This command is equivalent to pulling down **Window** and choosing one of the available windows. The following table lists the *window-name*s which `window manage forward` understands:

window-name	Stata window
`command`	Command window
`dialog`	Dialog window
`doeditor`	Do-file editor window
`graph`	Graph window
`help`	Help/search window
`log`	Log window
`results`	Results window
`review`	Review window
`variables`	Variables window

If a window would not have been available on Stata's **Window** menu (if it would have been grayed out), specifying that *window-name* after `window manage forward` will do nothing. For example, if there is no current log, `window manage forward log` will do nothing; it is not an error.

Example:

```
window manage forward results
```

brings the Results window to the top of the other Stata windows.

Also See

Background: [R] **window**

Title

> **window menu** — Create menus (Windows and Macintosh only)

Syntax

<u>win</u>dow <u>m</u>enu clear

<u>win</u>dow <u>m</u>enu append popout *"defined_menuname"* *"appending_menuname"*

<u>win</u>dow <u>m</u>enu append string *"defined_menuname"* *"entry_text"* *"command_to_execute"*

<u>win</u>dow <u>m</u>enu append separator *"defined_menuname"*

<u>win</u>dow <u>m</u>enu popout *"new_menuname"*

<u>win</u>dow <u>m</u>enu set *"defined_menuname"*

Note: the quotation marks above are required.

"defined_menuname" is the name of a previously defined menu or one of the system menus `"sysmenu"`, `"sFile"`, `"Edit"`, `"Prefs"`, or `"Window"`. The Macintosh also allows *"defined_menuname"* to be `"Search"` or `"Tools"`.

Description

window menu allows you to add new menu hierarchies. **window menu** is available only with Stata for Windows and Stata for Macintosh.

Remarks

Remarks are presented under the headings

> *Overview*
> *Clearing previously defined menu additions*
> *Defining menu items which invoke other menus*
> *Defining menu items which invoke actions*
> *Defining separator bars*
> *Declaring an orphan menu*
> *Activating a menu system*
> *Keyboard shortcuts (Windows only)*
> *Examples*
> *Advanced features: built-in actions*
> *Advanced features: Creating checked menu items*
> *Advanced features: Adding to other Stata menus*
> *Advanced features: Adding Stata's menus to yours*
> *Putting it all together*

Overview

A menu is a list of choices. Here are two menus:

The bar along the top is called the top-level menu. There is only one of these in all of Stata, but you can add to it or even replace it. The three choices below **Regression** form another menu—a submenu—called a popout.

A menu item is a word or phrase that appears in a menu that, when selected, causes something to happen. That something can be the popping out of yet another menu or the invocation of a Stata command or program. **Regression** is a menu item that invoked another menu. **Simple** is a menu item and we would guess that choosing it would cause something other than another menu to be displayed.

A menu hierarchy is the collection of menus and how they relate.

`window menu` allows you to create menu hierarchies, set the text that appears in each menu, and set the actions associated with each menu item.

Everything revolves around menu items. A menu is a collection of menu items. What happens when a menu item is chosen is defined by the menu item. There are three types of menu items,

1. Popouts, which is jargon for a menu item whose associated action is to display yet another menu.

2. Strings, which is jargon for a menu item whose associated action is to invoke a Stata command or program.

3. Separators, which are not exactly menu items at all. They are instead horizontal lines that separate items within a menu.

A menu is formally defined as an ordered list of menu items. The action of adding a new member to the end of the list is called appending a menu item. New menu hierarchies are defined from the top down, not the bottom up. Here is how you create a new menu hierarchy:

1. You append to some existing Stata menu a new popout item using `window menu append popout`. That the new item is itself an empty menu is of no consequence.

2. You append to the new popout item other items, which might be more popouts or strings or separators, all done with `window menu append`. In this way, you fill in the new popout menu you already appended in step 1.

3. If you appended popout items to the menu you defined in step 2, you append to each of them so that they are fully defined. This requires even more `window menu append` commands.

4. You keep going like this until all the popout items are defined. Then you tell Stata's menu manager that you are done using `window menu set`.

Everything you do up to step 4 is merely definitional. It is at step 4 that what you have done takes effect.

You can add menus to Stata. Then you can add more menus. Later, you can add even more menus. What you cannot do, however, is ever delete a little bit of what you have added. You can add some menus and `window menu set`, then add some more and `window menu set`, but you cannot go back and remove part of what you added earlier. What you can do is remove all the menus you have added, restoring Stata to its original configuration. `window menu clear` does this.

So, in our opening example, how did the **Regression** menu-item ever get defined? By typing

```
. window menu append popout "sysmenu" "Regression"
. window menu append string "Regression" "Simple" ...
. window menu append string "Regression" "Multiple" ...
. window menu append string "Regression" "Multivariate" ...
. window menu set "sysmenu"
```

`sysmenu` is the special name for Stata's top-level menu. The first command appended a popout menu item to `sysmenu` called **Regression**. At this point, **Regression** is an empty popout menu.

The next three commands filled in **Regression** by appending to it. All three items are strings, meaning items that when chosen, invoke some Stata command or program. (We have not shown you what the Stata commands are; we just put '...'.)

Finally, `window menu set sysmenu` told Stata we were done and to make our new additions available.

Clearing previously defined menu additions

    <u>win</u>dow <u>m</u>enu clear

clears any additions that have been made to Stata's menu system.

Defining menu items which invoke other menus

    <u>win</u>dow <u>m</u>enu append popout "*defined_menuname*" "*appending_menuname*"

defines items that appear in the top-level menu or which invoke other menus. This command creates a menu item with the text *appending_menuname* (the double-quote characters do not appear in the menu item when displayed) attached to the "*defined_menuname*" item. It also declares that the "*appending_menuname*" will invoke further menu items—that *appending_menuname* is a popout menu. Menus may be appended to Stata's top level menu using the command

    `window menu append popout "sysmenu" "`*appending_menuname*`"`

Example:

    `window menu append popout "sysmenu" "New Menu"`

appends **New Menu** to Stata's top-level menu.

Defining menu items which invoke actions

    <u>win</u>dow <u>m</u>enu append string "*defined_menuname*" "*entry_text*" "*command_to_execute*"

defines items that invoke actions. This command creates a menu item with the text "*entry_text*" which is attached to the "*defined_menuname*"

Example:

    `window menu append string "New Menu" "Describe" "describe"`

appends the menu item **Describe** to the **New Menu** item defined previously and specifies that if the user selects **Describe** the `describe` command is to be executed.

Defining separator bars

> <u>win</u>dow <u>m</u>enu append separator "*defined_menuname*"

defines a separator bar. The separator bar will appear in the position in which it is declared and is attached to an existing popout menu. You may not add separator bars to the top level menu.

Example:

> window append separator "New Menu"

adds a separator bar to **New Menu**.

Declaring an orphan menu

> <u>win</u>dow <u>m</u>enu popout "*new_menuname*"

declares an empty, orphan menu. By orphan we mean only that it has not been attached anywhere in the menu hierarchy yet. When you type

> window menu append popout *existing-menu new-menu*

it is really as if you typed

> window menu popout *new-menu*
> window menu append popout *existing-menu new-menu*

That is, **window menu append** declares the menu for you if it does not exist and attaches it somewhere in the hierarchy. When the menu does exist, it merely attaches it in the hierarchy.

As such, **window menu popout** does not look very useful. However, if you plan on replacing Stata's top-level menu in its entirety, you need to create a menu hierarchy that is in no way a part of the existing menu hierarchy and then use another command. You do that by starting with a **window menu popout**. Once you have the new hierarchy, you use **window menu set** to replace Stata's top-level menu.

Example:

> window menu popout "Top Level"

defines a new menu named **Top Level**.

Activating a menu system

> <u>win</u>dow <u>m</u>enu set "*defined_menuname*"

activates a menu system.

There are two cases. Consider first the case where you have added to Stata's existing menu structure. Thus, **sysmenu** will continue to be the top-level menu. 'window menu set "sysmenu"' reactivates the **sysmenu** and picks up all your additions.

Now consider the case where you wish to replace Stata's top-level menu. Then you previously created an orphan menu, say **Top Level**, and appended a hierarchy to it. 'window menu set "Top Level"' puts the new menu system in place.

These are actually both the same case from Stata's point of view. **window menu set** *name* sets the existing menu structure *name* to be the top level.

Example:

> window menu set "sysmenu"

will activate all the defined menus that were appended to the "sysmenu". If instead we were replacing Stata's top-level menu, we might code

```
window menu set "Top Level"
```

Keyboard shortcuts (Windows only)

When you define a menu item, you may assign a keyboard shortcut. A shortcut (or keyboard accelerator) is a key that allows a menu item to be selected via the keyboard in addition to the usual point-and-click method.

By placing an ampersand (**&**) immediately preceding a character, you define that character to be the shortcut. The ampersand will not appear in the menu item. Rather the character following the ampersand will be underlined to alert the user of the shortcut. The user may then choose the menu item by either clicking with the mouse or holding down *Alt* and pressing the shortcut key. Actually, you only have to hold down *Alt* for the top-level menu. For the submenus, once they are pulled down, holding down *Alt* is optional.

If you need to include an ampersand as part of the "*entry_text*", place two ampersands in a row.

It is your responsibility not to create conflicting keyboard shortcuts. When the user types in a keyboard shortcut, Stata finds the first item with the defined shortcut.

Example:

```
window menu append popout "sysmenu" "&Regression"
```

defines a new popout menu named **Regression** that will appear on the top-level menu bar and that users may access by pressing *Alt-R*.

Examples

▷ Example

Below we use the **window menu** commands to add to Stata's existing top-level menu. The following may be typed interactively:

```
window menu clear
window menu append popout "sysmenu" "&Data"
window menu append string "Data" "&Describe data" "describe"
window menu set "sysmenu"
```

`window menu clear`
    Clears any user-defined menu items and restores the menu system to the default.

`window menu append popout "sysmenu" "Data"`
    Appends to the system menu a new menu called **Data**. Note that you may name this new menu anything you like. You can capitalize its name or not. The new menu appears to the right of all the existing menu items since this is at the top level of the menu system.

`window menu append string "Data" "&Describe data" "describe"`
    Defines the name to be displayed (including a keyboard shortcut). This name is what the user will actually see. It also specifies the command to execute when the user selects the menu item. In this case we will run the **describe** command.

```
window menu set "sysmenu"
```
Causes all the menu items that have been defined and appended to the default system menu to become active and displayed.

◁

▷ Example

Instead of simply adding to Stata's existing menu system, you may replace it from the top-level on down. In the following, we define one menu item; you would presumably define more. This may be typed interactively.

```
window menu clear
window menu popout "MyTopLevel"
window menu append popout "MyTopLevel" "Commands"
window menu append string "Commands" "&Describe" "describe"
window menu set "MyTopLevel"
```

If we wanted to define the C of the "Commands" to act as a keyboard shortcut, we could instead specify the third command as

```
window menu append popout "MyTopLevel" "&Commands"
```

The reference name would remain Commands so that even with the keyboard shortcut, we do not alter the fourth command to include the & character.

◁

Advanced features: built-in actions

Recall that menu items can have associated actions:

<u>win</u>dow <u>m</u>enu append string "*defined_menuname*" "*entry_text*" "*command_to_execute*"

There are actions other than Stata commands and programs you write. In the course of designing a menu system, you may include menu items that will open a Stata dataset, save a Stata graph, or perform some other common Stata menu command.

You can specify "*command_to_execute*" as one of the following

"XEQ about"
displays Stata's About dialog box. The About dialog box is accessible from the default system menu by pulling down **File** and selecting **About**.

"XEQ save"
displays Stata's File Save dialog box in order to save the data in memory. This dialog box is accessible from the default system menu by pulling down **File** and selecting **Save**.

"XEQ saveas"
displays Stata's File Save As dialog box in order to save the data in memory. This dialog box is accessible from the default system menu by pulling down **File** and selecting **Save As...**.

"XEQ savegr"
displays the Save Stata Graph File dialog box that saves the currently displayed graph. This dialog box is accessible from the default system menu by pulling down **File** and selecting **Save Graph**.

"XEQ printgr"
prints the graph displayed in the graph window. This is available in the default menu system by pulling down the **File** menu and selecting **Print Graph**. See also [R] **window manage**.

`"XEQ use"`
> displays Stata's File Open dialog box that loads a Stata dataset. This is available in the default menu system by pulling down the **File** menu and selecting **Open...**.

`"XEQ exit"`
> exits Stata. This is available from the default menu system by pulling down the **File** menu and selecting **Exit**.

`"XEQ printlog"`
> prints the currently opened log to the default printer. This is available in the default menu system by pulling down the **File** menu and selecting **Print Log**.

`"XEQ conhelp"`
> opens the Stata help system to the default welcome topic. This is available by clicking on the **Help!** button in the help system.

Advanced features: Creating checked menu items

command_to_execute in

> <u>win</u>dow <u>m</u>enu append string *"defined_menuname"* *"entry_text"* *"command_to_execute"*

may also be specified as CHECK *macroname*.

Another detail that serious menu designers will want is the ability to create checked menu items. A checked menu item is one that appears in the menu system as either checked (includes a small check mark to the right) or not.

"CHECK *macroname*" specifies that the global macro *macroname* should contain the value as to whether or not the item is checked. If the global macro is not defined at the time that the menu item is created, Stata defines the macro to contain zero and the item is not checked. If the user selects the menu item in order to toggle the status of the item, Stata will place a check mark next to the item on the menu system and redefine the global macro to contain one. In this way, you may write programs that access information that you gather via the menu system.

Note that you should treat the contents of the global macro associated with the checked menu item as "read only". Changing the contents of the macro will not be reflected in the menu system.

Advanced features: Adding to other Stata menus

You can add items to many of Stata's menus, not just the top-level.

You may `window menu append` to **File** (specify `"sFile"`), **Edit** (specify `"Edit"`), **Prefs** (specify `"Prefs"`), and **Window** (specify `"Window"`). The Macintosh also allows appending to **Search** (specify `"Search"`) and **Tools** (specify `"Tools"`).

Advanced features: Adding Stata's menus to yours

You may `window menu append popout` to your menu name `"sFile"`, `"Edit"`, `"Prefs"`, and `"Window"`; the Macintosh also allows `"Search"` and `"Tools"`. When you append one of Stata's menus to yours, you obtain the full subhierarchy. For instance, if you append Stata's **File** menu by typing

> `. window menu append popout "mymenu" "sFile"`

You obtain all the items and submenus of Stata's **File** menu.

Putting it all together

In the following example, we create a larger menu system. Note how each of the items in the menu is defined using the `window menu append popout` if there are further items below it in the hierarchy. Other items are defined with `window menu append string` if the item does not have further items below it.

```
───────────────────────────────────────────────────────────── top of lgmenu.do ─────────
capture program drop mylgmenu
program define mylgmenu
        version 6.0
        win m clear
        win m append popout "sysmenu" "&Regression"
        win m append popout "sysmenu" "&Graphics"
        win m append popout "sysmenu" "&Tests"

        win m append string "Regression" "&Simple" "choose simple"
        win m append string "Regression" "&Multiple" "choose multiple"
        win m append string "Regression" "Multi&variate" "choose multivariate"

        win m append string "Graphics" "&Scatterplot" "choose scatterplot"
        win m append string "Graphics" "&Histogram" "myprog1"
        win m append string "Graphics" "Scatterplot &Matrix" "choose matrix"
        win m append string "Graphics" "&Pie chart" "choose pie"

        win m append popout "Tests" "Test of &mean"
        win m append string "Tests" "Test of &variance" "choose variance"

        win m append string "Test of mean" "&Unequal variances" "CHECK DB_uv"
        win m append separator "Test of mean"
        win m append string "Test of mean" "t-test &by variable" "choose by"
        win m append string "Test of mean" "t-test two &variables" "choose 2var"

        win m set "sysmenu"
end
capture program drop choose
program define choose
        version 6.0
        if "`1'" == "by" | "`1'" == "2var" {
                display in yellow "`1'" in green " from the menu system"
                if $DB_uv {
                        display in green "  use unequal variances"
                }
                else {
                        display in green "  use equal variances"
                }
        }
        else {
                display in yellow "`1'" in green " from the menu system"
        }
end
capture program drop myprog1
program define myprog1
        version 6.0
        display in yellow "myprog1" in green " from the menu system"
end
───────────────────────────────────────────────────────────── end of lgmenu.do ─────────
```

Running this do-file will define a program `mylgmenu` that we may use to set the menus. Note that the menu items will not run any interesting commands as the focus of the example is in the design of the menu interface only. To see the results, type `mylgmenu` in the Command window after you run the do-file. Below is an explanation of the example.

The command

```
win m append popout "sysmenu" "&Regression"
```

is a popout type menu because it has entries below it. If the user clicks on the **Regression** item, we will display another menu with items defined by

```
win m append string "Regression" "&Simple" "choose simple"
win m append string "Regression" "&Multiple" "choose multiple"
win m append string "Regression" "Multi&variate" "choose multivariate"
```

Since none of these entries open further menus, they use the `string` instead of `popout` version of the `window menu append` command. This part of the menu system appears as

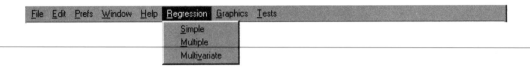

Similarly, the **Graphics** popout menu system is built first declaring that the **Graphics** menu item should be part of the system menu and that there will be items beneath it. In order to declare that there are further choices, we use the `popout` version of the command.

```
win m append popout "sysmenu" "&Graphics"
```

and then populate the menu items below **Graphics** using the `string` version of the `window menu append` command.

```
win m append string "Graphics" "&Scatterplot" "choose scatterplot"
win m append string "Graphics" "&Histogram" "myprog1"
win m append string "Graphics" "Scatterplot &Matrix" "choose matrix"
win m append string "Graphics" "&Pie chart" "choose pie"
```

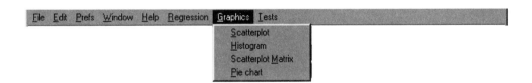

For the **Tests** menu, we decided to have one of the entries be another popout menu for illustration. First we declared the **Tests** menu to be a popout menu from the system menu using

```
win m append popout "sysmenu" "&Tests"
```

We then defined the entries that were to appear below the **Tests** menu. There are two items. One of them is another popout menu and the other is not. For the popout menu, we then defined the entries that are below it.

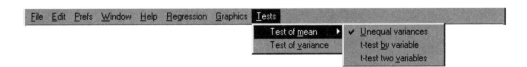

Finally, note how the commands that are run when the user makes a selection from the menu system are defined. For most cases, we simply call the same program and pass an argument that identifies the menu item that was selected. Each menu item may call a different program if you prefer. Also note how the global macro that was associated with the checked menu item is accessed in the programs that are run. When the item is checked the global macro will contain a 1. Otherwise it contains zero. Our program merely has to check the contents of the global macro to see if the item is checked or not.

Also See

Complementary:	[R] **window control**, [R] **window dialog**, [R] **window manage**
Background:	[R] **window**

Title

> **window push** — Copy command into Review window (Windows and Macintosh only)

Syntax

<u>win</u>dow push *command-line*

Description

window push copies the specified *command-line* onto the end of the command history. *command-line* will appear as the most recent command in the **#review** list, and will appear as the last command in the Review window.

Remarks

window push is useful when one Stata command creates another Stata command and executes it. Normally, commands inside ado-files are not added to the command history. But an ado-file such as a dialog interface to a Stata command might exist solely to create and execute another Stata command.

window push allows the interface to add the created command to the command history (and therefore to the Review window) after executing the command.

▷ Example

```
───────────────────────────────────────────────── top of example.ado ─────────
program define example
        version 6.0
        display "This display command is not added to the command history"
        display "This display command is added to the command history"
        window push display "This display command is added to the command history"
end
─────────────────────────────────────────────────── end of example.ado ─────────
. example
This display command is not added to the command history
This display command is added to the command history

. #review
3
2 example
1 display "This display command is added to the command history"

.
```

◁

Also See

Complementary:	[R] **#review**, [R] **window dialog**
Background:	[R] **window**

Title

window stopbox — Display message box (Windows and Macintosh only)

Syntax

window stopbox { stop | note | rusure } ["*line 1*" ["*line 2*" ["*line 3*" ["*line 4*"]]]]

Description

window stopbox allows Stata programs to display message boxes. Up to four lines of text may be displayed on a message box.

Remarks

There are three types of message boxes available to Stata programmers. The first is the stop message box. window stopbox stop displays a message box intended for error messages. This type of message box always exits with a return code of 1.

▷ Example

```
. window stopbox stop "You must type a variable name."  "Please try again."
```

```
--Break--
r(1);
```

◁

(*Continued on next page*)

The second message box is the `note` box. `window stopbox note` displays a message box intended for information messages, or notes. This type of message box always exits with a return code of 0.

▷ Example

. window stopbox note "You answered 3 of 4 questions correctly." "Press OK to continue."

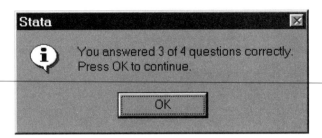

◁

The only way to close the first two types of message boxes is to click the **OK** button displayed at the bottom of the box.

The third message box is the **rusure** (say, "Are you sure?") box. This message box lets a Stata program ask the user a question. The user can close the box by clicking either **OK** or **Cancel**. The message box exits with a return code of 0 if the user clicks **OK** or exits with a return code of 1 if the user clicks **Cancel**.

A Stata program should use the `capture` command to determine whether the user clicked **OK** or Cancel.

▷ Example

. capture window stopbox rusure "Do you want to clear the current dataset from memory?"
"Press OK to clear or Cancel to abort."

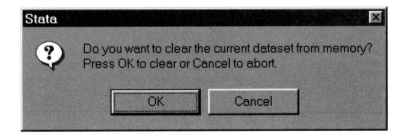

. if _rc == 0 { clear }

◁

Using the stopbox to warn of illegal input

If you program dialog boxes and wish to validate the user input collected by the dialog, you may warn of invalid input with a stopbox. Here we use `window stopbox` to display an error message if the information collected in the dialog box is not valid.

──────────────────────────────── top of sampdlg.do ────────────

```
capture program drop sampdlg
program define sampdlg
        version 6.0
        window control static "Please input a number between 0 and 1:" 10 10 40 10
        window control edit 55 10 15 10 DB_num
        window control button "OK" 20 20 10 15 DB_ok
        window control button "Cancel" 40 20 10 15 DB_ca
        global DB_ok "checknum"
        global DB_ca "exit 3000"
        capture noisily window dialog "Sample input check" 10 10 60 40
        if _rc>3000 {
                di "input was ok - can run program based on input"
        }
end

capture program drop checknum
program define checknum
        version 6.0
        capture confirm number $DB_num
        if _rc {
                window stopbox stop "Please input a number"
                exit    /* Do not close dialog */
        }
        if $DB_num < 0 | $DB_num > 1 {
                window stopbox stop "Number not between zero and one"
                exit    /* Do not close dialog */
        }
        exit 3001       /* Input OK, so close dialog */
end
```

──────────────────────────────── end of sampdlg.do ────────────

Run the `sampdlg.do` file and then type `sampdlg`. Try entering invalid data. If you click on the **Cancel** button, the program will exit, but if you click on the **OK** button, the program will verify that the information is correct. If it is not correct, a stopbox appears and you may try again.

Also See

Complementary:	[R] **beep**, [R] **capture**, [R] **window dialog**
Background:	[R] **window**

Title

wntestb — Bartlett's periodogram-based test for white noise

Syntax

wntestb *varname* [if *exp*] [in *range*] [, graph table level(#) *graph_options*]

wntestb is for use with time-series data; see [R] **tsset**. You must **tsset** your data before using wntestb. In addition, the time series must be dense (nonmissing and no gaps in the time variable) in the sample specified.

varname may contain time-series operators; see [U] **14.4.3 Time-series varlists**.

Description

wntestb performs Bartlett's periodogram-based test for white noise. The result is presented graphically by default, but may be optionally presented as text (table output).

Options

graph specifies that the results should be printed on the graph; this is the default.

table specifies that the test results should be printed as a table instead of the default graph.

level(#) specifies the confidence level, in percent, for the confidence bands included on the graph. The default is level(95) or as set by **set level**; see [U] **23.5 Specifying the width of confidence intervals**.

graph_options are any of the options allowed with **graph, twoway**; see [G] **graph options**.

Remarks

Bartlett's test is a test of the null hypothesis that the data come from a white noise process of uncorrelated random variables having a constant mean and a constant variance.

For a discussion of this test, see Bartlett (1955, 92–94), Newton (1988, 172), or Newton (1996).

▷ Example

In this example, we generate two time series and show the graphical and statistical tests that can be obtained from this command. The first time series is a white noise process and the second is a white noise process with an embedded deterministic cosine curve.

```
. drop _all
. set seed 12393
. set obs 100
. gen x1 = invnorm(uniform())
. gen x2 = invnorm(uniform()) + cos(2*_pi*(_n-1)/10)
. gen time = _n
. tsset time
```

We can then submit the white noise data to the **wntestb** command by typing

. wntestb x1

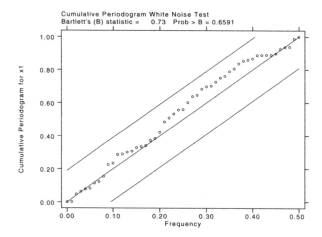

We can see in the graph that the values never appear outside of the confidence bands. We also note that the test statistic has a *p*-value of .66 so that we would conclude that the process is not different from white noise. If we had only wanted the statistic without the plot, we could have used the **table** option.

Turning our attention to the other series (**x2**), we type

. wntestb x2

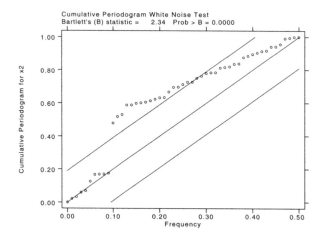

Here the process does appear outside of the bands. In fact, it steps out of the bands at a frequency of .1 (exactly as we synthesized this process). We also have confirmation from the test statistic at a *p*-value less than .0001, that the process is significantly different from white noise.

◁

Saved Results

wntestb saves in r():

Scalars

    r(stat)   Bartlett's statistic   r(p)   Probability value

Methods and Formulas

wntestb is implemented as an ado-file.

If $x(1), \ldots, x(T)$ is a realization from a white noise process with variance σ^2, the spectral distribution would be given by $F(\omega) = \sigma^2 \omega$ for $\omega \in [0, 1]$ and we would, thus, expect the cumulative periodogram (see [R] **cumsp**) of the data to be close to the points $S_k = k/q$ for $q = [n/2] + 1, k = 1, \ldots, q$. Here $[n/2]$ is the maximum integer less than or equal to $n/2$.

Except for $\omega = 0$ and $\omega = .5$, the random variables $2\widehat{f}(\omega_k)/\sigma^2$ are asymptotically independent and identically distributed as χ_2^2. Since a χ_2^2 is the same as twice a random variable distributed exponentially with mean 1, the cumulative periodogram has approximately the same distribution as the ordered values from a uniform (on the unit interval) distribution. Feller (1948) shows that this results in (where U_k is the ordered uniform quantile)

$$\lim_{q \to \infty} \Pr \left(\max_{1 \le k \le q} \sqrt{q} \left| U_k - \frac{k}{q} \right| \le a \right) = \sum_{j=-\infty}^{\infty} (-1)^j e^{-2a^2 j^2} = G(a)$$

The Bartlett statistic is computed as

$$B = \max_{1 \le k \le q} \sqrt{\frac{n}{2}} \left| \widehat{F}_k - \frac{k}{q} \right|$$

where $\widehat{F}_k$ is the cumulative periodogram defined in terms of the sample spectral density $\widehat{f}$ (see [R] **pergram**) as

$$\widehat{F}_k = \frac{\sum_{j=1}^{k} \widehat{f}(\omega_j)}{\sum_{j=1}^{q} \widehat{f}(\omega_j)}$$

The associated p-value for the Bartlett statistic and the confidence bands on the graph are computed as $1 - G(B)$ using Feller's result.

Acknowledgment

wntestb is based on the wntestf command by H. Joseph Newton (1996), Department of Statistics, Texas A&M University.

References

Bartlett, M. S. 1955. *An Introduction to Stochastic Processes with Special Reference to Methods and Applications.* Cambridge: Cambridge University Press.

Feller, W. 1948. On the Kolmogorov–Smirnov theorems for empirical distributions. *Annals of Mathematical Statistics* 19: 177–189.

Newton, H. J. 1988. *TIMESLAB: A Time Series Laboratory*. Pacific Grove, CA: Wadsworth & Brooks/Cole.

——. 1996. sts12: A periodogram-based test for white noise. *Stata Technical Bulletin* 34: 36–39. Reprinted in *Stata Technical Bulletin Reprints*, vol. 6, pp. 203–207.

Also See

Complementary:	[R] **tsset**
Related:	[R] **corrgram**, [R] **cumsp**, [R] **pergram**, [R] **wntestq**
Background:	*Stata Graphics Manual*

Title

wntestq — Portmanteau (Q) test for white noise

Syntax

wntestq *varname* [if *exp*] [in *range*] [, <u>l</u>ags(#)]

wntestq is for use with time-series data; see [R] **tsset**. You must **tsset** your data before using wntestq. In addition, the time series must be dense (nonmissing and no gaps in the time variable) in the sample specified.

varname may contain time-series operators; see [U] **14.4.3 Time-series varlists**.

Description

wntestq performs the portmanteau (or Q) test for white noise.

Options

<u>l</u>ags(#) specifies the number of autocorrelations to calculate. The default is to use $\min([n/2] - 2, 40)$ where $[n/2]$ is the greatest integer less than or equal to $n/2$.

Remarks

Box and Pierce (1970) developed a portmanteau test of white noise that was refined by Ljung and Box (1978). In addition to these two references, see Diggle (1990, section 2.5).

▷ Example

In the example shown in [R] **wntestb**, we generated two time series. One (**x1**) was a white noise process and the other (**x2**) was a white noise process with an embedded cosine curve. Here we compare the output of the two tests.

```
. wntestb x1, table
Cumulative periodogram white noise test
---------------------------------------
 Bartlett's (B) statistic  =    0.7311
 Prob > B                  =    0.6591
. wntestq x1
Portmanteau test for white noise
---------------------------------------
 Portmanteau (Q) statistic =   37.9027
 Prob > chi2(48)           =    0.8750
. wntestb x2, table
Cumulative periodogram white noise test
---------------------------------------
 Bartlett's (B) statistic  =    2.3364
 Prob > B                  =    0.0000
. wntestq x2
Portmanteau test for white noise
---------------------------------------
 Portmanteau (Q) statistic =  201.2912
 Prob > chi2(49)           =    0.0000
```

This example shows that both tests agree. For the first process, the Bartlett and portmanteau result in nonsignificant test statistics: a p-value of 0.6591 for **wntestb** and one of 0.8750 for **wntestq**.

For the second process, each of the tests has a significant result to less than 0.0001.

◁

Saved Results

wntestq saves in **r()**:

Scalars

r(stat)	Q statistic	r(p)	Probability value
r(df)	degrees of freedom		

Methods and Formulas

wntestq is implemented as an ado-file.

The portmanteau test relies on the fact that if $x(1), \ldots, x(n)$ is a realization from a white noise process, then

$$Q = n(n+2) \sum_{j=1}^{m} \frac{1}{n-j} \, \widehat{\rho}^2(j) \longrightarrow \chi_m^2$$

where m is the number of autocorrelations calculated (equal to the number of lags specified) and $\longrightarrow$ indicates convergence in distribution to a χ^2 distribution with m degrees of freedom. $\widehat{\rho}_j$ is the estimated autocorrelation for lag j; see [R] **corrgram** for details.

References

Box, G. E. P. and D. A. Pierce. 1970. Distribution of residual autocorrelations in autoregressive-integrated moving average time series models. *Journal of the American Statistical Association* 65, 1509–1526.

Diggle, P. J. 1990. *Time Series: A Biostatistical Introduction.* Oxford: Clarendon Press.

Ljung, G. M. and G. E. P. Box. 1978. On a measure of lack of fit in time series models. *Biometrika* 65: 297–303.

Also See

Complementary:	[R] **tsset**
Related:	[R] **corrgram**, [R] **cumsp**, [R] **wntestb**

Title

> **xcorr** — Cross-correlogram for bivariate time series

Syntax

> **xcorr** *varname*$_1$ *varname*$_2$ $\left[\right.$, **gen**(*newvarname*) **lags**(#) **needle** <u>table</u> **noplot**
>
> *graph_options* $\left.\right]$

xcorr is for use with time-series data; see [R] **tsset**. You must **tsset** your data before using **xcorr**. *varname*$_1$ and *varname*$_2$ may contain time-series operators; see [U] **14.4.3 Time-series varlists**.

Description

> xcorr plots the sample cross-correlation function.

Options

gen(*newvarname*) specifies a new variable to contain the cross-correlation values.

lags(#) indicates the number of lags and leads to include in the graph. The default is to use $\min([n/2]-2, 20)$.

needle specifies that the autocorrelations should be depicted with vertical lines from zero instead of a connected line between successive estimates.

table requests that the results be presented as a table rather than the default graph.

noplot requests that the tabular output not include the character based plot of the cross-correlations.

graph_options are any of the options allowed with **graph, twoway**; see [G] **graph options**.

Remarks

▷ Example

We have a bivariate time series (Series J from Box and Jenkins 1976) on the input and output of a gas furnace where 296 paired observations on the input gas rate and output percent CO_2 were recorded every 9 seconds. The cross-correlation function is given by

(Continued on next page)

```
. xcorr input output, xline(5) lags(40)
```

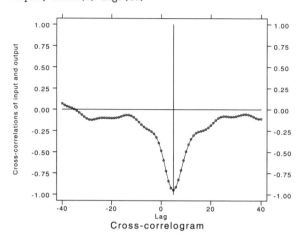

Cross-correlogram

Note that we included a vertical line at lag 5 as there is a well-defined peak at this value. This peak indicates that the output lags the input by 5 time periods. Further, the fact that the correlations are negative indicates that as input (coded gas rate) is increased, output ($\%CO_2$) decreases.

We may obtain the table of autocorrelations and the character-based plot of the cross-correlations (analogous to the univariate time-series command `corrgram`) by specifying the `table` option.

```
. xcorr input output, table lags(20)
                      -1      0      1
    LAG    CORR     [Cross-correlation]
    ------------------------------------
    -20   -0.1033           |
    -19   -0.1027           |
    -18   -0.0998           |
    -17   -0.0932           |
    -16   -0.0832           |
    -15   -0.0727           |
    -14   -0.0660           |
    -13   -0.0662           |
    -12   -0.0751           |
    -11   -0.0927           |
    -10   -0.1180           |
     -9   -0.1484          -|
     -8   -0.1793          -|
     -7   -0.2059          -|
     -6   -0.2266          -|
     -5   -0.2429          -|
     -4   -0.2604         --|
     -3   -0.2865         --|
     -2   -0.3287         --|
     -1   -0.3936        ---|
      0   -0.4845        ---|
      1   -0.5985       ----|
      2   -0.7251      -----|
      3   -0.8429     ------|
      4   -0.9246    -------|
      5   -0.9503    -------|
      6   -0.9146    -------|
      7   -0.8294     ------|
      8   -0.7166      -----|
      9   -0.5998       ----|
```

```
10     -0.4952      ---|
11     -0.4107      ---|
12     -0.3479       --|
13     -0.3049       --|
14     -0.2779       --|
15     -0.2632       --|
16     -0.2548       --|
17     -0.2463        -|
18     -0.2332        -|
19     -0.2135        -|
20     -0.1869        -|
```

Once again, the well-defined peak is apparent in the plot.

◁

Methods and Formulas

The cross-covariance function of lag k for time series x_1 and x_2 is given by

$$\text{Cov}\Big(x_1(t), x_2(t+k)\Big) = R_{12}(k)$$

Note that this function is not symmetric about lag zero, that is

$$R_{12}(k) \neq R_{12}(-k)$$

Define the cross-correlation function as

$$\rho_{ij}(k) = \text{Corr}\Big(x_i(t), x_j(t+k)\Big) = \frac{R_{ij}(k)}{\sqrt{R_{ii}(0)R_{jj}(0)}}$$

where ρ_{11} and ρ_{22} are the autocorrelation functions for x_1 and x_2 respectively. The sequence $\rho_{12}(k)$ is the cross-correlation function and is drawn for lags $k \in (-Q, -Q+1, \ldots, -1, 0, 1, \ldots, Q-1, Q)$.

Note that if $\rho_{12}(k) = 0$ for all lags, then we say that x_1 and x_2 are not cross-correlated.

References

Box, G. E. P. and G. J. Jenkins. 1976. *Time Series Analysis: Forecasting and Control*. Oakland, CA: Holden–Day.

Hamilton, J. 1994. *Time Series Analysis*. Princeton, NJ: Princeton University Press.

Newton, H. J. 1988. TIMESLAB: A Time Series Laboratory Pacific Grove, CA: Wadworth & Brooks/Cole.

Also See

Complementary: [R] **tsset**

Related: [R] **corrgram**, [R] **pergram**

Title

> **xi** — Interaction expansion

Syntax

> **xi** *term(s)*
>
> **xi:** *any_stata_command varlist_with_terms* ...

where a *term* is of the form

i.*varname*	or I.*varname*
i.*varname*$_1$*i.*varname*$_2$	I.*varname*$_1$*I.*varname*$_2$
i.*varname*$_1$**varname*$_3$	I.*varname*$_1$**varname*$_3$
i.*varname*$_1$|*varname*$_3$	I.*varname*$_1$|*varname*$_3$

varname, *varname*$_1$, and *varname*$_2$ denote categorical variables and may be numeric or string. *varname*$_3$ denotes a continuous, numeric variable.

Description

xi expands terms containing categorical variables into indicator (also called dummy) variable sets by creating new variables, and, in the second syntax (**xi:** *any_stata_command*), executes the specified command with the expanded terms. The dummy variables created are

i.*varname*	Creates dummies for categorical variable *varname*
i.*varname*$_1$*i.*varname*$_2$	Creates dummies for categorical variables *varname*$_1$ and *varname*$_2$: all interactions and main effects
i.*varname*$_1$**varname*$_3$	Creates dummies for categorical variable *varname*$_1$ and continuous variable *varname*$_3$: all interactions and main effects
i.*varname*$_1$|*varname*$_3$	Creates dummies for categorical variable *varname*$_1$ and continuous variable *varname*$_3$: all interactions and main effect of *varname*$_3$ but no main effect of *varname*$_1$

Remarks

Remarks are presented under the headings

Background
Indicator variables for simple effects
Controlling the omitted dummy
Categorical variable interactions
Interactions with continuous variables
Using xi: Interpreting output
How xi names variables
xi as a command rather than a command prefix
Warnings

xi provides a convenient way to include dummy or indicator variables when estimating a model (say with `regress`, `logistic`, etc.). For instance, assume the categorical variable `agegrp` contains 1 for ages 20–24, 2 for ages 25–39, 3 for ages 40–44, etc. Typing

```
. xi: logistic outcome weight i.agegrp bp
```

estimates a logistic regression of `outcome` on `weight`, dummies for each `agegrp` category, and `bp`. That is, `xi` searches out and expands terms starting with "`i.`" but leaves the other variables alone. `xi` will expand both numeric and string categorical variables, so if you had a string variable `race` containing "white", "black", and "other", typing

```
. xi: logistic outcome weight bp i.agegrp i.race
```

would include indicator variables for the race group as well.

The `i.` indicator variables `xi` expands may appear anywhere in the *varlist*, so

```
. xi: logistic outcome i.agegrp weight i.race bp
```

would estimate the same model.

You can also create interactions of categorical variables; typing

```
xi: logistic outcome weight bp i.agegrp*i.race
```

estimates a model with indicator variables for all `agegrp` and `race` combinations, including the `agegrp` and `race` main-effect terms (i.e., the terms that are created when you just type `i.agegrp i.race`).

You can interact dummy variables with continuous variables; typing

```
xi: logistic outcome bp i.agegrp*weight i.race
```

estimates a model with indicator variables for all `agegrp` categories interacted with `weight`, plus the main-effect terms `weight` and `i.agegrp`.

You can get the interaction terms without the `agegrp` main effect (but with the `weight` main effect) by typing

```
xi: logistic outcome bp i.agegrp|weight i.race
```

And, of course, you can include multiple interactions:

```
xi: logistic outcome bp i.agegrp*weight i.agegrp*i.race
```

We will now back up and describe the construction of dummy variables in more detail.

Background

The terms continuous, categorical, and indicator or dummy variables are used below. Continuous variables are variables that measure something—such as height or weight—and at least conceptually can take on any real number over some range. Categorical variables, on the other hand, take on a finite number of values each denoting membership in a subclass, for example, excellent, good, and poor—which might be coded 0, 1, 2 or 1, 2, 3 or even "Excellent", "Good", and "Poor". An indicator or dummy variable—the terms are used interchangeably—is a special type of two-valued categorical variable that contains values 0, denoting false, and 1, denoting true. The information contained in any k-valued categorical variable can be equally well represented by k indicator variables. Instead of a single variable recording values representing excellent, good, and poor, one can have three indicator variables, the first indicating the truth or falseness of "result is excellent", the second "result is good", and the third "result is poor".

xi provides a convenient way to convert categorical variables to dummy or indicator variables when estimating a model (say with regress, logistic, etc.).

For instance, assume the categorical variable agegrp contains 1 for ages 20–24, 2 for ages 25–39, and 3 for ages 40–44. (There is no one over 44 in our data.) As it stands, agegrp would be a poor candidate for inclusion in a model even if one thought age affected the outcome. It would be poor because the coding would force the restriction that the effect of being in the second age group must be twice the effect of being in the first and, similarly, the effect of being in the third must be three times the first. That is, if one estimated the model,

$$y = \beta_0 + \beta_1 \, \texttt{agegrp} + X\beta_2$$

the effect of being in the first age group is β_1, the second $2\beta_1$, and the third $3\beta_1$. If the coding 1, 2, 3 is arbitrary, we could just as well have coded the age groups 1, 4, and 9, and the effects would now be β_1, $4\beta_1$, and $9\beta_1$.

The solution to this arbitrariness is to convert the categorical variable agegrp to a set of indicator variables a_1, a_2, and a_3, where a_i is 1 if the individual is a member of the ith age group and 0 otherwise. We can then estimate the model:

$$y = \beta_0 + \beta_{11}a_1 + \beta_{12}a_2 + \beta_{13}a_3 + X\beta_2$$

The effect of being in age group 1 is now β_{11}; 2, β_{12}; and 3, β_{13}; and these results are independent of our (arbitrary) coding. The only difficulty at this point is that the model is unidentified in the sense that there are an infinite number of $(\beta_0, \beta_{11}, \beta_{12}, \beta_{13})$ that fit the data equally well.

To see this, pretend $(\beta_0, \beta_{11}, \beta_{12}, \beta_{13}) = (1, 1, 3, 4)$. Then the predicted values of y for the various age groups are

$$y = \begin{cases} 1 + 1 + X\beta_2 = 2 + X\beta_2 & \text{(age group 1)} \\ 1 + 3 + X\beta_2 = 4 + X\beta_2 & \text{(age group 2)} \\ 1 + 4 + X\beta_2 = 5 + X\beta_2 & \text{(age group 3)} \end{cases}$$

Now pretend $(\beta_0, \beta_{11}, \beta_{12}, \beta_{13}) = (2, 0, 2, 3)$. Then the predicted values of y are

$$y = \begin{cases} 2 + 0 + X\beta_2 = 2 + X\beta_2 & \text{(age group 1)} \\ 2 + 2 + X\beta_2 = 4 + X\beta_2 & \text{(age group 2)} \\ 2 + 3 + X\beta_2 = 5 + X\beta_2 & \text{(age group 3)} \end{cases}$$

These two sets of predictions are indistinguishable: for age group 1, $y = 2 + X\beta_2$ regardless of which coefficient vector is used, and similarly for age groups 2 and 3. This arises because we have 3 equations and 4 unknowns. Any solution is as good as any other and, for our purposes, we merely need to choose one of them. The popular selection method is to set the coefficient on the first indicator variable to 0 (as we have done in our second coefficient vector). This is equivalent to estimating the model:

$$y = \beta_0 + \beta_{12}a_2 + \beta_{13}a_3 + X\beta_2$$

How one selects a particular coefficient vector (identifies the model) does not matter. It does, however, affect the *interpretation* of the coefficients.

For instance, we could just as well choose to omit the second group. In our artificial example, this would yield $(\beta_0, \beta_{11}, \beta_{12}, \beta_{13}) = (4, -2, 0, 1)$ instead of $(2, 0, 2, 3)$. These coefficient vectors are the same in the sense that

$$y = \begin{cases} 2 + 0 + X\beta_2 = 2 + X\beta_2 = 4 - 2 + X\beta_2 & \text{(age group 1)} \\ 2 + 2 + X\beta_2 = 4 + X\beta_2 = 4 + 0 + X\beta_2 & \text{(age group 2)} \\ 2 + 3 + X\beta_2 = 5 + X\beta_2 = 4 + 1 + X\beta_2 & \text{(age group 3)} \end{cases}$$

but what does it mean that β_{13} can just as well be 3 or 1? We obtain $\beta_{13} = 3$ when we set $\beta_{11} = 0$, and so $\beta_{13} = \beta_{13} - \beta_{11}$ and β_{13} measures the difference between age groups 3 and 1.

In the second case, we obtain $\beta_{13} = 1$ when we set $\beta_{12} = 0$, so $\beta_{13} - \beta_{12} = 1$ and β_{13} measures the difference between age groups 3 and 2. There is no inconsistency. According to our $\beta_{12} = 0$ model, the difference between age groups 3 and 1 is $\beta_{13} - \beta_{11} = 1 - (-2) = 3$, exactly the same result we got in the $\beta_{11} = 0$ model.

The issue of interpretation, however, is important because it can affect the way one discusses results. Imagine you are studying recovery after a coronary bypass operation. Assume the age groups are (1) children under 13 (you have two of them), (2) young adults under 25 (you have a handful of them), (3) adults under 46 (of which you have more yet), (4) mature adults under 56, (5) older adults under 65, and (6) elder adults. You follow the prescription of omitting the first group, so all your results are reported relative to children under 13. While there is nothing statistically wrong with this, readers will be suspicious when you make statements like "compared with young children, older and elder adults ...". Moreover, it is likely that you will have to end each statement with "although results are not statistically significant" because you have only two children in your comparison group. Of course, even with results reported in this way, you can do reasonable comparisons (say with mature adults), but you will have to do extra work to perform the appropriate linear hypothesis test using Stata's **test** command.

In this case, it would be better if you forced the omitted group to be more reasonable, such as mature adults. There is, however, a generic rule for automatic comparison group selection that, while less popular, tends to work better than the omit-the-first-group rule. That rule is to omit the most prevalent group. The most prevalent is usually a reasonable baseline.

In any case, the prescription for categorical variables is

1. Convert each k-valued categorical variable to k indicator variables.

2. Drop one of the k indicator variables; any one will do but dropping the first is popular, dropping the most prevalent is probably better in terms of having the computer guess at a reasonable interpretation, and dropping a specified one often eases interpretation the most.

3. Estimate the model on the remaining $k - 1$ indicator variables.

It is this procedure that **xi** automates.

We will now consider each of **xi**'s features in detail.

Indicator variables for simple effects

When you type i.*varname*, **xi** internally tabulates *varname* (which may be a string or a numeric variable) and creates indicator (dummy) variables for each observed value, omitting the indicator for the smallest value. For instance, say **agegrp** takes on the values 1, 2, 3, and 4. Typing

```
xi: logistic outcome i.agegrp
```

creates indicator variables named **Iagegr_2**, **Iagegr_3**, and **Iagegr_4**. (**xi** chooses the names and tries to make them readable; **xi** guarantees that the names are unique.) The expanded logistic model then is

```
. logistic outcome Iagegr_2 Iagegr_3 Iagegr_4
```

Afterwards, you can drop the new variables **xi** leaves behind by typing 'drop I*' (note capitalization).

xi provides the following features when you type i.*varname*:

1. *varname* may be string or numeric.

2. Dummy variables are created automatically.

3. By default, the dummy-variable set is identified by dropping the dummy corresponding to the smallest value of the variable (how to specify otherwise is discussed below).

4. The new dummy variables are left in your dataset. You can drop them by typing 'drop I*'. You do not have to do this; each time you use the xi prefix or command, any previously created automatically generated dummies are dropped and new ones created.

5. The new dummy variables have variable labels so you can determine to what they correspond by typing 'describe' or 'describe I*'.

6. xi may be used with any Stata command (not just logistic).

Controlling the omitted dummy

By default, i.*varname* omits the dummy corresponding to the smallest value of *varname*; in the case of a string variable, this is interpreted as dropping the first in an alphabetical, case-sensitive sort. xi provides two alternatives to dropping the first: xi will drop the dummy corresponding to the most prevalent value of *varname* or xi will let you choose the particular dummy to be dropped.

To change xi's behavior to dropping the most prevalent, you type,

```
. char _dta[omit] prevalent
```

although whether you type "prevalent" or "yes" or anything else does not matter. Setting this characteristic affects the expansion of all categorical variables in the data. If you resave your data, the prevalent preference will be remembered. If you want to change the behavior back to the default drop-the-first-rule, you type

```
. char _dta[omit]
```

thus clearing the characteristic.

Once you set _dta[omit], i.*varname* omits the dummy corresponding to the most prevalent value of *varname*. Thus, the coefficients on the dummies have the interpretation of change from the most prevalent group. For example,

```
. char _dta[omit] prevalent
. xi: regress y i.agegrp
```

might create Iagegr_1 through Iagegr_4 and would result in Iagegr_2 being omitted if agegr = 2 is most common (as opposed to the default dropping of Iagegr_1). The model is then

$$y = b_0 + b_1 \, \texttt{Iagegr\_1} + b_3 \, \texttt{Iagegr\_3} + b_4 \, \texttt{Iagegr\_4} + u$$

Then,

Predicted y for agegrp $1 = b_0 + b_1$	Predicted y for agegrp $3 = b_0 + b_3$
Predicted y for agegrp $2 = b_0$	Predicted y for agegrp $4 = b_0 + b_4$

Thus, the model's reported t or Z statistics are for a test of whether each group is different from the most prevalent group.

Perhaps you wish to omit the dummy for agegrp 3 instead. You do this by setting the variable's omit characteristic:

```
. char agegrp[omit] 3
```

This overrides _dta[omit] if you have set it. Now when you type

. xi: regress y i.agegrp

Iagegr_3 will be omitted and you will estimate the model:

$$y = b'_0 + b'_1 \text{ Iagegr\_1} + b'_2 \text{ Iagegr\_2} + b'_4 \text{ Iagegr\_4} + u$$

Later, if you want to return to the default omission, you type

. char agegrp[omit]

thus clearing the characteristic.

In summary, i.*varname* omits the first group by default but if you define

. char _dta[omit] prevalent

then the default behavior changes to that of dropping the most prevalent group. Either way, if you define a characteristic of the form

. char *varname*[omit] #

or, if *varname* is a string,

. char *varname*[omit] *string-literal*

then the specified value will be omitted.

Examples: . char agegrp[omit] 1
              . char race[omit] White   (for race a string variable)
              . char agegrp[omit]   (to restore default for agegrp)

Categorical variable interactions

i.*varname*₁*i.*varname*₂ creates the dummy variables associated with the interaction of the categorical variables *varname*₁ and *varname*₂. The identification rules—which categories are omitted—are the same as for i.*varname*. For instance, assume agegrp takes on four values and race takes on three values. Typing

. xi: regress y i.agegrp*i.race

results in the model:

dummies for:

$$y = a + b_2 \text{ Iagegr\_2} + b_3 \text{ Iagegr\_3} + b_4 \text{ Iagegr\_4} \qquad \text{(agegrp)}$$
$$+ c_2 \text{ Irace\_2} + c_3 \text{ Irace\_3} \qquad \text{(race)}$$
$$+ d_{22} \text{ IaXr\_2\_2} + d_{23} \text{ IaXr\_2\_3} + d_{32} \text{ IaXr\_3\_2} + d_{33} \text{ IaXr\_3\_3} \quad \text{(agegrp*race)}$$
$$+ d_{42} \text{ IaXr\_4\_2} + d_{43} \text{ IaXr\_4\_3}$$
$$+ u$$

That is,

. xi: regress y i.agegrp*i.race

results in the same model as typing

. xi: regress y i.agegrp i.race i.agegrp*i.race

While there are lots of other ways the interaction could have been parameterized, this method has the advantage that one can test the joint significance of the interactions by typing

. testparm IaXr*

When you perform the estimation step, whether you specify i.agegrp*i.race or i.race*i.agegrp makes no difference (other than in the names given to the interaction terms; in the first case, the names will begin with IaXr; in the second, IrXa). Thus,

. xi: regress y i.race*i.agegrp

estimates the same model.

You may also include multiple interactions simultaneously:

. xi: regress y i.agegrp*i.race i.agegrp*i.sex

The model estimated is

$$
\begin{aligned}
y = a &+ b_2 \, \texttt{Iagegr\_2} + b_3 \, \texttt{Iagegr\_3} + b_4 \, \texttt{Iagegr\_4} && \text{(agegrp)}\\
&+ c_2 \, \texttt{Irace\_2} + c_3 \, \texttt{Irace\_3} && \text{(race)}\\
&+ d_{22} \, \texttt{IaXr\_2\_2} + d_{23} \, \texttt{IaXr\_2\_3} + d_{32} \, \texttt{IaXr\_3\_2} + d_{33} \, \texttt{IaXr\_3\_3} && \text{(agegrp*race)}\\
&+ d_{42} \, \texttt{IaXr\_4\_2} + d_{43} \, \texttt{IaXr\_4\_3}\\
&+ e_2 \, \texttt{Isex\_2} && \text{(sex)}\\
&+ f_{22} \, \texttt{IaXs\_2\_2} + f_{23} \, \texttt{IaXs\_2\_3} + f_{24} \, \texttt{IaXs\_2\_4} && \text{(agegrp*sex)}\\
&+ u
\end{aligned}
$$

Note that the agegrp dummies are (correctly) included only once.

Interactions with continuous variables

i.*varname*$_1$**varname*$_2$ (as distinguished from i.*varname*$_1$*i.*varname*$_2$, note the second i.) specifies an interaction of a categorical variable with a continuous variable. For instance,

. xi: regress y i.agegr*wgt

results in the model:

$$
\begin{aligned}
y = a &+ b_2 \, \texttt{Iagegr\_2} + b_3 \, \texttt{Iagegr\_3} + b_4 \, \texttt{Iagegr\_4} && \text{(agegrp dummies)}\\
&+ c \, \texttt{wgt} && \text{(continuous \texttt{wgt} effect)}\\
&+ d_2 \, \texttt{IaXwgt\_2} + d_3 \, \texttt{IaXwgt\_3} + d_4 \, \texttt{IaXwgt\_4} && \text{(agegrp*wgt interactions)}\\
&+ u
\end{aligned}
$$

A variation on this notation, using | rather than *, omits the agegrp dummies. Typing

. xi: regress y i.agegr|wgt

estimates the model:

$$
\begin{aligned}
y = a' &+ c' \, \texttt{wgt} && \text{(continuous \texttt{wgt} effect)}\\
&+ d_2' \, \texttt{IaXwgt\_2} + d_3' \, \texttt{IaXwgt\_3} + d_4' \, \texttt{IaXwgt\_4} && \text{(agegrp*wgt interactions)}\\
&+ u'
\end{aligned}
$$

The predicted values of y are

agegrp*wgt model	agegrp|wgt model	
$y = a + c\,\mathtt{wgt}$	$a' + c'\,\mathtt{wgt}$	if agegrp = 1
$a + c\,\mathtt{wgt} + b_2 + d_2\,\mathtt{wgt}$	$a' + c'\mathtt{wgt} + d'_2\,\mathtt{wgt}$	if agegrp = 2
$a + c\,\mathtt{wgt} + b_3 + d_3\,\mathtt{wgt}$	$a' + c'\mathtt{wgt} + d'_3\,\mathtt{wgt}$	if agegrp = 3
$a + c\,\mathtt{wgt} + b_4 + d_4\,\mathtt{wgt}$	$a' + c'\mathtt{wgt} + d'_4\,\mathtt{wgt}$	if agegrp = 4

That is, typing

```
. xi: regress y i.agegr*wgt
```

is equivalent to typing

```
. xi: regress y i.agegr i.agegr|wgt
```

Also note that in either case, it is not necessary to specify separately the continuous variable wgt; it is included automatically.

Using xi: Interpreting output

```
. xi: regress mpg i.rep78
i.rep78              Irep78_1-5    (naturally coded; Irep78_1 omitted)
    (output from regress appears )
```

Interpretation: i.rep78 expanded to the dummies Irep78_1, Irep78_2, ..., Irep78_5. The numbers on the end are "natural" in the sense that Irep78_1 corresponds to rep78 = 1, Irep78_2 to rep78 = 2, and so on. Finally, the dummy for rep78 = 1 was omitted.

```
. xi: regress mpg i.make
i.make               Imake_1-74    (Imake_1 for make==AMC Concord omitted)
    (output from regress appears )
```

Interpretation: i.make expanded to Imake_1, Imake_2, ..., Imake_74. The coding is not natural because make is a string variable. Imake_1 corresponds to one make, Imake_2 another, and so on. We can find out the coding by typing 'describe'. Imake_1 for the AMC Concord was chosen to be omitted.

How xi names variables

The names xi assigns to the dummy variables it creates are of the form

$$I\mathit{stub\_groupid}$$

You may subsequently refer to the entire set of variables by typing '$I\mathit{stub}*$'. For example:

name	= I +	stub	+ _ +	groupid	Entire set
Iagegr_1	I	agegr	_	1	Iagegr*
Iagegr_2	I	agegr	_	2	Iagegr*
IaXwgt_1	I	aXwgt	_	1	IaXwgt*
IaXr_1_2	I	aXr	_	1_2	IaXr*
IaXr_2_1	I	aXr	_	2_1	IaXr*

xi as a command rather than a command prefix

xi can be used as a command prefix or as a command by itself. In the latter form, xi merely creates the indicator and interaction variables. Equivalent to typing

```
. xi: regress y i.agegrp*wgt
  i.agegrp              Iagegr_1-4    (naturally coded; Iagegr_1 omitted)
  i.agegrp*wgt          IaXwgt_1-4    (coded as above)
    (output from regress appears )
```

is

```
. xi i.agegrp*wgt
  i.agegrp              Iagegr_1-4    (naturally coded; Iagegr_1 omitted)
  i.agegrp*wgt          IaXwgt_1-4    (coded as above)
. regress y Iagegr* IaXwgt*
    (output from regress appears )
```

Warnings

1. When you use xi, as either a prefix or a command by itself, xi first drops all previously created interaction variables—variables starting with capital I. Do not name your variables starting with this letter.

2. xi creates new variables in your data; most are bytes but interactions with continuous variables will have the storage type of the underlying continuous variable. You may get the message "insufficient memory". If so, you will need to increase the amount of memory allocated to Stata's data areas; see [U] **7 Setting the size of memory**.

3. When using xi with an estimation command, you may get the message "matsize too small". If so, see [R] **matsize**.

Methods and Formulas

xi is implemented as an ado-file.

Also See

Background: [U] **23 Estimation and post-estimation commands**

Title

xpose — Interchange observations and variables

Syntax

xpose, clear [varname]

Description

xpose transposes the data, changing variables into observations and observations into variables. All new variables—that is, after transposition—are made float. Thus, any original variables that were strings will result in observations containing missing values. (Transposing the data twice, therefore, will result in loss of the contents of string variables.)

Options

clear is not optional. This is supposed to remind you that the untransposed data will be lost (unless you have saved it previously).

varname adds the new variable _varname to the transposed data containing the original variable names. In addition, with or without the varname option, if the variable _varname exists in the data before transposition, those names will be used to name the variables after transposition. Thus, transposing the data twice will (almost) yield the original data.

Remarks

▷ Example

You have data on something by county and year; your data contains

```
. list
        county    year1    year2    year3
1.         1        57.2     11.3     19.5
2.         2        12.5      8.2     28.9
3.         3        18       14.2     33.2
```

Each observation reflects a county. To change this data so that each observation reflects a year:

```
. xpose, clear varname
. list
           v1        v2        v3    _varname
1.          1         2         3     county
2.       57.2      12.5        18     year1
3.       11.3       8.2      14.2     year2
4.       19.5      28.9      33.2     year3
```

315

It would now be necessary to drop the first observation (corresponding to the previous county variable) to make each observation correspond to one year. Had we not specified the **varname** option, the variable _varname would not have been created. The _varname variable is useful, however, if we want to transpose the data back to its original form:

```
. xpose, clear
. list
        county    year1    year2    year3
  1.         1     57.2     11.3     19.5
  2.         2     12.5      8.2     28.9
  3.         3       18     14.2     33.2
```

◁

Methods and Formulas

xpose is implemented as an ado-file.

Also See

Related: [R] **reshape**, [R] **stack**

Title

> **xt** — Cross-sectional time-series analysis

Syntax

$$\texttt{xt}cmd \; \ldots \; \big[\texttt{, i}(varname_i) \; \texttt{t}(varname_t) \; \ldots \big]$$

$$\texttt{iis} \; \big[varname_i \big]$$

$$\texttt{tis} \; \big[varname_t \big]$$

Description

The xt series of commands provide tools for analyzing cross-sectional time-series datasets. Cross-sectional time-series (longitudinal) datasets are of the form x_{it}, where x_{it} is a vector of observations for unit i and time t. The particular commands (such as xtdes, xtsum, xtreg, etc.) are documented in the [R] **xt** entries that follow this entry. This entry deals with concepts common across commands.

iis is related to the i() option on the other xt commands. Command iis or option i() sets the name of the variable corresponding to the unit index i. iis without an argument displays the current name of the unit variable.

tis is related to the t() option on the other xt commands. Command tis or option t() sets the name of the variable corresponding to the time index t. tis without an argument displays the current name of the time variable.

If your interest is in general time-series analysis see [U] **29.12 Models with time-series data**.

Options

i($varname_i$) specifies the variable name corresponding to index i in x_{it}. This must be a single, numeric variable, although whether it takes on the values 1, 2, 3 or 1, 7, 9, or even -2, $\sqrt{2}$, π is irrelevant. (If the identifying variable is a string, use egen's group() function to make a numeric variable from it; see [R] **egen**.)

For instance, if the cross-sectional time-series data is of persons in the years 1991–1994, each observation is a person in one of the years; there are four observations per person (assuming no missing data). $varname_i$ is the name of the variable that uniquely identifies the persons.

All xt commands require that i() be specified, but after i() has been specified once with any of the xt commands, it need not be specified again except to change the variable's identity. The identity can also be set and examined using the iis command.

t($varname_t$) specifies the variable name corresponding to index t in x_{it}. This must be a single, numeric variable, although whether it takes on the values 1, 2, 3 or 1, 7, 9, or even -2, $\sqrt{2}$, π is irrelevant.

For instance, if the cross-sectional time-series data is of persons in the years 1991–1994, each observation is a person in one of the years; there are four observations per person (assuming no missing data). $varname_t$ is the name of the variable recording the year.

Not all xt commands require that t() be specified. If the t() option is included in the syntax diagram for a command it must be specified, but after t() has been specified once with any of the xt commands, it need not be specified again except to change the variable's identity. The identity can also be set and examined using the tis command.

Remarks

Consider having data on n units—individuals, firms, countries, or whatever—over T time periods. The data might be income and other characteristics of n persons surveyed each of T years, or the output and costs of n firms collected over T months, or the health and behavioral characteristics of n patients collected over T years. Such cross-sectional time-series datasets are sometimes called longitudinal datasets or panels and we write x_{it} for the value of x for unit i at time t. The xt commands assume such datasets are stored as a sequence of observations on (i, t, x).

▷ Example

If we had data on pulmonary function (measured by forced expiratory volume or FEV) along with smoking behavior, age, sex, and height, a piece of the data might be

```
. list in 1/6

        pid  yr_visit   fev   age   sex   height   smokes
  1.   1071     1991    1.21   25    1       69        0
  2.   1071     1992    1.52   26    1       69        0
  3.   1071     1993    1.32   28    1       68        0
  4.   1072     1991    1.33   18    1       71        1
  5.   1072     1992    1.18   20    1       71        1
  6.   1072     1993    1.19   21    1       71        0
```

The other xt commands need to know the identities of the variables identifying patient and time. With this data, you would type

```
. iis pid
. tis yr_visit
```

Having made this declaration, you need not specify the i() and t() options on the other xt commands. If you resaved the data, you need not bother even respecifying iis and tis in future sessions.

◁

❑ Technical Note

Cross-sectional time-series data stored as shown above is said to be in the long form. Perhaps your data is in the wide form with one observation per unit and multiple variables for the value in each year. For instance, a piece of the pulmonary function data might be

```
 pid   sex   fev91   fev92   fev93   age91   age92   age93
1071    1     1.21    1.52    1.32     25      26      28
1072    1     1.33    1.18    1.19     18      20      21
```

Data in this form can be converted to the long form by reshape; see [R] reshape.

❑

▷ **Example**

Data for some of the time periods might be missing. That is, we have cross-sectional time-series data on $i = 1, \ldots, n$ and $t = 1, \ldots, T$, but only T_i of those observations are defined. With such missing periods—called unbalanced data—a piece of our pulmonary function data might be

```
. list in 1/6
         pid  yr_visit    fev   age   sex   height   smokes
  1.    1071      1991   1.21    25     1       69        0
  2.    1071      1992   1.52    26     1       69        0
  3.    1071      1993   1.32    28     1       68        0
  4.    1072      1991   1.33    18     1       71        1
  5.    1072      1993   1.19    21     1       71        0
  6.    1073      1991   1.47    24     0       64        0
```

Note that patient id 1072 is not observed in 1992. The xt commands are robust to this problem.

◁

❑ **Technical Note**

Throughout the [R] **xt** entries, we will use data from a subsample of the NLSY data (Center for Human Resource Research 1989) on young women aged 14–26 in 1968. Women were surveyed in each of the 21 years 1968 through 1988 except for the six years 1974, 1976, 1979, 1981, 1984, and 1986. We use two different subsets: `nlswork.dta` and `union.dta`.

For `nlswork.dta`, our subsample is of 4,711 women in years when employed, not enrolled in school and evidently having completed their education, and with wage in excess of $1/hour but less than $700/hour.

```
. use nlswork, clear
(National Longitudinal Survey.  Young Women 14-26 years of age in 1968)
. describe
Contains data from nlswork.dta
  obs:         28,534                    National Longitudinal Survey.
                                         Young Women 14-26 years of age
                                         in 1968
  vars:            21                    23 Aug 1998 10:39
  size:     1,027,224 (1.9% of memory free)
-------------------------------------------------------------------------------
    1. idcode     int     %8.0g          NLS id
    2. year       byte    %8.0g          interview year
    3. birth_yr   byte    %8.0g          birth year
    4. age        byte    %8.0g          age in current year
    5. race       byte    %8.0g          1=white, 2=black, 3=other
    6. msp        byte    %8.0g          1 if married, spouse present
    7. nev_mar    byte    %8.0g          1 if never yet married
    8. grade      byte    %8.0g          current grade completed
    9. collgrad   byte    %8.0g          1 if college graduate
   10. not_smsa   byte    %8.0g          1 if not SMSA
   11. c_city     byte    %8.0g          1 if central city
   12. south      byte    %8.0g          1 if south
   13. ind_code   byte    %8.0g          industry of employment
   14. occ_code   byte    %8.0g          occupation
   15. union      byte    %8.0g          1 if union
   16. wks_ue     byte    %8.0g          weeks unemployed last year
   17. ttl_exp    float   %9.0g          total work experience
   18. tenure     float   %9.0g          job tenure, in years
   19. hours      int     %8.0g          usual hours worked
   20. wks_work   byte    %8.0g          weeks worked last year
   21. ln_wage    float   %9.0g          ln(wage/GNP deflator)
-------------------------------------------------------------------------------
Sorted by:  idcode  year
```

```
. summarize

    Variable |     Obs        Mean    Std. Dev.       Min        Max
-------------+--------------------------------------------------------
      idcode |   28534    2601.284    1487.359         1       5159
        year |   28534    77.95865    6.383879        68         88
    birth_yr |   28534    48.08509    3.012837        41         54
         age |   28510    29.04511    6.700584        14         46
        race |   28534    1.303392    .4822773         1          3
         msp |   28518    .6029175    .4893019         0          1
     nev_mar |   28518    .2296795    .4206341         0          1
       grade |   28532    12.53259    2.323905         0         18
     collgrad |  28534    .1680451    .3739129         0          1
    not_smsa |   28526    .2824441    .4501961         0          1
      c_city |   28526     .357218    .4791882         0          1
       south |   28526    .4095562    .4917605         0          1
    ind_code |   28193    7.692973    2.994025         1         12
    occ_code |   28413    4.777672    3.065435         1         13
       union |   19238    .2344319    .4236542         0          1
      wks_ue |   22830    2.548095    7.294463         0         76
     ttl_exp |   28534    6.215316    4.652117         0   28.88461
      tenure |   28101    3.123836    3.751409         0   25.91667
       hours |   28467    36.55956    9.869623         1        168
    wks_work |   27831    53.98944     29.0325         0        104
     ln_wage |   28534    1.674907    .4780935         0   5.263916
```

For `union.dta`, our subset was sampled only from those with union membership information from 1970 to 1988. Our subsample is of 4,434 women. The important variables are `age` (16–46), `grade` (years of schooling completed, ranging from 0 to 18), `not_smsa` (28% of the person-time was spent living outside an SMSA—standard metropolitan statistical area), `south` (41% of the person-time was in the South), and `southXt` (`south` interacted with year, treating 1970 as year 0). You also have variable `union`. Overall, 22% of the person-time is marked as time under union membership and 44% of these women ever belonged to a union.

```
. describe
Contains data from union.dta
  obs:        26,200                          NLS Women 14-26 in 1968
  vars:           10                          16 Aug 1996 10:06
  size:      393,000 (86.9% of memory free)
-------------------------------------------------------------------------------
  1. idcode    int    %8.0g                   NLS id
  2. year      byte   %8.0g                   interview year
  3. age       byte   %8.0g                   age in current year
  4. grade     byte   %8.0g                   current grade completed
  5. not_smsa  byte   %8.0g                   1 if not SMSA
  6. south     byte   %8.0g                   1 if south
  7. union     byte   %8.0g                   1 if union
  8. t0        byte   %9.0g
  9. southXt   byte   %9.0g
 10. black     byte   %8.0g                   race black
-------------------------------------------------------------------------------
Sorted by:
```

```
. summarize
```

Variable	Obs	Mean	Std. Dev.	Min	Max
idcode	26200	2611.582	1484.994	1	5159
year	26200	79.47137	5.965499	70	88
age	26200	30.43221	6.489056	16	46
grade	26200	12.76145	2.411715	0	18
not_smsa	26200	.2837023	.4508027	0	1
south	26200	.4130153	.4923849	0	1
union	26200	.2217939	.4154611	0	1
t0	26200	9.471374	5.965499	0	18
southXt	26200	3.96874	6.057208	0	18
black	26200	.274542	.4462917	0	1
x	4434	1	0	1	1

With both datasets, we have typed

```
. iis idcode
. tis year
```

❏

❏ Technical Note

The `tis` and `iis` commands as well as other `xt` commands that set the t and i index for `xt` data do so by declaring them as characteristics of the data; see [R] **char**. In particular `tis` sets the characteristic `_dta[tis]` to the name of the t index variable. `iis` sets the characteristic `_dta[iis]` to the name of the i index variable.

❏

References

Center for Human Resource Research. 1989. *National Longitudinal Survey of Labor Market Experience, Young Women 14–26 years of age in 1968.* Ohio State University.

Also See

Complementary: [R] **xtclog**, [R] **xtdata**, [R] **xtdes**, [R] **xtgee**, [R] **xtgls**, [R] **xtintreg**, [R] **xtlogit**, [R] **xtnbreg**, [R] **xtpois**, [R] **xtprobit**, [R] **xtrchh**, [R] **xtreg**, [R] **xtsum**, [R] **xttab**, [R] **xttobit**

Title

> **xtclog** — Random-effects and population-averaged cloglog models

Syntax

Random-effects model

> xtclog *depvar* [*varlist*] [*weight*] [if *exp*] [in *range*] [, re i(*varname*) quad(*#*)
>
> noconstant noskip level(*#*) offset(*varname*) *maximize_options*]

Population-averaged model

> xtclog *depvar* [*varlist*] [*weight*] [if *exp*] [in *range*] , pa [i(*varname*) robust
>
> noconstant level(*#*) offset(*varname*) *xtgee_options maximize_options*]

iweights, aweights, and pweights are allowed for the population-averaged model and iweights are allowed for the random-effects model; see [U] **14.1.6 weight**. Note that weights must be constant within panels.

xtclog shares the features of all estimation commands; see [U] **23 Estimation and post-estimation commands**.

Syntax for predict

Random-effects model

> predict [*type*] *newvarname* [if *exp*] [in *range*] [, { xb | pu0 | stdp }
>
> nooffset]

Population-averaged model

> predict [*type*] *newvarname* [if *exp*] [in *range*] [, { mu | rate | xb | stdp }
>
> nooffset]

These statistics are available both in and out of sample; type predict ... if e(sample) ... if wanted only for the estimation sample.

Description

xtclog estimates population-averaged and random-effects complementary log-log (cloglog) models. There is no command for a conditional fixed-effects model as there does not exist a sufficient statistic allowing the fixed effects to be conditioned out of the likelihood. Unconditional fixed-effects cloglog models may be estimated with the cloglog command with indicator variables for the panels. The appropriate indicator variables can be generated using tabulate or xi. However, unconditional fixed-effects estimates are biased.

By default, the population-averaged model is an equal-correlation model; that is, xtclog, pa assumes corr(exchangeable). See [R] **xtgee** for details on how to fit other population-averaged models.

Note: xtclog, re, the default, is slow since it is calculated by quadrature; see *Methods and Formulas*. Computation time is roughly proportional to the number of points used for the quadrature. The default is quad(12). Simulations indicate that increasing it does not appreciably change the estimates for the coefficients or their standard errors. See [R] **quadchk**.

See [R] **logistic** for a list of related estimation commands.

Options

re requests the random-effects estimator. re is the default if neither re nor pa is specified.

pa requests the population-averaged estimator.

i(*varname*) specifies the variable name that contains the unit to which the observation belongs. You can specify the i() option the first time you estimate or use the iis command to set i() beforehand. After that, Stata will remember the variable's identity. See [R] **xt**.

quad(*#*) specifies the number of points to use in the quadrature approximation of the integral. The default is quad(12).

robust specifies the Huber/White/sandwich estimator of variance is to be used in place of the IRLS variance estimator; see [R] **xtgee**. This alternative produces valid standard errors even if the correlations within group are not as hypothesized by the specified correlation structure. It does, however, require that the model correctly specifies the mean. As such, the resulting standard errors are labeled "semi-robust" instead of "robust". Note that although there is no cluster() option, results are as if there were a cluster() option and you specified clustering on i().

noconstant suppresses the constant term (intercept) in the model.

noskip specifies that a full maximum-likelihood model with only a constant for the regression equation be estimated. This model is not displayed but is used as the base model to compute a likelihood-ratio test for the model test statistic displayed in the estimation header. By default, the overall model test statistic is an asymptotically equivalent Wald test of all the parameters in the regression equation being zero (except the constant). For many models, this option can significantly increase estimation time.

level(*#*) specifies the confidence level, in percent, for confidence intervals. The default is level(95) or as set by set level; see [U] **23.5 Specifying the width of confidence intervals**.

offset(*varname*) specifies that *varname* is to be included in the model with coefficient constrained to be 1.

xtgee_options specifies any other options allowed by xtgee for family(binomial) link(cloglog) such as corr(); see [R] **xtgee**.

maximize_options control the maximization process; see [R] **maximize**. Use the trace option to view parameter convergence. Use the ltol(*#*) option to relax the convergence criterion; default is 1e−6 during specification searches.

Options for predict

xb calculates the linear prediction. This is the default for the random-effects model.

pu0 calculates the probability of a positive outcome assuming that the random effect for that observation's panel is zero ($\nu = 0$). Note that this may not be similar to the proportion of observed outcomes in the group.

stdp calculates the standard error of the linear prediction.

mu and `rate` both calculate the predicted probability of *depvar*. mu takes into account the `offset()`. rate ignores those adjustments. mu and `rate` are equivalent if you did not specify `offset()`. mu is the default for the population-averaged model.

`nooffset` is relevant only if you specified `offset`(*varname*) for `xtclog`. It modifies the calculations made by `predict` so that they ignore the offset variable; the linear prediction is treated as $\mathbf{x}_{it}\mathbf{b}$ rather than $\mathbf{x}_{it}\mathbf{b} + \text{offset}_{it}$.

Remarks

`xtclog, pa` is a convenience command if you want the population-averaged model. Typing

    . xtclog ..., pa ...

is equivalent to typing

    . xtgee ..., ... family(binomial) link(cloglog) corr(exchangeable)

Thus, also see [R] **xtgee** for information about `xtclog`.

By default or when `re` is specified, `xtclog` estimates a maximum-likelihood random-effects model.

▷ Example

You are studying unionization of women in the United States and are using the `union` dataset; see [R] **xt**. You wish to estimate a random-effects model of union membership:

```
. xtclog union age grade not_smsa south southXt, re i(id) nolog
Random-effects complementary log-log          Number of obs      =      26200
Group variable (i) : idcode                   Number of groups   =       4434

Random effects u_i ~ Gaussian                 Obs per group: min =          1
                                                             avg =        5.9
                                                             max =         12

                                              Wald chi2(5)       =     540.31
Log likelihood  = -10559.721                  Prob > chi2        =     0.0000
```

union	Coef.	Std. Err.	z	P>|z|	[95% Conf. Interval]	
age	.0111755	.0021351	5.234	0.000	.0069908	.0153602
grade	.0577527	.0080725	7.154	0.000	.0419308	.0735745
not_smsa	-.2122546	.0402186	-5.278	0.000	-.2910817	-.1334275
south	-.8721779	.0552025	-15.800	0.000	-.9803728	-.7639829
southXt	.0173594	.0041862	4.147	0.000	.0091546	.0255641
_cons	-3.066762	.1223098	-25.074	0.000	-3.306485	-2.827039
/lnsig2u	1.158804	.0311211	37.235	0.000	1.097808	1.2198
sigma_u	1.784971	.0277751			1.731354	1.840247
rho	.7611153	.0056584			.7498491	.7720284

```
Likelihood ratio test of rho=0:      chi2(1) =  5968.96   Prob > chi2 = 0.0000
Note: 5811 completely determined observations
```

The output includes the additional panel-level variance component. This is parameterized as the log of the standard deviation $\ln \sigma_\nu$ (labeled lnsig2u in the output). The standard deviation σ_ν is also included in the output, labeled sigma_u, together with ρ (labeled rho)

$$\rho = \frac{\sigma_\nu^2}{\sigma_\nu^2 + 1}.$$

which is the proportion of the total variance contributed by the panel-level variance component.

When rho is zero, the panel-level variance component is unimportant and the panel estimator is no different from the pooled estimator (cloglog). A likelihood-ratio test of this is included at the bottom of the output. This test formally compares the pooled estimator with the panel estimator.

As an alternative to the random-effects specification, you might want to fit an equal-correlation population-averaged cloglog model by typing

```
. xtclog union age grade not_smsa south southXt, i(id) pa

Iteration 1: tolerance = .06579761
Iteration 2: tolerance = .00606811
Iteration 3: tolerance = .00032254
Iteration 4: tolerance = .00001657
Iteration 5: tolerance = 8.860e-07
```

GEE population-averaged model					Number of obs	=	26200
Group variable:			idcode		Number of groups	=	4434
Link:			cloglog		Obs per group: min =		1
Family:			binomial		avg =		5.9
Correlation:			exchangeable		max =		12
					Wald chi2(5)	=	232.45
Scale parameter:			1		Prob > chi2	=	0.0000

union	Coef.	Std. Err.	z	P>|z|	[95% Conf. Interval]	
age	.004578	.0021755	2.104	0.035	.000314	.008842
grade	.0544263	.0095095	5.723	0.000	.0357881	.0730645
not_smsa	-.1051874	.043052	-2.443	0.015	-.1895678	-.020807
south	-.6578935	.0618586	-10.635	0.000	-.7791341	-.5366529
southXt	.0142325	.0041332	3.443	0.001	.0061315	.0223334
_cons	-2.074678	.1357995	-15.278	0.000	-2.34084	-1.808515

◁

▷ Example

In [R] **cloglog** we showed the above results and compared them with cloglog, robust cluster(). xtclog with the pa option allows a robust option (the random-effects estimator does not allow the robust specification) and so we can obtain the population-averaged cloglog estimator with the robust variance calculation by typing

```
. xtclog union age grade not_smsa south southXt, i(id) pa robust nolog
GEE population-averaged model                Number of obs      =      26200
Group variable:                       idcode Number of groups   =       4434
Link:                                cloglog Obs per group: min =          1
Family:                             binomial                avg =        5.9
Correlation:                    exchangeable                max =         12
                                             Wald chi2(5)       =     153.65
Scale parameter:                           1 Prob > chi2        =     0.0000

                     (standard errors adjusted for clustering on idcode)
------------------------------------------------------------------------------
             |             Semi-robust
       union |      Coef.   Std. Err.      z    P>|z|     [95% Conf. Interval]
-------------+----------------------------------------------------------------
         age |    .004578   .0032609     1.404  0.160    -.0018134    .0109693
       grade |   .0544263   .0117508     4.632  0.000     .0313952    .0774573
    not_smsa |  -.1051874   .0548324    -1.918  0.055    -.2126569    .0022821
       south |  -.6578935   .0793593    -8.290  0.000    -.8134348   -.5023522
     southXt |   .0142325    .005975     2.382  0.017     .0025217    .0259432
       _cons |  -2.074678    .177018   -11.720  0.000    -2.421627   -1.727729
------------------------------------------------------------------------------
```

These standard errors are similar to those shown for `cloglog, robust cluster()` in [R] **cloglog**.

◁

Saved Results

`xtclog, re` saves in `e()`:

Scalars

e(N)	number of observations	e(g_avg)	average group size
e(N_g)	number of groups	e(chi2)	χ^2
e(df_m)	model degrees of freedom	e(chi2_c)	χ^2 for comparison test
e(ll)	log likelihood	e(rho)	ρ
e(ll_0)	log likelihood, constant-only model	e(sigma_u)	panel-level standard deviation
e(ll_c)	log likelihood, comparison model	e(N_cd)	number of completely determined obs.
e(g_max)	largest group size	e(n_quad)	number of quadrature points
e(g_min)	smallest group size		

Macros

e(cmd)	xtclog	e(chi2type)	Wald or LR; type of model χ^2 test
e(depvar)	name of dependent variable	e(chi2_ct)	Wald or LR; type of model χ^2 test
e(title)	title in estimation output		corresponding to e(chi2_c)
e(ivar)	variable denoting groups	e(distrib)	Gaussian; the distribution of the
e(wtype)	weight type		random effect
e(wexp)	weight expression	e(predict)	program used to implement predict
e(offset)	offset		

Matrices

e(b)	coefficient vector	e(V)	variance–covariance matrix of the
			estimators

Functions

e(sample)	marks estimation sample

`xtclog, pa` saves in `e()`:

Scalars

`e(N)`	number of observations	`e(deviance)`	deviance
`e(N_g)`	number of groups	`e(chi2_dev)`	χ^2 test of deviance
`e(df_m)`	model degrees of freedom	`e(dispers)`	deviance dispersion
`e(g_max)`	largest group size	`e(chi2_dis)`	χ^2 test of deviance dispersion
`e(g_min)`	smallest group size	`e(tol)`	target tolerance
`e(g_avg)`	average group size	`e(dif)`	achieved tolerance
`e(chi2)`	χ^2	`e(phi)`	scale parameter
`e(df_pear)`	degrees of freedom for Pearson χ^2		

Macros

`e(cmd)`	`xtgee`	`e(scale)`	x2, dev, phi, or #; scale parameter
`e(cmd2)`	`xtclog`	`e(ivar)`	variable denoting groups
`e(depvar)`	name of dependent variable	`e(vcetype)`	covariance estimation method
`e(family)`	`binomial`	`e(chi2type)`	Wald; type of model χ^2 test
`e(link)`	`cloglog`; link function	`e(offset)`	offset
`e(corr)`	correlation structure	`e(predict)`	program used to implement predict

Matrices

`e(b)`	coefficient vector	`e(R)`	estimated working correlation matrix
`e(V)`	variance–covariance matrix of the estimators		

Functions

`e(sample)`	marks estimation sample

Methods and Formulas

`xtclog` is implemented as an ado-file.

`xtclog` reports the population-averaged results obtained by using `xtgee, family(binomial)` `link(cloglog)` to obtain estimates.

Assuming a normal distribution, $N(0, \sigma_\nu^2)$, for the random effects ν_i, we have that

$$\Pr(y_i|x_i) = \int_{-\infty}^{\infty} \frac{e^{-\nu_i^2/2\sigma_\nu^2}}{\sqrt{2\pi}\sigma_\nu} \left[\prod_{t=1}^{n_i} F(x_{it}\beta + \nu_i) \right] d\nu_i$$

where

$$F(x_{it}\beta + \nu_i) = \begin{cases} 1 - \exp\left(- \exp(x_{it}\beta + \nu_i) \right) & \text{if } y_{it} \neq 0 \\ \exp\left(- \exp(x_{it}\beta + \nu_i) \right) & \text{otherwise} \end{cases}$$

and we can approximate the integral with M-point Gauss–Hermite quadrature

$$\int_{-\infty}^{\infty} e^{-x^2} f(x)dx \approx \sum_{m=1}^{M} w_m^* f(a_m^*)$$

where the w_m^* denote the quadrature weights and the a_m^* denote the quadrature abscissas. The log-likelihood L where $\rho = \sigma_\nu^2/(\sigma_\nu^2 + 1)$ is then calculated using the quadrature

$$L = \sum_{i=1}^{n} w_i \log\left(\Pr(y_i|x_i)\right)$$

$$\approx \sum_{i=1}^{n} w_i \log \frac{1}{\sqrt{\pi}} \sum_{m=1}^{M} w_m^* \prod_{t=1}^{n_i} F\left(x_{it}\beta + \sqrt{2\frac{\rho}{1-\rho}}\, a_m^*\right)$$

The quadrature formula requires that the integrated function be well-approximated by a polynomial. As the number of time periods becomes large (as panel size gets large)

$$\prod_{t=1}^{n_i} F(x_{it}\beta + \nu_i)$$

is no longer well-approximated by a polynomial. As a general rule-of-thumb, you should use this quadrature approach only for small-to-moderate panel sizes (based on simulations, 50 is a reasonably safe upper bound). However, if the data really come from random-effects cloglog and rho is not too large (less than say .3), then the panel size could be 500 and the quadrature approximation will still be fine. If the data is not random-effects cloglog or rho is large (bigger than say .7), then the quadrature approximation may be poor for panel sizes larger than 10. The quadchk command should be used to investigate the applicability of the numeric technique used in this command.

References

Liang, K.-Y. and S. L. Zeger. 1986. Longitudinal data analysis using generalized linear models. *Biometrika* 73: 13–22.

Neuhaus, J. M. 1992. Statistical methods for longitudinal and clustered designs with binary responses. *Statistical Methods in Medical Research* 1: 249–273.

Neuhaus, J. M., J. D. Kalbfleisch, and W. W. Hauck. 1991. A comparison of cluster-specific and population-averaged approaches for analyzing correlated binary data. *International Statistical Review* 59: 25–35.

Pendergast, J. F., S. J. Gange, M. A. Newton, M. J. Lindstrom, M. Palta, and M. R. Fisher. 1996. A survey of methods for analyzing clustered binary response data. *International Statistical Review* 64: 89–118.

Also See

Complementary:	[R] **lincom**, [R] **predict**, [R] **quadchk**, [R] **test**, [R] **testnl**, [R] **vce**, [R] **xtdata**, [R] **xtdes**, [R] **xtsum**, [R] **xttab**
Related:	[R] **cloglog**, [R] **xtgee**, [R] **xtlogit**, [R] **xtprobit**
Background:	[U] **16.5 Accessing coefficients and standard errors**, [U] **23 Estimation and post-estimation commands**, [U] **23.11 Obtaining robust variance estimates**, [R] **xt**

Title

xtdata — Faster specification searches with xt data

Syntax

xtdata [varlist] [if exp] [in range] [, be fe re ratio(#) clear i(varname_i)]

Description

If you have not read [R] **xt** and [R] **xtreg**, please do so.

xtdata produces a converted dataset of the variables specified or, if *varlist* is not specified, all the variables in the data. Once converted, Stata's ordinary `regress` command may be used to perform specification searches more quickly than use of xtreg; see [R] **regress** and [R] **xtreg**. In the case of xtdata, re, a variable named `constant` is also created. When using `regress` after xtdata, re, specify `nocons` and include `constant` in the regression. After xtdata, be and xtdata, fe, you need not include `constant` or specify `regress`'s `nocons` option.

Options

be specifies the data is to be converted into a form suitable for between estimation.

fe specifies the data is to be converted into a form suitable for fixed-effects (within) estimation.

re specifies the data is to be converted into a form suitable for random-effects estimation. re is the default if none of be, fe, or re is specified. ratio() must also be specified.

ratio(#), used with xtdata, re only, specifies the ratio $\sigma_\nu/\sigma_\epsilon$, the ratio of the random effect to the pure residual. Note, this is the ratio of the standard deviations, not the variances.

clear specifies that the data may be converted even though it has changed since it was last saved on disk.

i(varname_i) specifies the variable name corresponding to i in $\mathbf{x}_{it}$; see [R] **xt**.

Remarks

If you have not read [R] **xt**, please do so.

The formal estimation commands of xtreg—see [R] **xtreg**—are not instant, especially with large datasets. Equations (2), (3), and (4) of [R] **xtreg** provide a description of the data necessary to estimate each of the models with OLS. The idea here is to transform the data once to the appropriate form and then use `regress` to more quickly estimate such models.

▷ Example

Please see the example in [R] **xtreg** demonstrating between-effects regression. An alternative way to estimate the between equation is to convert the data in memory into the between data:

```
. use nlswork, clear
(National Longitudinal Survey.  Young Women 14-26 years of age in 1968)
. xtdata ln_w grade age* ttl_exp* tenure* black not_smsa south, be clear
. regress ln_w grade age* ttl_exp* tenure* black not_smsa south

    Source |       SS       df       MS                Number of obs =    4697
-----------+------------------------------             F( 10,  4686) =  450.23
     Model | 415.021612     10  41.5021612             Prob > F      =  0.0000
  Residual | 431.954992   4686  .092179896             R-squared     =  0.4900
-----------+------------------------------             Adj R-squared =  0.4889
     Total | 846.976604   4696  .180361287             Root MSE      =  .30361

-------------------------------------------------------------------------------
   ln_wage |     Coef.   Std. Err.      t    P>|t|     [95% Conf. Interval]
-----------+-------------------------------------------------------------------
     grade |   .0607602   .0020006    30.372  0.000     .0568381    .0646822
 (output omitted )
-------------------------------------------------------------------------------
```

The output is the same as produced by **xtreg, be**; the reported R^2 is the R^2 between. There are no time savings in using **xtdata** followed by just one **regress**. The use of **xtdata** is justified when you intend to explore the specification of the model by running many alternative regressions.

◁

❑ Technical Note

   It is important that when using **xtdata** you eliminate any variables you do not intend to use and that have missing values. **xtdata** follows a casewise deletion rule, which means that an observation is excluded from the conversion if it is missing on any of the variables. In the example above, we specified the variables to be converted on the command line. Alternatively, we could drop the variables first and it might even be useful to preserve our estimation sample:

```
. use nlswork, clear
(National Longitudinal Survey.  Young Women 14-26 years of age in 1968)
. keep id year ln_w grade age* ttl_exp* tenure* black not_smsa south
. save regsmpl
```

❑

▷ Example

   xtdata with the **fe** option converts the data so that results are equivalent to estimating with **xtreg** with the **fe** option.

```
. use regsmpl
(NLS Women 14-26 in 1968)
. xtdata, fe
. regress ln_w grade age* ttl_exp* tenure* black not_smsa south

    Source |       SS       df       MS                Number of obs =   28091
-----------+------------------------------             F(  8, 28082) =  732.64
     Model | 412.443883      8  51.5554854             Prob > F      =  0.0000
  Residual | 1976.12232  28082  .070369714             R-squared     =  0.1727
-----------+------------------------------             Adj R-squared =  0.1724
     Total | 2388.5662   28090  .085032617             Root MSE      =  .26527
```

```
-----------------------------------------------------------------------------
   ln_wage |      Coef.   Std. Err.       t    P>|t|     [95% Conf. Interval]
-----------+-----------------------------------------------------------------
     grade |  (dropped)
       age |   .0359987    .0030903    11.649   0.000     .0299415    .0420558
      age2 |   -.000723    .0000486   -14.876   0.000    -.0008183   -.0006277
  (output omitted)
-----------------------------------------------------------------------------
```

The coefficients reported by **regress** after **xtdata, fe** are the same as those reported by **xtreg, fe**, but the standard errors are slightly smaller. This is because no adjustment has been made to the estimated covariance matrix for the estimation of the person means. The difference is small, however, and results are adequate for a specification search.

◁

▷ Example

To use **xtdata, re**, you must specify the ratio $\sigma_\nu/\sigma_\epsilon$, the ratio of the standard deviations of the random effect and pure residual. Merely to show the relationship of **regress** after **xtdata, re** to **xtreg, re**, we will specify this ratio as $.2579053/.2906892 = .8872201$, which is the number **xtreg** reports when the model is estimated from the outset; see the random-effects example in [R] **xtreg**. For specification-search purposes, however, it is adequate to specify this number more crudely and, in fact, in performing the specification search for this manual entry, we used **ratio(1)**.

```
. xtdata, clear re ratio(.8872201)
------------------- theta --------------------
   min      5%      median      95%      max
 0.2520   0.2520    0.5499    0.7016   0.7206
```

xtdata reports the distribution of θ based on the specified ratio. If this were balanced data, θ would have been constant.

When running regressions with this data, you must specify the **nocons** option and include the variable **constant**:

```
. reg ln_w grade age* ttl_exp* tenure* black not_smsa south constant, nocons
      Source |       SS       df       MS              Number of obs =   28091
-------------+------------------------------          F( 11, 28080) =14302.56
       Model | 13271.7162     11  1206.51965          Prob > F      =  0.0000
    Residual | 2368.74211  28080  .084356913          R-squared     =  0.8486
-------------+------------------------------          Adj R-squared =  0.8485
       Total | 15640.4583  28091  .556778267          Root MSE      =  .29044

-----------------------------------------------------------------------------
   ln_wage |      Coef.   Std. Err.       t    P>|t|     [95% Conf. Interval]
-----------+-----------------------------------------------------------------
     grade |   .0646499    .0017812    36.296   0.000     .0611587    .0681411
  (output omitted)
  constant |   .2387207     .049469     4.826   0.000     .1417591    .3356823
-----------------------------------------------------------------------------
```

Results are the same coefficients and standard errors as **xtreg, re** previously estimated. The summaries at the top, however, should be ignored. These summaries are expressed in terms of equation (4) of [R] **xtreg** and, moreover, for a model without a constant.

◁

❏ Technical Note

Obviously, some caution is required in using `xtdata`. The following guidelines will help:

1. `xtdata` is intended for use during the specification search phase of analysis only. Final results should be estimated with `xtreg` on unconverted data.

2. After converting the data, you may use `regress` to obtain estimates of the coefficients and their standard errors. In the case of `regress` after `xtdata, fe`, the standard errors are too small, but only slightly.

3. You may loosely interpret the coefficient's significance tests and confidence intervals. However, for results after `xtdata, fe` and `re`, a wrong (but very close to correct) distribution is being assumed.

4. You should ignore the summary statistics reported at the top of `regress`'s output.

5. After converting the data, you may form linear, but not nonlinear, combinations of regressors; that is, if your data contained age, it would not be correct to convert the data and then form age squared. All nonlinear transformations should be done before conversion. (For `xtdata, be`, you can get away with forming nonlinear combinations *ex post*, but results will then not be exact.)
                                                                                                ❏

❏ Technical Note

The `xtdata` command can be used to assist in examining data, especially with `graph`. The graphs below were produced by typing

```
. use nlswork
. iis idcode
. tis year
. xtdata, be
. graph ln_wage age,   various options  saving(figure1)

. use nlswork, clear
. iis idcode
. tis year
. xtdata, fe
. graph ln_wage age,   various options  saving(figure2)

. use nlswork, clear
. graph ln_wage age,   various options  saving(figure3)
```

(Graphs on next page)

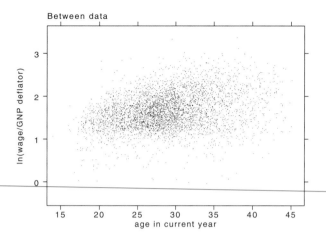

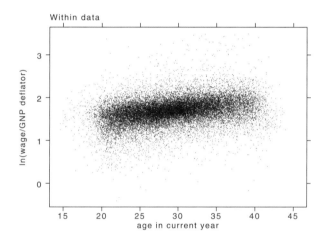

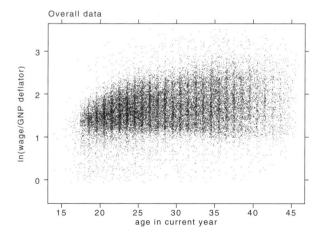

Methods and Formulas

xtdata is implemented as an ado-file.

(This is a continuation of the *Methods and Formulas* of [R] **xtreg**.)

xtdata, be, fe, and re transform the data according to equations (2), (3), and (4), respectively, of [R] **xtreg**, except that xtdata, fe adds back in the overall mean, thus forming the transformation $\mathbf{x}_{it} - \overline{x}_i + \overline{\overline{x}}$.

xtdata, re requires the user to specify r as an estimate of $\sigma_\nu / \sigma_\epsilon$. θ_i is calculated from

$$\theta_i = 1 - \frac{1}{\sqrt{T_i r^2 + 1}}$$

Also See

Complementary: [R] **xtreg**; [R] **regress**

Background: [R] **xt**

Title

xtdes — Describe pattern of xt data

Syntax

xtdes $\begin{bmatrix} \text{if } exp \end{bmatrix}$ $\begin{bmatrix} , & \underline{p}\text{atterns}(\#) & \text{i}(\textit{varname}_i) & \text{t}(\textit{varname}_t) \end{bmatrix}$

Description

xtdes describes the participation pattern of cross-sectional time-series (xt) data.

Options

patterns(#) specifies the maximum number of participation patterns to be reported; patterns(9) is the default. Specifying patterns(50) would list up to 50 patterns. Specifying patterns(1000) is taken to mean patterns(∞); all the patterns will be listed.

i(*varname*$_i$) specifies the variable name corresponding to i in $\mathbf{x}_{it}$; see [R] **xt**.

t(*varname*$_t$) specifies the variable name corresponding to t in $\mathbf{x}_{it}$; see [R] **xt**.

Remarks

If you have not read [R] **xt**, please do so.

xtdes does not have a simple-data counterpart. It describes the cross-sectional and time-series aspects of the data in memory.

▷ Example

In [R] **xt**, we introduced data based on a subsample of the NLSY data on young women aged 14–26 in 1968. Here is a description of the data used in many of the [R] **xt** examples:

(Continued on next page)

```
. use nlswork
(National Longitudinal Survey.  Young Women 14-26 years of age in 1968)
. xtdes, i(id) t(year)
   idcode:  1, 2, ..., 5159                                      n =      4711
     year:  68, 69, ..., 88                                      T =        15
            Delta(year) = 1; (88-68)+1 = 21
            (idcode*year uniquely identifies each observation)
Distribution of T_i:    min     5%    25%    50%    75%    95%    max
                          1      1      3      5      9     13     15

    Freq.  Percent    Cum. | Pattern
   ---------------------------+-------------------------
      136     2.89    2.89 | 1...................
      114     2.42    5.31 | ...................1
       89     1.89    7.20 | ................1.11
       87     1.85    9.04 | .................11
       86     1.83   10.87 | 111111.1.11.1.11.1.11
       61     1.29   12.16 | .............11.1.11
       56     1.19   13.35 | 11..................
       54     1.15   14.50 | ..............1.1.11
       54     1.15   15.64 | .......1.11.1.11.1.11
     3974    84.36  100.00 | (other patterns)
   ---------------------------+-------------------------
     4711   100.00         | XXXXXX.X.XX.X.XX.X.XX
```

xtdes tells us that we have 4,711 women in our data and that the idcode that identifies each ranges from 1 to 5,159. We are also told that the maximum number of individual years over which we observe any woman is 15. (The year variable, however, ranges over 21 years.) We are reassured that idcode and year, taken together, uniquely identify each observation in our data. We are also shown the distribution of T_i; 50% of our women are observed 5 years or less. Only 5% of our women are observed 13 years or more.

Finally, we are shown the participation pattern. A 1 in the pattern means one observation that year; a dot means no observation. The largest fraction of our women, but still only 2.89%, was observed in the single year 1968 and not thereafter; the next largest fraction was observed in 1988 but not before; and the next largest fraction was observed in 1985, 1987, and 1988.

At the bottom is the sum of the participation patterns, including the patterns that were not shown. We can see that none of the women were observed in six of the years (there are six dots). (The survey was not administered in those six years.)

If we wished, we could see more of the patterns by specifying the patterns() option and, in fact, we could see all the patterns by specifying patterns(1000).

◁

▷ Example

The strange participation patterns shown above have to do with our subsampling of the data and not with the administrators of the survey. As an aside, here is the data from which we drew the sample used in the [R] **xt** examples:

(Continued on next page)

```
. xtdes
  idcode:  1, 2, ..., 5159                                   n =        5159
    year:  68, 69, ..., 88                                   T =          15
           Delta(year) = 1; (88-68)+1 = 21
           (idcode*year does not uniquely identify observations)
Distribution of T_i:   min      5%     25%      50%     75%     95%     max
                         1       2      11       15      16      19      30

     Freq.  Percent   Cum. |  Pattern
   --------------------------+-----------------------
      1034    20.04   20.04 |  111111.1.11.1.11.1.11
       153     2.97   23.01 |  1..................
       147     2.85   25.86 |  112111.1.11.1.11.1.11
       130     2.52   28.38 |  111112.1.11.1.11.1.11
       122     2.36   30.74 |  111211.1.11.1.11.1.11
       113     2.19   32.93 |  11.................
        84     1.63   34.56 |  111111.1.11.1.11.1.12
        79     1.53   36.09 |  111111.1.12.1.11.1.11
        67     1.30   37.39 |  111111.1.11.1.11.1.1.
      3230    62.61  100.00 |  (other patterns)
   --------------------------+-----------------------
      5159   100.00         |  XXXXXX.X.XX.X.XX.X.XX
```

Note that we have multiple observations per year. In the pattern, 2 is used to indicate a woman appears twice in the year, 3 to indicate 3 times, and so on—X is used to mean 10 or more should that be necessary.

In fact, this is a dataset which was itself extracted from the NLSY in which t is not time but job number. In order to simplify exposition, we made a simpler dataset by selecting the last job in each year.

◁

Methods and Formulas

xtdes is implemented as an ado-file.

Also See

Related: [R] **xtsum**, [R] **xttab**

Background: [R] **xt**

Title

> **xtgee** — Estimate population-averaged panel-data models using GEE

Syntax

xtgee *depvar* [*varlist*] [*weight*] [if *exp*] [in *range*] [,

    <u>f</u>amily(*family*) <u>link</u>(*link*) <u>corr</u>(*correlation*)

    i(*varname*) t(*varname*) force <u>r</u>obust <u>score</u>(*newvar*) <u>ef</u>orm <u>level</u>(*#*)

    <u>e</u>xposure(*varname*) <u>off</u>set(*varname*) <u>nocon</u>stant <u>s</u>cale(x2 | dev | *#* | phi)

    tol(*#*) iter(*#*) <u>nolog</u>]

xtcorr

where *family* is one of { <u>b</u>inomial [*#* | *varname*] | <u>g</u>aussian | <u>gamma</u> | <u>ig</u>aussian |

                   <u>nb</u>inomial [*#*] | <u>p</u>oisson }

and *link* is one of { <u>i</u>dentity | <u>c</u>loglog | log | <u>logit</u> | <u>nb</u>inomial | <u>opower</u> [*#*] |

                  <u>power</u> [*#*] | <u>p</u>robit | <u>r</u>eciprocal }

and *correlation* is one of { <u>ind</u>ependent | <u>exc</u>hangeable | ar *#* | <u>s</u>tationary *#* |

                  <u>non</u>stationary *#* | <u>uns</u>tructured | <u>fixed</u> *matname* }

For example,

    . xtgee y x1 x2, family(gauss) link(ident) corr(exchangeable) i(id)

would estimate a random-effects linear regression—note that the corr(exchangeable) option does not in general provide random effects. It actually fits an equal-correlation population-averaged model that is equal to the random-effects model for linear regression.

iweights, aweights, and pweights are allowed; see [U] **14.1.6 weight**. Note that weights must be constant within panels.

xtgee shares the features of all estimation commands; see [U] **23 Estimation and post-estimation commands**.

Syntax for predict

predict [*type*] *newvarname* [if *exp*] [in *range*] [, { mu | <u>r</u>ate | xb | stdp }

    <u>nooff</u>set]

These statistics are available both in and out of sample; type predict ... if e(sample) ... if wanted only for the estimation sample.

Description

xtgee estimates cross-sectional time-series linear models. In particular, xtgee estimates general linear models and allows you to specify the within-group correlation structure for the panels.

xtcorr is for use after xtgee. It displays the estimated matrix of the within-group correlations.

See [R] **logistic** and [R] **regress** for lists of related estimation commands.

Options

family(*family*) specifies the distribution of *depvar*; family(gauss) is the default.

link(*link*) specifies the link function; the default is the canonical link for the family() specified.

corr(*correlation*) specifies the within-group correlation structure; the default corresponds to the equal-correlation model, corr(exchangeable).

When you specify a correlation structure that requires a lag, you indicate the lag after the structure's name with or without a blank, e.g., corr(ar 1) or corr(ar1).

If you specify the fixed correlation structure, you specify the name of the matrix containing the assumed correlations following the word fixed, e.g., corr(fixed myr).

i(*varname*) specifies the variable that contains the unit to which the observation belongs. You can specify the i() option the first time you estimate or use the iis command to set i() beforehand. After that, Stata will remember the variable's identity. See [R] **xt**.

t(*varname*) specifies the variable that contains the time at which the observation was made. You can specify the t() option the first time you estimate or use the tis command to set t() beforehand. After that, Stata will remember the variable's identity.

xtgee does not need to know t() for the corr(independent) and corr(exchangeable) correlation structures. Whether you specify t() makes no difference in these two cases.

force specifies that estimation is to be forced even though t() is not equally spaced. This is relevant only for correlation structures that require knowledge of t(). These correlation structures require observations be equally spaced so that calculations based on lags correspond to a constant time change. If you specify a t() variable that indicates observations are not equally spaced, xtgee will refuse to estimate the (time-dependent) model. If you also specify force, xtgee will estimate the model and assume that the lags based on the data ordered by t() are appropriate.

robust specifies the Huber/White/sandwich estimator of variance is to be used in place of the default IRLS variance estimator (see *Methods and Formulas* below). This produces valid standard errors even if the correlations within group are not as hypothesized by the specified correlation structure. It does, however, require that the model correctly specifies the mean. As such, the resulting standard errors are labeled "semi-robust" instead of "robust". Note that although there is no cluster() option, results are as if there were a cluster() option and you specified clustering on i().

score(*newvar*) creates *newvar* containing $u_{it} = \partial\ln L/\partial(\mathbf{x}_{it}\beta)$, where L is the quasi-likelihood function. Note that the scores for the independent panels can be obtained by $u_i = \sum_t u_{it}$ or, equivalently in Stata, egen ui=sum(uit), by(t) assuming you specified score(uit).

The score vector is $\partial\ln L/\partial\beta = \sum u_{it}\mathbf{x}_{it}$, the product of *newvar* with each covariate summed over observations. See [U] **23.12 Obtaining scores**.

eform displays the exponentiated coefficients and corresponding standard errors and confidence intervals as described in [R] **maximize**. For family(binomial) link(logit) (i.e., logistic regression), exponentiation results in odds ratios; for family(poisson) link(log) (i.e., Poisson regression), exponentiated coefficients are incidence rate ratios.

level(*#*) specifies the confidence level, in percent, for confidence intervals. The default is level(95) or as set by set level; see [U] **23.5 Specifying the width of confidence intervals**.

exposure(*varname*) and offset(*varname*) are different ways of specifying the same thing. exposure() specifies a variable that reflects the amount of exposure over which the *depvar* events were observed for each observation; ln(*varname*) with coefficient constrained to be 1 is entered into the log-link function. offset() specifies a variable that is to be entered directly into the log-link function with coefficient constrained to be 1; thus exposure is assumed to be $e^{varname}$. If you were estimating a Poisson regression model, family(poisson) link(log), for instance, you account for exposure time by specifying offset() containing the log of exposure time.

noconstant specifies that the linear predictor has no intercept term, thus forcing it through the origin on the scale defined by the link function.

scale(x2 | dev | *#* | phi) overrides the default scale parameter. By default, scale(1) is assumed for the discrete distributions (binomial, negative binomial, and Poisson) and scale(x2) is assumed for the continuous distributions (gamma, Gaussian, and inverse Gaussian).

scale(x2) specifies the scale parameter be set to the Pearson chi-squared (or generalized chi-squared) statistic divided by the residual degrees of freedom, as recommended by McCullagh and Nelder (1989) as a good general choice for continuous distributions.

scale(dev) sets the scale parameter to the deviance divided by the residual degrees of freedom. This provides an alternative to scale(x2) for continuous distributions and over- or underdispersed discrete distributions.

scale(*#*) sets the scale parameter to *#*. For example, using scale(1) in family(gamma) models results in exponential-errors regression (if you use assume independent correlation structure). Additional use of link(log) rather than the default power(-1) for family(gamma) essentially reproduces Stata's ereg command (see [R] **weibull**) if all the observations are uncensored (and you again assume independent correlation structure).

scale(phi) specifies the variance matrix should not be rescaled at all. The default scaling that xtgee applies makes results agree with other estimators and has been recommended by McCullagh and Nelder (1989) in the context of GLM. If you are comparing results with calculations made by other software, you may find that the other packages do not offer this feature. In such cases, specifying scale(phi) should match their results.

tol(*#*) specifies the convergence criterion for the maximum change in the estimated coefficient vector between iterations; tol(1e-6) is the default and you should never have to specify this option.

iter(*#*) specifies the maximum number of iterations allowed in estimating the model; iter(100) is the default. You should never have to specify this option.

nolog suppresses the iteration log.

Options for predict

mu, the default, and rate both calculate the predicted value of *depvar*. mu takes into account the offset() or exposure() together with the denominator if the family is binomial; rate ignores those adjustments. mu and rate are equivalent if (1) you did not specify offset() or exposure() when you estimated the xtgee model and (2) you did not specify family(binomial #) or family(binomial *varname*), which is to say, the binomial family and a denominator.

Thus mu and rate are the same for link(identity) family(gaussian).

mu and `rate` are not equivalent for `link(logit) family(binomial pop)`. In that case, mu would predict the number of positive outcomes and `rate` would predict the probability of a positive outcome.

mu and `rate` are not equivalent for `link(log) family(poisson) exposure(time)`. In that case, `mu` would predict the number of events given exposure time and `rate` would calculate the incidence rate—the number of events given an exposure time of 1.

`xb` calculates the linear prediction.

`stdp` calculates the standard error of the linear prediction.

`nooffset` is relevant only if you specified `offset(varname)` or `exposure(varname)` or `family(binomial #)` or `family(binomial varname)` when you estimated the model. It modifies the calculations made by `predict` so that they ignore the offset or exposure variable and ignore the binomial denominator. Thus `predict ..., mu nooffset` produces the same results as `predict ..., rate`.

Remarks

For a thorough introduction to GEE in the estimation of GLM, see Liang and Zeger (1986). Further information on linear models is presented in Nelder and Wedderburn (1972). Finally, there have been a number of illuminating articles on various applications of GEE in Zeger, Liang, and Albert (1988), Zeger and Liang (1986), and Liang (1987). Pendergast et al. (1996) provide a nice survey of the current methods for analyzing clustered data in regard to binary response data. Our implementation follows that of Liang and Zeger (1986).

`xtgee` fits generalized linear models of y_{it} with covariates $\mathbf{x}_{it}$:

$$g\big(E(y_{it})\big) = \mathbf{x}_{it}\boldsymbol{\beta}, \qquad y \sim F \text{ with parameters } \theta_{it}$$

for $i = 1, \ldots, m$ and $t = 1, \ldots, n_i$ where there are n_i observations for each group identifier i. In the above, $g(\ )$ is called the link function and F the distributional family. Substituting various definitions for $g(\ )$ and F results in a surprising array of models. For instance, if y_{it} is distributed Gaussian (normal) and $g(\ )$ is the identity function, we have

$$E(y_{it}) = \mathbf{x}_{it}\boldsymbol{\beta}, \qquad y \sim N(\ )$$

yielding linear regression, random-effects regression, or other regression-related models depending on what we assume for the correlation structure.

If $g(\ )$ is the logit function and y_{it} is distributed Bernoulli (binomial), we have

$$\operatorname{logit}\big(E(y_{it})\big) = \mathbf{x}_{it}\boldsymbol{\beta}, \qquad y \sim \text{Bernoulli}$$

or logistic regression. If $g(\ )$ is the natural log function and y_{it} is distributed Poisson, we have

$$\ln\big(E(y_{it})\big) = \mathbf{x}_{it}\boldsymbol{\beta}, \qquad y \sim \text{Poisson}$$

or Poisson regression, also known as the log-linear model. Other combinations are possible.

You specify the link function using the `link()` option, the distributional family using `family()`, and the assumed within-group correlation structure using `corr()`. The allowed link functions are

Link function	xtgee option	Min. abbreviation
cloglog	link(cloglog)	l(cl)
identity	link(identity)	l(i)
log	link(log)	l(log)
logit	link(logit)	l(logi)
negative binomial	link(nbinomial)	l(nb)
odds power	link(opower)	l(opo)
power	link(power)	l(pow)
probit	link(probit)	l(p)
reciprocal	link(reciprocal)	l(rec)

Link function cloglog is defined as $\ln\bigl(-\ln(1-y)\bigr)$.

Link function identity is defined as $y = y$.

Link function log is defined as $\ln(y)$.

Link function logit is defined $\ln\bigl(y/(1-y)\bigr)$, the natural log of the odds.

Link function nbinomial α is defined as $\ln\bigl(y/(y+\alpha)\bigr)$.

Link function opower k is defined as $\bigl[(y/(1-y))^k - 1\bigr]/k$. If $k = 0$, then this link is the same as the logit link.

Link function power k is defined as y^k. If $k = 0$, then this link is the same as the log link.

Link function probit is defined $\Phi^{-1}(y)$, where $\Phi^{-1}(\,)$ is the inverse Gaussian cumulative.

Link function reciprocal is defined as $1/y$.

The allowed distributional families are

Family	xtgee option	Min. abbreviation
Bernoulli/binomial	family(binomial)	f(b)
gamma	family(gamma)	f(gam)
Gaussian (normal)	family(gaussian)	f(gau)
inverse Gaussian	family(igaussian)	f(ig)
negative binomial	family(nbinomial)	f(nb)
Poisson	family(poisson)	f(p)

family(normal) is allowed as a synonym for family(gaussian).

The binomial distribution can be specified as (1) family(binomial), (2) family(binomial #), or (3) family(binomial varname). In case 2, # is the value of the binomial denominator N, the number of trials. Specifying family(binomial 1) is the same as specifying family(binomial); both mean that y has the Bernoulli distribution with values 0 and 1 only. In case 3, varname is the variable containing the binomial denominator, thus allowing the number of trials to vary across observations.

The negative binomial distribution must be specified as family(nbinomial #) where # denotes the value of the parameter α in the negative binomial distribution. The results will be conditional on this value.

You do not have to specify both family() and link(); the default link() is the canonical link for the specified family():

Family	Default link
family(binomial)	link(logit)
family(gamma)	link(reciprocal)
family(gaussian)	link(identity)
family(igaussian)	link(power -2)
family(nbinomial)	link(log)
family(poisson)	link(log)

If you do specify both `family()` and `link()`, note that not all combinations make sense. You may choose among the following combinations:

	cloglog	identity	log	logit	nbinom	opower	power	probit	reciprocal
binomial	x	x	x	x	x	x	x	x	x
gamma		x	x				x		x
Gaussian		x	x			x	x		x
inverse Gaussian		x	x				x		x
negative binomial		x	x		x		x		x
Poisson		x	x				x		x

You specify the assumed within-group correlation structure using the `corr()` option. The allowed correlation structures are

Correlation structure	xtgee option	Min. abbreviation
Independent	corr(independent)	c(ind)
Exchangeable	corr(exchangeable)	c(exc)
Autoregressive	corr(ar #)	c(ar #)
Stationary	corr(stationary #)	c(sta #)
Non-stationary	corr(nonstationary #)	c(non #)
Unstructured	corr(unstructured)	c(uns)
User-specified	corr(fixed *matname*)	c(fix *matname*)

Let us explain.

Call $\mathbf{R}$ the working correlation matrix for modeling the within-group correlation, a square $\max\{n_i\} \times \max\{n_i\}$ matrix. Option `corr()` specifies the structure of $\mathbf{R}$. Let $\mathbf{R}_{t,s}$ denote the t, s element.

The `independent` structure is defined as

$$\mathbf{R}_{t,s} = \begin{cases} 1 & \text{if } t = s \\ 0 & \text{otherwise} \end{cases}$$

The `corr(exchangeable)` structure (corresponding to equal-correlation models) is defined as

$$\mathbf{R}_{t,s} = \begin{cases} 1 & \text{if } t = s \\ \rho & \text{otherwise} \end{cases}$$

The `corr(ar g)` structure is defined as the usual correlation matrix for an AR(g) model. This is sometimes called multiplicative correlation. For example, an AR(1) model is given by

$$\mathbf{R}_{t,s} = \begin{cases} 1 & \text{if } t = s \\ \rho^{|t-s|} & \text{otherwise} \end{cases}$$

The `corr(stationary g)` structure is a stationary(g) model. For example, a stationary(1) model is given by

$$\mathbf{R}_{t,s} = \begin{cases} 1 & \text{if } t = s \\ \rho & \text{if } |t - s| = 1 \\ 0 & \text{otherwise} \end{cases}$$

The `corr(nonstationary g)` structure is a nonstationary(g) model which imposes only the constraints that the elements of the working correlation matrix along the diagonal are 1 and the elements outside of the gth band are zero,

$$\mathbf{R}_{t,s} = \begin{cases} 1 & \text{if } t = s \\ \rho_{ts} & \text{if } 0 < |t - s| \leq g, \, \rho_{ts} = \rho_{st} \\ 0 & \text{otherwise} \end{cases}$$

The corr(unstructured) imposes only the constraint that the diagonal elements of the working correlation matrix are 1.

$$\mathbf{R}_{t,s} = \begin{cases} 1 & \text{if } t = s \\ \rho_{ts} & \text{otherwise, } \rho_{ts} = \rho_{st} \end{cases}$$

The corr(fixed *matname*) specification is taken from the user-supplied matrix, so that

$$\mathbf{R} = matname$$

In this case, the correlations are not estimated from the data. The user-supplied matrix must be a valid correlation matrix with 1s on the diagonal.

Full formulas for all the correlation structures are provided in the *Methods and Formulas* below.

❑ Technical Note

Some family(), link(), and corr() combinations result in models already estimated by Stata. These are

family()	link()	corr()	Other Stata estimation command
gaussian	identity	independent	regress
gaussian	identity	exchangeable	xtreg, re (see note 1)
gaussian	identity	exchangeable	xtreg, pa
binomial	cloglog	independent	cloglog (see note 2)
binomial	cloglog	exchangeable	xtclog, pa
binomial	logit	independent	logit or logistic
binomial	logit	exchangeable	xtlogit, pa
binomial	probit	independent	probit (see note 3)
binomial	probit	exchangeable	xtprobit, pa
nbinomial	nbinomial	independent	nbreg (see note 4)
poisson	log	independent	poisson
poisson	log	exchangeable	xtpois, pa
gamma	log	independent	ereg (see note 5)
family	*link*	independent	glm (see note 6)

Notes:

1. These methods produce the same results only in the case of balanced panels; see [R] **xt**.

2. For cloglog estimation, xtgee with corr(independent) and cloglog (see [R] **cloglog**) will produce the same coefficients, but the standard errors will be only asymptotically equivalent because cloglog is not the canonical link for the binomial family.

3. For probit estimation, xtgee with corr(independent) and probit will produce the same coefficients, but the standard errors will be only asymptotically equivalent because probit is not the canonical link for the binomial family. If the binomial denominator is not 1, the equivalent maximum-likelihood command is bprobit; see [R] **probit** and [R] **glogit**.

4. Fitting a negative binomial model using xtgee (or using glm) will yield results conditional on the specified value of α. The nbreg command, however, fits that parameter as well as providing unconditional estimates; see [R] **nbreg**.

5. xtgee with corr(independent) can be used to estimate exponential regressions, but this requires specifying scale(1). As with probit, the xtgee-reported standard errors will be only asymptotically equivalent to those produced by ereg (see [R] **weibull**) because log is not the canonical link for the gamma family. xtgee cannot be used to estimate exponential regressions on censored data.

Using the `independent` correlation structure, the `xtgee` command will estimate the same model as estimated with the `glm` command provided the family-link combination is the same.

6. If the `xtgee` command is equivalent to another command, then the use of `corr(independent)` and the `robust` option with `xtgee` corresponds to using both the `robust` option and the `cluster(`*varname*`)` option in the equivalent command where *varname* corresponds to the i() group variable.

❏

`xtgee` is a direct generalization of the `glm` command and will give the same output whenever the same family and link are specified together with an independent correlation structure. What makes `xtgee` useful is

1. the number of statistical models that it generalizes for use with panel data, many of which are not otherwise available in Stata;

2. the richer correlation structure `xtgee` allows even when models are available through other xt commands; and

3. the availability of robust standard errors (see [U] **23.11 Obtaining robust variance estimates**) even when the model and correlation structure is available through other xt commands.

In the following examples, we illustrate the relationships of `xtgee` with other Stata estimation commands. It is important to remember that although `xtgee` generalizes many other commands, the computational algorithm is different: therefore, the answers that you obtain will not be identical. The dataset we are using is a subset of the `nlswork` data (see [R] **xt**); we are looking at observations prior to 1980.

▷ Example

We can use `xtgee` to perform ordinary least squares performed by `regress`:

```
. gen age2 = age^2
(9 missing values generated)
. regress ln_w grade age age2

    Source |       SS       df       MS              Number of obs =   16085
-----------+------------------------------           F(  3, 16081) = 1413.68
     Model |  597.54468     3   199.18156            Prob > F      =  0.0000
  Residual |  2265.74584 16081    .14089583          R-squared     =  0.2087
-----------+------------------------------           Adj R-squared =  0.2085
     Total |  2863.29052 16084   .178021047          Root MSE      =  .37536

-----------------------------------------------------------------------------
   ln_wage |      Coef.   Std. Err.       t    P>|t|     [95% Conf. Interval]
-----------+-----------------------------------------------------------------
     grade |   .0724483   .0014229    50.915   0.000     .0696592    .0752374
       age |   .1064874   .0083644    12.731   0.000     .0900922    .1228825
      age2 |  -.0016931   .0001655   -10.233   0.000    -.0020174   -.0013688
     _cons |  -.8681487   .1024896    -8.471   0.000    -1.06904    -.6672577
-----------------------------------------------------------------------------

. xtgee ln_w grade age age2, i(id) corr(indep)
Iteration 1: tolerance = 1.299e-12

GEE population-averaged model                 Number of obs      =     16085
Group variable:                   idcode      Number of groups   =      3913
Link:                           identity      Obs per group: min =         1
Family:                         Gaussian                     avg =       4.1
Correlation:                 independent                     max =         9
                                              Wald chi2(3)       =   4241.04
Scale parameter:                 .1408958     Prob > chi2        =    0.0000
Pearson chi2(16081):             2265.75      Deviance           =   2265.75
Dispersion (Pearson):            .1408958     Dispersion         =  .1408958
```

```
------------------------------------------------------------------------------
 ln_wage |     Coef.   Std. Err.      z    P>|z|    [95% Conf. Interval]
---------+--------------------------------------------------------------------
   grade |   .0724483   .0014229    50.915   0.000    .0696594    .0752372
     age |   .1064874   .0083644    12.731   0.000    .0900935    .1228812
    age2 |  -.0016931   .0001655   -10.233   0.000   -.0020174   -.0013688
   _cons |  -.8681487   .1024896    -8.471   0.000   -1.069025   -.6672728
------------------------------------------------------------------------------
```

Note that the scale parameter estimate from the **xtgee** command equals the MSE calculation from **regress**; both are estimates of the variance of the residuals.

◁

▷ Example

The identity link and Gaussian family produce regression-type models. With the independent correlation structure, we reproduce ordinary least squares. With the exchangeable correlation structure, we produce an equal-correlation linear regression estimator.

xtgee, fam(gauss) link(ident) corr(exch) is asymptotically equivalent to the weighted-GLS estimator provided by **xtreg, re** and to the full maximum-likelihood estimator provided by **xtreg, mle**. Nevertheless, in finite samples results will differ among all three of these estimators. In balanced data, all three produce very similar results. Below we demonstrate the use of the three estimators with unbalanced data. We begin with **xtgee**, then show the maximum likelihood estimator **xtreg, mle**, then show the GLS estimator **xtreg, re**, and finally show **xtgee** with the **robust** option.

```
. xtgee ln_w grade age age2, i(id) nolog
GEE population-averaged model            Number of obs      =     16085
Group variable:                   idcode  Number of groups   =      3913
Link:                           identity  Obs per group: min =         1
Family:                         Gaussian                 avg =       4.1
Correlation:                exchangeable                 max =         9
                                          Wald chi2(3)       =   2917.46
Scale parameter:                .1416937  Prob > chi2        =    0.0000

------------------------------------------------------------------------------
 ln_wage |     Coef.   Std. Err.      z    P>|z|    [95% Conf. Interval]
---------+--------------------------------------------------------------------
   grade |   .0717731   .0021102    34.013   0.000    .0676373    .075909
     age |   .1077644   .0068863    15.649   0.000    .0942675    .1212613
    age2 |  -.0016381   .0001362   -12.027   0.000   -.0019051   -.0013712
   _cons |  -.9480374   .0869426   -10.904   0.000   -1.118442   -.7776331
------------------------------------------------------------------------------

. xtreg ln_w grade age age2, i(id) mle
Fitting constant-only model:

Iteration 0:   log likelihood = -6035.2751
Iteration 1:   log likelihood = -5870.6718
Iteration 2:   log likelihood = -5858.9478
Iteration 3:   log likelihood = -5858.8244

Fitting full model:

Iteration 0:   log likelihood = -4591.9241
Iteration 1:   log likelihood = -4562.4406
Iteration 2:   log likelihood = -4562.3526
```

```
Random-effects ML regression              Number of obs      =     16085
Group variable (i) : idcode               Number of groups   =      3913
Random effects u_i ~ Gaussian             Obs per group: min =         1
                                                         avg =       4.1
                                                         max =         9
                                          LR chi2(3)         =   2592.94
Log likelihood  = -4562.3526              Prob > chi2        =    0.0000
------------------------------------------------------------------------
 ln_wage |     Coef.   Std. Err.      z    P>|z|     [95% Conf. Interval]
---------+--------------------------------------------------------------
   grade |   .0717747   .0021419    33.510  0.000     .0675766    .0759728
     age |   .1077899   .0068265    15.790  0.000     .0944102    .1211696
    age2 |  -.0016364    .000135   -12.120  0.000    -.0019011   -.0013718
   _cons |  -.9500833   .0863831   -10.998  0.000    -1.119391   -.7807755
---------+--------------------------------------------------------------
 /sigma_u |   .2689639    .004085    65.841  0.000     .2609574    .2769704
 /sigma_e |   .2669944   .0017113   156.022  0.000     .2636404    .2703484
---------+--------------------------------------------------------------
     rho |   .5036748   .0086443                       .486734    .5206089
------------------------------------------------------------------------
Likelihood ratio test of sigma_u=0:  chi2(1) =  4996.22   Prob > chi2 = 0.0000

. xtreg ln_w grade age age2, i(id) re
Random-effects GLS regression             Number of obs      =     16085
Group variable (i) : idcode               Number of groups   =      3913
R-sq:  within  = 0.0983                    Obs per group: min =         1
       between = 0.2946                                  avg =       4.1
       overall = 0.2076                                  max =         9
Random effects u_i ~ Gaussian             Wald chi2(3)       =   2875.02
corr(u_i, X)      = 0 (assumed)            Prob > chi2        =    0.0000
------------------------------------------------------------------------
 ln_wage |     Coef.   Std. Err.      z    P>|z|     [95% Conf. Interval]
---------+--------------------------------------------------------------
   grade |   .0717757   .0021666    33.129  0.000     .0675294    .0760221
     age |   .1078043   .0068125    15.824  0.000     .0944519    .1211566
    age2 |  -.0016355   .0001347   -12.138  0.000    -.0018996   -.0013714
   _cons |  -.9512122   .0863139   -11.020  0.000    -1.120384   -.7820401
---------+--------------------------------------------------------------
 sigma_u |  .27383747
 sigma_e |  .26624266
     rho |  .51405959   (fraction of variance due to u_i)
------------------------------------------------------------------------

. xtgee ln_w grade age age2, i(id) nolog robust
GEE population-averaged model             Number of obs      =     16085
Group variable:                    idcode Number of groups   =      3913
Link:                            identity  Obs per group: min =         1
Family:                          Gaussian                 avg =       4.1
Correlation:                  exchangeable                 max =         9
                                          Wald chi2(3)       =   2030.91
Scale parameter:                 .1416937 Prob > chi2        =    0.0000
                    (standard errors adjusted for clustering on idcode)
------------------------------------------------------------------------
         |             Semi-robust
 ln_wage |     Coef.   Std. Err.      z    P>|z|     [95% Conf. Interval]
---------+--------------------------------------------------------------
   grade |   .0717731   .0023343    30.747  0.000     .0671979    .0763483
     age |   .1077644   .0098105    10.985  0.000     .0885362    .1269926
    age2 |  -.0016381   .0001964    -8.342  0.000     -.002023   -.0012532
   _cons |  -.9480374   .1195109    -7.933  0.000    -1.182274   -.7138004
------------------------------------------------------------------------
```

In [R] **regress** we noted the ability of `regress, robust cluster()` to produce inefficient coefficient estimates with valid standard errors for random-effects models. These standard errors are robust to model misspecification. The `robust` option of `xtgee`, on the other hand, requires that the model correctly specifies the mean.

◁

▷ Example

One of the features of `xtgee` is being able to estimate richer correlation structures. In the previous example, we estimated the model

```
. xtgee ln_w grade age age2, i(id)
```

After estimation, `xtcorr` will report the working correlation matrix **R**:

```
. xtcorr

Estimated within-idcode correlation matrix R:

        c1      c2      c3      c4      c5      c6      c7      c8      c9
r1  1.0000
r2  0.4851  1.0000
r3  0.4851  0.4851  1.0000
r4  0.4851  0.4851  0.4851  1.0000
r5  0.4851  0.4851  0.4851  0.4851  1.0000
r6  0.4851  0.4851  0.4851  0.4851  0.4851  1.0000
r7  0.4851  0.4851  0.4851  0.4851  0.4851  0.4851  1.0000
r8  0.4851  0.4851  0.4851  0.4851  0.4851  0.4851  0.4851  1.0000
r9  0.4851  0.4851  0.4851  0.4851  0.4851  0.4851  0.4851  0.4851  1.0000
```

The equal-correlation model corresponds to an exchangeable correlation structure, meaning the correlation of observations within person is a constant. The working correlation estimated by `xtgee` is 0.4851. (`xtreg, re`, by comparison, reports .5141.) We constrained the model to have this simple correlation structure. What if we relaxed the constraint? To go to the other extreme, let's place no constraints on the matrix (other than it being symmetric). This we do by specifying `correlation(unstructured)`, although we can abbreviate the option.

```
. xtgee ln_w grade age age2, i(id) t(year) corr(unstr) nolog

GEE population-averaged model                   Number of obs      =       16085
Group and time vars:                idcode year  Number of groups   =        3913
Link:                                  identity  Obs per group: min =           1
Family:                                Gaussian                 avg =         4.1
Correlation:                       unstructured                 max =           9
                                                 Wald chi2(3)       =     2501.18
Scale parameter:                        .1415121  Prob > chi2        =      0.0000

------------------------------------------------------------------------------
  ln_wage |      Coef.   Std. Err.      z    P>|z|     [95% Conf. Interval]
----------+-------------------------------------------------------------------
    grade |   .0721459   .001987    36.309   0.000     .0682515    .0760403
      age |   .1016351   .0089667   11.335   0.000     .0840607    .1192095
     age2 |  -.0015526   .000178    -8.724   0.000    -.0019013   -.0012038
    _cons |  -.8549129   .1100937   -7.765   0.000    -1.070693   -.6391333
------------------------------------------------------------------------------
```

```
. xtcorr
Estimated within-idcode correlation matrix R:
          c1        c2        c3        c4        c5        c6        c7        c8        c9
r1    1.0000
r2    0.2936    1.0000
r3    0.2841    0.4509    1.0000
r4    0.2343    0.3587    0.4209    1.0000
r5    0.1907    0.2900    0.2941    0.4445    1.0000
r6    0.1880    0.2659    0.2968    0.3864    0.6053    1.0000
r7    0.1416    0.1971    0.2340    0.2538    0.3371    0.3882    1.0000
r8    0.1479    0.1758    0.2319    0.2539    0.3068    0.3603    0.4895    1.0000
r9    0.0838    0.1355    0.1546    0.1791    0.2727    0.2734    0.4083    0.6126    1.0000
```

This correlation matrix looks quite different from the previously constrained one and shows, in particular, that the serial correlation of the residuals diminishes as the lag increases although residuals separated by small lags are more correlated than, say, AR(1) would imply.

◁

▷ Example

In [R] **xtprobit**, we showed a random-effects model of unionization using the union data described in [R] **xt**. We estimated using `xtprobit` but said it could be estimated using `xtgee` as well and here we estimate a population-averaged (equal-correlation) model for comparison:

```
. xtgee union age grade not_smsa south southXt, i(id) fam(bin) link(probit)
Iteration 1: tolerance = .0479535
Iteration 2: tolerance = .0035256
Iteration 3: tolerance = .00017879
Iteration 4: tolerance = 8.649e-06
Iteration 5: tolerance = 4.147e-07

GEE population-averaged model              Number of obs      =      26200
Group variable:                   idcode   Number of groups   =       4434
Link:                             probit   Obs per group: min =          1
Family:                         binomial                  avg =        5.9
Correlation:                exchangeable                  max =         12
                                           Wald chi2(5)       =     241.67
Scale parameter:                       1   Prob > chi2        =     0.0000

------------------------------------------------------------------------------
    union |      Coef.   Std. Err.      z    P>|z|     [95% Conf. Interval]
----------+-------------------------------------------------------------------
      age |   .0031599   .0014679     2.153   0.031     .0002829    .0060369
    grade |   .0329988   .0062332     5.294   0.000     .0207819    .0452156
 not_smsa |  -.0721893   .0275194    -2.623   0.009    -.1261262   -.0182523
    south |  -.4090316   .0372223   -10.989   0.000     -.481986   -.3360772
  southXt |   .0081824   .0025452     3.215   0.001      .003194    .0131709
    _cons |  -1.184792   .0890111   -13.311   0.000    -1.359251   -1.010334
------------------------------------------------------------------------------
```

Let us look at the correlation structure and then relax it:

```
. xtcorr
```

Estimated within-idcode correlation matrix R:

	c1	c2	c3	c4	c5	c6	c7	c8	c9
r1	1.0000								
r2	0.4629	1.0000							
r3	0.4629	0.4629	1.0000						
r4	0.4629	0.4629	0.4629	1.0000					
r5	0.4629	0.4629	0.4629	0.4629	1.0000				
r6	0.4629	0.4629	0.4629	0.4629	0.4629	1.0000			
r7	0.4629	0.4629	0.4629	0.4629	0.4629	0.4629	1.0000		
r8	0.4629	0.4629	0.4629	0.4629	0.4629	0.4629	0.4629	1.0000	
r9	0.4629	0.4629	0.4629	0.4629	0.4629	0.4629	0.4629	0.4629	1.0000
r10	0.4629	0.4629	0.4629	0.4629	0.4629	0.4629	0.4629	0.4629	0.4629
r11	0.4629	0.4629	0.4629	0.4629	0.4629	0.4629	0.4629	0.4629	0.4629
r12	0.4629	0.4629	0.4629	0.4629	0.4629	0.4629	0.4629	0.4629	0.4629

	c10	c11	c12
r10	1.0000		
r11	0.4629	1.0000	
r12	0.4629	0.4629	1.0000

We estimate the fixed correlation between observations within person to be 0.4629. We have a lot of data (an average of 5.9 observations on 4,434 women) and so estimating the full correlation matrix is feasible. Let's do that and then examine the results:

```
. xtgee union age grade not_smsa south southXt, i(id) t(t) fam(bin)
> link(probit) corr(unstr) nolog
```

GEE population-averaged model				Number of obs	=	26200
Group and time vars:		idcode t0		Number of groups	=	4434
Link:		probit		Obs per group: min =		1
Family:		binomial		avg =		5.9
Correlation:		unstructured		max =		12
				Wald chi2(5)	=	229.49
Scale parameter:		1		Prob > chi2	=	0.0000

union	Coef.	Std. Err.	z	P>|z|	[95% Conf. Interval]	
age	.0025502	.002001	1.274	0.202	-.0013716	.0064721
grade	.0326872	.0060324	5.419	0.000	.0208638	.0445106
not_smsa	-.1035074	.0290902	-3.558	0.000	-.1605232	-.0464916
south	-.3989208	.0429111	-9.296	0.000	-.483025	-.3148167
southXt	.0069737	.003508	1.988	0.047	.0000981	.0138493
_cons	-1.158885	.0948613	-12.217	0.000	-1.34481	-.9729601

(Continued on next page)

```
. xtcorr

Estimated within-idcode correlation matrix R:
           c1       c2       c3       c4       c5       c6       c7       c8       c9
  r1   1.0000
  r2   0.4741   1.0000
  r3   0.3950   0.4625   1.0000
  r4   0.3163   0.3661   0.4477   1.0000
  r5   0.2025   0.2328   0.2736   0.3466   1.0000
  r6   0.1430   0.1807   0.2242   0.2693   0.5517   1.0000
  r7   0.1379   0.1719   0.1979   0.2435   0.3840   0.4687   1.0000
  r8   0.1436   0.1634   0.1832   0.2283   0.3391   0.4232   0.5888   1.0000
  r9   0.1443   0.1497   0.1595   0.2138   0.3372   0.3604   0.4649   0.5858   1.0000
 r10   0.1253   0.1474   0.1607   0.2228   0.2674   0.3433   0.4349   0.4520   0.5113
 r11   0.1280   0.1302   0.1573   0.1988   0.2379   0.3058   0.3688   0.4158   0.4447
 r12   0.1242   0.1260   0.1391   0.1816   0.2300   0.2520   0.3270   0.3481   0.3942

          c10      c11      c12
 r10   1.0000
 r11   0.4661   1.0000
 r12   0.4095   0.5522   1.0000
```

As before, we find that the correlation of residuals decreases as the lag increases, but more slowly than an AR(1) process, and then quickly decreases toward zero.

◁

▷ Example

In this example, we examine injury incidents among 20 airlines in each of 4 years. The data is fictional and, as a matter of fact, really is from a random-effects model.

```
. gen lnpm = ln(pmiles)

. xtgee i_cnt inprog, f(pois) i(airline) t(time) eform off(lnpm) nolog

GEE population-averaged model          Number of obs      =         80
Group variable:               airline  Number of groups   =         20
Link:                             log  Obs per group: min =          4
Family:                       Poisson                 avg =        4.0
Correlation:              exchangeable                 max =          4
                                       Wald chi2(1)       =       5.23
Scale parameter:                    1  Prob > chi2        =     0.0222

------------------------------------------------------------------------------
     i_cnt |        IRR   Std. Err.      z    P>|z|     [95% Conf. Interval]
-----------+------------------------------------------------------------------
    inprog |   .9060927   .0390813    -2.286   0.022     .8326431    .9860214
      lnpm |   (offset)
------------------------------------------------------------------------------
```

```
. xtcorr

Estimated within-airline correlation matrix R:
           c1       c2       c3       c4
  r1   1.0000
  r2   0.4567   1.0000
  r3   0.4567   0.4567   1.0000
  r4   0.4567   0.4567   0.4567   1.0000
```

Now, there is not really enough data here to reliably estimate the correlation without any constraints of structure, but here is what happens if we try:

```
. xtgee i_cnt inprog, f(pois) i(airline) t(time) eform off(lnpm)
> corr(unstr) nolog
GEE population-averaged model          Number of obs      =        80
Group and time vars:        airline time   Number of groups   =        20
Link:                              log   Obs per group: min =         4
Family:                        Poisson                  avg =       4.0
Correlation:             unstructured                  max =         4
                                          Wald chi2(1)       =      0.52
Scale parameter:                     1   Prob > chi2        =    0.4716

------------------------------------------------------------------------------
     i_cnt |       IRR   Std. Err.      z    P>|z|     [95% Conf. Interval]
---------+--------------------------------------------------------------------
    inprog |  .9741657   .0354228    -0.720   0.472    .9071545    1.046127
      lnpm |  (offset)
------------------------------------------------------------------------------

. xtcorr

Estimated within-airline correlation matrix R:

          c1      c2      c3      c4
r1   1.0000
r2   0.5524  1.0000
r3   0.6993  0.4102  1.0000
r4   0.2369  0.3754  0.3463  1.0000
```

There is no sensible pattern to the correlations.

We admitted previously that we created this data from a random-effects Poisson model. We reran our data-creation program and this time had it create 400 airlines rather than 20, still with 4 years of data each. Here is the equal-correlation model and estimated correlation structure

```
. xtgee i_cnt inprog, f(pois) i(airline) eform off(lnpm) nolog
GEE population-averaged model          Number of obs      =      1600
Group variable:                 airline   Number of groups   =       400
Link:                              log   Obs per group: min =         4
Family:                        Poisson                  avg =       4.0
Correlation:             exchangeable                  max =         4
                                          Wald chi2(1)       =    111.75
Scale parameter:                     1   Prob > chi2        =    0.0000

------------------------------------------------------------------------------
     i_cnt |       IRR   Std. Err.      z    P>|z|     [95% Conf. Interval]
---------+--------------------------------------------------------------------
    inprog |  .8915318   .0096828   -10.571   0.000    .8727545    .9107132
      lnpm |  (offset)
------------------------------------------------------------------------------

. xtcorr

Estimated within-airline correlation matrix R:

          c1      c2      c3      c4
r1   1.0000
r2   0.5289  1.0000
r3   0.5289  0.5289  1.0000
r4   0.5289  0.5289  0.5289  1.0000
```

and here are the estimation results assuming unstructured correlation:

```
. xtgee i_cnt inprog, f(pois) i(airline) corr(unstr) t(time) eform
> off(lnpm) nolog
GEE population-averaged model              Number of obs      =      1600
Group and time vars:        airline time   Number of groups   =       400
Link:                                 log   Obs per group: min =         4
Family:                           Poisson                  avg =       4.0
Correlation:                 unstructured                  max =         4
                                            Wald chi2(1)       =    113.26
Scale parameter:                        1   Prob > chi2        =    0.0000
------------------------------------------------------------------------------
    i_cnt |       IRR   Std. Err.      z    P>|z|     [95% Conf. Interval]
----------+-------------------------------------------------------------------
   inprog |  .8914202   .0096273  -10.643   0.000     .8727492    .9104905
     lnpm |  (offset)
------------------------------------------------------------------------------
```

```
. xtcorr
Estimated within-airline correlation matrix R:
        c1      c2      c3      c4
r1  1.0000
r2  0.4727  1.0000
r3  0.5234  0.5742  1.0000
r4  0.5133  0.5043  0.5833  1.0000
```

The equal-correlation model estimated a fixed .5289 and above we have correlations ranging between .4727 and .5833 with little pattern in their structure.

◁

Saved Results

xtgee saves in e():

Scalars

e(N)	number of observations	e(deviance)	deviance
e(N_g)	number of groups	e(chi2_dev)	χ^2 test of deviance
e(df_m)	model degrees of freedom	e(dispers)	deviance dispersion
e(g_max)	largest group size	e(chi2_dis)	χ^2 test of deviance dispersion
e(g_min)	smallest group size	e(tol)	target tolerance
e(g_avg)	average group size	e(dif)	achieved tolerance
e(chi2)	χ^2	e(phi)	scale parameter
e(df_pear)	degrees of freedom for Pearson χ^2		

Macros

e(cmd)	xtgee	e(ivar)	variable denoting groups
e(depvar)	name of dependent variable	e(chi2type)	Wald; type of model χ^2 test
e(family)	distribution family	e(disp)	deviance dispersion
e(link)	link function	e(offset)	offset
e(corr)	correlation structure	e(predict)	program used to implement **predict**
e(scale)	x2, dev, phi, or #; scale parameter		

Matrices

e(b)	coefficient vector	e(R)	estimated working correlation matrix
e(V)	variance–covariance matrix of the estimators		

Functions

e(sample)	marks estimation sample

Methods and Formulas

xtgee is implemented as an ado-file.

xtgee estimates general linear models for panel data using the GEE approach described in Liang and Zeger (1986). Below we present the derivation of that estimator. A related method, referred to as GEE2, is described in Zhao and Prentice (1990) and Prentice and Zhao (1991). The GEE2 method attempts to gain efficiency in the estimation of β by specifying a parametric model for α and then relies on assuming the models for both the mean and dependency parameters are correct. Thus, there is a tradeoff in robustness for efficiency. The preliminary work of Liang, Zeger, and Qaqish (1987), however, indicates that there is little efficiency gained with this alternate approach.

In the GLM approach (see McCullagh and Nelder 1989), we assume that

$$h(\boldsymbol{\mu}_{i,j}) = x_{i,j}^{\mathrm{T}}\boldsymbol{\beta}$$
$$\mathrm{Var}(y_{i,j}) = g(\mu_{i,j})\phi$$
$$\boldsymbol{\mu}_i = E(\mathbf{y}_i) = \{h^{-1}(x_{i,1}^{\mathrm{T}}\boldsymbol{\beta}), \ldots, h^{-1}(x_{i,n_i}^{\mathrm{T}}\boldsymbol{\beta})\}^{\mathrm{T}}$$
$$\mathbf{A}_i = \mathrm{diag}\{g(\mu_{i,1}), \ldots, g(\mu_{i,n_i})\}$$
$$\mathrm{Cov}(\mathbf{y}_i) = \phi\mathbf{A}_i \quad \text{for independent observations.}$$

In the absence of a convenient likelihood function with which to work, one can rely on a multivariate analog of the quasi-score function introduced by Wedderburn (1974)

$$\mathbf{S}_{\boldsymbol{\beta}}(\boldsymbol{\beta}, \boldsymbol{\alpha}) = \sum_{i=1}^{m}\left(\frac{\partial\boldsymbol{\mu}_i}{\partial\boldsymbol{\beta}}\right)^{\mathrm{T}}\mathrm{Var}(\mathbf{y}_i)^{-1}(\mathbf{y}_i - \boldsymbol{\mu}_i) = 0$$

The correlation parameters $\boldsymbol{\alpha}$ can be solved for simultaneously solving

$$\mathbf{S}_{\boldsymbol{\alpha}}(\boldsymbol{\beta}, \boldsymbol{\alpha}) = \sum_{i=1}^{m}\left(\frac{\partial\boldsymbol{\eta}_i}{\partial\boldsymbol{\alpha}}\right)^{\mathrm{T}}\mathbf{H}_i^{-1}(\mathbf{W}_i - \boldsymbol{\eta}_i) = 0$$

In the GEE approach to GLM, we let $\mathbf{R}_i(\boldsymbol{\alpha})$ be a "working" correlation matrix depending on the parameters in $\boldsymbol{\alpha}$ (see the *Correlation structures* section for the number of parameters) and estimate β by solving the generalized estimating equation

$$\mathbf{U}(\boldsymbol{\beta}) = \sum_{i=1}^{m}\frac{\partial\boldsymbol{\mu}_i}{\partial\boldsymbol{\beta}}\mathbf{V}_i^{-1}(\boldsymbol{\alpha})(\mathbf{y}_i - \boldsymbol{\mu}_i) = 0$$
$$\text{where} \quad \mathbf{V}_i(\boldsymbol{\alpha}) = \mathbf{A}_i^{1/2}\mathbf{R}_i(\boldsymbol{\alpha})\mathbf{A}_i^{1/2}.$$

To solve the above, we need only a crude approximation to the variance matrix. We can obtain one from a Taylor's series expansion where

$$\mathrm{Cov}(\mathbf{y}_i) = \mathbf{L}_i\mathbf{Z}_i\mathbf{D}_i\mathbf{Z}_i^{\mathrm{T}}\mathbf{L}_i + \phi\mathbf{A}_i = \widetilde{\mathbf{V}}_i$$
$$\mathbf{L}_i = \mathrm{diag}\{\partial h^{-1}(u)/\partial u, u = x_{i,j}^{\mathrm{T}}\boldsymbol{\beta}, j = 1, \ldots, n_i\}.$$

which allows that

$$\widehat{\mathbf{D}}_i \approx (\mathbf{Z}_i^{\mathrm{T}}\mathbf{Z}_i)^{-1}\mathbf{Z}_i\widehat{\mathbf{L}}_i^{-1}\left[(\mathbf{y}_i - \widehat{\boldsymbol{\mu}}_i)(\mathbf{y}_i - \widehat{\boldsymbol{\mu}}_i)^{\mathrm{T}} - \widehat{\phi}\widehat{\mathbf{A}}_i\right]\widehat{\mathbf{L}}_i^{-1}\mathbf{Z}_i^{\mathrm{T}}(\mathbf{Z}_i'\mathbf{Z}_i)^{-1}$$
$$\widehat{\phi} = \sum_{i=1}^{m}\sum_{j=1}^{n_i}\frac{(y_{i,j} - \widehat{\mu}_{i,j})^2 - (\widehat{\mathbf{L}}_{i,j})^2\mathbf{Z}_{i,j}^{\mathrm{T}}\widehat{\mathbf{D}}_i\mathbf{Z}_{i,j}}{g(\widehat{\mu}_{i,j})}$$

Calculation of GEE for GLM

Using the notation from Liang and Zeger (1986), let $\mathbf{y}_i = (y_{i,1}, \ldots, y_{i,n_i})^{\mathrm{T}}$ be the $n_i \times 1$ vector of outcome values and $\mathbf{X}_i = (x_{i,1}, \ldots, x_{i,n_i})^{\mathrm{T}}$ be the $n_i \times p$ matrix of covariate values for the ith subject $i = 1, \ldots, m$. We assume that the marginal density for $y_{i,j}$ may be written in exponential family notation as

$$f(y_{i,j}) = \exp\left[\{y_{i,j}\theta_{i,j} - a(\theta_{i,j}) + b(y_{i,j})\}\,\phi\right]$$

where $\theta_{i,j} = h(\eta_{i,j})$, $\eta_{i,j} = x_{i,j}\beta$. Under this formulation, the first two moments are given by

$$E(y_{i,j}) = a'(\theta_{i,j}), \qquad \mathrm{Var}(y_{i,j}) = a''(\theta_{i,j})/\phi$$

We define the quantities (assuming that we have an $n \times n$ working correlation matrix $\mathbf{R}(\alpha)$),

$$
\begin{aligned}
\boldsymbol{\Delta}_i &= \mathrm{diag}(d\theta_{i,j}/d\eta_{i,j}) & n \times n \text{ matrix} \\
\mathbf{A}_i &= \mathrm{diag}\{a''(\theta_{i,j})\} & n \times n \text{ matrix} \\
\mathbf{S}_i &= \mathbf{y}_i - a'(\boldsymbol{\theta}_i) & n \times 1 \text{ matrix} \\
\mathbf{D}_i &= \mathbf{A}_i\boldsymbol{\Delta}_i\mathbf{X}_i & n \times p \text{ matrix} \\
\mathbf{V}_i &= \mathbf{A}_i^{1/2}\mathbf{R}(\alpha)\mathbf{A}_i^{1/2} & n \times n \text{ matrix}
\end{aligned}
$$

such that the GEE becomes

$$\sum_{i=1}^{m}\mathbf{D}_i^{\mathrm{T}}\mathbf{V}_i^{-1}\mathbf{S}_i = 0$$

We then have that

$$\widehat{\beta}_{j+1} = \widehat{\beta}_j - \left\{\sum_{i=1}^{m}\mathbf{D}_i^{\mathrm{T}}(\widehat{\beta}_j)\widetilde{\mathbf{V}}_i^{-1}(\widehat{\beta}_j)\mathbf{D}_i(\widehat{\beta}_j)\right\}^{-1}\left\{\sum_{i=1}^{m}\mathbf{D}_i^{\mathrm{T}}(\widehat{\beta}_j)\widetilde{\mathbf{V}}_i^{-1}(\widehat{\beta}_j)\mathbf{S}_i(\widehat{\beta}_j)\right\}$$

where the term,

$$\left\{\sum_{i=1}^{m}\mathbf{D}_i^{\mathrm{T}}(\widehat{\beta}_j)\widetilde{\mathbf{V}}_i^{-1}(\widehat{\beta}_j)\mathbf{D}_i(\widehat{\beta}_j)\right\}^{-1}$$

is what we call the IRLS variance estimate (iteratively reweighted least squares) and is used to calculate the standard errors if the **robust** option is not specified. See Liang and Zeger (1986) for the calculation of the robust variance estimator.

Define

$$
\begin{aligned}
\mathbf{D} &= (\mathbf{D}_1^{\mathrm{T}}, \ldots, \mathbf{D}_m^{\mathrm{T}}) \\
\mathbf{S} &= (\mathbf{S}_1^{\mathrm{T}}, \ldots, \mathbf{S}_m^{\mathrm{T}})^{\mathrm{T}} \\
\widetilde{\mathbf{V}} &= nm \times nm \text{ block diagonal matrix with } \widetilde{\mathbf{V}}_i \\
\mathbf{Z} &= \mathbf{D}\beta - \mathbf{S}
\end{aligned}
$$

At a given iteration, the correlation parameters α and scale parameter ϕ can be estimated from the current Pearson residuals defined by

$$\widehat{r}_{i,j} = \{y_{i,j} - a'(\widehat{\theta}_{i,j})\}/\{a''(\widehat{\theta}_{i,j})\}^{1/2}$$

where $\widehat{\theta}_{i,j}$ depends on the current value for $\widehat{\beta}$. We can then estimate ϕ by

$$\widehat{\phi}^{-1} = \sum_{i=1}^{m} \sum_{j=1}^{n_i} \widehat{r}_{i,j}^2 / (N - p)$$

As the above general derivation is complicated, let's follow the derivation of the Gaussian family with the identity link (regression) to illustrate the generalization. After making appropriate substitutions, we will see a familiar updating equation. First, we rewrite the updating equation for β as

$$\widehat{\beta}_{j+1} = \widehat{\beta}_j - \mathbf{Z}_1^{-1} \mathbf{Z}_2$$

and then derive for $\mathbf{Z}_1$ and $\mathbf{Z}_2$.

$$\mathbf{Z}_1 = \sum_{i=1}^{m} \mathbf{D}_i^{\mathrm{T}}(\widehat{\beta}_j) \widetilde{\mathbf{V}}_i^{-1}(\widehat{\beta}_j) \mathbf{D}_i(\widehat{\beta}_j) = \sum_{i=1}^{m} \mathbf{X}_i^{\mathrm{T}} \Delta_i^{\mathrm{T}} \mathbf{A}_i^{\mathrm{T}} (\mathbf{A}_i^{1/2} \mathbf{R}(\alpha) \mathbf{A}_i^{1/2})^{-1} \mathbf{A}_i \Delta_i \mathbf{X}_i$$

$$= \sum_{i=1}^{m} \mathbf{X}_i^{\mathrm{T}} \operatorname{diag}\left(\frac{\partial \theta_{i,j}}{\partial (\mathbf{X}\beta)}\right) \operatorname{diag}\left(a''(\theta_{i,j})\right) \left[\operatorname{diag}\left(a''(\theta_{i,j})\right)^{1/2} \mathbf{R}(\alpha) \operatorname{diag}\left(a''(\theta_{i,j})\right)^{1/2}\right]^{-1}$$

$$\operatorname{diag}\left(a''(\theta_{i,j})\right) \operatorname{diag}\left(\frac{\partial \theta_{i,j}}{\partial (\mathbf{X}\beta)}\right) \mathbf{X}_i$$

$$= \sum_{i=1}^{m} \mathbf{X}_i^{\mathrm{T}} \mathbf{II}[\mathbf{III}]^{-1} \mathbf{IIX}_i = \sum_{i=1}^{m} \mathbf{X}_i^{\mathrm{T}} \mathbf{X}_i = \mathbf{X}^{\mathrm{T}} \mathbf{X}$$

$$\mathbf{Z}_2 = \sum_{i=1}^{m} \mathbf{D}_i^{\mathrm{T}}(\widehat{\beta}_j) \widetilde{\mathbf{V}}_i^{-1}(\widehat{\beta}_j) \mathbf{S}_i(\widehat{\beta}_j) = \sum_{i=1}^{m} \mathbf{X}_i^{\mathrm{T}} \Delta_i^{\mathrm{T}} \mathbf{A}_i^{\mathrm{T}} (\mathbf{A}_i^{1/2} \mathbf{R}(\alpha) \mathbf{A}_i^{1/2})^{-1} \left(\mathbf{y}_i - \mathbf{X}_i \widehat{\beta}_j\right)$$

$$= \sum_{i=1}^{m} \mathbf{X}_i^{\mathrm{T}} \operatorname{diag}\left(\frac{\partial \theta_{i,j}}{\partial (\mathbf{X}\beta)}\right) \operatorname{diag}\left(a''(\theta_{i,j})\right) \left[\operatorname{diag}\left(a''(\theta_{i,j})\right)^{1/2} \mathbf{R}(\alpha) \operatorname{diag}\left(a''(\theta_{i,j})\right)^{1/2}\right]^{-1}$$

$$\left(\mathbf{y}_i - \mathbf{X}_i \widehat{\beta}_j\right)$$

$$= \sum_{i=1}^{m} \mathbf{X}_i \mathbf{II}[\mathbf{III}]^{-1} (\mathbf{y}_i - \mathbf{X}_i \widehat{\beta}_j) = \sum_{i=1}^{m} \mathbf{X}_i^{\mathrm{T}} (\mathbf{y}_i - \mathbf{X}_i \widehat{\beta}_j) = \mathbf{X}^{\mathrm{T}} \widehat{s}_j$$

So, that means that we may write the update formula as

$$\widehat{\beta}_{j+1} = \widehat{\beta}_j - (\mathbf{X}^{\mathrm{T}} \mathbf{X})^{-1} \mathbf{X}^{\mathrm{T}} \widehat{s}_j$$

which is the same formula for IRLS in regression.

Correlation structures

The working correlation matrix $\mathbf{R}$ is a function of α and more accurately written as $\mathbf{R}(\alpha)$. Depending on the assumed correlation structure, α might be

Independent	No parameters to estimate
Exchangeable	α is a scalar
Autoregressive	α is a vector
Stationary	α is a vector
Nonstationary	α is a matrix
Unstructured	α is a matrix

Also note that throughout the estimation of a general unbalanced panel, it is more proper to discuss $\mathbf{R}_i$ which is the upper left $n_i \times n_i$ submatrix of the ultimately saved matrix in `e(R)` which is $\max\{n_i\} \times \max\{n_i\}$.

The only panels that enter into the estimation for a lag-dependent correlation structure are those with $n_i > g$ (assuming a lag of g). `xtgee` drops panels with too few observations (and mentions the fact when it does so).

Independent

The working correlation matrix $\mathbf{R}$ is an identity matrix.

Exchangeable

$$\alpha = \sum_{i=1}^{m} \left[\frac{\sum_{j=1}^{n_i} \sum_{k=1}^{n_i} \widehat{r}_{i,j} \widehat{r}_{i,k} - \sum_{j=1}^{n_i} \widehat{r}_{i,j}^2}{n_i(n_i - 1)} \right] \Bigg/ \left[\sum_{i=1}^{m} \frac{\sum_{j=1}^{n_i} \widehat{r}_{i,j}^2}{n_i} \right]$$

and the working correlation matrix is given by

$$\mathbf{R}_{s,t} = \begin{cases} 1 & s = t \\ \alpha & \text{otherwise} \end{cases}$$

Autoregressive and stationary

These two structures require g parameters to be estimated so that α is a vector of length $g + 1$ (the first element of α is 1).

$$\alpha = \sum_{i=1}^{m} \left[\frac{\sum_{j=1}^{n_i} \widehat{r}_{i,j}^2}{n_i} , \frac{\sum_{j=1}^{n_i-1} \widehat{r}_{i,j} \widehat{r}_{i,j+1}}{n_i} , \ldots , \frac{\sum_{j=1}^{n_i-g} \widehat{r}_{i,j} \widehat{r}_{i,j+g}}{n_i} \right] \Bigg/ \left[\sum_{i=1}^{m} \frac{\sum_{j=1}^{n_i} \widehat{r}_{i,j}^2}{n_i} \right]$$

The working correlation matrix for the AR model is calculated as a function of Toeplitz matrices formed from the α vector. See Newton (1988) for a discussion of the algorithm. The working correlation matrix for the stationary model is given by

$$\mathbf{R}_{s,t} = \begin{cases} \alpha_{1,|s-t|} & \text{if } |s - t| \leq g \\ 0 & \text{otherwise} \end{cases}$$

Nonstationary and Unstructured

These two correlation structures require a matrix of parameters. α is estimated (where we replace $\widehat{r}_{i,j} = 0$ whenever $i > n_i$ or $j > n_i$) as

$$
\alpha = \sum_{i=1}^{m} m
\begin{bmatrix}
N_{1,1}^{-1}\widehat{r}_{i,1}^2 & N_{1,2}^{-1}\widehat{r}_{i,1}\widehat{r}_{i,2} & \cdots & N_{1,n}^{-1}\widehat{r}_{i,1}\widehat{r}_{i,n} \\
N_{2,1}^{-1}\widehat{r}_{i,2}\widehat{r}_{i,1} & N_{2,2}^{-1}\widehat{r}_{i,2}^2 & \cdots & N_{2,n}^{-1}\widehat{r}_{i,2}\widehat{r}_{i,n} \\
\vdots & \vdots & \ddots & \vdots \\
N_{n,1}^{-1}\widehat{r}_{i,n_i}\widehat{r}_{i,1} & N_{n,2}^{-1}\widehat{r}_{i,n_i}\widehat{r}_{i,2} & \cdots & N_{n,n}^{-1}\widehat{r}_{i,n}^2
\end{bmatrix}
\bigg/ \left[\left(\sum_{i=1}^{m} \frac{\sum_{j=1}^{n_i} \widehat{r}_{i,j}^2}{n_i} \right) \right]
$$

where $N_{i,j} = \min(N_i, N_j)$ and N_i = number of panels observed at time i, and $n = \max(n_1, n_2, \ldots, n_m)$.

The working correlation matrix for the nonstationary model is given by

$$
\mathbf{R}_{s,t} = \begin{cases} 1 & \text{if } s = t \\ \alpha_{s,t} & \text{if } 0 < |s - t| \leq g \\ 0 & \text{otherwise} \end{cases}
$$

The working correlation matrix for the unstructured model is given by

$$
\mathbf{R}_{s,t} = \begin{cases} 1 & \text{if } s = t \\ \alpha_{s,t} & \text{otherwise} \end{cases}
$$

such that the unstructured model is equal to the nonstationary model at lag $g = n - 1$ where the panels are balanced with $n_i = n$ for all i.

References

Hosmer, D. W., Jr., and S. Lemeshow. 1989. *Applied Logistic Regression*. New York: John Wiley & Sons.

Liang, K.-Y. and S. L. Zeger. 1986. Longitudinal data analysis using generalized linear models. *Biometrika* 73: 13–22.

Liang, K.-Y. 1987. Estimating functions and approximate conditional likelihood. *Biometrika* 4: 695–702.

Liang, K.-Y., Zeger, S. L. and B. Qaqish. 1987. Multivariate regression analyses for categorical data. *Journal of the Royal Statistical Society*, Series B 54: 3–40.

McCullagh, P. and J. A. Nelder. 1989. *Generalized Linear Models*. 2d ed. London: Chapman & Hall.

Nelder, J. A. and R. W. M. Wedderburn. 1972. Generalized linear models. *Journal of the Royal Statistical Society*, Series A 135: 370–384.

Newton, H. J. 1988. *TIMESLAB: A Time Series Analysis Laboratory*, Belmont, CA: Wadsworth & Brooks/Cole.

Pendergast, J. F., S. J. Gange, M. A. Newton, M. J. Lindstrom, M. Palta, and M. R. Fisher. 1996. A survey of methods for analyzing clustered binary response data. *International Statistical Review* 64: 89–118.

Prentice, R. L. and L. P. Zhao. 1991. Estimating equations for parameters in means and covariances of multivariate discrete and continuous responses. *Biometrics* 47: 825–839.

Wedderburn, R. W. M. 1974. Quasi-likelihood functions, generalized linear models, and the Gauss–Newton method. *Biometrika* 61: 439–447.

Zeger, S. L. and K.-Y. Liang. 1986. Longitudinal data analysis for discrete and continuous outcomes. *Biometrics* 42: 121–130.

Zeger, S. L., Liang, K.-Y., and P. S. Albert. 1988. Models for longitudinal data: a generalized estimating equation approach *Biometrics* 44: 1049–1060.

Zhao, L. P. and R. L. Prentice. 1990. Correlated binary regression using a quadratic exponential model. *Biometrika* 77: 642–648.

Also See

Complementary:	[R] **lincom**, [R] **predict**, [R] **test**, [R] **testnl**, [R] **vce**, [R] **xtdata**, [R] **xtdes**, [R] **xtsum**, [R] **xttab**
Related:	[R] **logistic**, [R] **prais**, [R] **regress**, [R] **svy estimators**, [R] **xtclog**, [R] **xtgls**, [R] **xtintreg**, [R] **xtlogit**, [R] **xtnbreg**, [R] **xtpois**, [R] **xtprobit**, [R] **xtreg**, [R] **xttobit**
Background:	[U] **16.5 Accessing coefficients and standard errors**, [U] **23 Estimation and post-estimation commands**, [U] **23.11 Obtaining robust variance estimates**, [U] **23.12 Obtaining scores**, [R] **xt**

Title

---
xtgls — Estimate panel-data models using GLS

Syntax

xtgls *depvar* [*varlist*] [*weight*] [if *exp*] [in *range*] [, i(*varname*) t(*varname*)

    force igls ols pcse nmk p̲anels({i̲id|h̲eteroscedastic|c̲orrelated})

    c̲orr({independent|a̲r1|p̲sar1}) level(#) t̲ol(#) i̲terate(#) nolog

    r̲hotype({regress|dw|freg|n̲agar|t̲heil|t̲scorr})]

aweights are allowed; see [U] **14.1.6 weight**.

xtgls shares the features of all estimation commands; see [U] **23 Estimation and post-estimation commands**.

Syntax for predict

predict [*type*] *newvarname* [if *exp*] [in *range*] [, { xb | stdp }]

These statistics are available both in and out of sample; type predict ... if e(sample) ... if wanted only for the estimation sample.

Description

xtgls estimates cross-sectional time-series linear models using feasible generalized least squares. This command allows estimation in the presence of AR(1) autocorrelation within panels and cross-sectional correlation and/or heteroscedasticity across panels.

Options

i(*varname*) specifies the variable that identifies the panel to which the observation belongs. You can specify the i() option the first time you estimate or use the iis command to set i() beforehand. After that, Stata will remember the variable's identity. See [R] **xt**.

t(*varname*) specifies the variable that contains the time at which the observation was made. You can specify the t() option the first time you estimate or use the tis command to set t() beforehand. After that, Stata will remember the variable's identity. See [R] **xt**.

xtgls does not need to know t() in all cases and, in those cases, whether you specify t() makes no difference. We note in the descriptions of the panels() and corr() options when t() is required. When t() is required, it is also required that the observations be spaced equally over time; however, see option force below.

force specifies that estimation is to be forced even though t() is not equally spaced. This is relevant only for correlation structures that require knowledge of t(). These correlation structures require observations be equally spaced so that calculations based on lags correspond to a constant time change. If you specify a t() variable that indicates observations are not equally spaced, xtgls will refuse to estimate the (time-dependent) model. If you also specify force, xtgls will estimate the model and assume that the lags based on the data ordered by t() are appropriate.

igls requests an iterated GLS estimator instead of the two step GLS estimator in the case of a
   nonautocorrelated model or instead of the three step GLS estimator in the case of an autocorrelated
   model. The iterated GLS estimator converges to the MLE for the corr(independent) models,
   but does not for the other corr() models.

ols and pcse are synonyms; either requests the OLS parameter estimates but with appropriate model
   based estimates of variance, also known as OLS with Panel-Corrected Standard Errors. Beck and
   Katz (1995) show that when the number of time periods is small relative to the number of panels,
   the coverage probabilities based on the OLS point estimates with panel-corrected standard errors are
   closer to the nominal levels than the coverage probabilities of the GLS estimators with associated
   model-based GLS standard errors.

   The default is to present the GLS parameter estimates. Note that when there is only one group,
   the OLS and GLS estimates are the same.

nmk specifies standard errors are to be normalized by $n - k$, where k is the number of parameters
   estimated, rather than n, the number of observations. Different authors have used one or the other
   normalization. Greene (1997, 659) recommends n and reminds that whether you use n or $n - k$
   does not make the variance calculation unbiased in these models.

panels(*pdist*) specifies the error structure across panels.

   panels(iid) specifies a homoscedastic error structure with no cross-sectional correlation. This
   is the default.

   panels(heteroscedastic) $\big($typically abbreviated p(h)$\big)$ specifies a heteroscedastic error structure with no cross-sectional correlation.

   panels(correlated) (abbreviation p(c)) specifies heteroscedastic error structure with cross-
   sectional correlation. If p(c) is specified, you must also specify t(). Note that the results will
   be based on a generalized inverse of a singular matrix unless $T \geq n$ (the number of time periods
   is greater than or equal to the number of panels).

corr(*corr*) specifies the assumed autocorrelation within panels.

   corr(independent) (abbreviation c(i)) specifies that there is no autocorrelation. This is the
   default.

   corr(ar1) (abbreviation c(a)) specifies that, within panels, there is AR(1) autocorrelation and
   that the coefficient of the AR(1) process is common to all the panels. If c(ar1) is specified, you
   must also specify t().

   corr(psar1) (abbreviation c(p)) specifies that, within panels, there is AR(1) autocorrelation and
   that the coefficient of the AR(1) process is specific to each panel. psar1 stands for panel-specific
   AR(1). If c(psar1) is specified, t() must also be specified.

level(#) specifies the confidence level, in percent, for confidence intervals. The default is level(95)
   or as set by set level; see [U] **23.5 Specifying the width of confidence intervals**.

tol(#) specifies the convergence criterion for the maximum change in the estimated coefficient
   vector between iterations; tol(1e-6) is the default.

iterate(#) specifies the maximum number of iterations allowed in estimating the model; iter-
   ate(100) is the default. You should never have to specify this option.

nolog suppresses the iteration log.

rhotype(*calc*) specifies the method to be used to calculate the autocorrelation parameter. Allowed strings for *calc* are

regress	regression using lags (the default)
dw	Durbin–Watson calculation
freg	regression using leads
nagar	Nagar calculation
theil	Theil calculation
tscorr	time series autocorrelation calculation

All the calculations are asymptotically equivalent and all are consistent; this is a rarely used option.

Options for predict

xb, the default, calculates the linear prediction.

stdp calculates the standard error of the linear prediction.

Remarks

Information on GLS can be found in Greene (1997), Maddala (1992), Davidson and MacKinnon (1993), and Judge et al. (1985).

If you have a large number of panels relative to time periods, see [R] **xtreg** and [R] **xtgee**. xtgee, in particular, provides similar capabilities as **xtgls** but does not allow cross-sectional correlation. On the other hand, **xtgee** will allow a richer description of the correlation within panels subject to the constraint that the same correlations apply to all panels. That is, **xtgls** provides two unique features:

1. Cross-sectional correlation may be modeled (panels(correlated)).

2. Within panels, the AR(1) correlation coefficient may be unique (corr(psar1)).

It is also true that **xtgls** allows models with heteroscedasticity and no cross-sectional correlation whereas, strictly speaking, **xtgee** does not, but **xtgee** with the **robust** option relaxes the assumption of equal variances at least as far as the standard-error calculation is concerned.

In addition,

1. xtgls, panels(iid) corr(independent) nmk is equivalent to regress.

2. xtgls, ols panels(heteroscedastic) nmk when there is only one panel is equivalent to either newey with the lag(0) option or regress with the robust option.

The nmk option uses $n - k$ to normalize the variance calculation rather than n.

In order to estimate a model with autocorrelated errors (corr(ar1) or corr(psar1)), the data must be equally spaced in time. In order to estimate a model with cross-sectional correlation (panels(correlated)), panels must have the same number of observations (be balanced).

The equation from which the models are developed is given by

$$y_{i,t} = \mathbf{x}_{i,t}\boldsymbol{\beta} + \epsilon_{i,t}$$

where $i = 1, \ldots, m$ is the number of units (or panels) and $t = 1, \ldots, n_i$ is the number of observations for panel i. This model can equally well be written

$$\begin{bmatrix} \mathbf{y}_1 \\ \mathbf{y}_2 \\ \vdots \\ \mathbf{y}_m \end{bmatrix} = \begin{bmatrix} \mathbf{X}_1 \\ \mathbf{X}_2 \\ \vdots \\ \mathbf{X}_m \end{bmatrix} \boldsymbol{\beta} + \begin{bmatrix} \epsilon_1 \\ \epsilon_2 \\ \vdots \\ \epsilon_m \end{bmatrix}$$

The variance matrix of the disturbance terms can be written

$$
E[\epsilon\epsilon'] = \Omega =
\begin{bmatrix}
\sigma_{1,1}\Omega_{1,1} & \sigma_{1,2}\Omega_{1,2} & \cdots & \sigma_{1,m}\Omega_{1,m} \\
\sigma_{2,1}\Omega_{2,1} & \sigma_{2,2}\Omega_{2,2} & \cdots & \sigma_{2,m}\Omega_{2,m} \\
\vdots & \vdots & \ddots & \vdots \\
\sigma_{m,1}\Omega_{m,1} & \sigma_{m,2}\Omega_{m,2} & \cdots & \sigma_{m,m}\Omega_{m,m}
\end{bmatrix}
$$

In order for the $\Omega_{i,j}$ matrices to be parameterized to model cross-sectional correlation, they must be square (balanced panels).

In these models, we assume that the coefficient vector β is the same for all panels and consider a variety of models by changing the assumptions on the structure of Ω.

For the classic OLS regression model, we have

$$
E[\epsilon_{i,t}] = 0
$$
$$
\text{Var}[\epsilon_{i,t}] = \sigma^2
$$
$$
\text{Cov}[\epsilon_{i,t}, \epsilon_{j,s}] = 0 \qquad \text{if } t \neq s \text{ or } i \neq j
$$

This amounts to assuming that Ω has the structure given by

$$
\Omega =
\begin{bmatrix}
\sigma^2 I & 0 & \cdots & 0 \\
0 & \sigma^2 I & \cdots & 0 \\
\vdots & \vdots & \ddots & \vdots \\
0 & 0 & \cdots & \sigma^2 I
\end{bmatrix}
$$

whether or not the panels are balanced (the **0** matrices may be rectangular). The classic OLS assumptions are the default `panels(uncorrelated)` and `corr(independent)` options for this command.

Heteroscedasticity across panels

In many cross-sectional datasets, the variance for each of the panels will differ. It is common to have data on countries, states, or other units that have variation of scale. The heteroscedastic model is specified by including the `panels(heteroscedastic)` option, which assumes

$$
\Omega =
\begin{bmatrix}
\sigma_1^2 I & 0 & \cdots & 0 \\
0 & \sigma_2^2 I & \cdots & 0 \\
\vdots & \vdots & \ddots & \vdots \\
0 & 0 & \cdots & \sigma_m^2 I
\end{bmatrix}
$$

▷ Example

Greene (1997, 650) reprints data in a classic study of investment demand by Grunfeld and Griliches (1960). Below we allow the variances to differ for each of the five companies.

```
. xtgls invest market stock, i(company) panels(hetero)

Cross-sectional time-series FGLS regression

Coefficients:  generalized least squares
Panels:        heteroscedastic
Correlation:   no autocorrelation

Estimated covariances      =      5       Number of obs      =       100
Estimated autocorrelations =      0       Number of groups   =         5
Estimated coefficients     =      3       No. of time periods=        20
                                          Wald chi2(2)       =    865.38
Log likelihood            =  -523.293     Pr > chi2          =    0.0000

------------------------------------------------------------------------------
  invest |      Coef.   Std. Err.      z    P>|z|     [95% Conf. Interval]
---------+--------------------------------------------------------------------
  market |   .0949905    .007409    12.821   0.000     .0804692    .1095118
   stock |   .3378129   .0302254    11.176   0.000     .2785722    .3970535
   _cons |   -36.2537   6.124363    -5.920   0.000    -48.25723   -24.25017
------------------------------------------------------------------------------
```

The coefficient estimates reported above are the GLS estimates. In comparing the properties of the OLS and GLS estimators, Beck and Katz (1995) show that when the number of time periods is small relative to the number of panels, the coverage probabilities for the OLS point estimates with associated model-based standard errors are much closer to the nominal levels than the coverage probabilities for the GLS estimators with associated model-based standard errors.

xtgls with the ols or pcse options (they mean the same thing) will produce the results they suggest. Beck and Katz refer to this as OLS with panel-corrected standard errors:

```
. xtgls invest market stock, i(company) panels(hetero) pcse

Cross-sectional time-series FGLS regression

Coefficients:  ordinary least squares
Panels:        heteroscedastic
Correlation:   no autocorrelation

Estimated covariances      =      5       Number of obs      =       100
Estimated autocorrelations =      0       Number of groups   =         5
Estimated coefficients     =      3       No. of time periods=        20
                                          Wald chi2(2)       =    720.01
Log likelihood            = -524.0017     Pr > chi2          =    0.0000

------------------------------------------------------------------------------
         |           Panel-Corrected
  invest |      Coef.   Std. Err.      z    P>|z|     [95% Conf. Interval]
---------+--------------------------------------------------------------------
  market |   .1050854   .0090625    11.596   0.000     .0873232    .1228476
   stock |   .3053655   .0409468     7.458   0.000     .2251113    .3856198
   _cons |  -48.02974   14.20367    -3.382   0.001    -75.86841   -20.19106
------------------------------------------------------------------------------
```

◁

❑ Technical Note

The groupwise heteroscedastic models (no autocorrelation) estimated by (1) xtgls, ols; (2) regress, robust; and (3) regress, robust cluster are not the same. While the estimated variance matrices can be written in the general form

$$(\mathbf{X}'\mathbf{X})^{-1}\mathbf{X}\mathbf{W}\mathbf{X}(\mathbf{X}'\mathbf{X})^{-1}$$

the **W** matrix differs in each of the three approaches. Obviously regress without cluster() does not use the group information, but xtgls, ols and regress, robust cluster() use the group information differently:

$$\mathbf{W_1} = \sum_i \mathbf{x}'_i \bar{\epsilon}_{i\cdot} \bar{\epsilon}_{i\cdot} \mathbf{x}_i$$

$$\mathbf{W_2} = \sum_i \sum_j x_{ij} \epsilon_{ij} \epsilon_{ij} x_{ij}$$

$$\mathbf{W_3} = \sum_i (\overline{\mathbf{x}_i \epsilon_i})' (\overline{\mathbf{x}_i \epsilon_i})$$

❑

Correlation across panels (cross-sectional correlation)

We may wish to assume that the error terms of panels are correlated in addition to having different scale variances. This variance structure is specified by including the panels(correlated) option and is given by

$$
\Omega = \begin{bmatrix}
\sigma_1^2 \mathbf{I} & \sigma_{1,2}\mathbf{I} & \cdots & \sigma_{1,m}\mathbf{I} \\
\sigma_{2,1}\mathbf{I} & \sigma_2^2 \mathbf{I} & \cdots & \sigma_{2,m}\mathbf{I} \\
\vdots & \vdots & \ddots & \vdots \\
\sigma_{m,1}\mathbf{I} & \sigma_{m,2}\mathbf{I} & \cdots & \sigma_m^2 \mathbf{I}
\end{bmatrix}
$$

Note that since we must estimate cross-sectional correlation in this model, the panels must be balanced (and $T \geq n$ for valid results). In addition, we must now specify the t() option so that xtgls knows how the observations within panels are ordered.

▷ Example

```
. xtgls invest market stock, i(company) t(time) panels(correlated)

Cross-sectional time-series FGLS regression

Coefficients:  generalized least squares
Panels:        heteroscedastic with cross-sectional correlation
Correlation:   no autocorrelation

Estimated covariances      =        15        Number of obs       =        100
Estimated autocorrelations =         0        Number of groups    =          5
Estimated coefficients     =         3        No. of time periods=         20
                                              Wald chi2(2)        =    1600.89
Log likelihood             = -488.2793        Pr > chi2           =     0.0000

------------------------------------------------------------------------------
   invest |      Coef.   Std. Err.      z    P>|z|     [95% Conf. Interval]
----------+-------------------------------------------------------------------
   market |   .0891009   .0050723     17.566   0.000     .0791595    .0990424
    stock |    .334015   .0167125     19.986   0.000     .3012591     .366771
    _cons |  -28.24669   4.888238     -5.779   0.000    -37.82746   -18.66592
------------------------------------------------------------------------------
```

◁

▷ Example

We can obtain the MLE results by specifying the igls option, which iterates the GLS estimation technique to convergence:

```
. xtgls invest market stock, i(company) t(time) panels(correlated) igls

Iteration 1: tolerance = .27778881
Iteration 2: tolerance = .1701293
 (output omitted)
Iteration 13: tolerance = 3.458e-08

Cross-sectional time-series FGLS regression

Coefficients:  generalized least squares
Panels:        heteroscedastic with cross-sectional correlation
Correlation:   no autocorrelation

Estimated covariances      =         15      Number of obs      =        100
Estimated autocorrelations =          0      Number of groups   =          5
Estimated coefficients     =          3      No. of time periods=         20
                                             Wald chi2(2)       =    1615.32
Log likelihood                =  -485.1033   Pr > chi2          =     0.0000

------------------------------------------------------------------------------
     invest |      Coef.   Std. Err.      z    P>|z|     [95% Conf. Interval]
------------+-----------------------------------------------------------------
     market |    .086832   .0051569    16.838   0.000     .0767247    .0969392
      stock |    .333665   .0171446    19.462   0.000     .3000622    .3672677
      _cons |  -15.58819   4.202578    -3.709   0.000    -23.82509   -7.351291
------------------------------------------------------------------------------
```

◁

Autocorrelation within panels

The individual identity matrices along the diagonal of Ω may be replaced with more general structures in order to allow for serial correlation. xtgls allows three options so that you may assume a structure with corr(independent) (no autocorrelation); corr(ar1) (serial correlation where the correlation parameter is common for all panels); or corr(psar1) (serial correlation where the correlation parameter is unique for each panel).

The restriction of a common autocorrelation parameter is reasonable when the individual correlations are nearly equal and the time series are short.

If the restriction of a common autocorrelation parameter is reasonable, this allows us to use more information in estimating the autocorrelation parameter and thus produce a more reasonable estimate of the regression coefficients.

▷ Example

If corr(ar1) is specified, each group is assumed to have errors that follow the same AR(1) process; that is, the autocorrelation parameter is the same for all groups.

(Continued on next page)

```
. xtgls invest market stock, i(company) t(time) panels(hetero) corr(ar1)

Cross-sectional time-series FGLS regression

Coefficients:  generalized least squares
Panels:        heteroscedastic
Correlation:   common AR(1) coefficient for all panels  (0.8651)

Estimated covariances      =     5        Number of obs      =       100
Estimated autocorrelations =     1        Number of groups   =         5
Estimated coefficients     =     3        No. of time periods=        20
                                          Wald chi2(2)       =    119.69
Log likelihood             = -459.3317    Pr > chi2          =    0.0000

------------------------------------------------------------------------------
      invest |     Coef.   Std. Err.      z    P>|z|     [95% Conf. Interval]
-------------+----------------------------------------------------------------
      market |   .0744315   .0097937     7.600   0.000     .0552362    .0936268
       stock |   .2874294   .0475391     6.046   0.000     .1942545    .3806043
       _cons |  -18.96238   17.64943    -1.074   0.283    -53.55463    15.62988
------------------------------------------------------------------------------
```

◁

▷ Example

If `corr(psar1)` is specified, each group is assumed to have errors that follow a different AR(1) process.

```
. xtgls invest market stock, i(company) t(time) panels(iid) corr(psar1)

Cross-sectional time-series FGLS regression

Coefficients:  generalized least squares
Panels:        homoscedastic
Correlation:   panel-specific AR(1)

Estimated covariances      =     1        Number of obs      =       100
Estimated autocorrelations =     5        Number of groups   =         5
Estimated coefficients     =     3        No. of time periods=        20
                                          Wald chi2(2)       =    252.93
Log likelihood             = -498.6388    Pr > chi2          =    0.0000

------------------------------------------------------------------------------
      invest |     Coef.   Std. Err.      z    P>|z|     [95% Conf. Interval]
-------------+----------------------------------------------------------------
      market |   .0934343   .0097783     9.555   0.000     .0742693    .1125993
       stock |   .3838814   .0416775     9.211   0.000      .302195    .4655677
       _cons |   -10.1246   34.06675    -0.297   0.766     -76.8942    56.64499
------------------------------------------------------------------------------
```

◁

(Continued on next page)

Saved Results

xtgls saves in e():

Scalars

e(N)	number of observations	e(df)	degrees of freedom
e(N_g)	number of groups	e(ll)	log likelihood
e(N_t)	number of time periods	e(g_max)	largest group size
e(N_miss)	number of missing observations	e(g_min)	smallest group size
e(n_cf)	number of estimated coefficients	e(g_avg)	average group size
e(n_cv)	number of estimated covariances	e(chi2)	χ^2
e(n_cr)	number of estimated correlations	e(df_pear)	degrees of freedom for Pearson χ^2

Macros

e(cmd)	xtgls	e(tvar)	variable denoting time
e(depvar)	name of dependent variable	e(wtype)	weight type
e(title)	title in estimation output	e(wexp)	weight expression
e(corr)	correlation structure	e(chi2type)	Wald; type of model χ^2 test
e(vt)	panel option	e(predict)	program used to implement predict
e(rhotype)	type of estimated correlation	e(rho)	ρ
e(ivar)	variable denoting groups		

Matrices

e(b)	coefficient vector	e(Sigma)	$\widehat{\Sigma}$ matrix
e(V)	variance–covariance matrix of the estimators		

Functions

e(sample)	marks estimation sample

Methods and Formulas

xtgls is implemented as an ado-file.

We may investigate our data using either the GLS or the OLS results.

The OLS results are given by

$$\widehat{\beta}_{OLS} = (\mathbf{X'X})^{-1}\mathbf{X'y}$$
$$\widehat{\mathrm{Var}}(\widehat{\beta}_{OLS}) = (\mathbf{X'X})^{-1}\mathbf{X'}\widehat{\Omega}\mathbf{X}(\mathbf{X'X})^{-1}$$

and the GLS results are given by

$$\widehat{\beta}_{GLS} = (\mathbf{X'}\widehat{\Omega}^{-1}\mathbf{X})^{-1}\mathbf{X'}\widehat{\Omega}^{-1}\mathbf{y}$$
$$\widehat{\mathrm{Var}}(\widehat{\beta}_{GLS}) = (\mathbf{X'}\widehat{\Omega}^{-1}\mathbf{X})^{-1}$$

For all our models, the Ω matrix may be written in terms of the Kronecker product

$$\Omega = \Sigma_{m \times m} \otimes \mathbf{I}_{n_i \times n_i}$$

The estimated variance matrix is then obtained by substituting the estimator $\widehat{\Sigma}$ for Σ where

$$\widehat{\Sigma}_{i,j} = \frac{\widehat{\epsilon}_i{}' \widehat{\epsilon}_j}{n}$$

The residuals used in estimating Σ are first obtained from OLS regression. If the estimation is iterated, then residuals are obtained from the last estimated model.

Maximum likelihood estimates may be obtained by iterating the FGLS estimates to convergence (for models with no autocorrelation—corr(0)).

Note that the GLS estimates and their associated standard errors are calculated using $\widehat{\Sigma}^{-1}$. As Beck and Katz (1995) point out, the Σ matrix is of rank at most $\min(n, m)$ when you use the panels(correlated) option, so for the GLS results to be valid (not based on a generalized inverse), n must be at least as large as m (you need at least as many time period observations as there are panels). The OLS results do not rely on inverting $\widehat{\Sigma}$ which is why these authors recommend them over the GLS results. The fact that the standard errors do include the $\widehat{\Sigma}$ matrix estimated under the panel assumptions of the error terms explains the term "panel-corrected standard errors".

References

Beck, N. and Katz, J. N. 1995. What to do (and not to do) with time-series cross-section data. *American Political Science Review* 89: 634–647.

Davidson, R. and J. G. MacKinnon. 1993. *Estimation and Inference in Econometrics.* New York: Oxford University Press.

Greene, W. H. 1997. *Econometric Analysis.* 3d ed. Upper Saddle River, NJ: Prentice–Hall.

Grunfeld, Y. and Z. Griliches. 1960. Is aggregation necessarily bad? *Review of Economics and Statistics* 42: 1–13.

Judge, G. G., W. E. Griffiths, R. C. Hill, H. Lütkepohl, and T.-C. Lee. 1985. *The Theory and Practice of Econometrics.* 2d ed. New York: John Wiley & Sons.

Maddala, G. S. 1992. *Introduction to Econometrics.* 2d ed. New York: Macmillan.

Also See

Complementary: [R] **lincom**, [R] **predict**, [R] **test**, [R] **testnl**, [R] **vce**, [R] **xtdata**, [R] **xtdes**, [R] **xtsum**, [R] **xttab**

Related: [R] **newey**, [R] **prais**, [R] **regress**, [R] **svy estimators**, [R] **xtgee**, [R] **xtreg**

Background: [U] **16.5 Accessing coefficients and standard errors**, [U] **23 Estimation and post-estimation commands**, [R] **xt**

Title

> **xtintreg** — Random-effects interval data regression models

Syntax

Random-effects model

> xtintreg *depvar*$_{lower}$ *depvar*$_{upper}$ [*varlist*] [*weight*] [if *exp*] [in *range*]
>
> [, i(*varname*) quad(*#*) noconstant noskip level(*#*) offset(*varname*)
>
> intreg *maximize_options*]

iweights are allowed; see [U] **14.1.6 weight**. Note that weights must be constant within panels.

xtintreg shares the features of all estimation commands; see [U] **23 Estimation and post-estimation commands**.

Syntax for predict

> predict [*type*] *newvarname* [if *exp*] [in *range*] [, { xb | stdp } nooffset]

These statistics are available both in and out of sample; type predict ... if e(sample) ... if wanted only for the estimation sample.

Description

xtintreg estimates random-effects interval regression models. There is no command for a conditional fixed-effects model as there does not exist a sufficient statistic allowing the fixed effects to be conditioned out of the likelihood. Unconditional fixed-effects intreg models may be estimated with the intreg command with indicator variables for the panels. The appropriate indicator variables can be generated using tabulate or xi. However, unconditional fixed-effects estimates are biased.

Note: xtintreg is slow since it is calculated by quadrature; see *Methods and Formulas*. Computation time is roughly proportional to the number of points used for the quadrature. The default is quad(12). Simulations indicate that increasing it does not appreciably change the estimates for the coefficients or their standard errors. See [R] **quadchk**.

Options

i(*varname*) specifies the variable name that contains the unit to which the observation belongs. You can specify the i() option the first time you estimate or use the iis command to set i() beforehand. After that, Stata will remember the variable's identity. See [R] **xt**.

quad(*#*) specifies the number of points to use in the quadrature approximation of the integral.

The default is quad(12). The number specified must be an integer between 4 and 30, and also be no greater than the number of observations.

`noconstant` suppresses the constant term (intercept) in the model.

`noskip` specifies that a full maximum-likelihood model with only a constant for the regression equation be estimated. This model is not displayed but is used as the base model to compute a likelihood-ratio test for the model test statistic displayed in the estimation header. By default, the overall model test statistic is an asymptotically equivalent Wald test of all the parameters in the regression equation being zero (except the constant). For many models, this option can significantly increase estimation time.

`level(#)` specifies the confidence level, in percent, for confidence intervals. The default is `level(95)` or as set by `set level`; see [U] **23.5 Specifying the width of confidence intervals**.

`offset(varname)` specifies that *varname* is to be included in the model with coefficient constrained to be 1.

`intreg` specifies that a likelihood-ratio test comparing the random-effects model with the pooled (intreg) model should be included in the output. By default, a Wald test is included.

maximize_options control the maximization process; see [R] **maximize**. Use the `trace` option to view parameter convergence. Use the `ltol(#)` option to relax the convergence criterion; default is 1e−6 during specification searches.

Options for predict

`xb`, the default, calculates the linear prediction.

`stdp` calculates the standard error of the linear prediction.

`nooffset` is relevant only if you specified `offset(varname)` for `xtintreg`. It modifies the calculations made by `predict` so that they ignore the offset variable; the linear prediction is treated as $\mathbf{x}_{it}\mathbf{b}$ rather than $\mathbf{x}_{it}\mathbf{b} + \text{offset}_{it}$.

Remarks

▷ Example

We begin with the dataset `nlswork` described in [R] **xt**, and we create two fictional dependent variables where the wages are instead reported sometimes as ranges. The wages have been adjusted by a GNP deflator such that they are in terms of 1988 dollars and have further been recoded such that some of the observations are known exactly, some are left censored, some are right censored, and some are known only in an interval.

We wish to estimate a random-effects interval regression model of adjusted (log) wages:

```
. xtintreg ln_wage1 ln_wage2 union age grade not_smsa south southXt occ_code,
> i(id) noskip intreg nolog
Random-effects interval regression              Number of obs     =      19095
Group variable (i) : idcode                     Number of groups  =       4139

Random effects u_i ~ Gaussian                   Obs per group: min =          1
                                                               avg =        4.6
                                                               max =         12

                                                LR chi2(7)        =    3549.47
Log likelihood  = -14856.934                    Prob > chi2       =     0.0000

------------------------------------------------------------------------------
             |     Coef.   Std. Err.      z    P>|z|     [95% Conf. Interval]
---------+--------------------------------------------------------------------
       union |  .1409746   .0068364    20.621   0.000     .1275755    .1543737
         age |   .012631   .0005148    24.534   0.000     .0116219    .0136401
       grade |   .078379   .0020912    37.480   0.000     .0742802    .0824777
    not_smsa |  -.133309   .0089209   -14.943   0.000    -.1507937   -.1158243
       south | -.1218995   .0121087   -10.067   0.000     -.145632   -.0981669
     southXt |  .0021033   .0008314     2.530   0.011     .0004738    .0037328
    occ_code | -.0185603    .001033   -17.967   0.000     -.020585   -.0165355
       _cons |  .4567544    .032493    14.057   0.000     .3930693    .5204395
---------+--------------------------------------------------------------------
    /sigma_u |   .282881   .0038227    74.000   0.000     .2753887    .2903734
    /sigma_e |  .2696118   .0015957   168.958   0.000     .2664843    .2727394
---------+--------------------------------------------------------------------
         rho |  .5240031   .0075625                       .5091677    .5388053
------------------------------------------------------------------------------
Likelihood ratio test of sigma_u=0:  chi2(1) =  6549.28   Prob > chi2 = 0.0000
          Obs. summary:      14372 uncensored observations
                              157 left-censored observations
                              718 right-censored observations
                             3848 interval observations
   Note: 22 completely determined observations
```

The output includes the overall and panel-level variance components (labeled `sigma_e` and `sigma_u`, respectively) together with ρ (labeled `rho`)

$$\rho = \frac{\sigma_\nu^2}{\sigma_\epsilon^2 + \sigma_\nu^2}$$

which is the proportion of the total variance contributed by the panel-level variance component.

When `rho` is zero, the panel-level variance component is unimportant and the panel estimator is not different from the pooled estimator. A likelihood-ratio test of this is included at the bottom of the output. This test formally compares the pooled estimator (intreg) with the panel estimator.

◁

❑ Technical Note

The random-effects model is calculated using quadrature. As the panel sizes (or ρ) increase, the quadrature approximation becomes less accurate. We can use the `quadchk` command to see if changing the number of quadrature points affects the results. If the results do change, then the quadrature approximation is not accurate and the results of the model should not be interpreted. See [R] **quadchk** for details and [R] **xtprobit** for an example.

❑

Saved Results

xtintreg saves in e():

Scalars

e(N)	number of observations	e(g_min)	smallest group size
e(N_g)	number of groups	e(g_avg)	average group size
e(N_unc)	number of uncensored observations	e(chi2)	χ^2
e(N_lc)	number of left-censored observations	e(chi2_c)	χ^2 for comparison test
e(N_rc)	number of right-censored observations	e(rho)	ρ
e(N_int)	number of interval observations	e(sigma_u)	panel-level standard deviation
e(df_m)	model degrees of freedom	e(sigma_e)	standard deviation of ϵ_{it}
e(ll)	log likelihood	e(N_cd)	number of completely determined obs.
e(ll_0)	log likelihood, constant-only model	e(n_quad)	number of quadrature points
e(g_max)	largest group size		

Macros

e(cmd)	xtintreg	e(chi2type)	Wald or LR; type of model χ^2 test
e(depvar)	names of dependent variables	e(chi2_ct)	Wald or LR; type of model χ^2 test
e(title)	title in estimation output		corresponding to e(chi2_c)
e(ivar)	variable denoting groups	e(distrib)	Gaussian; the distribution of the
e(wtype)	weight type		random effect
e(wexp)	weight expression	e(predict)	program used to implement predict
e(offset1)	offset		

Matrices

e(b)	coefficient vector	e(V)	variance–covariance matrix of the
			estimators

Functions

e(sample)	marks estimation sample

Methods and Formulas

xtintreg is implemented as an ado-file.

Assuming a normal distribution, $N(0, \sigma_\nu^2)$, for the random effects ν_i, we have that

$$\Pr(y_i|x_i) = \int_{-\infty}^{\infty} \frac{e^{-\nu_i^2/2\sigma_\nu^2}}{\sqrt{2\pi}\sigma_\nu} \left[\prod_{t=1}^{n_i} F(x_{it}\beta + \nu_i) \right] d\nu_i$$

where

$$F(\Delta_{it}) = \begin{cases} -1/\sqrt{2\pi\sigma_\epsilon^2}e^{-(y_{1it}-\Delta_{it})^2/(2\sigma_\epsilon^2)} & \text{if } (y_{1it}, y_{2it}) \in C \\ \Phi\left(\frac{y_{2it}-\Delta_{it}}{\sigma_\epsilon}\right) & \text{if } (y_{1it}, y_{2it}) \in L \\ 1 - \Phi\left(\frac{y_{1it}-\Delta_{it}}{\sigma_\epsilon}\right) & \text{if } (y_{1it}, y_{2it}) \in R \\ \Phi\left(\frac{y_{1it}-\Delta_{it}}{\sigma_\epsilon}\right) - \Phi\left(\frac{y_{2it}-\Delta_{it}}{\sigma_\epsilon}\right) & \text{if } (y_{1it}, y_{2it}) \in I \end{cases}$$

where C is the set of noncensored observations ($y_{1it} = y_{2it} \neq .$), L is the set of left-censored observations ($y_{1it} = .$ and $y_{2it} \neq .$), R is the set of right-censored observations ($y_{1it} \neq .$ and $y_{2it} = .$), I is the set of interval observations ($y_{1it} < y_{2it}, y_{1it} \neq ., y_{2it} \neq .$) and $\Phi()$ is the cumulative normal distribution. We can approximate the integral with M-point Gauss–Hermite quadrature

$$\int_{-\infty}^{\infty} e^{-x^2} f(x) dx \approx \sum_{m=1}^{M} w_m^* f(a_m^*)$$

where the w_m^* denote the quadrature weights and the a_m^* denote the quadrature abscissas. The log-likelihood L where $\rho = \sigma_\nu^2 / (\sigma_\epsilon^2 + \sigma_\nu^2)$ is then calculated using the quadrature

$$L = \sum_{i=1}^{n} w_i \log\left(\Pr(y_i | x_i) \right)$$

$$\approx \sum_{i=1}^{n} w_i \log \frac{1}{\sqrt{\pi}} \sum_{m=1}^{M} w_m^* \prod_{t=1}^{n_i} F\left(x_{it}\beta + \sqrt{2\frac{\rho}{1-\rho}} \, a_m^* \right)$$

The quadrature formula requires that the integrated function be well-approximated by a polynomial. As the number of time periods becomes large (as panel size gets large)

$$\prod_{t=1}^{n_i} F(x_{it}\beta + \nu_i)$$

is no longer well-approximated by a polynomial. As a general rule-of-thumb, you should use this quadrature approach only for small-to-moderate panel sizes (based on simulations, 50 is a reasonably safe upper bound). However, if the data really comes from random-effects intreg and rho is not too large (less than say .3), then the panel size could be 500 and the quadrature approximation will still be fine. If the data is not random-effects intreg or rho is large (bigger than say .7), then the quadrature approximation may be poor for panel sizes larger than 10. The quadchk command should be used to investigate the applicability of the numeric technique used in this command.

References

Neuhaus, J. M. 1992. Statistical methods for longitudinal and clustered designs with binary responses. *Statistical Methods in Medical Research* 1: 249–273.

Pendergast, J. F., S. J. Gange, M. A. Newton, M. J. Lindstrom, M. Palta, and M. R. Fisher. 1996. A survey of methods for analyzing clustered binary response data. *International Statistical Review* 64: 89–118.

Also See

Complementary:	[R] **lincom**, [R] **predict**, [R] **quadchk**, [R] **test**, [R] **testnl**, [R] **vce**, [R] **xtdata**, [R] **xtdes**, [R] **xtsum**, [R] **xttab**
Related:	[R] **tobit**, [R] **xtgee**, [R] **xtreg**, [R] **xttobit**
Background:	[U] **16.5 Accessing coefficients and standard errors**, [U] **23 Estimation and post-estimation commands**, [U] **23.11 Obtaining robust variance estimates**, [R] **xt**

Title

> **xtlogit** — Fixed-effects, random-effects, and population-averaged logit models

Syntax

Random-effects model

> xtlogit *depvar* [*varlist*] [*weight*] [if *exp*] [in *range*] [, re i(*varname*)
>
> quad(*#*) noconstant noskip level(*#*) offset(*varname*) *maximize_options*]

Conditional fixed-effects model

> xtlogit *depvar* [*varlist*] [*weight*] [if *exp*] [in *range*] , fe [i(*varname*)
>
> noskip level(*#*) offset(*varname*) *maximize_options*]

Population-averaged model

> xtlogit *depvar* [*varlist*] [*weight*] [if *exp*] [in *range*] , pa [i(*varname*) robust
>
> noconstant level(*#*) offset(*varname*) *xtgee_options* *maximize_options*]

iweights, aweights, and pweights are allowed for the population-averaged model and iweights are allowed for the fixed-effects and random-effects models; see [U] **14.1.6 weight**. Note that weights must be constant within panels.

xtlogit shares the features of all estimation commands; see [U] **23 Estimation and post-estimation commands**.

Syntax for predict

Random-effects model

> predict [*type*] *newvarname* [if *exp*] [in *range*] [, { xb | pu0 | stdp }
>
> nooffset]

Fixed-effects model

> predict [*type*] *newvarname* [if *exp*] [in *range*] [, { p | xb | stdp }
>
> nooffset]

Population-averaged model

> predict [*type*] *newvarname* [if *exp*] [in *range*] [, { mu | rate | xb | stdp }
>
> nooffset]

These statistics are available both in and out of sample; type predict ... if e(sample) ... if wanted only for the estimation sample.

Note that the predicted probability for the fixed-effects model is conditional on there being only one outcome per group. See [R] **clogit** for details.

Description

xtlogit estimates random-effects, conditional fixed-effects, and population-averaged logit models. Whenever we refer to a fixed-effects model, we mean the conditional fixed-effects model.

Note: xtlogit, re is slow since it is calculated by quadrature; see *Methods and Formulas*. Computation time is roughly proportional to the number of points used for the quadrature. The default is quad(12). Simulations indicate that increasing it does not appreciably change the estimates for the coefficients or their standard errors. See [R] **quadchk**.

By default, the population-averaged model is an equal-correlation model; xtlogit assumes corr(exchangeable). See [R] **xtgee** for details on how to fit other population-averaged models.

See [R] **logistic** for a list of related estimation commands.

Options

re requests the random-effects estimator. re is the default if none of re, fe, and pa is specified.

fe requests the fixed-effects estimator.

pa requests the population-averaged estimator.

i(*varname*) specifies the variable name that contains the unit to which the observation belongs. You can specify the i() option the first time you estimate or use the iis command to set i() beforehand. After that, Stata will remember the variable's identity. See [R] **xt**.

quad(*#*) specifies the number of points to use in the quadrature approximation of the integral. The default is quad(12). See [R] **quadchk**.

robust specifies the Huber/White/sandwich estimator of variance is to be used in place of the IRLS variance estimator; see [R] **xtgee**. This alternative produces valid standard errors even if the correlations within group are not as hypothesized by the specified correlation structure. It does, however, require that the model correctly specifies the mean. As such, the resulting standard errors are labeled "semi-robust" instead of "robust". Note that although there is no cluster() option, results are as if there were a cluster() option and you specified clustering on i().

noconstant suppresses the constant term (intercept) in the model.

noskip specifies that a full maximum-likelihood model with only a constant for the regression equation be estimated. This model is not displayed but is used as the base model to compute a likelihood-ratio test for the model test statistic displayed in the estimation header. By default, the overall model test statistic is an asymptotically equivalent Wald test of all the parameters in the regression equation being zero (except the constant). For many models, this option can significantly increase estimation time.

level(*#*) specifies the confidence level, in percent, for confidence intervals. The default is level(95) or as set by set level; see [U] **23.5 Specifying the width of confidence intervals**.

offset(*varname*) specifies that *varname* is to be included in the model with coefficient constrained to be 1.

xtgee_options specifies any other options allowed by xtgee for family(binomial) link(logit) such as corr(); see [R] **xtgee**.

maximize_options control the maximization process; see [R] **maximize**. Use the trace option to view parameter convergence. Use the ltol(*#*) option to relax the convergence criterion; default is 1e−6 during specification searches.

Options for predict

xb calculates the linear prediction. This is the default for the random-effects model.

p calculates the predicted probability of a positive outcome conditional on one positive outcome within group. This is the default for the fixed-effects model.

pu0 calculates the probability of a positive outcome assuming that the random effect for that observation's panel is zero ($\nu = 0$). Note that this may not be similar to the proportion of observed outcomes in the group.

stdp calculates the standard error of the linear prediction.

mu and rate both calculate the predicted probability of *depvar*. mu takes into account the offset(). rate ignores those adjustments. mu and rate are equivalent if you did not specify offset(). mu is the default for the population-averaged model.

nooffset is relevant only if you specified offset(*varname*) for xtlogit. It modifies the calculations made by predict so that they ignore the offset variable; the linear prediction is treated as $\mathbf{x}_{it}\mathbf{b}$ rather than $\mathbf{x}_{it}\mathbf{b} + \text{offset}_{it}$.

Remarks

xtlogit is a convenience command if you want the population-averaged model. Typing

        . xtlogit ..., pa ...

is equivalent to typing

        . xtgee ..., ... family(binomial) link(logit) corr(exchangeable)

It is also a convenience command if you want the fixed-effects model. Typing

        . xtlogit ..., fe i(*varname*) ...

is equivalent to typing

        . clogit ..., group(*varname*) ...

Thus, also see [R] **xtgee** and [R] **clogit** for information about xtlogit.

By default, or when re is specified, xtlogit estimates a maximum-likelihood random-effects model.

▷ Example

You are studying unionization of women in the United States and are using the union dataset; see [R] **xt**. You wish to estimate a random-effects model of union membership:

```
. xtlogit union age grade not_smsa south southXt, i(id) nolog
Random-effects logit                    Number of obs     =      26200
Group variable (i) : idcode             Number of groups  =       4434

Random effects u_i ~ Gaussian           Obs per group: min =          1
                                                       avg =        5.9
                                                       max =         12

                                        Wald chi2(5)      =     221.95
Log likelihood  = -10556.294            Prob > chi2       =     0.0000
```

```
------------------------------------------------------------------------------
       union |      Coef.   Std. Err.      z    P>|z|     [95% Conf. Interval]
-------------+----------------------------------------------------------------
         age |   .0092401   .0044368     2.083   0.037     .0005441    .0179361
       grade |   .0840066   .0181622     4.625   0.000     .0484094    .1196038
    not_smsa |  -.2574574   .0844771    -3.048   0.002    -.4230294   -.0918854
       south |  -1.152854   .1108294   -10.402   0.000    -1.370075   -.9356323
     southXt |   .0237933   .0078548     3.029   0.002     .0083982    .0391884
       _cons |   -3.25016   .2622898   -12.391   0.000    -3.764238   -2.736081
-------------+----------------------------------------------------------------
    /lnsig2u |   1.669888   .0430016    38.833   0.000     1.585607     1.75417
-------------+----------------------------------------------------------------
     sigma_u |   2.304685   .0495526                       2.209582    2.403882
         rho |   .8415609   .0057337                       .8299971     .852478
------------------------------------------------------------------------------
Likelihood ratio test of rho=0:        chi2(1) =  5978.89    Prob > chi2 = 0.0000
```

The output includes the additional panel-level variance component. This is parameterized as the log of the standard deviation $\ln(\sigma_\nu)$ (labeled `lnsig2u` in the output). The standard deviation σ_ν is also included in the output labeled `sigma_u` together with ρ (labeled `rho`)

$$\rho = \frac{\sigma_\nu^2}{\sigma_\nu^2 + 1}$$

which is the proportion of the total variance contributed by the panel-level variance component.

When `rho` is zero, the panel-level variance component is unimportant and the panel estimator is not different from the pooled estimator. A likelihood ratio test of this is included at the bottom of the output. This test formally compares the pooled estimator (logit) with the panel estimator.

As an alternative to the random-effects specification, you might want to fit an equal-correlation logit model:

```
. xtlogit union age grade not_smsa south southXt, i(id) pa
Iteration 1: tolerance = .07493929
Iteration 2: tolerance = .00626292
Iteration 3: tolerance = .00030974
Iteration 4: tolerance = .00001431
Iteration 5: tolerance = 6.695e-07

GEE population-averaged model           Number of obs      =        26200
Group variable:                idcode    Number of groups   =         4434
Link:                           logit    Obs per group: min =            1
Family:                      binomial                   avg =          5.9
Correlation:              exchangeable                   max =           12
                                         Wald chi2(5)       =       233.60
Scale parameter:                   1     Prob > chi2        =       0.0000

------------------------------------------------------------------------------
       union |      Coef.   Std. Err.      z    P>|z|     [95% Conf. Interval]
-------------+----------------------------------------------------------------
         age |   .0053244   .0024989     2.131   0.033     .0004266    .0102221
       grade |   .0595071   .0108308     5.494   0.000     .0382791    .0807351
    not_smsa |  -.1225117   .0483146    -2.536   0.011    -.2172066   -.0278169
       south |  -.7270912   .0675539   -10.763   0.000    -.8594943    -.594688
     southXt |   .0151978   .0045588     3.334   0.001     .0062627     .024133
       _cons |    -2.0111   .1543886   -13.026   0.000    -2.313696   -1.708504
------------------------------------------------------------------------------
```

◁

▷ Example

xtlogit with the pa option allows a robust option so we can obtain the population-averaged logit estimator with the robust variance calculation by typing

```
. xtlogit union age grade not_smsa south southXt, i(id) pa robust nolog
GEE population-averaged model          Number of obs      =       26200
Group variable:                idcode  Number of groups   =        4434
Link:                           logit  Obs per group: min =           1
Family:                      binomial                 avg =         5.9
Correlation:             exchangeable                 max =          12
                                       Wald chi2(5)       =      152.03
Scale parameter:                    1  Prob > chi2        =      0.0000
```

(standard errors adjusted for clustering on idcode)

union	Coef.	Semi-robust Std. Err.	z	P>|z|	[95% Conf. Interval]	
age	.0053244	.0037493	1.420	0.156	-.0020242	.0126729
grade	.0595071	.0133478	4.458	0.000	.0333459	.0856683
not_smsa	-.1225117	.0613625	-1.997	0.046	-.24278	-.0022435
south	-.7270912	.087025	-8.355	0.000	-.8976569	-.5565254
southXt	.0151978	.0066129	2.298	0.022	.0022367	.0281589
_cons	-2.0111	.2016343	-9.974	0.000	-2.406296	-1.615904

These standard errors are somewhat larger than those obtained without the robust option.

◁

Finally, we can also fit a fixed-effects model to this data (see also [R] **clogit** for details):

```
. xtlogit union age grade not_smsa south southXt, i(id) fe
Note: multiple positive outcomes within groups encountered.
Note: 2744 groups (14165 obs) dropped due to all positive or negative outcomes.
Iteration 0:   log likelihood = -4541.9044
Iteration 1:   log likelihood = -4511.1353
Iteration 2:   log likelihood = -4511.1042
Conditional fixed-effects logit        Number of obs      =       12035
Group variable (i) : idcode            Number of groups   =        1690

                                       Obs per group: min =           2
                                                     avg =         7.1
                                                     max =          12

                                       LR chi2(5)         =       78.16
Log likelihood  = -4511.1042           Prob > chi2        =      0.0000
```

union	Coef.	Std. Err.	z	P>|z|	[95% Conf. Interval]	
age	.0079706	.0050283	1.585	0.113	-.0018848	.0178259
grade	.0811808	.0419137	1.937	0.053	-.0009686	.1633302
not_smsa	.0210368	.113154	0.186	0.853	-.2007411	.2428146
south	-1.007318	.1500491	-6.713	0.000	-1.301409	-.7132271
southXt	.0263495	.0083244	3.165	0.002	.010034	.0426649

Saved Results

`xtlogit, re` saves in `e()`:

Scalars

`e(N)`	number of observations	`e(g_avg)`	average group size
`e(N_g)`	number of groups	`e(chi2)`	χ^2
`e(df_m)`	model degrees of freedom	`e(chi2_c)`	χ^2 for comparison test
`e(ll)`	log likelihood	`e(rho)`	ρ
`e(ll_0)`	log likelihood, constant-only model	`e(sigma_u)`	panel-level standard deviation
`e(ll_c)`	log likelihood, comparison model	`e(N_cd)`	number of completely determined obs.
`e(g_max)`	largest group size	`e(n_quad)`	number of quadrature points
`e(g_min)`	smallest group size		

Macros

`e(cmd)`	xtlogit	`e(chi2type)`	Wald or LR; type of model χ^2 test
`e(depvar)`	name of dependent variable	`e(chi2_ct)`	Wald or LR; type of model χ^2 test
`e(title)`	title in estimation output		corresponding to `e(chi2_c)`
`e(ivar)`	variable denoting groups	`e(distrib)`	Gaussian; the distribution of the
`e(wtype)`	weight type		random effect
`e(wexp)`	weight expression	`e(predict)`	program used to implement predict
`e(offset)`	offset		

Matrices

`e(b)`	coefficient vector	`e(V)`	variance–covariance matrix of the estimators

Functions

`e(sample)`	marks estimation sample

`xtlogit, pa` saves in `e()`:

Scalars

`e(N)`	number of observations	`e(deviance)`	deviance
`e(N_g)`	number of groups	`e(chi2_dev)`	χ^2 test of deviance
`e(df_m)`	model degrees of freedom	`e(dispers)`	deviance dispersion
`e(g_max)`	largest group size	`e(chi2_dis)`	χ^2 test of deviance dispersion
`e(g_min)`	smallest group size	`e(tol)`	target tolerance
`e(g_avg)`	average group size	`e(dif)`	achieved tolerance
`e(chi2)`	χ^2	`e(phi)`	scale parameter
`e(df_pear)`	degrees of freedom for Pearson χ^2		

Macros

`e(cmd)`	xtgee	`e(scale)`	x2, dev, phi, or #; scale parameter
`e(cmd2)`	xtlogit	`e(ivar)`	variable denoting groups
`e(depvar)`	name of dependent variable	`e(vcetype)`	covariance estimation method
`e(family)`	binomial	`e(chi2type)`	Wald; type of model χ^2 test
`e(link)`	logit; link function	`e(offset)`	offset
`e(corr)`	correlation structure	`e(predict)`	program used to implement predict

Matrices

`e(b)`	coefficient vector	`e(R)`	estimated working correlation matrix
`e(V)`	variance–covariance matrix of the estimators		

Functions

`e(sample)`	marks estimation sample

`xtlogit, fe` saves in `e()`:

Scalars

`e(N)`	number of observations	`e(g_max)`	largest group size
`e(N_g)`	number of groups	`e(g_min)`	smallest group size
`e(df_m)`	model degrees of freedom	`e(g_avg)`	average group size
`e(ll)`	log likelihood	`e(chi2)`	χ^2
`e(ll_0)`	log likelihood, constant-only model		

Macros

`e(cmd)`	`clogit`	`e(offset)`	offset
`e(cmd2)`	`xtlogit`	`e(wtype)`	weight type
`e(depvar)`	name of dependent variable	`e(wexp)`	weight expression
`e(title)`	title in estimation output	`e(chi2type)`	LR; type of model χ^2 test
`e(ivar)`	variable denoting groups	`e(predict)`	program used to implement `predict`

Matrices

`e(b)`	coefficient vector	`e(V)`	variance–covariance matrix of the estimators

Functions

`e(sample)`	marks estimation sample

Methods and Formulas

`xtlogit` is implemented as an ado-file.

`xtlogit` reports the population-averaged results obtained by using `xtgee, family(binomial) link(logit)` to obtain estimates. The fixed-effects results are obtained using `clogit`. See [R] **xtgee** and [R] **clogit** for details on the methods and formulas.

Assuming a normal distribution, $N(0, \sigma_\nu^2)$, for the random effects ν_i, we have that

$$\Pr(y_i|x_i) = \int_{-\infty}^{\infty} \frac{e^{-\nu_i^2/2\sigma_\nu^2}}{\sqrt{2\pi}\sigma_\nu} \left[\prod_{t=1}^{n_i} F(x_{it}\beta + \nu_i) \right] d\nu_i$$

where

$$F(x_{it}\beta + \nu_i) = \begin{cases} \dfrac{1}{1 + \exp(x_{it}\beta + \nu_i)} & \text{if } y_{it} \neq 0 \\ 1 - \dfrac{1}{1 + \exp(x_{it}\beta + \nu_i)} & \text{otherwise} \end{cases}$$

and we can approximate the integral with M-point Gauss–Hermite quadrature

$$\int_{-\infty}^{\infty} e^{-x^2} f(x)dx \approx \sum_{m=1}^{M} w_m^* f(a_m^*)$$

where the w_m^* denote the quadrature weights and the a_m^* denote the quadrature abscissas. The log-likelihood L where $\rho = \sigma_\nu^2/(\sigma_\nu^2 + 1)$ is then calculated using the quadrature

$$L = \sum_{i=1}^{n} w_i \log \Big(\Pr(y_i|x_i) \Big)$$

$$\approx \sum_{i=1}^{n} w_i \log \frac{1}{\sqrt{\pi}} \sum_{m=1}^{M} w_m^* \prod_{t=1}^{n_i} F \left(x_{it}\beta + \sqrt{2\frac{\rho}{1-\rho}} \, a_m^* \right)$$

The quadrature formula requires that the integrated function be well-approximated by a polynomial. As the number of time periods becomes large (as panel size gets large)

$$\prod_{t=1}^{n_i} F(x_{it}\beta + \nu_i)$$

is no longer well-approximated by a polynomial. As a general rule-of thumb, you should use this quadrature approach only for small-to-moderate panel sizes (based on simulations, 50 is a reasonably safe upper bound). However, if the data really come from random-effects logit and rho is not too large (less than say .3), then the panel size could be 500 and the quadrature approximation will still be fine. If the data is not random-effects logit or rho is large (bigger than say .7), then the quadrature approximation may be poor for panel sizes larger than 10. The quadchk command should be used to investigate the applicability of the numeric technique used in this command.

References

Conway, M. R. 1990. A random effects model for binary data. *Biometrics* 46: 317–328.

Liang, K.-Y. and S. L. Zeger. 1986. Longitudinal data analysis using generalized linear models. *Biometrika* 73: 13–22.

Neuhaus, J. M. 1992. Statistical methods for longitudinal and clustered designs with binary responses. *Statistical Methods in Medical Research* 1: 249–273.

Neuhaus, J. M., J. D. Kalbfleisch, and W. W. Hauck. 1991. A comparison of cluster-specific and population-averaged approaches for analyzing correlated binary data. *International Statistical Review* 59: 25–35.

Pendergast, J. F., S. J. Gange, M. A. Newton, M. J. Lindstrom, M. Palta, and M. R. Fisher. 1996. A survey of methods for analyzing clustered binary response data. *International Statistical Review* 64: 89–118.

Also See

Complementary:	[R] **lincom**, [R] **predict**, [R] **quadchk**, [R] **test**, [R] **testnl**, [R] **vce**, [R] **xtdata**, [R] **xtdes**, [R] **xtsum**, [R] **xttab**
Related:	[R] **clogit**, [R] **logit**, [R] **xtclog**, [R] **xtgee**, [R] **xtprobit**
Background:	[U] **16.5 Accessing coefficients and standard errors**, [U] **23 Estimation and post-estimation commands**, [U] **23.11 Obtaining robust variance estimates**, [R] **xt**

Title

| xtnbreg — Fixed-effects, random-effects, & population-averaged negative binomial models |

Syntax

Random-effects and conditional fixed-effects overdispersion models

> xtnbreg *depvar* [*varlist*] [*weight*] [if *exp*] [in *range*] [, { re | fe } i(*varname*)
>
> irr noconstant noskip exposure(*varname*) offset(*varname*) level(#)
>
> *maximize_options*]

Population-averaged model

> xtnbreg *depvar* [*varlist*] [*weight*] [if *exp*] [in *range*] , pa [i(*varname*)
>
> irr robust noconstant exposure(*varname*) offset(*varname*) level(#)
>
> *xtgee_options maximize_options*]

iweights, aweights, and pweights are allowed for the population-averaged model and iweights are allowed in the random-effects and fixed-effects models; see [U] **14.1.6 weight**. Note that weights must be constant within panels.

xtnbreg shares the features of all estimation commands; see [U] **23 Estimation and post-estimation commands**.

Syntax for predict

Random-effects and conditional fixed-effects overdispersion models

> predict [*type*] *newvarname* [if *exp*] [in *range*] [, { xb | stdp } nooffset]

Population-averaged model

> predict [*type*] *newvarname* [if *exp*] [in *range*] [, { mu | rate | xb | stdp }
>
> nooffset]

These statistics are available both in and out of sample; type predict ... if e(sample) ... if wanted only for the estimation sample.

Description

xtnbreg estimates random-effects overdispersion models, conditional fixed-effects overdispersion models, and population-averaged negative binomial models. Here "random-effects" and "fixed-effects" apply to the distribution of the dispersion parameter, and not to the $\mathbf{x}\beta$ term in the model. In the random-effects and fixed-effects overdispersion models, the dispersion is the same for all elements in the same group (i.e., elements with the same value of the i() variable). In the random-effects model, the dispersion varies randomly from group to group such that the inverse of the dispersion has a $\text{Beta}(r, s)$ distribution. In the fixed-effects model, the dispersion parameter in a group can take on any value, since a conditional likelihood is used in which the dispersion parameter drops out of the estimation.

By default, the population-averaged model is an equal-correlation model; xtnbreg assumes corr(exchangeable). See [R] **xtgee** for details on this option to fit other population-averaged models.

Options

re requests the random-effects estimator. re is the default if none of re, fe, and pa is specified.

fe requests the conditional fixed-effects estimator.

pa requests the population-averaged estimator.

i(*varname*) specifies the variable name that contains the unit to which the observation belongs. You can specify the i() option the first time you estimate or use the iis command to set i() beforehand. After that, Stata will remember the variable's identity. See [R] **xt**.

irr reports exponentiated coefficients e^b rather than coefficients b. For the negative binomial model, exponentiated coefficients have the interpretation of incidence rate ratios.

robust (pa only) specifies the Huber/White/sandwich estimator of variance is to be used in place of the IRLS variance estimator; see [R] **xtgee**. This alternative produces valid standard errors even if the correlations within group are not as hypothesized by the specified correlation structure. It does, however, require that the model correctly specifies the mean. As such, the resulting standard errors are labeled "semi-robust" instead of "robust". Note that although there is no cluster() option, results are as if there were a cluster() option and you specified clustering on i().

noconstant suppresses the constant term (intercept) in the model.

noskip specifies that a full maximum-likelihood model with only a constant for the regression equation be estimated. This constant-only model is used as the base model to compute a likelihood-ratio χ^2 statistic for the model test. By default, the model test uses an asymptotically equivalent Wald χ^2 statistic. For many models, this option can significantly increase estimation time.

exposure(*varname*) and offset(*varname*) are different ways of specifying the same thing. exposure() specifies a variable that reflects the amount of exposure over which the *depvar* events were observed for each observation; ln(*varname*) with coefficient constrained to be 1 is entered into the regression equation. offset() specifies a variable that is to be entered directly into the regression equation with coefficient constrained to be 1; thus exposure is assumed to be $e^{varname}$.

level(#) specifies the confidence level, in percent, for confidence intervals. The default is level(95) or as set by set level; see [U] **23.5 Specifying the width of confidence intervals**.

xtgee_options specifies any other options allowed by xtgee for family(nbinom) link(log); see [R] **xtgee**.

maximize_options control the maximization process; see [R] **maximize**. Use the trace option to view parameter convergence.

Options for predict

xb calculates the linear prediction. This is the default for the random-effects and fixed-effects models.

stdp calculates the standard error of the linear prediction.

mu and rate both calculate the predicted probability of *depvar*. mu takes into account the offset(). rate ignores those adjustments. mu and rate are equivalent if you did not specify offset(). mu is the default for the population-averaged model.

`nooffset` is relevant only if you specified `offset`(*varname*) for `xtnbreg`. It modifies the calculations made by `predict` so that they ignore the offset variable; the linear prediction is treated as $\mathbf{x}_{it}\mathbf{b}$ rather than $\mathbf{x}_{it}\mathbf{b} + \text{offset}_{it}$.

Remarks

`xtnbreg` is a convenience command if you want the population-averaged model. Typing

```
. xtnbreg ..., ... pa exposure(time)
```

is equivalent to typing

```
. xtgee ..., ... family(nbinom) link(log) corr(exchangeable) exposure(time)
```

Thus, also see [R] **xtgee** for information about `xtnbreg`.

By default, or when `re` is specified, `xtnbreg` estimates a maximum-likelihood random-effects overdispersion model.

▷ Example

You have (fictional) data on injury "incidents" incurred among 20 airlines in each of 4 years. (Incidents range from major injuries to exceedingly minor ones.) The government agency in charge of regulating airlines has run an experimental safety training program and, in each of the years, some airlines have participated and some have not. You now wish to analyze whether the "incident" rate is affected by the program. You choose to estimate using random-effects negative binomial regression because the dispersion might vary across the airlines because of unidentified airline-specific reasons. Your measure of exposure is passenger miles for each airline in each year.

```
. xtnbreg i_cnt inprog, i(airline) exposure(pmiles) irr nolog
Random-effects negative binomial          Number of obs      =        80
Group variable (i) : airline              Number of groups   =        20

Random effects u_i ~ Beta                 Obs per group: min =         4
                                                         avg =       4.0
                                                         max =         4

                                          Wald chi2(1)       =      2.04
Log likelihood  = -265.38202              Prob > chi2        =    0.1532
------------------------------------------------------------------------------
     i_cnt |       IRR   Std. Err.      z    P>|z|     [95% Conf. Interval]
-----------+------------------------------------------------------------------
    inprog |   .911673   .0590278   -1.428   0.153     .8030204    1.035027
    pmiles | (exposure)
-----------+------------------------------------------------------------------
     /ln_r |  4.794971    .951754    5.038   0.000     2.929567    6.660374
     /ln_s |  3.268055   .4709027    6.940   0.000     2.345103    4.191007
-----------+------------------------------------------------------------------
         r |  120.9008   115.0679                      18.71953    780.8432
         s |  26.26022   12.36601                      10.43435    66.08933
------------------------------------------------------------------------------
Likelihood ratio test versus pooled: chi2(1) =      18.34   Prob > chi2 = 0.0000
```

In the output above, the `/ln_r` and `/ln_s` lines refer to $\ln(r)$ and $\ln(s)$, where the inverse of the dispersion is assumed to follow a $\text{Beta}(r, s)$ random distribution. The output also includes a likelihood-ratio test which compares the panel estimator with the pooled estimator (i.e., a negative binomial estimator with constant dispersion).

You find that the incidence rate for accidents is not significantly different for participation in the program and that the panel estimator is significantly different from the pooled estimator.

We may alternatively estimate a fixed-effects overdispersion model:

```
. xtnbreg i_cnt inprog, i(airline) exposure(pmiles) irr fe nolog
Conditional fixed-effects negative binomial     Number of obs      =        80
Group variable (i) : airline                    Number of groups   =        20

                                                Obs per group: min =         4
                                                               avg =       4.0
                                                               max =         4

                                                Wald chi2(1)       =      2.11
Log likelihood  = -174.25143                    Prob > chi2        =    0.1463
------------------------------------------------------------------------------
      i_cnt |       IRR   Std. Err.      z    P>|z|     [95% Conf. Interval]
---------+--------------------------------------------------------------------
     inprog |  .9062668   .0613916    -1.453   0.146     .7935872    1.034946
     pmiles | (exposure)
------------------------------------------------------------------------------
```

◁

▷ Example

Rerunning our previous example in order to fit a robust equal-correlation population-averaged model:

```
. xtnbreg i_cnt inprog, i(airline) exposure(pmiles) eform robust pa
Iteration 1: tolerance = .02488289
Iteration 2: tolerance = .00004846
Iteration 3: tolerance = 2.914e-07
GEE population-averaged model                   Number of obs      =        80
Group variable:                        airline  Number of groups   =        20
Link:                                      log  Obs per group: min =         4
Family:            negative binomial(k=1)                       avg =       4.0
Correlation:                       exchangeable                 max =         4
                                                Wald chi2(1)       =      1.28
Scale parameter:                             1  Prob > chi2        =    0.2578
                  (standard errors adjusted for clustering on airline)
------------------------------------------------------------------------------
            |             Semi-robust
      i_cnt |       IRR   Std. Err.      z    P>|z|     [95% Conf. Interval]
---------+--------------------------------------------------------------------
     inprog |  .9273828   .0617892    -1.131   0.258     .8138524     1.05675
     pmiles | (exposure)
------------------------------------------------------------------------------
```

We may compare this with a pooled estimator with cluster robust variance estimates:

```
. nbreg i_cnt inprog, exposure(pmiles) robust cluster(airline) irr nolog
Negative binomial regression                    Number of obs   =         80
                                                Wald chi2(1)    =       0.60
Log likelihood = -274.55077                     Prob > chi2     =     0.4369
                        (standard errors adjusted for clustering on airline)
------------------------------------------------------------------------------
             |             Robust
      i_cnt  |      IRR   Std. Err.      z    P>|z|     [95% Conf. Interval]
-------------+----------------------------------------------------------------
      inprog |  .9429015   .0713091    -0.777  0.437     .8130031    1.093554
      pmiles |  (exposure)
-------------+----------------------------------------------------------------
    /lnalpha | -2.835089   .3351784    -8.458  0.000    -3.492027   -2.178152
-------------+----------------------------------------------------------------
       alpha |  .0587133   .0196794                      .0304391    .1132507
------------------------------------------------------------------------------
```

Saved Results

xtnbreg, re saves in e():

Scalars

e(N)	number of observations	e(ll_c)	log likelihood, comparison model
e(k)	number of estimated parameters	e(df_m)	model degrees of freedom
e(k_eq)	number of equations	e(chi2)	model χ^2
e(k_dv)	number of dependent variables	e(p)	model significance
e(N_g)	number of groups	e(chi2_c)	χ^2 for comparison test
e(g_min)	smallest group size	e(r)	value of r in Beta(r,s)
e(g_avg)	average group size	e(s)	value of s in Beta(r,s)
e(g_max)	largest group size	e(ic)	number of iterations
e(ll)	log likelihood	e(rc)	return code
e(ll_0)	log likelihood, constant-only model		

Macros

e(cmd)	xtnbreg	e(opt)	type of optimization
e(cmd2)	xtn_re	e(chi2type)	Wald or LR; type of model χ^2 test
e(depvar)	name of dependent variable	e(chi2_ct)	Wald or LR; type of model χ^2 test
e(title)	title in estimation output		corresponding to e(chi2_c)
e(ivar)	variable denoting groups	e(offset)	offset
e(wtype)	weight type	e(distrib)	Beta; the distribution of the
e(wexp)	weight expression		random effect
e(method)	estimation method	e(predict)	program used to implement predict
e(user)	name of likelihood-evaluation program		

Matrices

e(b)	coefficient vector	e(V)	variance–covariance matrix of the estimators

Functions

e(sample)	marks estimation sample

`xtnbreg, fe` saves in `e()`:

Scalars

e(N)	number of observations	e(ll)	log likelihood
e(k)	number of estimated parameters	e(ll_0)	log likelihood, constant-only model
e(k_eq)	number of equations	e(df_m)	model degrees of freedom
e(k_dv)	number of dependent variables	e(chi2)	model χ^2
e(N_g)	number of groups	e(p)	model significance
e(g_min)	smallest group size	e(ic)	number of iterations
e(g_avg)	average group size	e(rc)	return code
e(g_max)	largest group size		

Macros

e(cmd)	xtnbreg	e(method)	requested estimation method
e(cmd2)	xtn_fe	e(user)	name of likelihood-evaluator program
e(depvar)	name of dependent variable	e(opt)	type of optimization
e(title)	title in estimation output	e(chi2type)	Wald or LR; type of model χ^2 test
e(ivar)	variable denoting groups	e(offset)	offset
e(wtype)	weight type	e(predict)	program used to implement predict
e(wexp)	weight expression		

Matrices

e(b)	coefficient vector	e(V)	variance–covariance matrix of the estimators

Functions

e(sample)	marks estimation sample

`xtnbreg, pa` saves in `e()`:

Scalars

e(N)	number of observations	e(deviance)	deviance
e(N_g)	number of groups	e(chi2_dev)	χ^2 test of deviance
e(g_min)	smallest group size	e(dispers)	deviance dispersion
e(g_avg)	average group size	e(chi2_dis)	χ^2 test of deviance dispersion
e(g_max)	largest group size	e(tol)	target tolerance
e(df_m)	model degrees of freedom	e(dif)	achieved tolerance
e(chi2)	model χ^2	e(phi)	scale parameter
e(df_pear)	degrees of freedom for Pearson χ^2		

Macros

e(cmd)	xtgee	e(ivar)	variable denoting groups
e(cmd2)	xtnbreg	e(vcetype)	covariance estimation method
e(depvar)	name of dependent variable	e(chi2type)	Wald; type of model χ^2 test
e(family)	negative binomial($k=1$)	e(offset)	offset
e(link)	log; link function	e(nbalpha)	α
e(corr)	correlation structure	e(predict)	program used to implement predict
e(scale)	x2, dev, phi, or #; scale parameter		

Matrices

e(b)	coefficient vector	e(V)	variance–covariance matrix of the estimators
e(R)	estimated working correlation matrix		

Functions

e(sample)	marks estimation sample

Methods and Formulas

`xtnbreg` is implemented as an ado-file.

`xtnbreg` reports the population-averaged results obtained by using `xtgee, family(nbreg)` `link(log)` to obtain estimates. See [R] **xtgee** for details on the methods and formulas.

For the random-effects and fixed-effects overdispersion models, we let y_{it} be the count for the tth observation in the ith group. We begin with the model $y_{it} \mid \gamma_{it} \sim \text{Poisson}(\gamma_{it})$, where $\gamma_{it} \mid \delta_i \sim \text{Gamma}(\lambda_{it}, 1/\delta_i)$ with $\lambda_{it} = \exp(\mathbf{x}_{it}\beta + \text{offset}_{it})$ and δ_i is the dispersion parameter. This yields the model

$$\Pr(Y_{it} = y_{it} \mid \delta_i) = \frac{\Gamma(\lambda_{it} + y_{it})}{\Gamma(\lambda_{it})\Gamma(y_{it} + 1)} \left(\frac{1}{1 + \delta_i}\right)^{\lambda_{it}} \left(\frac{\delta_i}{1 + \delta_i}\right)^{y_{it}}$$

Looking at within-group effects only, this specification yields a negative binomial model for the ith group with dispersion (variance divided by the mean) equal to $1 + \delta_i$; i.e., constant dispersion within group. Note that this parameterization of the negative binomial model differs from the default parameterization of `nbreg`, which has dispersion equal to $1 + \alpha \exp(\mathbf{x}\beta + \text{offset})$; see [R] **nbreg**.

For a random-effects overdispersion model, we allow δ_i to vary randomly across groups; namely, we assume that $1/(1 + \delta_i) \sim \text{Beta}(r, s)$. The joint probability of the counts for the ith group is

$$\Pr(Y_{i1} = y_{i1}, \ldots, Y_{in_i} = y_{in_i}) = \int \prod_{t=1}^{n_i} \Pr(Y_{it} = y_{it} \mid \delta_i) \, f(\delta_i) \, d\delta_i$$

$$= \frac{\Gamma(r + s)\Gamma(r + \sum_{t=1}^{n_i} \lambda_{it})\Gamma(s + \sum_{t=1}^{n_i} y_{it})}{\Gamma(r)\Gamma(s)\Gamma(r + s + \sum_{t=1}^{n_i} \lambda_{it} + \sum_{t=1}^{n_i} y_{it})} \prod_{t=1}^{n_i} \frac{\Gamma(\lambda_{it} + y_{it})}{\Gamma(\lambda_{it})\Gamma(y_{it} + 1)}$$

The resulting log likelihood is

$$\ln L = \sum_{i=1}^{n} w_i \left\{ \ln \Gamma(r + s) + \ln \Gamma\left(r + \sum_{k=1}^{n_i} \lambda_{ik}\right) + \ln \Gamma\left(s + \sum_{k=1}^{n_i} y_{ik}\right) - \ln \Gamma(r) - \ln \Gamma(s) \right.$$

$$\left. - \ln \Gamma\left(r + s + \sum_{k=1}^{n_i} \lambda_{ik} + \sum_{k=1}^{n_i} y_{ik}\right) + \sum_{t=1}^{n_i} \left[\ln \Gamma(\lambda_{it} + y_{it}) - \ln \Gamma(\lambda_{it}) - \ln \Gamma(y_{it} + 1)\right] \right\}$$

where $\lambda_{it} = \exp(\mathbf{x}_{it}\beta + \text{offset}_{it})$ and w_i is the weight for the ith group.

For the fixed-effects overdispersion model, we condition the joint probability of the counts for each group on the sum of the counts for the group (i.e., the observed $\sum_{t=1}^{n_i} y_{it}$). This yields

$$\Pr(Y_{i1} = y_{i1}, \ldots, Y_{in_i} = y_{in_i} \mid \textstyle\sum_{t=1}^{n_i} Y_{it} = \sum_{t=1}^{n_i} y_{it})$$

$$= \frac{\Gamma(\sum_{t=1}^{n_i} \lambda_{it})\Gamma(\sum_{t=1}^{n_i} y_{it} + 1)}{\Gamma(\sum_{t=1}^{n_i} \lambda_{it} + \sum_{t=1}^{n_i} y_{it})} \prod_{t=1}^{n_i} \frac{\Gamma(\lambda_{it} + y_{it})}{\Gamma(\lambda_{it})\Gamma(y_{it} + 1)}$$

The conditional log likelihood is

$$\ln L = \sum_{i=1}^{n} w_i \left\{ \ln \Gamma\left(\sum_{t=1}^{n_i} \lambda_{it}\right) + \ln \Gamma\left(\sum_{t=1}^{n_i} y_{it} + 1\right) - \ln \Gamma\left(\sum_{t=1}^{n_i} \lambda_{it} + \sum_{t=1}^{n_i} y_{it}\right) \right.$$

$$\left. + \sum_{t=1}^{n_i} \left[\ln \Gamma(\lambda_{it} + y_{it}) - \ln \Gamma(\lambda_{it}) - \ln \Gamma(y_{it} + 1)\right] \right\}$$

See Hausman et al. (1984) for a more thorough development of the random-effects and fixed-effects models. Note that Hausman et al. (1984) use a δ that is the inverse of the δ we have used here.

References

Hausman, J., B. H. Hall, and Z. Griliches. 1984. Econometric models for count data with an application to the patents–R & D relationship. *Econometrica* 52: 909–938.

Liang, K.-Y. and S. L. Zeger. 1986. Longitudinal data analysis using generalized linear models. *Biometrika* 73: 13–22.

Also See

Complementary:	[R] **lincom**, [R] **predict**, [R] **test**, [R] **testnl**, [R] **vce**, [R] **xtdata**, [R] **xtdes**, [R] **xtsum**, [R] **xttab**
Related:	[R] **nbreg**, [R] **xtgee**, [R] **xtpois**
Background:	[U] **16.5 Accessing coefficients and standard errors**, [U] **23 Estimation and post-estimation commands**, [U] **23.11 Obtaining robust variance estimates**, [R] **xt**

Title

> **xtpois** — Fixed-effects, random-effects, and population-averaged Poisson models

Syntax

Random-effects model

> xtpois *depvar* [*varlist*] [*weight*] [if *exp*] [in *range*] [, re i(*varname*) <u>irr</u>
>
> <u>q</u>uad(#) noskip <u>noncon</u>stant <u>level</u>(#) normal <u>off</u>set(*varname*) *maximize_options*]

Conditional fixed-effects model

> xtpois *depvar* [*varlist*] [*weight*] [if *exp*] [in *range*] , fe [i(*varname*) <u>irr</u>
>
> noskip <u>level</u>(#) <u>off</u>set(*varname*) *maximize_options*]

Population-averaged model

> xtpois *depvar* [*varlist*] [*weight*] [if *exp*] [in *range*] , pa [i(*varname*) <u>irr</u>
>
> <u>noncon</u>stant <u>level</u>(#) <u>r</u>obust <u>off</u>set(*varname*)
>
> *xtgee_options* *maximize_options*]

iweights, aweights, and pweights are allowed for the population-averaged model and iweights are allowed in the random-effects and fixed-effects models; see [U] **14.1.6 weight**. Note that weights must be constant within panels.

xtpois shares the features of all estimation commands; see [U] **23 Estimation and post-estimation commands**.

Syntax for predict

Random-effects and fixed-effects models

> predict [*type*] *newvarname* [if *exp*] [in *range*] [, { xb | stdp } <u>nooff</u>set]

Population-averaged model

> predict [*type*] *newvarname* [if *exp*] [in *range*] [, { mu | rate | xb | stdp }
>
> <u>nooff</u>set]

These statistics are available both in and out of sample; type predict ... if e(sample) ... if wanted only for the estimation sample.

Description

xtpois estimates random-effects, conditional fixed-effects, and population-averaged Poisson models. Whenever we refer to a fixed-effects model we mean the conditional fixed-effects model.

Note: `xtpois, re normal`, is slow since it is calculated by quadrature; see *Methods and Formulas*. Computation time is roughly proportional to the number of points used for the quadrature. The default is `quad(12)`. Simulations indicate that increasing it does not appreciably change the estimates for the coefficients or their standard errors. See [R] **quadchk**.

By default, the population-averaged model is an equal-correlation model; `xtpois` assumes `corr(exchangeable)`. See [R] **xtgee** for information on how to fit other population-averaged models.

Options

`re`, the default, requests the random-effects estimator.

`fe` requests the fixed-effects estimator.

`pa` requests the population-averaged estimator.

`i(varname)` specifies the variable name that contains the unit to which the observation belongs. You can specify the `i()` option the first time you estimate or use the `iis` command to set `i()` beforehand. After that, Stata will remember the variable's identity. See [R] **xt**.

`irr` reports exponentiated coefficients e^b rather than coefficients b. For the Poisson model, exponentiated coefficients have the interpretation of incidence rate ratios.

`quad(#)` specifies the number of points to use in the quadrature approximation of the integral. This option is relevant only if you are estimating a random-effects model; if you specify `quad(#)` with `pa`, the `quad(#)` is ignored.

The default is `quad(12)`. The number specified must be an integer between 4 and 30, and also be no greater than the number of observations.

`robust` specifies the Huber/White/sandwich estimator of variance is to be used in place of the IRLS variance estimator; see [R] **xtgee**. This alternative produces valid standard errors even if the correlations within group are not as hypothesized by the specified correlation structure. It does, however, require that the model correctly specifies the mean. As such, the resulting standard errors are labeled "semi-robust" instead of "robust". Note that although there is no `cluster()` option, results are as if there were a `cluster()` option and you specified clustering on `i()`.

`noconstant` suppresses the constant term (intercept) in the model.

`noskip` specifies that a full maximum-likelihood model with only a constant for the regression equation be estimated. This model is not displayed but is used as the base model to compute a likelihood-ratio test for the model test statistic displayed in the estimation header. By default, the overall model test statistic is an asymptotically equivalent Wald test of all the parameters in the regression equation being zero (except the constant). For many models, this option can significantly increase estimation time.

`level(#)` specifies the confidence level, in percent, for confidence intervals. The default is `level(95)` or as set by `set level`; see [U] **23.5 Specifying the width of confidence intervals**.

`normal` specifies that the random effects follow a normal distribution instead of a gamma distribution.

`offset(varname)` specifies that *varname* is to be included in the model with coefficient constrained to be 1.

xtgee_options specifies any other options allowed by `xtgee` for `family(poisson) link(log)`; see [R] **xtgee**.

maximize_options control the maximization process; see [R] **maximize**. Use the `trace` option to view parameter convergence. Use the `ltol(#)` option to relax the convergence criterion; default is 1e−6 during specification searches.

Options for predict

xb calculates the linear prediction. This is the default for the random-effects and fixed-effects models.

stdp calculates the standard error of the linear prediction.

mu and rate both calculate the predicted probability of *depvar*. mu takes into account the offset(). rate ignores those adjustments. mu and rate are equivalent if you did not specify offset(). mu is the default for the population-averaged model.

nooffset is relevant only if you specified offset(*varname*) for xtpois. It modifies the calculations made by predict so that they ignore the offset variable; the linear prediction is treated as $x_{it}b$ rather than $x_{it}b + \text{offset}_{it}$.

Remarks

xtpois is a convenience command if you want the population-averaged model. Typing

. xtpois ..., ... pa exposure(time)

is equivalent to typing

. xtgee ..., ... family(poisson) link(log) corr(exchangeable) exposure(time)

Thus, also see [R] **xtgee** for information about xtpois.

By default, or when re is specified, xtpois estimates a maximum-likelihood random-effects model.

▷ Example

You have data on the number of ship accidents for 5 different types of ships (McCullagh and Nelder 1989, 205). You wish to analyze whether the "incident" rate is affected by the period in which the ship was constructed and operated. Your measure of exposure is months of service for the ship and in this model we assume that the random effects are distributed as $\text{gamma}(\theta, \theta)$.

```
. xtpois accident op_75_79 co_65_69 co_70_74 co_75_79, i(ship) ex(service) irr
> nolog
Random-effects poisson                          Number of obs      =         34
Group variable (i) : ship                       Number of groups   =          5
Random effects u_i ~ Gamma                      Obs per group: min =          6
                                                               avg =        6.8
                                                               max =          7
                                                LR chi2(4)         =      54.92
Log likelihood  = -74.811217                    Prob > chi2        =     0.0000
```

accident	IRR	Std. Err.	z	P>|z|	[95% Conf. Interval]	
op_75_79	1.466305	.1734005	3.237	0.001	1.162957	1.848777
co_65_69	2.032543	.304083	4.741	0.000	1.515982	2.72512
co_70_74	2.356853	.3999259	5.052	0.000	1.690033	3.286774
co_75_79	1.641913	.3811398	2.136	0.033	1.04174	2.58786
service	(exposure)					
/invln_a	2.368406	.8474597	2.795	0.005	.7074155	4.029397
alpha	.0936298	.0793475			.0177851	.4929165

```
Likelihood ratio test of alpha=0:      chi2(1) =     10.61   Prob > chi2 = 0.0011
```

In the output above, the `alpha` output line refers to $\alpha = 1/\theta$. The `alpha` parameter is parameterized as $1/\log(\alpha)$ and presented in the output as `/invln_a`.

The output also includes a likelihood-ratio test of $\alpha = 0$ which compares the panel estimator with the pooled (Poisson) estimator.

You find that the incidence rate for accidents is significantly different for the periods of construction and operation of the ships and that the random-effects model is significantly different from the pooled model.

We may alternatively fit a fixed-effects specification instead of a random-effects specification:

```
. xtpois accident op_75_79 co_65_69 co_70_74 co_75_79, i(ship) ex(service) irr
> fe
Fitting comparison model:
Iteration 0:   log likelihood = -48087.775
Iteration 1:   log likelihood =  -46867.52
Iteration 2:   log likelihood = -46840.487
Iteration 3:   log likelihood = -46840.242
Iteration 4:   log likelihood = -46840.242

Fitting full model:
Iteration 0:   log likelihood = -1724.2412
Iteration 1:   log likelihood = -757.20797
Iteration 2:   log likelihood = -529.94286
Iteration 3:   log likelihood = -186.70307
Iteration 4:   log likelihood = -69.047591
Iteration 5:   log likelihood =  -54.69344
Iteration 6:   log likelihood = -54.641864
Iteration 7:   log likelihood = -54.641859
```

```
Conditional fixed-effects poisson          Number of obs      =         34
Group variable (i) : ship                  Number of groups   =          5

                                           Obs per group: min =          6
                                                          avg =        6.8
                                                          max =          7

                                           LR chi2(4)         =   93571.20
Log likelihood  = -54.641859               Prob > chi2        =     0.0000
```

accident	IRR	Std. Err.	z	P>|z|	[95% Conf. Interval]	
op_75_79	1.468831	.1737218	3.251	0.001	1.164926	1.852019
co_65_69	2.008002	.3004803	4.659	0.000	1.497577	2.692398
co_70_74	2.26693	.384865	4.821	0.000	1.625274	3.161912
co_75_79	1.573695	.3669393	1.945	0.052	.9964273	2.485397
service	(exposure)					

Both of these models estimate the same thing. The difference will be in efficiency depending on whether the assumptions of the random-effects model are true.

Note that we could have assumed that the random effects followed a normal distribution, $N(0, \sigma_\nu^2)$, instead of a gamma distribution and obtained

```
. xtpois accident op_75_79 co_65_69 co_70_74 co_75_79, i(ship) ex(service) irr
> normal nolog

Random-effects poisson                          Number of obs      =         34
Group variable (i) : ship                       Number of groups   =          5

Random effects u_i ~ Gaussian                   Obs per group: min =          6
                                                               avg =        6.8
                                                               max =          7

                                                LR chi2(4)         =    6920.48
Log likelihood  = -74.225924                    Prob > chi2        =     0.0000

------------------------------------------------------------------------------
 accident |       IRR   Std. Err.       z    P>|z|     [95% Conf. Interval]
----------+-------------------------------------------------------------------
 op_75_79 |  1.470182   .1737941     3.260   0.001     1.166134    1.853505
 co_65_69 |  2.025867   .3030043     4.720   0.000     1.511119    2.715959
 co_70_74 |  2.336483   .3960783     5.006   0.000     1.675976    3.257298
 co_75_79 |  1.640625   .3777039     2.150   0.032     1.044831    2.576158
  service | (exposure)
----------+-------------------------------------------------------------------
 /lnsig2u |  -1.42662   .5613596    -2.541   0.011    -2.526865   -.3263758
----------+-------------------------------------------------------------------
  sigma_u |  .4900195   .1375386                       .2826821    .8494315
      rho |  .1936258   .0876478                       .0739962    .4191227
------------------------------------------------------------------------------
Likelihood ratio test of rho=0:      chi2(1) =    11.78   Prob > chi2 = 0.0006
Note: 2 completely determined observations
```

The output includes the additional panel-level variance component. This is parameterized as the log of the standard deviation $\ln(\sigma_\nu)$ (labeled lnsig2u in the output). The standard deviation σ_ν is also included in the output labeled sigma_u together with ρ (labeled rho)

$$\rho = \frac{\sigma_\nu^2}{\sigma_\nu^2 + 1}$$

which is the proportion of the total variance contributed by the panel-level variance component.

When rho is zero, the panel-level variance component is unimportant and the panel estimator is not different from the pooled estimator. A likelihood-ratio test of this is included at the bottom of the output. This test formally compares the pooled estimator (poisson) with the panel estimator. In this case, rho is not zero so a panel estimator is indicated.

◁

▷ Example

Rerunning our previous example in order to fit a robust equal-correlation population-averaged model:

```
. xtpois accident op_75_79 co_65_69 co_70_74 co_75_79, i(ship) ex(service)
> pa robust eform
Iteration 1: tolerance = .03834503
Iteration 2: tolerance = .00247597
Iteration 3: tolerance = .00025959
Iteration 4: tolerance = .00002721
Iteration 5: tolerance = 2.835e-06
Iteration 6: tolerance = 2.949e-07
```

GEE population-averaged model   Number of obs   =   34
Group variable: ship   Number of groups =   5
Link: log   Obs per group: min =   6
Family: Poisson   avg =   6.8
Correlation: exchangeable   max =   7
                                     Wald chi2(3)   =   176.82
Scale parameter: 1   Prob > chi2   =   0.0000

                      (standard errors adjusted for clustering on ship)

accident	IRR	Semi-robust Std. Err.	z	P>|z|	[95% Conf. Interval]	
op_75_79	1.482795	.1204125	4.851	0.000	1.264614	1.738618
co_65_69	2.044468	.1873073	7.806	0.000	1.708426	2.446609
co_70_74	2.657415	.4221873	6.152	0.000	1.946381	3.628198
co_75_79	1.885471	.3355286	3.564	0.000	1.330284	2.672362
service	(exposure)					

We may compare this with a pooled estimator with cluster robust variance estimates:

```
. poisson accident op_75_79 co_65_69 co_70_74 co_75_79, ex(service) robust
> cluster(ship) irr nolog
```

Poisson regression   Number of obs   =   34
                                     Wald chi2(3)   =   32.59
Log likelihood = -80.115916   Prob > chi2   =   0.0000

                      (standard errors adjusted for clustering on ship)

accident	IRR	Robust Std. Err.	z	P>|z|	[95% Conf. Interval]	
op_75_79	1.47324	.1287036	4.435	0.000	1.2414	1.748377
co_65_69	2.125914	.2850531	5.625	0.000	1.634603	2.764897
co_70_74	2.860138	.6213563	4.837	0.000	1.868384	4.378325
co_75_79	2.021926	.4265285	3.337	0.001	1.337221	3.057227
service	(exposure)					

◁

Saved Results

xtpois, re saves in e():

Scalars

e(N)	number of observations	e(g_min)	smallest group size
e(k)	number of variables	e(g_avg)	average group size
e(k_eq)	number of equations	e(rc)	return code
e(k_dv)	number of dependent variables	e(chi2)	χ^2
e(N_g)	number of groups	e(chi2_c)	χ^2 for comparison test
e(df_m)	model degrees of freedom	e(p)	significance
e(ll)	log likelihood	e(ic)	number of iterations
e(ll_0)	log likelihood, constant-only model	e(n_quad)	number of quadrature points
e(ll_c)	log likelihood, comparison model	e(alpha)	α
e(g_max)	largest group size		

Macros

e(cmd)	xtpois	e(opt)	type of optimization
e(depvar)	name of dependent variable	e(chi2type)	Wald or LR; type of model χ^2 test
e(title)	title in estimation output	e(chi2_ct)	Wald or LR; type of model χ^2 test
e(ivar)	variable denoting groups		corresponding to e(chi2_c)
e(wtype)	weight type	e(distrib)	Gamma; the distribution of the
e(wexp)	weight expression		random effect
e(user)	name of likelihood-evaluator program	e(predict)	program used to implement predict
e(offset1)	offset		

Matrices

e(b)	coefficient vector	e(V)	variance–covariance matrix of the estimators

Functions

e(sample)	marks estimation sample

(Continued on next page)

xtpois, re normal saves in e():

Scalars

e(N)	number of observations	e(g_avg)	average group size
e(N_g)	number of groups	e(chi2)	χ^2
e(df_m)	model degrees of freedom	e(chi2_c)	χ^2 for comparison test
e(ll)	log likelihood	e(rho)	ρ
e(ll_0)	log likelihood, constant-only model	e(sigma_u)	panel-level standard deviation
e(ll_c)	log likelihood, comparison model	e(N_cd)	number of completely determined obs.
e(g_max)	largest group size	e(n_quad)	number of quadrature points
e(g_min)	smallest group size		

Macros

e(cmd)	xtpois	e(chi2type)	Wald or LR; type of model χ^2 test
e(depvar)	name of dependent variable	e(chi2_ct)	Wald or LR; type of model χ^2 test
e(title)	title in estimation output		corresponding to e(chi2_c)
e(ivar)	variable denoting groups	e(distrib)	Gaussian; the distribution of the
e(wtype)	weight type		random effect
e(wexp)	weight expression	e(predict)	program used to implement predict
e(offset1)	offset		

Matrices

e(b)	coefficient vector	e(V)	variance–covariance matrix of the estimators

Functions

e(sample)	marks estimation sample

xtpois, fe saves in e():

Scalars

e(N)	number of observations	e(g_max)	largest group size
e(k)	number of variables	e(g_min)	smallest group size
e(k_eq)	number of equations	e(g_avg)	average group size
e(k_dv)	number of dependent variables	e(rc)	return code
e(N_g)	number of groups	e(chi2)	χ^2
e(df_m)	model degrees of freedom	e(p)	significance
e(ll)	log likelihood	e(ic)	number of iterations
e(ll_0)	log likelihood, constant-only model	e(n_quad)	number of quadrature points

Macros

e(cmd)	xtpois	e(user)	name of likelihood-evaluator program
e(depvar)	name of dependent variable	e(opt)	type of optimization
e(title)	title in estimation output	e(chi2type)	LR; type of model χ^2 test
e(ivar)	variable denoting groups	e(offset1)	offset
e(wtype)	weight type	e(predict)	program used to implement predict
e(wexp)	weight expression		

Matrices

e(b)	coefficient vector	e(V)	variance–covariance matrix of the estimators

Functions

e(sample)	marks estimation sample

`xtpois, pa` saves in `e()`:

Scalars

`e(N)`	number of observations	`e(deviance)`	deviance
`e(N_g)`	number of groups	`e(chi2_dev)`	χ^2 test of deviance
`e(df_m)`	model degrees of freedom	`e(dispers)`	deviance dispersion
`e(g_max)`	largest group size	`e(chi2_dis)`	χ^2 test of deviance dispersion
`e(g_min)`	smallest group size	`e(tol)`	target tolerance
`e(g_avg)`	average group size	`e(dif)`	achieved tolerance
`e(chi2)`	χ^2	`e(phi)`	scale parameter
`e(df_pear)`	degrees of freedom for Pearson χ^2		

Macros

`e(cmd)`	`xtgee`	`e(scale)`	x2, dev, phi, or #; scale parameter
`e(cmd2)`	`xtpois`	`e(ivar)`	variable denoting groups
`e(depvar)`	name of dependent variable	`e(vcetype)`	covariance estimation method
`e(family)`	Poisson	`e(chi2type)`	Wald; type of model χ^2 test
`e(link)`	log; link function	`e(offset)`	offset
`e(corr)`	correlation structure	`e(predict)`	program used to implement `predict`

Matrices

`e(b)`	coefficient vector	`e(V)`	variance–covariance matrix of the
`e(R)`	estimated working correlation matrix		estimators

Functions

`e(sample)`	marks estimation sample

Methods and Formulas

`xtpois` is implemented as an ado-file.

`xtpois` reports the population-averaged results obtained by using `xtgee, family(poisson) link(log)` to obtain estimates. See [R] **xtgee** for details on the methods and formulas.

For a random-effects specification, we know that

$$\Pr(y_{i1}, \ldots, y_{in_i} | \alpha_i, x_i) = \left[\prod_{t=1}^{n_i} \frac{\lambda_{it}^{y_{it}}}{y_{it}!} \right] \exp\left(- \exp(\alpha_i) \sum_{t=1}^{n_i} \lambda_{it} \right) \exp\left(\alpha_i \sum_{t=1}^{n_i} y_{it} \right)$$

where $\lambda_{it} = \exp(x_{it}\beta)$. We may rewrite the above as

$$\Pr(y_{i1}, \ldots, y_{in_i} | \epsilon_i, x_i) = \left[\prod_{t=1}^{n_i} \frac{(\lambda_{it}\epsilon_i)^{y_{it}}}{y_{it}!} \right] \exp\left(- \sum_{t=1}^{n_i} (\lambda_{it}\epsilon_i) \right)$$

$$= \left[\prod_{t=1}^{n_i} \frac{\lambda_{it}^{y_{it}}}{y_{it}!} \right] \exp\left(-\epsilon_i \sum_{t=1}^{n_i} \lambda_{it} \right) \epsilon_i^{\sum_{t=1}^{n_i} y_{it}}$$

We now assume that ϵ_i follows a gamma distribution with expected value equal to 1 such that

$$
\Pr(y_{i1}, \ldots, y_{in_i}|x_i) = \frac{\theta^\theta}{\Gamma(\theta)} \left[\prod_{t=1}^{n_i} \frac{\lambda_{it}^{y_{it}}}{y_{it}!} \right] \int_0^\infty \exp\left(-\epsilon_i \sum_{t=1}^{n_i} \lambda_{it} \right) \epsilon_i^{\sum_{t=1}^{n_i} y_{it}} \epsilon_i^{\theta-1} \exp(-\theta\epsilon_i) d\epsilon_i
$$

$$
= \frac{\theta^\theta}{\Gamma(\theta)} \left[\prod_{t=1}^{n_i} \frac{\lambda_{it}^{y_{it}}}{y_{it}!} \right] \int_0^\infty \exp\left(-\epsilon_i \left(\theta + \sum_{t=1}^{n_i} \lambda_{it} \right) \right) \epsilon_i^{\theta + \sum_{t=1}^{n_i} y_{it} - 1} d\epsilon_i
$$

$$
= \left[\prod_{t=1}^{n_i} \frac{\lambda_{it}^{y_{it}}}{y_{it}!} \right] \frac{\Gamma\left(\theta + \sum_{t=1}^{n_i} y_{it} \right)}{\Gamma(\theta)} \left(\frac{\theta}{\theta + \sum_{t=1}^{n_i} \lambda_{it}} \right)^\theta \left(\frac{1}{\theta + \sum_{t=1}^{n_i} \lambda_{it}} \right)^{\sum_{t=1}^{n_i} y_{it}}
$$

The log likelihood (assuming Gamma(θ, θ) heterogeneity) is then derived using

$$
u_i = \frac{\theta}{\theta + \sum_{t=1}^{n_i} \lambda_{it}} \qquad \lambda_{it} = \exp(x_{it}\beta)
$$

$$
\Pr(Y_{i1} = y_{i1}, \ldots, Y_{in_i} = y_{in_i}) = \frac{\prod_{t=1}^{n_i} \lambda_{it}^{y_{it}} \Gamma\left(\theta + \sum_{t=1}^{n_i} y_{it} \right)}{\prod_{t=1}^{n_i} y_{it}! \Gamma(\theta) \left(\sum_{t=1}^{n_i} \lambda_{it} \right)^{\sum_{t=1}^{n_i} y_{it}}} u_i^\theta (1 - u_i)^{\sum_{t=1}^{n_i} y_{it}}
$$

such that the log likelihood may be written as

$$
L = \sum_{i=1}^n w_i \left\{ \log \Gamma\left(\theta + \sum_{t=1}^{n_i} y_{it} \right) - \sum_{t=1}^{n_i} \log \Gamma\left(1 + y_{it} \right) - \log \Gamma(\theta) + \theta \log u_i \right.
$$
$$
\left. + \log(1 - u_i) \sum_{t=1}^{n_i} y_{it} + \sum_{t=1}^{n_i} y_{it}(x_{it}\beta) - \left(\sum_{t=1}^{n_i} y_{it} \right) \log \left(\sum_{t=1}^{n_i} \lambda_{it} \right) \right\}
$$

Alternatively, if we assume a normal distribution, $N(0, \sigma_\nu^2)$, for the random effects ν_i, we have that

$$
\Pr(y_i|x_i) = \int_{-\infty}^\infty \frac{e^{-\nu_i^2/2\sigma_\nu^2}}{\sqrt{2\pi}\sigma_\nu} \left[\prod_{t=1}^{n_i} F(x_{it}\beta + \nu_i) \right] d\nu_i
$$

where

$$
F(x_{it}\beta + \nu_i) = \exp\left(-\exp(x_{it}\beta + \nu_i) + (x_{it}\beta + \nu_i)y_{it} - \log(y_{it}!) \right)
$$

and we can approximate the integral with M-point Gauss–Hermite quadrature

$$
\int_{-\infty}^\infty e^{-x^2} f(x)dx \approx \sum_{m=1}^M w_m^* f(a_m^*)
$$

where the w_m^* denote the quadrature weights and the a_m^* denote the quadrature abscissas. The log-likelihood L where $\rho = \sigma_\nu^2/(\sigma_\nu^2 + 1)$ is then calculated using the quadrature

$$L = \sum_{i=1}^{n} w_i \log\left(\Pr(y_i | x_i)\right)$$

$$\approx \sum_{i=1}^{n} w_i \log \frac{1}{\sqrt{\pi}} \sum_{m=1}^{M} w_m^* \prod_{t=1}^{n_i} F\left(x_{it}\beta + \sqrt{2\frac{\rho}{1-\rho}}\, a_m^*\right)$$

The quadrature formula requires that the integrated function be well-approximated by a polynomial. As the number of time periods becomes large (as panel size gets large)

$$\prod_{t=1}^{n_i} F(x_{it}\beta + \nu_i)$$

is no longer well-approximated by a polynomial. As a general rule-of thumb, you should use this quadrature approach only for small-to-moderate panel sizes (based on simulations, 50 is a reasonably safe upper bound). However, if the data really come from random-effects poisson and rho is not too large (less than say .3), then the panel size could be 500 and the quadrature approximation will still be fine. If the data is not random-effects poisson or rho is large (bigger than say .7), then the quadrature approximation may be poor for panel sizes larger than 10. The quadchk command should be used to investigate the applicability of the numeric technique used in this command.

For a fixed-effects specification, we know that

$$\Pr(Y_{it} = y_{it}) = \exp(-\exp(\alpha_i + x_{it}\beta)) \exp(\alpha_i + x_{it}\beta)^{y_{it}} / y_{it}!$$

$$= \frac{1}{y_{it}!} \exp(-\exp(\alpha_i) \exp(x_{it}\beta) + \alpha_i y_{it}) \exp(x_{it}\beta)^{y_{it}}$$

$$= F_{it}$$

Since we know that the observations are independent, we may write the joint probability for the observations within a panel as

$$\Pr(Y_{i1} = y_{i1}, \ldots, Y_{in_i} = y_{in_i}) = \prod_{t=1}^{n_i} \frac{1}{y_{it}!} \exp(-\exp(\alpha_i) \exp(x_{it}\beta) + \alpha_i y_{it}) \exp(x_{it}\beta)^{y_{it}}$$

$$= \prod_{t=1}^{n_i} \frac{\exp(x_{it}\beta)^{y_{it}}}{y_{it}!} \exp\left(-\exp(\alpha_i) \sum_t \exp(x_{it}\beta) + \alpha_i \sum_t y_{it}\right)$$

and we also know that the sum of n_i Poisson independent random variables each with parameter λ is distributed as Poisson with parameter $n_i \lambda$ so that we have

$$\Pr\left(\sum_t y_{it}\right) = \frac{1}{\sum_t (y_{it})!} \exp\left(-\exp(\alpha_i) \sum_t \exp(x_{it}\beta) + \alpha_i \sum_t y_{it}\right) \left[\sum_t \exp(x_{it}\beta)\right]^{\sum_t y_{it}}$$

So, the conditional likelihood is conditioned on the sum of the outcomes in the set (panel). The appropriate function is given by

$$\Pr\left(Y_{i1} = y_{i1}, \ldots, Y_{in_i} = y_{in_i} \big| \alpha_i, \beta, \sum_t y_{it}\right) =$$

$$\left\{ \prod_{t=1}^{n_i} \frac{\exp(x_{it}\beta)^{y_{it}}}{y_{it}!} \exp\left(-\exp(\alpha_i)\sum_t \exp(x_{it}\beta) + \alpha_i \sum_t y_{it}\right) \right\} \Bigg/$$

$$\left\{ \frac{1}{\sum(y_{it})!} \exp\left(-\exp(\alpha_i)\sum_t \exp(x_{it}\beta) + \alpha_i \sum_t y_{it}\right) \left[\sum_t \exp(x_{it}\beta)\right]^{\sum_t y_{it}} \right\}$$

$$= \left(\sum_t y_{it}\right)! \prod_{t=1}^{n_i} \frac{\exp(x_{it}\beta)^{y_{it}}}{y_{it}! \left[\sum_k \exp(x_{ik}\beta)\right]^{y_{it}}}$$

which is free of α.

So, the conditional log-likelihood is given by

$$L = \log\left\{ \prod_{i=1}^{n} w_i \left(\sum_{t=1}^{n_i} y_{it}\right)! \prod_{t=1}^{n_i} \frac{\exp(x_{it}\beta)^{y_{it}}}{y_{it}! \left[\sum_{\ell=1}^{n_\ell} \exp(x_{i\ell}\beta)\right]^{y_{it}}} \right\}$$

$$= \log\left\{ \prod_{i=1}^{n} w_i \frac{(\sum_t y_{it})!}{\prod_{t=1}^{n_i} y_{it}!} \prod_{t=1}^{n_i} p_{it}^{y_{it}} \right\}$$

$$= \sum_{i=1}^{n} w_i \left\{ \log\Gamma(\sum_{t=1}^{n_i} y_{it} + 1) - \sum_{t=1}^{n_i} \log\Gamma(y_{it} + 1) + \right.$$

$$\left. \sum_{t=1}^{n_i} \left[y_{it}(x_{it}\beta) - y_{it}\log\left(\sum_{\ell=1}^{n_i} \exp(x_{i\ell}\beta)\right) \right] \right\}$$

$$p_{it} = e^{x_{it}\beta} \Bigg/ \sum_{\ell} e^{x_{i\ell}\beta}$$

References

Greene, W. H. 1997. *Econometric Analysis*. 3d ed. Upper Saddle River, NJ: Prentice–Hall.

Liang, K.-Y. and S. L. Zeger. 1986. Longitudinal data analysis using generalized linear models. *Biometrika* 73: 13–22.

McCullagh, P. and J. A. Nelder. 1989. *Generalized Linear Models*. 2d ed. London: Chapman & Hall.

Also See

Complementary:	[R] **lincom**, [R] **predict**, [R] **quadchk**, [R] **test**, [R] **testnl**, [R] **vce**, [R] **xtdata**, [R] **xtdes**, [R] **xtsum**, [R] **xttab**
Related:	[R] **poisson**, [R] **xtgee**, [R] **xtnbreg**
Background:	[U] **16.5 Accessing coefficients and standard errors**, [U] **23 Estimation and post-estimation commands**, [U] **23.11 Obtaining robust variance estimates**, [R] **xt**

Title

xtprobit — Random-effects and population-averaged probit models

Syntax

Random-effects model

> xtprobit *depvar* [*varlist*] [*weight*] [if *exp*] [in *range*] [, re i(*varname*) quad(#)
>
> noconstant noskip level(#) offset(*varname*) *maximize_options*]

Population-averaged model

> xtprobit *depvar* [*varlist*] [*weight*] [if *exp*] [in *range*] , pa [i(*varname*) robust
>
> noconstant level(#) offset(*varname*) *xtgee_options maximize_options*]

iweights, aweights, and pweights are allowed for the population-averaged model and iweights are allowed in the random-effects model; see [U] **14.1.6 weight**. Note that weights must be constant within panels.

xtprobit shares the features of all estimation commands; see [U] **23 Estimation and post-estimation commands**.

Syntax for predict

Random-effects model

> predict [*type*] *newvarname* [if *exp*] [in *range*] [, { xb | pu0 | stdp }
>
> nooffset]

Population-averaged model

> predict [*type*] *newvarname* [if *exp*] [in *range*] [, { mu | rate | xb | stdp }
>
> nooffset]

These statistics are available both in and out of sample; type predict ... if e(sample) ... if wanted only for the estimation sample.

Description

xtprobit estimates random-effects and population-averaged probit models. There is no command for a conditional fixed-effects model as there does not exist a sufficient statistic allowing the fixed effects to be conditioned out of the likelihood. Unconditional fixed-effects probit models may be estimated with the probit command with indicator variables for the panels. The appropriate indicator variables can be generated using tabulate or xi. However, unconditional fixed-effects estimates are biased.

Note: `xtprobit, re`, the default, is slow since it is calculated by quadrature; see *Methods and Formulas*. Computation time is roughly proportional to the number of points used for the quadrature. The default is `quad(12)`. Simulations indicate that increasing it does not appreciably change the estimates for the coefficients or their standard errors. See [R] **quadchk**.

By default, the population-averaged model is an equal-correlation model; `xtprobit` assumes the within-group correlation structure `corr(exchangeable)`. See [R] **xtgee** for information on how to fit other population-averaged models.

See [R] **logistic** for a list of related estimation commands.

Options

re requests the random-effects estimator. `re` is the default if neither `re` nor `pa` is specified.

pa requests the population-averaged estimator.

i(*varname*) specifies the variable name that contains the unit to which the observation belongs. You can specify the `i()` option the first time you estimate or use the `iis` command to set `i()` beforehand. After that, Stata will remember the variable's identity. See [R] **xt**.

quad(*#*) specifies the number of points to use in the quadrature approximation of the integral. This option is relevant only if you are estimating a random-effects model; if you specify `quad(#)` with `pa`, the `quad(#)` is ignored.

The default is `quad(12)`. The number specified must be an integer between 4 and 30, and also be no greater than the number of observations.

robust specifies the Huber/White/sandwich estimator of variance is to be used in place of the IRLS variance estimator; see [R] **xtgee**. This alternative produces valid standard errors even if the correlations within group are not as hypothesized by the specified correlation structure. It does, however, require that the model correctly specifies the mean. As such, the resulting standard errors are labeled "semi-robust" instead of "robust". Note that although there is no `cluster()` option, results are as if there were a `cluster()` option and you specified clustering on `i()`.

noconstant suppresses the constant term (intercept) in the model.

noskip specifies that a full maximum-likelihood model with only a constant for the regression equation be estimated. This model is not displayed but is used as the base model to compute a likelihood-ratio test for the model test statistic displayed in the estimation header. By default, the overall model test statistic is an asymptotically equivalent Wald test of all the parameters in the regression equation being zero (except the constant). For many models, this option can significantly increase estimation time.

level(*#*) specifies the confidence level, in percent, for confidence intervals. The default is `level(95)` or as set by `set level`; see [U] **23.5 Specifying the width of confidence intervals**.

offset(*varname*) specifies that *varname* is to be included in the model with coefficient constrained to be 1.

xtgee_options specifies any other options allowed by `xtgee` for `family(binomial) link(probit)` such as `corr()`; see [R] **xtgee**.

maximize_options control the maximization process; see [R] **maximize**. Use the `trace` option to view parameter convergence. Use the `ltol(#)` option to relax the convergence criterion; default is 1e−6 during specification searches.

Options for predict

xb calculates the linear prediction. This is the default for the random-effects model.

pu0 calculates the probability of a positive outcome assuming that the random effect for that observation's panel is zero ($\nu = 0$). Note that this may not be similar to the proportion of observed outcomes in the group.

stdp calculates the standard error of the linear prediction.

mu and rate both calculate the predicted probability of *depvar*. mu takes into account the offset(). rate ignores those adjustments. mu and rate are equivalent if you did not specify offset(). mu is the default for the population-averaged model.

nooffset is relevant only if you specified offset(*varname*) for xtprobit. It modifies the calculations made by predict so that they ignore the offset variable; the linear prediction is treated as $\mathbf{x}_{it}\mathbf{b}$ rather than $\mathbf{x}_{it}\mathbf{b} + \text{offset}_{it}$.

Remarks

xtprobit is a convenience command if you want the population-averaged model. Typing

    . xtprobit ..., pa ...

is equivalent to typing

    . xtgee ..., ... family(binomial) link(probit) corr(exchangeable)

Thus, also see [R] **xtgee** for information about xtprobit.

By default, or when re is specified, xtprobit estimates a maximum-likelihood random-effects model.

▷ Example

You are studying unionization of women in the United States and are using the union dataset; see [R] **xt**. You wish to estimate a random-effects model of union membership:

```
. xtprobit union age grade not_smsa south southXt, i(id) nolog
Random-effects probit                           Number of obs      =      26200
Group variable (i) : idcode                     Number of groups   =       4434

Random effects u_i ~ Gaussian                   Obs per group: min =          1
                                                               avg =        5.9
                                                               max =         12

                                                Wald chi2(5)       =     218.90
Log likelihood  = -10561.065                    Prob > chi2        =     0.0000

------------------------------------------------------------------------------
       union |      Coef.   Std. Err.      z    P>|z|     [95% Conf. Interval]
-------------+----------------------------------------------------------------
         age |   .0044483   .0025027     1.777   0.076    -.000457    .0093535
       grade |   .0482482   .0100413     4.805   0.000     .0285677    .0679287
    not_smsa |  -.1370699   .0462961    -2.961   0.003    -.2278087   -.0463312
       south |  -.6305824   .0614827   -10.256   0.000    -.7510863   -.5100785
     southXt |   .0131853   .0043819     3.009   0.003      .004597    .0217737
       _cons |  -1.846838   .1458222   -12.665   0.000    -2.132644   -1.561032
------------------------------------------------------------------------------
```

```
---------+-----------------------------------------------------------------
/lnsig2u |   .5612193   .0431875   12.995   0.000     .4765733    .6458653
---------+-----------------------------------------------------------------
 sigma_u |   1.323937   .0285888                      1.269073    1.381172
     rho |   .6367346   .0099894                      .6169384    .6560781
---------------------------------------------------------------------------
Likelihood ratio test of rho=0:          chi2(1) =  5972.49   Prob > chi2 = 0.0000
```

The output includes the additional panel-level variance component. This is parameterized as the log of the standard deviation $\ln(\sigma_\nu)$ (labeled `lnsig2u` in the output). The standard deviation σ_ν is also included in the output labeled `sigma_u` together with ρ (labeled `rho`)

$$\rho = \frac{\sigma_\nu^2}{\sigma_\nu^2 + 1}$$

which is the proportion of the total variance contributed by the panel-level variance component.

When `rho` is zero, the panel-level variance component is unimportant and the panel estimator is not different from the pooled estimator. A likelihood ratio test of this is included at the bottom of the output. This test formally compares the pooled estimator (probit) with the panel estimator.

◁

❏ Technical Note

The random-effects model is calculated using quadrature. As the panel sizes (or ρ) increase, the quadrature approximation becomes less accurate. We can use the `quadchk` command to see if changing the number of quadrature points affects the results. If the results do change, then the quadrature approximation is not accurate and the results of the model should not be interpreted.

```
. quadchk, nooutput
Refitting model quad() =  8
Refitting model quad() = 16
                     Quadrature check
```

	Fitted quadrature 12 points	Comparison quadrature 8 points	Comparison quadrature 16 points	
Log likelihood	-10561.065	-10574.78 -13.714764 .00129862	-10555.853 5.2126898 -.00049358	Difference Relative difference
union: age	.00444829	.00478943 .00034115 .07669143	.00451117 .00006288 .01413662	Difference Relative difference
union: grade	.04824822	.05629525 .00804704 .16678412	.04411081 -.00413741 -.0857525	Difference Relative difference
union: not_smsa	-.13706993	-.1314541 .00561584 -.04097061	-.14109796 -.00402803 .02938665	Difference Relative difference
union: south	-.63058241	-.62309654 .00748587 -.01187136	-.64546968 -.01488727 .02360876	Difference Relative difference

```
union:         .01318534      .01194434      .01341723
  southXt                     -.001241       .00023189   Difference
                             -.09411977      .01758658   Relative difference
    ----------------------------------------------------------
union:       -1.8468379      -1.9306422     -1.8066853
  _cons                      -.08380426      .0401526    Difference
                              .04537716     -.02174127   Relative difference
    ----------------------------------------------------------
lnsig2u:      .56121927       .49078989      .58080961
  _cons                      -.07042938      .01959034   Difference
                             -.12549352      .03490674   Relative difference
    ----------------------------------------------------------
```

Note that the results obtained for 12 quadrature points were closer to the results using 18 points than to the results using 6 points. However, since the convergence point seems to be sensitive to the number of quadrature points, we should not use this output. Since there is no alternative method for calculating the random-effects model in Stata, we may either fit a different model or use a different command. We should not use the output of a random-effects specification when there is evidence that the numeric technique for calculating the model is not stable (as shown by quadchk).

A subjective rule of thumb is that the relative differences in the coefficients should not change by more than 1% if the quadrature technique is stable. See [R] **quadchk** for details. The important point to remember is that when the quadrature technique is not stable, you can not merely increase the number of quadrature points to fix the problem.

❑

▷ Example

As an alternative to the random-effects specification, we can fit an equal-correlation probit model:

```
. xtprobit union age grade not_smsa south southXt, i(id) pa
Iteration 1: tolerance = .0479535
  (output omitted )
Iteration 5: tolerance = 4.147e-07
GEE population-averaged model               Number of obs      =     26200
Group variable:                    idcode   Number of groups   =      4434
Link:                              probit   Obs per group: min =         1
Family:                          binomial                  avg =       5.9
Correlation:                 exchangeable                  max =        12
                                            Wald chi2(5)       =    241.67
Scale parameter:                        1   Prob > chi2        =    0.0000

    union |    Coef.    Std. Err.      z      P>|z|     [95% Conf. Interval]
 ---------+------------------------------------------------------------------
      age |  .0031599   .0014679     2.153   0.031     .0002829    .0060369
    grade |  .0329988   .0062332     5.294   0.000     .0207819    .0452156
 not_smsa | -.0721893   .0275194    -2.623   0.009    -.1261262   -.0182523
    south | -.4090316   .0372223   -10.989   0.000    -.481986    -.3360772
  southXt |  .0081824   .0025452     3.215   0.001     .003194     .0131709
    _cons | -1.184792   .0890111   -13.311   0.000    -1.359251   -1.010334
```

◁

▷ Example

In [R] **probit**, we showed the above results and compared them with probit, robust cluster(). xtprobit with the pa option allows a robust option (the random-effects estimator does not allow the robust specification) and so we can obtain the population-averaged probit estimator with the robust variance calculation by typing

```
. xtprobit union age grade not_smsa south southXt, i(id) pa robust nolog
GEE population-averaged model              Number of obs      =      26200
Group variable:                  idcode    Number of groups   =       4434
Link:                            probit    Obs per group: min =          1
Family:                        binomial                   avg =        5.9
Correlation:               exchangeable                   max =         12
                                           Wald chi2(5)       =     154.01
Scale parameter:                      1    Prob > chi2        =     0.0000
                     (standard errors adjusted for clustering on idcode)
```

		Semi-robust				
union	Coef.	Std. Err.	z	P>|z|	[95% Conf.	Interval]
age	.0031599	.0022027	1.435	0.151	-.0011572	.0074771
grade	.0329988	.0076629	4.306	0.000	.0179799	.0480177
not_smsa	-.0721893	.034876	-2.070	0.038	-.140545	-.0038336
south	-.4090316	.0482529	-8.477	0.000	-.5036056	-.3144577
southXt	.0081824	.0037108	2.205	0.027	.0009095	.0154554
_cons	-1.184792	.1164535	-10.174	0.000	-1.413037	-.9565476

These standard errors are similar to those shown for `probit, robust cluster()` in [R] **probit**.

◁

▷ Example

In a previous example, we showed how `quadchk` indicated that the quadrature technique was numerically unstable. Here we present an example where the quadrature is stable.

In this example, we have (synthetic) data on whether workers complain to managers at a fast-food restaurant. The covariates are `age` (in years of the worker), `grade` (years of schooling completed by worker), `south` (equal to 1 if restaurant located in the South), `tenure` (number of years spent on the job by the worker), `gender` (of worker), `race` (of work), `income` (in thousands of dollars by the restaurant), `genderm` (gender of manager), `burger` (equal to 1 if restaurant specializes in hamburgers), and `chicken` (equal to 1 if restaurant specializes in chicken). The model is given by

```
. xtprobit complain age grade south tenure gender race income genderm
> burger chicken, i(person) nolog
Random-effects probit                      Number of obs      =       5952
Group variable (i) : person                Number of groups   =       1076
Random effects u_i ~ Gaussian              Obs per group: min =          3
                                                        avg =        5.5
                                                        max =          8
                                           Wald chi2(10)      =      65.03
Log likelihood  =  -2574.115               Prob > chi2        =     0.0000
```

complain	Coef.	Std. Err.	z	P>|z|	[95% Conf.	Interval]
age	-.0003157	.0762518	-0.004	0.997	-.1497665	.1491351
grade	-.0411126	.0647728	-0.635	0.526	-.1680649	.0858396
south	-.0346366	.0723753	-0.479	0.632	-.1764896	.1072163
tenure	-.3836063	.0550447	-6.969	0.000	-.491492	-.2757206
gender	.0667994	.0734596	0.909	0.363	-.0771787	.2107775
race	.0834963	.0557731	1.497	0.134	-.0258169	.1928095
income	-.2111629	.0730127	-2.892	0.004	-.3542651	-.0680607
genderm	.1306497	.0557134	2.345	0.019	.0214535	.2398459
burger	-.0616544	.0729739	-0.845	0.398	-.2046807	.0813718
chicken	.0635842	.0557645	1.140	0.254	-.0457122	.1728806
_cons	-1.123845	.0330159	-34.039	0.000	-1.188556	-1.059135

```
/lnsig2u |  -1.030313    .129242    -7.972   0.000    -1.283622   -.777003
---------+------------------------------------------------------------------
 sigma_u |   .5974072    .038605                        .5263383    .6780722
     rho |   .2630235   .0250525                        .2169343    .3149662
---------------------------------------------------------------------------
Likelihood ratio test of rho=0:        chi2(1) =     166.88   Prob > chi2 = 0.0000
```

Again, we would like to check the stability of the quadrature technique of the model before interpreting the results. Given the estimate of ρ and the small size of the panels (between 3 and 8), we should find that the quadrature technique is numerically stable.

```
. quadchk, nooutput

Refitting model quad() =  8
Refitting model quad() = 16
```

	Fitted quadrature 12 points	Comparison quadrature 8 points	Comparison quadrature 16 points	
Log likelihood	-2574.115	-2574.1293	-2574.1164	
		-.01424246	-.00132579	Difference
		5.533e-06	5.150e-07	Relative difference
complain: age	-.00031569	-.00013111	-.00031858	
		.00018459	-2.891e-06	Difference
		-.58470325	.00915831	Relative difference
complain: grade	-.04111263	-.04100666	-.04111079	
		.00010597	1.839e-06	Difference
		-.0025776	-.00004474	Relative difference
complain: south	-.03463663	-.03469524	-.03462929	
		-.00005861	7.341e-06	Difference
		.0016922	-.00021193	Relative difference
complain: tenure	-.38360629	-.38351811	-.38360047	
		.00008818	5.820e-06	Difference
		-.00022987	-.00001517	Relative difference
complain: gender	.06679944	.06655282	.0668029	
		-.00024662	3.455e-06	Difference
		-.003692	.00005172	Relative difference
complain: race	.0834963	.08340258	.08349099	
		-.00009373	-5.311e-06	Difference
		-.00112252	-.00006361	Relative difference
complain: income	-.21116286	-.21100203	-.21115631	
		.00016083	6.556e-06	Difference
		-.00076164	-.00003105	Relative difference
complain: genderm	.13064966	.1305605	.13064386	
		-.00008916	-5.804e-06	Difference
		-.00068243	-.00004442	Relative difference
complain: burger	-.06165444	-.06168062	-.06164754	
		-.00002618	6.903e-06	Difference
		.0004246	-.00011195	Relative difference

Quadrature check

```
complain:      .0635842      .06359848      .06358665
 chicken                     .00001428      2.452e-06    Difference
                             .00022456      .00003856    Relative difference
-------------------------------------------------------------
complain:    -1.1238455     -1.1237932     -1.1238278
  _cons                      .00005231      .00001769    Difference
                            -.00004654     -.00001574    Relative difference
-------------------------------------------------------------
lnsig2u:     -1.0303127     -1.0317132     -1.0304345
  _cons                     -.00140056     -.0001218     Difference
                             .00135936      .00011821    Relative difference
-------------------------------------------------------------
```

The relative differences are all very small between the default 12 quadrature points and the result with 16 points. We have only one coefficient that has a large relative difference between the default 12 quadrature points and 8 quadrature points. In looking again at the absolute differences, we see also that the absolute differences between 12 and 16 quadrature points were also small.

We conclude that the quadrature technique is stable. We may wish to rerun the above model with quad(16) or even higher (but we do not have to since the results will not significantly differ) and interpret those results for our presentation.

◁

Saved Results

xtprobit, re saves in e():

Scalars

e(N)	number of observations	e(g_avg)	average group size
e(N_g)	number of groups	e(chi2)	χ^2
e(df_m)	model degrees of freedom	e(chi2_c)	χ^2 for comparison test
e(ll)	log likelihood	e(rho)	ρ
e(ll_0)	log likelihood, constant-only model	e(sigma_u)	panel-level standard deviation
e(ll_c)	log likelihood, comparison model	e(N_cd)	number of completely determined obs.
e(g_max)	largest group size	e(n_quad)	number of quadrature points
e(g_min)	smallest group size		

Macros

e(cmd)	xtprobit	e(chi2type)	Wald or LR; type of model χ^2 test
e(depvar)	name of dependent variable	e(chi2_ct)	Wald or LR; type of model χ^2 test
e(title)	title in estimation output		corresponding to e(chi2_c)
e(ivar)	variable denoting groups	e(distrib)	Gaussian; the distribution of the
e(wtype)	weight type		random effect
e(wexp)	weight expression	e(predict)	program used to implement predict
e(offset)	offset		

Matrices

e(b)	coefficient vector	e(V)	variance–covariance matrix of the estimators

Functions

e(sample)	marks estimation sample

xtprobit, pa saves in **e()**:

Scalars

e(N)	number of observations	e(deviance)	deviance
e(N_g)	number of groups	e(chi2_dev)	χ^2 test of deviance
e(df_m)	model degrees of freedom	e(dispers)	deviance dispersion
e(g_max)	largest group size	e(chi2_dis)	χ^2 test of deviance dispersion
e(g_min)	smallest group size	e(tol)	target tolerance
e(g_avg)	average group size	e(dif)	achieved tolerance
e(chi2)	χ^2	e(phi)	scale parameter
e(df_pear)	degrees of freedom for Pearson χ^2		

Macros

e(cmd)	xtgee	e(scale)	x2, dev, phi, or #; scale parameter
e(cmd2)	xtprobit	e(ivar)	variable denoting groups
e(depvar)	name of dependent variable	e(vcetype)	covariance estimation method
e(family)	binomial	e(chi2type)	Wald; type of model χ^2 test
e(link)	probit; link function	e(offset)	offset
e(corr)	correlation structure	e(predict)	program used to implement predict

Matrices

e(b)	coefficient vector	e(R)	estimated working correlation matrix
e(V)	variance–covariance matrix of the estimators		

Functions

e(sample)	marks estimation sample

Methods and Formulas

xtprobit is implemented as an ado-file.

xtprobit reports the population-averaged results obtained by using **xtgee, family(binomial) link(probit)** to obtain estimates.

Assuming a normal distribution, $N(0, \sigma_\nu^2)$, for the random effects ν_i, we have that

$$\Pr(y_i|x_i) = \int_{-\infty}^{\infty} \frac{e^{-\nu_i^2/2\sigma_\nu^2}}{\sqrt{2\pi}\sigma_\nu} \left[\prod_{t=1}^{n_i} F(x_{it}\beta + \nu_i) \right] d\nu_i$$

where

$$F(x_{it}\beta + \nu_i) = \begin{cases} \Phi(x_{it}\beta + \nu_i) & \text{if } y_{it} \neq 0 \\ 1 - \Phi(x_{it}\beta + \nu_i) & \text{otherwise} \end{cases}$$

(where Φ is the cumulative normal distribution) and we can approximate the integral with M-point Gauss–Hermite quadrature

$$\int_{-\infty}^{\infty} e^{-x^2} f(x)dx \approx \sum_{m=1}^{M} w_m^* f(a_m^*)$$

where the w_m^* denote the quadrature weights and the a_m^* denote the quadrature abscissas. The log-likelihood L where $\rho = \sigma_\nu^2/(\sigma_\nu^2 + 1)$ is then calculated using the quadrature

$$L = \sum_{i=1}^{n} w_i \log\Big(\Pr(y_i|x_i)\Big)$$

$$\approx \sum_{i=1}^{n} w_i \log \frac{1}{\sqrt{\pi}} \sum_{m=1}^{M} w_m^* \prod_{t=1}^{n_i} F\left(x_{it}\beta + \sqrt{2\frac{\rho}{1-\rho}}\, a_m^*\right)$$

The quadrature formula requires that the integrated function be well-approximated by a polynomial. As the number of time periods becomes large (as panel size gets large)

$$\prod_{t=1}^{n_i} F(x_{it}\beta + \nu_i)$$

is no longer well-approximated by a polynomial. As a general rule-of thumb, you should use this quadrature approach only for small-to-moderate panel sizes (based on simulations, 50 is a reasonably safe upper bound). However, if the data really comes from random-effects probit and rho is not too large (less than say .3), then the panel size could be 500 and the quadrature approximation will still be fine. If the data is not random-effects probit or rho is large (bigger than say .7), then the quadrature approximation may be poor for panel sizes larger than 10. The quadchk command should be used to investigate the applicability of the numeric technique used in this command.

References

Conway, M. R. 1990. A random effects model for binary data. *Biometrics* 46: 317–328.

Guilkey, D. K. and J. L. Murphy. 1993. Estimation and testing in the random effects probit model. *Journal of Econometrics* 59: 301–317.

Liang, K.-Y. and S. L. Zeger. 1986. Longitudinal data analysis using generalized linear models. *Biometrika* 73: 13–22.

Neuhaus, J. M. 1992. Statistical methods for longitudinal and clustered designs with binary responses. *Statistical Methods in Medical Research* 1: 249–273.

Neuhaus, J. M., J. D. Kalbfleisch, and W. W. Hauck. 1991. A comparison of cluster-specific and population-averaged approaches for analyzing correlated binary data. *International Statistical Review* 59: 25–35.

Pendergast, J. F., S. J. Gange, M. A. Newton, M. J. Lindstrom, M. Palta, and M. R. Fisher. 1996. A survey of methods for analyzing clustered binary response data. *International Statistical Review* 64: 89–118.

Also See

Complementary:	[R] **lincom**, [R] **predict**, [R] **quadchk**, [R] **test**, [R] **testnl**, [R] **vce**, [R] **xtdata**, [R] **xtdes**, [R] **xtsum**, [R] **xttab**
Related:	[R] **probit**, [R] **xtclog**, [R] **xtgee**, [R] **xtlogit**
Background:	[U] **16.5 Accessing coefficients and standard errors**, [U] **23 Estimation and post-estimation commands**, [U] **23.11 Obtaining robust variance estimates**, [R] **xt**

Title

> **xtrchh** — Hildreth–Houck random coefficients model

Syntax

> **xtrchh** *depvar varlist* [**if** *exp*] [**in** *range*] [**,** i(*varname*) t(*varname*) <u>level</u>(#)
>
> <u>off</u>set(*varname*) *maximize_options*]

xtrchh shares the features of all estimation commands; see [U] **23 Estimation and post-estimation commands**.

Syntax for predict

> **predict** [*type*] *newvarname* [**if** *exp*] [**in** *range*] [**,** { xb | stdp } <u>nooff</u>set]

These statistics are available both in and out of sample; type predict ... if e(sample) ... if wanted only for the estimation sample.

Description

xtrchh estimates the Hildreth–Houck random coefficients linear regression model.

Options

i(*varname*) specifies the variable that contains the unit to which the observation belongs. You can specify the i() option the first time you estimate or use the iis command to set i() beforehand. After that, Stata will remember the variable's identity. See [R] **xt**.

t(*varname*) specifies the variable that contains the time at which the observation was made. You can specify the t() option the first time you estimate or use the tis command to set t() beforehand. After that, Stata will remember the variable's identity.

level(#) specifies the confidence level, in percent, for confidence intervals. The default is level(95) or as set by set level; see [U] **23.5 Specifying the width of confidence intervals**.

offset(*varname*) specifies that *varname* is to be included in the model with coefficient constrained to be 1.

maximize_options control the maximization process; see [R] **maximize**. Use the trace option to view parameter convergence. Use the ltol(#) option to relax the convergence criterion; default is 1e−6 during specification searches.

Options for predict

xb calculates the linear prediction.

stdp calculates the standard error of the linear prediction.

nooffset is relevant only if you specified offset(*varname*) for xtrchh. It modifies the calculations made by predict so that they ignore the offset variable; the linear prediction is treated as $\mathbf{x}_{it}\mathbf{b}$ rather than $\mathbf{x}_{it}\mathbf{b} + \text{offset}_{it}$.

Remarks

In random coefficients models, we wish to treat the parameter vector as a realization (in each panel) of a stochastic process.

Interested readers should see Greene (1997) for information on this and other panel data models.

▷ Example

Greene (1997, 650) reprints data from a classic study of investment demand by Grunfeld and Griliches (1960). In [R] **xtgls**, we use this data to illustrate many of the possible models that may be estimated with the **xtgls** command. While the models included in the **xtgls** command offer considerable flexibility, they all assume that there is no parameter variation across firms (the cross-sectional units).

To take a first look at the assumption of parameter constancy, we should **reshape** our data so that we may estimate a simultaneous equation model using **sureg**; see [R] **sureg**. Since there are only 5 panels here, it is not too difficult.

```
. reshape wide invest market stock, i(time) j(company)
(note:  j = 1 2 3 4 5)

Data                               wide   -> long
---------------------------------------------------------------------
Number of obs.                      100   ->     20
Number of variables                   5   ->     16
j variable (5 values)           company   ->   (dropped)
xij variables:
                                 invest   ->   invest1 invest2 ... invest5
                                 market   ->   market1 market2 ... market5
                                  stock   ->   stock1 stock2 ... stock5
---------------------------------------------------------------------

. sureg (invest1 market1 stock1) (invest2 market2 stock2) (invest3 market3 stock3)
> (invest4 market4 stock4) (invest5 market5 stock5)

Seemingly unrelated regression
---------------------------------------------------------------------
Equation    Obs  Parms      RMSE    "R-sq"      Chi2        P
---------------------------------------------------------------------
invest1      20      2   84.94729   0.9207   261.3219   0.0000
invest2      20      2   12.36322   0.9119   207.2128   0.0000
invest3      20      2   26.46612   0.6876    46.88498  0.0000
invest4      20      2   9.742303   0.7264    59.14585  0.0000
invest5      20      2   95.85484   0.4220    14.9687   0.0006
```

```
-------------------------------------------------------------------------
             |    Coef.    Std. Err.        z      P>|z|    [95% Conf. Interval]
-------------+-----------------------------------------------------------
invest1      |
    market1  |   .120493    .0216291      5.571    0.000     .0781007    .1628853
     stock1  |  .3827462     .032768     11.680    0.000      .318522    .4469703
      _cons  | -162.3641    89.45922     -1.815    0.070    -337.7009    12.97279
-------------+-----------------------------------------------------------
invest2      |
    market2  |  .0695456    .0168975      4.116    0.000     .0364271    .1026641
     stock2  |  .3085445    .0258635     11.930    0.000     .2578529    .3592362
      _cons  |  .5043112    11.51283      0.044    0.965    -22.06042    23.06904
-------------+-----------------------------------------------------------
invest3      |
    market3  |  .0372914    .0122631      3.041    0.002     .0132561    .0613268
     stock3  |   .130783    .0220497      5.931    0.000     .0875663    .1739997
      _cons  | -22.43892    25.51859     -0.879    0.379    -72.45443    27.57659
-------------+-----------------------------------------------------------
invest4      |
    market4  |  .0570091    .0113623      5.017    0.000     .0347395    .0792788
     stock4  |  .0415065    .0412016      1.007    0.314    -.0392472    .1222602
      _cons  |  1.088878    6.258805      0.174    0.862    -11.17815    13.35591
-------------+-----------------------------------------------------------
invest5      |
    market5  |  .1014782    .0547837      1.852    0.064    -.0058958    .2088523
     stock5  |  .3999914    .1277946      3.130    0.002     .1495186    .6504642
      _cons  |  85.42324    111.8774      0.764    0.445    -133.8525    304.6989
-------------------------------------------------------------------------
```

Here we instead estimate a random coefficients model:

```
. use invest, clear

. xtrchh invest market stock, i(company) t(time)

Hildreth-Houck random-coefficients regression    Number of obs      =       100
Group variable (i) : company                      Number of groups   =         5

                                                  Obs per group: min =        20
                                                                 avg =      20.0
                                                                 max =        20

                                                  Wald chi2(2)       =     17.55
                                                  Prob > chi2        =    0.0002

-------------------------------------------------------------------------
    invest   |    Coef.    Std. Err.        z      P>|z|    [95% Conf. Interval]
-------------+-----------------------------------------------------------
    market   |  .0807646    .0250829      3.220    0.001     .0316031    .1299261
     stock   |  .2839885    .0677899      4.189    0.000     .1511229    .4168542
     _cons   | -23.58361    34.55547     -0.682    0.495    -91.31108    44.14386
-------------------------------------------------------------------------

Test of parameter constancy:     chi2(12) =    603.99       Prob > chi2 = 0.0000
```

Just as a subjective examination of the results of our simultaneous-equation model does not support the assumption of parameter constancy, the test included with the random coefficients model also indicates that assumption is not valid for this data. With large panel datasets, obviously we would not want to take the time to look at a simultaneous-equations model (aside from the fact that our doing so was very subjective).

◁

Saved Results

xtrchh saves in e():

Scalars

e(N)	number of observations	e(g_avg)	average group size
e(N_g)	number of groups	e(chi2)	χ^2
e(df_m)	model degrees of freedom	e(chi2_c)	χ^2 for comparison test
e(g_max)	largest group size	e(df_chi2)	degrees of freedom for model χ^2
e(g_min)	smallest group size		

Macros

e(cmd)	xtrchh	e(chi2type)	Wald; type of model χ^2 test
e(depvar)	name of dependent variable	e(offset)	offset
e(title)	title in estimation output	e(predict)	program used to implement predict
e(ivar)	variable denoting groups		

Matrices

e(b)	coefficient vector	e(V)	variance–covariance matrix of the estimators
e(Sigma)	$\widehat{\Sigma}$ matrix		

Functions

e(sample)	marks estimation sample

Methods and Formulas

xtrchh is implemented as an ado-file.

In a random coefficients model, the parameter heterogeneity is treated as stochastic variation. Assume that we write

$$\mathbf{y}_i = \mathbf{X}_i \boldsymbol{\beta}_i + \boldsymbol{\epsilon}_i$$

where $i = 1, \ldots, m$, and $\boldsymbol{\beta}_i$ is the coefficient vector $(k \times 1)$ for the ith cross-sectional unit such that

$$\boldsymbol{\beta}_i = \boldsymbol{\beta} + \boldsymbol{\nu}_i \qquad E(\boldsymbol{\nu}_i) = \mathbf{0} \qquad E(\boldsymbol{\nu}_i \boldsymbol{\nu}_i') = \boldsymbol{\Gamma}$$

Our goal is to find $\widehat{\boldsymbol{\beta}}$ and $\widehat{\boldsymbol{\Gamma}}$.

The derivation of the estimator assumes that the cross-sectional specific coefficient vector $\boldsymbol{\beta}_i$ is the outcome of a random process with mean vector $\boldsymbol{\beta}$ and covariance matrix $\boldsymbol{\Gamma}$.

$$\mathbf{y}_i = \mathbf{X}_i \boldsymbol{\beta}_i + \boldsymbol{\epsilon}_i = \mathbf{X}_i(\boldsymbol{\beta} + \boldsymbol{\nu}_i) + \boldsymbol{\epsilon}_i = \mathbf{X}_i \boldsymbol{\beta} + (\mathbf{X}_i \boldsymbol{\nu}_i + \boldsymbol{\epsilon}_i) = \mathbf{X}_i \boldsymbol{\beta} + \boldsymbol{\omega}_i$$

where $E(\boldsymbol{\omega}_i) = \mathbf{0}$ and

$$E(\boldsymbol{\omega}_i \boldsymbol{\omega}_i') = E\Big((\mathbf{X}_i \boldsymbol{\nu}_i + \boldsymbol{\epsilon}_i)(\mathbf{X}_i \boldsymbol{\nu}_i + \boldsymbol{\epsilon}_i)'\Big) = E(\boldsymbol{\epsilon}_i \boldsymbol{\epsilon}_i') + \mathbf{X}_i E(\boldsymbol{\nu}_i \boldsymbol{\nu}_i') \mathbf{X}_i' = \sigma_i^2 \mathbf{I} + \mathbf{X}_i \boldsymbol{\Gamma} \mathbf{X}_i' = \boldsymbol{\Pi}_i$$

The covariance matrix for the panel-specific coefficient estimator $\boldsymbol{\beta}_i$ can then be written

$$\mathbf{V}_i + \boldsymbol{\Gamma} = (\mathbf{X}_i' \mathbf{X}_i)^{-1} \mathbf{X}_i' \boldsymbol{\Pi}_i \mathbf{X}_i (\mathbf{X}_i' \mathbf{X}_i)^{-1} \qquad \text{where} \qquad \mathbf{V}_i = \sigma_i^2 (\mathbf{X}_i' \mathbf{X}_i)^{-1}$$

We may then compute a weighted average of the panel-specific coefficient estimates as

$$\widehat{\boldsymbol{\beta}} = \sum_{i=1}^m \mathbf{W}_i \boldsymbol{\beta}_i \qquad \text{where} \qquad \mathbf{W}_i = \left\{ \sum_{i=1}^m [\boldsymbol{\Gamma} + \mathbf{V}_i]^{-1} \right\}^{-1} [\boldsymbol{\Gamma} + \mathbf{V}_i]^{-1}$$

such that the resulting GLS estimator is a matrix-weighted average of the panel-specific (OLS) estimators.

To calculate the above estimator $\widehat{\beta}$ for the unknown Γ and $\mathbf{V}_i$ parameters, we use the two-step approach suggested by Swamy (1971):

$$\widehat{\beta}_i = \text{OLS panel} - \text{specific estimator}$$

$$\widehat{\mathbf{V}}_i = \frac{\widehat{\epsilon}_i'\widehat{\epsilon}_i}{n_i - k}$$

$$\bar{\beta} = \frac{1}{m}\sum_{i=1}^{m}\widehat{\beta}_i$$

$$\widehat{\Gamma} = \frac{1}{m-1}\left(\sum_{i=1}^{m}\widehat{\beta}_i\widehat{\beta}_i' - m\bar{\beta}\bar{\beta}\right) - \frac{1}{m}\sum_{i=1}^{m}\widehat{\mathbf{V}}_i$$

The two-step procedure begins with the usual OLS estimate of β. With an estimate of β, we may proceed by (1) obtaining estimates of $\widehat{\mathbf{V}}_i$ and $\widehat{\Gamma}$ (and, thus, $\widehat{\mathbf{W}}_i$) and then (2) obtain an updated estimate of β.

Swamy (1971) further points out that the matrix $\widehat{\Gamma}$ may not be positive definite and that since the second term is of order $1/(mT)$, it is negligible in large samples. A simple and asymptotically expedient solution is to simply drop this second term and instead use

$$\widehat{\Gamma} = \frac{1}{m-1}\left(\sum_{i=1}^{m}\widehat{\beta}_i\widehat{\beta}_i' - m\bar{\beta}\bar{\beta}\right)$$

As a test of the model, we may look at the difference between the OLS estimate of β ignoring the panel structure of the data and the matrix-weighted average of the panel-specific OLS estimators. The test statistic suggested by Swamy (1971) is given by

$$\chi^2_{k(m-1)} = \sum_{i=1}^{m}[\widehat{\beta}_i - \bar{\beta}^*]'\widehat{\mathbf{V}}_i^{-1}[\widehat{\beta}_i - \bar{\beta}^*] \quad \text{where} \quad \bar{\beta}^* = \left[\sum_{i=1}^{m}\widehat{\mathbf{V}}_i^{-1}\right]^{-1}\sum_{i=1}^{m}\widehat{\mathbf{V}}_i^{-1}\widehat{\beta}_i$$

Johnston (1984) has shown that the test is algebraically equivalent to testing

$$H_0 : \beta_1 = \beta_2 = \cdots = \beta_m$$

in the generalized (groupwise heteroscedastic) `xtgls` model where $\mathbf{V}$ is block diagonal with ith diagonal element Π_i.

References

Greene, W. H. 1997. *Econometric Analysis*. 3d ed. Upper Saddle River, NJ: Prentice–Hall.

Grunfeld, Y. and Z. Griliches. 1960. Is aggregation necessarily bad? *Review of Economics and Statistics* 42: 1–13.

Hardin, J. W. 1996. sg62: Hildreth–Houck random coefficients model. *Stata Technical Bulletin* 33: 21–23. Reprinted in *Stata Technical Bulletin Reprints*, vol. 6, pp. 158–162.

Hildreth, C. and C. Houck. 1968. Some estimators for a linear model with random coefficients. *Journal of the American Statistical Association* 63: 584–595.

Johnston, J. 1984. *Econometric Methods*. New York: McGraw–Hill.

Swamy, P. 1970. Efficient inference in a random coefficient regression model. *Econometrica* 38: 311–323.

———. 1971. *Statistical Inference in Random Coefficient Regression Models*. New York: Springer-Verlag.

Also See

Complementary:	[R] **lincom**, [R] **predict**, [R] **test**, [R] **testnl**, [R] **vce**, [R] **xtdata**, [R] **xtdes**, [R] **xtsum**, [R] **xttab**
Related:	[R] **xtgee**, [R] **xtgls**, [R] **xtreg**
Background:	[U] **16.5 Accessing coefficients and standard errors**, [U] **23 Estimation and post-estimation commands**, [R] **xt**

Title

> **xtreg** — Fixed-, between-, and random-effects, and population-averaged linear models

Syntax

GLS Random-effects model

> xtreg *depvar* [*varlist*] [if *exp*] [, re level(*#*) i(*varname*) theta]

> xttest0

> xthaus

Between-effects model

> xtreg *depvar* [*varlist*] [if *exp*] , be [level(*#*) wls i(*varname*)]

Fixed-effects model

> xtreg *depvar* [*varlist*] [if *exp*] , fe [level(*#*) i(*varname*)]

ML Random-effects model

> xtreg *depvar* [*varlist*] [*weight*] [if *exp*] , mle [level(*#*) i(*varname*)]

Population-averaged model

> xtreg *depvar* [*varlist*] [*weight*] [if *exp*] , pa [level(*#*) i(*varname*)

> offset(*varname*) *xtgee_options*]

iweights, aweights, and pweights are allowed for the population-averaged model and iweights are allowed for the maximum likelihood (ML) random-effects model; see [U] **14.1.6 weight**. Note that weights must be constant within panels.

xtreg shares the features of all estimation commands; see [U] **23 Estimation and post-estimation commands**.

(Continued on next page)

Syntax for predict

For all but the population-averaged model

> predict [*type*] *newvarname* [if *exp*] [in *range*] [, *statistic* <u>nooff</u>set]

where *statistic* is

xb	$\mathbf{x}_j\mathbf{b}$, fitted values (the default)
stdp	standard error of the fitted values
ue	$u_i + e_{it}$, the combined residual
* xbu	$\mathbf{x}_j\mathbf{b} + u_i$, prediction including effect
* u	u_i, the fixed or random error component
* e	e_{it}, the overall error component

Unstarred statistics are available both in and out of sample; type predict ... if e(sample) ... if wanted only for the estimation sample. Starred statistics are calculated only for the estimation sample even when if e(sample) is not specified.

Population-averaged model

> predict [*type*] *newvarname* [if *exp*] [in *range*] [, { mu | rate | xb | stdp }
>
> <u>nooff</u>set]

These statistics are available both in and out of sample; type predict ... if e(sample) ... if wanted only for the estimation sample.

Description

xtreg estimates cross-sectional time-series regression models. In particular, **xtreg** with the **be** option estimates random-effects models using the between regression estimator; with the **fe** option, fixed-effects models (using the within regression estimator); and with the **re** option, random-effects models using the GLS estimator (producing a matrix-weighted average of the between and within results). (Also see [R] **xtdata** for a faster way to estimate fixed- and random-effects models.)

xttest0, for use after **xtreg, re**, presents the Breusch and Pagan (1980) Lagrange multiplier test for random effects, a test that $\mathrm{Var}(\nu_i) = 0$.

xthaus, for use after **xtreg, re**, presents Hausman's (1978) specification test. If one believes the model is correctly specified and the test returns a significant result, then this can be interpreted as evidence that the random effects, ν_i, and the regressors, $\mathbf{x}_{it}$, are correlated. Thus, under the assumption of correct specification, **xthaus** tests the appropriateness of the random-effects estimator **xtreg, re** applied to this data.

Options

re requests the GLS random-effects estimator. **re** is the default.

be requests the between regression estimator.

fe requests the fixed-effects (within) regression estimator.

mle requests the maximum-likelihood random-effects estimator. Note that the utility commands **xttest0** and **xthaus** may not be used after **xtreg, mle**.

pa requests the population-averaged estimator. For linear regression this is the same as a random-effects estimator (both interpretations hold). Note that the utility commands **xttest0**, and **xthaus** may not be used after **xtreg, pa**.

> **xtreg, pa** is equivalent to **xtgee, family(gaussian) link(id) corr(exchangeable)**, which are the defaults for the **xtgee** command. **xtreg, pa** allows all the relevant **xtgee** options such as **robust**. Whether you use **xtreg, pa** or **xtgee** makes no difference. See [R] **xtgee**.

level(#) specifies the confidence level, in percent, for confidence intervals. The default is **level(95)** or as set by **set level**; see [U] **23.5 Specifying the width of confidence intervals**.

theta, used with **xtreg, re** only, specifies that the output should include the estimated value of θ used in combining the between and fixed estimators. For balanced data, this is a constant, and for unbalanced data a summary of the values is presented in the header of the output.

wls, used with **xtreg, be** only, specifies that, in the case of unbalanced data, weighted least squares be used rather than the default OLS. Both methods produce consistent estimates. The true variance of the between-effects residual is $\sigma_\nu^2 + T_i\sigma_\epsilon^2$ (see *Methods and Formulas* below). WLS produces a "stabilized" variance of $\sigma_\nu^2/T_i + \sigma_\epsilon^2$ which is also not constant. The choice between OLS and WLS thus amounts to which is more stable.

> Comment: **xtreg, be** is not much used anyway, but between estimates are an ingredient in the random-effects estimate. Our implementation of **xtreg, re** uses the OLS estimates for this ingredient based on our judgment that σ_ν^2 is large relative to σ_ϵ^2 in most models. Formally, any consistent estimate of the between estimates is all that is required.

i(varname**)** specifies the variable name that contains the unit to which the observation belongs. You can specify the **i()** option the first time you estimate or use the **iis** command to set **i()** beforehand. After that, Stata will remember the variable's identity. See [R] **xt**.

offset(varname**)** specifies that *varname* is to be included in the model with coefficient constrained to be 1.

xtgee_options specifies any other options allowed by **xtgee** for **family(gaussian) link(id)** such as **corr()**; see [R] **xtgee**.

Options for predict

xb calculates the linear prediction; that is, $a + \mathbf{b}\mathbf{x}_{it}$. This is the default for all except the population-averaged model.

mu and **rate** both calculate the predicted probability of *depvar*. **mu** takes into account the **offset()**. **rate** ignores those adjustments. **mu** and **rate** are equivalent if you did not specify **offset()**. **mu** is the default for the population-averaged model.

stdp calculates the standard error of the linear prediction. Note that in the case of the fixed-effects model, this excludes the variance due to uncertainty about the estimate of u_i.

ue calculates the prediction of $u_i + e_{it}$.

xbu calculates the prediction of $a + \mathbf{b}\mathbf{x}_{it} + u_i$, the prediction including the fixed or random component.

u calculates the prediction of u_i, the estimated fixed or random effect.

e calculates the prediction of e_{it}.

`nooffset` is relevant only if you specified `offset`(*varname*) for `xtreg, pa`. It modifies the calculations made by `predict` so that they ignore the offset variable; the linear prediction is treated as $\mathbf{x}_{it}\mathbf{b}$ rather than $\mathbf{x}_{it}\mathbf{b} + \text{offset}_{it}$.

Remarks

If you have not read [R] **xt**, please do so.

Consider estimating models of the form

$$y_{it} = \alpha + \mathbf{x}_{it}\boldsymbol{\beta} + \nu_i + \epsilon_{it} \tag{1}$$

In this model, $\nu_i + \epsilon_{it}$ is the residual in the sense that we have little interest in it; we want estimates of $\boldsymbol{\beta}$. ν_i is the unit-specific residual; it differs between units but, for any particular unit, its value is constant. In the pulmonary data of [R] **xt**, a person who exercises less would presumably have a lower FEV year after year and so would have a negative ν_i.

ϵ_{it} is the "usual" residual with the usual properties (mean 0, uncorrelated with itself, uncorrelated with $\mathbf{x}$, uncorrelated with ν, and homoscedastic) although in a more thorough development, we could decompose $\epsilon_{it} = \upsilon_t + \omega_{it}$, assume ω_{it} is a standard residual, and better describe υ_t.

Before making the assumptions necessary for estimation, let us perform some useful algebra on equation (1). Whatever the properties of ν_i and ϵ_{it}, if equation (1) is true, it must also be true that

$$\overline{y}_i = \alpha + \overline{\mathbf{x}}_i\boldsymbol{\beta} + \nu_i + \overline{\epsilon}_i \tag{2}$$

where $\overline{y}_i = \sum_t y_{it}/T_i$, $\overline{\mathbf{x}}_i = \sum_t \mathbf{x}_{it}/T_i$, and $\overline{\epsilon}_i = \sum_t \epsilon_{it}/T_i$. Subtracting equation (2) from (1), it must be equally true that

$$(y_{it} - \overline{y}_i) = (\mathbf{x}_{it} - \overline{\mathbf{x}}_i)\boldsymbol{\beta} + (\epsilon_{it} - \overline{\epsilon}_i) \tag{3}$$

These three equations provide the basis for estimating $\boldsymbol{\beta}$. In particular, `xtreg, fe` provides what is known as the fixed-effects estimator—also known as the within estimator—and amounts to using OLS to estimate equation (3). `xtreg, be` provides what is known as the between estimator and amounts to using OLS to estimate equation (2). `xtreg, re` provides the random-effects estimator and is a (matrix) weighted average of the estimates produced by the between and within estimators. In particular, the random-effects estimator turns out to be equivalent to estimation of

$$(y_{it} - \theta\overline{y}_i) = (1 - \theta)\alpha + (\mathbf{x}_{it} - \theta\overline{\mathbf{x}}_i)\boldsymbol{\beta} + [(1 - \theta)\nu_i + (\epsilon_{it} - \theta\overline{\epsilon}_i)] \tag{4}$$

where θ is a function of σ_ν^2 and σ_ϵ^2. If $\sigma_\nu^2 = 0$, meaning ν_i is always 0, $\theta = 0$ and equation (1) can be estimated by OLS directly. Alternatively, if $\sigma_\epsilon^2 = 0$, meaning ϵ_{it} is 0, $\theta = 1$ and the within estimator returns all the information available (which will, in fact, be an $R^2 = 1$ regression).

Returning to more reasonable cases, few assumptions are required to justify the fixed-effects estimator of equation (3). The estimates are, however, conditional on the sample in that ν_i are not assumed to have a distribution but are instead treated as fixed and estimable. This statistical fine point can lead to difficulty when making out-of-sample predictions but, that aside, the fixed-effects estimator has much to recommend it.

More is required to justify the between estimator of equation (2), but the conditioning on the sample is not assumed since $\nu_i + \overline{\epsilon}_i$ is treated as a residual. Newly required is that we assume ν_i and $\overline{\mathbf{x}}_i$ are uncorrelated. This follows from the assumptions of the OLS estimator but is also transparent: Were ν_i and $\overline{\mathbf{x}}_i$ correlated, the estimator could not determine how much of the change in $\overline{y}_i$ associated with an increase in $\overline{\mathbf{x}}_i$ to assign to $\boldsymbol{\beta}$ versus how much to attribute to the unknown correlation. (This of course suggests the use of an instrumental-variable estimator—the use of $\overline{\mathbf{z}}_i$ that is correlated with $\overline{\mathbf{x}}_i$ but uncorrelated with ν_i, but that approach is not implemented here.)

The random-effects estimator of equation (4) requires the same no-correlation assumption. In comparison with the between estimator, the random-effects estimator produces more efficient results, albeit ones with unknown small-sample properties. The between estimator is less efficient because it discards the over-time information in the data in favor of simple means; the random-effects estimator uses both the within and the between information.

All of this would seem to leave the between estimator of equation (2) with no role (except for a minor, technical part it plays in helping to estimate σ_ν^2 and σ_ϵ^2 used in the calculation of θ on which the random-effects estimates depend). Let us, however, consider a variation on equation (1):

$$y_{it} = \alpha + \overline{\mathbf{x}}_i\boldsymbol{\beta}_1 + (\mathbf{x}_{it} - \overline{\mathbf{x}}_i)\boldsymbol{\beta}_2 + \nu_i + \epsilon_{it} \tag{1$'$}$$

In this model, we postulate that changes in the average value of $\mathbf{x}$ for an individual have a different effect than temporary departures from the average. In an economic situation, y might be purchases of some item and $\mathbf{x}$ income; a change in average income should have more effect than a transitory change. In a clinical situation, y might be a physical response and $\mathbf{x}$ the level of a chemical in the brain; the model allows a different response to permanent rather than transitory changes.

The variations of equations (2) and (3) corresponding to equation (1$'$) are

$$\overline{y}_i = \alpha + \overline{\mathbf{x}}_i\boldsymbol{\beta}_1 + \nu_i + \overline{\epsilon}_i \tag{2$'$}$$
$$(y_{it} - \overline{y}_i) = (\mathbf{x}_{it} - \overline{\mathbf{x}}_i)\boldsymbol{\beta}_2 + (\epsilon_{it} - \overline{\epsilon}_i) \tag{3$'$}$$

That is, the between estimator estimates $\boldsymbol{\beta}_1$ and the within $\boldsymbol{\beta}_2$ and, moreover, neither estimates the other. Thus, even when estimating equations like (1), it is worth comparing the within and between estimators. Differences in results can suggest models like (1$'$) or, at the least, some other specification error.

Finally, it is worth understanding the role of the between and within estimators with regressors that are constant over time or constant over units. Consider the model:

$$y_{it} = \alpha + \mathbf{x}_{it}\boldsymbol{\beta}_1 + \mathbf{s}_i\boldsymbol{\beta}_2 + \mathbf{z}_t\boldsymbol{\beta}_3 + \nu_i + \epsilon_{it} \tag{1$''$}$$

This model is the same as (1) except that we explicitly identify the variables that vary over both time and i ($\mathbf{x}_{it}$, such as output or FEV); variables that are constant over time ($\mathbf{s}_i$, such as race or sex); and variables that vary solely over time ($\mathbf{z}_t$, such as the consumer price index or age in a cohort study). The corresponding between and within equations are

$$\overline{y}_i = \alpha + \overline{\mathbf{x}}_i\boldsymbol{\beta}_1 + \mathbf{s}_i\boldsymbol{\beta}_2 + \overline{\mathbf{z}}\boldsymbol{\beta}_3 + \nu_i + \overline{\epsilon}_i \tag{2$''$}$$
$$(y_{it} - \overline{y}_i) = (\mathbf{x}_{it} - \overline{\mathbf{x}}_i)\boldsymbol{\beta}_1 + (\mathbf{z}_t - \overline{\mathbf{z}})\boldsymbol{\beta}_3 + (\epsilon_{it} - \overline{\epsilon}_i) \tag{3$''$}$$

In the between estimator of equation (2$''$), no estimate of $\boldsymbol{\beta}_3$ is possible because $\overline{\mathbf{z}}$ is a constant across the i observations; the regression-estimated intercept will be an estimate of $\alpha + \overline{\mathbf{z}}\boldsymbol{\beta}_3$. On the other hand, it is able to provide estimates of $\boldsymbol{\beta}_1$ and $\boldsymbol{\beta}_2$. It is able to estimate effects of factors that are constant over time, such as race and sex, but in order to do so, it must assume that ν_i is uncorrelated with those factors.

The within estimator of equation (3$''$), like the between estimator, provides an estimate of $\boldsymbol{\beta}_1$, but provides no estimate of $\boldsymbol{\beta}_2$ for time-invariant factors. Instead, it provides an estimate of $\boldsymbol{\beta}_3$, the effects of the time-varying factors. The between estimator can also provide estimates u_i for ν_i. More correctly, the estimator u_i is an estimator of $\nu_i + \mathbf{s}_i\boldsymbol{\beta}_2$. Thus, u_i is an estimator of ν_i only if there are no time-invariant variables in the model. If there are time-invariant variables, u_i is an estimate of ν_i plus the effects of the time-invariant variables.

Assessing goodness of fit

R^2 is a popular measure of goodness of fit in ordinary regression. In our case, given $\widehat{\alpha}$ and $\widehat{\beta}$ estimates of α and β, we can assess the goodness of fit with respect to equation (1), (2), or (3). The prediction equations are respectively

$$\widehat{y}_{it} = \widehat{\alpha} + \mathbf{x}_{it}\widehat{\beta} \tag{1'''}$$

$$\widehat{\overline{y}}_i = \widehat{\alpha} + \overline{\mathbf{x}}_i\widehat{\beta} \tag{2'''}$$

$$\widehat{\widetilde{y}}_{it} = (\widehat{y}_{it} - \widehat{\overline{y}}_i) = (\mathbf{x}_{it} - \overline{\mathbf{x}}_i)\widehat{\beta} \tag{3'''}$$

xtreg reports "R-squareds" corresponding to these three equations. R-squareds is in quotes because the R-squareds reported do not have all the properties of the OLS R^2.

The ordinary properties of R^2 include being equal to the squared correlation between $\widehat{y}$ and y and being equal to the fraction of the variation in y explained by $\widehat{y}$—formally defined as $\mathrm{Var}(\widehat{y})/\mathrm{Var}(y)$. The identity of the definitions is due to a special property of the OLS estimates; in general, given a prediction $\widehat{y}$ for y, the squared correlation is not equal to the ratio of the variances and the ratio of the variances is not required to be less than 1.

xtreg reports R^2 values calculated as correlations squared, calling them R^2 overall, corresponding to equation (1'''); R^2 between, corresponding to equation (2'''); and R^2 within, corresponding to equation (3'''). In fact, you can think of each of these three numbers as having all the properties of ordinary R^2s if you bear in mind that the prediction being judged is not $\widehat{y}_{it}$, $\widehat{\overline{y}}_i$, and $\widehat{\widetilde{y}}_{it}$, but $\gamma_1\widehat{y}_{it}$ from the regression $y_{it} = \gamma_1\widehat{y}_{it}$; $\gamma_2\widehat{\overline{y}}_i$ from the regression $\overline{y}_i = \gamma_2\widehat{\overline{y}}_i$; and $\gamma_3\widehat{\widetilde{y}}_{it}$ from $\widetilde{y}_{it} = \gamma_3\widehat{\widetilde{y}}_{it}$.

In particular, xtreg, be obtains its estimates by performing OLS on equation (2) and therefore its reported R^2 between is an ordinary R^2. The other two reported R^2s are merely correlations squared or, if you prefer, R^2s from the second-round regressions $y_{it} = \gamma_{11}\widehat{y}_{it}$ and $\widetilde{y}_{it} = \gamma_{13}\widehat{\widetilde{y}}_{it}$.

xtreg, fe obtains its estimates by performing OLS on equation (3) and so its reported R^2 within is an ordinary R^2. As with be, the other R^2s are correlations squared or, if you prefer, R^2s from the second-round regressions $\overline{y}_i = \gamma_{22}\widehat{\overline{y}}_i$ and, as with be, $\widetilde{y}_{it} = \gamma_{23}\widehat{\widetilde{y}}_{it}$.

xtreg, re obtains its estimates by performing OLS on equation (4); none of the R^2s corresponding to equations (1'''), (2'''), or (3''') corresponds directly to this estimator (the "relevant" R^2 is the one corresponding to equation (4)). All three reported R^2s are correlations squared or, if you prefer, from second-round regressions.

xtreg and associated commands

▷ Example

Using the nlswork dataset described in [R] xt, we will model ln_wage in terms of completed years of schooling (grade), current age and age squared, current years worked (experience) and experience squared, current years of tenure on the current job and tenure squared, whether black, whether resides in an area not designated an SMSA (standard metropolitan statistical area), and whether resides in the South. Most of these variables are in the data, but we need to construct a few:

```
. gen age2 = age^2
(24 missing values generated)
. gen ttl_exp2 = ttl_exp^2
```

```
. gen tenure2 = tenure^2
(433 missing values generated)
. gen byte black = race==2
```

To obtain the between-effects estimates, we use `xtreg, be`:

```
. xtreg ln_w grade age* ttl_exp* tenure* black not_smsa south, be
Between regression (regression on group means)   Number of obs      =       28091
Group variable (i) : idcode                      Number of groups   =        4697
R-sq:   within  = 0.1591                          Obs per group: min =           1
        between = 0.4900                                         avg =         6.0
        overall = 0.3695                                         max =          15
                                                 F(10,4686)         =      450.23
sd(u_i + avg(e_i.))=  .3036114                    Prob > F           =      0.0000
------------------------------------------------------------------------------
   ln_wage |      Coef.   Std. Err.      t    P>|t|     [95% Conf. Interval]
-----------+------------------------------------------------------------------
     grade |   .0607602   .0020006    30.372   0.000     .0568381    .0646822
       age |   .0323158   .0087251     3.704   0.000     .0152105    .0494211
      age2 |  -.0005997   .0001429    -4.195   0.000    -.0008799   -.0003194
   ttl_exp |   .0138853   .0056749     2.447   0.014     .0027598    .0250108
  ttl_exp2 |   .0007342   .0003267     2.247   0.025     .0000936    .0013747
    tenure |   .0698419   .0060729    11.501   0.000     .0579361    .0817476
   tenure2 |  -.0028756   .0004098    -7.017   0.000    -.0036789   -.0020722
     black |  -.0564167   .0105131    -5.366   0.000    -.0770272   -.0358061
  not_smsa |  -.1860406   .0112495   -16.538   0.000    -.2080949   -.1639862
     south |  -.0993378   .010136     -9.800   0.000    -.1192091   -.0794665
     _cons |   .3339112   .1210434     2.759   0.006     .0966092    .5712132
------------------------------------------------------------------------------
```

The between-effects regression is estimated on person averages, so it is the "n = 4697" that is relevant. `xtreg, be` reports the "number of observations" and group-size information; to wit: `describe` in [R] **xt** showed that we have 28,534 "observations"—person-years, really—of data. Taking the subsample that has no missing values in `ln_wage`, `grade`, ..., `south`, this leaves us with 28,091 observations on person-years, reflecting 4,697 persons each observed for an average of 5.98 years.

In terms of goodness of fit, it is the R^2 between that is directly relevant; our R^2 is .4900. If, however, we used these estimates to predict the within model, we have an R^2 of .1591. If we used these estimates to fit the overall data, our R^2 is .3695.

The F statistic is a test that the coefficients on the regressors `grade`, `age`, ..., `south` are all jointly zero. Our model is significant.

The root mean square error of the estimated regression, which is an estimate of the standard deviation of $\nu_i + \bar{\epsilon}_i$, is .3036.

In terms of our coefficients, we find that each year of schooling increases hourly wages by 6.1%; that age increases wages up to age 26.9 and thereafter decreases them (because quadratic $ax^2 + bx + c$ turns over at $x = -b/2a$, which for our `age` and `age2` coefficients is $.0323158/(2 \times .0005997) \approx 26.9$); that total experience increases wages at an increasing rate (which is surprising and bothersome); that tenure on the current job increases wages up to a tenure of 12.1 years and thereafter decreases them; that wages of blacks are, these things held constant, (approximately) 5.6% below that of nonblacks (approximately because `black` is an indicator variable); that residing in a nonSMSA (rural area) reduces wages by 18.6%; and that residing in the South reduces wages by 9.9%.

◁

▷ Example

To estimate the same model with the fixed-effects estimator, we specify the `fe` option.

```
. xtreg ln_w grade age* ttl_exp* tenure* black not_smsa south, fe
Fixed-effects (within) regression              Number of obs     =       28091
Group variable (i) : idcode                    Number of groups  =        4697

R-sq:  within  = 0.1727                         Obs per group: min =           1
       between = 0.3505                                        avg =         6.0
       overall = 0.2625                                        max =          15

                                                F(8,23386)        =      610.12
corr(u_i, Xb)  = 0.1936                          Prob > F          =      0.0000
```

ln_wage	Coef.	Std. Err.	t	P>|t|	[95% Conf. Interval]	
grade	(dropped)					
age	.0359987	.0033864	10.630	0.000	.0293611	.0426362
age2	-.000723	.0000533	-13.575	0.000	-.0008274	-.0006186
ttl_exp	.0334668	.0029653	11.286	0.000	.0276545	.039279
ttl_exp2	.0002163	.0001277	1.693	0.090	-.0000341	.0004666
tenure	.0357539	.0018487	19.340	0.000	.0321303	.0393775
tenure2	-.0019701	.000125	-15.762	0.000	-.0022151	-.0017251
black	(dropped)					
not_smsa	-.0890108	.0095316	-9.339	0.000	-.1076933	-.0703282
south	-.0606309	.0109319	-5.546	0.000	-.0820582	-.0392036
_cons	1.03732	.0485546	21.364	0.000	.9421496	1.13249

```
sigma_u |  .35562203
sigma_e |  .29068923
    rho |  .59946283   (fraction of variance due to u_i)
------------------------------------------------------------------------------
F test that all u_i=0:     F(4696,23386) =      5.13       Prob > F = 0.0000
```

The observation summary at the top is the same as for the between-effects model although this time it is the "Number of obs" that is relevant.

Our three R^2s are not too different from those reported previously; the R^2 within is slightly higher (.1727 vs .1591) and the R^2 between a little lower (.3505 vs .4900), which is as expected since the between estimator maximizes R^2 between and the within estimator R^2 within. In terms of overall fit, these estimates are somewhat worse (.2625 vs .3695).

`xtreg, fe` is able to provide estimates of σ_ν and σ_ϵ, although how you interpret these estimates depends on whether you are using `xtreg` to estimate a fixed-effects model or random-effects model. To clarify this fine point, in the fixed-effects model, ν_i are formally fixed—they have no distribution. If you subscribe to this view, think of the reported $\widehat\sigma_\nu$ as merely an arithmetic way to describe the range of the estimated but fixed ν_i. If, however, you are employing the fixed-effects estimator of the random-effects model—as is likely—then .355622 is an estimate of σ_ν, or it would be if there were no dropped variables in the estimation.

In our case, note that both `grade` and `black` were dropped from the model. They were dropped because they do not vary over time. Since `grade` and `race` are time-invariant, our estimate u_i is an estimate of ν_i plus the effects of `grade` and `race` and so our estimate of the standard deviation is based on the variation in ν_i, `grade`, and `race`. On the other hand, had `race` and `grade` been dropped merely because they were collinear with the other regressors in our model, u_i would be an estimate of ν_i and .3556 would be an estimate of σ_ν. (`xtsum` and `xttab` allow determining whether a variable is time-invariant; see [R] **xtsum** and [R] **xttab**.)

Regardless of the status of our estimator u_i, our estimate of the standard deviation of ϵ_{it} is valid (and, in fact, is the estimate that would be used by the random-effects estimator in producing its results).

Our estimate of the correlation of u_i with $\mathbf{x}_{it}$ suffers from the problem of what u_i measures. We find correlation, but whether this is correlation of ν_i with $\mathbf{x}_{it}$ or merely correlation of grade and race we cannot say. In any case, the fixed-effects estimator is robust to such correlation and the other estimates it produces are unbiased.

So, while this estimator produces no estimates of the effects of grade and race, it does predict that age has a positive effect on wages up to age 24.9 years (as compared with 26.9 years estimated by the between estimator); that total experience still increases wages at an increasing rate (which is still bothersome); that tenure increases wages up to 9.1 years (as compared with 12.1); that living in a nonSMSA reduces wages by 8.9% (as compared with a more drastic 18.6%); and that living in the South reduces wages by 6.1% (as compared with 9.9%).

◁

▷ Example

Reestimating our log-wage model with the random-effects estimator, we obtain

```
. xtreg ln_w grade age* ttl_exp* tenure* black not_smsa south, re
```

Random-effects GLS regression   Number of obs   =   28091
Group variable (i) : idcode   Number of groups   =   4697

R-sq: within   = 0.1715   Obs per group: min =   1
      between = 0.4784   avg =   6.0
      overall = 0.3708   max =   15

Random effects u_i ~ Gaussian   Wald chi2(10)   =   9244.74
corr(u_i, X)   = 0 (assumed)   Prob > chi2   =   0.0000

ln_wage	Coef.	Std. Err.	z	P>|z|	[95% Conf. Interval]	
grade	.0646499	.0017812	36.296	0.000	.0611589	.0681409
age	.0368059	.0031195	11.799	0.000	.0306918	.0429201
age2	-.0007133	.00005	-14.268	0.000	-.0008113	-.0006153
ttl_exp	.0290208	.002422	11.982	0.000	.0242739	.0337678
ttl_exp2	.0003049	.0001162	2.623	0.009	.000077	.0005327
tenure	.0392519	.0017554	22.360	0.000	.0358113	.0426925
tenure2	-.0020035	.0001193	-16.796	0.000	-.0022373	-.0017697
black	-.053053	.0099926	-5.309	0.000	-.0726381	-.0334679
not_smsa	-.1308252	.0071751	-18.233	0.000	-.1448881	-.1167622
south	-.0868922	.0073032	-11.898	0.000	-.1012062	-.0725781
_cons	.2387207	.049469	4.826	0.000	.1417633	.3356781
sigma_u	.25790526					
sigma_e	.29068923					
rho	.44045273	(fraction of variance due to u_i)				

According to the R^2s, this estimator performs worse within than the within/fixed-effects estimator and worse between than the between estimator, as it must, and slightly better overall.

We estimate that σ_ν is .2579 and σ_ϵ is .2907 and, by assertion, assume the correlation of ν and $\mathbf{x}$ is zero.

All that is known about the random-effects estimator is its asymptotic properties, so rather than reporting an F statistic for overall significance, xtreg, re reports a χ^2. Taken jointly, our coefficients are significant.

Also reported is a summary of the distribution of θ_i, an ingredient in the estimation of equation (4). θ is not a constant in this case because we observe women for unequal periods of time.

In terms of interpretation, we estimate that schooling has a rate of return of 6.5% (compared with 6.1% between and no estimate within); the increase of wages with age turns around at 25.8 years (compared with 26.9 between and 24.9 within); total experience yet again increases wages increasingly; the effect of job tenure turns around at 9.8 years (compared with 12.1 between and 9.1 within); being black reduces wages by 5.3% (compared with 5.6% within and no estimate between); living in a nonSMSA reduces wages 13.1% (compared with 18.6% between and 8.9% within); and living in the South reduces wages 8.7% (compared with 9.9% between and 6.1% within).

◁

▷ Example

Alternatively, we could have estimated this random-effects model using the maximum likelihood estimator:

```
. xtreg ln_w grade age* ttl_exp* tenure* black not_smsa south, mle

Fitting constant-only model:
Iteration 0:   log likelihood = -13690.161
Iteration 1:   log likelihood = -12819.317
Iteration 2:   log likelihood = -12662.039
Iteration 3:   log likelihood = -12649.744
Iteration 4:   log likelihood = -12649.614

Fitting full model:
Iteration 0:   log likelihood =  -8922.145
Iteration 1:   log likelihood = -8853.6409
Iteration 2:   log likelihood = -8853.4255
Iteration 3:   log likelihood = -8853.4254

Random-effects ML regression            Number of obs      =     28091
Group variable (i) : idcode             Number of groups   =      4697

Random effects u_i ~ Gaussian           Obs per group: min =         1
                                                       avg =       6.0
                                                       max =        15

                                        LR chi2(10)        =   7592.38
Log likelihood  = -8853.4254            Prob > chi2        =    0.0000
```

ln_wage	Coef.	Std. Err.	z	P>|z|	[95% Conf. Interval]	
grade	.0646093	.0017372	37.191	0.000	.0612044	.0680142
age	.0368531	.0031226	11.802	0.000	.030733	.0429732
age2	-.0007132	.0000501	-14.243	0.000	-.0008113	-.000615
ttl_exp	.0288196	.0024143	11.937	0.000	.0240877	.0335515
ttl_exp2	.000309	.0001163	2.657	0.008	.0000811	.0005369
tenure	.0394371	.0017604	22.402	0.000	.0359868	.0428875
tenure2	-.0020052	.0001195	-16.773	0.000	-.0022395	-.0017709
black	-.0533394	.0097338	-5.480	0.000	-.0724172	-.0342615
not_smsa	-.1323433	.0071322	-18.556	0.000	-.1463221	-.1183644
south	-.0875599	.0072143	-12.137	0.000	-.1016998	-.0734201
_cons	.2390837	.0491902	4.860	0.000	.1426727	.3354947
/sigma_u	.2485556	.0035017	70.982	0.000	.2416925	.2554187
/sigma_e	.2918458	.001352	215.869	0.000	.289196	.2944956
rho	.4204033	.0074828			.4057959	.4351212

```
Likelihood ratio test of sigma_u=0:  chi2(1) =  7339.84   Prob > chi2 = 0.0000
```

The estimates are very nearly the same as those produced by xtreg, re—the GLS estimator. For instance, xtreg, re estimated the coefficient on grade to be .0646499; xtreg, mle estimated .0646093; the ratio is .0646499/.0646093 = 1.001 to three decimal places. Similarly, the standard errors are nearly equal: .0017812/.0017372 = 1.025. Below we compare all 11 coefficients:

Estimator	Coefficient ratio			SE ratio		
	mean	min.	max.	mean	min.	max.
xtreg, mle (ML)	1.	1.	1.	1.	1.	1.
xtreg, re (GLS)	.997	.987	1.007	1.006	.997	1.027

◁

▷ Example

We could also have estimated this model using the population-averaged estimator:

```
. xtreg ln_w grade age* ttl_exp* tenure* black not_smsa south, i(idcode) pa
Iteration 1: tolerance = .03104898
Iteration 2: tolerance = .00074865
Iteration 3: tolerance = .00001469
Iteration 4: tolerance = 2.877e-07

GEE population-averaged model            Number of obs      =      28091
Group variable:                  idcode  Number of groups   =       4697
Link:                          identity  Obs per group: min =          1
Family:                        Gaussian                 avg =        6.0
Correlation:               exchangeable                 max =         15
                                         Wald chi2(10)      =    9595.07
Scale parameter:                .1437269  Prob > chi2       =     0.0000

------------------------------------------------------------------------------
 ln_wage |     Coef.   Std. Err.      z    P>|z|     [95% Conf. Interval]
---------+--------------------------------------------------------------------
   grade |   .0645425   .0016831    38.346   0.000     .0612436    .0678414
     age |   .0369323   .0031517    11.718   0.000      .030755    .0431096
    age2 |  -.0007129   .0000506   -14.094   0.000    -.0008121   -.0006138
 ttl_exp |   .0284866   .0024175    11.784   0.000     .0237485    .0332248
 ttl_exp2 |  .0003158   .0001173     2.693   0.007      .000086    .0005457
  tenure |   .0397479   .0017784    22.350   0.000     .0362623    .0432336
 tenure2 |   -.002008   .0001209   -16.609   0.000     -.002245   -.0017711
   black |  -.0538333   .0094097    -5.721   0.000    -.0722759   -.0353906
not_smsa |  -.1347875   .0070557   -19.103   0.000    -.1486165   -.1209585
   south |  -.0886005   .0071145   -12.453   0.000    -.1025448   -.0746563
   _cons |   .2396305   .0491577     4.875   0.000     .1432831    .3359779
------------------------------------------------------------------------------
```

These results differ from those produced by xtreg, re and xtreg, mle. Coefficients are larger and standard errors smaller. xtreg, pa is simply another way to run the xtgee command. That is, we would have obtained the same output had we typed

```
. xtgee ln_w grade age* ttl_exp* tenure* black not_smsa south, i(idcode)
(output omitted because it is the same as above )
```

See [R] **xtgee**. In the language of **xtgee**, the random-effects model corresponds to an **exchangeable** correlation structure and **identity** link, and **xtgee** has the advantage that it will allow other correlation structures as well. Let us stay with the random-effects model, however. **xtgee** will also produce robust estimates of variance, and we reestimated this model that way by typing

. xtgee ln_w grade age* ttl_exp* tenure* black not_smsa south, i(idcode) robust
(*output omitted, coefficients the same, standard errors different*)

In the previous example, we presented a table comparing **xtreg, re** with **xtreg, mle**. Below we add the results from the estimates shown and the ones we did with **xtgee, robust**:

Estimator		Coefficient ratio			SE ratio		
		mean	min.	max.	mean	min.	max.
~~xtreg, mle~~	~~(ML)~~	~~1.~~	~~1.~~	~~1.~~	~~1.~~	~~1.~~	~~1.~~
xtreg, re	(GLS)	.997	.987	1.007	1.006	.997	1.027
xtreg, pa	(PA)	1.060	.847	1.317	.853	.626	.986
xtgee, robust	(PA)	1.060	.847	1.317	1.306	.957	1.545

So which are right? This is real data and we do not know. However, in the example after the next we will present evidence that the assumptions underlying the **xtreg, re** and **xtreg, mle** results are not met. Our suspicion is that the **xtgee, robust** results are more correct because those standard errors do not hinge on the assumptions.

◁

▷ Example

After **xtreg, re** estimation, **xttest0** will report a test of $\nu_i = 0$ in case we had any doubts:

```
. xttest0
Breusch and Pagan Lagrangian multiplier test for random effects:
        ln_wage[idcode,t] = Xb + u[idcode] + e[idcode,t]
        Estimated results:
                           Var      sd = sqrt(Var)
                ---------+-----------------------------
            ln_wage |    .2283326       .4778416
                  e |    .0845002       .29068923
                  u |    .0665151       .25790526
    Test:   Var(u) = 0
                          chi2(1) =  14779.98
                          Prob>chi2 =     0.0000
```

◁

▷ Example

More importantly, after **xtreg, re** estimation, **xthaus** will perform the Hausman specification test. If our model is correctly specified and if ν_i is uncorrelated with $\mathbf{x}_{it}$, then the (subset of) coefficients that are estimated by the fixed-effects estimator and the same coefficients that are estimated here should not statistically differ:

```
. xthaus

Hausman specification test

                ---- Coefficients ----
            |     Fixed       Random
   ln_wage  |    Effects      Effects      Difference
------------+-------------------------------------------
       age  |   .0359987     .0368059       -.0008072
      age2  |   -.000723     -.0007133      -9.68e-06
   ttl_exp  |   .0334668     .0290208        .0044459
  ttl_exp2  |   .0002163     .0003049       -.0000886
    tenure  |   .0357539     .0392519        -.003498
   tenure2  |  -.0019701     -.0020035       .0000334
  not_smsa  |  -.0890108     -.1308252       .0418144
     south  |  -.0606309     -.0868922       .0262613

Test:  Ho:  difference in coefficients not systematic

            chi2( 8) = (b-B)'[S^(-1)](b-B), S = (S_fe - S_re)
                     =    149.43
             Prob>chi2 =     0.0000
```

We can reject the hypothesis that the coefficients are the same. Before turning to what this means, note that **xthaus** listed the coefficients estimated by the two models. It did not, however, list **grade** and **race**. **xthaus** did not make a mistake; in the Hausman test, one compares only the coefficients estimated by both techniques.

What does this mean? We have an unpleasant choice: we can admit that our model is misspecified—that we have not parameterized it correctly—or we can hold to our specification being correct, in which case the observed differences must be due to the zero-correlation of ν_i and $\mathbf{x}_{it}$ assumption.

◁

❑ Technical Note

We can also mechanically explore the underpinnings of the test's dissatisfaction. In the comparison table, note that it is the coefficients on **not_smsa** and **south** that exhibit the largest differences. In equation $(1')$, we showed how to decompose a model into within and between effects. Let us do that with these two variables, assuming that changes in the average have one effect while transitional changes have another:

```
. egen avgnsmsa = mean(not_smsa), by(id)

. gen devnsma = not_smsa - avgnsmsa
(8 missing values generated)

. egen avgsouth = mean(south), by(id)

. gen devsouth = south - avgsouth
(8 missing values generated)

. xtreg ln_w grade age* ttl_exp* tenure* black avgnsm devnsm avgsou devsou

Random-effects GLS regression            Number of obs      =     28091
Group variable (i) : idcode              Number of groups   =      4697

R-sq:  within  = 0.1723                   Obs per group: min =         1
       between = 0.4809                                  avg =       6.0
       overall = 0.3737                                  max =        15

Random effects u_i ~ Gaussian             Wald chi2(12)      =   9319.56
corr(u_i, X)       = 0 (assumed)          Prob > chi2        =    0.0000
```

ln_wage	Coef.	Std. Err.	z	P>|z|	[95% Conf. Interval]	
grade	.0631716	.0017903	35.285	0.000	.0596627	.0666805
age	.0375196	.0031186	12.031	0.000	.0314072	.043632
age2	-.0007248	.00005	-14.504	0.000	-.0008228	-.0006269
ttl_exp	.0286543	.0024207	11.837	0.000	.0239098	.0333989
ttl_exp2	.0003222	.0001162	2.773	0.006	.0000945	.0005499
tenure	.0394423	.001754	22.486	0.000	.0360044	.0428801
tenure2	-.0020081	.0001192	-16.850	0.000	-.0022417	-.0017746
black	-.0545936	.0102101	-5.347	0.000	-.074605	-.0345821
avgnsmsa	-.1833237	.0109339	-16.767	0.000	-.2047537	-.1618937
devnsma	-.0887596	.0095071	-9.336	0.000	-.1073931	-.070126
avgsouth	-.1011234	.0098789	-10.236	0.000	-.1204858	-.0817611
devsouth	-.0598538	.0109054	-5.488	0.000	-.081228	-.0384797
_cons	.2682987	.0495778	5.412	0.000	.171128	.3654694

sigma_u	.2579182	
sigma_e	.29068923	
rho	.44047745	(fraction of variance due to u_i)

We will leave the reinterpretation of this model to you except to note that if we were really going to sell this model, we would have to explain why the between and within effects are different. Focusing on residence in a nonSMSA, we might tell a story about rural folk being paid less and continuing to get paid less when they move to the SMSA. As such, however, it is just a story. Given our cross-sectional time-series data, we could create variables to measure this (an indicator for moved from nonSMSA to SMSA) and measure the effects. In our assessment of this model, we should think about women in the cities moving to the country and their relative productivity in a bucolic setting.

In any case, the Hausman test now is

```
. xthaus
```

Hausman specification test

	---- Coefficients ----		
ln_wage	Fixed Effects	Random Effects	Difference
age	.0359987	.0375196	-.0015209
age2	-.000723	-.0007248	1.84e-06
ttl_exp	.0334668	.0286543	.0048124
ttl_exp2	.0002163	.0003222	-.0001059
tenure	.0357539	.0394423	-.0036884
tenure2	-.0019701	-.0020081	.000038
devnsma	-.0890108	-.0887596	-.0002512
devsouth	-.0606309	-.0598538	-.0007771

Test: Ho: difference in coefficients not systematic

$$\text{chi2(8)} = (b-B)'[S^{(-1)}](b-B), S = (S\_fe - S\_re)$$
$$= 92.52$$
$$\text{Prob>chi2} = 0.0000$$

We have mechanically succeeded in greatly reducing the χ^2, but not by enough. The major differences now are in the age, experience, and tenure effects. We already knew this problem existed because of the ever-increasing effect of experience. More careful parameterization work needs to be done than simply including squares.

❏

Acknowledgments

We thank Richard Goldstein, who wrote the first draft of the routine that estimates random-effects regressions, and Badi Baltagi and Manuelita Ureta of Texas A&M University, who assisted us in working our way through the literature.

Saved Results

`xtreg, re` saves in `e()`:

Scalars

e(N)	number of observations	e(r2_o)	R-squared for overall model
e(N_g)	number of groups	e(r2_b)	R-squared for between model
e(df_m)	model degrees of freedom	e(sigma)	ancillary parameter (gamma, lnormal)
e(g_max)	largest group size	e(sigma_u)	panel-level standard deviation
e(g_min)	smallest group size	e(sigma_e)	standard deviation of ϵ_{it}
e(g_avg)	average group size	e(thta_min)	minimum θ
e(chi2)	χ^2	e(thta_5)	θ, 5th percentile
e(rho)	ρ	e(thta_50)	θ, 50th percentile
e(Tbar)	harmonic mean of group sizes	e(thta_95)	θ, 95th percentile
e(Tcon)	1 if T is constant	e(thta_max)	maximum θ
e(r2_w)	R-squared for within model		

Macros

e(cmd)	xtreg	e(ivar)	variable denoting groups
e(depvar)	name of dependent variable	e(chi2type)	Wald; type of model χ^2 test
e(model)	re	e(predict)	program used to implement predict

Matrices

e(b)	coefficient vector	e(Vf)	VCE for fixed-effects model
e(theta)	θ	e(bf)	coefficient vector for fixed-effects model
e(V)	variance–covariance matrix of the estimators		

Functions

e(sample)	marks estimation sample

(Continued on next page)

`xtreg, be` saves in `e()`:

Scalars

e(N)	number of observations	e(ll)	log likelihood
e(N_g)	number of groups	e(ll_0)	log likelihood, constant-only model
e(mss)	model sum of squares	e(g_max)	largest group size
e(df_m)	model degrees of freedom	e(g_min)	smallest group size
e(rss)	residual sum of squares	e(g_avg)	average group size
e(df_r)	residual degrees of freedom	e(Tbar)	harmonic mean of group sizes
e(r2)	R-squared	e(Tcon)	1 if T is constant
e(r2_a)	adjusted R-squared	e(r2_w)	R-squared for within model
e(F)	F statistic	e(r2_o)	R-squared for overall model
e(rmse)	root mean square error	e(r2_b)	R-squared for between model

Macros

e(cmd)	xtreg	e(ivar)	variable denoting groups
e(depvar)	name of dependent variable	e(predict)	program used to implement `predict`
e(model)	be		

Matrices

e(b)	coefficient vector	e(V)	variance–covariance matrix of the estimators

Functions

e(sample)	marks estimation sample

`xtreg, fe` saves in `e()`:

Scalars

e(N)	number of observations	e(g_max)	largest group size
e(N_g)	number of groups	e(g_min)	smallest group size
e(mss)	model sum of squares	e(g_avg)	average group size
e(tss)	total sum of squares	e(rho)	ρ
e(df_m)	model degrees of freedom	e(Tbar)	harmonic mean of group sizes
e(rss)	residual sum of squares	e(Tcon)	1 if T is constant
e(df_r)	residual degrees of freedom	e(r2_w)	R-squared for within model
e(r2)	R-squared	e(r2_o)	R-squared for overall model
e(r2_a)	adjusted R-squared	e(r2_b)	R-squared for between model
e(F)	F statistic	e(sigma)	ancillary parameter (gamma, lnormal)
e(rmse)	root mean square error	e(corr)	corr(u_i, Xb)
e(ll)	log likelihood	e(sigma_u)	panel-level standard deviation
e(ll_0)	log likelihood, constant-only model	e(sigma_e)	standard deviation of ϵ_{it}
e(df_a)	degrees of freedom for absorbed effect	e(F_f)	F for $u_i=0$

Macros

e(cmd)	xtreg	e(ivar)	variable denoting groups
e(depvar)	name of dependent variable	e(predict)	program used to implement `predict`
e(model)	fe		

Matrices

e(b)	coefficient vector	e(V)	variance–covariance matrix of the estimators

Functions

e(sample)	marks estimation sample

xtreg, mle saves in e():

Scalars

e(N)	number of observations	e(g_min)	smallest group size
e(N_g)	number of groups	e(g_avg)	average group size
e(df_m)	model degrees of freedom	e(chi2)	χ^2
e(ll)	log likelihood	e(chi2_c)	χ^2 for comparison test
e(ll_0)	log likelihood, constant-only model	e(rho)	ρ
e(ll_c)	log likelihood, comparison model	e(sigma_u)	panel-level standard deviation
e(g_max)	largest group size	e(sigma_e)	standard deviation of ϵ_{it}

Macros

e(cmd)	xtreg	e(wexp)	weight expression
e(depvar)	name of dependent variable	e(chi2type)	Wald or LR; type of model χ^2 test
e(title)	title in estimation output	e(chi2_ct)	Wald or LR; type of model χ^2 test
e(model)	ml		corresponding to e(chi2_c)
e(ivar)	variable denoting groups	e(distrib)	Gaussian; the distribution of the re
e(wtype)	weight type	e(predict)	program used to implement predict

Matrices

e(b)	coefficient vector	e(V)	variance–covariance matrix of the estimators

Functions

e(sample)	marks estimation sample

xtreg, pa saves in e():

Scalars

e(N)	number of observations	e(deviance)	deviance
e(N_g)	number of groups	e(chi2_dev)	χ^2 test of deviance
e(df_m)	model degrees of freedom	e(dispers)	deviance dispersion
e(g_max)	largest group size	e(chi2_dis)	χ^2 test of deviance dispersion
e(g_min)	smallest group size	e(tol)	target tolerance
e(g_avg)	average group size	e(dif)	achieved tolerance
e(chi2)	χ^2	e(phi)	scale parameter
e(df_pear)	degrees of freedom for Pearson χ^2		

Macros

e(cmd)	xtgee	e(scale)	x2, dev, phi, or #; scale parameter
e(cmd2)	xtreg	e(ivar)	variable denoting groups
e(depvar)	name of dependent variable	e(vcetype)	covariance estimation method
e(model)	pa	e(chi2type)	Wald; type of model χ^2 test
e(family)	Gaussian	e(disp)	deviance dispersion
e(link)	identity; link function	e(offset)	offset
e(corr)	correlation structure	e(predict)	program used to implement predict

Matrices

e(b)	coefficient vector	e(V)	variance–covariance matrix of the estimators
e(R)	estimated working correlation matrix		

Functions

e(sample)	marks estimation sample

Methods and Formulas

The model to be estimated is

$$y_{it} = \alpha + \mathbf{x}_{it}\boldsymbol{\beta} + \nu_i + \epsilon_{it}$$

for $i = 1, \ldots, n$ and, for each i, $t = 1, \ldots, T$, of which T_i periods are actually observed.

xtreg, fe

`xtreg, fe` produces estimates by running OLS on

$$(y_{it} - \overline{y}_i + \overline{\overline{y}}) = \alpha + (\mathbf{x}_{it} - \overline{\mathbf{x}}_i + \overline{\overline{\mathbf{x}}})\boldsymbol{\beta} + [\epsilon_{it} - \overline{\epsilon}_i + \overline{\nu}] + \overline{\overline{\epsilon}}$$

where $\overline{y}_i = \sum_{t=1}^{T_i} y_{it}/T_i$, and similarly, $\overline{\overline{y}} = \sum_i \sum_t y_{it}/(nT_i)$. The covariance matrix of the estimators is adjusted for the extra $n - 1$ estimated means, so results are the same as using OLS on equation (1) to estimate ν_i directly.

From the estimates $\widehat{\alpha}$ and $\widehat{\boldsymbol{\beta}}$, estimates u_i of ν_i are obtained as $u_i = \overline{y}_i - \widehat{\alpha} - \overline{\mathbf{x}}_i\widehat{\boldsymbol{\beta}}$. Reported from the calculated u_i is its standard deviation and its correlation with $\overline{\mathbf{x}}_i\widehat{\boldsymbol{\beta}}$. Reported as the standard deviation of e_{it} is the regression's estimated root mean square error, s^2, which is adjusted (as previously stated) for the $n - 1$ estimated means.

Reported as R^2 within is the R^2 from the mean-deviated regression.

Reported as R^2 between is $\mathrm{corr}(\overline{\mathbf{x}}_i\widehat{\boldsymbol{\beta}}, \overline{y}_i)^2$.

Reported as R^2 overall is $\mathrm{corr}(\mathbf{x}_{it}\widehat{\boldsymbol{\beta}}, y_{it})^2$.

xtreg, be

`xtreg, be` estimates the model:

$$\overline{y}_i = \alpha + \overline{\mathbf{x}}_i\boldsymbol{\beta} + \nu_i + \overline{\epsilon}_i$$

Estimation is via OLS unless T_i is not constant and the `wls` option is specified. Otherwise, the estimation is performed via WLS. The estimation is performed by `regress` for both cases, but in the case of WLS, `[aweight=`T_i`]` is specified.

Reported as R^2 between is the R^2 from the estimated regression.

Reported as R^2 within is $\mathrm{corr}\left((\mathbf{x}_{it} - \overline{\mathbf{x}}_i)\widehat{\boldsymbol{\beta}}, y_{it} - \overline{y}_i\right)^2$.

Reported as R^2 overall is $\mathrm{corr}(\mathbf{x}_{it}\widehat{\boldsymbol{\beta}}, y_{it})^2$.

xtreg, re

First, a fixed-effects model is estimated via `xtreg, fe`. Let $(a_f, \mathbf{b}_f)$ be the estimated coefficients; $\mathbf{V}_f$, the estimated covariance matrix; and s_f^2, the estimated mean square error. s_f^2 is an estimate of σ_ϵ^2, so define $s_e^2 = s_f^2$.

Second, a model on averages over time, $\overline{y}_i = \alpha + \overline{\mathbf{x}}_i\boldsymbol{\beta} + (\nu_i + \overline{\epsilon}_i)$, is estimated via OLS. Note that the variance of the combined residual $\mathrm{Var}(\nu_i + \overline{\epsilon}_i) = \sigma_\nu^2 + T_i\sigma_\epsilon^2$ is not constant in unbalanced data. Regardless, the mean square error s_*^2 provides a consistent estimate of $\sigma_\nu^2 + \overline{T}\sigma_\epsilon^2$, where (the harmonic mean) $\overline{T} = n/\sum_i(1/T_i)$. Whether T_i varies or not, s_u^2, an estimate of σ_ν^2, is calculated as

$$s_u^2 = \max\left(0, s_*^2 - \frac{s_e^2}{\overline{T}}\right)$$

Note the use of $\overline{T}$ in the denominator. The quantity

$$\widehat{\theta}_i = 1 - \sqrt{\frac{s_e^2}{T_i s_u^2 + s_e^2}}$$

is calculated and then the regression

$$(y_{it} - \widehat{\theta}_i \overline{y}_i) = \alpha(1 - \widehat{\theta}_i) + (\mathbf{x}_{it} - \widehat{\theta}_i \overline{\mathbf{x}}_i)\boldsymbol{\beta} + [(1 - \widehat{\theta}_i)u_i + e_{it} - \widehat{\theta}_i \overline{e}_i]$$

is estimated via OLS. If the data is balanced, θ_i does not vary with i and the equation reduces to the form given by Hausman (1978). The generalization for unbalanced data is due to Baltagi (1985).

The estimated coefficients $(a_r, \mathbf{b}_r)$ and their covariance matrix $\mathbf{V}_r$ are reported together with the previously calculated quantities s_e and s_u. The standard deviation of $u_i + e_{it}$ is calculated as $\sqrt{s_e^2 + s_u^2}$.

Reported as R^2 between is $\mathrm{corr}(\overline{\mathbf{x}}_i \widehat{\boldsymbol{\beta}}, \overline{y}_i)^2$.

Reported as R^2 within is $\mathrm{corr}\big((\mathbf{x}_{it} - \overline{\mathbf{x}}_i)\widehat{\boldsymbol{\beta}}, y_{it} - \overline{y}_i\big)^2$.

Reported as R^2 overall is $\mathrm{corr}(\mathbf{x}_{it}\widehat{\boldsymbol{\beta}}, y_{it})^2$.

xtreg, mle

The log likelihood for the ith unit is

$$l_i = -\frac{1}{2}\left\{\frac{1}{\sigma_e^2}\left[\sum_{t=1}^{T_i}(y_{it} - \mathbf{x}_{it}\boldsymbol{\beta})^2 - \frac{\sigma_u^2}{T_i\sigma_u^2 + \sigma_e^2}\left(\sum_{t=1}^{T_i}(y_{it} - \mathbf{x}_{it}\boldsymbol{\beta})\right)^2\right]\right.$$
$$\left. + \ln\left(T_i\frac{\sigma_u^2}{\sigma_e^2} + 1\right) + T_i\ln(2\pi\sigma_e^2)\right\}$$

The mle and re options yield essentially the same results except when total $N = \sum_i T_i$ is small (200 or less) and the data is unbalanced.

xtreg, pa

See [R] xtgee for details on the methods and formulas used to calculate the population-averaged model using a generalized estimating equations approach.

xttest0

xttest0 reports the Lagrange multiplier test for random effects developed by Breusch and Pagan (1980) and as modified by Baltagi and Li (1990). The model

$$y_{it} = \alpha + \mathbf{x}_{it}\boldsymbol{\beta} + \nu_{it}$$

is estimated via OLS and then the quantity

$$\lambda_{\mathrm{LM}} = \frac{(n\overline{T})^2}{2}\left(\frac{A_1^2}{(\sum_i T_i^2) - n\overline{T}}\right)$$

calculated, where

$$A_1 = 1 - \frac{\sum_{i=1}^{n}(\sum_{t=1}^{T_i} v_{it})^2}{\sum_i \sum_t v_{it}^2}$$

The Baltagi and Li modification allows for unbalanced data and reduces to the standard formula

$$\lambda_{\text{LM}} = \frac{nT}{2(T-1)} \left(\frac{\sum_i (\sum_t v_{it})^2}{\sum_i \sum_t v_{it}^2} - 1 \right)^2$$

when $T_i = T$ (balanced data). Under the null hypothesis, λ_{LM} is distributed $\chi^2(1)$.

xthaus

xthaus reports Hausman's (1978) specification test. This test is formally a test of the equality of the coefficients estimated by the fixed- and random-effects estimators. If the coefficients differ significantly, either the model is misspecified or the assumption that the random effects v_i are uncorrelated with the regressors $\mathbf{x}_{it}$ is incorrect. Thus, under the assumption of a correctly specified model, Hausman's test examines the appropriateness of the random-effects estimator; see Greene (1997, 443–444) and Judge et al. (1985, 527). The test statistic is

$$W = (\boldsymbol{\beta}_f - \boldsymbol{\beta}_r)'(\mathbf{V}_f - \mathbf{V}_r)^{-1}(\boldsymbol{\beta}_f - \boldsymbol{\beta}_r)$$

where all vectors and matrices have the row and column corresponding to the intercept removed along with any row and column corresponding to a parameter that cannot be estimated by the fixed-effects estimator (regressors that are constant over time). Under the null hypothesis, W is distributed $\chi^2(k)$, where k is the number of estimated coefficients in $\boldsymbol{\beta}$ excluding the intercept and time-invariant regressors.

References

Baltagi, B. H. 1985. Pooling cross-sections with unequal time-series lengths. *Economics Letters* 18: 133–136.

——. 1995. *Econometric Analysis of Panel Data*. New York: John Wiley & Sons.

Baltagi, B. H. and Qi Li. 1990. A Lagrange multiplier test for the error components model with incomplete panels. *Econometric Reviews* 9(1): 103–107.

Breusch, T. and A. Pagan. 1980. The Lagrange multiplier test and its applications to model specification in econometrics. *Review of Economic Studies* 47: 239–253.

Dwyer, J. and M. Feinleib. 1992. Introduction to statistical models for longitudinal observation. In *Statistical Models for Longitudinal Studies of Health*, ed. J. Dwyer, M. Feinleib, P. Lippert, and H. Hoffmeister, 3–48. New York: Oxford University Press.

Greene, W. H. 1983. Simultaneous estimation of factor substitution, economies of scale, and non-neutral technical change. In *Econometric Analyses of Productivity*, ed. A. Dogramaci. Boston: Kluwer-Nijhoff.

——. 1997. *Econometric Analysis*. 3d ed. Upper Saddle River, NJ: Prentice–Hall.

Hausman, J. A. 1978. Specification tests in econometrics. *Econometrica* 46: 1251–1271.

Judge, G. G., W. E. Griffiths, R. C. Hill, H. Lütkepohl, and T.-C. Lee. 1985. *The Theory and Practice of Econometrics*. 2d ed. New York: John Wiley & Sons.

Lee, L. and W. Griffiths. 1979. The prior likelihood and best linear unbiased prediction in stochastic coefficient linear models. University of New England Working Papers in Econometrics and Applied Statistics No. 1, Armidale, Australia.

Taub, A. J. 1979. Prediction in the context of the variance-components model. *Journal of Econometrics* 10: 103–108.

Also See

Complementary:	[R] **lincom**, [R] **predict**, [R] **test**, [R] **testnl**, [R] **vce**, [R] **xtdata**, [R] **xtdes**, [R] **xtsum**, [R] **xttab**
Related:	[R] **xtgee**, [R] **xtintreg**, [R] **xttobit**
Background:	[U] **16.5 Accessing coefficients and standard errors**, [U] **23 Estimation and post-estimation commands**, [R] **xt**

Title

xtsum — Summarize xt data

Syntax

xtsum [*varlist*] [if *exp*] [, i(*varname*)]

Description

xtsum, a generalization of summarize, reports means and standard deviations for cross-sectional time-series (xt) data; it differs from summarize in that it decomposes the standard deviation into between and within components.

Options

i(*varname*) specifies the variable name that contains the unit to which the observation belongs. You can specify the i() option the first time you estimate or use the iis command to set i() beforehand. After that, Stata will remember the variable's identity. See [R] xt.

Remarks

If you have not read [R] xt, please do so.

xtsum provides an alternative to summarize. For instance, in the nlswork dataset described in [R] xt, hours contains the number of hours worked last week:

```
. summarize hours

Variable |     Obs      Mean   Std. Dev.       Min        Max
---------+-----------------------------------------------------
   hours |   28467   36.55956   9.869623         1        168

. xtsum hours

Variable          |     Mean   Std. Dev.       Min        Max |   Observations
------------------+-----------------------------------------------+----------------
hours     overall |  36.55956   9.869623         1        168 |   N =    28467
          between |             7.846585         1       83.5 |   n =     4710
          within  |             7.520712  -2.154726   130.0596 |   T-bar = 6.04395
```

xtsum provides the same information as summarize and more. It decomposes the variable x_{it} into a between ($\bar{x}_i$) and within ($x_{it} - \bar{x}_i + \bar{\bar{x}}$; the global mean $\bar{\bar{x}}$ being added back in make results comparable). The overall and within are calculated over 28,467 person-years of data. The between is calculated over 4,710 persons. And, for your information, the average number of years a person was observed in the hours data is 6.

xtsum also reports minimums and maximums: Hours worked last week varied between 1 and (unbelievably) 168. Average hours worked last week for each woman varied between 1 and 83.5. "Hours worked within" varied between −2.15 and 130.1, which is not to say any woman actually worked negative hours. The within number refers to deviation from each individual's average and naturally, some of those deviations must be negative. In that case, it is not the negative value that is disturbing but the positive value. Did some woman really deviate from her average by +130.1 hours? No; in our definition of within, we add back in the global average of 36.6 hours. Some woman did deviate from her average by 130.1 − 36.6 = 93.5 hours, which is still quite large.

The reported standard deviations tell us something that may surprise you. They say that the variation in hours worked last week across women is very nearly equal to that observed within a woman over time. That is, if you were to draw two women randomly from our data, the difference in hours worked is expected to be nearly equal to the difference for the same woman in two randomly selected years.

If a variable does not vary over time, its within standard deviation will be zero:

```
. xtsum birth_yr
Variable         |      Mean   Std. Dev.       Min        Max |    Observations
-----------------+--------------------------------------------+----------------
birth_yr overall |  48.08509   3.012837         41         54 |   N =    28534
         between |             3.051795         41         54 |   n =     4711
         within  |                    0   48.08509   48.08509 | T-bar = 6.05689
```

Also See

Related: [R] **xtdes**, [R] **xttab**

Background: [R] **xt**

Title

> **xttab** — Tabulate xt data

Syntax

xttab *varname* [if *exp*] [, i(*varname$_i$*)]

xttrans *varname* [if *exp*] [, i(*varname$_i$*) t(*varname$_t$*) freq]

Description

xttab, a generalization of tabulate, performs one-way tabulations and decomposes counts into between and within components in cross-sectional time-series (xt) data.

xttrans, another generalization of tabulate, reports transition probabilities (the change in a single categorical variable over time).

Options

i(*varname$_i$*) specifies the variable name that contains the unit to which the observation belongs. You can specify the i() option the first time you estimate or use the iis command to set i() beforehand. After that, Stata will remember the variable's identity. See [R] **xt**.

t(*varname$_t$*) specifies the variable that contains the time at which the observation was made. You can specify the t() option the first time you estimate or use the tis command to set t() beforehand. After that, Stata will remember the variable's identity. See [R] **xt**.

freq, allowed with xttrans only, specifies that frequencies as well as transition probabilities are to be displayed.

Remarks

If you have not read [R] **xt**, please do so.

▷ Example

Using the nlswork dataset described in [R] **xt**, variable msp is 1 if a woman is married and her spouse resides with her and 0 otherwise:

```
. xttab msp
```

| | Overall | | Between | | Within |
msp	Freq.	Percent	Freq.	Percent	Percent
0	11324	39.71	3113	66.08	55.06
1	17194	60.29	3643	77.33	71.90
Total	28518	100.00	6756	143.41	64.14

(n = 4711)

443

The overall part of the table summarizes results in terms of person-years. We have 11,324 person-years of data in which msp is 0 and 17,194 in which it is 1—in 60.3% of our data the woman is married with her spouse present. Between repeats the breakdown, but this time in terms of women rather than woman-years: 3,113 of our women ever had msp 0 and 3,643 ever had msp 1, for a grand total of 6,756 as ever having either. We have in our data, however, only 4,711 women. This means there are women who sometimes have msp 0 and at other times, msp 1.

The within percent tells us the fraction of the time a woman has the specified value of msp. Taking the first line, conditional on a woman ever having a value of msp 0, 55.1% of her observations have msp 0. Similarly, conditional on a woman ever having msp 1, 71.9% of her observations have msp 1. These two numbers are a measure of the stability of the msp values and, in fact, msp 1 is more stable among these younger women than msp 0, meaning that they tend to marry more than they divorce. The total within of 64.14 percent is the normalized between weighted average of the within percents, to wit: $(3113 \times 55.06 + 3643 \times 71.90)/6756$. It is a measure of the overall stability of the msp variable.

A time-invariant variable will have a tabulation with within percents of 100:

```
. xttab race

             Overall              Between           Within
   race |   Freq.   Percent     Freq.  Percent      Percent
--------+----------------------------------------------------
      1 |   20180    70.72       3329    70.66       100.00
      2 |    8051    28.22       1325    28.13       100.00
      3 |     303     1.06         57     1.21       100.00
--------+----------------------------------------------------
  Total |   28534   100.00       4711   100.00       100.00
                              (n = 4711)
```

▷ Example

xttrans shows the transition probabilities. In cross-sectional time-series data, one can estimate the probability that $x_{i,t+1} = v_2$ given that $x_{it} = v_1$ by counting transitions. For instance:

```
. xttrans msp
     1 if |
  married, | 1 if married, spouse
   spouse |       present
  present |      0         1 |    Total
----------+---------------------+----------
        0 |   80.49     19.51 |   100.00
        1 |    7.96     92.04 |   100.00
----------+---------------------+----------
    Total |   37.11     62.89 |   100.00
```

The rows reflect the initial values and the columns reflect the final values. Each year, some 80% of the msp 0 persons in the data remained msp 0 in the next year; the remaining 20% became msp 1. While msp 0 had a 20% chance of becoming msp 1 in each year, the msp 1 had only an 8% chance of becoming (or returning to) msp 0. The freq option displays the frequencies that go into the calculation:

```
. xttrans msp, freq

     1 if |
  married, | 1 if married, spouse
    spouse |       present
   present |       0          1 |    Total
-----------+----------------------+----------
         0 |    7697       1866 |     9563
           |   80.49      19.51 |   100.00
-----------+----------------------+----------
         1 |    1133      13100 |    14233
           |    7.96      92.04 |   100.00
-----------+----------------------+----------
     Total |    8830      14966 |    23796
           |   37.11      62.89 |   100.00
```

◁

❑ Technical Note

The transition probabilities reported by **xttrans** are not necessarily the transition probabilities in a Markov sense. **xttrans** counts transition from one observation to the next once the observations have been put in t order within i. It does not normalize for missing time periods. **xttrans** does pay attention to missing values of the variable being tabulated, however, and does not count transitions from nonmissing to missing and missing to nonmissing. Thus, if the data is fully rectangularized, **xttrans** does produce (inefficient) estimates of the Markov transition matrix. **fillin** will rectangularize datasets; see [R] **fillin**. Thus, the Markov transition matrix could be estimated by typing

```
. fillin idcode year
. xttrans msp
```

❑

Also See

Related: [R] **xtdes**, [R] **xtsum**

Background: [R] **xt**

Title

> **xttobit** — Random-effects tobit models

Syntax

Random-effects model

> xttobit *depvar* [*varlist*] [*weight*] [*if exp*] [*in range*] [, i(*varname*) quad(*#*)
>
> noconstant noskip level(*#*) offset(*varname*) ll(*varname* | *#*) ul(*varname* | *#*)
>
> tobit *maximize_options*]

iweights are allowed; see [U] **14.1.6 weight**. Note that weights must be constant within panels.

xttobit shares the features of all estimation commands; see [U] **23 Estimation and post-estimation commands**.

Syntax for predict

> predict [*type*] *newvarname* [*if exp*] [*in range*] [, { xb | stdp } nooffset]

These statistics are available both in and out of sample; type predict ... if e(sample) ... if wanted only for the estimation sample.

Description

xttobit estimates random-effects tobit models. There is no command for conditional fixed-effects model as there does not exist a sufficient statistic allowing the fixed effects to be conditioned out of the likelihood. Unconditional fixed-effects tobit models may be estimated with the tobit command with indicator variables for the panels. The appropriate indicator variables can be generated using tabulate or xi. However, unconditional fixed-effects estimates are biased.

Note: xttobit is slow since it is calculated by quadrature; see *Methods and Formulas*. Computation time is roughly proportional to the number of points used for the quadrature. The default is quad(12). Simulations indicate that increasing it does not appreciably change the estimates for the coefficients or their standard errors. See [R] **quadchk**.

Options

i(*varname*) specifies the variable name that contains the unit to which the observation belongs. You can specify the i() option the first time you estimate or use the iis command to set i() beforehand. After that, Stata will remember the variable's identity. See [R] **xt**.

quad(*#*) specifies the number of points to use in the quadrature approximation of the integral.

The default is quad(12). The number specified must be an integer between 4 and 30, and also be no greater than the number of observations.

noconstant suppresses the constant term (intercept) in the model.

noskip specifies that a full maximum-likelihood model with only a constant for the regression equation be estimated. This model is not displayed but is used as the base model to compute a likelihood-ratio test for the model test statistic displayed in the estimation header. By default, the overall model test statistic is an asymptotically equivalent Wald test of all the parameters in the regression equation being zero (except the constant). For many models, this option can significantly increase estimation time.

level(#) specifies the confidence level, in percent, for confidence intervals. The default is level(95) or as set by set level; see [U] **23.5 Specifying the width of confidence intervals**.

offset(*varname*) specifies that *varname* is to be included in the model with coefficient constrained to be 1.

ll(*varname*|#) and ul(*varname*|#) indicate the censoring points. You may specify one or both. ll() indicates the lower limit for left censoring. Observations with *depvar* ≤ ll() are left-censored; observations with *depvar* ≥ ul() are right-censored; remaining observations are not censored. See [R] **tobit** for a more detailed description.

tobit specifies that a likelihood-ratio test comparing the random-effects model with the pooled (tobit) model should be included in the output. By default, a Wald test is included.

maximize_options control the maximization process; see [R] **maximize**. Use the trace option to view parameter convergence. Use the ltol(#) option to relax the convergence criterion; default is 1e−6 during specification searches.

Options for predict

xb, the default, calculates the linear prediction.

stdp calculates the standard error of the linear prediction.

nooffset is relevant only if you specified offset(*varname*) for xttobit. It modifies the calculations made by predict so that they ignore the offset variable; the linear prediction is treated as $x_{it}b$ rather than $x_{it}b + \text{offset}_{it}$.

Remarks

▷ Example

Using the nlswork data described in [R] **xt**, we estimate a random-effects tobit model of adjusted (log) wages. We use the ul() option to impose an upper limit on the recorded log of wages.

(*Continued on next page*)

```
. xttobit ln_wage union age grade not_smsa south southXt occ_code, i(id) ul(1.9)
> nolog tobit

Random-effects tobit regression              Number of obs      =       19151
Group variable (i) : idcode                  Number of groups   =        4140

Random effects u_i ~ Gaussian                Obs per group: min =           1
                                                            avg =         4.6
                                                            max =          12

                                             LR chi2(7)         =     3128.23
Log likelihood  = -6665.7878                 Prob > chi2        =      0.0000

------------------------------------------------------------------------------
     ln_wage |     Coef.   Std. Err.      z    P>|z|     [95% Conf. Interval]
-------------+----------------------------------------------------------------
       union |  .1539529   .0069077    22.287   0.000     .140414    .1674918
         age |  .0086198   .0005423    15.895   0.000    .0075569    .0096826
       grade |  .0789552   .0022067    35.780   0.000    .0746303    .0832802
    not_smsa | -.1269592     .00889   -14.281   0.000   -.1443833    -.109535
       south | -.1182003   .0120556    -9.805   0.000   -.1418287   -.0945718
     southXt |  .0031335   .0008385     3.737   0.000    .0014901    .0047769
    occ_code |  -.018946   .0010936   -17.325   0.000   -.0210894   -.0168026
       _cons |  .5596518   .0332332    16.840   0.000    .4945159    .6247877
-------------+----------------------------------------------------------------
     /sigma_u |  .2838666   .0043967    64.563   0.000    .2752492     .292484
     /sigma_e |  .2495757   .0018144   137.553   0.000    .2460196    .2531319
-------------+----------------------------------------------------------------
         rho |  .5640177   .0082238                       .5478505    .5800786
------------------------------------------------------------------------------
Likelihood ratio test of sigma_u=0:  chi2(1) =  5921.31   Prob > chi2 = 0.0000
```

```
        Obs. summary:     12288 uncensored observations
                              0 left-censored observations
                           6863 right-censored observations
```

Note: 31 completely determined observations

The output includes the overall and panel-level variance components (labeled `sigma_e` and `sigma_u`, respectively) together with ρ (labeled `rho`)

$$\rho = \frac{\sigma_\nu^2}{\sigma_\epsilon^2 + \sigma_\nu^2}$$

which is the percent contribution to the total variance of the panel-level variance component.

When `rho` is zero, the panel-level variance component is unimportant and the panel estimator is not different from the pooled estimator. A likelihood ratio test of this is included at the bottom of the output. This test formally compares the pooled estimator (tobit) with the panel estimator.

◁

❑ Technical Note

The random-effects model is calculated using quadrature. As the panel sizes (or ρ) increase, the quadrature approximation becomes less accurate. We can use the `quadchk` command to see if changing the number of quadrature points affects the results. If the results do change, then the quadrature approximation is not accurate and the results of the model should not be interpreted. See [R] **quadchk** for details and [R] **xtprobit** for an example.

❑

Saved Results

xttobit saves in e():

Scalars

e(N)	number of observations	e(g_min)	smallest group size
e(N_g)	number of groups	e(g_avg)	average group size
e(N_unc)	number of uncensored observations	e(chi2)	χ^2
e(N_lc)	number of left-censored observations	e(chi2_c)	χ^2 for comparison test
e(N_rc)	number of right-censored observations	e(rho)	ρ
e(df_m)	model degrees of freedom	e(sigma_u)	panel-level standard deviation
e(ll)	log likelihood	e(sigma_e)	standard deviation of ϵ_{it}
e(ll_0)	log likelihood, constant-only model	e(N_cd)	number of completely determined obs.
e(ll_c)	log likelihood, comparison model	e(n_quad)	number of quadrature points
e(g_max)	largest group size		

Macros

e(cmd)	xttobit	e(chi2type)	Wald or LR; type of model χ^2 test
e(depvar)	name of dependent variable	e(chi2_ct)	Wald or LR; type of model χ^2 test
e(title)	title in estimation output		corresponding to e(chi2_c)
e(ivar)	variable denoting groups	e(distrib)	Gaussian; the distribution of the
e(wtype)	weight type		random effect
e(wexp)	weight expression	e(predict)	program used to implement predict
e(offset)	offset		

Matrices

e(b)	coefficient vector	e(V)	variance–covariance matrix of the estimators

Functions

e(sample)	marks estimation sample

Methods and Formulas

xttobit is implemented as an ado-file.

Assuming a normal distribution, $N(0, \sigma_\nu^2)$, for the random effects ν_i, we have that

$$\Pr(y_i | x_i) = \int_{-\infty}^{\infty} \frac{e^{-\nu_i^2/2\sigma_\nu^2}}{\sqrt{2\pi}\sigma_\nu} \left[\prod_{t=1}^{n_i} F(x_{it}\beta + \nu_i) \right] d\nu_i$$

where

$$F(\Delta_{it}) = \begin{cases} \left(-1/\sqrt{2\pi\sigma_\epsilon^2} \right) e^{-(y_{it} - \Delta_{it})^2/(2\sigma_\epsilon^2)} & \text{if } y_{it} \in C \\ \Phi\left(\frac{y_{it} - \Delta_{it}}{\sigma_\epsilon} \right) & \text{if } y_{it} \in L \\ 1 - \Phi\left(\frac{y_{it} - \Delta_{it}}{\sigma_\epsilon} \right) & \text{if } y_{it} \in R \end{cases}$$

where C is the set of noncensored observations, L is the set of left-censored observations, R is the set of right-censored observations, and $\Phi()$ is the cumulative normal distribution. We can approximate the integral with M-point Gauss–Hermite quadrature

$$\int_{-\infty}^{\infty} e^{-x^2} f(x) dx \approx \sum_{m=1}^{M} w_m^* f(a_m^*)$$

where the w_m^* denote the quadrature weights and the a_m^* denote the quadrature abscissas. The log-likelihood L where $\rho = \sigma_\nu^2/(\sigma_\epsilon^2 + \sigma_\nu^2)$ is then calculated using the quadrature

$$L = \sum_{i=1}^{n} w_i \log\Big(\Pr(y_i|x_i)\Big)$$

$$\approx \sum_{i=1}^{n} w_i \log \frac{1}{\sqrt{\pi}} \sum_{m=1}^{M} w_m^* \prod_{t=1}^{n_i} F\left(x_{it}\beta + \sqrt{2\frac{\rho}{1-\rho}}\, a_m^*\right)$$

The quadrature formula requires that the integrated function be well-approximated by a polynomial. As the number of time periods becomes large (as panel size gets large)

$$\prod_{t=1}^{n_i} F(x_{it}\beta + \nu_i)$$

is no longer well-approximated by a polynomial. As a general rule-of thumb, you should use this quadrature approach only for small-to-moderate panel sizes (based on simulations, 50 is a reasonably safe upper bound). However, if the data really comes from random-effects tobit and rho is not too large (less than say .3), then the panel size could be 500 and the quadrature approximation will still be fine. If the data is not random-effects tobit or rho is large (bigger than say .7), then the quadrature approximation may be poor for panel sizes larger than 10. The quadchk command should be used to investigate the applicability of the numeric technique used in this command.

References

Neuhaus, J. M. 1992. Statistical methods for longitudinal and clustered designs with binary responses. *Statistical Methods in Medical Research* 1: 249–273.

Pendergast, J. F., S. J. Gange, M. A. Newton, M. J. Lindstrom, M. Palta, and M. R. Fisher. 1996. A survey of methods for analyzing clustered binary response data. *International Statistical Review* 64: 89–118.

Also See

Complementary:	[R] **lincom**, [R] **predict**, [R] **quadchk**, [R] **test**, [R] **testnl**, [R] **vce**, [R] **xtdata**, [R] **xtdes**, [R] **xtsum**, [R] **xttab**
Related:	[R] **tobit**, [R] **xtgee**, [R] **xtintreg**, [R] **xtreg**
Background:	[U] **16.5 Accessing coefficients and standard errors**, [U] **23 Estimation and post-estimation commands**, [U] **23.11 Obtaining robust variance estimates**, [R] **xt**

Title

| zip — Zero-inflated Poisson and negative binomial models |

Syntax

Zero-inflated Poisson model

zip *depvar* $\left[\textit{indepvars}\right]$ $\left[\textit{weight}\right]$ $\left[\texttt{if } \textit{exp}\right]$ $\left[\texttt{in } \textit{range}\right]$ $\left[\texttt{, irr } \underline{\texttt{level}}(\#) \ \underline{\texttt{nocon}}\texttt{stant}\right.$

$\underline{\texttt{inf}}\texttt{late}(\textit{varlist}\left[, \ \underline{\texttt{off}}\texttt{set}(\textit{varname})\right]) \ \underline{\texttt{r}}\texttt{obust} \ \underline{\texttt{cl}}\texttt{uster}(\textit{varname}) \ \underline{\texttt{score}}(\textit{newvarlist})$

$\underline{\texttt{e}}\texttt{xposure}(\textit{varname}) \ \underline{\texttt{off}}\texttt{set}(\textit{varname}) \ \texttt{poisson } \texttt{probit } \textit{maximize\_options} \left.\right]$

Zero-inflated negative binomial model

zinb *depvar* $\left[\textit{indepvars}\right]$ $\left[\textit{weight}\right]$ $\left[\texttt{if } \textit{exp}\right]$ $\left[\texttt{in } \textit{range}\right]$ $\left[\texttt{, irr } \underline{\texttt{level}}(\#) \ \underline{\texttt{nocon}}\texttt{stant}\right.$

$\underline{\texttt{inf}}\texttt{late}(\textit{varlist}\left[, \ \underline{\texttt{off}}\texttt{set}(\textit{varname})\right]) \ \underline{\texttt{r}}\texttt{obust} \ \underline{\texttt{cl}}\texttt{uster}(\textit{varname}) \ \underline{\texttt{score}}(\textit{newvarlist})$

$\underline{\texttt{e}}\texttt{xposure}(\textit{varname}) \ \underline{\texttt{off}}\texttt{set}(\textit{varname}) \ \texttt{nbreg } \texttt{zip } \texttt{probit } \textit{maximize\_options} \left.\right]$

fweights, iweights, and pweights are allowed; see [U] **14.1.6 weight**.

zip and zinb share the features of all estimation commands; see [U] **23 Estimation and post-estimation commands**.

Syntax for predict

predict $\left[\textit{type}\right]$ *newvarname* $\left[\texttt{if } \textit{exp}\right]$ $\left[\texttt{in } \textit{range}\right]$ $\left[, \ \{ \ \texttt{n} \ | \ \texttt{ir} \ | \ \texttt{p} \ | \ \texttt{xb} \ | \ \texttt{stdp} \ \}\right.$

$\underline{\texttt{noo}}\texttt{ffset} \left.\right]$

Description

zip estimates a zero-inflated Poisson maximum-likelihood regression of *depvar* on *indepvars*, where *depvar* is a nonnegative count variable.

zinb estimates a zero-inflated negative binomial maximum-likelihood regression of *depvar* on *indepvars*, where *depvar* is a nonnegative count variable.

Options

irr reports estimated coefficients transformed to incidence rate ratios, i.e., e^b rather than b. Standard errors and confidence intervals are similarly transformed. This option affects how results are displayed, not how they are estimated. irr may be specified at estimation or when replaying previously estimated results.

level(#) specifies the confidence level, in percent, for confidence intervals. The default is level(95) or as set by set level; see [U] **23.5 Specifying the width of confidence intervals**.

noconstant suppresses the constant term (intercept) in the model.

inflate(*varlist*[, offset(*varname*)]) specifies the *varlist* that determines the binary outcome of whether an observed count is zero. You may optionally include an offset. Note that if you do not specify the inflate() option, the result is a model fit by poisson.

robust specifies that the Huber/White/sandwich estimator of variance is to be used in place of the traditional calculation; see [U] **23.11 Obtaining robust variance estimates**. robust combined with cluster() allows observations which are not independent within cluster (although they must be independent between clusters).

cluster(*varname*) specifies that the observations are independent across groups (clusters) but not necessarily within groups. *varname* specifies to which group each observation belongs; e.g., cluster(personid) in data with repeated observations on individuals. cluster() affects the estimated standard errors and variance–covariance matrix of the estimators (VCE), but not the estimated coefficients; see [U] **23.11 Obtaining robust variance estimates**.

cluster() implies robust; specifying robust cluster() is equivalent to typing cluster() by itself.

score(*newvarlist*) creates *newvar* containing $u_j^b = \partial \ln L_j / \partial(\mathbf{x}_j \mathbf{b})$ for each observation j in the sample. The score vector is $\sum \partial \ln L_j / \partial \mathbf{b} = \sum u_j^b \mathbf{x}_j$; i.e., the product of *newvar* with each covariate summed over observations. If a second variable is specified in the *newvarlist*, then another variable is created containing $u_j^g = \partial \ln L_j / \partial(\mathbf{z}_j \mathbf{g})$ for each observation j in the sample. See [U] **23.12 Obtaining scores**.

exposure(*varname*) and offset(*varname*) are different ways of specifying the same thing. exposure() specifies a variable that reflects the amount of exposure over which the *depvar* events were observed for each observation; ln(*varname*) with coefficient constrained to be 1 is entered into the log-link function. offset() specifies a variable that is to be entered directly into the log-link function with coefficient constrained to be 1; thus exposure is assumed to be $e^{varname}$.

poisson requests a likelihood-ratio test comparing the zero-inflated Poisson model with the (nested) Poisson model. By default, a Wald test is included. Note that if you specify robust, then the test will always be a Wald test; the poisson option will be ignored.

probit requests that a probit, instead of logit, model be used to characterize the excess zeros in the data.

nbreg requests that likelihood-ratio tests comparing the zero-inflated negative binomial model with the negative binomial and Poisson models be included in the output. The default is to include only a Wald test against the uninflated negative binomial model.

zip requests that a likelihood-ratio test comparing the zero-inflated negative binomial model with the zero-inflated Poisson model be included in the output.

maximize_options control the maximization process; see [R] **maximize**. You should never have to specify them.

Options for predict

n, the default, calculates the number of events.

ir calculates the incidence rate.

p calculates the probability of a zero outcome.

xb calculates the linear prediction.

stdp calculates the standard error of the linear prediction.

nooffset is relevant only if you specified offset(*varname*) for zip (or zinb). It modifies the calculations made by predict so that they ignore the offset variable; the linear prediction is treated as $\mathbf{x}_j \mathbf{b}$ rather than $\mathbf{x}_j \mathbf{b} + \text{offset}_j$.

Remarks

See Long (1997, 242–247) and Greene (1997, 943–945) for a discussion of zero-modified count models.

Poisson regression and negative binomial regression are used to estimate models of the number of occurrences (counts) of an event. We could use poisson or nbreg for this (see [R] **poisson** and [R] **nbreg**), but in some count data models, we would like to account for the prevalence of zero counts in the data.

For instance, we may count how many fish each visitor to a park catches. A large number of visitors may catch zero as they do not fish (as opposed to being unsuccessful). We may be able to model whether a person fishes depending on a number of covariates related to fishing activity and we may model how many fish a person catches depending on a number of covariates having to do with the success of catching fish (type of lure/bait, time of day, temperature, season, etc.). This is the type of data for which the zip command is useful.

The zero-inflated (or zero-altered) Poisson model, or negative binomial model, allows overdispersion via the introduction of the splitting process which models the outcomes as zero or nonzero.

▷ Example

We have data on the number of fish caught by visitors to a national park. Some of the visitors do not fish, but we do not have the data on whether a person fished or not; we merely have data on how many fish were caught together with several covariates. As our data have a preponderance of zeros (142 out of 250), we use the zip command to model the outcome.

```
. zip count persons livebait, inf(child camper) nolog
Zero-inflated poisson regression              Number of obs   =       250
                                              Nonzero obs     =       108
                                              Zero obs        =       142
Inflation model = logit                       LR chi2(2)      =    506.48
Log likelihood  = -850.7014                   Prob > chi2     =    0.0000
------------------------------------------------------------------------------
      count |      Coef.   Std. Err.      z    P>|z|     [95% Conf. Interval]
------------+-----------------------------------------------------------------
count       |
    persons |   .8068853   .0453288   17.801   0.000    .7180424    .8957281
   livebait |   1.757289   .2446082    7.184   0.000    1.277866    2.236713
      _cons |  -2.178472   .2860289   -7.616   0.000   -2.739078   -1.617865
------------+-----------------------------------------------------------------
inflate     |
      child |   1.602571   .2797719    5.728   0.000    1.054228    2.150913
     camper |  -1.015698    .365259   -2.781   0.005   -1.731593   -.2998038
      _cons |  -.4922872   .3114562   -1.581   0.114    -1.10273    .1181558
------------------------------------------------------------------------------
Wald test of inflate=0:             chi2(3) =    34.81   Prob > chi2 = 0.0000
```

The output includes a Wald test comparing the zero-inflated Poisson model with the Poisson model which shows the significance of the additional modeling of the splitting process for zero and nonzero counts.

We could also estimate this model using `zinb`:

```
. zinb count persons livebait, inf(child camper) nolog
Zero-inflated negative binomial regression          Number of obs   =       250
                                                    Nonzero obs     =       108
                                                    Zero obs        =       142

Inflation model = logit                             LR chi2(2)      =     82.23
Log likelihood  = -401.5478                         Prob > chi2     =    0.0000

------------------------------------------------------------------------------
     count |      Coef.   Std. Err.      z    P>|z|     [95% Conf. Interval]
-----------+------------------------------------------------------------------
count      |
   persons |   .9742984   .1034938     9.414   0.000     .7714543    1.177142
  livebait |   1.557523   .4124424     3.776   0.000     .7491503    2.365895
     _cons |  -2.730064    .476953    -5.724   0.000    -3.664874   -1.795253
-----------+------------------------------------------------------------------
inflate    |
     child |   3.185999   .7468551     4.266   0.000      1.72219    4.649808
    camper |  -2.020951   .872054     -2.317   0.020    -3.730146   -.3117567
     _cons |  -2.695385   .8929071    -3.019   0.003     -4.44545   -.9453189
-----------+------------------------------------------------------------------
  /lnalpha |   .5110429   .1816816     2.813   0.005     .1549535    .8671323
-----------+------------------------------------------------------------------
     alpha |   1.667029   .3028685                       1.167604    2.380076
------------------------------------------------------------------------------
Wald test of inflate=0:                   chi2(3) =    18.21   Prob > chi2 = 0.0004
```

The Wald test appearing at the bottom of the model is a test that the inflation parameters are all zero (a test comparing against a negative binomial model without zero inflation). By default, this is a Wald test. If you would like to see a likelihood-ratio (LR) test, then specify the `nbreg` option. In addition to an LR test for inflation, you will get an LR test vs. a simple Poisson model without inflation. Option `zip` may also be specified to obtain an LR test vs. a zero-inflated Poisson model—the test that $\alpha = 0$.

◁

Methods and Formulas

zip

There are several models in the literature that are all (correctly) described as zero-inflated. The `zip` command maximizes the log-likelihood L defined by

$$\xi_i^\beta = x_i\beta + \text{offset}_i^\beta$$
$$\xi_i^\gamma = z_i\gamma + \text{offset}_i^\gamma$$
$$L = \sum_{i \in S} w_i \ln \left[F(\xi_i^\gamma) + \left(1 - F(\xi_i^\gamma)\right) \exp(-\lambda_i) \right] +$$
$$\sum_{i \notin S} \left[w_i \ln \left(1 - F(\xi_i^\gamma)\right) - w_i \lambda_i + w_i \xi_i^\beta y_i - w_i \ln(y_i!) \right]$$

where w_i are the weights, F is the logit link (or probit link if `probit` was specified), and S is the set of observations for which the outcome $y_i = 0$.

zinb

There are several models in the literature that are all (correctly) described as zero-inflated. The `zinb` command maximizes the log-likelihood L defined by

$$m = 1/\alpha$$

$$p_i = 1/(1 + \alpha\mu_i)$$

$$\xi_i^\beta = x_i\beta + \text{offset}_i^\beta$$

$$\xi_i^\gamma = z_i\gamma + \text{offset}_i^\gamma$$

$$\mu_i = \exp(\xi_i^\beta)$$

$$L = \sum_{i \in S} w_i \ln \left[F(\xi_i^\gamma) + \left(1 - F(\xi_i^\gamma)\right)p_i^m \right]$$

$$+ \sum_{i \notin S} \left[w_i \ln \left(1 - F(\xi_i^\gamma)\right) + w_i \ln \Gamma(m + y_i) - w_i \Gamma(y_i + 1) - \right.$$

$$\left. w_i \ln \Gamma(m) + w_i m \ln p_i + w_i y_i \ln(1 - p_i) \right]$$

where w_i are the weights, F is the logit link (or probit link if `probit` was specified), and S is the set of observations for which the outcome $y_i = 0$.

(Continued on next page)

Saved Results

zip and zinb save in e():

Scalars

e(N)	number of observations
e(k)	number of variables
e(k_eq)	number of equations
e(k_dv)	number of dependent variables
e(N_zero)	number of zero observations
e(df_m)	model degrees of freedom
e(ll)	log likelihood
e(ll_0)	log likelihood, constant-only model
e(ll_c)	log likelihood, comparison model (zip only)
e(df_c)	degrees of freedom for comparison test
e(N_clust)	number of clusters
e(rc)	return code
e(chi2)	χ^2
e(chi2_c)	χ^2 for comparison test
e(p)	significance of model test
e(chi2_p)	χ^2 test against Poisson model (zinb only)
e(chi2_cp)	χ^2 for test of $\alpha = 0$ (zinb only)
e(ic)	number of iterations

Macros

e(cmd)	zip or zinb
e(depvar)	name of dependent variable
e(title)	title in estimation output
e(inflate)	logit or probit
e(wtype)	weight type
e(wexp)	weight expression
e(clustvar)	name of cluster variable
e(vcetype)	covariance estimation method
e(user)	name of likelihood-evaluator program
e(opt)	type of optimization
e(chi2type)	Wald or LR; type of model χ^2 test
e(chi2_ct)	Wald or LR; type of model χ^2 test corresponding to e(chi2_c)
e(chi2_cpt)	Wald or LR; type of model χ^2 test corresponding to e(chi2_cp) (zinb only)
e(chi2_pt)	Wald or LR; type of model χ^2 test corresponding to e(chi2_p) (zinb only)
e(offset1)	offset
e(offset2)	offset for inflate()
e(predict)	program used to implement predict

Matrices

e(b)	coefficient vector
e(V)	variance–covariance matrix of the estimators

Functions

e(sample)	marks estimation sample

References

Greene, W. H. 1997. *Econometric Analysis.* 3d ed. Upper Saddle River, NJ: Prentice–Hall.

Lambert, D. 1992. Zero-inflated Poisson regression, with an application to defects in manufacturing. *Technometrics* 34: 1–14.

Long, J. S. 1997. *Regression Models for Categorical and Limited Dependent Variables.* Thousand Oaks, CA: Sage Publications.

Mullahy, J. 1986 Specification and testing of some modified count data models. *Journal of Econometrics* 33: 341–365.

Also See

Complementary:	[R] **lincom**, [R] **linktest**, [R] **lrtest**, [R] **predict**, [R] **test**, [R] **testnl**, [R] **vce**, [R] **xi**
Related:	[R] **glm**, [R] **nbreg**, [R] **poisson**, [R] **xtpois**
Background:	[U] **16.5 Accessing coefficients and standard errors**, [U] **23 Estimation and post-estimation commands**, [U] **23.11 Obtaining robust variance estimates**, [U] **23.12 Obtaining scores**

Author Index

This is the combined author index for the *Stata Reference Manual* and the *Stata User's Guide*.

A

Aalen, O. O., [R] st sts
Abramowitz, M., [U] **16 Functions and expressions**, [R] **orthog**
Afifi, A. A., [R] **anova**, [R] **sw**
Agresti, A., [R] **tabulate**
Aitchison, J., [R] ologit, [R] oprobit
Aitken, A. C., [R] **reg3**
Akaike, H., [R] **st streg**
Aldrich, J. H., [R] **logit**, [R] **mlogit**, [R] **probit**
Allen, M. J., [R] **alpha**
Altman, D. G., [R] **anova**, [R] **fracpoly**, [R] **kappa**, [R] **kwallis**, [R] **meta**, [R] **nptrend**, [R] **oneway**, [R] **st stcox**
Ambler, G., [R] **regress**
Amemiya, T., [R] **glogit**, [R] **tobit**
Anagnoson, J. T., [U] **2 Resources for learning and using Stata**
Andersen, E. B., [R] **clogit**
Anderson, J. A., [R] **ologit**
Andrews, D. F., [R] **ml**, [R] **rreg**
Arbuthnott, J., [R] **signrank**
Armitage, P., [R] **ltable**, [R] **means**
Armstrong, R. D., [R] **qreg**
Arthur, B. S., [R] **symmetry**
Atkinson, A. C., [R] **boxcox**, [R] **nl**
Azen, S. P., [R] **anova**

B

Baker, R. J., [R] **glm**
Balanger, A., [R] **sktest**
Baltagi, B. H., [R] **hausman**, [R] **ivreg**, [R] **xtreg**
Bancroft, T. A., [R] **sw**
Bartlett, M. S., [R] **factor**, [R] **oneway**, [R] **wntestb**
Barnwell, B. G., [R] **svytab**
Basmann, R. L. [R] **ivreg**
Bassett, G., Jr., [R] **qreg**
Beale, E. M. L., [R] **sw**, [R] **test**
Beaton, A. E., [R] **rreg**
Beck, N., [R] **xtgls**
Becketti, S., [R] **corrgram**, [R] **fracpoly**, [R] **pause**, [R] **runtest**, [R] **spearman**
Begg, C. B., [R] **meta**
Belle, G. van, [R] **dstdize**, [R] **epitab**
Belsley, D. A., [R] **regression diagnostics**
Bendel, R. B., [R] **sw**
Beniger, J. R., [R] **cumul**,
Berk, K. N., [R] **sw**
Berk, R. A., [R] **rreg**
Berkson, J., [R] **logit**, [R] **probit**
Bernstein, I. H., [R] **alpha**, [R] **loneway**

Berry, G., [R] **ltable**, [R] **means**
Beyer, W. H., [R] **qc**
Bickel, P. J., [R] **ml**, [R] **rreg**
Bickenböller, H., [R] **symmetry**
Bieler, G. S., [R] **svytab**
Binder, D. A., [U] **23 Estimation and post-estimation commands**, [R] **_robust**, [R] **svy estimators**
Birdsall, T. G., [R] **logistic**
Bland, M., [R] **signrank**
Bliss, C. I., [R] **probit**
Bloch, D. A., [R] **brier**
Bloomfield, P., [R] **qreg**
BMDP, [R] **symmetry**
Boice, J. D., [R] bitest, [R] epitab
Bollen, K. A., [R] regression diagnostics
Bollerslev, T., [R] **arch**
Bortkewitsch, L. von, [R] **poisson**
Bowker, A. H., [R] **symmetry**
Box, G. E. P., [R] **anova**, [R] **arima**, [R] **boxcox**, [R] **corrgram**, [R] **lnskew0**, [R] **pergram**, [R] **wntestq**, [R] **xcorr**
Boyd, N. F., [R] **kappa**
Bradburn, M. J., [R] **meta**
Brady, A. R., [R] **logistic**, [R] **spikeplt**
Brant, R., [R] **ologit**
Breslow, N. E., [R] **clogit**, [R] **dstdize**, [R] **epitab**, [R] **st stcox**, [R] **st sts test**, [R] **symmetry**
Breusch, T., [R] **mvreg**, [R] **sureg**, [R] **xtreg**
Brier, G. W., [R] **brier**
Brook, R., [R] **brier**
Brown, D. R., [R] **anova**, [R] **oneway**
Brown, S. E., [R] **symmetry**
Buchner, D. M., [R] **ladder**
Burnam, M. A., [R] **lincom**, [R] **mlogit**
Burr, I. W., [R] **qc**

C

Campbell, M. J., [R] **logistic**
Carlile, T., [R] **kappa**
Carlin, J., [R] **means**
Carroll, R. J., [R] **rreg**
Chadwick, J., [R] **poisson**
Chamberlain, G., [R] **clogit**
Chambers, J. M., [U] **9 Stata's on-line tutorials and sample datasets**, [R] **diagplots**, [R] **grmeanby**, [R] **ksm**
Charlett, A., [R] **fracpoly**
Chatfield, C., [R] **corrgram**, [R] **pergram**
Chatterjee, S., [R] **eivreg**, [R] **poisson**, [R] **prais**, [R] **regress**, [R] **regression diagnostics**
Chiang, C. L., [R] **ltable**
Clark, V. A., [R] **ltable**
Clarke, M. R. B., [R] **factor**
Clarke, R. D., [R] **poisson**
Clayton, D., [R] **cloglog**, [R] **epitab**, [R] **st strate**, [R] **st stsplit**, [R] **st sttocc**
Clerget-Darpoux, [R] **symmetry**

I

J

K

Subject Index

This is the combined subject index for the *Stata Reference Manual* and the *Stata User's Guide*. Readers interested in graphics topics should see the index in the *Stata Graphics Manual*.

Semicolons set off the most important entries from the rest. Sometimes no entry will be set off with semicolons; this means all entries are equally important.

& (and), *see* logical operators
| (or), *see* logical operators
~ (not), *see* logical operators
! (not), *see* logical operators
!, *see* shell command
== (equality), *see* relational operators
!= (not equal), *see* relational operators
~= (not equal), *see* relational operators
< (less than), *see* relational operators
<= (less than or equal), *see* relational operators
> (greater than), *see* relational operators
>= (greater than or equal), *see* relational operators

A

Aalen–Nelson cumulative hazard, [R] **st sts**, [R] **st sts generate**, [R] **st sts graph**, [R] **st sts list**
abbreviations, [U] **14.2 Abbreviation rules**; [U] **14.1.1 varlist**, [U] **14.4 varlists**
unabbreviating variable list, [R] **syntax**, [R] **unab**
aborting command execution, [U] **12 The Break key**, [U] **13 Keyboard use**
about command, [R] **about**
abs() function, [U] **16.3.1 Mathematical functions**, [R] **functions**
absolute value function, *see* abs() function
absorption in regression, [R] **areg**
ac command, [R] **corrgram**
accelerated failure-time model, [R] **st streg**
Access, Microsoft, reading data from, [U] **24.4 Transfer programs**
accum matrix subcommand, [R] **matrix accum**
acos() function, [U] **16.3.1 Mathematical functions**, [R] **functions**
acprplot command, [R] **regression diagnostics**
actuarial tables, [R] **ltable**
added-variable plots, [R] **regression diagnostics**
addition across observations, [U] **16.3.6 Special functions**, [R] **egen**
addition across variables, [R] **egen**
addition operator, *see* arithmetic operators
adjust command, [R] **adjust**
adjusted Kaplan–Meier survivor function, [R] **st sts**
adjusted partial residual plot, [R] **regression diagnostics**

.ado filename suffix, [U] **14.6 File-naming conventions**
ado-files, [U] **2.4 The Stata Technical Bulletin**, [U] **20 Ado-files**, [U] **21.11 Ado-files**; [R] **sysdir**, [R] **version**, *also see* programs
editing, [R] **doedit**
display version of, [R] **which**
downloading, [U] **32 Using the Internet to keep up to date**
installing, [U] **20.8 How do I obtain and install STB updates?**, [R] **net**
location, [U] **20.5 Where does Stata look for ado-files?**
long lines, [U] **21.11.2 Comments and long lines in ado-files**, [R] **#delimit**
official, [U] **32 Using the Internet to keep up to date**, [R] **update**
verifying installation, [R] **which**, *also see* verinst command
adopath command, [U] **20.5 Where does Stata look for ado-files?**, [R] **sysdir**
adosize parameter, [R] **sysdir**; [U] **21.11 Ado-files**, [R] **macro**
aggregate functions, [R] **egen**
aggregate statistics, dataset of, [R] **collapse**
agreement, interrater, [R] **kappa**
algebraic expressions, functions, and operators, [U] **16 Functions and expressions**, [U] **16.3 Functions**, [R] **matrix define**
_all, [U] **14.1.1 varlist**
alpha coefficient, Cronbach's, [R] **alpha**
alpha command, [R] **alpha**
alphabetizing
observations, [R] **sort**; [R] **gsort**
variable names, [R] **order**
alphanumeric variables, *see* string variables
analysis of covariance, *see* ANCOVA
analysis of variance, *see* ANOVA
analysis-of-variance test of normality, [R] **swilk**
analytic weights, [U] **14.1.6 weight**, [U] **23.13.2 Analytic weights**
and operator, [U] **16.2.4 Logical operators**
ANCOVA, [R] **anova**
ANOVA, [R] **anova**, [R] **loneway**, [R] **oneway**
Kruskal–Wallis, [R] **kwallis**
repeated measures, [R] **anova**
anova command, [R] **anova**; *also see* estimation commands
with string variables, [R] **encode**
aorder command, [R] **order**
append command, [R] **append**; [U] **25 Commands for combining data**
_append variable, [R] **append**
appending data, [R] **append**; [U] **25 Commands for combining data**
appending files, [R] **copy**
appending rows and columns to matrix, [R] **matrix define**
AR, *see* autocorrelation

Continued on next page

M

Continued on next page

R

r() saved results, [U] **21.8 Accessing results calculated by other programs**, [U] **21.10.1 Saving results in r()**, [R] **discard**, [R] **return**, [R] **saved results**

r-class command, [U] **21.8 Accessing results calculated by other programs**, [R] **program**, [R] **return**, [R] **saved results**

radians, [U] **16.3.1 Mathematical functions**

raise to a power function, [U] **16.2.1 Arithmetic operators**

Ramsey test, [R] **regression diagnostics**

random number function, [U] **16.3.2 Statistical functions**, [R] **functions**, [R] **generate**

random numbers, normally distributed, *see* random number function

random order, test for, [R] **runtest**

random sample, [R] **bstrap**, [R] **sample**; [U] **24.3 If you run out of memory**

random-effects models, [R] **anova**, [R] **xtclog**, [R] **xtgee**, [R] **xtintreg**, [R] **xtlogit**, [R] **xtnbreg**, [R] **xtpois**, [R] **xtprobit**, [R] **xtreg**, [R] **xttobit**; [R] **loneway**

range chart, [R] **qc**

range command, [R] **range**

range of data, [R] **summarize**, [R] **table**; [R] **codebook**, [R] **inspect**, [R] **lv**, [R] **xtsum**

rank correlation, [R] **spearman**

rank() egen function, [R] **egen**

rank-order statistics, [R] **signrank**, [R] **spearman**; [R] **egen**

ranks of observations, [R] **egen**

ranksum command, [R] **signrank**

ratios, survey data, [R] **svymean**

raw data, [U] **15 Data**

.raw filename suffix, [U] **14.6 File-naming conventions**

rc (return codes), *see* error messages and return codes

_rc built-in variable, [U] **16.4 System variables (_variables)**, [R] **capture**

rchart command, [R] **qc**

reading console input in programs, *see* console

reading data from disk, [U] **24 Commands to input data**, [U] **24.4 Transfer programs**, [R] **infile**; *also see* inputting data interactively; combining datasets

real number to string conversion, [U] **16.3.5 String functions**, [R] **functions**

real() string function, [U] **16.3.5 String functions**, [R] **functions**

recase string function, [U] **16.3.5 String functions**, [R] **functions**

recast command, [R] **recast**

receiver operating characteristic (ROC) curves, [R] **logistic**

recode command, [R] **recode**

recode() function, [U] **16.3.6 Special functions**, [U] **28.1.2 Converting continuous to categorical variables**

recoding data autocode() function, [U] **16.3.6 Special functions**, [R] **functions**

record I/O versus stream I/O, [U] **24 Commands to input data**

recording sessions, [U] **18 Printing and preserving output**

rectangularize dataset, [R] **fillin**

reexpression, [R] **boxcox**, [R] **ladder**, [R] **lnskew0**

reg3 command, [R] **reg3**; *also see* estimation commands

regress command, [R] **regress**; [U] **28.2 Using indicator variables in estimation**; *also see* estimation commands

regression (in generic sense)

    accessing coefficients and standard errors, [U] **16.5 Accessing coefficients and standard errors**, [R] **matrix get**

    basics, *also see* estimation commands

    creating orthogonal polynomials for, [R] **orthog**

    diagnostics, [R] **predict**; [R] **logistic**, [R] **regression diagnostics**

    dummy variables, with, [U] **28.2 Using indicator variables in estimation**, [R] **anova**, [R] **areg**, [R] **xi** [R] **xtreg**

    fixed-effects, [R] **xtreg**; [R] **areg**

    fractional polynomial, [R] **fracpoly**

    graphing, [R] **logistic**, [R] **regression diagnostics**

    grouped data, [R] **tobit**

    increasing number of variables allowed, [R] **matsize**

    instrumental variables, [R] **ivreg**

    linear, *see* linear regression

    random-effects, [R] **xtgee**, [R] **xtreg**

    system, [R] **mvreg**, [R] **reg3**, [R] **sureg**

    also see estimation commands

relational operators, [U] **16.2.3 Relational operators**

relative risk, [R] **epitab**; *also see* survival analysis

reldiff() function, [U] **16.3.1 Mathematical functions**, [R] **functions**

release marker, [R] **version**

reliability, [R] **alpha**, [R] **eivreg**, [R] **factor**, [R] **loneway**

reliability theory, *see* survival analysis

remainder function, [U] **16.3.6 Special functions**, [R] **functions**

removing files, [R] **erase**

rename command, [R] **rename**

rename matrix subcommand, [R] **matrix utility**

renpfix command, [R] **rename**

reorganizing data, [R] **reshape**, [R] **xpose**

repeated measures anova, [R] **anova**

repeating and editing commands, [U] **13 Keyboard use**, [R] **for**, [R] **#review**

replace command, [R] **generate**

replace option, [U] **14.2 Abbreviation rules**

replay() function, [R] **estimates**, [R] **functions**

S

string functions, expressions, and operators,
[U] **16.3.5 String functions**; [U] **15.4 Strings**,
[U] **26 Commands for dealing with strings**
string variables, [U] **15.4 Strings**, [U] **26 Commands
for dealing with strings**
converting to numbers, [U] **16.3.5 String functions**
encoding, [R] **encode**
formatting, [R] **format**
inputting, [U] **24 Commands to input data**,
[R] **infile**
making from value labels, [R] **encode**
mapping to numbers, [R] **encode**, [R] **label**
parsing, [R] **gettoken**, [R] **tokenize**
sort order, [U] **16.2.3 Relational operators**
string() function, [U] **16.3.5 String functions**,
[R] **functions**
sts command, [R] **st sts**, [R] **st sts generate**, [R] **st sts
graph**, [R] **st sts list**, [R] **st sts test**, [R] **st stset**,
[R] **st stsum**
sts generate command, [R] **st sts**, [R] **st sts generate**
sts graph command, [R] **st sts**, [R] **st sts graph**
sts list command, [R] **st sts**, [R] **st sts list**
sts test command, [R] **st sts**, [R] **st sts test**
stset command, [R] **st stset**
stsplit command, [R] **st stsplit**
sttocc command, [R] **st sttocc**
sttoct command, [R] **st st_is**
Student's *t* distribution
cdf, [U] **16.3.2 Statistical functions**, [R] **functions**
confidence interval for mean, [R] **ci**
testing equality of means, [R] **ttest**; [R] **hotel**
student version of Stata, [U] **2.7 Books and other
support materials**
studentized residuals, [R] **predict**, [R] **regression
diagnostics**
stvary command, [R] **st stvary**
subdirectories, [U] **14.6 File-naming conventions**
subscripting matrices, [R] **matrix define**
subscripts in expressions, [U] **16.7 Explicit
subscripting**
substr() function, [U] **16.3.5 String functions**,
[R] **functions**
substring function, [U] **16.3.5 String functions**,
[R] **functions**
subtraction operator, *see* arithmetic operators
sum() function, [U] **16.3.6 Special functions**,
[R] **functions**
sum() egen function, [R] **egen**
summarize command, [R] **summarize**; [R] **format**,
[R] **tabsum**
summarizing data, [R] **summarize**; [R] **codebook**,
[R] **inspect**, [R] **lv**, [R] **svytab**, [R] **tabdisp**,
[R] **table**, [R] **tabsum**, [R] **tabulate**, [R] **xtsum**
summary statistics, *see* descriptive statistics
summative (Likert) scales, [R] **alpha**
sums
creating dataset containing, [R] **collapse**
over observations, [U] **16.3.6 Special functions**,
[R] **egen**, [R] **functions**, [R] **summarize**

sums, *continued*
over variables, [R] **egen**
support of Stata, [U] **2 Resources for learning and
using Stata**
suppressing terminal output, [R] **quietly**
sureg command, [R] **sureg**; *also see* estimation
commands
survey data, [U] **30 Overview of survey estimation**,
[R] **svy**, [R] **svy estimators**, [R] **svydes**,
[R] **svylc**, [R] **svymean**, [R] **svyset**, [R] **svytab**,
[R] **svytest**, *also see* survey sampling
survey sampling, [U] **30 Overview of survey
estimation**, [R] **areg**, [R] **biprobit**, [R] **cloglog**,
[R] **cox**, [R] **heckprob**, [R] **hetprob**, [R] **ivreg**,
[R] **logistic**, [R] **logit**, [R] **probit**, [R] **regress**,
[R] **_robust**, [R] **st stcox**, [R] **st streg**, [R] **svy**,
[R] **svy estimators**, [R] **svydes**, [R] **svylc**,
[R] **svymean**, [R] **svyset**, [R] **svytest**, [R] **scobit**,
[R] **tobit**, [R] **weibull**
survival analysis, [R] **st**, [R] **st st_is**, [R] **st stbase**,
[R] **st stcox**, [R] **st stdes**, [R] **st stfill**, [R] **st
stgen**, [R] **st stir**, [R] **st stphplot**, [R] **st strate**,
[R] **st streg**, [R] **st sts**, [R] **st sts generate**, [R] **st
sts graph**, [R] **st sts list**, [R] **st sts test**, [R] **st
stset**, [R] **st stsplit**, [R] **st stsum**, [R] **st sttocc**,
[R] **st sttoct**, [R] **st stvary**; [R] **ct**, [R] **ct ctset**,
[R] **ct cttost**; [R] **ltable**, [R] **nbreg**, [R] **oprobit**,
[R] **poisson**, [R] **snapspan**, [R] **svy estimators**,
[R] **tobit**, [R] **xtnbreg**, [R] **xtpois**, [R] **zip**
survival-time data, *see* survival analysis
survivor function, [R] **st sts**, [R] **st sts generate**, [R] **st
sts list**, [R] **st sts test**
graph of, [R] **st streg**, [R] **st sts graph**
svd matrix subcommand, [R] **matrix svd**
svmat command, [R] **matrix mkmat**
svydes command, [R] **svydes**
svyintrg command, [R] **svy estimators**; *also see*
estimation commands
svyivreg command, [R] **svy estimators**; *also see*
estimation commands
svylc command, [R] **svylc**
svylogit command, [R] **svy estimators**; *also see*
estimation commands
svymean command, [R] **svymean**
svymlog command, [R] **svy estimators**; *also see*
estimation commands
svyolog command, [R] **svy estimators**; *also see*
estimation commands
svyoprob command, [R] **svy estimators**; *also see*
estimation commands
svypois command, [R] **svy estimators**; *also see*
estimation commands
svyprobt command, [R] **svy estimators**; *also see*
estimation commands
svyreg command, [R] **svy estimators**; *also see*
estimation commands
svyset command, [R] **svyset**
svytab command, [R] **svytab**
svytest command, [R] **svytest**

U